DATE DUE

STUDIES IN THE HISTORY OF ACCOUNTING

Studies in the
History of Accounting

Edited on behalf of
The Association of University Teachers of Accounting
and the American Accounting Association

by

A. C. LITTLETON, Ph.D.

Emeritus Professor of Accounting, University of Illinois

and

B. S. YAMEY, B.Com.

Reader in Economics, London School of Economics and
Political Science, University of London

1956

RICHARD D. IRWIN, INC.

HOMEWOOD, ILLINOIS

PRINTED IN THE UNITED STATES OF AMERICA

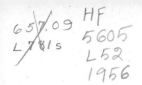
Preface

MODERN accountancy differs from most branches of professional
activity in that one of its major techniques—double-entry book-
keeping—goes back as far as the fourteenth, perhaps even the
thirteenth, century. This technique has proved to be serviceable and
effective in the changing circumstances and with the changing business
requirements of over five centuries. It has also had an intellectual
interest sufficient to attract the active attention down the centuries of
distinguished mathematicians and scientists such as Luca Pacioli,
Simon Stevin, Charles Hutton and Augustus de Morgan.

It is one of the objectives of this book to illumine some aspects
of the long history of double entry. Its early origins as revealed in
surviving accounting records; some of its earliest expositors, their
eminence and achievements in wider fields, and their treatises on
accounting; the evolution of particular practices associated with double
entry; the methods of teaching double entry and the emergence of
theories of accounting; the spread of the practice—these are among
the subjects considered in this collection of studies. In many instances
the authors of the essays in question break new ground, provide new
interpretations, or conveniently bring together and analyse material
otherwise available only in scattered places.

But the history of accounting, of course, is more than the history
of double entry. The need to keep records of financial and other
business transactions is an ancient one, and it is perhaps no accident
that the earliest surviving examples of writing are in the records of
temple incomes kept by priests in Sumeria. We have therefore
included some essays on accounting practices and records before the
appearance of double entry. Thus the first essay is on accounting in
classical antiquity; besides its thorough and comprehensive review and
interpretation of surviving records, the essay also includes discussions
on several related topics, notably on numeral systems. We have also
included, for example, a short essay on the oldest known business
records of the Middle Ages—three scraps of paper, dating from 1157,
inserted in the records of a Genoese notary. This contribution illustrates the skill of the historian in making use of fragmentary material;
it also serves to show, as do other essays also, that simple accounting
records have often adequately met the needs of their owners.

Double entry did not immediately displace all other systems—or
practices which cannot be dignified with the name of system. We

have included a number of essays which deal with post-Paciolian accounting records untouched by the teachings of Pacioli and his numerous successors. For example, there is an essay on a bookseller in seventeenth-century London who kept track of his varied activities by means of simple records, and others on traders in Colonial America and pioneering merchants in Australia whose account-books reveal much of early trading conditions and practices, though displaying a low level of technical accounting attainment.

The fascination of old accounts stems from at least two sources. Those familiar with present-day accounting practices may be interested to find similarities and differences in earlier accounting, and to see the germs of modern techniques and procedures in centuries-old records. The other main source of interest is the contents of old account-books as distinct from the accounting technique displayed in them. Historians working in a variety of branches of history have found useful or entertaining material in account-books which often have little to offer the historian interested in accounting techniques as such. Entries in the account-books of patrons showing payments to artists have sometimes helped art historians to settle difficult problems of attribution and of dating works of art. Accounting records of business firms have similarly helped to shed light on a wide range of subjects of interest to economic and social historians; thus they have provided useful information, for example, on the profitability of the eighteenth-century slave trade, or added lively detail to established generalisations on matters such as the direction of international trade or the degree of specialisation in trading activities in earlier centuries.

In our selection we have included a variety of essays, some likely to appeal more especially to readers who are interested in the development of accounting technique, and others also likely to attract those with other or less-specialised interests. And the dichotomy between the two sorts of interest is not a sharp one; the economic historian, for example, may well wish to speculate on the influence of changes in accounting techniques on the organisation of business firms or on business practices generally. The majority of the essays, we believe, are likely to be useful to the historians of accounting (in the narrow sense) without having their interest confined to this specialised field.

The historian of accounting can have recourse to two main kinds of material: surviving accounting records, and the textbooks and treatises on accounting. The precise relation between practice and pedagogic exposition is debatable; but it is clear that both sources are of use and of interest to the historian, and we have therefore included studies based on both kinds of material.

We have chosen the year 1900 as our rough terminal date, and

there are no essays on " contemporary history." Two of the contributions relating to the nineteenth century, however, are directly concerned with issues that are still prominent today—the definition and
periodic calculation of the profits of an enterprise, the contents of
accounting statements to be furnished to absentee shareholders, and
the role of the State in regulating company accounting practices. But
our terminal date does not permit the inclusion of material, for
example, on mechanised accounting, which is already bringing about
major changes in the organisation of accounting procedures and in
the processing of raw data to make them useful for administrative
purposes. But even here, as in other developments also, there is
some historical continuity; the abortive revolt against double entry
some 150 years ago, described in one of the essays, was at least partly
inspired by the wish to minimise clerical work in the keeping of
accounts, to accelerate the production of required data, and to reduce
the possibility of human error.

The studies in this book span a period of roughly two-and-a-half
thousand years, from about 600 B.C. to the end of the Victorian era.
It is almost superfluous to say that the collection does not pretend to
present a comprehensive record of the development of accounting
practices and techniques during this long period. Some of the
inevitable gaps indicate areas or periods in the history of accounting
which, so far as we know, have not attracted attention; the examination of double-entry records of the seventeenth and eighteenth
centuries is a case in point. We would like to think that the publication of this collection of studies will help to arouse more active interest
in the history of accounting, and that parts of the story, at present
inadequately understood, will be elucidated. We have also
deliberately excluded a number of aspects of the development of
accounting so that the remaining field could be more satisfactorily
represented; for this reason our selection does not attempt to cover
the history of cost accounting, auditing, and government accounting.

We are very grateful to our contributors for making our task as
editors both easy and pleasant. Requests for contributions—well
over half the studies in this book have not been published before—
did not meet with a single refusal, and our contributors both agreed
to work, and in fact did work, within a fairly tight time-schedule. We
are also much indebted to the following for their generous permission
to reprint published material: American Institute Publishing Co., Inc.,
Accountants Publishing Company Limited (of Australia), and the
Editors of *Accounting Research, The Bulletin of the Business Historical Society, The Economic History Review, The Three Banks
Review,* and *The Westminster Bank Review.* The inclusion of eight

pages of photographic reproductions has been made possible by the courteous co-operation of the following: British Library of Political and Economic Science; Delegates of the Clarendon Press, Oxford; Professor Raymond de Roover; Electa Editrice of Milan and Florence; Institute of Chartered Accountants; Library of the Harvard Business School; Mercers' Company; Public Records Office; and Society for the Promotion of Hellenic Studies. We also wish to thank our publishers, colleagues and contributors for much helpful advice and assistance.

This is the third in a series of volumes of collected studies on accounting subjects, the first two volumes being *Studies in Accounting*, edited by Professor W. T. Baxter, and *Studies in Costing*, edited by Professor David Solomons. However, the initiation of the present work differs from that of its predecessors in an important respect. In its sponsorship of this third volume the Association of University Teachers of Accounting has been joined by the American Accounting Association, a form of Anglo-American co-operation which it is hoped will continue in the future.

THE EDITORS.

DENVER and LONDON,

July, 1956.

Contents

Illustrations

(facing page 1)

(a)

(b)

I. IN THE COUNTING-HOUSE

(a) A PANNONIAN BANKER. Lower part of a funeral *stele* found in Serbia. The
office of a banker or business man. The banker (in Roman dress) is seated
on a chair near a folding wall-table. In his left hand he holds a triptych,
no doubt his *codex accepti et expensi*, and on the table before him lies a large
bag of coin—the day's takings. In front of the table stands a slave reading
his daily report from the *adversaria* or *ephemerides* (the daily record-book).
Museum, Belgrade. (M. Rostovtzeff, *Social and Economic History of the
Roman Empire*: Oxford, at The Clarendon Press, 1926.)

(Courtesy of The Clarendon Press.)

(b) ADMINISTRATOR AND SCRIBE IN THEIR OFFICE. A painting by an unknown
artist on the cover of an account-book of the Commune of Sienna, 1394.
(*Catalogo delle Tavolette della Biccherna e di altri uffici dello Stato di Siena*,
ed. Enzo Carli: Electa Editrice, Milan and Florence, 1950.)

(Courtesy of Electa Editrice.)

(a)

(b)

II. IN THE COUNTING-HOUSE

(a) Engraving by P. Serwouter on title-page of H. Waningen, *'tRecht Gebruyck van't Italiaens Boeck-houden* . . . , Amsterdam, 1672.

(*Courtesy of Institute of Chartered Accountants, London.*)

(b) Detail of frontispiece engraving, by J. Goeree, in S. Ricard, *Traité general du commerce* . . . , Amsterdam, 1700.

(*Courtesy of British Library of Political and Economic Science, London.*)

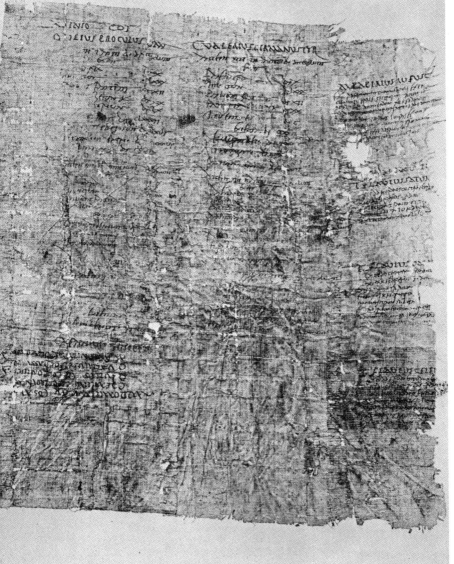

III. ROMAN ARMY PAY-SHEETS
(see pp. 39-40)

(From J. Nicole and Ch. Morel, *Archives Militaires du Ier siècle*: W. Kündig
& Fils, Geneva, 1900.)

(*Courtesy of the Society for the Promotion of Hellenic Studies, London.*)

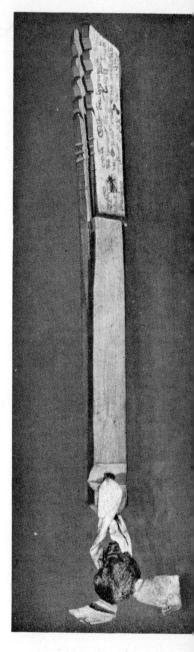

(a)

(b)

IV. TALLIES

(a) Stock of a tally with £2,000 scored on lower edge; believed to have been a receipt for money issued to Edward of Westminster, an important financier in the reign of Henry III, possibly for work on Westminster Abbey. (Public Record Office: Exchequer of Receipt. E 402. Case 3A. File 3.)

(b) Stock and foil of a private tally dating back to the reign of Edward III, with £3 13. 4. on the lower edge. The parties were William de Hynton, a baillif, and Nicholas Raunche, a reeve. (Public Record Office: Queen's Remembrancer, Accounts Various. E. 101/684/4.)

(*Courtesy of Public·Record Office, London.*)

**V. LAST PAGE OF BALANCE SHEET OF FRANCESCO DATINI & CO.
IN BARCELONA, 1399**

(see p. 143)

The entries listed include an item of £80, Barcelonese currency, set aside as a reserve for unpaid expenses and taxes (*Riserbo di spese e di lelde restano a paghare*), and another item of £751 10s. 7d. representing the balance of Profit and Loss (*Pro di merchatantie*). At first there was a gap of £101 9s. 1d. between total debits and credits, but it was reduced to £11 9s. 1d., by making several adjustments.

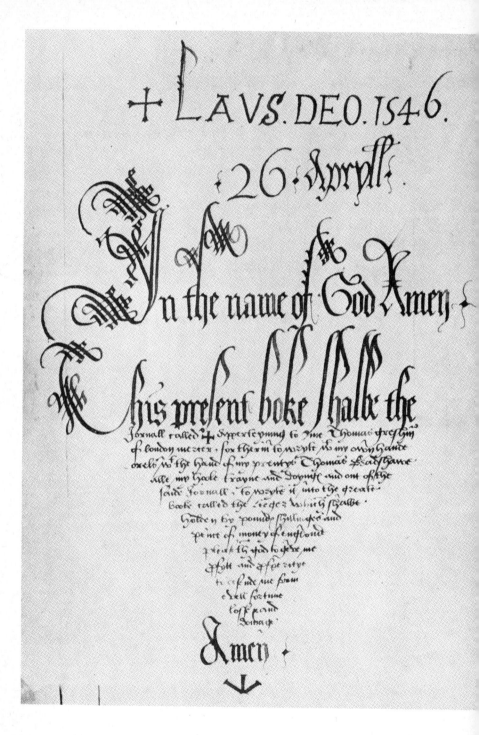

VI. JOURNAL OF SIR THOMAS GRESHAM, 1546: DEDICATION

(see p. 189)

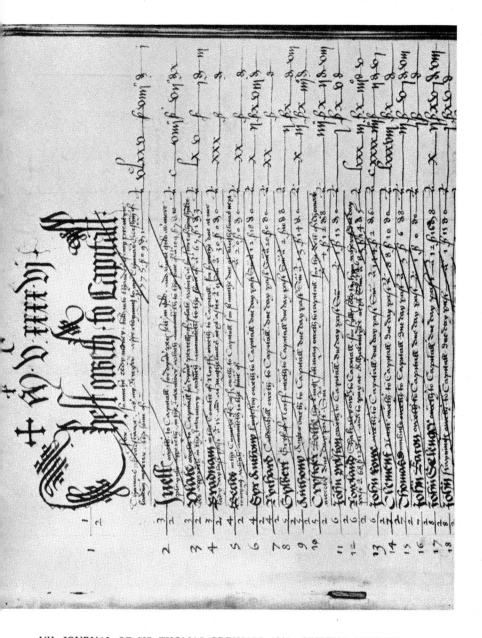

VII. JOURNAL OF SIR THOMAS GRESHAM, 1546: OPENING ENTRIES
(see p. 190)

(*Courtesy of the Mercers' Company, London.*)

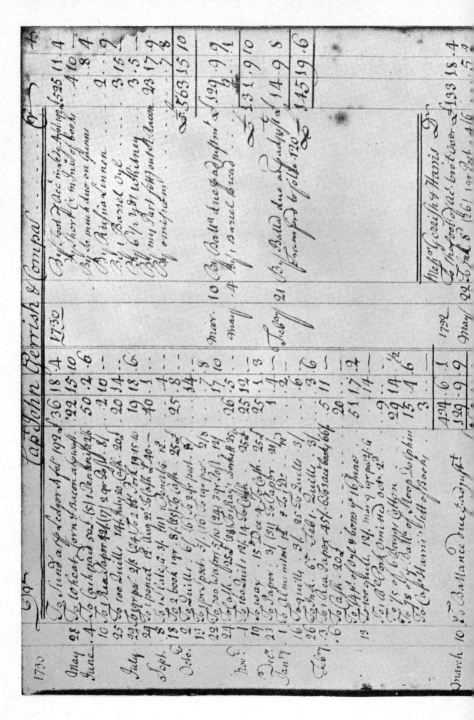

VIII. A PERSONAL ACCOUNT IN DANIEL HENCHMAN'S LEDGER, 1730
(see p. 278)
(*Courtesy of The Library, Harvard Business School.*)

Introduction

B. S. Yamey*

IN introducing this collection of twenty-three essays dealing with a diversity of subjects I could have prepared a descriptive catalogue of all the items in the volume, even though the result was likely to be reminiscent of some early account-books in which a miscellany of entries are strung together with little order or continuity. Or I could have considered a few selected themes on which several but not all of the essays throw some light. I have taken this second course, choosing for discussion the origins and spread of double-entry book-keeping and the development of accounting " principles " concerning the calculation of profits and the valuation of assets.

Mr. de Ste. Croix in his essay shows conclusively that the Romans neither knew nor used the double-entry system or anything approximating at all closely to it. It is therefore possible to assert with more confidence than has hitherto been possible that it has its origins in medieval Italy,[1] though despite, or perhaps because of, the researches of a number of historians it is still not possible to be more precise concerning the date or place of its birth. The results of this research are admirably summarised and explained in this volume by Professor de Roover, who himself has participated notably in the exploration of documentary resources. This research suggests that there may have been double-entry accounts before those of the *Massari* of Genoa of the year 1340, which for a long time were thought to have been the earliest. It is perhaps better to place the origins somewhere in the second half of the thirteenth century or the first decades of the next; the birthplace is also uncertain, and there are several rival claimants for this honour—Genoa, Lombardy and Tuscany.

We know a good deal more now than fifty years ago about the

---

* Reader in Economics, London School of Economics and Political Science.
[1] It should be added that the " invention " of double entry has sometimes been attributed to other countries and periods. For example, it has been claimed that Spain is its birthplace, largely on the ground that the use of Arabic numerals was introduced into Europe by the Moors in Spain. This claim has little support today. Again, Alexander Hamilton, F.R.S., a noted orientalist, wrote in 1798: " We would remark that the Banians of India have been, from time immemorial, in possession of the method of book-keeping by double entry, and that Venice was the emporium of Indian commerce at the time at which Friar Lucas's [Pacioli's] treatise appeared." (Book review in *Monthly Review*, 26 [1798], p. 129.) The attribution of this unsigned review to Hamilton is due to B. C. Nangle, *The Monthly Review, Second Series, 1790-1815*; *Indexes of Contributors and Articles* [Oxford, 1955]). Unfortunately, Hamilton did not indicate the basis for his remarks.

1

general chronology of the development of double entry. But in the nature of things we are on less sure ground when trying to explain the process by which the earlier collections of incomplete and unorganised commercial accounting records became transformed into a systematised and simple yet elegant arrangement of inter-locking accounts comprehending personal, real and nominal accounts. When one seeks for causes and predisposing circumstances one leaves, perforce, the more secure foundation of surviving records, though here too their value is evident. It is therefore following the path of caution, and perhaps also of wisdom, if I attempt no more than to present four possible approaches to the origins of double entry, with some comments on each, and on its practice in the first three or four centuries of its use. The emergence of double entry may be conceived either as, first, the work of a single gifted inventor, or second, the product or reflection of the spirit of the Renaissance, or third, the resultant of accidental or chance influences, or fourth, the necessary outcome of a purposive evolution—in the context, 'a sort of economic determinism. Let us look at each of these four possibilities in turn.

Augspurg, writing in 1897, came to the romantic conclusion that " the scientific system [double entry] based on mathematical principles could have had no other source than the genius of one individual (and he a mathematician well acquainted with commerce) from whose pen it must have flowed forth in one gush." [2] Augspurg identified this genius with Luca Pacioli,[3] whose life and achievement are described by Professor Taylor in this volume. Pacioli was an eminent mathematician and also conversant with the world of trade. However, the error of Augspurg's views is easily demonstrated, since[Pacioli himself wrote that he was describing Venetian practice as he found it, and we now know that the practice was probably two centuries old when he wrote his famous *Summa.*] Whether there was another genius with the necessary combination of learning and business knowledge who invented double entry in the thirteenth century must remain a conjecture. Perhaps there were several innovators who came upon the same idea independently: the practice appears to have started in different parts of Italy at roughly the same time; moreover regional differences in the details of practice suggest independent development.

The early date of the earliest double-entry records does not permit us to seek the impetus of the development of the practice in one or other manifestation of the *Zeitgeist* of the Renaissance. This is unfortunate, for it would not be altogether fanciful to see in double

[2] G. D. Augspurg in *Zeitschrift für Buchhaltung* (1897).
[3] In this volume the version *Pacioli* is used throughout. For a discussion of the correct spelling of the name, see R. de Roover, " Paciolo or Pacioli?," *Accounting Review*, XIX (1944), pp. 68–69.

entry the application of science in the form of mathematics, that is, the application of scientific measurement, to phenomena in the world of trade. The attractiveness of this line of approach is strengthened by the fact that Pacioli, as Professor Taylor shows, was closely associated with some of the leading figures in Renaissance art in whose work the ideas of proportion, symmetry and scientific precision (for example, in the rendering of perspective) find their practical expression; and—if the comparison is permissible—could one not claim that in double entry the ideas of balance, symmetry and precision are central? But the harsh facts of chronology are against this pleasant hypothesis. Equally, and for the same reason, one must discard the idea that the emergence of double entry represents the triumph of the Renaissance search for breadth and simplicity over the meticulous medieval concern with detail—implying, in our field, the emergence of an integrating system producing synoptic business statements in place of more-or-less discrete and particularised records. Moreover, the meticulous concern with detail in accounting records seems to have persisted generally even with those who adopted and used the double-entry system. Indeed, it is the early practice of making detailed entries in journals and ledgers—detailed, that is, by the yardstick of modern practice—which makes these books and records so useful as source-material for economic, social and business historians. One may venture to suggest (though, as will be shown below, this interpretation is not generally accepted) that the merchants who first kept their records by double entry valued as the main virtue of the system the greater comprehensiveness of their detailed records rather than the summary statements of financial position, and of periodic changes therein, which the system facilitates.

The thesis considered in the preceding paragraph—that double entry is a product of the spirit of the Renaissance—may seem to some to be so unplausible or unrealistic as not to warrant discussion. Be this as it may, if I had to offer an excuse for having considered it, it would be that the emergence of double entry has on occasions been described as an event of some considerable general cultural significance, and as being representative of important historical tendencies. The German economic historian, Werner Sombart, for example, wrote in his study of modern capitalism [4]: " Double-entry book-keeping is

---

[4] W. Sombart, *Der Moderne Kapitalismus* (6th ed., Munich and Leipzig, 1924), vol. 2, part 1, p. 119. (" Die doppelte Buchhaltung ist aus demselben Geiste geboren wie die Systeme Galileis und Newtons, wie die Lehren der modernen Physik und Chemie. Mit denselben Mitteln wie diese ordnet sie die Erscheinungen zu einem kunstvollen System, und man kann sie als den ersten, auf dem Grundsatz des mechanischen Denkens aufgebauten Kosmos bezeichnen.")

Sombart goes on to claim that one can see in double entry the germs of the ideas of the force of gravity, the circulation of the blood and the conservation of energy.

born of the same spirit as the systems of Galileo and Newton.' . . .
Using the same means as these, it orders the phenomena into an
elegant system, and it may be described as the first cosmos built up on
the basis of mechanistic thought." The book-keepers, merchants and
others who in the first four or five centuries of double-entry practice
laboriously matched each credit entry with its corresponding debit in
their ledgers—and also Pacioli, who first described the system—would
perhaps have been surprised to learn how much was one day to be
read into their oft-times irksome activity. However, it is undoubtedly
true that the double-entry system appears to have been of much
interest to some eminent scientists and mathematicians, of whom
Pacioli was the first. Dr. ten Have, in his essay in this volume, writes
of another, Simon Stevin, whose place in the history of science and
mathematics is secure and significant. And the names of others will
be found in the late Professor Hatfield's delightful essay " An
Historical Defense of Book-keeping." [5] Again, the development of
national income accounting and social accounting during the last few
decades shows that economic statisticians have found the technique of
double entry to have utility as well as a certain elegance.

   The third possible line of approach is to regard double entry as a
technique which grew by chance or accident, and by a gradual process
of accretion and adaptation, out of earlier book-keeping techniques. This process, if it was at work, bridged a wide gap, for there
are big differences between double entry and earlier book-keeping
methods. This is so even though it seems that the recognition of
positive and negative entries, the grouping of items under appropriate
heads, and the use of bilateral accounts or of other forms of account
separating positive and negative entries, ante-date the first double-
entry records.[6] However, it is possible that the accounting needs of
agents or factors may have led to some system of more-or-less
mutually inter-related accounts, including, for example, cash accounts,
goods accounts (probably recording quantities and not values), personal accounts and an account in the name of the principal. When
so many accounts were kept, some types of transaction may have
required *contra* entries in two different accounts. Similarly, in the
accounts of bankers many transactions would give rise to both a
positive and negative entry even without a formal double-entry system.
And as Professor Littleton has suggested: " Once the practice of dual

[5] *Journal of Accountancy*, 37 (1924); reprinted in W. T. Baxter (ed.), *Studies in
    Accounting* (London, 1950).
[6] The periodic " account " in medieval manorial administration and its separation
    of " charge " and " discharge " items are considered in the contributions by
    Dr. Oschinsky and Miss Myatt-Price in this volume.

entries upon opposing sides of bilateral accounts had become established, it would not be difficult to extend it by analogy to new accounts. No one would have to stop and reason out the philosophy of the matter first." [7]

The fourth line of approach is to see in the emergence and development of double entry the response to new or growing business needs not satisfied by earlier methods of record-keeping. This approach carries with it the implication that the "invention" of double entry, by solving or helping to solve previously intractable business problems, facilitated the development of individual concerns and of business enterprise generally, and in this manner contributed to economic growth. As I have written previously on this subject with a somewhat unsympathetic approach, it is perhaps necessary at the start to indicate that it is not at all unlikely that accounting techniques may have some (possibly significant) influence on business organisation and methods, or that new business requirements may call forth improvements in business techniques. [8] My lack of sympathy is only towards

---

[7] A. C. Littleton, *Accounting Evolution to 1900* (New York, 1933), pp. 38–39. See also P. G. A. de Waal, *De Leer van het Boekhouden in de Nederlanden tijdens de 16e Eeuw* (Roermond, 1927), p. 282. Note also the remark by R. de Roover: " Since trade rests on the exchange of goods and services, the duality which forms the basis of double-entry book-keeping is rooted in the nature of things." (" New Perspectives on the History of Accounting," *Accounting Review*, XXX [1955], p. 405). This points to the possibility—which Professor de Roover rejects—that double entry may have evolved almost by chance.

[8] Three examples, widely separated in time, may be considered here.
    (i) The connection between economic organisation and accounting is indicated in the following discussion of the origins of *writing*: " The motive which brought about this invention of writing [by the Sumerians] was economic. By the middle of the fourth millennium B.C., men in lower Mesopotamia had passed beyond Neolithic barbarism. The region of Sumer and the neighbouring region of Akkad were already divided into many small city-states. Each of the cities contained one or more temples with a large staff of priests. The city god was regarded as the owner of all the state lands. Dues were payable to the temple in the form of products of the soil. Hence arose the need for a system of accounts, or records of dues owing or paid. It is generally agreed that these earliest tablets from Erech, Jemdet Nasr, and other Sumerian cities are records, kept by the priests, of the temple incomes." (S. H. Hooke, " Reading and Writing," in C. Singer, E. J. Holmyard and A. R. Hall (eds.), *A History of Technology*, vol. 1 [Oxford, 1954], p. 745, with ill. on p. 746.)
    (ii) H. van Werveke has attempted to show that the development of the Flemish cloth industry in the eleventh century as an *urban* industry may be accounted for largely in terms of the organising merchants' illiteracy and inability to keep written accounts. According to him this meant that the merchant could not work through distant intermediaries, and also that he had to be in close touch with weavers and fullers, who therefore had to live in his town. When merchants acquired schooling and became conversant with book-keeping, the need for proximity disappeared and the industry was able to spread to town suburbs and villages. (" Industrial Growth in the Middle Ages: the Cloth Industry in Flanders," *Economic History Review*, second series, VI [1954], pp. 237-245.) This explanation, though of interest, would carry more conviction if the author had shown that no literate clerks were available in the eleventh century to keep the simple records required, and also had explained how the merchants were able to keep track of the materials put out to each of a number of urban workers. If, as is likely, there were clerks, the explanation is not cogent since an illiterate merchant could have employed them. And if a merchant in fact was able to

what appear to me to be exaggerated statements concerning the inter-
connections between accounting techniques, double entry in particular,
and the conduct and motivation of business enterprise.

A major difficulty is that even where accounting records have
survived it is not always possible to be sure how they were used or
what their owners expected from them.   The available evidence can
be interpreted in a variety of ways: some may be more readily
prepared than others to discern revealing clues in particular pieces of
evidence; and while some may lay stress on one sort of evidence others
may find significance elsewhere.   A further difficulty is that very few
double-entry records of the sixteenth, seventeenth and eighteenth
centuries have been subjected to scrutiny from the point of view which
is relevant for present purposes, that is, the discovery of the uses to
which they were put.   In this volume there is Mr. Ramsey's study of
some Tudor merchants' account-books, a contribution which itself is
suggestive of the light which accounting records can throw on the use
which was made of them.   It is to be hoped that similar studies will
be made of many other double-entry records after Pacioli, so that in
time it will be possible for someone to draw them all together in a
careful and illuminating survey, just as Professor de Roover has done
in this volume for records before Pacioli.

The present lack of knowledge about double-entry practice after
Pacioli inevitably leads one to study the other main likely source of
information, the book-keeping textbooks or treatises which appeared
in a growing stream after 1494.   This at once raises the question of
the reliability of these books as descriptions of contemporary practices
or of the attitudes of businessmen to their accounts.   The books vary
a good deal in quality, as is apparent after even cursory examination
of their texts.   However, an examination of what appear to be the
better works reveals a marked degree of uniformity, particularly in
their discussion of such key topics as the periodic calculation of
profits and the balancing of the ledger.   This could be the result of
copying a common model, or a few similar models.   But this explanation will not do.   Several of the works were written by merchants
and their descriptions and discussions of double entry do not differ
significantly from those of other writers, many of whom were so-called

---

memorise the details of his dealings with each town worker, it is difficult to see
why he could not have used rural intermediaries by memorising the facts of his
essentially similar dealings with them; each agent could in the same way have
supervised the issue of materials, etc., in his locality.

(iii) The last example is provided by W. T. Baxter in his *The House of
Hancock* (Cambridge, Mass., 1945) and in his essay in this volume.   The shortage
of sound currency and the narrowness of markets in Colonial America made it
necessary for trade to be conducted in large part in the form of " book-keeping
barter "; this was only possible if there were some accounting records, though
a rather simple " system " seems to have been adequate for the purpose.
Without such records, trade would have been far more difficult and laborious.

schoolmasters. Moreover, writers like de la Porte and Malachy Postlethwayt were closely acquainted with the world of commerce even though they may not have been in business themselves. It is thus not possible to dismiss all the treatises as the work of hack writers or impractical schoolmasters. Many of the self-styled " teachers " were also practising book-keepers employed by merchants. Richard Dafforne described himself as " Accountant and Teacher of the Same "; he is only one of many.

Again, though my acquaintance with double-entry ledgers in the three centuries after Pacioli is decidedly small, I have not discovered anything which would make me abandon such faith as I have in the treatises—and I am most familiar with the ones in English—as acceptable reflections of the contemporary practice of double entry.[9] Of course, the treatises were not written to describe in detail the book-keeping arrangements of such exceptional concerns as the Bank of England or the East India Company, though even here a knowledge of the treatises helps one to find one's way about their voluminous account-books. Moreover, in a sense most of the treatises were simplifications in that they were meant to instruct generally without necessarily providing a blue-print directly applicable to a particular firm; but the simplification, I suggest, concerns detail and elaboration rather than more basic matters.[10]

Double entry has three main advantages over the earlier methods of record-keeping. First, the records are more comprehensive and orderly; second, the duality of entries provides a convenient check on the accuracy or completeness of the ledger; third, the ledger including as it does personal, real and nominal accounts in an integrated whole, contains the materials for developing, as part of the system, statements of profit-and-loss and of capital, assets and liabilities.[11] Did, indeed, the need for any or all of these attributes provide the spur for the development of double entry, and did the

[9] A systematic survey of the main books on accounting in English published up to, say, 1800, would, I am sure, be of much interest and value. The books by de Waal (cited in note 7, above) and O. ten Have (*De Leer van het Boekhouden in de Nederlanden tijdens de Zeventiende en Achttiende Eeuw* [Delft, 1934]) on works published in the Netherlands provide worthy models to emulate. Mr. Coomber's essay on Oldcastle and Mellis in this volume makes a good start to such a project.

[10] Even then some of the texts contain much instruction on the keeping of subsidiary books, for example, and the withering away of the journal can be traced in the better textbooks.

[11] Some words of explanation may be necessary for readers who are not acquainted with the details of double entry. The entries in a set of books may be sufficient to enable the book-keeper to draw up statements of profits and financial position. But such statements will be based on book values of assets which, at the time of balancing, may not reflect the commercial values of the assets. If these latter are to be used in the final accounts, some process of valuation or inventorisation, external to the book-keeping system, has to be undertaken and its results incorporated in the books. This process is, however, also available if books are kept

possession of these qualities commend the double-entry system, once in existence, to merchants for its adoption?　As the first half of the question is obviously even more speculative than the second, the discussion will be concerned mainly with the latter.

There can be little doubt that the first two qualities were much appreciated.　The greater comprehensiveness of double-entry records must have been very acceptable to merchants with growing or more complex interests; the old need for records of individual transactions, amounts owed to or by the firm, cash balances, goods in stock or on consignment, etc., would be met, with a margin to spare, in an orderly way.[12]　Double-entry records are necessarily organised and disciplined, though here, I suspect, the treatises may give a somewhat false picture since it is easier to be methodical in a textbook example than in a busy counting-house, particularly when account-books have to be ruled by hand.　Then, too, the trial balance check, whose history in the early treatises is traced by Professor Peragallo in this volume, must have been appreciated, even though the merchant or book-keeper may not always have thought it necessary to find the error when his books did not balance.　The textbook writers were loud in their praises of the check, and Stephen Monteage, writing in 1682, claimed: " This way of accounting which we Treat of, carries with it its own Proof: And here lies the supreme Excellency and Usefulness of this mystery."　It may be added that it is these two qualities, the comprehensiveness of the records and the presence of an arithmetical or consistency check, which seem to be most relevant in commending the double-entry system for use in national income accounting.

This leaves the third quality of double entry, the fact that it makes possible the development, as part of the system, of summary statements of profit-and-loss and of proprietary interests and assets.　Was double entry greatly valued for this quality by its practitioners in its first few centuries?　In seeking to answer this question two opposing points of view are encountered concerning the role of the profit-and-loss account and of the balance account in early double entry.　On the one hand there are those who hold that these synoptic statements, expressing profits and capital in precise quantitative terms, were highly prized end-products of double entry, that through their instrumentality the double-entry system made possible or sharpened the

---

by a simple system of single entry.　Statements of profits and capital are not products peculiar to double entry, and historically precede that system; partnership accounting, which normally requires statements of profits, is older than double entry.

[12] It may be noted, however, that for several centuries after Pacioli's treatise even complicated business affairs were managed without double entry.　Mr. Blagden's essay in this volume shows that a simple arrangement of records was sufficient for the needs of the small but quite involved business of a seventeenth century publisher-bookseller.

so-called " rationalistic pursuit of profit," and that mainly in this way, though also in some other ways, the system was essential to the development of nascent capitalism. On the other hand, there is the more prosaic view that the profit-and-loss account and the whole process of balancing the ledger primarily served narrow book-keeping purposes related to the first two qualities already discussed. The choice between the two points of view, or, perhaps better, the relative distribution of emphasis between the two points of view, must depend essentially on one's interpretation of the significance of early double-entry techniques and the use to which early double-entry records were put. This is not a proper occasion to attempt to set out the arguments and evidence, and, since I am a proponent of the second point of view, perhaps I may not be a proper person to attempt a detached presentation of the matters at issue or the cogency of the opposing contentions. The reader who is interested in this issue is advised to turn to the writings of the contending parties.[13] Here it must be sufficient to state that, if the first point of view be accepted, double entry would have been both a manifestation of the spirit of capitalism in its formative decades as well as a propulsive agency furthering a significant economic and cultural development. Sombart, who put forward these views, wrote as follows [14]: " One can scarcely conceive of capitalism without double-entry book-keeping: they are related as are form and content. It is difficult to decide, however, whether in double-entry book-keeping capitalism provided itself with a tool to make it more effective, or whether capitalism derives from the ' spirit ' of double-entry book-keeping." I would prefer a far more modest appraisal of the role and significance of double entry, related more particularly to the first two qualities of the system considered in this section.

The spread of double-entry book-keeping from Italy to the rest of Europe, and thence further afield, was largely the result of the influence of treatises describing and explaining the system and its practice, and of business practices in Italy and those of Italian merchants elsewhere, which were copied by others who came into contact with them. It is interesting to see, in Dr. Nishikawa's essay in this volume, the similar influence of books and of foreigners in the introduction and spread of double entry in modern Japan. An historical parallel for

13 For a general discussion of sources and views, and a critical examination of the Sombartian thesis, see my " Scientific Bookkeeping and the Rise of Capitalism," *Economic History Review*, second series, I (1949), reprinted in W. T. Baxter (ed.), *Studies in Accounting*. Professor de Roover's essay in the present volume has some observations on the role of double entry in early economic development.
14 Sombart, *ibid.*, p. 118. (" Man kann schlechthin Kapitalismus ohne doppelte Buchhaltung nicht denken: sie verhalten sich wie Form und Inhalt zueinander. Und man kann im Zweifel sein, ob sich der Kapitalismus in der doppelten Buchhaltung ein Werkzeug, um seine Kräfte zu betätigen, geschaffen oder ob die doppelte Buchhaltung erst den Kapitalismus aus ihrem Geiste geboren habe.")

the peculiar twist given to early Japanese double entry by local influences may be found in the first treatises published in German in the sixteenth century; the works of both Schreiber and Gottlieb display features which are not encountered in Italian practice or teaching (for example, the use of a separate " ledger " for merchandise accounts, and the profit calculation derived from but not fully integrated with the double-entry records), and suggest a lingering influence of earlier book-keeping practices in Germany.[15]

The fact that textbooks played their part in spreading knowledge of double entry lends more than specialist interest to Mr. Jackson's account, in this volume, of the ways in which double entry was elucidated and taught. Explanation by way of personification of accounts,[16] the memorising of rules and examples, and the copying of models were probably the most important methods of instruction. Examples have survived of exercises from textbooks copied out by neophyte book-keepers; these " documents " provide some hazard—though usually not a serious one—to the historian searching for documentary records: the copy-book of the struggling student may be mistaken for the records of a business enterprise.[17]

It is difficult, however, to assess the relative importance of the printed word and direct commercial contacts in developing familiarity with the double-entry system. It is also difficult to arrive at a just view of the role of Pacioli's treatise in particular. It seems that those who first investigated the history of accounting were apt to over-state the importance of his work. The tendency now is to believe that Pacioli's writing was based on a manuscript circulating in Venice, and that this manuscript was only one of several which all contributed to the spread of double entry in Italy, and from thence to other countries.

A question which has rarely been asked is how widespread the

---

[15] On these early works, see my " Notes on the Origin of Double-Entry Book-keeping," *Accounting Review*, XXII (1947), pp. 266–268. The division of the ledger into two parts is found in the second example in Matthäus Schwarz's early sixteenth century manuscript work on book-keeping; this example, he writes, is kept according to German usage. Schwarz's example also resembles the other works in that not all the debits appear on the left-hand side of the accounts; the authors, however, make the necessary adjustments when combining the accounts. On Schwarz's work, see A. Weitnauer, *Venezianischer Handel der Fugger* (Munich and Leipzig, 1931).

[16] An example of personification of accounts in practice is given in the article " Mr. Chest and Mr. Box " in this volume.

[17] The German historian Penndorf examined an account-book in a German collection which was described as the book of a business-man, Lohn. He ascertained that this was mistaken, and that the book was the exercise book of a student of a German schoolmaster in Antwerp, Mennher, who published several treatises. One of the clues which helped to establish the nature of the records was an entry for some sugar given to an advocate (Gelltlieb) to make him act more energetically; the same entry appears in one of Mennher's works. (B. Penndorf, *Geschichte der Buchhaltung in Deutschland* [Leipzig, 1913], p. 139).

Another example of a copy-book preserved for 150 years is mentioned by Mr. Goldberg in his contribution in this volume.

practice of double entry had become by, say, the end of the eighteenth century. The spate of treatises and the work of " professional " book-keepers no doubt were responsible for the use of double entry in some cases where a less complete system would have been quite adequate. On the other hand, the " mystery " of double entry might have militated against its use in other cases. In general, it may be suggested that, in England at least, double entry was practised at that time mainly by merchants engaged in wholesale trade, and by no means by all of them. The final triumph of double entry as a system practised by the vast majority of firms, large and small, came later when the proliferation of joint stock companies and the attentions of income-tax authorities gave rise to the growing influence of professional accountants to whom, not unnaturally, double entry is synonymous with a sound book-keeping system.[18]

Double entry is basically a classifying device or technique of considerable efficacy, adaptability and versatility. As such the system itself does not determine what transactions or items should fall within its sway.[19] The system remains intact, for example, whether or not unrealised increases or decreases in the value of assets are recorded in the ledger. Again, the system does not determine how a particular item should be classified, for example, whether a particular debit should be transferred as a negative item to the profit-and-loss account or retained as an " asset " in the balance sheet. As a classifying technique, the system of double entry has little, if any, influence on profit calculations and balance sheet valuations, issues which are central to the work of the modern accountant; in a sense, all the system does in this field is to ensure consistency between the profit calculation and net changes in recorded asset values.

The early accounting treatises have very little to say about the conventions and rules governing profit calculations and asset valuations. These conventions and rules were hammered out in large part during the nineteenth century though earlier traces of them can be found. Their development was intimately connected with the growth of the joint stock company, and the consequential increasing importance of absentee shareholders on the one hand, and " professional " management on the other.

One suspects that there must be a mass of records in private and public archives which, if carefully studied, would yield clues to

---

[18] Double-entry book-keeping was prescribed in Table A of the 1856 Companies Act in England (see p. 362, below); this appendix to the Act was not binding on all companies, but could be adopted as articles of association by any company.

[19] Several of the early treatises on double entry give examples which exclude fixed assets; these are examined in P. Kats, " Early History of Book-keeping," *Journal of Accountancy*, XLVII (1929). The exclusion of certain assets from the books of Sir Thomas Gresham is discussed by Mr. Ramsey (p. 196, below).

establish the chronology of the development of present-day accounting " principles " and practices and to explain how they came about. Unfortunately, it seems that very little use has been made of this material. It is all the more welcome, therefore, to include in this volume the essay by Mr. Pollins, an economic historian, which summarises and illustrates the results of his work on early railway accounts. One of the main conclusions reached is that considerations of financial policy affected the rules or procedures used for the calculation of periodic profits presented in the published accounts. It seems that this conclusion applies also to company accounting generally in the nineteenth century and even later. The practice of the " secret reserve " is merely the most obvious illustration of the tendency for the statement of profits in published accounts to be conditioned by managements' ideas on how the interests of their companies were best served.[20] The published accounts were used to give information to absentee shareholders and other interested parties; but it was generally conceded that it was proper to make such adjustments in the calculation of profits and in the presentation of accounts as were considered in good faith to be necessary in the interests of the company.

The accounting conventions and rules which developed in the nineteenth century were not unnaturally characterised by the wide latitude that was left to business men in drawing up the final accounts of their enterprises. A further development in the history of financial accounting is the growth of influences and attitudes which have tended to narrow somewhat the area of discretion as well as to inject a high degree of responsibility in the making of accounting decisions affecting published accounts. These influences and their effectiveness have varied from country to country. In England the strength and rising status of the accountancy profession, the growing vigilance of the stock exchange authorities and the initiative of government have all made their contribution. Messrs. Edey and Panikpakdi in their essay in this volume trace the story of the interest of the legislature in company accounting during the nineteenth century.

The exercise of judgment and discretion still plays a large part in decisions affecting entries in the periodic final accounts of companies.[1]

---

[20] One example must suffice. The annual report of the London Brick Co., Ltd., for 1938 includes the following: " It will be readily appreciated that the effectiveness of present and future depreciation is much enhanced because of the exceptionally low figures to which our fixed assets have already been written down. Thus from past prosperity have we provided for possible future adversity, a policy designed . . . ."

[1] It would be interesting in this connection to trace the origins of differences in British and American accounting rules and conventions. To what extent do such differences reflect differences in the objectives and outlook of company management in the two countries? On this, see Kenneth L. Smith, " Capital Gains and Losses in Accounting," *Accounting Review*, XIV (1939), esp. pp. 131 *et seq.*

This is probably inevitable. However, the question may be posed whether, if published accounts are designed to convey information to shareholders and potential investors, the usual published accounts might not with advantage be supported by other accounting data more objective in character than profit figures and balance sheet values.[2] Would not some return of the main heads of receipts and expenditures be a valuable adjunct to the usual financial statements in the published accounts of companies? This is not a question for the historian to answer, though he may be permitted to point out that it may have been pure chance which in the nineteenth century required the final accounts of companies to serve in several possibly incompatible capacities—as accounts of stewardship (in a narrow sense) rendered to absentee owners, as statements of profitability and financial condition for the information of shareholders as well as of potential investors and creditors, and as statements of divisible profits which were inevitably influenced by considerations of financial and general managerial policy.

Another question suggests itself to a student of the history of accounting. The accounting rules and conventions which are now widely followed were developed in the nineteenth century. Can we be sure that they are appropriate in the changed circumstances of today, and more particularly in the so-called age of inflation? Already a voice has been raised in the British House of Commons, protesting that current accounting practice is hamstrung by rules worked out five centuries ago on the plains of Lombardy, and a writer in the *Journal of Accountancy* has pronounced " a plague on Pacioli." These historical allusions may not be very relevant, for double entry is not the culprit; but they express a growing sentiment that the traditional practices of company accounting may be in some respects anachronistic.

---

[2] Thus a leading company chairman of the 1930's (Arthur Chamberlain): " The items [in final accounts] on which different views can be taken, sometimes with perfect honesty and sometimes with less, sometimes with prudent foresight and sometimes with light-hearted lack of it, are legion, and between the two extremes I would almost undertake to draw up two balance-sheets for the same company, both coming within an auditor's statutory certificate, in which practically the only recognisable items would be the name and the capital authorised and issued." (Reprinted in Baxter, *op. cit.*, p. 203).

Howard C. Greer made some calculations for eighteen American corporations with total reported profits of about 185 million dollars. Recalculated on the most " liberal " basis compatible with contemporary practices the total rose to 218 million dollars, and on the most " conservative " basis was reduced to 98 million dollars. (" Application of Accounting Rules and Standards to Financial State ments," *Accounting Review*, XIII [1938], pp. 341–345.)

Greek and Roman Accounting

G. E. M. de Ste. Croix*

(*Note.*—At the request of the editors of this volume I have done my best to
make the text of this essay easily intelligible to those who cannot read Greek
or Latin and have little or no knowledge of the ancient world. At the same
time I have tried to interest specialists in Greek and Roman history, law and
literature: the footnotes, giving references to sources and to the modern
literature, and the Appendices, are intended mainly for them. Standard abbreviations have been employed in citing ancient and modern works. Any which
are unfamiliar to the reader can be identified by a glance at the lists of
abbreviations in, *e.g.,* the *Oxford Classical Dictionary*, Liddell and Scott's
Greek-English Lexicon, Lewis and Short's *Latin Dictionary*, or the *Cambridge
Ancient History*.)

THE question has often been asked in modern times how far the
Greeks and Romans developed systematic book-keeping, and in
particular whether they employed double entry. It will help to put
the subject-matter of this essay in better perspective if I make it clear
from the start that the Greeks and Romans, far from reaching the
advanced stage of accounting at which double entry becomes possible,
thought, and kept their books, mainly in terms of receipts and
expenditure rather than debit and credit; and furthermore that they
never even got as far as the habitual separation of what we should
call debit and credit entries by writing them in two separate columns,
let alone on opposite pages of an account. That the Romans, at any
rate, regularly wrote debit and credit entries on opposite pages of
their accounts has been asserted again and again, without ever (as far
as I know) being contradicted; but the whole conception is false, as I
shall show. Ancient accounts are not disposed in double columns:
they are not even placed precisely in single columns. If, as sometimes
happens, the figures are written approximately underneath each other,
this is done, as we shall see, not in order to assist computation but
merely to give a neater appearance, or to make it easier and less
fatiguing to follow the account and trace individual items within it.
The Greeks and Romans did develop some quite advanced institutions
in the fields of property law and commercial practice; but their book-
keeping, minutely detailed as it often was, remained rudimentary in
method and never grew into an integrated double-entry complex, with
interlocking accounts, or even into a unified single-entry system.
Greek and Roman accounting took the form of individual records of

---

* Fellow of New College, Oxford.

debts and of receipts and payments, and miscellaneous inventories, rather than accounts in the modern sense. The fundamental reason for this was, of course, that the Greek and Roman economy failed to develop to the point at which an advanced system of book-keeping would have become generally necessary. However, a subsidiary reason for the backwardness of Greek and Roman accounting— important in its own right, in my opinion—was the systems of numeral notation employed in the Graeco-Roman world, a question which will be discussed in detail towards the end of this essay.

A word of warning is necessary at the outset about terminology. If we thoughtlessly use as equivalent to the Greek and Latin terms modern expressions associated with a much more highly developed system of book-keeping, we shall tend to form our ideas of ancient practice after the model of contemporary accounting methods, and this would be a serious handicap. It is above all essential to realise that the very conceptions of debit and credit in the technical modern sense are alien to the thought and practice of the Greek and Roman world. Various Latin words such as *acceptum* and *expensum, lucrum* and *damnum,* are often translated " credit " and " debit," and sometimes this is convenient and harmless enough; but we must always remember that the words in question really mean " receipts " and " expenditure," " profit " and " loss." Expressions like *lucro apponere, in lucris ponere*,[1] which are often used figuratively, mean " treat it as gain," rather than " enter it to credit." I hope I have said enough, by way of introduction, to indicate that what I have to say here is going to be pitched, so to speak, in a very low key. I must emphasise that I have not tried to give anything like a complete picture of Greek and Roman accounting, but only a general summary, with special attention to some points which have not previously received the attention they deserve.

I. The Sources

The first thing we have to do is to consider the nature of the sources from which our knowledge of Greek and Roman accounting is derived. They are written partly in Greek, partly in Latin. When in this essay I use the expressions " the Greeks " and " the Romans," I shall mean those who wrote in Greek and those who wrote in Latin respectively. For my purposes the Apostle Paul would count as a Greek because he wrote in Greek, although he could also claim to be a Roman citizen and may well have spoken Aramaic at times when in purely Jewish circles. Under the Roman Empire, Greek was the predominant language, for purposes of writing at any rate, in the Asiatic provinces, in the eastern and southern Balkans, and in Egypt,

---

[1] Hor., *Od.* 1.9.14–15; Cic., *ad Fam.* 7.24.1.

Cyrenaica and Sicily; Latin was the predominant language in the rest of the Empire.

We know very little of Greek civilisation before about 600 B.C., and it is not until the fifth and fourth centuries that our information becomes really plentiful. Nearly all of it, at this period, relates principally to Athens, the most civilised and brilliant of the hundreds of little " city-states " which dotted the shores and islands of the Mediterranean (especially, of course, the Aegean), the Sea of Marmora and the Black Sea. I shall speak of the fifth and fourth centuries B.C. as " the Classical Greek period." So far as the eastern Mediterranean world is concerned, the last three centuries B.C. are always referred to as " the Hellenistic period." At this time Rome was under a republican form of government. With the last generation before Christ, when Augustus consolidated an essentially monarchical rule, there begins the Roman Imperial period.

For convenience I am going to divide the evidence for Greek and Roman accounting into three main branches: legal, literary and documentary. The legal sources, which are partly documentary in character but have been transmitted to us along with the literary texts, are predominantly Roman; we do not possess the texts of many Greek laws dealing with economic questions. By far the most important of the legal sources, for present purposes, is the *Digest*, a compilation of mainly disconnected excerpts from the treatises of the Roman jurists of earlier days, arranged under subject-headings. The *Digest* was issued in 533 and forms part of the Emperor Justinian's great *Corpus Juris Civilis*. It contains a large number of references to accounts. Another of the legal sources which is constantly cited by modern writers on ancient accounting—mainly owing to misunderstanding of a particular passage [2]—is the *Institutes* of Gaius, a textbook of Roman law written in the mid-second century.

My second branch of evidence, the literary, includes all kinds of published literature. For the general history of the Graeco-Roman world, the literary evidence is on the whole the most important; but for economic history it is relatively much less helpful. The Greek and Roman authors in general were not interested in the economic processes of everyday life; they were content, one might say, to take their economics for granted, and even when they were writing history they were much more concerned with political, diplomatic and military affairs—with wars, court intrigues, the exploits of great men, political and dynastic struggles, and so forth. There are a few literary works, however, which give us a certain amount of evidence about financial practices: the most important of these are the speeches of the

---

[2] See Appendix C, below.

Athenian orators of the fourth century B.C., above all Demosthenes. The speeches of Cicero, from the middle of the last century B.C., deal mainly with political matters, but I shall have occasion to refer to some interesting and illuminating passages in some of his speeches concerning the keeping of accounts.

The last of the three main kinds of evidence, the documentary, is much the most varied. I shall divide it into two branches, and say a little about each: epigraphic evidence (that provided by inscriptions —words written on stone or other durable material), and papyrological evidence (that of papyri and ostraca, almost entirely from Egypt). Epigraphy [3] is the study of verbal inscriptions, most of which, so far as the Graeco-Roman world is concerned, are on stone, although a few are on wood or on metal, mainly bronze or lead. Inscriptions were collected by more than one ancient Greek, and from Renaissance times onwards they have been copied and studied more and more carefully. It is difficult to give an accurate estimate of the total number of Latin and Greek inscriptions which have been edited and published in modern times, but the number runs well into six figures, the Latin inscriptions probably outnumbering the Greek by something like three to one. These inscriptions range from a few words or even letters to hundreds of lines. Comparatively few Latin inscriptions, or Greek inscriptions of the Roman Imperial period, give us much information about financial matters of any sort, but from the Classical Greek and Hellenistic periods (the last five centuries B.C.) we have a mass of material, very useful for our subject, in the form of temple and state accounts and other documents.

The other branch of documentary evidence, and perhaps the most important of all kinds of evidence for our immediate purposes, is the papyrological.[4] In this category are generally classed together the papyri and ostraca (with some parchments) which have been found in modern times in great quantities in Upper Egypt (southern and central Egypt, including for present purposes the Fayum) and also at a few other places. Ostraca, the Greek term for potsherds (broken pieces of

---

[3] Those unacquainted with the subject who wish for an elementary introduction to it' might consult the articles " Epigraphy, Greek " (by M. N. Tod) and " Epigraphy, Latin " (by R. H. Barrow), on pp. 327-331 of the *Oxford Classical Dict.* (1949), where bibliographies will also be found.

[4] There is an excellent short introduction to this subject, *ibid.*, 645-646 (" Papyrology, Greek," by C. H. Roberts). An admirable recent book by Sir Harold Bell (H. Idris Bell, *Egypt from Alexander the Great to the Arab Conquest*, 1948) has an introductory chapter on " Papyri and the Science of Papyrology," and the Biliography at the end gives a very useful list of the principal editions of Greek papyri and ostraca, with the standard abbreviations by which they are commonly cited. Most of the numerous editions of papyri by English-speaking scholars (*e.g.*, *P. Oxy.*, *P. Ryl.*, *P. Fay.*, *P. Tebt.*) give translations of at least the more important papyri. A handy selection of Greek papyri, with facing English translations, prepared by two leading papyrologists, will be found in the Loeb *Select Papyri* (2 vols., 1932-1934, ed. A. S. Hunt and C. C. Edgar).

pottery), were much used as a writing material in Egypt, after its conquest by Alexander the Great in 332, and inscribed ostraca have been found in large numbers in Upper Egypt. Tax receipts are particularly common, but there are a fair number of accounts, necessarily brief. Very much more important are the papyri—a term which is often used in this connection to include parchments. From at least the sixth century B.C. until the fourth century of the Christian era, papyrus was the main writing material of Greek and Roman civilisation. Pliny the Elder [5] could say that it was papyrus which preserved human achievement from oblivion, and that without it mankind would have little culture and no history. Papyrus had been used in Egypt from at least the third millennium B.C., and our oldest inscribed papyrus is something like 4,000 years old.[6] The papyrus used as a writing material—the manufacture of which was an Egyptian monopoly—was made from the pith in the stem of the papyrus plant, which used to flourish in the swamps of the Nile Delta (where it is now extinct) and grew also in one or two other places, though on a very much smaller scale.[7] There have been a couple of finds of papyri in the Delta and a few outside Egypt. Apart from these, the whole mass of the papyri have come from Upper Egypt, where alone the sandy soil is dry enough to preserve great quantities of this perishable material for centuries; and the great majority have been found in rubbish heaps, ruined buildings, or tombs. Greek papyri have been known since 1778, but the regular flow of publication did not begin until the 1890's, and it is only since then that papyrology has really come into its own. The range of dates of the Greek papyri covers roughly a thousand years, from the late fourth century B.C. until after the Arab conquest of Egypt in A.D. 642. Latin papyri also occur, but they are far fewer in number than those written in Greek, which in Egypt was spoken at first only by the relatively small immigrant Greek population, but long before the Roman conquest in 30 B.C. had become the regular language of the educated upper classes. The known Greek and Latin papyri (including very many fragmentary ones) already number tens of thousands, of which well over 20,000 have been published. Some of the papyri are literary texts, but by far the greater number are documentary, and the variety of these is very great— almost as great as that of ancient inscriptions, but covering a different range of subjects.

And here we come right to the heart of our subject, the nature of

---

[5] *NH* 13.68–70: papyrus is the thing " qua constat immortalitas hominum " (§ 70); and " cum chartae usu maxime humanitas vitae constet, certe memoria " (§ 68).
[6] *Papyrus Prisse*, now in Paris.
[7] See F. G. Kenyon, *Books and Readers in Ancient Greece and Rome*[2] (1951) 47 *et seq.*; also 121–125, containing part of the text of Pliny, *NH* 13.68–78 (with trans.), the *locus classicus* on the manufacture of papyrus.

ancient accounting methods, because among the documentary papyri are very large numbers of actual accounts, both public and private. The great majority of the modern writers who have discussed ancient accounting have concentrated entirely upon the literary and legal sources and have tried to infer from them what ancient accounts must have been like, oblivious of the fact that we actually have preserved among the papyri hundreds of pages of accounts kept by the Greeks and Romans over a period of a thousand years, in the exact form in which they were written—not to mention a very large quantity of Greek public accounts recorded in inscriptions on stone. Making false inferences from the legal and literary sources, and ignoring (or at best imperfectly understanding) the massive and conclusive evidence provided by the inscriptions and papyri, these writers have given an entirely false picture of Greek and Roman accounting, which they have represented as much more advanced and nearer to modern practice than in fact it was.

In Appendix A (pp. 66–68 below) I have given an outline of modern work on the subject of Greek and Roman accounting. Most of it is of very little value, but there are a few useful studies of limited scope and one article of outstanding interest.

II. The Absence of " Bilateral Form "

It is a fundamental error to imagine, as writers on this subject habitually have done since at least the seventeenth century,[8] that in Greek and (more especially) Roman accounts receipts and payments were placed on opposite pages. In all Greek and Latin literature, there is just one passage which does appear at first sight to support this conception. It occurs in Pliny the Elder's *Natural History*,[9] written in the seventies of the first century. Emphasising the sovereign power of Fortune, Pliny says, " Huic omnia expensa, huic omnia feruntur accepta, et in tota ratione mortalium sola utramque paginam facit." (" To her account all expenditure and all receipts are entered, and in the account-book of every mortal she alone makes out both pages.") Certainly, *utramque paginam* means not just " each page," but " each of two pages." Taken in conjunction with

---

[8] Richard Dafforne, in *The Merchants Mirrour* (1635; 3rd ed., 1660), quotes with approval the statement of Simon Stevin, the Dutch mathematician of the early 17th cent., " That the one side of their [the Romans'] Book was used for Debtor, the other for Creditor, is manifest "—from Pliny, *NH* 2.22 (see below). Among many recent writers who have made the same assumption are F. de Zulueta, *The Insts. of Gaius* II 163; P. F. Girard, *Man. élém. de droit rom.*[8] 527; and various authors whose works are cited in Appendix A below, *viz.*: Melis 367, 436; Voigt 531–532, *etc.*; Beigel 173–181; Früchtl 32; Roby II 291; Murray 126. And see T. Zerbi, *Le origini della partita doppia* (1952) 64, where the passage in Pliny is taken as a reference to " conti a sezioni divise."

[9] 2.22.

the reference to expenditure and receipts in the first part of the sentence, these words have created the almost universal impression that the Romans entered their receipts on one page of their account-books and their payments on the other, as we do today.   That is a reasonable enough inference from the wording of this passage alone; but in the light of all our other evidence I can say categorically that it is a wrong inference.   I will not enter into details here regarding the physical form of Greek and Roman accounts, a subject which I have treated at some length in Appendix B (pp. 68–72 below): it will be sufficient if I say that in Pliny's day Romans apparently still kept their more formal accounts mainly on waxed tablets, although papyrus, in sheets and rolls, was also used.   When he remarks that Fortune makes out " both pages " [10] in the account-book of every mortal, Pliny must mean simply the two pages of an open set of tablets, without there being any implication that one page consists of debit and the other of credit entries.   In the whole of Greek and Latin literature, as far as I am aware, there is nothing whatever to suggest that receipts and payments were placed on opposite pages of an account, nor, as far as I have been able to discover, does this particular variety of " bilateral form " appear in any Greek or Latin inscription, tablet or papyrus. The only writing tablet I know containing actual accounts which has survived from antiquity is one from Verespatak in Transylvania (Alburnum Maius in the Roman province of Dacia) [11] giving a list of sums of money received and articles purchased: here there are quite neat columns, and in general the receipts happen to appear on the left-hand leaf, the payments on the right; but the total sum in hand on the last day of April (166 denarii or a little more) is placed at the head of the right-hand leaf, and there is no question of an account with two " sides."   Occasionally, as in the case of the Verespatak tablet, we may find some attempt at tabulation in a single column,[12] to assist the eye in running over the account, or a tendency to group together receipts and payments respectively [13]; but such practices, when they do occur, are not carried out rigorously.

As far as my knowledge goes, it is only in one surviving document, a unique papyrus roll of the Roman period from Karanis in the

---

[10] *Pagina* is used indifferently in Latin for one side of a leaf of a codex or tablet, as here, and for a single column (σελίς in Greek) in a papyrus roll (as in Pliny, *NH* 13.80 ; Mart. 2.6.2, with 3)—and perhaps also for one side of a single sheet of papyrus.

[11] *CIL* III ii, p. 953, no. xv, presumably dating from the early or middle 2nd cent.

[12] It will be well to give some examples, among many others which might be quoted, of papyri containing figures placed in column: *P. Cairo Masp.* I 67,056–67,059 (see pl. xxv–xxvi in that volume); *P. Hamb.* 56 ; *P. Mich.* IV (" Tax Rolls from Karanis ") ; *P. Ryl.* IV 627, 629, 630–637, 640–641 ; *P. Oxy.* IV 737 (see pl. viii in that vol.), a Latin papyrus containing a list of wages paid ; and papyri (also Latin) nos. 1 (lines 59-65), 2 (lines 9–13) and 3 in J. O. Tjäder, *Die nichtliterar. latein. Pap. Italiens aus der Zeit 445–700* (1955).

[13] See Fig. I on p. 24 below, also p. 37 below.

Fayum, to be further discussed later,[14] that we find an ancient account drawn up in " bilateral form"; and here we have the other variety of bilateral form [15]—receipts and payments not on opposite " pages " (the successive columns of a papyrus roll do not naturally fall into pairs) but separately aligned vertically side by side within each column of writing. The peculiar form of this papyrus account is not to be taken as a fundamental advance in book-keeping method, because it can only have been adopted for convenience in perusing the account and identifying individual items within it. Now it may be said that if a particular book-keeper in Egypt was sensible enough to devise one type of bilateral form, suited to accounts kept in independent columns on papyrus, Roman book-keepers may very well have adopted the other type of bilateral form, suited to accounts kept on tablets with pairs of facing " pages." I believe, however, that such an inference would be quite unjustified. Because writing materials in antiquity were not nearly as easy to obtain and as cheap as they are today, the variety of bilateral form in which receipts and payments appear on opposite pages was surely much less likely to be adopted than the variety which we find in the papyrus from Karanis, for the former necessarily takes up more space vertically, except where receipts and payments happen to be recorded in equal quantities of writing—if there are more entries of one sort than of the other, whole pages on one side of the account may be left blank and wasted. This would have been intolerable to ancient book-keepers, who were in general obliged to be more economical of space than are their modern counterparts.

III. THE CLASSICAL GREEK PERIOD

My next task is to discuss some of the more important pieces of detailed evidence for accounting practices which have survived from the ancient world, beginning with the Classical Greek period. I ought first to explain that it was among the Greeks, and as late as the sixth century B.C., that coined money came into general use for the first time in human history. The adoption of money as the normal medium of valuation and exchange made it possible for book-keeping to rise to an entirely new level: all possessions and all transactions could at last be recorded not as so many fields, so many slaves, so many bushels of grain, or the exchange of so many casks of wine against so many pounds of silver, but in every case as so many units of a particular system of currency. All possessions and transactions, then, could be so recorded; but it does not by any means follow that in practice they always were. Although the Greeks and Romans

---

14 *P. Goodsp. Cair.* 30. See pp. 35–36 below.
15 *Cf.* p. 64 below.

usually did reduce all items in their accounts to a common monetary denominator, they often failed to do so. Property might still be hoarded in kind, and reckoned in public or private accounts simply as measures of wheat or units of a foreign currency, instead of being expressed in terms of the prevailing monetary system. There are examples of this among the inscriptions of the Classical Greek period and many among the papyri from Hellenistic and even Roman Egypt: we shall be noticing some of these later.[16] When the units of entry are different from the standard monetary ones, the items concerned are normally placed by themselves in separate accounts, but occasionally (as in the building accounts of the Parthenon, to be considered presently) a few such entries intrude into accounts which are otherwise kept in terms of the local system of currency.

Before coined money existed, trading was done by barter or in terms of some universally valued unit such as the ox; and when the precious metals were used for purposes of exchange, they were reckoned by weight. The standard measure of value for Homer's Achaeans was the ox, as it was for the early Romans, whose very word for money, *pecunia*, is derived from *pecus*, cattle. At the all-in wrestling match between Ajax and Odysseus at the funeral games of Patroclus in the *Iliad*,[17] the winner was to receive a large tripod, said to be worth twelve oxen, and the loser a woman, worth four oxen.[18] Even the most civilised peoples of the Near East—the Sumerians, Babylonians, Assyrians, Egyptians, Hittites and Phoenicians—had never used coins, in the sense of lumps of metal stamped with the mark of some individual or State as a guarantee of their purity and weight, and intended to be used as currency. Such stamps on pieces of metal from Babylonia and Assyria seem to have attested only the purity of the metal, not its weight, and these pieces therefore are not true coins. No one now disputes that the place of the introduction of coinage was western Asia Minor, but some scholars, for no very good reason, have preferred to credit the Ionian Greeks with the invention, rather than the Lydians, to whom it is attributed not only by Herodotus [19] but also by the philosopher Xenophanes,[20] who wrote at least as early as 500 B.C. The date of the innovation has been the subject of considerable dispute, but E. S. G. Robinson [1] of the British Museum has recently advanced very strong arguments for thinking that the invention of coinage took place not much earlier than about 630 B.C. The evidence is mainly the foundation deposit and later deposits in

---

[16] See pp. 24 and 31–32 below.
[17] XXIII 700–705.
[18] *Cf. Od.* I 428–433.
[19] 1.94.1.
[20] Fr. 4 in Diels⁶ I 130, *ap.* Poll. 9.83.
[1] In *JHS* 71 (1951) 156–167 ; *cf.* P. Jacobsthal, *ibid.* 85–95.

the temple of Artemis at Ephesus—" Diana of the Ephesians," as our Biblical translators call her. These deposits include a series of extremely primitive coins, some Lydian, some probably Greek, in examining which, as Robinson happily puts it, " one has the feeling of assisting at the very birth of coinage." If, then, we assign the earliest coins of Lydia and the Ionian Greek cities to about 630 B.C. and just after, we shall have to put the coinages of the towns of mainland Greece later still, since the earliest of these are clearly less primitive than the earliest issues from Asia Minor and must have been copied from the latter when they had already passed the rudimentary stage. The earliest coins are of the precious metals, particularly electrum (mixed gold and silver). Small change was slower to appear, and the universal use of coins in the Greek world developed only slowly during the sixth century.

We can now examine some of the evidence for accounting in the Classical Greek period. It is of course too early for documentary papyri, but we have a formidable body of public and sacred accounts on stone [2] and some informative literary passages. The epigraphic evidence at first sight looks quite varied in character, the accounts apparently taking many different forms; but everyone who goes through the material observantly will soon find that the variations are not very important and their range not really very wide. It has not been easy to find representative specimens suitable for reproduction here: most of the accounts are incomplete or fragmentary, and in many cases it is impossible to convey an adequate notion of their form and content without giving long extracts. I have chosen two accounts, the second of which, in pure narrative form, is a much more characteristic specimen than the first, which shows perhaps the highest degree of tabulation I have discovered in any Greek account carved on stone.

The first document [3] is an extract from the building accounts of the Parthenon, covering the Attic (*i.e.,* Athenian) year 434–433 B.C. The erection of this temple of Athena took place between the years 447–446 and 433–432 B.C., and the accounts were then inscribed on a large marble stele, which was set up on the Acropolis of Athens.

---

[2] Representative specimens of 5th and 4th cent. public accounts of different kinds, mainly but not exclusively Athenian, will be found in M. N. Tod, *Sel. of Gk. Historical Inscr.* I² nos. 30, 38, 46–47, 50, 52–56, 62, 64, 69–71, 75, 78–81, 83, 85, 92; II nos. 125, 140, 160, 169, 172. Almost all the 331 quarto pages of *IG* II², Pars ii, Fasc. 1, are devoted to Athenian public accounts of the 4th cent. Vol. II of *The Athenian Tribute Lists,* by B. D. Meritt, H. T. Wade-Gery and M. F. McGregor, gives the texts of all the surviving documents dealing with the finances of the Athenian Empire of the 5th cent. The accounts of the temple of Delphi in the 4th cent., which survive in considerable quantities, are published in *Fouilles de Delphes* III, Fasc. v (ed. E. Bourguet, 1932); there are lengthy selections in *SIG*³ I nos. 239–253; and see Bourguet, *L'admin. financière du sanct. pythique au IVe siècle av. J.-C.* (1905).
[3] Tod I² 52=*IG* I² 352.

24 *Greek and Roman Accounting*

Fragments of this inscription have survived, the best preserved portion being that for the year 434–433, of which we have the greater part of the record. I give it in a literal translation which also reproduces the arrangement of the original as closely as possible (Figure I). I have substituted Arabic numerals for the " old Attic " numeral signs. Square brackets indicate restorations of fragmentary passages, and the sign [– – –] represents portions which cannot safely be restored at all. The monetary units are Attic silver talents, drachmae and obols (6 ob. = 1 dr.; 6,000 dr. = 1 tal.).

Figure 1

The following were the receipts of the fourteenth board of Overseers, whose Secretary was Anticles, the first Secretary of the Council in this year being Metagenes, and Crates being Athenian Archon (i.e., the date is 434–433 B.C.):

1,470 dr.	balance remaining from the preceding year.
70	gold staters of Lampsacus.
27 1/6	gold staters of Cyzicus.
25,000 dr.	from the Treasurers of the Goddess whose Secretary was Crates of Lamptra (i.e., those of 434–433 B.C.).
1,372 dr.	proceeds of sale of gold, weight 98? dr.
1,305 dr., } *4 ob.*	proceeds of sale of ivory, weight ?3? tal., 60 dr.

Expenditure :

[– – –] [– – –]	purchases.
[– – –]	payments under contract.
[– – –]	to quarrymen at Pentelicus and men loading stones on the carts.
16,392 dr.	wages to sculptors of the pediment-reliefs.
1,800? dr.	to employees paid by the month.
[– – –]	balance remaining from this year.
[70	gold staters of Lampsacus.]
[27 1/6	gold staters of Cyzicus.]

The Lampsacene and Cyzicene staters, which were coins foreign to the Athenian monetary system, are recorded in effect as bullion and not in terms of the Attic silver coinage, and they appear unchanged throughout the Parthenon building accounts. Here we have a good example of the tendency referred to earlier, for a Greek account occasionally to express the value of a particular piece of property in units other than those of the system of currency in terms of which the account is being kept.

The second document [4] is a small part of a very long inscription on marble, found at Eleusis in Attica, containing the accounts for the year 329–328 B.C. of the Eleusinian Overseers and the Treasurers of the Two Goddesses (Demeter and Persephone), who were public officials, elected by the Athenian general assembly. The inscription consists of 312 lines, each of 81 letters. It deals separately with each

---

[4] *IG* II² (ii 1) 1672, lines 1, 114–137.

of the ten " prytanies " into which the Attic year was divided.   I can
do no more than give extracts from the record of the fifth prytany,
which I have again translated literally, following the narrative form
of the original (Figure II).

Figure II

(Line 1) *Account of the Eleusinian Overseers and the Treasurers of the
Two Goddesses, in the archonship of Cephisophon (i.e., 329–328 B.C.) . . .
(lines 114–116) in the fifth prytany, that of the tribe Cecropis : balance in
the hands of the Treasurers of the Two Goddesses 1,565 dr., 2 3/8 ob.;
balance in the hands of the Treasurer of the Two Goddesses Nicophilus
of Alopece 42 dr., 3 ob.; balance in the hands of the Eleusinian Overseers
1 5/8 ob.; and the amount distributed to the Overseers by the Apodectae
850 dr. Of this the following has been spent : . . .* (There are now 18
lines, nos. 116–134, containing particulars of expenditure, including)
4 faggots, price 2 ob. . . . (The account for the prytany ends) *Total of
expenditure 950 dr., 1 5/8 ob. Total of money received from the
Apodectae 850 dr. Balance in the hands of the Treasurers of the Two
Goddesses 1,565 dr., 2 3/8 ob., and in the hands of the Treasurer of the
Two Goddesses Nicophilus of Alopece 32 dr. 3 ob. . . .* (line 137) *Account
of the Eleusinian Overseers . . . in the sixth prytany* (etc.).

This document, in its complete lack of tabulation and the minute
details it gives of most items of expenditure, is unfortunately more
typical of fifth and fourth century public accounts than the briefer and
much better arranged Parthenon account.   The two documents represent almost the extremes which are to be found in public accounts of
the Classical Greek period.   Various intermediate stages appear in
other sets of accounts.[5]

Now there can be little doubt that the main reason for recording
all this material in permanent form and " publishing " it in expensive
inscriptions on stone (usually, as here, marble) was to prove to
everyone's satisfaction that the respective treasurers, public or sacred,[6]
could account for everything which had passed through their hands,
down to the very last fraction of an obol.   In some accounts, those
of the Parthenon for instance, quite substantial payments are recorded
for wages or purchases without much circumstantial detail; but in the
fourth century the three main bodies of surviving accounts (from
Athens, Delos and Delphi) are almost uniformly detailed, with very
few lapses.   The Eleusinian accounts nearly always give the most
minute particulars of expenditure, including for example details of the
clothing bought for the public slaves working under the direction of
the Overseers, and even the exact amounts spent on repairing these
slaves' sandals, with the price of the studs or nails used, at a mere

---

[5] *e.g.*, the accounts of the Athenian Amphictyons of Delos in the 4th cent. B.C.: see
esp. Tod II 125=*IG* II² 1635.
[6] It was sacred accounts which were most likely to be preserved in permanent form,
but at Athens in particular a large number of non-sacred public accounts were
also cut on stone, esp. in the 4th cent. B.C.—the navy lists, for example (*IG* II²
1604–1632).

obol per pair of sandals.[7] The concept of "petty cash," in the modern sense, which can be spent up to a certain limit without the necessity for detailed accounting by the person concerned, never really established itself as a regular feature of ancient accounts, although, as we shall see,[8] we do come across items labelled "petty cash" in a few papyrus accounts of Roman times. Greek accounts of the Classical period are normally set out in narrative form, in what seems to us a clumsy and confusing manner: receipts and payments are often intermingled and flow in a continuous stream. If a number of payments follow each other in immediate succession, as they commonly do, this may often be accidental and due to the fact that most treasurers would receive money on only a few occasions, in relatively large amounts, and between each receipt would make many small payments. There is never more than rough tabulation, as in the Parthenon accounts; and even this is infrequent.

One feature of Athenian public finance of the fifth century deserves special mention here. The Athenians in the second half of the fifth century made a habit of depositing surplus public funds with their patron goddess, Athena, under two of her aspects, Athena Polias and Athena Nike, and with the "Other Gods" collectively—"Treasurers of the Other Gods" (that was their official title: ταμίαι τῶν ἄλλων θεῶν) were appointed in 434.[9] The Athenian State then borrowed the money back from the obliging deities at low rates of interest, and ultimately, it would seem, without interest. The evidence for the loans is entirely epigraphic.[10] These borrowings were essentially book-keeping transactions, a mere transferring of public money from one treasury controlled by the State to another. It was the Athenian general assembly, the supreme governing body of the city, which appointed the sacred as well as the ordinary public treasurers, and gave instructions about the making and repayment of the loans. Transactions which in theory were loans were in practice analogous to what we should call transfers from deposit account to current account. The whole policy of building up a large reserve fund in the hands of the gods, upon which the city might draw in an emergency, seems to have been an innovation of the mid-fifth century, the work of Pericles. That statesman himself was surely a sceptic, but what he evidently wanted was to ensure that Athens' reserve fund should become as sacrosanct as possible, and not subject to indiscriminate raids by the general assembly. The best way of doing this, in a world in which most people still had a superstitious reverence for the old gods, was

---

[7] *IG* II² 1673, lines 45–51. *Cf.* 1672, lines 70–71, 102–105, 190–191, 230.

[8] See below, pp. 34–35.

[9] Tod I² 51A = *ATL*, D 1.

[10] See Tod I² 51, 64 (with the Addenda, pp. 262–263); *cf.* 75, 81, 83, 92, etc.

to entrust the gods with the money. Once that was done, the money would not in practice be simply reappropriated and spent: that would be impiety. It might, however, be borrowed at interest—of course with the proclaimed intention of repaying it; but the gods could not protect their own property save in so far as the Athenian general assembly chose to do so on their behalf. The Athenian State was the real creditor as well as the debtor. All this explains the very curious Athenian method of State book-keeping (for that is what it really amounts to): only by pretending that they were using borrowed sacred money and had to repay it with interest were the Athenians able to provide themselves with a permanent reminder of the need to put back their funds into reserve as soon as they could possibly afford to do so. They put themselves on their honour, as it were, to pay back to the gods the money they had borrowed. Unfortunately, the vast expenditure occasioned by the Peloponnesian War of 431–404 B.C., followed by the loss of their tribute-paying empire, made it hardly possible for the reserve fund to be built up anew, and in due course the debts to the gods were conveniently forgotten. Some of the more pious Athenians might well have jibbed at borrowing the money at all had they realised that it would never be repaid.

I know of few records of genuine borrowing by the Athenian State from outside sources on any appreciable scale.[11] I may add that public loans in the Greek world were infrequent and seldom important and were never funded. They played no regular part in Greek city finance.

The literary sources give us one or two useful pieces of information about private accounts—which throughout antiquity, there is every reason to believe, were not significantly better kept, from our point of view, than public accounts. The most important passage, from a forensic speech delivered soon after 370 B.C.,[12] gives us the actual text of an entry in the books of a prominent fourth-century Athenian banker, the ex-slave Pasion. The speaker, Apollodorus son of Pasion, describes how a certain merchant, Lycon of Heraclea, a customer of Pasion's bank, cast up his account (διαλογισάμενος) with Pasion in the presence of two witnesses, before setting off on a voyage to North Africa (on which he was killed by pirates), and left instructions for the money standing to his credit, 1,640 drachmae, to be paid out to his partner, Cephisiades, who was away on a voyage at the time. The speech gives the very words of the entry made on that occasion in Pasion's accounts (γραμματεῖον or writing tablet—apparently the

---

[11] See Tod. II 175 (Tenedos, 339 B.C.); *IG* VII 1737–1738 (Thespiae, 229 B.C.: see W. S. Ferguson, *Hellenistic Athens* 206–207).
[12] Ps.-Dem. 52.6, *cf.* 4.

standard term for a banker's account-books)[13]: "Lycon of Heraclea, 1,640 drachmae, to be paid to Cephisiades. Archebiades of Lamptra will introduce him." Explaining this entry, the speaker says that it is customary with bankers, if they know by sight the person to whom money is to be paid out, just to write down, "To be paid to so-and-so"; but if they do not know him by sight, they add the name of the person who is to identify the payee. This certainly exposes the primitive character of Greek banking, and it is entirely consistent with what we know of Classical Greek financial and commercial practice. All the bankers kept account-books, and would have to be prepared to produce them if they became involved in litigation.[14] All business, however, was done in person and not by writing, and a number of witnesses would attend any important transaction, the details of which would be established in court, not by any written record which might have been made, but by personal testimony. The speaker of Isocrates' *Trapeziticus*[15] says that contracts with bankers were made without witnesses, and many modern writers have innocently repeated this statement as if it were perfectly true. No doubt in practice many banking transactions would take place without anyone except the parties themselves being present. But in the *Trapeziticus* the speaker, who is the plaintiff in a lawsuit against Pasion the banker, is seeking to establish the existence of an alleged contract between himself and Pasion of which there were no witnesses, and anything he says on such a point must be regarded with grave suspicion. His statement is not borne out by what happened at Lycon's settlement with Pasion, at which, as we have seen, two witnesses were present. If Apollodorus was speaking the truth in the action he brought in the 360's B.C. against Timotheus (a leading Athenian general and statesman), Pasion had lent Timotheus various sums of money privately, without requiring witnesses or security[16]; but it is noticeable that Apollodorus, whose case is seriously weakened by the absence of witnesses, does not venture to repeat the assertion of the plaintiff in the *Trapeziticus* that it was normal for bankers' dealings to be carried out without witnesses. Certainly other contracts, loans, repayments and so forth were always made before witnesses. Demosthenes, in one of his private speeches, actually claims the fact that a man had never been to the Crimea as

---

13 See also Ps.-Dem. 45.33. *Cf.* 49.59 (ἐν τοῖς γράμμασιν τοῖς τραπεζιτικοῖς). An individual account, as distinct from what it is written on, is a λόγος (Latin *ratio*): see, *e.g.*, Tod. I² 51A.25; II 125.77; Hdts. III 142.5; 143.1; Dem. 8.47; Ps.-Dem. 49.16; *Ev. Matt.* 18.23.
14 See Ps.-Dem. 49.43 & 59. The entries included ὑπομνήματα (memoranda) giving particulars of each transaction: see *ibid.* 5, 8, 30. Despite κελεύοντος in Ps.-Dem. 49.43, I know of no positive evidence that anyone concerned in litigation against a banker had a legal right to demand production of his books; but refusal or failure to produce them would naturally prejudice the banker's case.
15 Isocr. 17.2, *c.* 390 B.C.
16 Ps.-Dem. 49.2.

evidence that he could not possibly have collected a debt payable there.[17]   In other ways, too, Greek bankers of the Classical period were quite different from modern ones: for example, there is no clear evidence that they paid interest on money deposited with them. (Roman bankers sometimes did, but those who deposited money with bankers without any agreement for the payment of interest ranked as preferential creditors if the banker suffered *venditio bonorum*, a process which involved the sale of all the property of a debtor and corresponded roughly to bankruptcy in English law.   If interest was payable on the deposit, the customer was not given preferential treatment over the creditors.) [18]

No doubt some men of business other than bankers would find it necessary to keep detailed accounts of their operations, if only to make sure that they were not cheated by their slaves or their associates. But to me it seems most unlikely that the ordinary Greek would have felt the need to keep regular books.   He was certainly never required to do so for taxation purposes: at no time in the ancient world were taxes assessed upon money incomes.   Indeed, as I have already argued elsewhere,[19] it is probable that no Greek ever had occasion to reckon his total income in money; and I see no reason to suppose that the situation was different in the Roman world.   Wealth in antiquity was conceived in terms of capital, not income, and the unit of taxation, when it was not the annual produce of a man's land (reckoned in kind and not money), or simply his body (for a poll tax), was his total capital.

One form of account which the ordinary Greek might often keep was a note of debts owing to him or owed by him.   In the opening scene of the *Clouds* of Aristophanes, produced in 423 B.C., Strepsiades calls for his list of debts and reads out the records of two of them,[20] the second of which is " Three minas for a chariot and wheels to Amynias."   This is doubtless a typical entry, in narrative form.   The account-book is spoken of as a γραμματεῖον, a wooden tablet.

In a world which did not recognise signatures as having any special value, it might be dangerous to allow one's debtor to pay the money to anyone not specifically designated at the outset.   In the *Curculio* [1] of Plautus (the Greek original of which seems to date from the very end of the fourth century B.C.), a banker has arranged with his customer to pay over the money deposited with him to the person who brings a letter sealed with the customer's ring.   Curculio steals the ring, writes out a letter of authorisation on a tablet, seals it with the ring,

---

[17] Dem. 38.11, *cf*. 12–14.   See also 30.19–23 ; Ps.-Dem. 34.30–32 ; 49.51–52.
[18] See esp. *Dig*. 16.3.7.2 ; 42.5.24.2.   *Cf*. 16.3.24, 28.
[19] In *Classica et Mediaevalia* 14 (1953), at p. 41.
[20] Lines 21–23, 31.
[1] II iii 61–69 ; III 36–84 ; IV iii, esp. 19–20.

and gets the money from the banker. The customer tells the banker he is a fool to pay any regard to tablets, but the banker retorts that all public and private business is transacted by means of them [2]—and the customer evidently realises he has no claim.

This raises the whole question of signatures in Greek and Roman documents—or rather, their absence.[3] The Greeks and Romans never signed letters or documents with their names: a man dictating a letter to his slave or subordinate might write some formula of farewell at the end with his own hand (*subscripsi, vale,* ἔρρωσο), but he might not do even this, and in any event the genuineness of the letter would be guaranteed not at all by the style of the handwriting but by other means—doubtless in many cases by the personality of the man bringing the letter. Seals were often used to authenticate documents,[4] but it is difficult to tell just how common this practice was. We may often be puzzled as to how the recipient of a letter authorising him, for example, to pay out money deposited with him could be certain that the letter came from the right person. Various expedients might be adopted by cautious business men. For example, in a Berlin papyrus [5] of A.D. 277–278 we find an order to a banker to pay out a sum of money to a third person. The document purports to be an idiograph of the writer—that is, a document written entirely in his own hand. In place of a signature, there is what appears to be a certificate by a man named Sarapion, described as a διαστολεύς and probably an accredited agent of the writer, that the order was genuine. We must remember, too, that many humble folk in the ancient world were illiterate; and although most of these may have had few possessions, there were certainly some illiterates who were property-owners [6] and might therefore need to enter into transactions involving written documents. In

---

[2] An exaggeration, of course. Probably the great majority of business transactions at Athens in *c.* 300 B.C., as at Rome in Plautus's day, a hundred years later, were personal and not written. During the Hellenistic period business practices certainly developed to some extent, and banking in particular attained a higher level of organisation, especially perhaps in Ptolemaic Egypt; but I cannot understand the statement of M. Rostovtzeff (*Soc. & Econ. Hist. of the Hellenistic World* I 405) that " one of the most striking novelties [in Ptolemaic banking] in comparison with the practice of the Greek banks was the *complete change* from oral management (*partly* used in the Greek cities) to written management of banking business " [my italics].
[3] See H. Steinacker, *Die antiken Grundlagen der frühmittelalterlichen Privaturkunde* (1927) 106–122; H. F. Jolowicz, *Historical Introd. to the Study of Roman Law*[2] 430–431.
[4] See Pliny, *NH* 33.8 *et seq.*, esp. 21, 23, 25, 28; 37.8–10.
[5] *BGU* IV 1064. See F. Preisigke, *Girowesen im griech. Aegypten* (1910) 204–205; Kiessling in Pauly-Wissowa, *Realenc.*, Suppl. IV (1924) 707–708.
[6] See *Cod. Just.* 10.32(31).6, of A.D. 293, stating that there was nothing to prevent illiterates from being conscripted for the duties of the decurionate (" expertes litterarum decurionis munera peragere non prohibent jura "). The decurions were those members of the curial class (see p. 48 below) who actually became local councillors.

the Egyptian papyri we very often find documents subscribed on behalf of illiterates, especially by husbands for their wives.

It is also interesting to find that when a debt or other liability is discharged or remitted, any written evidence of it is normally destroyed altogether, instead of a receipt or acknowledgment being indorsed on or annexed to the original document or given separately. This is true even of public debts due to the Athenian State.[7] The principal evidence of the discharge of the liability would be the personal testimony of eye-witnesses who saw payment being made. Written receipts do not seem to have become usual until the Hellenistic age. By at any rate the Roman period (and no doubt in fact earlier) it was quite usual to acknowledge the discharge of an obligation by drawing lines criss-cross (χιάζειν) over the face of the document embodying the original contract,[8] and that document itself was often handed back to the person who had undertaken the obligation.[9]

IV. The Hellenistic Period

For accounting in the Hellenistic period further epigraphic evidence is available,[10] not significantly different from that provided by the earlier inscriptions, and in addition we begin to have papyrus accounts from Ptolemaic Egypt in considerable numbers.[11] By far the most important single body of private accounts from the Hellenistic period is contained in the "Zenon archive" from the mid-third century B.C.: here we find the extraordinarily detailed accounts of the great private estate in the Fayum of the chief finance minister of Ptolemy II, Apollonius, whose personal agent Zenon was.[12] Zenon's accounts are far more elaborate and varied than any earlier ones we have, but the system of accounting remains essentially the same as in former times. We may notice that just as the Ptolemaic State collected its revenue and stored its surpluses in grain as well as money, and its accounts are therefore divided into those relating to

---

[7] Arist., *Ath. Pol.* 47.5; 48.1; 59.3; Ps.-Dem. 58.50–51.

[8] A good example is *P. Ryl.* IV 601, as shown in the photograph (pl. 3) in that vol.

[9] As, *e.g.*, in *P.Ryl.* II 174, lines 9–14, 21–25; 174a, lines 9–15. The document is usually said to be given up εἰς ἀθέτησιν καὶ ἀκύρωσιν.

[10] For the great series of temple accounts from Delos, from the late 4th cent. to 166 B.C., see J. A. O Larsen in *Econ. Survey of Ancient Rome* (ed. Tenney Frank) IV 334–357, where detailed references will be found. See also W. A. Laidlaw, *Hist of Delos* (1933) 139 (with 161, note 1), 153–157 (with 163, note 13). Most of the extant material (ed. F. Durrbach) is in *IG* XI ii (1912); and *Inscr. de Délos : Comptes des hiéropes* nos. 290–371 (1926), 372–498 (1929), 1400–1479 (1935).

[11] Among many interesting papyrus accounts it is worth mentioning *P. Tebt.* III ii 890 (2nd cent. B.C.), part of the accounts of a bank: see on this Rostovtzeff, *op. cit.* (in note 2 above) II 1276–1277, 1284–1285.

[12] See Elizabeth Grier, *Accounting in the Zenon Papyri* (*cf.* p. 68 below). For useful descriptions of the background of the Zenon papyri, see Claire Préaux, *Les grecs en Égypte* (1947); Rostovtzeff, *A Large Estate in Egypt in the 3rd Cent. B.C.* (1922).

the State granaries and those relating to the State banks, so in the Zenon accounts we can distinguish between accounts kept in terms of money and accounts kept in terms of grain (ἀργυρικοὶ λόγοι and σιτικοὶ λόγοι).[13]

It has been suggested [14] that Zenon may have kept " ledgers " which were taken over by his successor, or the State, and were thus separated from the remaining records which Zenon retained among his personal papers. There may conceivably have been some special accounts with individuals which have not come down to us, distinct from Zenon's general accounts and corresponding roughly to what we call ledger accounts. We do find occasional evidence of such accounts in other papyri of the Hellenistic and Roman periods.[15] It would be a mistake, however, to think of these as " ledger accounts " in anything like our sense of the term, for they certainly did not form part of a unified system of book-keeping. The essential point is that even if a banker or merchant or estate owner did think it worth while to keep separate individual accounts for particular persons, the existence of any such accounts would necessitate no special entries in his other accounts. At all costs we must avoid the tendency to think in terms of an integrated system: that is just what was lacking in all ancient accounting. Elaborate and minutely detailed as the Zenon accounts are, their purpose was very much more limited than that of comparable estate accounts today: it was not to enable Apollonius to draw up at regular intervals complete " profit and loss accounts " and " balance sheets " (nothing of this sort appears in antiquity), not to assist him to obtain the highest possible rate of profit out of his estate, but simply to prevent theft, embezzlement, fraudulent conversion and other avoidable losses due to carelessness and the like. This, indeed, was the one major aim of all ancient accounting. The great man might occasionally make a snap check of cash in hand, and in one papyrus [16] we find a correspondent warning Zenon that Apollonius, finding seven talents missing from a chest, had ordered two of his clerks to produce their accounts for his inspection. Evidently large numbers of clerks were employed in the accounting offices on Apollonius's estate. The wages of some of them seem to have been little higher than those paid to unskilled labourers.[17]

In one or two papyri of the Hellenistic period containing lists of payments due from or made by different individuals there is some attempt to put the names in alphabetical order—a feature which we

[13] *Cf.* pp. 21-22 above.
[14] Grier, *op. cit.*, 14.
[15] See, *e.g.*, *UPZ* I 83, 97, 99, 101, 103-105 ; *P. Oxy.* X 1289; IV 739; *P. Tebt.* I 241, 250.
[16] *PSI* IV 411.
[17] Grier, *op. cit.*, 11-12.

also find in some papyrus accounts of the Roman period, but which I rather think took some time to re-emerge after the Dark Ages.[18] The practice, however, is sometimes conspicuous by its absence just where we might reasonably have expected to find it; and even where it does occur, the order is not rigorously kept.

Bureaucracy, always endemic in Egyptian State administration even under the Pharaohs, grew steadily during the Hellenistic age, both in Ptolemaic Egypt and (if to a smaller extent) in the kingdoms of the other successors of Alexander. The Greek cities, in which bureaucracy never really flourished before the Roman period, developed quasi-bureaucratic features in their attempts to check corruption in public administration. Cicero,[19] in his speech for Flaccus, delivered in 59 B.C., permits himself some heavy sarcasm— which has a curiously modern ring—about the municipal bank of the city of Temnos, in north-west Asia Minor: the town, he says, is " very businesslike, and most proficient in paper-work (*acerrima et conficientissima litterarum*). Not a farthing can change hands without the intervention of five praetors, three quaestors and four bankers, elected there by the people."

The fact that I have devoted very little space to accounting in the Hellenistic age, compared with the Classical Greek and Roman periods, must not be taken to imply that our knowledge of accounting in Hellenistic times is relatively small or that Hellenistic accounting is relatively uninteresting. On the contrary, owing to the survival from the Hellenistic period of so many accounts (mainly private) on papyrus, in addition to sacred or public accounts on stone, we have a far greater variety of actual accounts from Hellenistic than from Classical Greek times; and, as we shall see, no very important general advances in method can be traced in the Roman period.

V. Roman Accounting

We can conveniently consider at one time accounting at Rome during the late Republic (the last two centuries B.C.) and throughout the Graeco-Roman world in the Roman Imperial period (the early centuries of the Christian era). Our sources of information in this field are rather different in character from the sources for the Hellenistic period. The epigraphic evidence becomes negligible, but we have documentary papyri from Egypt in even greater numbers than before, including now a few in Latin,[20] the legal sources become

---

[18] The Hellenistic examples are *P. Tebt.* I 93, 94 (c. 112 B.C.). The Roman ones are *P. Fay.* 153 (1st cent. C.E.); *BGU* II 659 (A.D. 228–229); *P. Lond.* I p. 142, no. 119 (2nd cent.); *P. Col.* II₁ (2nd cent.). See Preisigke in *Arch. Pap.* 4 (1908), at p. 103.

[19] *Pro Flacc.* 19.44.

[20] See esp. pp. 38–40 and Figure IV below.

available, and the literary evidence is richer again. Our main texts are now the papyri, the Roman law books (especially of course the *Digest*), some speeches and other works of Cicero, and the *scriptores rei rusticae,* the writers on estate management—Cato, Varro and Columella. The information we can derive from these sources is fragmentary, but surprisingly copious when all the little pieces are put together. It is impossible in this outline of Greek and Roman accounting to give more than a brief summary of it, and draw attention to some of the more important pieces of evidence.

Although there is perhaps some advance in method and precision during the period we are now considering, there is no fundamental change. Bureaucracy continues to increase, and with it the further multiplication of public accounts. (In the year 194 we even find a local scribe and acting *strategus* writing an official letter [1] from himself in one capacity to himself in another capacity: he addresses himself as " my dearest friend " and politely says goodbye to himself at the end.) Certain improvements in method are visible here and there: some of them will be described presently. However, in accounts of the Roman period in general there is no really significant advance in the system of accounting: capital and income are still not properly separated; the conceptions of credit and debit, although they may seem to make fitful appearances now and again, especially in records of debts, never actually materialise as permanent features of accounting; a system of interlocking accounts with double entry, of course, is undreamt of; and the basic purpose of accounting remains what it always was in antiquity—to expose losses due to fraud or inefficiency on the part of the proprietor's servants and others. For this purpose ancient book-keeping was probably quite efficient, if at a great cost in clerical manpower. We must not belittle the intelligence of the Greeks and Romans because they did not try to do what the nature of their economic system made it unnecessary for them to attempt.

Improvements in methods of accounting during the Roman period, when they do appear, are not consistently maintained and are confined to isolated papyri or groups of papyri. Three such improvements are worth special mention. In a few accounts from Roman Egypt we find certain small items of expenditure described by some such term as λεπτὴ δαπάνη,[2] which we may fairly translate " petty cash." However, this does not mean that the modern notion of petty cash which can be spent as such without detailed explanation has become a regular

---

[1] *W. Chr.* 52 = A. S. Hunt and C. C. Edgar, *Select Papyri* (Loeb) II no. 301, pp. 312–314.

[2] *e.g.,* λεπτῆς δαπάνης in *P. Goodsp. Cair.* 30, col. xxxvii, line 17; and probably in *P. Oxy.* III 522, line 29. *Cf.* λεπτῶν in *P. Oxy.* VI 920, line 4. Contrast pp. 25–26 above.

feature of Graeco-Roman accounting: the papyri in question are exceptional, and the more usual practice is still to insert separately every individual disbursement, however small.   Again, in at least one papyrus,[3] of the first century, we find what must be cross-references to another account.   Our papyrus contains a banker's list of tax-payers, arranged more or less alphabetically, with the instalments of tax paid through the bank entered against the names.   Preisigke has demonstrated that the abbreviation K° with a numeral, against each entry, must stand for κολλήματος[4] and must denote the appropriate numbered column of the " cash-book " (if we may call it that—it would actually have been a papyrus roll) in which the banker evidently entered up all payments of this particular tax in chronological order.[5]   But the presence of cross-references in the papyrus we are considering does not imply that the account it contains was in any way integrated with others in a unified system of accounts: as I have said before, that was a stage of development which ancient accounting never reached, even if occasionally two or more individual accounts are found to be connected in one way or another.

The third and most interesting of the advances in accounting method which are observable in the Roman period is the adoption of bilateral form in the account from Karanis referred to above,[6] dating apparently from the years 191–192 and contained in a papyrus roll having forty-seven columns of writing, each of which must be a little under four inches wide.   Unfortunately the editor, Goodspeed, did not provide a photograph of any part of the papyrus, but we must assume that his text is a faithful transcription of the original, in form as well as substance.   The particulars given against each entry are mostly very brief indeed: " From Arches " or " For meat," or at most " To Pamounis, for the rope-makers " or " Food for 5 asses to Memphis."   The account was evidently drawn up not as each transaction occurred but on the basis of other material, apparently consisting of some general day-to-day records, described in a marginal note[7] as χειριστικά, supplemented by odd memoranda, one of which is also referred to in the same note as a πιττάκιον, presumably a tablet. The existence of further details in the rough records, so long as these were preserved, would make up for the brevity of the entries in the roll; but I should mention that very many other papyrus accounts have similarly imprecise and uninformative entries.

The unique characteristic of this account, which is the private cash

---

[3] *P. Fay.* 153: see Preisigke, *op. cit.* in note 18, p. 33 above; *cf.* C. Wessely, *Stud. Pal.* IV (1905) 119–121.

[4] See p. 69 below.

[5] *P. Cornell* 21 is a specimen of this kind of " cash-book."

[6] *P. Goodsp. Cair.* 30: see pp. 20–21 above.

[7] Col. iv, line 5.

account of the manager of an estate in the Fayum, is that all the figures representing receipts and payments respectively, and the explanatory verbal entries, are separately aligned vertically within each column of writing on the roll. Another interesting feature of the same account is the fact that entries in the receipts column are frequently balanced by the entry or entries next following in the payments column. I have set out, in a literal translation (Figure III),

Figure III

From Dioscorus	36 dr.	
To Antonas for the price of [- - -]		36 dr.
From Dioscorus	72 dr.	
To Paseinicus		12 dr.
,, me for a symbole		8 dr.
,, Sempronius for wheat		52 dr.
From Dioscorus	100 dr.	
To Agrippinus for vegetables		100 dr.
From Dioscorus	18 dr. 2 ob.	
To Pamounis		18 dr. 2 ob.
(Date) From Dioscorus	56 dr.	
To Soterichus for Antinous		?56 dr.
(Date) From Dioscorus	124 dr.	
To Soterichus for Copres		124 dr.
From Dioscorus for 4 jars of wine 64 dr.		
To Antonas for 2 (measures) of oil		32 dr.
,, Agrippinus for 2 (measures) of vegetables		32 dr.
From Dioscorus for 10 jars of wine for me at 16 dr. each		
160 dr. To me for drink		160 dr.

the first nineteen lines of column xxiv, the portion of the account in which this procedure is most consistently employed. Elsewhere in the account, although there are plenty of similarly corresponding entries, there are also many independent items which appear in one column only, without our being able to connect them with any particular entries in the other column; and I can see no trace of any attempt to make the two columns " balance." There are no totals in the body of the account: whether there were at the end we cannot tell, as the final column is entirely illegible. The editor of the papyrus jumped to quite unwarrantable conclusions when he used the expressions " a method much like modern double-entry bookkeeping," and " spasmodic double-entry accounting." Before we can speak of " double entry," of course, we must have entries in two different accounts, not merely two sides of a single account.

Nevertheless, this papyrus does seem to me to represent in some ways the high-water-mark of ancient book-keeping. The disposition of the figures in two separate columns could only have been a matter of convenience, not a point of principle, as in modern accounting; but it would obviously have been a great help to anyone checking the account or trying to identify particular entries, even if, for reasons arising out of the nature of the Greek numeral system (to be explained in section VI of this essay), the alignment of the figures in columns would not make it any easier to add up the figures, as it would if Arabic numerals had been employed. As I have said, I know of no other example of bilateral form in any other ancient account, among the hundreds which have survived. Our papyrus cannot, of course, have been the only one of its kind; but even if a few others should turn up, it would still be true to say that bilateral form was an exceptional and incidental feature found in only an insignificant proportion of ancient accounts. Often one finds a tendency to group together receipts and payments respectively, but the arrangement is seldom rigorous, and as a rule all that happens is that little blocks of receipts and payments follow each other, with totals given at the end of each block.[8]

The complete difference between ancient and modern objectives and methods in estate accounting has been emphasised by the Finnish scholar, Gunnar Mickwitz, in a brief but profound analysis [9] of the aims and achievements of the book-keeping of Graeco-Roman landowners, a study based upon a thorough knowledge of the papyri and of the treatises on farming methods of Cato, Varro and Columella. Mickwitz points out that it was hardly possible for a large Roman landowner who went in for different kinds of agricultural activity to tell which kinds paid best, because his inadequate accounting system did not permit separate costing. The corn grown on the estate which was given as wages to hired vine-dressers, or fed to slaves doing this work, would not be entered in the vineyard accounts, and hence the landowner would not know the net income attributable to vine-growing and corn-growing respectively, nor could he assess the financial consequences of employing less or more labour in his vineyard. In the elaborate estate accounts included in the Heroninus papyri of the third century, for instance, the wine produced on the estate is treated as an item of stock and records are kept of the quantities sold or given to employees as wages; but the wine accounts do not contain any information about the value of wine given to employees or even the amounts realised from the sale of the wine, which must have been entered separately; and thus the landowner could never properly estimate the profitability of his vine-growing

---

[8] See, *e.g.*, *P. Oxy.* XVIII 2195. (For the many errors of calculation in this account, see the editors' notes on pp. 166–167 of *P. Oxy.* XVIII.) Another interesting example is *P. Amh.* II 126–127. Here the ultimate balances are right (126) or only 1 obol out (127), but in each case the individual totals both of receipts and of payments are wrong. I suggest that the reason for this is that the clerk concerned always kept running balances checked against the cash in hand, and hence got his final results right, and that only when he was completing the accounts did he give individual totals of receipts and expenditure, which remained unchecked.

[9] " Economic Rationalism in Graeco-Roman Agriculture," in *Eng. Hist. Rev.* 52 (1937) 577–589. The neglect of this important paper, especially by historians of accounting, may be due partly to its rather unfortunate title.

from the information in his accounts.[10]   It is not surprising to find
that the Roman agricultural writers never think of advising a man
who is buying a farm to examine the vendor's accounts.[11]

Columella,[12] who wrote about A.D. 60, tries to make a conservative
estimate of the profits to be derived from vine-growing; but he takes
into account, in making his calculations, nothing but the cost of the
land, of the slave vine-dresser, and of vines and stakes and setting
them out, with interest at 6 per cent. on this expenditure—he ignores
the amortisation of the vine-dresser, the cost of maintaining him, and
of fertilisation, the hiring of casual labour, and all other current
expenses.   It is interesting to find that the items which Columella
ignores are just those which the ancient accounting system ignored.
Even the distinction, elementary to us, between capital and income,
without which profits and losses cannot be accurately computed, was
never thoroughly understood in ancient times, and only to a limited
extent do ancient accounts recognise the distinction.[13]   It would be
impossible for the ancient landowner to estimate in advance, or even
calculate in retrospect, from the material contained in his accounts,
the profitability of making capital improvements.   Mickwitz is certainly right, in my view, in claiming that recent opinion has tended
to overestimate the extent to which Graeco-Roman farming can be
considered to have been " scientifically managed."   We must always
remember, however, that the whole purpose of ancient accounting was
not to measure the rate of profit or loss but to keep accurate records
of acquisitions and outgoings, in money and kind, and to expose any
losses due to dishonesty or negligence.[14]   In this respect, private
accounts came much closer to public accounting than a modern
accountant would have expected; and indeed the methods of Greek
and Roman public and private accounting are strikingly similar, in
the main indistinguishable, their objectives being much more nearly
identical than in modern times.

Of the scores of public and private accounts of the Roman period
preserved on papyrus the vast majority are in Greek, but there are a
few in Latin, and fortunately one of these [15] is particularly suitable
for reproduction here.   A photograph of the original papyrus is given

[10] Mickwitz (pp. 580, 588–589) claims that there was no fundamental change in
accounting method in these respects until after the appearance in 1770 of Arthur
Young's *A Course of Experimental Agriculture.*
[11] And see Mickwitz, *op. cit.*, 583–584.
[12] *RR* 3.3.
[13] And see p. 29 above.
[14] See Cic., *pro Font.* 2.3: " res ipsa tamen ac ratio litterarum confectioque tabu-
larum habet hanc vim, ut ex acceptis et datis quidquid fingatur aut surripiatur
aut non constet appareat."
[15] *P. Gen. Lat.* 1=J. Nicole and Ch. Morel, *Archives militaires du Ier siècle* (1900).
See also Th. Mommsen, *Ges. Schr.* VI 118–127 (=*Hermes* 35, 1900, 443–452);
A. von Premerstein, in *Klio* 3 (1903) 1–46. Premerstein's date, A.D. 80–81, may
be right.

in Plate III. The document contains, among other things, the official pay-sheets of two Roman soldiers (almost certainly legionaries) stationed in Egypt, probably in 83–84, the third year of the reign of the emperor Domitian. I give in Figure IV first a transcript of the two pay-sheets as they appear in the papyrus. I have restored the passages which are now illegible, relying at many points on the original editors of the papyrus. Nearly all the entries are repeated several times over, and in most cases an indecipherable entry can be restored with certainty by comparison with similar ones which can still be read. In the transcript a full stop after a word indicates that it is an abbreviation. Next I give a separate translation of each soldier's account, with Arabic numerals in place of the Roman ones, and with the three successive instalments of pay placed side by side instead of vertically, to save repetition of the explanatory entries. It will be seen that the method of accounting is elementary, each instalment of pay being treated separately. I may add that in regard to both method and lay-out this account is if anything an improvement on most papyrus accounts: with the exception of the papyrus roll from Karanis which has been discussed above, I know of none which is significantly better in either respect, and few are as good.

Figure IV

Q. IULIUS PROCULUS ?DAM.?		C. VALERIUS GERMANUS TYR.	
Accepit stip. I an. III Do.	*dr. ccxlviii*	*Accepit stip. I an. III Do.*	*dr. ccxlviii*
ex eis		*ex eis*	
faenaria	*dr. x*	*faenaria*	*dr. x*
in victum	*dr. lxxx*	*in victum*	*dr. lxxx*
caligas fascias	*dr. xii*	*caligas fascias*	*dr. xii*
Saturnalicium k.	*dr. xx*	*Saturnalicium k.*	*dr. xx*
in vestitorium	*dr. lx*	*in vestimentum*	*dr. c*
expensas	*dr. clxxxii*	*expensas*	*dr. ccxxii*
reliquas deposuit	*dr. lxvi*	*reliquas deposuit*	*dr. xxvi*
et habuit ex priore	*dr. cxxxvi*	*et habuit*	*dr. xx*
fit summa	*dr. ccii*	*fit summa omnis*	*dr. xlvi*
Accepit stip. II anni eiusd.	*dr. ccxlviii*	*Accepit stip. II anni eiusd.*	*dr. ccxlviii*
ex eis		*ex eis*	
faenaria	*dr. x*	*faenaria*	*dr. x*
in victum	*dr. lxxx*	*in victum*	*dr. lxxx*
caligas fascias	*dr. xii*	*caligas fascias*	*dr. xii*
ad signa	*dr. iv*	*ad signa*	*dr. iv*
expensas	*dr. cvi*	*expensas*	*dr. cvi*
reliquas deposuit	*dr. cxlii*	*reliquas deposuit*	*dr. cxlii*
et habuit ex priore	*dr. ccii*	*habuit ex priore*	*dr. xlvi*
fit summa omnis	*dr. cccxliv*	*fit summa omnis*	*dr. clxxxviii*
Accepit stip. III anni eiusd.	*dr. ccxlviii*	*Accepit stip. III anni eiusd.*	*dr. ccxlviii*
ex eis		*ex eis*	
faenaria	*dr. x*	*faenaria*	*dr. x*
in victum	*dr. lxxx*	*in victum*	*dr. lxxx*
caligas fascias	*dr. xii*	*caligas fascias*	*dr. xii*
in vestimentis	*dr. cxlvi*	*in vestimentis*	*dr. cxlvi*
expensas	*dr. ccxlviii*	*habet in deposito*	*dr. clxxxviii*
habet in deposito	*dr. cccxliv*		

Q. Julius Proculus, from ?Damascus?

First instalment of pay, third year of Domitian		Second instalment	Third instalment
	dr. 248	dr. 248	dr. 248
Deduct			
hay	dr. 10	dr. 10	dr. 10
food	„ 80	„ 80	„ 80
boots and straps	„ 12	„ 12	„ 12
camp Saturnalia(?)	„ 20	– –	– –
clothing	„ 60	– –	„ 146
?burial club?	– –	„ 4	– –
Total deductions	„ 182	„ 106	„ 248
Balance deposited	„ 66	„ 142	– –
Brought forward	„ 136	„ 202	
Total on deposit	„ 202	„ 344	„ 344

C. Valerius Germanus, from Tyre

First instalment of pay, third year of Domitian		Second instalment	Third instalment
	dr. 248	dr. 248	dr. 248
Deduct			
hay	dr. 10	dr. 10	dr. 10
food	„ 80	„ 80	„ 80
boots and straps	„ 12	„ 12	„ 12
camp Saturnalia(?)	„ 20	– –	– –
clothing	„ 100	– –	„ 146
?burial club?	– –	„ 4	– –
Total deductions	„ 222	„ 106	(„ 248)
Balance deposited	„ 26	„ 142	– –
Brought forward	„ 20	„ 46	
Total on deposit	„ 46	„ 188	„ 188

In what follows more use will be made of the legal and literary sources than of the papyri, from which it is difficult to extract more than negative generalisations.

First, it will be desirable to clear out of the way a misconception which has appeared again and again in the works of modern writers on Roman accounting [16]: the supposed evidence for double-entry book-keeping in the form of the Roman " literal contract " (*obligatio litteris* or *litterarum*). As this subject involves some highly technical questions of Roman law, I have dealt with it separately in Appendix C (pp. 72–74 below) and need not enter into any discussion here. I will only say that the literal contract certainly provides no evidence of the existence in Roman times of double-entry book-keeping or any anticipation thereof.

---

[16] Most recently C. A. Smith, " Speculations on Roman Influence on the Theory of Double-Entry Book-keeping," in *Accounting Research* 5 (1954) 335–342.

It is worth spending a little time on some of the references in Cicero to the keeping of accounts in his own day. His speech for Q. Roscius, the famous actor, dating from about 77 B.C., is concerned with a financial transaction; and here we have an interesting description—the only one I know of in ancient literature—of the accounts which the ordinary well-to-do Roman would keep.[17] It seems that two kinds of account-books were distinguished—if not as emphatically as Cicero makes out: he has particular reasons in this speech for exaggerating the difference between the two varieties of record and for belittling one variety.[18] First, there were *adversaria*[19] (the Greek ἐφημερίδες), which were rough records or memoranda. There is no harm in referring to them as " day-books " or " waste-books," but in order to avoid inapposite comparisons with modern accounting practices it is better to keep to some non-technical term like " memoranda." I know of no certain evidence as to what the memoranda were written on: waxed tablets often, no doubt, and possibly parchment codices, but usually, I fancy, papyrus, in loose sheets or rolls, probably as a rule the back (*verso*) of sheets or rolls already used on the front (*recto*) for other purposes. In a sculptured relief (see Plate I) on a funeral monument from Serbia (Pannonia)[20] we find a slave reading from a papyrus roll to his master, a banker perhaps, who sits holding a writing-tablet at a table on which lies a bag of coins. It seems very likely that both the papyrus roll and the writing-tablet were intended to represent accounts, the papyrus perhaps containing the *adversaria*. Secondly, there were the *tabulae* proper, which are referred to indifferently by Cicero in the same passage (not to mention many others) as *tabulae,*[1] *tabulae accepti et expensi,*[2] *codex,*[3] *codices,*[4] *codex accepti et expensi.*[5] Obviously a man's permanent accounts might be called by any of these names; they might equally well be referred to as *rationes,* a term which Cicero and other writers tend to employ more in the abstract sense (corresponding to the Greek λόγοι), using *tabulae* and *codex* for the actual physical objects on which the accounts were kept. It is quite fantastic to try to distinguish, as Voigt

---

[17] Cic., *pro Q. Rosc. com.* 1.1 to 3.9.
[18] See the latter part of note 14, p. 74 below.
[19] For which see Corn. Nep., *Attic.* 13.6 ; Propert. III xxiii (*Ergo tam doctae*) 19–20 ; Ovid, *Am.* 1.12.25–26 ; Sen., *Ep.* 123.10. *Diarium* in this sense appears only in Asellio *ap.* Gell. 5.18.8. *Cf.* perhaps the χειριστικά mentioned on p. 35 above ; also in *P. Mich.* IV i 225, lines 3024, 3350 ; *P. Oxy.* X 1257, line 10 ; *Stud. Pal.* IV p. 57 (col. IV, line 1) ; XX 85ᵛ, line 1 (p. 76).
[20] See M. Rostovtzeff, *Soc. and Econ. Hist. of the Roman Emp.,* pl. xxxiii 1. The original is in the Belgrade Museum.
[1] *Pro Q. Rosc. com.* 1.1 (4 times) ; 1.2 ; 1.3 ; 1.4 (twice) ; 2.5 (twice) ; 2.6 ; 2.7 (twice) ; 3.8 (twice) ; 3.9 ; 4.12 ; 4.13 (twice)=19 times.
[2] *Ibid.,* 1.2 only.
[3] *Ibid.,* 1.1 ; 1.4 ; 2.5 ; 2.6 (twice) ; 2.7=6 times.
[4] *Ibid.,* 1.4 ; 5.14=twice.
[5] *Ibid.,* 1.4 ; 2.5 ; 3.8 ; 3.9=4 times.

did,[6] between a *codex rationum* or *tabulae rationum* on the one hand and on the other a special *codex accepti et expensi*—an expression found nowhere but in the speech for Roscius,[7] although the term *tabulae accepti et expensi* also occurs once in that speech and in one or two other places.[8] It is abundantly clear that *codex* (or *tabulae*) *accepti et expensi* was simply another name for the permanent accounts kept by a Roman, or the portion of those accounts recording the receipt and payment of money—as distinct, for example, from special accounts with individuals, schedules of property and the like, which might also form part of a man's account-books. The terminology is untechnical and indiscriminate: no Latin word or phrase is known to us as having been consistently applied in a technical sense to any particular kind of account or account-book, except *kalendarium* (*kalendarii liber*),[9] an expression which seems always to have denoted a man's record of outstanding debts, the name being derived from the fact that the date at which the debt became due would be specified in the record. As we have just seen, Voigt would oppose to the *codex* (*tabulae*) *accepti et expensi* a *codex* (*tabulae*) *rationum*, as the general account-book of every Roman. But the expression *codex rationum*, as far as I can discover, never occurs at all in Latin literature and is found only once in the legal sources [10]: there it refers to the accounts of bankers (*argentarii*), who would always need to keep accounts on a considerable scale, as the ordinary Roman would not. There is in fact no reason to believe that all Romans kept detailed accounts.[11] Voigt's *codex rationum domesticarum*,[12] the private account-book which he believed every Roman kept, appears to be entirely his own invention: the expression seems not to be used in any surviving source. If we take the earliest surviving portion [13] of Cicero's speech for Q. Roscius, we find the term *tabulae* by itself used nineteen times, *codex* by itself six times, *codex accepti et expensi* four times, *codices* twice, *tabulae accepti et expensi*

---

[6] See pp. 66–67 below. According to Voigt (pp. 541 *et seq.*) the *codex accepti et expensi* was nothing but " das Litteralgeschäfts-Journal des Bürgers," *i.e.*, it recorded only transactions coming under the heading of *obligatio litteris* (on which see Appendix C below). The unwary reader who does not verify Voigt's references may not realise that his theory about the *codex accepti et expensi* is entirely devoid of foundation.

[7] 1.4; 2.5; 3.8; 3.9.

[8] *Ibid.*, 1.2; *II Verr.* ii 76.186; Auson., *Grat. actio ad Gratian. imp. pro cons.* 23 (ed. R. Peiper, p. 359). In Plaut., *Most.* I iii 147 we find " ratio accepti atque expensi," but this is a metaphor (" bene igitur ratio accepti atque expensi inter nos convenit: tu me amas, ego te amo ").

[9] See Mart. 8.44.11, and many passages in the *Digest, e.g.*, 31.1.88.pr.; 33.8.23.pr.; XXXII 34.1; 41.6; 64; 91.pr. An action for interest might be called *actio kalendarii*: *ibid.*, 26.7.39.14.

[10] In *Dig.* 2.13.10.2.

[11] *Cf.* p. 44 below.

[12] Voigt, *op. cit.*, 533–535.

[13] 1.1 to 5.15.

once.[14]   Except as I have already indicated in regard to the use of
codex (*tabulae*) *accepti et expensi* in a sense roughly equivalent to our
" cash book," it is impossible to draw any general distinction between
these terms, in the speech for Q. Roscius or elsewhere, and I shall
translate them all " accounts " or " account-books," sometimes using
" cash book " for *codex* (*tabulae*) *accepti et expensi*.

In the lawsuit in which Cicero was briefed for the defence of
Roscius the actor, the plaintiff C. Fannius Chaerea claimed that
Roscius owed him a large sum of money.   " We demand your
accounts," Cicero [15] says to Fannius, " and we don't object to having
the action decided by them.   Why don't you produce them?   Doesn't
he keep accounts?   Indeed he does, most diligently.   Doesn't he enter
even trifling accounts in his books?   He does indeed: everything.   Is
this a small and trivial account?   It's 100,000 sesterces."   And so on.
Fannius claimed, it appears, that the vital entry was in his memoranda,
his *adversaria*, though not in his permanent cash book, his *codex
accepti et expensi*.   Cicero pours scorn on this.   " Have you such an
overblown conceit of yourself," he asks, " that you expect people to
pay money on the strength not of your account-books but of your
memoranda? . . .   If memoranda have the same force, precision and
authority as proper accounts, what's the use of keeping books? . . .
Why do we write up our memoranda carelessly, but keep our accounts
diligently?   Why?   Because the former are intended to last for a
month only, the latter for ever; the former are expunged immediately,
the latter religiously preserved "—and so forth.   " Therefore," Cicero
goes on, " no one ever produced his memoranda at a trial; one pro-
duces one's books and reads out the accounts. . . .   I ask you,
Fannius, how long is it since you made this entry in your memoranda?
He blushes.   He doesn't know what to answer.   He's at a loss for
anything to invent offhand.   ' It's two months ago,' you will say.
Still, it ought to have been entered in your cash book.   ' It's more
than six months.'   Why then is it left so long in your memoranda?
What if it is more than three years ago?   How is it that when everyone who keeps accounts enters up his books more or less monthly,
you let this entry remain in your memoranda more than three years? "

It is nearly always dangerous to accept the statements of a Greek
or Roman forensic orator at their face value; but here it seems fairly
safe to conclude that men of property at Rome often did write up
their permanent account-books (or rather, get their slaves to do this,
and then check the result) about every month, from their *adversaria*,
as indeed Cicero's friend Atticus apparently did.[16]

---

[14] See notes 1–5 above.
[15] *Pro Q. Rosc. com.* 1.3–3.8.
[16] See Corn. Nep., *Attic.* 13.6.   *Cf. P. Ryl.* IV 629, 630–638, part of the private
accounts of Theophanes, a Roman civil servant of fairly high position in Egypt

There are some interesting references to book-keeping in the
"Verrine orations," Cicero's great speeches dating from 70 B.C.
against Verres, the iniquitous governor of the province of Sicily during
the years 73 to 70. In the first of the five speeches of the so-called
Actio Secunda in Verrem,[17] Cicero is accusing Verres of having appropriated and not bought certain statues which he had somehow acquired
during his governorship. He lays great stress on the fact that Verres
cannot show any entry in his accounts relating to the purchase of the
statues. "Show in your accounts (*in tabulis*), or in your father's,
that any one of them was bought, and you have proved your case."
Cicero speaks as if Verres had claimed that he had kept personal
accounts up to the year 73 but had then ceased to do so. Naturally
Cicero makes great play with this, claiming it as proof of the concealment of villainy. "We hear," he says, "that some men have never
kept accounts. There may be people who behave like this, but it's
not at all proper (*minime probandum*)." But to keep accounts for a
time and then suddenly stop—Cicero finds it easy to ridicule this.

It is often asserted that every Roman *paterfamilias*[18] was legally
bound to keep proper accounts. The passage I have just quoted[19]
shows that this is an exaggeration: Cicero simply says it is "not
done" not to keep accounts, and there is nothing in the sources to
make one think that there was any legal duty in this respect, except
of course as regards bankers (*argentarii*), who in practice were obliged
to keep books, properly dated, and to produce them in legal proceedings whenever they were required to do so. There were quite
elaborate and very sensible rules governing the production of bankers'
books, which will be found in the chapter of the *Digest* headed "De
Edendo."[20] Only a banker, then, would be certain to keep formal
accounts. Other people might be equally strict, however; and we
find Cato[1] advising the landowner to go over the cash accounts and
the inventories[2] of grain, fodder, wine and oil every time he arrived

---

in the early 4th century: here we find totals of expenditure given for each day,
each period of five days, and each month, a procedure which seems to be without
parallel among known papyri. There is another interesting feature of the accounts
in the Theophanes archive: in addition to the fair copies, rough drafts of some
of the accounts (nos. 630–638) also survive, not significantly different from the
final versions in form or content. There are no financial memoranda belonging
to a preliminary stage in the accounting.

[17] Cic., *II Verr.* i 23.60–61. The speeches of the *Actio Secunda* were not actually
delivered, and they now appear in the form in which Cicero afterwards wrote
them up for publication.

[18] No one *in potestate* would keep accounts, according to Cic., *pro Cael.* 7.17.

[19] Cic., *II Verr.* i 23.60.

[20] *Dig.* II xiii: see in particular 4 (esp. pr., 1, 4); 6 (esp. 3, 6, 7, 8); 8 pr.; 9.2;
10.pr., 1, 2. And see *Cod. Just.* 2.1.

[1] *RR* 2.5; 5.4. It was Cato, according to Plutarch (*Cato Maj.* 21), who declared
that a man showed admirable and indeed positively godlike qualities if it appeared
from his accounts at his death (ὃς ἀπολείπει . . . ἐν τοῖς λόγοις) that he had
acquired even more property than he had inherited.

[2] Cato, of course, uses the same word: *rationes*.

on his farm, and frequently to check the account of his slave steward (*vilicus*). Sometimes we hear of special accounts: for instance, a master's private account,[3] an account as between guardian and ward,[4] or husband and wife.[5] A wealthy man would have an inventory or inventories of his property in which different possessions were entered up under different headings [6]: these inventories might be collectively known as the *libellus familiae*.[7] The owner of a large estate might have a running record kept for him in narrative form, containing notes of interesting occurrences on the estate as well as matters of financial importance [8]: this would probably go by the name of *commentarii*. Anyone who had money out on loan would keep records of it in a *kalendarium* (*kalendarii liber*).[9] Practice evidently varied greatly, however, from person to person, and each man kept only such accounts as he felt to be necessary.

In the second speech of the *Actio Secunda in Verrem* there is a brilliant denunciation of Verres for having entered into shady transactions with tax-farmers under a false name.[10] While examining the accounts of Carpinatius, local manager in Sicily of a tax-farming company, Cicero came across a number of entries in which the name C. Verrutius appeared. "Holding the accounts in my hands," says Cicero, "I suddenly noticed entries which bore the traces of recent wounds inflicted upon them (*quaedam vulnera tabellarum recentia*)"; and he goes on to show that C. Verrutius is an afterthought, replacing the name of the wicked governor himself. "Come out into the middle of the court," he says to the clerk, "and open up the copy of the accounts, so that everyone can see, not merely the traces of that man's avarice, but the very bed in which it lay."

Perhaps the most important of all the passages in the *Verrines* which have to do with accounting is the one in which Cicero reads out, with a scornful commentary, the accounts which Verres gave in to the Roman State, as required by law, in respect of his quaestorship in 84 B.C., when he was attached to the consul Cn. Papirius Carbo, operating in Gaul. This is an extraordinary document. It gives no details at all, but simply says, "I received 2,235,417 sesterces. I spent on army pay, corn, the legates, the proquaestor and the praetorian cohort 1,635,417 sesterces. I left at Ariminum 600,000 sesterces. The account rendered to P. Lentulus and L. Triarius,

---

[3] *Dig.* 40.1.6.
[4] *Dig.* 26.7.46.5.
[5] *Dig.* 23.3.9.3 (really an inventory).
[6] See esp. *Dig.* 33.10.7.2.
[7] *Dig.* 32.99.pr.; *cf.* 33.10.3.5.
[8] See Petron., *Sat.* 53—an entertaining passage.
[9] See p. 42 above.
[10] Cic., *II Verr.* ii 76.186 to 77.190.

urban quaestors, in accordance with a decree of the Senate." [11]   It is true that this account was handed in during a confused and revolutionary period, and that Cicero inveighs bitterly against the extraordinary impudence of a man who çould hand in accounts as brief as this—" Is this rendering accounts?   Did you or I, Hortensius, or anyone else ever submit accounts in this fashion?   What have we here?   What impertinence!   What audacity!   What parallel is there for this among all the accounts that have ever been rendered? " Nevertheless, some thirteen or fourteen years had passed, and Verres' accounts had evidently been accepted.

More than one writer, including Beigel,[12] has speculated about the form in which these accounts were actually handed in.   This is absurd.   There is no doubt about the form of the account: it was submitted and filed in the exact words which appear in the speech. Cicero is reading from the document itself or an office copy: this is clear from the inclusion of the official formula at the end of the account: " P. Lentulo, L. Triario quaestoribus urbanis, res rationum relatarum, ex Senatus consulto."   The document is in narrative and not tabular form—but that is exactly what we must expect of Greek and Roman accounts.

Before we go on to our last section, dealing with Greek and Roman numerals, we may glance at the terminology of Roman book-keeping and notice some of the expressions which habitually recur in the sources.   A few references must suffice for illustration, out of a far greater number of almost equal interest which might be given.

The usual expression for making what we should call a credit entry is *acceptum* (or *accepto*) *referre*,[13] or *ferre* [14]; for a debit entry *expensum* (or *expenso*) *ferre* [15]—not (or very rarely) *referre*, although at least once [16] we have *nomen referre* in the sense of *expensum referre*.   An account is a *nomen*,[17] and the same term can be applied to any individual entry in an account.[18]   *Nomen* can also mean a

---

[11] *II Verr.* i 14.36–37.   *Cf.* Cic., *ad Att.* 7.1.6, from which it appears that Cicero's staff expected him to distribute among them the whole surplus (HS 1,000,000) of the official funds he had received as proconsul of Cilicia.   Evidently these official accounts would give only the most general particulars of expenditure, and nothing like " vouchers " would be required.

[12] *Op. cit.*, ón p. 67 below, 177 *et seq.*

[13] Cic., *II Verr.* i 36.92,93 ; 39.100,102 ; ii 70.170 ; *pro Caec.* 6.17 ; *pro Font.* 2.3 ; Suet., *Tib.* 15.2 ; *Dig.* 23.3.48.1 ; 32.29.2 ; 35.1.82 ; 40.1.6.

[14] *Dig.* 13.7.35 ; 20.5.12.1 ; 21.2.4.1 ; 26.7.39.18 ; 26.7.56 ; 32.91.4,6 ; XLVI iii 1 ; 3 ; 5.2 ; 102.2 ; *Cod. Just.* 5.37.3.

[15] Cic., *pro Q. Rosc. com.* 1.1,2 ; 4.13 ; 5.14 ; *II Verr.* i 39.102 ; ii 70.170 ; *pro Caec.* 6.17 ; Corn. Nep., *Attic.* 13.6 ; *Auctor ad Herenn.* 2.13.19 ; Livy 6.20.6 ; Val. Max. 8.2.2 ; *Dig.* 20.4.12.5 ; 33.10.10 ; 36.1.23.4 ; *CIL* II 5042.7–8.

[16] Cic., *pro Q. Rosc. com.* 2.5.

[17] What is " in nominibus " is what is owed " in tabulis ": Cic., *Top.* 3.16. " Nomine liberare " is to discharge a debtor : *Dig.* 34.3.28.9.

[18] Cic., *II Verr.* ii 77.188.

debt,[19] and so a debtor: a good debt or debtor can be called a *bonum nomen*,[20] and *nomina facere* can mean " make loans," " give credit," as well as " make entries." [1] An account, but not an individual entry therein, is also a *ratio*.[2] And so we have *rationem computare* or *putare*,[3] or *subducere*,[4] or *dispungere*,[5] to complete an account and obtain what we should call a " balance "—although of course the notion of " balancing " two " sides " of an account is misleading if applied to Greek and Roman accounting. Ulpian [6] put it very nicely when he said that *dispungere* was " to compare receipts and payments." When a man examined and agreed accounts with another he was said *parem rationem facere* [7] or *adscribere*,[8] or *paria facere*,[9] *pariare*.[10] When a man was satisfied with accounts so dealt with, he might make a note on them accordingly, for future reference: he was then said *subscribere rationes*.[11] To close an account was literally to expunge it: *rationem expungere*.[12]

Carefully kept accounts were of course dated.[13] Anything left out could be inserted later, with the note *AFPR* [14] or *AGPR* [15] (*ante factum*, or *gestum, post relatum*).

The heyday of Roman book-keeping was evidently the last two centuries B.C. and the first two of our era. After that, references become thinner, even when we make allowance for the smaller quantity of later literature in which we might expect to find mention of book-keeping. From the fifth century we have a very interesting

---

[19] From the point of view of creditor (Cic., *ibid.* i 10.28) or debtor (Cic., *ad Att.* 5.6.2). See also *Dig.* 40.7.40.8.

[20] Cic., *ad Fam.* 5.6.2 ; *Dig.* 14.6.1.pr. ; 17.1.26.2.

[1] Cic., *ad Fam.* 7.23.1 ; *de Offic.* III 14.59 ; *II Verr.* i 36.92 ; Colum., *RR* 3.3.9 ; Sen., *de Vit. Beat.* 24.1 ; *de Benef.* 1.1.2 ; 2.23.2 ; 3.15.2 ; *Dig.* 2.14.9.pr. ; 15.1.4.1 ; 15.1.52.pr. ; 26.7.16 ; 40.5.41.17.

[2] Defined in *Dig.* 2.13.6.3. For a *ratio implicita* (an involved account), see 2.14.47.1. *Rationibus inferre* is to make entries in one's accounts: Suet., *Div. Jul.* 47 ; *Dig.* 40.7.40.pr. A well-known passage is Plaut., *Trinumm.* II iv 18: " ratio . . . apparet, argentum οἴχεται." For the diminutive *ratiuncula*, see, *e.g.*, Plaut., *Curc.* III 1.

[3] Gell. 7.5.7 ; Plaut., *Aul.* III v 53, *cf.* 55 ; *Most.* I iii 142 (*cf.* 147) ; *Trin.* II iv 16 ; Cato, *RR* 2.5 ; 5.4 ; Cic., *ad Att.* 4.11.1 ; *Dig.* 2.14.47.1 ; 18.1.7.pr. ; 40.5.47.2 ; *Cod. Just.* 2.5.1.

[4] Plaut., *Capt.* I ii 83–84 ; *Curc.* III i ; Cic., *ad Att.* 5.21.12 ; *Dig.* 34.9.17.

[5] Sen., *de Benef.* 4.32.4 ; *Dig.* 40.7.6.7 ; 50.16.56.pr. ; also 42.5.15.1 (*dispunctio*).

[6] In *Dig.* 50.16.56.pr.

[7] Sen., *Ep.* 19.10 ; *Dig.* 44.4.17.3.

[8] *Dig.* 40.4.22.

[9] Colum., *RR* 1.8.13 ; 11.1.24 ; *Dig.* 40.7.40.8. Frequent in metaphor, as, *e.g.*, Sen., *de Benef.* 2.30.2 ; 3.9.3 ; *de Tranq. An.* 7.2 ; *Ep.* 9.6 ; 81.3.

[10] *Dig.* 40.1.4.5. Also *pariatio* (12.6.67.3), *pariator* (35.1.81), *pararius* (Sen., *de Benef.* 2.23.2 ; 3.15.2).

[11] *Dig.* 34.3.12 ; 35.1.82 ; 40.5.41.10,17 ; 40.7.40.3—all particularly interesting.

[12] Plaut., *Cist.* I iii 41 ; *Dig.* 44.3.13.1 ; 50.8.10(8).

[13] Cic., *II Verr.* ii 77.188 ; *Dig.* II xiii 1.2 ; 6.6.

[14] Cic., *de Orat.* II 69.280.

[15] Fronto, *Ep. ad Ant. imp.* 1.5.1 (ed. van den Hout, I p. 94).

statement by the anonymous scholar known to us as Pseudo-
Asconius,[16] who wrote a commentary on Cicero's *Verrines*, to the
effect that the custom of keeping full and exact accounts, which used
to flourish once, had entirely ceased. The reason given is interesting:
men were condemned in the courts on the evidence of their own
account-books (*ex suis quisque tabulis damnari coepit*). This is
plausible enough but requires explanation here. The local units of
the Roman Empire were the *civitates*, sometimes mere tribal areas,
but normally and increasingly towns, with their surrounding territory.
Each *civitas* was administered by magistrates and a council (*senatus*,
βουλή), who came eventually to be drawn from a hereditary class of
curiales, consisting of all the wealthiest members of the *civitas* who
were not members of the senatorial and equestrian orders, the imperial
aristocracy. Now of all those inhabitants of the Empire who had
sufficient property to need to keep regular accounts, the vast majority
would belong to the curial class. And by a gradual process extending
from the second to the sixth century the *curiales* were squeezed dry
by taxation and the imposition of hereditary burdens attaching to their
property, from which there was no legal escape.[17] Concealment of
property became a necessity, and accounts revealing the extent of
one's "invisible property" (loans on mortgage or bottomry, for
instance) might prove a serious embarrassment, and lead to con-
demnation in the courts, or at least to the acquisition of new fiscal
burdens. It is not surprising if formal private accounts came to be
kept less and less, except by bankers.

The question is often asked how far the Greeks and Romans made
use of cheques, or of book transfers of credit (*giro*). This is a very
difficult problem,[18] and it is impossible to deal with it adequately
here, although something must be said about it, if only because at
least one of the texts which is sometimes quoted as evidence of book
transfer is actually part of the accounts of a bank in Ptolemaic
Egypt.[19] The more important evidence is almost entirely papyrological,[20] but there are one or two inscriptions [1] and some literary

---

[16] Ps.-Ascon., *in Verr. II* i 60 (p. 175 Baiter).

[17] See A. H. M. Jones, *The Greek City from Alexander to Justinian* (1940) 179–210.

[18] The most useful modern works on the subject are F. Preisigke, *Girowesen im griech. Aegypten* (1910); Kiessling, *s.v.* "Giroverkehr," in Pauly-Wissowa, *Realenc.*, Suppl. IV (1924) 696–709; W. L. Westermann, "Warehousing and Trapezite Banking in Antiquity," in *Jnl. of Econ. and Business Hist.* 3 (1930–1931) 30–54; E. H. Vogel, "Zur Gesch. des Giralverkehres im Altertum," in *Vierteljahrschr. für Soz.- u. Wirtschaftsgesch.* 29 (1936) 337–359.

[19] *P. Tebt.* III ii 890; see Rostovtzeff, as cited in note 11, p. 31 above.

[20] See the works of Preisigke and Kiessling cited in note 18 above.

[1] *IG* VII 3172 (the Nikareta inscription from Orchomenus, of *c.* 200 B.C., on which see Kiessling, as cited); XI ii 287 A 134–135 (Delos, 249 B.C.).

passages,[2] virtually all relating to individual transactions, the real nature of which is often not fully known to us. It was evidently a not uncommon practice for depositors in banks to give the banker written instructions (διαστολικόν) for money standing to their credit to be paid over to a third party [3]; and it also seems to have been possible for a depositor to give a written order to his banker for money to be transferred from his own account to the credit of a third party.[4] We cannot tell, however, how usual such transactions were. There is perhaps no harm in our referring loosely to the διαστολικά mentioned above as "cheques" [5]; but although they did to a very limited extent perform the same function as the modern cheque, they were fundamentally different from our cheques, in that there was no question of endorsement or negotiability—concepts which were entirely unknown in the ancient world.[6]

In the sphere of Roman State finance we find payments being made on written warrant. Transporting coin for long distances was a risky business, and so the government preferred to arrange for tax-money to be used locally as far as possible. Warrants were issued, authorising officials and others to draw upon money in the provincial treasuries or in the hands of tax-farmers; these warrants were known in the late Republic as *publicae permutationes* and in the later Empire

---

[2] *e.g.*, Ps.-Dem. 52.6, *cf.* 4; Polyb. 32.13.7 (31.27.7); and the passages referring to *permutatio*, *e.g.*, Cic., *ad Att.* XII 24.1 and 27.2 (Cicero's son); V 13.2; 15.2; XI 1.2; 24.3; XV 15.4; XVI 1.5; *ad Q. fr.* I 3.7; *pro Rab. Post.* 14.40; *Dig.* 50.16.76.

[3] Among the best examples are *P. Fay.* 100 and *BGU* IV 1063 (A.D. 99 and 100). The same practice is even better attested in relation to deposits in the state granaries of Egypt: see esp. Westermann, as cited in note 18, p. 48 above.

[4] The clearest example is *BGU* IV 1064 (A.D. 277-278). The verb used is μεταβάλλειν. There is again evidence of the same practice in connection with deposits in granaries: see, *e.g.*, *P. Lips.* I 114-115 (A.D. 133).

[5] *P. Gen.* 2 is said to be "almost a cheque" by Preisigke, *op. cit.* (in note 18, p. 48 above), 209-210; but he is probably right in thinking it was not addressed to a banker. If we are to confine the class of "cheques" strictly to those instructions to bankers which are handed over to the payees, then I know of no example of a "money-cheque" to equal the surviving "grain-cheques" (see notes 3 and 4 above), *e.g.*, *P. Oxy.* III 516 (A.D. 160).

[6] Mr. C. H. Roberts (to whom I am grateful for making several valuable suggestions) has drawn my attention to two papyri of the last century B.C., one of which (*P. Mich. Inv.* 6051: see A. E. R. Boak in *Aegyptus* 13, 1933, 107-112) records a loan but leaves the name of the lender blank, and the other (*P. Ryl.* IV 580) apparently assigns a funeral benefit (ταφικόν) without naming the assignee. The editors of both documents suggest that they were intended to be "negotiable." This, however, is surely misleading: the word "negotiable" is a technical legal term, and no document can properly be called negotiable unless it is one of a class of negotiable instruments recognised as such by statute or by mercantile usage. Negotiability is far from being the same thing as assignability: see, *e.g.*, W. R. Anson, *Principles of the Eng. Law of Contract* (19th ed., by J. L. Brierly, 1945) 275-284; G. C. Cheshire and C. H. S. Fifoot, *The Law of Contract*[5] (1952) 421-424.

as *litterae delegatoriae.*[7] We might expect such transactions to involve rather complicated book-keeping entries, but I should be surprised if in practice they did. Unfortunately I know of no evidence on the point. It is sometimes said that Roman bankers transacted " discount business," one of the elements in the " classical " definition of a banker in modern times. This seems to have no better foundation than Cicero's statement [8] that a man named Vettienus had offered to purchase at half its value a debt due to Cicero from some unfortunate whose property had been confiscated by the State—a debt which was likely to prove partly if not wholly irrecoverable.

VI. Greek and Roman Numerals

I said at the very beginning that the Greeks and Romans never reached the stage of separating what we should call debit and credit entries by putting them in separate columns or on two " sides " of an account, and I went on to say that they never even put their figures in precise columns at all. Here, it seems to me, we have our best clue to one important contributory reason for the backwardness of Graeco-Roman accounting. I shall now try to show that this lies in the nature of the systems of numeral notation used by the Greeks and Romans.

I must first make it clear that when I distinguish between the various numeral notations (or scripts) of the Greeks and Romans and our own I do not imply that the Greeks and Romans used a different system of numbers from ours. It was only their way of writing down their numbers which was different from our own. They counted in exactly the same way as we do, on the decimal system: that is to say, they took the number ten and its multiples as their basic units. The decimal system is, of course, the most common numerical system the world over, simply because all men have ten fingers and find it useful to count on them, and hence tend to construct their number systems in such a way as to make the fullest use of the digital reckoning apparatus which nature has conveniently provided.[9] If man had twelve fingers, we should doubtless now be thinking numerically in terms of a duodecimal system, in which numbers would be grouped in twelves, with the numbers 12, 144 and 1,728 filling the role given in our decimal system to 10, 100 and 1,000. Our numeral script would also have been fashioned differently, to fit the duodecimal system, with two additional symbols of one digit each for 10 and 11, the number 12 represented by the unit sign combined with the zero,

---

[7] Cic., *ad Fam.* 3.5.4 (*publica permutatio*); *cf. II Verr.* iii 70/71. 163–165; Plut., *Pomp.* 25. See A. H. M. Jones in *JRS* 40 (1950) 22 *et seq.* For the later Empire, see, *e.g.,* Cassiod., *Var.* XI 33, 35; *Cod. Theod.* 7.4.22; *cf.* Marc. Diac., *Vit. Porph.* 54.

[8] *ad Att.* 12.3.2.   [9] This was realised by Aristotle (*Probl.* 15.3, 910b23–911a4).

the number 144 by the unit sign combined with two zeros, and so on—but that is an entirely different matter.

Any given numerical system can of course be written down in various notations, some of which will be more efficient than others. An inefficient notation will tend to obstruct all calculations not simple enough to be performed without the aid of writing, by making it unnecessarily difficult to write them down easily and quickly. The notation, however, can have no direct effect upon the purely mental part of our calculations, or upon operations performed with the aid of an abacus. This simple fact is often overlooked. We reckon not with numeral signs but with the words for the numbers they represent.[10] Thus, whether we are adding 1,011 and 1,309, or MXI and MCCCIX (or, for that matter, ,αια and ,ατθ, in the Greek alphabetic notation), what we do is to say, " Nine and one are ten and ten are *twenty*; and *three hundred*; and one and one are *two thousand* " —2,320, or MMCCCXX (or ,βτκ). We disregard the notation and— our numerical system being a decimal one—mentally grasp the numbers according to powers of ten. If we are not very good at mental arithmetic, and find a calculation too difficult to be done entirely in the head, with or without the aid of the fingers, we may use an abacus of some kind: this will provide a frame, so to speak, in which the different powers of ten can be kept distinct.

About the Roman numeral notation I need say little, as it is very well known to everyone. Its one great advantage, compared with the alphabetic Greek system, is that it uses very few different signs —only seven basic ones, in fact: those for 1, 5, 10, 50, 100, 500 and 1,000, although other symbols, in bewildering variety, were added in ancient times for larger numbers.[11] We ourselves, of course, use ten different signs, including the zero. In the acrophonic Greek notation, which we shall come to next, there are also ten signs (six simple and four compound), while in the other Greek system, the alphabetic, there are twenty-eight. The Roman system, like the Greek acrophonic, is very clumsy indeed. The number 4,999, for example, which we write with four digits, requires no less than nineteen (MMMMDCCCCLXXXXVIIII) in the standard Roman system, and ten (MMMMCMXCIX) even in the abbreviated form—which, incidentally, is much rarer than the other in inscriptions, though not in papyri, which sometimes use the longer forms, sometimes the shorter, and sometimes both.[12] The worst defect of the Roman

[10] See T. L. Heath, *Hist. of Gk. Mathematics* (1921) I 38–39.
[11] See R. Cagnat, *Cours d'épigr. lat.*⁴ (1914) 30–32. For fractions, see *ibid.* 32–34.
[12] For instance, to mention only military accounts: (a) only the shorter forms are used in *P. Gen. Lat.* 1 (see note 15, p. 38 above), A.D. 83–84; (b) both forms in the rather later *P. Gen. Lat.* 4 (see J. Nicole in *Arch. Pap.* 2, 1903, 63–69), and in *P. Berl.* 6,866 (see R. Marichal, *L'occupation rom. de la Basse Egypte*, 1945), of the 190's; (c) only the longer in *P. Fay.* 105 (see Marichal, *op. cit.*), c. 180.

system, compared with ours, is that it knows nothing of place-value (position-value). A numeral notation which lacks place-value must inevitably have at least one of two defects: either, like the Roman and the Greek acrophonic scripts, it will repeat individual symbols with much greater frequency than is necessary in using a script possessing place-value; or, like the Greek alphabetic notation, it will use a far greater number of different symbols than the ten which suffice, on a decimal system, for a script in which place-value is present.

We can now turn to the Greek numeral scripts.[13] Quite a number of these are known from inscriptions, but if we ignore some unimportant local aberrations such as the peculiar script of Cyrene[14] we can divide all the notations into two main varieties: acrophonic and alphabetic. The first, the acrophonic, consists of a whole related group of scripts, but one of these appears in our surviving records very much more frequently than the rest, and I shall treat it as representative of the group and ignore the others.[15] This notation bears a very striking family resemblance to the Roman, although it must have developed entirely independently. It is sometimes called the " old Attic " notation, because it is best known in inscriptions from Attica, the district of Athens; sometimes the "Herodianic," because it is described in a passage attributed to Herodian, a Greek grammarian of the second century of the Christian era; and sometimes the "acrophonic" (the most suitable name), because the symbols it employs, other than the 1, are the initial letters (in an early form) of the Greek names of the respective numbers—a *delta* (Δ) for ten, for instance, because the Greek word for ten, δέκα (in the original capitals, ΔΕΚΑ), begins with a *delta*, and so on. This script may go back to the earliest days of Greek writing, in the eighth century B.C., but the date of its origin does not concern us here. The earliest precisely datable document containing this notation which I know of is the first Athenian tribute quota-list,[16] of 453 B.C., but there are one or two others[17] which may be earlier. The acrophonic script was

---

[13] See esp. Sterling Dow, " Gk. Numerals," in *AJA* 56 (1952) 21–23, with bibliography; W. Larfeld, *Griech. Epigraphik*[3] (=Iwan von Müller's *Handb. d. Altertumswissenschaft* I v, 1914) 290 *et seq.*; M. N. Tod, "The Gk. Numeral Notation," in *BSA* 18 (1911–1912) 98–132; "Three Gk. Numl. Systems," in *JHS* 33 (1913) 27–34; " Further Notes on the Gk. Acroph. Numls.," in *BSA* 28 (1926–1927) 141–157; "The Gk. Acroph. Numls.," in *BSA* 37 (1936–1937) 236–258; "The Alphabetic Numl. Syst. in Attica," in *BSA* 45 (1950) 126–139.

[14] See Tod in *BSA* 37 (1936–1937), at pp. 255–257.

[15] They are mostly less efficient. See, *e.g.*, the clumsy script employed in *IG* IV[2] i 102, an inscription of the early 4th cent. B.C., from Epidaurus, where 9,800 appears as ΧΧΧΧΧΧΧΧΧ⊟⊟⊟⊟⊟⊟⊟⊟ (line 47). In the old Attic script this would have been ⋈ΧΧΧΧⲠΗΗΗ—nine instead of seventeen digits.

[16] Tod I[2] 30.

[17] *IG* IV 553, from the Argolid. *SIG*[3] 46 can hardly be earlier than *c.* 450 B.C. and is probably later.

used to express cardinal numbers only, not ordinals.[18]   It works on exactly the same principles as the Roman, except that it lacks the abbreviated forms, and 4,999 cannot be written with less than nineteen digits (ΧΧΧΧΓ͞ΗΗΗΗΓ͞ΔΔΔΔΓΙΙΙΙ).   Place-value is absent. To express sums of money, the symbols were sometimes slightly modified: sums in talents, for instance, might incorporate the letter T in each sign, so that 161 talents would be Η Γ͞ Δ Τ.   The longest individual set of figures I have been able to find in a Greek inscription contains no fewer than twenty-nine digits.   It occurs in a long Athenian inscription [19] of the year 422 B.C., recording in talents, drachmae and obols the loans made to the Athenian State treasury during the years 426–422 by the gods of the city. ́ The Greek figures are Γ͞Γ͞Γ͞ΔΔΔΔΓ͞ΤΤΤΤΧΧΧΧΓ͞ΗΗΗΗΓ͞ΔΔΔΔΓΗΗΙ.   We should write this as 5,599 t., 4,897 dr., 1 ob.

The acrophonic script is known to have been used in Attica and (with various modifications) in many other parts of the Greek world from before the middle of the fifth century until the last century B.C.[20] In this notation were inscribed on stone the great series of Athenian public and sacred accounts, large portions of which have been recovered in modern times and reconstructed by epigraphists.   In the quota-lists and assessment decrees relating to the tribute of the Athenian Empire in the fifth century B.C., the sums of money are often arranged in columns with what seems at first sight great precision; but this is done purely for aesthetic reasons and not at all for convenience of addition, as can be seen from the following specimen,[1] opposite which I have given the value of each of the sums of money concerned: —

Χ	=	1,000 dr.
Γ͞	=	500 dr.
Γ͞Τ	=	6 tal. (36,000 dr.)
ΤΤ	=	2 tal. (12,000 dr.)
ΧΧΧΧ	=	4,000 dr.
Η	=	100 dr.

The other main variety of Greek numeral script, the alphabetic, which was used for ordinal as well as cardinal numbers,[2] seems to me a very much better notation than either the Roman or the Greek acrophonic, although I must admit that this is a matter of dispute among mathematicians.[3]   Some scholars believe the alphabetic system

---

[18] See Tod in *BSA* 45 (1950), at pp. 129–134.
[19] Tod I² 64, line 122. *Cf.* pp. 26–27 above.
[20] There are a few later archaizing survivals: see, *e.g.*, *P. Ryl.* III 540.
[1] Extracted from A 9 in *ATL* II p. 43, col. II, lines 138–152.
[2] *Cf.* above and note 18.
[3] Against the alphabetic notation are Moritz Cantor, *Vorlesungen über der Gesch. der Mathematik I³* (1907) 129–130; Jas. Gow, *Short Hist. of Gk. Mathematics* (1884) 46; H. Hankel, *Zur Gesch. der Math.* (1874) 36; W. W. Rouse Ball, *Short Account of the Hist. of Maths.³* (1901) 131–132; Florian Cajori, *Hist. of*

was invented at Miletus (or at any rate in south-west Asia Minor) in the eighth or seventh century B.C.; but this is disputed, and again we need not concern ourselves with the origin of the script. The two earliest surviving occurrences of the alphabetic numerals that I have been able to discover in formal documents are in a rather mysterious Athenian inscription [4] which seems to date from about the third quarter of the fifth century B.C., and an inscription of Halicarnassus in Caria (south-west Asia Minor), dating from the latter part of the same century.[5] (The latter document is also, as it happens, one of our earliest pieces of evidence for the acrophonic system: it uses both notations.) Even earlier than these inscriptions are certain odd scribblings on Athenian vases, apparently recording quantities and prices,[6] some of which appear to be of the early fifth century. There is little evidence for the use of the alphabetic notation during the Classical Greek period, but during the third century it came into general use in the Greek world, and in the last century B.C. it entirely replaced the acrophonic system, even at Athens, where the old notation lingered longest.

The alphabetic notation takes the twenty-four letters of the Greek alphabet, with three other letters which in Classical times had become obsolete, for the digits from 1 to 9, the tens up to 90 and the hundreds up to 900. Intermediate numbers are represented by combinations of these letters, and thousands by the same letters with strokes against them. Thus the first three letters of the alphabet, α, β and γ, are 1, 2 and 3, while $_{/}\alpha$, $_{/}\beta$, $_{/}\gamma$ [7] are 1,000, 2,000, 3,000; ι, κ, λ are 10, 20, 30; and ρ, σ, τ are 100, 200, 300; so that 111 is $\rho\iota\alpha$ (three different letters, it will be noticed), 2,323 is $_{/}\beta\tau\kappa\gamma$, and 3,232 is $_{/}\gamma\sigma\lambda\beta$. The letter M was usually borrowed from the acrophonic notation to represent 10,000, the number of tens of thousands being then given by putting the appropriate letter above the M (*e.g.*, $\overset{\delta}{M} = 40,000$). Sometimes the letters might appear in a different order, but we need not confuse the issue now by taking notice of this or the many other variations which are to be found in the papyri. The highest figure

---

Maths. (1894) 64; *Hist. of Mathl. Notations* I (1928) 25–26. More favourable is Heath, *op. cit.* I 37–39. The best defence of the alphabetic system is by J. G. Smyly, "The Employment of the Alphabet in Gk. Logistic," in *Mél. J. Nicole* (1905) 515–530.

4 *IG* I² 760.   5 *SIG*³ 46.

6 See R. Hackl, "Merkantile Inschriften auf attischen Vasen," in *Münchener archäol. Studien dem Andenken A. Furtwänglers gewidmet* (1909) 1–106. Even if some of the *graffiti* are of 6th cent. date, I do not think that those letters which are certainly numerals need be older than the 5th cent. One of the *graffiti* is illustrated in J. Kirchner, *Imagines Inscr. Attic.* (2nd ed. by G. Klaffenbach, 1948), pl. 11, no. 23. See also Mabel Lang, "Numerical Notation on Greek Vases," in *Hesp.* 25 (1956) 1–24, with references to other recent publications, including those of Amyx and Jongkees.

7 Distinguish figures with strokes against them in a different position, to the right and above: this was the commonest way of representing fractions ($\gamma' = 1/3$, $\iota'\beta' = 1/12$, etc.).

which could be represented in the ordinary Greek alphabetic notation was 99,999,999.[8] The number of the hundred million angels of *Revelation* V, 11,[9] was therefore literally inexpressible—by ordinary symbols: it could be stated only in words, as " ten thousand times ten thousand" (μυριάδες μυριάδων, literally " ten thousands of ten thousands "), an expression which consequently became a standard phrase for " a number which no man could count." Whenever a number up to 9,999 can be represented in our notation without using a zero, it will be expressed by exactly the same number of digits in the Greek alphabetic notation. The number 3,333, for example, is ,γτλγ. Whenever we have to use a zero, however, the two sets of symbols are visibly different. In the Greek notation there is nothing corresponding to our zero, so that 100, for instance, is ρ alone, 103 is ργ, and 40,001 is Μα.

Thus the Greek alphabetic notation has a minor drawback peculiar to itself and a major defect which it shares with the Roman and the Greek acrophonic systems. The minor failing is that it has as many as twenty-eight different signs, three or four times as many as the other two ancient scripts and our own—enough to make it distinctly harder to learn, but not so many (when we remember that our alphabet has twenty-six letters) as to present any real difficulty to a person of reasonable intelligence. The serious defect is that the alphabetic notation (like the other two ancient systems) knows nothing of place-value. However, as will become apparent shortly, this notation has certain qualities which to some extent compensate for this defect—sufficiently so, at any rate, to prevent the Greeks from becoming aware that the defect existed.

It is the practical consequences (especially for accounting) of the lack of place-value in the three numeral scripts of the Greeks and Romans and its presence in our own that I now wish to discuss. I intend to put forward two theses: first, that the habitual arrangement of figures in columns in our notation is not an intrinsic virtue of that notation but, on the contrary, an incidental defect, due, somewhat paradoxically, to the combination of its two greatest virtues, namely place-value and the small number of symbols it employs; but secondly, that this very defect (the necessity for the arrangement of figures in columns) has, paradoxically again, provided a very useful stimulus towards the evolution of the advanced concepts of debit and credit (positive and negative entries), by producing accounts kept first in one

---

[8] Apollonius of Perga (late 3rd cent. B.C.), however, devised an extension of the system, covering all numbers which can be expressed by anything up to 40,000 digits in our notation. His elder contemporary Archimedes went far beyond this, producing a further extension which at a fairly early stage, it seems, would provide an equivalent for some nine hundred million digits in our notation (Smyly, *op. cit.* in note 3 above, 527–530).

[9] And see *Daniel* VII 10.

column and then in two, the separation of the figures into columns
being of material assistance in bringing about that distinction between
two " sides " of an account which was an essential preliminary to a
co-ordinated system of book-keeping by double or even single entry.

I cannot proceed any further without undertaking a criticism of
the conception of Greek numerals which seems to prevail generally
nowadays, and is stated clearly in Sir Thomas Heath's *History of
Greek Mathematics* (1921),[10] the standard work on its subject. After
saying that the real defect of the alphabetic notation is the absence of
a zero symbol, Heath goes on to assert that " if there had been a sign
or signs to indicate the absence in a number of a particular denomination, *e.g.,* units or tens or hundreds, the Greek symbols could have
been made to serve as a position-value system scarcely less effective
than ours "; and he then proceeds to show how the Greeks must have
tried to compensate for the lack of place-value in their numeral
notation. He takes it for granted that the Greeks, when they were
operating with their alphabetic numerals, wrote down the units, tens,
hundreds, thousands and ten-thousands in separate vertical columns.
Thus Heath assumes, for instance, that in adding together 12,281
and 30,030, to make 42,311, a Greek would have proceeded to write
the sum as follows: —

$$M_{\prime}\ \beta\sigma\pi\alpha$$
$$\overset{\gamma}{M}\quad \lambda$$
$$\overline{\overset{\delta}{M_{\prime}}\ \beta\tau\iota\alpha}$$

He gives no authority for this statement: he simply says, " There is
no doubt that, in writing down numbers for the purpose of these
operations, the Greeks would keep the several powers of ten separate
in a manner practically corresponding to our system of numerals." [11]
Now in relation to the ancient world the expression " there is no
doubt that " is often a kind of euphemism for " there is no evidence
that "; and so it is here. Heath, I should say, was trying in effect to
smuggle into Greek arithmetic (of course without the slightest intention to deceive) a partial substitute for the place-value which is missing
from the numeral notation, involving the use of a blank space corresponding to our zero. The whole conception, however, is fundamentally wrong, both on factual grounds and because it is based on a
misconception of the functioning of the alphabetic numeral notation.

First, Heath is wrong on the facts. We cannot simply take it for
granted that the Greeks " must have " adopted the procedure he so
confidently describes; we must look for evidence as to whether they

actually did so or not. As far as I can discover, there is no trace of
any such arrangement as Heath postulates, with gaps between the
alphabetical digits, or any other substitute for a zero, in any Greek
inscription or papyrus. It may be dangerous to assert a negative in
such a case as this, where the field of possible evidence is very large;
but it can at least be said with absolute confidence that no such practice as Heath assumes was at all usual or characteristic. The Greeks,
like the Babylonians, did have zero-signs, including an 0 just like our
nought, but they seem to have employed these symbols only in sexagesimal fractions,[12] which could have been known only to a limited
circle of mathematicians and were not used consistently except in
astronomy and pure mathematics.[13] The very fact that the figures in
Greek inscriptions and papyri are never—or not normally—arranged
in precise columns is dead against Heath's theory. And there is a
valuable piece of evidence from a literary source, the only ancient
treatise I know of in which multiplication sums [14] are set out in full
in the text, in figures.[15] This is a commentary written in the sixth
century by Eutocius of Ascalon on Archimedes' *Measurement of a
Circle* (κύκλου μέτρησις, third century B.C.). In the standard Teubner
text, edited by Heiberg, there is no attempt to arrange the numerals in
strict columns, and it seems quite certain that they cannot be so
arranged in the manuscripts. This, with the other evidence, seems
conclusive.

Secondly, Heath was mistaken about the way the alphabetic
notation operated. It may be rash for one who is not a mathematician to suggest that one of the highest authorities on Greek
mathematics did not fully grasp the simple structure of the Greek
alphabetic numeral system; but mathematicians are often uninterested
in elementary arithmetical questions, and in any event we are dealing
here with plain matters of common sense. The essential point which
Heath failed to see is that the symbols in the Greek alphabetic
notation have a quality which is in many respects a substitute for
place-value and prevented the Greeks from even noticing the absence
of place-value in the full sense, let alone regretting it and trying to
compensate for it. In a most valuable article which was published
sixteen years before the appearance of Heath's *History of Greek*

[12] See Heath, *Hist. of Gk. Maths.* I 44–45 ; O. Neugebauer, *The Exact Sciences in
Antiquity* (1951) 10–22, and pl. II, showing part of an astronomical papyrus:
P. Lund Inv. 35a.
[13] Neugebauer, *op. cit.* 17.
[14] I believe that similarly there is only a single surviving example of a division sum
worked out at length, in Theon's *Commentary* on the *Syntaxis* of Ptolemy, and
this is in the sexagesimal notation: see the text and trans. in Ivor Thomas,
Gk. Mathl. Works (Loeb) I 50–53 ; *cf.* Smyly, *op. cit.* (in note 3 above) 526–527.
[15] There are nice examples of multiplication sums written out in words in Dem. 22,
Hypoth. 2. 4–6: *e.g.* (§ 5) $12 \times 29\frac{1}{2}$ is solemnly written out (in words) as $10 \times 20 =
200$, $2 \times 20 = 40$, $10 \times 9 = 90$, $2 \times 9 = 18$, $\frac{1}{2} \times 12 = 6$.

Mathematics but apparently remained unknown to Heath, the classical scholar and papyrologist J. G. Smyly demonstrated [16] that the symbols of the alphabetic numeral system (twenty-seven in number, if we ignore the extraneous M which is 10,000) were conceived as arranged in four rows (*versus* [17] in Latin; the original Greek term is not known), each containing nine symbols, the fourth *versus* being of course a repetition of the symbols of the first, with the addition of a short stroke against each. The symbols of the first *versus* represent units up to nine, those of the second *versus* tens, of the third hundreds and of the fourth thousands. In the minds of the Greeks the symbols would naturally arrange themselves in this order, just as our figures fall into place in our minds in " rows " of ten. For the Greeks, ten was the first number of the second row, one hundred the first of the third row, and one thousand of the fourth, whereas with us ten completes the first row, and so on, there being ten numbers in each row instead of nine. Here, it seems to me, the alphabetic notation can be harshly criticised. It is at the very least inelegant, and I should say clumsy and muddling, for a decimal numerical system to be expressed by symbols grouped in nines. The only way out, for the Greeks, would have been to employ a symbol corresponding to our zero; and this they never did, in ordinary arithmetic. (The absence of the zero from the alphabetic notation is not as strange as many people might think. The zero, however natural it may appear to us, is actually an advanced concept which very few numeral systems have evolved.) But the Greek did have one advantage over us: he never needed to write down his figures in columns. If this had been suggested to him, the Greek might reasonably have retorted that it was quite superfluous: he, like the Roman, could add numbers in any position equally well. (We need not consider multiplication and division separately: if one knows one's tables, multiplication and division then resolve themselves into mere addition and subtraction— and it appears from a chance remark of Aristotle's that in his day it was considered advisable to know the multiplication tables up to " ten times." [18]) To the Greek, a number was immediately recognisable as a member of a particular *versus*. Smyly [19] is surely right in saying that when adding numbers together a Greek first added up mentally any numbers belonging to the first *versus,* and then went up through the other *versus* in turn. Thus, in adding 281, 30 and 8 ($\sigma\pi\alpha$, λ and η) a Greek would instantly pick out the α and η, add one to eight, and write down θ (9). He would next take the π and λ, and

---

[16] *Op. cit.* 516–518.
[17] Smyly (*loc. cit.*) refers to the use of this term by Martianus Capella 7.745 (ed. Eyssenhardt, p. 265) and Favonius Eulogius, *in Somn. Scip.* p. 22.
[18] *Topica* 8.14, 163b. The procedure in multiplication and division is explained by Smyly, *op. cit.* 522–525.   [19] *Op. cit.* (in note 3, p. 54 above) 520–521.

add eighty to thirty, making a hundred and ten ($\rho\iota$): of this he would write down the ι (10) and carry a hundred (ρ), adding it to σ (200) to make three hundred, *i.e.*, τ. His answer would be $\tau\iota\theta$ (319).[20] Operating in this way, one would obviously never think of writing down the numbers of each *versus* underneath each other—it would have been a waste of time. The Greek was not liable to confuse hundreds with thousands or tens or units: he used a completely different set of symbols for each denomination. He might reasonably have told us that the difficulty most people experience in adding Arabic numerals, in any quantity, without first writing them down in a column, is a minor defect and not a virtue of our notation. This is true, but against this we must set the far smaller number of numeral signs which we have to learn, and the very much greater flexibility of our notation, which is decidedly superior to the Greek alphabetic script in the range of calculations for which it can be used. Decimals, as far as I can see, could not be expressed at all in the alphabetic notation without some radical departure from its principles. And fractions evidently created great difficulties in practice for the users of the alphabetic script: they were dealt with in a clumsy manner [1] and must have made calculation much more difficult. Mistakes in operating with fractions are particularly common in papyri. But it is sometimes difficult to tell how far deficiencies observable in ancient arithmetical calculations are due to the nature of the scripts used and how far to the comparative indifference of the Greeks and Romans to extreme precision in such matters as the calculation of interest on loans.[2]

It has often been asserted that the Greeks and Romans could hardly have performed even the simplest arithmetical calculations without recourse to an abacus.[3] This has been flatly denied by

---

[20] There is just one text which makes me a little uneasy about this reconstruction: Hdts. 2.36.4 says, " Greeks write, and reckon with counters ($\kappa\alpha\grave{\iota}$ $\lambda o\gamma\acute{\iota}\zeta o\nu\tau\alpha\iota$ $\psi\acute{\eta}\phi o\iota\sigma\iota$), by moving the hand from left to right, Egyptians from right to left." The $\psi\tilde{\eta}\phi o\iota$ are undoubtedly the counters used with the abacus, as in Aristoph., *Vesp.* 656; Dem. 18.227; Polyb. 5.26.13 (and see Liddell & Scott, *Gk.-Eng. Lexicon*[9], *s.v.* $\psi\tilde{\eta}\phi o\varsigma$ II 1 a). Now the surviving abaci (see note 3 below) must surely have been operated from right to left, from smaller to larger numbers The reverse would have entailed going back unnecessarily, to add on figures which had to be carried over. I cannot understand what H. means, unless 5th-cent. abaci had the column representing units on the left.

[1] It seems to me that the Greeks were quite unnecessarily clumsy in expressing fractions in their alphabetic script. I cannot see that fractions need have created such difficulties for them.

[2] For the inexact reckoning of interest in the records of the loans made to the Athenian State by the sacred treasuries in the late 5th cent. B.C. (pp. 26–27 above), see B. D. Meritt, *The Athenian Calendar in the 5th Cent.* (1928) 30–37. See also *ibid.* 48–50, 69–70 for mistakes in calculation in these accounts. *Cf.* G. Glotz in *REG* 23 (1910) 280–281 for inaccuracies in the Delian accounts.

[3] On the abacus in general, see D. E. Smith, *Hist. of Mathematics* II (1925) 156–192. On the abacus in antiquity, see A. Nagl, " Die Rechentafel der Alten "= *Sb. Ak. Wien* 177.5 (1914), and *s.v.* " Abacus " in Pauly-Wissowa, *Realenc.*, Suppl. III (1918) 4–18.

Smyly,[4] for the Greeks who used the alphabetic notation; and there can be no doubt that he is right. Certainly, the abacus is referred to occasionally in Greek and Latin literature,[5] and it is quite possible that it was widely used by the Greeks as well as the Romans. But this does not of itself prove that Smyly has overrated the Greek alphabetic numeral system. Abaci are regularly used to this day in certain countries (Russia, for example) by people who reckon with Arabic figures. The fact—if it is a fact—that the Greeks often used abaci does not prove that they could not have managed quite well without them.

Now one might think that through the use of the abacus, with its natural arrangement in columns according to powers of ten, and an empty column to represent zero in each denomination, the idea of place-value, in our sense, might have spilled over, so to speak, into the Greek numeral notation; but as I have already shown, the evidence of the papyri and inscriptions proves that it did not. The figures in a numeral script need not correspond individually, as ours would, with the columns of an abacus: this is very obvious in regard to Roman numerals.

At last we can go back to Greek and Roman accounting. My argument, in a nutshell, is that owing to the absence of place-value from their numeral notations the Greeks and Romans never needed to put the figures of an account in a precise column. We have discussed the question of simple calculation with the Greek alphabetic notation. The facts are even plainer in regard to the Roman and the Greek acrophonic notations. If one wants to add, say, 1,011 and 1,309, writing down MXI and MCCCIX, or XΔI and XHHHΓIIII, one underneath the other does not help in the slightest degree. As the Greeks and Romans did not use even one column, of course they did not normally separate debits and credits (or receipts and payments) into two columns. This surely helped to prevent the advanced anti-thetical concepts of debit and credit from emerging. And without the fully developed notions of debit and credit there can of course be no question of double entry. I would not claim that this is the principal reason for the failure of the Greeks and Romans to devise a more advanced system of book-keeping. Much more fundamental was the relatively primitive character of the Graeco-Roman economy, in which

4 *Op. cit.* (in note 3, p. 54 above) 521.
5 *e.g.*, the passages cited in note 20, p. 59 above, also Diog. Laert. 1.59; Plut., *Cat. Min.* 70; Juv., *Sat.* 9.40–41; probably also Aesch., *Agam.* 570; Eurip. *Rhes.* 309–310; Dem. 18.227, 229; Plut., *Mor.* 812e. Apart from references to abaci in connection with the more advanced kind of mathematical calculation (as in Plut., *Cat. Min.* 70, cited above; also Pers. 1.131; Apul., *Apol.* 16) or the learning of arithmetic by children, I have found surprisingly few passages in Greek or Latin literature in which the abacus is mentioned. This makes me suspect that even the users of the much more cumbrous Roman numeral notation may not have been so dependent upon the abacus as many moderns have supposed.

credit was not highly developed. In a system which dealt largely in cash and in kind, the need for a technique such as double entry would seldom arise, and the small men who carried on most of the trade of the ancient world managed quite well without it. Even they, however, would obviously have benefited from a better numeral notation and the separation of debit and credit items; and owners of great estates, tax-farmers, large-scale moneylenders, bankers, and the few important merchants, might even have been glad to use double entry, had it been available to them.

VII. ARABIC NUMERALS AND THE RISE OF MODERN ACCOUNTING

It seems appropriate that I should conclude by saying something about the subsequent history of the Greek and Roman numeral systems and their ultimate supersession by our own numerals, commonly called Arabic, but sometimes, more properly, Hindu-Arabic, since their origin was Indian, although their diffusion towards the West was due to the Arabs. A most interesting passage in the *Chronicle* of the Byzantine historian Theophanes [6] tells us that in A.D. 699, more than half a century after Egypt and Syria had fallen under Muslim rule, the Ummayad Caliph Walid ordered the scribes of the public treasury to use only Arabic instead of Greek characters, except for numerals, the Greek signs for which might still be employed owing to the poverty of the Arabic numeral notation—which at this time, then, was evidently not the modern one. Theophanes adds that for this reason Christian clerks were still serving under the Muslims in his own day, the early ninth century.

At this point my knowledge of the sources fails, as I am not a medievalist, and for the rest of this section I have had to rely largely on the works of modern scholars, although I have examined as much published source material as possible, including all the documents I have mentioned here. The notation we use today, complete with place-value and a zero symbol (certainly taken over by the Arabs from India),[7] began to come into use in the Muslim world during the ninth century, just after the time of Theophanes. In the first half of that century the Persian mathematician Al-Khwarazmi wrote an arithmetical treatise in Arabic in which the modern numeral notation, expressly attributed by him to the Hindus, is said to appear complete [8];

---

[6] *Chronographia, s.a.* A.D. 699 (ed. Classen, in the Bonn *Corp. script. hist. byzant.* XXVI, i, p. 575).
[7] See esp. the admirable work of D. E. Smith and L. C. Karpinski, *The Hindu-Arabic Numls.* (1911), particularly Chaps. i, vi.
[8] *Ibid.* 4–5, 97.

and ninth-century Arabic manuscripts [9] are known which use the zero, the great innovation of this script. The new system seems to have been slow to prevail in the Muslim area: as late as about 1025 we hear that most people still preferred to use the old Arabic notation.[10]

The introduction of the Hindu-Arabic numerals into Christian Europe, through Muslim Spain, was even longer delayed. So far as I can discover, the oldest extant documents of Christian Europe using the new numerals (the *gobar* numerals,[11] as they were called at first) are Spanish manuscripts of the later tenth century, the earliest datable one being of 976.[12]   About this very time, Gerbert (later Pope Sylvester II) was the first man in Christendom to give a proper description of the new numerals; but it appears that he did not know the zero—usually represented in Arabic script then, as now in Arab lands, by a dot.[13]   In the first half of the twelfth century Al-Khwarazmi's arithmetical treatise was translated into Latin by an Englishman, possibly Adelard of Bath or Robert of Chester,[14] under the name " Algoritmi de numero Indorum "; and from about the same time, in 1138, we have the earliest known official document inscribed with the new numerals: a coin of Roger, the Norman king of Sicily [15] —where, however, the date occurs as part of an Arabic inscription. It was another three to five hundred years before the Arabic notation became general throughout Europe, and accounts seem to have been kept mainly in Roman figures until at least the sixteenth century.

Now it appears to be universally agreed that double-entry book-keeping had made its appearance beyond any doubt before 1340, by which time the system—wherever it may have been invented—had established itself in the official books of the *Massari* at Genoa.[16] Recently two Italian scholars, the philologist Castellani and the historian of accounting Melis, have traced the origin of double entry

---

[9] The earliest seems to be of 873: *ibid.* 56 and note 2, *cf.* 138, note 3.

[10] *Ibid.* 98.

[11] *Ibid.* 65–70.

[12] *Ibid.* 116 and note 2, 137–138, 140; G. F. Hill, *The Development of Arabic Numls. in Europe* (1915) 28–29; " On the Early Use of Arabic Numls. in Eur.," in *Archaeologia* 62 (1910) 137–190, at p. 170.

[13] See Smith and Karpinski, *op. cit.* (in note 7 above) 112–117, *cf.* 53–56.

[14] Each of whom translated into Latin a work of Al-Khwarazmi's: see L. C. Karpinski, *Robert of Chester's Latin Trans. of the Algebra of Al-Khowarizmi* (1915).   According to Karpinski, the Latin translation of the arithmetical work (the *Algoritmi*) was published in 1857 by B. Boncompagni, *Trattati d'aritmetica* I 1–23 ; but I have not been able to find a copy of this in any library to which I have had access.   See also Smith and Karpinski, *op. cit.,* 5, 97, 126.   A. Clerval, *Les Écoles de Chartres au Moyen-Âge* (– *Méms. de la soc. archéol. d'Eure-et-Loir* 11, 1895) 238, mentions the appearance of the zero in the *Heptateuchon* of Thierry of Chartres (before 1150).   But see C. H. Haskins, *Stud. in the Hist. of Mediaeval Science*[2] (1927) 90–91.

[15] Hill, *DANE* (see note 12 above) 16, note 1=*EUANE* 146, note 1.

[16] For these accounts, see F. Melis, *Storia della ragioneria* 527 *et seq.,* with refs.

still further back. Both Melis [17] and Castellani [18] believe that the
system can be found in the accounts of the Florentine merchant
Rinieri Fini and his brothers, whose books relating to dealings at the
fairs of Champagne survive for the years 1296 to 1305 [19]; and Melis
(who also believes that the books of other Florentine merchants, from
the year 1299 onwards, are in double entry) is a strong advocate of the
view that double entry actually originated in the towns of Tuscany.[20]
However that may be, we shall be safe in concluding that book-keeping
by double entry had established itself in the towns of northern Italy
by the very end of the thirteenth century or the first half of the
fourteenth century at the latest.   This was the climax of a process of
evolution the earlier stages of which we cannot trace with any
certainty, owing to the extreme paucity of material.   We need consider
only commercial accounts, for it seems to be a fact (which I have not
been able to verify at first hand except to a very limited extent) that
no significant advances in technique took place independently in non-
commercial accounts, such as (in England) those of manors, religious
houses and colleges, and the Pipe Rolls and other financial records
kept by departments of State and other authorities, specimens of
which survive from as early as the twelfth century and are quite
plentiful from the thirteenth century onwards.   Apart from a few
fragments dating from the year 1157,[1] the earliest commercial account
which has survived from the European Middle Ages seems to belong
to 1211.[2]   Not very many commercial accounts of any sort have
survived from the thirteenth century; but by the late thirteenth and
early fourteenth centuries two kinds of evolution in commercial
accounting can be traced [3]: in some accounts, debit and credit entries
respectively are arranged together in groups, and the two groups are
placed either one below the other or in two different parts of the
book [4]; and in some other accounts debit and credit entries are posted

---

[17] Melis, *op. cit.* 381 *et seq.*

[18] Arrigo Castellani, *Nuovi testi fiorentini del Dugento* (1952) I 8-10; II 674-696,
no. 22.   Raymond de Roover, in his review-article, " New Perspectives in the
Hist. of Accounting," in *Accounting Review* 30 (1955) 405-420, at pp. 406-407,
discusses this work and Melis's and also Tommaso Zerbi, *Le origini della partita
doppia.   Gestioni aziendali e situazioni di mercato nei secoli XIV e XV* (1952).
This last is a long and difficult book, which I was not able to consult until this
essay was completed.   As far as I could see at a brief inspection, it contains
little that is relevant to what has been said here.

[19] See Castellani, *loc. cit.*; Melis, *op. cit.* 481-485 and pl. xxxiii.

[20] An earlier article by de Roover on the origin of double entry is still valuable:
" Aux origines d'une technique intellectuelle: la formation et l'expansion de la
comptabilité à partie double," in *Annales d'hist. écon. et soc.* 44 (1937) 171-193;
45 (1937) 270-298.

[1] From Genoa.   See de Roover, *op. cit.* in the preceding note, 174.

[2] From Florence.   See Melis, *op. cit.* 392-395, with photograph, pl. xxviii.

[3] See de Roover, *op. cit.* in note 20 above, 179-182; Melis, *op. cit.* 385-437.

[4] Italian *conti a sezioni sovrapposte.*   For the accounts of the Peruzzi of Florence,
1282-1343, see de Roover, *op. cit.* in note 20 above, 179-181; Melis, *op. cit.*
405-411, and 387, note 10.   De Roover, *op. cit.* in note 18 above, 411-412, agrees
with Melis that these books (at any rate those of 1335-1343) are in double entry.

in columns side by side, in " bilateral form." [5]   The earliest known "bilateral" accounts appear in two different varieties: the two "sides" of the account may be placed either on the same page or on opposite pages.   The former type of " bilateral " account, with debits and credits on the same page, is that of our earliest surviving examples, which happen to come from towns of Tuscany other than Florence,[6] and it seems to have been adopted also in Genoa and the towns of Lombardy and Emilia.[7]   The latter type, with debits and credits on opposite pages, was evidently associated particularly with Venice (whether or not it was actually invented there), for it is described in the late fourteenth and in the fifteenth century as accounting " alla veneziana." [8]   There is no evidence that, as Besta [9] maintained, double entry was first evolved at Venice: unfortunately no Venetian commercial documents seem to be extant of an earlier date than the beginning of the fifteenth century.[10]

The idea that the rise of the advanced modern form of book-keeping was closely connected with the introduction of Arabic numerals has found no advocates for a long time, as far as I am aware, and nowadays it is generally rejected out of hand,[11] apparently on two grounds.   First, although double-entry book-keeping makes its appearance not later than the first half of the fourteenth century, virtually all [12] the surviving accounts down to about the end of the fifteenth century are kept in Roman numerals, even where dates and folio numbers are in Arabic figures.[13]   (It seems to have been thought, rightly or wrongly, that Roman numerals are less easy to alter.)   Secondly, it is claimed that with the aid of an abacus calculations could be made very efficiently and quickly, so that a person doing the

---

[5] Italian *conti a sezioni contrapposte*, German *Gegenüberstellung*, Dutch *scontro-vorm* (de Roover, *op. cit.* in note 20 above, 181, note 2).   *Cf.* pp. 19–21 above.

[6] These are (a) the cash accounts of a firm of merchants and bankers at Siena, 1281; (b) the cash accounts of Cepperello Diotaiuti of Prato, 1288; (c) the accounts of the Gallerani company of Siena, 1305–1308; and (d) the accounts of Princivalle Manni, Geri Burlamacchi and company, silk merchants of Lucca, 1332–1336: see Melis, *op. cit.* in note 16 above, 429–433; *cf.* de Roover, *op. cit.* in note 20 above, 181–182.

[7] See Melis, *op. cit.* 433, 435, 527–531.

[8] See de Roover, *op. cit.* in note 20 above, 181; F. Besta, *La ragioneria*² III 328–329; Melis *op. cit.* 427–437, 535–537.   The earliest known occurrence of this expression, as far as I can discover, is in the account-books, opened in 1382, of the Florentine merchant Paliano di Falco, where we read, " Questo libro . . . scriverollo alla viniziana, cioè nell'una carta dare e a rimpetto l'avere " (Melis, *op. cit.* 427).

[9] *Op. cit.* III 342–349.

[10] See de Roover, *op. cit.* in note 20 above, 181–182; Melis, *op. cit.* 532–535.

[11] As by Melis, *op. cit.* 382 (" assai poco influenti "); Besta, *op. cit.* III 338.

[12] The earliest exception I know of is the Badoer accounts of 1436–1439, a product of the commercial intercourse between Venice and Constantinople: see Besta, *op. cit.* II 434; III 310–313; Zerbi, *op. cit.* (in note 18 above) 396–412; Melis, *op. cit.* 534–535 and note 354; T. Bertelè, " Il libro dei conti di Giacomo Badoer," in *Byzantion* 21 (1951) 123–126.

[13] As in the Barbarigo accounts of 1430: see Melis, *op. cit.* 533–534, with photograph, pl. xliii.   See also Besta, *op. cit.* II 434; III 297.

sums would not have felt the lack of a place-value system with figures disposed in precise columns and added or subtracted on the actual page itself. Both these points are valid, but to my mind they are not decisive. I should like to draw attention to two pieces of evidence which have made me suspect that the rise of modern book-keeping may in fact be bound up with the introduction of Arabic figures.

First, as early as 1299 the rules of the *Arte dei cambi* (the guild of moneychangers) at Florence forbade the use of Arabic numerals in accounts.[14] This shows that Arabic figures were in fact being used in accounting at Florence in the thirteenth century, the very time when commercial accounting was evidently making a great advance, and double-entry was on the point of emerging. if indeed it had not already appeared, in the accounting practice of merchants of Florence itself.

My second piece of evidence is a very remarkable and highly original book, the *Liber Abbaci*,[15] written as early as 1202 by the greatest mathematician of the time, Leonardo Fibonacci of Pisa (Leonardo Pisano, or Leonard of Pisa). Leonardo was the son of a man who acted as official notary to the merchants of Pisa operating on the Barbary coast, at a place which must be the modern Bougie in Algeria; and in his youth he himself had travelled as a merchant from end to end of the Mediterranean.[16] He was taught the Hindu-Arabic numerals (which he calls *figurae Indorum*) by his father, and his express aim in writing the *Liber Abbaci* was to encourage their general use for all purposes, including commercial accounting, a subject to which he devotes a great deal of attention in this book. He actually sets out an account,[17] with a full explanation, in both Roman and Arabic numerals, the Roman figures in the text and the Arabic ones drawn out in columns in the right-hand margin—a most striking demonstration of the superior value of the new system for accounting purposes. Leonardo has justly been recognised as a major figure in the history of accounting.[18] His admirers, however, have paid scant

---

[14] *Rubrica* 101 of the *Statuto dell'arte dei cambi in Firenze*: see Besta, *op. cit.* II 434; de Roover, *op. cit.* in note 20, p. 63 above, 191, note 3.

[15] The standard edition is that of B. Boncompagni (1857). For a discussion of this fascinating work from the point of view of an historian of accounting, see Melis, *op. cit.* (in note 16, p. 62 above) 585–592.

[16] *Liber Abbaci*, p. 1: " Cum genitor meus a patria publicus scriba in duana Bugee pro Pisanis mercatoribus ad eam confluentibus constitutus preesset, me in pueritia mea ad se venire faciens, . . . ibi me studio abbaci per aliquot dies stare voluit et doceri. Ubi ex mirabili magisterio in arte per novem figuras Indorum introductus, scientia artis in tantum mihi pre ceteris placuit, et intellexi ad illam, quod quicquid studebatur ex ea apud Egyptum, Syriam, Greciam, Siciliam et Provinciam cum suis variis modis, ad que loca negotiationis tam postea peragravi per multum studium et disputationis didici conflictum."

[17] *Liber Abbaci*, 21–22.

[18] Melis, *op. cit.* 591, agrees with P. Bariola (*Storia della ragioneria ital.* 48) that the *Liber Abbaci* is " l'opera che delineò l'orizzonte della moderna computisteria."

attention to his insistence on the great superiority of Arabic over Roman numerals as the medium of accounting.

Leonardo's father was using the Arabic notation well before the end of the twelfth century. At that time, and even more of course during the thirteenth century, there must have been many other merchants who, like Leonardo and his father, perceived the usefulness of the Arabic numerals for purposes of book-keeping. I suggest that it was these men who were responsible for the introduction into Europe of the practice of arranging figures—Arabic figures—in accounts in regular columns, a practice which was surely important in its own right, in that it would lead naturally to further developments as the economy of the high Middle Ages expanded and made them increasingly desirable. Once figures began to be disposed in a *single* column, instead of being scattered all over the page and reduced to order only outside the account-book, on the abacus or in the mind, the advantages of having *two* clearly separated columns, simply to facilitate computation, would very quickly become apparent; and this would of itself result in the emergence of the bilateral form of account, with debits and credits visibly distinguished. The final step, the further advance to double entry, could then equally well be made by those (no doubt still the large majority) who continued to employ Roman numerals. All that I am claiming for the users of Arabic figures is a very probable priority in disposing figures regularly and visibly on the page first in one and then in two columns, a procedure which, as I see it, would have been a decided stimulus to the emergence of the developed concepts of debit and credit, and which the more conservative users of Roman (or Greek) numerals would be far less likely to initiate, because the nature of their script did not invite it, their tabulation being done (if at all) separately on the abacus, although once they did adopt it they might be responsible for further developments just as easily as the others. I believe that this whole question would repay thorough investigation by a medievalist.

APPENDIX A.   RECENT WORK ON ANCIENT ACCOUNTING

Moritz Voigt's *Über die Bankiers, die Buchführung und die Litteral-obligation der Römer*,[19] published in 1887 and translated into Italian four years later,[20] at a time when documentary papyri had scarcely begun to come to general notice among scholars, is impressive on a superficial reading, if only by the mere number and length of its laborious footnotes, and it has been cited again and again as one of the standard works on Roman book-keeping. Voigt's main theses, however, were fundamentally

---

[19] *Abhandl. der phil.-hist. Classe der Königl. Sächsischen Gesellschaft der Wissenschaften* [Leipzig] X vii (1887) 515–577.
[20] *I banchieri, la tenuta dei libri e l'obbligazione letterale dei Romani*, tr. G. Carnazza (Catania, 1891).

mistaken. They were conclusively refuted by Th. Niemeyer in a long review published in 1890,[1] and no serious Roman historian would now accept them. It is a great pity that Voigt's conclusions should have been taken over entire by (among others) Federigo Melis, in his recent *Storia della ragioneria* (1950),[2] an impressive work which is now, and is likely to remain for some time to come, the standard book on the history of accounting. Melis's volume deals only summarily with Greek accounting of the Classical period (pp. 349–359), in a chapter which, curiously enough, comes after instead of before the section on accounting in Hellenistic and Roman Egypt (pp. 314–348) ; and unfortunately the latter subject is discussed quite separately from Roman accounting (pp. 360–373), although of course a very large part of the evidence for Roman accounts consists precisely of Greek and Latin papyri from the Roman province of Egypt. However, Melis does give in translation the text of several papyri ; his conclusions, except when he is reproducing Voigt on Roman Accounting, are on the whole cautious and reasonable; and his long bibliography is useful, if hardly complete.

Before the appearance of Melis's book the best general work on the history of accounting was Fabio Besta's *La ragioneria*.[3] This deals briefly in its second and third volumes with aspects of Greek and Roman accounting, but Besta seems to have known nothing of Greek and Latin inscriptions and he shows very little acquaintance with the papyri: he refers to only two collections and makes poor use of them.

R. Beigel's *Rechnungswesen und Buchführung der Römer* (1904), the only full-length study of Roman book-keeping to appear since Voigt's, is based on an altogether inadequate acquaintance with the original sources and is quite unscholarly in method.[4] The other general books on the history of accounting have very little to say about our subject that is both true and significant, and they all over-estimate the extent to which the Greeks and more especially the Romans developed systematic book-keeping. David Murray, *Chapters in the History of Bookkeeping, Accountancy and Commercial Arithmetic* (1930), and A. C. Littleton, *Accounting Evolution to 1900* (1933), make no reference to papyri or inscriptions. Edward Boyd, in his chapter on " Ancient Systems of Accounting " in the *History of Accounting and Accountants*, edited by Richard Brown in 1905, does show awareness of the existence of one or two inscriptions, but he evidently had no real understanding of the possibilities of epigraphic and papyrological evidence. Albert Dupont, *La partie double avant Paciolo* (1926), pp. 1–19, is entirely inadequate. Plinio Bariola, dealing briefly with Roman book-keeping in his *Storia della ragioneria italiana* (1897), pp. 229–240, merely follows Voigt ; and

---

[1] In *Zeitschr. der Savigny-Stiftung für Rechtsgesch.* XI (=*Zeitschr. für Rechtsgesch.* XXIV), 1890, ii (*Rom. Abt.*) 312–326.

[2] For an appraisement by a leading authority of the later portions of this book, dealing with accounting in medieval and modern times, see de Roover, *op. cit.* in note 18, p. 63 above. The remarks about Roman book-keeping on p. 410 of that article, however, are not based (as is the remainder of the article) on first-hand knowledge of the original sources, and the erroneous view is accepted there (as by Melis) from Voigt, that Roman account-books included a *codex accepti et expensi* as well as a *codex rationum*. Against this, see Niemeyer, *op. cit.*, and pp. 42–43 above.

[3] 2nd ed., 3 vols., Milan, 1920–1932.

[4] See esp. the crushing review by C. Bardt in *Wochenschr. für klass. Philol.* 22 (1905) cols. 14–21. And Bardt does not even mention Beigel's inexcusable failure to use other forms of evidence than that of the literary and legal sources!

Alois Früchtl, *Die Geldgeschäfte bei Cicero* (1912), in his section on "Buchführung" (pp. 31–41), simply reproduces Beigel. Perhaps the least misleading treatment of Roman book-keeping, which does at any rate utilise the evidence of the literary and legal sources in a sensible manner, is the short section on "Litterarum obligatio" in H. J. Roby's *Roman Private Law*" (1902) [5]; and even this takes no account whatever of the papyri.

Of a quite different character are some scholarly studies of particular papyri. Friedrich Preisigke's *Zur Buchführung der Banken* [6] is excellent so far as it goes, but it is of much more limited character than its title might lead one to suppose: in fact it is little more than a study of certain special accounts relating to a particular tax, kept by a particular banker in the Fayum area in the first century. Another special monograph, *Accounting in the Zenon Papyri* (1934), by an American classical scholar, Elizabeth Grier, disappoints by its failure to deal adequately with some of the fundamental questions of ancient accounting method.[7] Other publications, notably a long article by Lydia Bandi [8] on the private accounts in the papyri, and an article by M. Schnebel [9] on the papyrus accounts of a large estate in Egypt dating from the seventh century, have made useful contributions to our knowledge of specific accounts in the papyri,[10] without giving much information about Greek and Roman accounting methods in general.

The one study in modern times which has some really penetrating things to say about the ancient system of accounting and its economic consequences is the article by Mickwitz to which reference has already been made.[11]

APPENDIX B. THE PHYSICAL FORM OF ANCIENT ACCOUNTS

Many of the problems presented by ancient writing materials which have long been obscure are now being gradually elucidated as a result of discoveries in various parts of the Graeco-Roman world and the persistent researches of papyrologists and palaeographers.[12]

Papyrus (βύβλος or βίβλος, *charta*) came first in importance among ancient writing materials until well into the Roman Imperial period, when

---

[5] II 279–296.

[6] In *Arch. Pap.* 4 (1908) 95–114, on *P. Fay.* 153.

[7] Miss Grier's statement (p. 7) that "there is very little progress over the Greek and Roman systems shown in accounting until the 19th cent. after Christ" is quite mistaken: for example, a great advance was made in the 13th–15th cents.— see pp. 62–64 above.

[8] "I conti privati nei papiri dell'Egitto greco-romano," in *Aegyptus* 17 (1937) 349–451. This contains a list of ninety relevant documents (pp. 351–353, and see 353–354).

[9] "An Agricultural Ledger in *P. Bad.* 95," in *JEA* 14 (1928) 34–45.

[10] Among other works of this kind is E. R. Hardy, *The Large Estates of Byzantine Egypt* (=*Columbia Univ. Stud. in Hist., Econ. & Public Law*, no. 354, 1951) 94–101.

[11] pp. 37–38 above.

[12] The most authoritative and scholarly work on the subject is a recent article by a leading papyrologist, C. H. Roberts, "The Codex," in *Proc. of the Brit. Acad.* 40 (1954) 169–204, where references to the earlier literature will be found. Sir Fredk. G. Kenyon has given useful introductions to the subject in his article, "Books, Greek and Latin," in the *Oxford Class. Dict.* 141–143 and his short book, *Books and Readers in Ancient Greece and Rome*² (1951)—cited below as *BRAGR.*² W. Schubart, *Das Buch bei den Griechen u. Römern*² (1921) is less up to date, but still useful.

it was superseded by parchment,[13] or vellum (διφθέρα, *membrana*), made from the skins of animals,[14] the transition taking place by degrees during the third and fourth centuries. When more than one sheet of papyrus (κόλλημα, *charta*) was required for single purposes, the sheets [15] were stuck together to form a roll (τόμος, *scapus*; when written upon, βυβλίον or βιβλίον, *volumen*). Until the papyrus codex began to come into use, from about the early second century onwards, the roll was the regular form in which papyrus was employed in bulk, for ordinary documents as well as literary texts. A literary roll might be anything up to about 40 feet long,[16] a size sufficient for, say, Luke's Gospel, written in an average hand; documentary rolls might sometimes be even longer. The writing is in columns (σελίδες, *paginae*) which are often independent of the sheets and can vary greatly in width, especially in documentary (*i.e.*, non-literary) papyri.

For accounts papyrus was undoubtedly much used, but wooden tablets were employed probably even more often, except in Egypt. The wood was either whitened to receive ink from a pen or, more usually, covered with wax on which writing could be scratched with a *stilus* [17]—and then if necessary obliterated, and the tablet used again and again. A complete set of tablets would be made up of two or more wooden leaves, pierced at the edges and held together by thongs: two or three leaves were particularly common, but four or five were not unusual, and we know of tablets with as many as ten leaves,[18] though not more. Various expressions are used for a set of tablets: in Greek they are often δέλτος, δελτάριον, γραμματεῖον, γράμματα, in Latin *tabulae, tabellae, pugillares*,[19] even (because wax was normally employed) *cerae*,[20] and sometimes *codex* (originally, it seems, *caudex*), an expression which was being used as equivalent to *tabulae* at least as early as the first half of the second

---

[13] The origin of parchment used to be attributed to Eumenes I (263–241 B.C.) or II (197–160/159) of Pergamum, on the strength of Varro, *ap*. Plin. *NH* 13.70; but the discovery at Dura Europus of parchments dating from the earliest years of the 2nd cent. B.C. has made many scholars think that (to quote Kenyon) " what Eumenes did was to develop for literary purposes the use of a material already in existence."

[14] Esp. lambs, calves and kids. The process of preparation is quite different from the making of leather, which was not used for writing purposes by the Greeks and Romans but was widely employed by other peoples of antiquity (*cf*. Hdts. 5.58.3), notably those of Syria and Palestine.

[15] Of about 9–13 inches in height and 5–10 inches in width: Kenyon, *BRAGR²* 49 *et seq*.

[16] " The extreme limit of a normal Greek literary roll " is about 35 feet, according to Kenyon, *BRAGR²* 53–55, 64–65; but see *P. Oxy*. XXII 2333, 2336. According to Pliny (*NH* 13.77) there were never more than twenty sheets in a roll, and the roll would therefore not exceed 10–15 feet in length (acc. to the width of the individual sheets); but Pliny must be referring to rolls which could be purchased in Italy—it was always possible to stick together two or more rolls.

[17] For a contrast between the two types of γραμματεῖον, see Ps.-Dem. 46.11 (where the emphasis, of course, is on οἴκοθεν κατεσκευασμένον).

[18] See, *e.g.*, Mart. 14.6.1 (*triplices nostros*); 14.4.2 (*quinciplici cera*); *P. Fouad* 74 (δελτάριον . . . δεκάπτυχον, 4th cent.); G. Plaumann, " Antike Schultafeln aus Ägypten," in *Amtl. Berichte aus d. königl. Kunstsammlungen* (Berlin) 34 (1912–1913) 210–223, where a wooden tablet of nine (originally, it seems, ten) leaves, each about 7 inches by 4 inches, is illustrated in figs. 96, 98–100. For an early (5th cent. B.C.) reference to many-leaved tablets, see Eurip., *Iph. in Taur*. 727.

[19] See, *e.g.*, Pliny, *NH* 13.69.

[20] As in Plaut., *Curc*. III 40; Cic., *II Verr*. i 36.92; Quint., *Inst. Or*. 10.3.31–32; Gai. 2.104; *Dig*. 48.10.1.4.

century B.C.[1] and is often found in Cicero, applied in particular to business documents, including accounts. The Greeks and Romans made extensive use of wooden tablets, especially as papyrus was not cheap enough to be used for ephemeral scribblings and could not be re-used indefinitely as tablets could. Waxed tablets, too, owing to the ease with which alterations could be made, were particularly convenient for drafting.[2] And they were used for very diverse purposes: for accounts, memoranda,[3] letters, *billets-doux*,[4] wills,[5] and official documents such as dispatches from the Roman Senate to a foreign king.[6] In Cicero's day (roughly the second quarter of the last century B.C.) it would appear that the great majority of accounts at Rome, public [7] as well as private, were written on waxed tablets; and this was probably true of most of the Graeco-Roman world at that time, apart from Egypt. A fair number of legible wooden tablets have survived from the ancient world,[8] but as I said earlier, I know of only one,[9] from Verespatak in Transylvania, containing actual accounts.

Tablets made of wood, however, were very clumsy: there were physical limitations not only to the number of leaves which could be bound together and used conveniently as one, but also to the size of individual leaves. Tablets of fair dimensions are sometimes pictured in ancient sculpture, reliefs or painting,[10] but all the actual specimens surviving which are known to me are quite small: a tablet 7 inches by 5 or 6

---

1 See Cato, *ap.* Front., *Ep. ad Ant. imp.* 1.2.11 ("jussi caudicem proferri . . . tabulae prolatae." The expression which follows, "usque istuc ad lignum dele," confirms that the *tabulae* were wooden). *Cf.* Sen., *de Brev. Vit.* 13.4. For an explanation of Suet., fr. 104 (Reifferscheid, pp. 133-134), see Roberts, *op. cit.* (in note 12, p. 68 above) 171, note 4.

2 See Quint., *Inst. Or.* 10.3.31: "scribi optime ceris, in quibus facillime est ratio delendi."

3 See, *e.g.*, Pliny, *Ep.* 3.5.15: a "notarius cum libro [a papyrus roll, to be read from] et pugillaribus" [tablets for memoranda] always attended the Elder Pliny when he was journeying.

4 See Mart. 14.8; 14.9; Plut., *Cat. Min.* 24.1-2.

5 Suet., *Div. Jul.* 83.2; *Nero* 17; Gai. 2.104. Suet., *Div. Aug.* 101, records that Augustus at his death left (a) a will in two *codices* (two sets of tablets) and (b) three *volumina* (papyrus rolls), containing (i) directions for his funeral, (ii) his *res gestae*, and (iii) a *breviarium totius imperii*—which was not an "imperial balance sheet" but rather an inventory of financial assets and military strength.

6 As in Polyb. 29.27.2 (168 B.C.).

7 See Cic., *pro Flacc.* 18.43 (*aerarii nostri tabulas*); Ascon., *in Milonian.* 29 (p. 33 Clark: *codices librariorum* were burnt on the improvised funeral pyre of Clodius). The accounts torn up by Scipio Africanus in the Senate in 187 B.C. (Polyb. 23.14.8) were not public accounts but the private accounts of Scipio himself or his brother Lucius: they were apparently written on a papyrus roll (βυβλίον).

8 For the 155 tablets found at Pompeii, mostly in the house of the banker, L. Caecilius Jucundus, see *CIL* IV, Suppl. i, 3340. For the tablets from Verespatak, see *CIL* III ii, pp. 921-960, 1058, 2215. Facsimiles are given in both cases. For the tablets found recently at Herculaneum, see G. Pugliese Carratelli in *La parola del passato*, fasc. 3 (1946) 373-385; 8 (1948) 165-184. *Cf.* Paul, *Sent.* 5.25.6.

9 See p. 20 above.

10 In particular the large tablets depicted in the reliefs on one of the balustrades of the Roman Forum—if this scene really does refer, as most people have thought, to the remission of debts owed to the Roman State, by order of Trajan or Hadrian, in which case the objects being piled up (for burning) must be the wooden tablets on which the debts were recorded. (*Cf.* p. 31 above.) For a reproduction and notes, see Rostovtzeff, *op. cit.* in note 20, p. 41 above, pl. 50.2. A tablet composed of several leaves, of more normal size, is represented in a relief from Sens (Agedincum), now in the local museum: see Rostovtzeff, *op. cit.* 206 and

inches would be if anything rather larger than most. In the *Curculio* of Plautus the banker Lyco complains that he filled up four whole pages of his tablets, writing down the absurd name "Therapontigonus Plata-gidorus"[11]; and although this is of course comic exaggeration, it may serve to remind us that we are dealing with something much nearer the size of the schoolboy's slate than a modern ledger. And it is difficult to write small on wax. A real step forward was made by the Romans, probably in the last century B.C.,[12] when some of them began to employ, to a limited extent, a *codex* made up of leaves of parchment instead of wood,[13] at first for those everyday purposes for which wooden tablets had been used, and then occasionally (by any rate A.D. 84–85)[14] for works of literature, in place of the papyrus roll. Quintilian,[15] writing in the early nineties of the first century of the Christian era, specially recommends the parchment notebook (*membranae*) for drafting purposes to those having poor sight (who might well find scratchings on wax difficult to read), although at the same time he deplores the necessity—unknown when waxed tablets were being used—for constant dipping of the pen, which tended to shatter the *cogitationis impetum*. Neratius Priscus, an early second-century lawyer, gave the title "Membranae" to one of his

---

pl. xxix 2. A tablet of typical dimensions (to judge by those which have survived) is shown in Plate I in this book. A charming ancient picture of "a poetess with tablets and stylus" is reproduced in Kenyon, *BRAGR*[2] (note 12, p. 68 above), opp. p. 16.

[11] Plaut., *Curc.* III 39–40: "nam mihi istoc nomine, dum scribo, explevi totas ceras quattuor."

[12] The evidence is scanty but just sufficient. I cannot agree with Roberts, *op. cit.* in note 12, p. 68 above) 173 and note 3, that "in palimpsestos" in Catull. 22.5 (not 12.5) probably refers to parchment, since (a) the only other time this word appears in Latin in the last cent. B.C. (Cic., *ad Fam.* 7.18.2) it clearly means papyrus (*cf.* "in illa chartula" in the next sentence), as Roberts himself says; and (b) Catullus is speaking here of a great quantity of verses, 10,000 lines or more, evidently a finished product, and the contrast he draws is not between the completed roll and "the poet's jottings" (which might reasonably have been written on poor material) but between the splendid papyri (*chartae*, line 6) on which Suffenus's verses were actually written and the twice-used papyrus to which other people so often ("ut fit," line 5) committed their poetry. However, Hor., *Sat.* 2.3.2 and *Ars Poet.* 389 can only refer to a parchment notebook used for drafting poems. These two passages are sufficient to establish the familiar use of the parchment codex at Rome before the end of the last cent. B.C. See also Pers. 3.10 (*c.* A.D. 55–60); the jurist C. Cassius Longinus (cos. A.D. 30, died *c.* 70) *ap.* Ulp. in *Dig.* 32.52.pr.,3 ("membranae" are included in a bequest of "libri"); *Epist. II ad Tim.* 4.13 (here, as Roberts, *op. cit.* 174, 190–191, acutely points out, the writer "uses the Latin word μεμβράνας because he is referring to a Latin object for which there was no simple equivalent in Greek"). It is quite possible that the parchment notebook (*membranae*, in the plural) was already widely used in Cicero's day: see Roberts, *op. cit.* 174, citing Cic., *ad Att.* 13.24.2. However, I cannot find any suggestion in the sources that the parchment codex was yet employed for accounts—it may have been, but the language of the sources rather suggests the contrary.

[13] We seem to have no definite evidence for the use of the word "codex" for anything except wooden tablets before Gaius (A.D. 160's–170's—see *Dig.* 2.13.10.2: "totum . . . codicem rationum totasque membranas," of the *argentarius*), his contemporary Q. Cervidius Scaevola (*Dig.* 32.102.pr.: "membranulis . . . mem-branis"), and Ulpian (*c.* A.D. 211–217—see *Dig.* 32.52.pr.: "in codicibus . . . membraneis vel chartaceis . . . vel in ceratis codicillis"; also 2.13.6.7). And see Paul, *Sent.* 3.6.87. "Tabulae," so far as I know, was never used except of wooden tablets.

[14] Mart. XIV 7; 184; 186; 188; 190; 192.

[15] *Inst. Or.* 10.3.31–32.

works,[16] as today he might have called it "Jottings from a Lawyer's Notebook." [17]

Nor was it only in Italy that parchment was used in codex form: an isolated parchment diptych fastened with a leather thong, containing a document believed to date from the last century B.C. or the first of the Christian era, has been found at Dura-Europus on the Middle Euphrates [18]; and one of the comparatively few early Latin literary documents from Egypt,[19] dating apparently from about A.D. 100, once formed part of a parchment codex. During the first two centuries of our era the use of the parchment codex by the Romans seems not to have developed very greatly: at any rate, there appears to be no obvious allusion to it in the works of such writers as Pliny the Elder, Pliny the Younger, or Lucian, and only one in Galen [20]; and I do not myself know of any specific surviving reference during those two centuries to the keeping of accounts on parchment codices instead of wooden tablets, except in the lawyers of the mid-second century, Gaius and Scaevola,[1] from whose language, however, it is clear that accounts kept on parchment were by no means exceptional, even if the use of wooden tablets was still much more common.[2] In Egypt the papyrus codex [3] must have appeared soon after the parchment codex arrived—from the West, if we may accept Roberts's plausible reconstruction of the sequence of events, and hardly later than the end of the first century.[4] The codex form, applied to papyrus, was much favoured by the Christian communities in Egypt. A high proportion of the Biblical papyri from about the first four centuries of the Christian era are codices or fragments of codices, whereas for pagan literature the roll was almost invariable until well into the third century.[5]

APPENDIX C. THE ROMAN " LITERAL CONTRACT "

The Roman literal contract [6] (*obligatio litteris* or *litterarum*) certainly existed in late Republican times.[7] It was probably obsolescent, however, even in the mid-second century of our era, from which period there survives the only reliable description of it we have, in the *Institutes* of Gaius,[8] and it had entirely fallen out of use before Justinian codified

---

16 *Dig.* 1.3.21.

17 So Roberts, *op. cit.* (in note 12, p. 68 above) 196.

18 F. Cumont, *Fouilles de Doura-Europos* (1926) 296–304; and see Roberts, *op. cit.* 173, note 1.

19 *P. Oxy.* I 30: see Roberts, *op. cit.* 180.

20 See Roberts, *op. cit.* 170–171, 180.

1 As cited in note 13, p. 71 above.

2 It would be interesting to know what Juvenal (*Sat.* 7.110) had in mind when he wrote of a creditor coming to collect a debt " grandi cum codice."

3 Note Roberts, *op. cit.* 182–183 : " There is no essential connection between format and material." Papyrus could be made up in codex form and parchment in roll form (see *Dig.* 32.52.pr.), although the reverse was of course much more common.

4 See above and note 19.

5 See Roberts, *op. cit.* 183–191.

6 On the literal contract, see the brief and clear commentary of F. de Zulueta, *The Institutes of Gaius* II (1953) 163–166; also H. F. Jolowicz, *Historical Introd. to the Study of Roman Law*[2] 295–297, 564–565; W. W. Buckland, *Textbook of Rn. Law*[2] 459–461; P. F. Girard, *Manuel élém. de droit rom.*[8] 527–532.

7 I do not regard Livy 35.7 as conclusive evidence of the existence of the literal contract in the early 2nd cent. B.C.; but Cic., *de Offic.* 3.14.58–60 shows that it was well established by the later years of that cent. (I assume that the C. Canius, *eques Romanus*, in this passage and *de Orat.* 2.69.280 are identical.)

8 3.128–134, 137–138. Theoph., *Paraphr. Inst.* 3.21 can be ignored.

Roman law in the sixth century.[9] The literal contract was the only
" formal " or " abstract " [10] written contract known to Roman law: that
is to say, it was the only type of contract recognised by Roman law in
which the writing actually *was* the contract, as distinct from merely
providing *evidence* of the contract. It was a highly technical affair, and
nothing could be more mistaken than to infer from the name, as the
layman might, that any written contract could create an *obligatio litteris*.
On the contrary, the only two forms which we can be sure the literal
contract could take are as follows [11] : —

(a) *Transcriptio a persona in personam*.[12] If a debt was owing from
B to A, C might by agreement be substituted as A's debtor *litteris* in
place of B, who then dropped out entirely. The essential writing was an
entry by A of a fictitious loan to C, equivalent to the amount of the
existing debt.

(b) *Transcriptio a re in personam*. If a debt was owing from B to A,
the debt could with the agreement of the parties be converted into an
obligatio litteris by an entry in writing by A of a fictitious loan to B.
This was, of course, a plain form of novation of an existing debt.

From the creditor's point of view the superiority of a contract *litteris*
to an ordinary contract (of sale, for example) was that it might greatly
improve his own legal position by providing him with a more effective
form of action *stricti juris*, by *condictio*,[13] free from the counterclaims
and other features of an action *bonae fidei* which, but for the literal
contract, might have been his only remedy at law.

That is virtually all we know about the Roman literal contract.[14]

---

[9] See *Inst. J.* 3.21. It has been very plausibly suggested that creditors came to
prefer the *constitutum* (on which see Buckland, *op. cit.* 529–531), since on this
could be based the *actio de pecunia constituta*, with its higher penal *sponsio
pecuniae partis dimidiae* (Gai. 4.171 ; *Inst. J.* 4.6.8,9).

[10] It may be that in strictness these terms are inapplicable to the literal contract :
see de Zulueta, *op. cit.* (in note 6 above) II 165.

[11] From these two forms of *nomina transcripticia* Gaius (3.131–132) distinguishes
real entries recording the payment of money (*nomina arcaria*), where the contract
is brought into existence by the actual payment (*numeratio pecuniae*) and not by
the making of the entry, which can do no more than supply evidence of the
payment.

[12] An inscription apparently illustrating this is *FIRA* III² no. 124=Bruns, *Fontes'*
no. 156. See also P. F. Girard, *Textes de droit rom.*⁶ 846–847.

[13] See de Zulueta, *op. cit.* (in note 6 above) II 164–165 ; and, for the *condictio*,
Jolowicz, *op. cit.* (in note 6 above) 221–223, with 197–200 (see esp. 198–199 on the
sponsio et restipulatio tertiae partis). The literal contract was inferior in some
respects to *stipulatio*, but unlike *stipulatio* it could be concluded *cum absentis*
(Gai. 3.138 ; and note the words " apsente [de]bitore " in the inscription mentioned
in the preceding note).

[14] Our three main pieces of literary evidence for the literal contract do not take us
much further :—(a) Val. Max. 8.2.2 does not make clear the grounds on which
the *judex* gave judgment against Otacilia: he may simply have refused to enforce
a contract which could well be regarded as contrary to morality. (b) Cic., *de
Offic.* 3.14.58–60 is evidently describing a literal contract: Pythius had swindled
Canius, but Canius had become his debtor by novation under a literal contract,
and it appears that at that time. the Roman courts would not go behind a
literal contract, even to investigate a case of alleged fraud. This, however, took
place (see note 7 above) at a time before C. Aquilius Gallus had devised
the *exceptio doli*, *c.* 66 B.C. (see Jolowicz, *op. cit.* 292 and note 6). Presumably Canius was shown to have consented, by words or actions if not by
writing, to the making of the all-important *nomina* by Pythius, and this was
sufficient to bind him. (c) Cic., *pro Q. Rosc. com.* (see pp. 41–43 above) is a
real puzzle, mainly perhaps because Cic. may have had a bad case and may have˙

There is no reason to suppose that any writing on the debtor's part was necessary,[15] although of course there would be no *obligatio* unless the debtor had consented to the making by the creditor of the *nomen* which created the literal contract.[16]   Nor is there the slightest evidence that it was necessary, or even customary, for the creditor to make a " counter-entry " recording the discharge of the debt which was being replaced by the literal contract.   In my opinion it is not even quite certain, whatever Cicero may say in his speech for Q. Roscius, that the *nomen* had to appear *in the account-books* of the creditor. Fannius, the plaintiff against Roscius, evidently believed the entry in his *adversaria* to be sufficient ; and I think that possibly the *nomen* might appear in any document, although an entry in the formal account-book may in practice have been almost invariable.[17]

It is usual to speak of the entry creating the literal contract as *expensilatio*, but this expression never occurs in Classical Latin except once in Aulus Gellius,[18] where it may not be a technical term and indeed is probably two words, *expensi latio*.   Certainly the word one might have expected to provide its antithesis, *acceptilatio*,[19] is a technical term belonging to an entirely different legal context: it denotes only the verbal release of a verbal contract (*verbis obligatio*, including *stipulatio*).   Any obligation created otherwise than verbally might, with the agreement of the parties, be transformed by a novating *stipulatio* into an *obligatio verbis*, and then released by *acceptilatio*[20] ; but the *acceptilatio* itself was purely verbal and required no book-keeping entries or other writing.

When we remember that Roman accounts were kept in narrative rather than tabular form, and above all that separate debit and credit columns were unknown, we shall not be tempted to try to find in the *nomina transcripticia* of the literal contract any anticipation of double-entry book-keeping.

---

confused the issue deliberately.   Fannius Chaerea, the plaintiff, was surely claiming under a literal contract (see esp. 4.13 ; 5.14), the evidence for which was in his *adversaria* (1.2 to 3.9).   Cic. ridicules this evidence, but we do not know whether he was justified.   Evidently Fannius believed he had a good case.   Cic. claims that Roscius had made no corresponding entry in his own accounts ; but Roscius, of course, might have made the entries originally and afterwards destroyed the accounts.   Cic. invites the court (1.2) to treat the absence of entries in Roscius's books as evidence at least equal in force to the entries made by Fannius: evidently the absence of writing on the part of Roscius was not at all a serious legal flaw in Fannius's case, or Cic. would have made very much more of the point.

15 See the last part of the preceding note.
16 " Nuda ratio non facit aliquem debitorem ": *Dig.* 39.5.26 ; 15.1.49.2.   And see Cic., *pro Q. Rosc. com.* 1.2 (" jussu hujus ").
17 I have not been able to read the article by V. Arangio-Ruiz in *Studi Enrico Redenti* I (1950) 115–123, which is not available to me.   I know of it only through Jolowicz, *op. cit.* (in note 6 above) 564–565.
18 14.2.7.
19 Gai. 3.169–172 ; *Dig.* 46.4.
20 Gai. 3.170 ; *Dig.* 46.4.19.pr.

A Short History of Tallies*

Rudolph Robert †

THE notched stick, which later developed into the wooden tally, is perhaps the first accounting aid ever employed in the history of man. At a time when the "electronic brain" is stealing the limelight by reason of its fantastic capacities, there is a certain interest in looking back at the remote and curious beginnings, if only to marvel at the length of the road traversed.

Of the antiquity of the tally there is not the slightest doubt, and the scoring of sticks as a means of recording numbers may be traced back to neolithic, and even, according to the experts, to palaeolithic times, though with these extremely primitive instruments we can scarcely concern ourselves. Exactly how they were used is pure speculation.

Indeed, even when we come to study the *modus operandi* of the tallies in medieval England, at the Court of the Exchequer, where they attained an importance unequalled in any other country in the world, certain things still remain obscure and conjectural. This is largely due to the fact that, owing to a disastrous accident which will be mentioned later, the great bulk of the Exchequer tallies was destroyed.

However, much extremely interesting matter has been unearthed about them, as a result of the patient labours of Sir Hilary Jenkinson and the officials of the Public Record Office, as well as by a number of independent inquirers into the subject.

Before giving a brief résumé of what is known about the tallies, it is as well to clear the ground by defining precisely what they were, how they were made, and why their adoption in medieval England attained such widespread popularity.

First as to the definition. The tally as used in the twelfth century Exchequer was an instrument made of wood, usually hazel wood, and has been more fully described as "a primitive form of chirograph, or indented writing, recommended for its superior durability." (Hubert Hall in *Antiquities and Curiosities of the Exchequer*.) The definition could, of course, be elaborated upon, but is probably sufficiently concise for all practical purposes.

---

* From *Accounting Research*, vol. 3, no. 3 (July, 1952), pp. 220–229, with amendments by the author.
† Company Secretary and Accountant, Welwyn Garden City, Hertfordshire.

For the details as to the method of cutting—and this was a ritual, meticulously observed—we are indebted to the literary proclivities of a Bishop of London, Richard Fitznigel, who was both a great cleric and a man of wide learning. Member of a family which was to be closely connected with the royal household for nearly 150 years, well acquainted with the legal and financial problems of his day, he left a " famous and inestimable treatise " from which scholars have derived almost the whole of their knowledge of early Government tallies.

His *Dialogus de Scaccario* was written about 1176. One cannot do better than quote from it the passage on the actual technique of cutting:

> The cutting is done thus: At the top they put thousands of pounds so that the cut for it will take the thickness of the palm of the hand. £100 the breadth of the thumb, £20 that of the little finger. The cut for £1 is of the thickness of a grain of ripe barley; for 1s. less, yet so that by the two converging cuts something is removed and a small notch made; a penny is marked by a single cut, nothing being removed. On the edge where a thousand is cut you shall put no other number save the half of a thousand, in fashion so that you remove the half of the cut. . . .

The description goes on at some length, becoming increasingly involved, and we need continue no further with it. The worthy Bishop himself remarks " you will understand all this better by seeing than being told."

In size these early tallies were quite short, extending, according to the *Dialogus,* from the tip of the index finger to the tip of the thumb (some 8 or 9 inches), and in addition to the notching, details of the transaction were inscribed on both of the flattened sides.

The wording (which was, of course, in Latin) followed a similar formula to the cutting and was copied from the tally into the Receipt Roll, or in the Receipt Book of a century later. Properly cut and inscribed, the tally was then complete, apart from the very important procedure of splitting it down its length, though not, it should be noted, down its entire length. The notches were identical on both segments, but one, the " stock," retained the solid stump of the original block of wood at its end, while the other, known as the " foil," was much smaller in size. (See Plate IV.)

There, then, in outline we have sketched in for us the actual methods of tally-production and it is only necessary to round off by adding something to the definition which was quoted. The tally, we read, is a " primitive form of chirograph or indented writing," that is, an acknowledgment made in two parts, and in such a way that, when rejoined, it constituted proof of the parties' responsibility in the transaction.

The tally was, in effect—and this is the key to a comprehension of it, even in its later uses—a form of receipt. It acknowledged the receipt of a certain sum of money (or of goods), the stock remaining in the hands of the creditor, the foil being given to the debtor. It was a notched stick, fashioned in a way prescribed by long tradition and according to a set of highly complex rules, which admitted a financial liability on the part of one person to another.

Despite subsequent developments in the use to which the tally was put, it was never any more, nor less, than this—simply a receipt.

Now for the dynamics and the historical explanations. For what reason did tally-making reach the proportions that it did, not only in the age when Bishop Fitznigel was penning the famous *Dialogus de Scaccario* but in the seven hundred years that were to supervene?

There is, of course, the superior durability of wood and the greater availability of this material as against parchment or paper. But the fundamental *raison d'être* of the tally is to be found in the fact that this tangible wooden object, with its careful scoring, was a comprehensible record to the untutored men of that distant past. There is, indeed, some reason for supposing that, in addition to the monks in the monasteries, there was a not entirely negligible laity versed in the arts of reading, writing and arithmetic, but the mass of the population, whether of high or low degree, was illiterate. Henry I stands out as one of the first monarchs of medieval times who had acquired learned accomplishments, and that he put them to good use is evidenced in his organisation of the Exchequer, and in his management of finance. But the nobles, and, of even more importance, the sheriffs responsible for collecting his revenues in the counties, were men who often could not count without the aid of their ten fingers.

Receipts in the forms of scraps of parchment would have been anathema to them. But the notched stick, known to them and to their fathers before them, the wooden tally, which they could interpret by rough and ready inspection, and which threw no great strain on the intellect, was at least acceptable. An incision of the breadth of a thumb represented £100, a simple cut involving no removal of wood from the tally represented one penny, a punched hole (as has since been discovered) one half-penny.

Not only was this method of recording legible, but there was in all probability a general appreciation of the safeguard against fraud which it provided. In any settling of accounts both parties would be obliged to produce their portions of the tally, and the notches and the cuttings would have to correspond. Neither side could falsify the account and " get away with it " as we might now say. That attempts at fraud were sometimes made by dishonest persons, however, will astonish no one, and Sir Hilary Jenkinson, in one of his papers in

Archaeologia, mentions the case of a man who was entrusted by the sheriff with 60s. in cash and a tally showing 5 marks already paid into the Exchequer. Very foolishly, as it turned out, this man cut notches equivalent to 60s. on the foil and kept the cash. He evidently was unaware of the procedure, for when compared with the stock the fraud was immediately discovered, and he was sentenced to prison for a year and day.

Finally, we may mention the " proffer " system, as practised in the twelfth century at the Exchequer, as setting an example, and popularising the use of the tally in connection with both public and private transactions throughout the country.

Not only are we indebted to Bishop Fitznigel for information on the mysteries of Government tally-cutting but for an account of how affairs were managed at the Exchequer, of its division into Upper and Lower Departments, and the responsibilities of the officials.

The way in which the proffer system operated is an illustration of how much can sometimes be accomplished with comparatively simple means. In essence it was a system through which the King's taxes could be collected from the counties without all the paraphernalia of forms, returns and demands to which we, in the twentieth century, have become conditioned. The intermediary between the monarch and his subjects in the matter of feudal dues was, of course, the sheriff. Usually a person of importance in his own part of the country, and charged with heavy responsibilities, he was not necessarily, in fact he was but rarely, a skilled accountant. But upon him devolved the duty of collecting for the King the rents of the Crown lands, import and export taxes, tributes from the towns, fines and penalties, and a whole miscellany of other revenue.

It was the custom for the sheriff to journey to Westminster each year at Easter and pay into the Lower Exchequer, or Exchequer of Receipt, approximately one-half of the total amount for which his region was liable. The Treasurer, having accepted the sheriff's proffer, or payment on account, issued instructions for a tally to be cut, one half being given to the sheriff as his receipt, the other finding its way into the Exchequer archives.

Later in the year, at Michaelmas, came the final reckoning. Once again the sheriff made his way to Westminster to render a full account of his stewardship, and to pay over the balance of the " ferms " and other county dues. The proceedings were presided over by the Justiciar, and took place in the Upper Exchequer, or Exchequer of Account. The " chequer cloth " was laid out on a table, and the sheriff submitted himself to audit.

An official known as the Calculator produced a set of counters which he set up on the squares, like draughtsmen, in such a way as to exhibit the total amount due from the sheriff to the king.   When this operation had been completed, and agreed by both parties, the Calculator laid out another row of counters, which recorded the sum which the sheriff had paid on account at the Easter session.   This would be checked by reference to the tally which he had received. The two halves would be fitted together, after which the *Ludus Scaccorum* or Counter Game, continued until a balance had been struck.

A fuller account of these audit proceedings cannot be given, as it would constitute at least a minor digression.   Enough has probably been said to prove the main point—to demonstrate how important the tally was, how large a part it played at the Exchequer and in the system of royal accounting.   Its role was indeed an essential one.

A certain emphasis has been laid upon the fact that the tally was primarily a form of receipt, and that it remained, in essence, a receipt until the time eventually came, early in the nineteenth century, for it to be abolished.   But the Plantagenet kings, running a State apparatus with revenues that seemed always inadequate, found that this very convenient accessory, the tally, had possibilities in other directions. Not only was it a means of acknowledging payments, but with a little ingenuity it could be made to meet present financial difficulties by drawing on the future.   This employment of the tally as a means of anticipating revenue was a most significant development, and must now briefly engage our attention.

It was, no doubt, discovered at quite an early stage that a debt could be assigned.   If, for example, the King borrowed £100 from a moneylender and was owed £100 by one of his barons, he could instruct the latter to pay the former, and thus discharge his liability. Presently this convenient arrangement was improved upon.   Money was raised upon the security of tallies which gave the lender the right to collect certain taxes, or to receive the proceeds of taxes, at a later date.

Sir Hilary Jenkinson, in his second monograph, published in *Archaeologia* in 1925, mentions a specific instance of repayment by assignment.   The debtor was Henry II, and the creditor a Flemish moneylender named William Cade.   Cade was given the customary form of receipt, a tally, and at the same time invested with an authority to draw upon some specified third party, a royal debtor in the provinces.   When the debtor paid, he in turn received a tally, one which had already been " levied " at the Exchequer and entered upon the Receipt Roll (which latter was, in effect, a register of tallies). Subsequently, it is thought, the written authority, or writ, may have been considered superfluous in transactions of this kind, and full reliance placed upon the tally.

Nothing is fundamentally changed, and yet something in the nature of a metamorphosis has taken place. The tally remains, what it had always been, a receipt, but in addition it takes on some of the characteristics of a negotiable instrument, a bill of exchange, a post-dated cheque payable to bearer. Several hundreds of years later a similar thing happened to the goldsmiths' receipts, which were passed from hand to hand, and evolved into an early type of bank note.

At first, it may be assumed that this system of assignment through the medium of the tallies was resorted to in only a minority of cases, for its dangers, as well as its undoubted advantages, will have been apparent to the king's advisers. But there is reason to believe that eventually assignments became the rule rather than the exception. Revenue, anticipated at first only occasionally, was later drawn upon in advance with unfailing regularity, and the levying of tallies settled into a routine.

The economic consequences we are not concerned with, but from an accounting angle there are several interesting points to be observed. Payment by assignment reduced the amount of money paid into, and out of, the Exchequer, for obviously, with increasing numbers of tallies " in circulation," smaller amounts of metal coinage would be required. At the same time, the book-keeping, by which is meant the recording of the issue of tallies on the Receipt Roll, tended to become so complicated that there is evidence of its having at times failed lamentably to cope with the burdens placed upon it. This is hardly to be wondered at, for there would be difficulty even today in operating an extensive system of settling accounts by assignment only. Most important repercussion of all, however, was the coming into existence, as the volume of Exchequer business mounted, of machinery for discounting.

Whether the facilities existed, or were used on a large scale, during the reign of Henry II, when Fitznigel wrote, is not known, but as we begin to leave medieval times behind, the facts are more easily ascertained, and the picture gains in clarity. The discounting of tallies was undoubtedly an important part of the goldsmiths' business in Restoration days, a fact borne out by Pepys, who has an entry dated June 21, 1665, which reads:

> I find our tallies will not be money in less than sixteen months, which is a sad thing for the king to pay all that interest for every penny he spends; and which is strange, the goldsmiths with whom I spoke do declare that they will not be moved to part with money upon the increase of their consideration of ten per cent. which they have.

The goldsmiths' rates, it will be seen, were high, but probably only commensurate with the risks they ran. Two of the most famous, Vyner and Backwell, it may be mentioned, were virtually put out of business by the Exchequer Stop of 1672, an action which, among other things, involved repudiation of the tallies.

It was during the days of Charles II that a further, and last, development in tally technique occurred. As is well known, the troubles of this monarch were considerable, and he was perpetually in debt. In the year prior to the Stop, he had anticipated a full year's revenue, partly by the issue, in 1667, of " tallies of loan." The tallies of assignment had already been made to serve their turn from 1660 onwards, and were simple orders on customs farmers to remit to third parties. But the loan tallies, ostensibly issued to help build the navy, were mere charges against such taxation as Parliament might, at its leisure, be pleased to sanction. The temptation to overdo them was very great, and in the face of temptation Charles was always more inclined to yield than to resist. Tally cutting, under his direction, was raised to the status of a royal sport—even, it might be said, to an art!

But his reckless utilisation of the wooden marvels as a method of mortgaging the future also discredited them, and sowed the seeds of their eventual decline. Confidence in the royal finances was badly shaken by the events of 1672 and the unsatisfactoriness of the tallies as a security was everywhere being felt. They were quoted at a heavy discount, and apart from all this, were criticised on the grounds of their size, which had shown a decided tendency to increase, and their clumsiness. Even the Government officials grumbled at their inconvenience. The notched sticks, in fact, were already an anachronism. Wood, even the most durable, was on the point of being superseded by scrip.

Pepys, secretary of the Navy Board, the reader may be reminded, has a number of references in his Diary to the tallies, many of them in the nature of complaints. A favourite theme is the dilatoriness of the men responsible for their cutting.

" To the Exchequer," he writes on May 16, 1666, " where the lazy rogues have not yet done my tallies."

In actual fact the " rogues " at that time were most industriously engaged: for it was precisely in the days of the famous diarist that the tallies reached the climacteric of their long career. Both by weight of numbers, and in physical dimension, they surpassed anything that had been known before. A whole branch of the civil service was engaged in dealing with them. There were, indeed, certain Exchequer officials, the Chamberlains and other recipients of salaries and fees, for whom tally cutting constituted not only a hallowed ritual, governed by an immutable code of laws, but a vested interest. These were the men, oblivious to the passing of the years, hostile to any suggestion of change, who helped to keep the tallies going for at least another hundred years.

So far as the City and the middle-class public was concerned, one may perhaps draw a comparison between the late seventeenth-century tallies and certain bonds and equities of the present day. They were regarded as a speculative form of investment, yielding a not unsatisfactory rate of interest, part of the Government " stocks." The student interested in etymology may speculate upon, and become absorbed in quite interesting research into the derivation of that word " stocks," as current now as it was then. He will be in the best of company in concluding that at least one plausible answer is provided by the tallies, which consisted, as we saw, of a wooden stump, or " stock," and a " foil." " Tally " itself, it may be mentioned in passing, stems either from the Latin *talea*, stick, or the French, *tailler*, to cut, or possibly both.

There we must leave the assignment system, and its variations, employed so recklessly by Charles II and his immediate successors. It is necessary to return, for a moment, to the twelfth and thirteenth centuries, for we have not yet glanced at an important field in which the primitive accounting auxiliary, which provides our subject-matter, was found most useful.

England, in Henry II's time, was still a feudal State, backward economically when compared with other European countries, but the foundations of her future commercial greatness were already being laid. Wool was being exported, and there was a fair amount of internal trading. Business, whether it involved the use of money or was merely conducted on a barter basis, could not be confined entirely to the royal court. The merchants, lords-of-the-manor, and in particular the moneylenders, found themselves obliged to give and to accept receipts. And a receipt, in medieval times, was invariably equated with the tally.

There are, in fact, ample reasons for believing, despite the paucity of concrete evidence, that the private tally, like the Exchequer tally, enjoyed a considerable vogue. It was probably a less elaborate instrument: the abracadabra surrounding it not so formalised, the rules simpler and less rigid, whilst the individual responsible for its issue was free to indulge his own idiosyncrasies in the manner of cutting and inscribing. Since the private tally, like a token coin, would have only a limited currency, this would create no difficulties. But the nearer a person was to the king's court, and the more familiar he was with its customs, the more likely his tallies were to be modelled on those struck by the Exchequer officials.

In actual size and general appearance the private tallies (of which a hoard was discovered in three leather bags in the Public Record Office some years ago) differed only slightly from the ones in official use. They were notched in similar if not quite the same manner, and split in half to form two equal portions. But whereas the Exchequer tallies were destined to remain accounting records without a break for at least seven successive centuries, the private tallies seem to have enjoyed but an ephemeral existence. As soon as parchment and paper became more freely available as a substitute for wood the private tallies fell out of favour and were discarded. In its functioning the private tally, so far as is known, was confined to the acknowledgment of money or of goods. It remained simply a receipt.

Before leaving this part of the subject, one other point merits brief reference—the employment, by Henry II, of a special kind of Exchequer tally, known as the *dividenda* tally, which had the effect of stimulating the use of private tallies. Its *modus operandi* can be explained quite quickly, for it was nothing more than a device for devolving detail work from Westminster to the counties. Overloaded by the vast number of payments, the Exchequer officials invented this procedure of the *dividenda*, whereby the collection and acknowledgment of trifling sums was thrown upon the local sheriff.

This was a commendably common sense course to take, one which should have worked well in practice. The sheriff, remitting to the Exchequer, was given one tally, the *dividenda* tally, covering the multiplicity of petty receipts. It was left to him to satisfy the individual debtors from whom he had collected. The implication of this is that he issued his own private tallies from his local office, complete with accounting system and clerks. Further, one is entitled to make the assumption that the monarch had by now succeeded in gathering round him a body of reliable men—officials at the Exchequer and tax-collectors in the counties—who were not only literate but had acquired some degree of skill as accountants. The extra duties included the submission by the sheriffs of accurate lists to the centre for audit. Subsidiary Receipt Rolls had also to be kept locally.

The tally *dividenda*, clearing an entire bloc of small remittances, amercements, fines and debts, seems to have been replaced by another, almost identical in the way it functioned, known as the tally *debitus pluriam*, and numbers of the Public Record Office discoveries, alluded to above, were of this latter type, as the inscriptions on them show.

If there is any single event which, looking back, we can see dealt the tallies a blow, not indeed immediately mortal but ultimately so, it is the founding of the Bank of England in 1694, six years after the Whig revolution had placed William of Orange on the throne.

A war against France was in progress. Money was urgently

needed, but there was difficulty in borrowing it, for the public credit was at a low ebb. William Patterson's scheme for the formation of a bank seemed to offer a way out of the crisis. The sum of £1,200,000 was loaned to the Government, and the Old Lady of Threadneedle Street received acknowledgment in the usual form—tallies. But no ordinary tallies! These tallies, which remain in existence today, owing to the fact that they have never been redeemed—unless the act of nationalisation may be said to have done so—set up a record no less for their amounts than for their outsize proportions. Where the early tallies described by Bishop Fitznigel were mere hazel wands eight inches in length, these were solid trunks, the longest exceeding *eight feet*!

This, however, is in parenthesis. Of more importance here are the dealings in tallies which took place in 1696, dealings in which the Bank of England was deeply involved. The war was continuing to act as a drain on the Exchequer, and the Government's financial standing was no higher. Large numbers of tallies-of-loan were in private hands, and there were no funds from which to pay them as they fell due. The consequence was that they were quoted at a heavy discount, as much as 40 per cent. on occasions, and the Government felt obliged to do something about them if public confidence was to be restored.

Fairly full details of what actually happened are to be found in several of the authorities (for example, in Sir John Clapham's *History of the Bank of England*), but the crux of the matter was that the Bank " ingrafted " the tallies, that is to say, took them over from the holders in exchange for Bank stock. The directors were by no means enthusiastic about the scheme, as they considered it would not enhance the Bank's credit. Since the tallies were often forward-dated to such an extent as to be practically non-negotiable anywhere else, and as the security, usually consisting of a charge against a specific tax or duty, had not infrequently been cancelled by Act of Parliament, the reluctance of the court of the Bank to take over the tallies was natural. However, the much-abused chirographs, when the " ingrafting " had for patriotic reasons been accepted, carried interest at 8 per cent., and the principal sum being considerable, the Bank did very well out of the bargain!

The tally as a means of raising public loans was, nevertheless, passing into desuetude. Other and simpler means of anticipating revenue were thought out, one very effective method being the Exchequer " bill." Funds could be raised on alternative, and more acceptable, securities, and in the eighteenth century the gradual withering away of the tallies as accounting and financial instruments was an observable process. Towards the end of that astonishing century, in 1782, an Act of Parliament was in fact introduced for their abolition. But it was not to become effective until the decease of the last of the Exchequer Chamberlains, and as this historic event did not take place until 1826, the tallies continued to be used well into the nineteenth century.

What people had by then come to think of them is magnificently expressed in a famous Dickens diatribe (taken from his *Letters and Speeches*, volume 2) which it would be cheating the reader not to quote. The passage is as under:

> Ages ago a savage mode of keeping accounts on notched sticks was introduced into the Court of Exchequer, and the accounts were kept, much as Robinson Crusoe kept his calendar on the desert island. . . . A multitude of accountants, book-keepers, and actuaries were born, and died. Still official routine inclined to these notched sticks, as if they were pillars of the constitution, and still the Exchequer accounts continued to be kept on certain splints of elm-wood called tallies. In the reign of George III an enquiry was made by some revolutionary spirit whether pens, ink and paper, slates and pencils, being in existence, this obstinate adherence to an obsolete custom ought to be continued, and whether a change ought not to be effected.
>
> All the red tape in the country grew redder at the bare mention of this bold and original conception, and it took till 1826 to get these sticks abolished.

But then, at long last, the tallies were returned to Westminster in such volume that the old Star Chamber had to be cleared to accommodate them, and, when this was packed to the ceiling, much other valuable space was taken up. They ceased to have any validity, and their place at the Exchequer was taken by indented cheque receipts.

Had this great accumulation of ancient tallies come down to us, it would undoubtedly have been a mine from which infinitely interesting matter might have been hewed for antiquarians and economic historians, as well as for accountants. Unfortunately, a statute of William IV ordered a holocaust. The tallies were condemned to be destroyed. Consequently, in 1834, they were thrown into the heating stoves of the House of Commons, with results that could scarcely have been foreseen. So excessive was the zeal of the stokers that the historic Parliament buildings were set on fire and razed to the ground!

The tallies perished in a blaze of defiant glory, leaving, as far as was then known, not a wrack behind. And but for the accidental discovery of various hoards, including an important one in the Chapel of the Pyx at Westminster, early in the present century, our knowledge of them, imperfect and incomplete as it still is, would have been even less.

Existing only as isolated specimens here and there, or as enigmatic fragments, the tallies would have been little more than curiosities; things noted down in the pages of old books, and left to be puzzled over by the *littérateurs* and the investigators of a future age.

Partnership Accounts in Twelfth Century Genoa*

Florence Edler de Roover †

IN a sketch of the activities of a Genoese public notary of the late twelfth century, which appeared in this *Bulletin* some time ago,[1] it was pointed out that his records included a considerable number of partnership contracts. Such contracts were almost always concluded for the purpose of trading overseas. As we know, the Genoese merchants of the twelfth century were chiefly engaged in the trade with North Africa, Romania (the Byzantine Empire), the Levant, and also Spain, southern France, Sicily, and Sardinia.

Since there are thousands of partnership agreements in the extant cartularies of medieval Genoese notaries, we are well informed about all the legal aspects of such contracts, but we know little about the way in which these partnerships actually carried on their business, because hardly any accounting records of the twelfth century have survived. The existence, therefore, of accounts relating to the winding up of three partnerships between Genoese merchants for the years 1156–1158 provides us with information as valuable as it is rare.

These partnerships for overseas trade were not formed for a period of years but for a single venture, that is to say, each partnership was dissolved at the close of each voyage. There were two principal types of contract: the *commenda* and the *societas maris*. Both involved co-operation between a travelling partner and an investing partner. In the *commenda* the venture was financed entirely by the investing partner; the travelling partner did not supply any capital, but he had to run the risk of a dangerous sea voyage and to endure all the discomforts that went with it. As a reward for his labours and hardships he usually received one-fourth of the profits; and the investing partner, who ran only the risk of losing his money, received the remaining three-fourths.

In the *societas maris* an opportunity was given the travelling partner to invest some of his profits made on previous voyages. Usually he supplied one-third of the capital and the investing partner,

* From *Bulletin of the Business Historical Society*, vol. xv (December, 1941), pp. 87–92.
† Former Professor of Medieval History, Cedar Crest College, Allentown, Pennsylvania.
1 Florence Edler de Roover, " The Business Records of an Early Genoese Notary, 1190–1192," *Bulletin of the Business Historical Society*, xiv (1940), pp. 41–46.

two-thirds; profits were shared equally. The *societas maris* was practically the same contract as the *commenda*, because profits in both
cases were really divided according to the same rules. The active
partner always received one-fourth of the profits for his labour; three-
fourths always went to the investors of capital. Because in the
societas maris the travelling partner supplied one-third of the capital,
he received an additional one-fourth of the profits for his share as an
investor of capital.

The travelling partner was frequently a young merchant with an
adventurous and enterprising spirit but with little or no money to
invest. The investing partner very often had been a travelling merchant in his early years who was now content to stay at home and to
speculate with his accumulated profits. A part of these profits he
usually devoted to the purchase of real estate and a part he entrusted
to younger merchants.

The investing partner should not, however, be regarded as a silent
or dormant partner who was interested only in a return on his capital
and who shunned any responsibilities. In reality he had an important
role to play and should perhaps, in order to emphasise the contrast
between him and the " travelling " partner, be designated as the
" stay-at-home " partner. It was the older partner who usually
decided where the travelling partner should go, whether he should
take with him money or goods, and which foreign wares he should
buy in exchange. The investing partner also took charge of the sale
of the goods which were brought back by the travelling partner.

The notarial records of Genoa show that not all the investing
partners were retired travelling merchants. Some of them were
nobles, clerics, widows, guardians of orphans, artisans, and shopkeepers, but it is likely that those people, in making venturesome
investments, followed the advice of some experienced relative or
acquaintance who looked after their interests for a consideration or
out of real friendship. (Just as in the gay twenties, kind-hearted
business men gave market tips to the elevator-boy, to their widowed
sisters, and to their favourite clergymen.)

Of course, the investing partner had to use his judgment in the
choice of a travelling associate, because the latter had to assume a
great deal of managerial responsibility in foreign parts. There being
no rapid means of communication, the travelling merchant had to be
given a free hand, in case the instructions received could not be
carried out. Naturally it was impossible to foresee everything, such
as price fluctuations, scarcity of certain goods, special bargains, and
so forth.

The administrative problems in the age of the travelling merchant
were still very simple. Most sales and purchases, chiefly in the

Levant, were either cash transactions or barter agreements. Consequently, they involved little book-keeping. Nevertheless, since he had to render account to the investing partner, the travelling merchant must have kept some kind of record of his business transactions and of his expenses. Another reason for keeping careful accounts was that one single travelling merchant frequently had contracts with several investing partners. Of course, a separate account had to be kept for each of them.

In spite of this minor complication, twelfth-century accounts were rather simple in comparison with modern accounting. Nothing shows this better than the three sheets of paper which contain the figures relating to the winding up of three successive temporary partnerships between two Genoese—an investing partner, Ingo da Volta, and a travelling partner, Ansaldo Baialardo.

Those three sheets were found slipped in between the pages of the cartulary of the Genoese notary, John the Scribe (Giovanni Scriba). The acts of this notary are the oldest that are extant and cover the years 1155 to 1164. The importance of these insignificant-looking scraps of paper was first discovered by the late Professor Eugene H. Byrne. A careful study of them was eventually published by a young Italian scholar, Guido Astuti.[2] To decipher the three sheets was a very difficult task because the accounts were jotted down in a disorderly way. Italian book-keeping in the middle of the twelfth century was still in a primitive stage of development. With such unsystematic methods of book-keeping it would have been quite impossible to disentangle any business situation that was in the least complicated, which confirms our statement that administrative problems were relatively simple. Even so, the lack of system is responsible for some minor errors, which Dr. Astuti has pointed out; because of these errors, it is not always possible to give exact figures.

The first partnership was formed in the autumn of 1156, probably for a coastal voyage to Provence, Montpellier, or Catalonia. This partnership was a *commenda*; accordingly the active partner, Ansaldo Baialardo, did not put in any money. All the capital, amounting to £205 4s. 1d., was contributed by Ingo da Volta. Accounts showed, at the termination of the voyage, several months later, that a profit of £74 had been made. In accordance with the usual rules of the *commenda*, this profit had to be shared in the proportion of three-fourths to the investor and one-fourth to the traveller. Consequently, Ingo received £55 10s. and Ansaldo, £18 10s. Ingo's capital was thus raised from £205 4s. 1d. to £260 14s. 1d. or an increase of about 27 per cent.

---

[2] Guido Astuti, *Rendiconti mercantili inediti del cartolare di Giovanni Scriba* (Turin, 1933).

In October, 1157, Ansaldo set out on another voyage, likewise to the western part of the Mediterranean, and entered into a new *commenda* agreement with Ingo da Volta. The latter invested £254 14s. 1d., that is to say his original capital, plus the major part of the profits from the preceding venture. This time Ansaldo carried with him £18 10s. of his own. This sum remained, however, outside the *commenda* agreement, and Ansaldo was consequently entitled to the full profit of his own investment. We know these details from the notarial records of John the Scribe, for it was he who drafted the contract of this second *commenda*.

The total profits on the second voyage amounted to £244 15s. 11d., of which £17 9s. 11d. were produced by Ansaldo's investment of £18 10s. The remainder of £227 6s. represents the profits of the *commenda* and was divided between the two partners in the customary proportion.

The account of each partner was made up as follows:

INGO DA VOLTA	£	s.	d.
Original investment	254	14	1
¾ of *commenda* profit (£227 6s.)	170	9	6
	£425	3	7

ANSALDO BAIALARDO	£	s.	d.
¼ of *commenda* profit (£227 6s.)	56	16	6
His private investment	18	10	0
Profit on private investment	17	9	11
	£92	16	5

On the original sheet the allocation of profits is computed in two different ways with a difference of £1 between the two computations and with some other minor mistakes. The editor has tried in vain to reconcile the discrepancies.

This second venture was very profitable—the most profitable of the three. Ingo's investment was increased by approximately 67 per cent., and Ansaldo, who had started out with a capital of only £18 10s., was now in possession of over £92.

The third partnership was formed on August 3, 1158, for a voyage to Syria, Palestine, and Egypt. This time Ansaldo had enough money to make a new kind of agreement, which was a combination of both the *commenda* and the *societas maris* contracts. Ansaldo invested £64 8s. 8d. and Ingo invested twice this amount, or £128 17s. 4d., under a *societas maris* contract: profits to be shared equally between the partners. In addition to this amount Ingo invested £284 9s. 10d. under a *commenda* agreement: three-fourths of the profits were to go to him and one-fourth, not to Ansaldo, but to the *societas maris*. Consequently, each partner would get one-half of this fourth, that is to say, one-eighth. This was a common arrangement when a travelling merchant, who was already a party to a *societas maris* contract, received additional funds under the form of a *commenda.*

The third venture proved to be profitable, but not quite so profitable as the second. The proceeds from the sale of the goods brought back from the Levant amounted to about £760. This figure, less the original investment of £477 15s. 10d., gives a profit of approximately £282. This amount was divided between the *commenda* and the *societas maris* in proportion to the total capital invested in each. As a result, £114 was allocated to the *societas maris* and £168 to the *commenda.*

The £168 was further divided as follows: three-fourths or £126 to Ingo, and one-fourth or £42 to the *societas maris.* The total profits of the latter were consequently £114 plus £42, or a total of £156. The division of the profits between the partners was as follows: Ingo received the above mentioned £126 plus one-half of the total profits of the *societas maris* or £78, and Ansaldo got only £78 for his share.

This last venture added about 50 per cent. to the capital of Ingo, inasmuch as he received £204 on an investment of £403. Ansaldo's capital was more than doubled, having swollen from £64 to £142.

The sheets give more information about the goods brought back from the Levant than about those of the first two voyages. The list includes pepper for the value of £465; cotton for £176 14s.; sugar for £77; cardamon for £3; brazilwood (?) for £21 11s. 3d.

The three documents also show how the profits were determined. Settlement between the partners apparently took place before all the goods had been sold. Unsold goods were presumably appraised at the market price. If the selling price later differed from this market price, some kind of adjustment became necessary. Once the aggregate proceeds of the venture had been determined, the expenses of the travelling partner were deducted. The difference thus obtained represented the net proceeds of the venture. From these net proceeds each partner was repaid his original investment. The remaining balance, representing profit, was then divided in accordance with the provisions of the partnership agreement.

Overseas trade in the Middle Ages was at times tremendously profitable, but the risks were great and ventures sometimes ended in such disaster as a shipwreck or the death of the travelling partner. As these records show, Ingo da Volta tripled his capital in three years. Ansaldo Baialardo, who started with nothing, accumulated a capital of £142 in the same period of time. There is no doubt that capital invested in real estate did not yield so much. The documents inserted in the cartulary of John the Scribe seem, therefore, to indicate that the accumulation of capital originated in the profits of trade rather than in income derived from landed property.

Medieval Treatises
on Estate Accounting[*]

D. Oschinsky †

No survey of estate accounting in England in the Middle Ages has yet been made; there exists so far only the fine study of the financial organisation of the manor by A. E. Levett.[1] In order to write such a survey it would be necessary to turn both to the wealth of manorial accounts preserved in archives all over the country and to the didactic treatises on the subject.

Of these two sources the actual accounts, extant from the early thirteenth century, are at present best known. These show that, notwithstanding the variety of accounting methods in use, there were certain salient features which were common to all accounts. Before turning to the didactic treatises it may be helpful to summarise these features and to give a short characterisation of the account itself. It was a record on which the accountant stated all the goods both in kind and in money which had been received by him or had been paid out by him during the period of account, together with his liabilities at the beginning and at the end of the period. Thus it was essentially a statement of the receipts and expenses of the accountant and not of the manor.

The account, as we know it best, consisted of two parts: the money account and the corn and stock account, the latter comprising the entries for corn, beasts and dairy produce. This division tends to obscure a very characteristic feature of the manorial account, that is that each of the entries in the corn and stock account represents as much an independent account as the money account itself. Because of the importance of money in the working of the manor the money account had many subdivisions and subheadings—such as rents, moneys from sales or for purchases, court-dues, money liveries to the head of the estate, etc.—for which there was no necessity in the corn and stock account. For each accountable item—money as well as corn, oats, rye, horses, cattle, poultry, etc.—we have first a statement of the arrears at the beginning of the year and then the receipts during

---

[*] From *The Economic History Review*, vol. XVII (1947), pp. 52–57. The Appendix, "Short Description of Extant Treatises" (pp. 58–61), has been omitted.
† Lecturer in Medieval History, University of Liverpool.
[1] A. E. Levett, *Studies in Manorial History*, ed. by H. M. Cam, M. Coate and L. S. Sutherland (Oxford, 1938).

the year and a total of both; from this the expenses are deducted and
the remainder at the end of the year completes the picture. The
heading gives the name of the manor for which the account was
drawn up, the names of the accountants, that is the reeve, the bailiff
or both, and sometimes also of the auditors. It gives the place and
possibly the date of the audit and, most important of all, the period
of the account, which with few exceptions runs from Michaelmas to
Michaelmas. The cash arrears seldom meant cash in hand but more
often moneys which the reeve owed through his default or because
he had not yet received them; both cash and stock arrears showed
what should have been in the possession of the accountant. The
manor was an economic unit; therefore any receipts or expenditure for
which neither produce nor services were rendered or received are
described as " foreign." The foreign receipts comprised money or
goods received from other manors within the same estate, from the
central authority of the estate, or from a person not connected with
the estate at all. Foreign expenses included payments for transport of
goods, travelling expenses of the reeve, fees and expenses on behalf
of the household officials—the bailiff, steward, auditors and guests—
and any accounting expenses. If, for example, a distinguished guest
of the lord stayed at a manor the money expenses which had been
incurred during his stay would be entered as foreign expenses in the
money account while the oats for his horses would be entered as
foreign expenses in the oats account.

The accounts were examined at a yearly audit by the lord or his
representatives—the steward, the receiver or a specially appointed
auditor. The audit might take place at the centre of the estate, thus
relieving the auditors from going round from manor to manor, or it
might be itinerant, although for most of the big estates it was only
partly so in that all the accounts of one geographical district were
audited at one manor of that group.

The knowledge of manorial accountancy gained from these actual
accounts has a valuable supplement in didactic works both on estate
management in general and on accountancy in particular. The former
include four treatises, all well known: *Walter of Henley's Husbandry,*
the *Seneschaucie,* the anonymous *Husbandry* and the *Rules of
Robert Grossetête.*[2] These four treatises are concerned primarily
with matters of agriculture and the general running of an estate but
incidentally give information about keeping accounts. Thus it is
stated by the author of the *Seneschaucie* that the accounts should be
heard every year,[3] that the audit should take place on the different

2 E. Lamond, *Henley (Walter de) Husbandry together with an anonymous Husbandry, Seneschaucie and Robert Grosseteste's rules* (1890).
3 E. Lamond, *op. cit.,* p. 107.

manors, and that the lord should look through the rolls in order to satisfy himself that everything has been done correctly [4]; elsewhere the steward is asked to be careful to see that the bailiff knows where, when and to whom to deliver the money.[5] Similarly, in injunctions as to practices to be followed in managing particular estates the express references to accountancy are few. One such is to be found, however, in the injunctions contained in the Cartulary of St. Peter's of Gloucester,[6] where the reeves are told to draw up their expenditure at least once a month on account rolls. These rolls must have resembled a weekly ledger rather than an annual account [7] and may be compared with the rolls which, according to one treatise on accounting, the clerk had to examine before he drew up the final account.[8] The reeves are also asked not to write their notes on wax tables but on parchment, and the author goes on to say that nothing should be allowed but the sums actually entered in the parchment rolls [9]—an interesting point which shows that wax tables were then common; the objection to their use was doubtless that the reeve sometimes forget to copy out certain items and, once the writing on the tables had been erased, there was then no proof at the audit as to how the money had been spent.

In order to find out more about accounting systems we must turn from these injunctions and treatises on estate management in general, compiled primarily for the lord or his steward, to the treatises on accounting which were compiled for clerks and auditors. About twenty such treatises on manorial accounting are known to exist, four on rolls and the others in books.

Some of these treatises on accounting are included in manuscripts whose general character entitles them to be described as reference books. Such manuscripts had been compiled, for instance, for the use of the monastery of St. Albans and for Ramsey Abbey. They contain notes of matters which the compiler found it important to remember, such as names of bishops and abbots, tables for finding Easter, and formularies for various kinds of letters,[10] but the main part of the contents is usually the law remembrancer, containing a *registrum brevium*, statutes and legal treatises. The importance of

---

4 *Ibid.*, pp. 107 and 131.
5 Dd VII 6, fol. 52*b* (Cambridge University Library).
6 W. H. Hart and P. A. Lyons, *Cartularium Monasterii Petri Gloucestriae.* Rolls Ser. (1863–1867), vol. iii, pp. 213 *et seq.*
7 M. L. Lacour, " Traité inédit d'économie rurale composé en Angleterre au XIIIe siècle " (*Bibl. de l'École des Chartes*, Paris, 1856), p. 28.
8 Ee I 1, fol. 231, col. 1 (Cambridge University Library): " *Cum quis compotum ordinare debuerit primo faciat uenire ante se omnia monumenta ballivi et prepositi, tallias, rotulos, memorandas, breuia, litteras acquietationes vel tallias acquietationis* "
9 W. H. Hart and P. A. Lyons, *op. cit.* iii, p. 213.
10 *e.g.*, Ee IV 20 (Cambridge University Library), and Ashmolean MS. 1524 (Oxford University Library).

estate accounting cannot be better illustrated than by the fact that some of these reference books included treatises on that subject.

Not much is known about the authors of the treatises. Most of them indeed are anonymous. In some, however, the compiler is mentioned in the introduction. Thus, for instance, we know that the treatise which was in the possession of the Church of York was written by a certain J. de Morbiria. While this name conveys nothing to us, there are two compilers about whom we know more. One is John of Oxford,[11] a monk of Luffield Priory and an Oxford teacher. The other is Robert Carpenter,[12] who started as bailiff in the service of William de Insula, one of the greatest military tenants in the Isle of Wight and later guardian of the vacant Bishopric of Winchester.

The dating of treatises presents considerable difficulties. Very often we find no date at all, the treatise simply using some such phrase as *anno regni regis Edwardi*, etc. Sometimes the date of the compilation of the manuscript in which the treatise is included will throw light on the date of the treatise itself, and sometimes there is some internal evidence. But even if a specimen account inserted in the treatise bears a date this is not necessarily the date of the treatise itself. If, however, we assume that the dates of the compilation of the treatises roughly approximate to the dates given in the forms of account included in the treatises, then we may conclude that only four treatises were compiled prior to 1270.[13]

Two main types of treatise may be distinguished—those based on the accounting system in use on one particular estate (although in no case is it certain which estate served as a model) and those which contain specimens of more than one form of account. The latter served as formularies and they prove—a fact which is borne out by the extant Ministers' accounts—that there existed more than one form of account. In these formularies the compilers copied parts of tracts on accounting as they had found them, regardless of repetitions, and we get the impression that it was their aim to collect as many examples as possible. The account form is sometimes presented in the shape of a blank enumeration of the different headings; in other cases figures are inserted, sums are totted up, the heading gives full particulars of place and of accountant, and the specimen account is in fact so complete that it is clear that an original had been used as

---

[11] H. G. Richardson, " An Oxford Teacher of the fifteenth century," *Bulletin of the John Rylands Library*, xxiii (1939), p. 16.

[12] 205/111, MS. 3, 1138 (Caius College, Cambridge), and Mm I 27 (Cambridge University Library). For Robert Carpenter see N. Denholm Young, " Robert Carpenter and the Provisions of Westminster," *English Historical Review*, L (1935), p. 22.

[13] Add. MS. 8167 (British Museum); Rawlinson MS. C 775, fol. 117 (Oxford University Library); Mm I 27 (Cambridge University Library); MS. 205/111, CMA 1138 (Caius College, Cambridge).

a model. In yet other cases the forms are fragmentary or the sums have been left out. Arrears are sometimes accounted for separately, without including them in the total of the receipt, while in other cases they are not distinguished from other items of the accountant's charges. Acquittances and loss of rent may be entered as the first or as the last item of the accountant's discharge or they may come directly after the rent and be subtracted from it. We may find the liveries added to the general expenses, but there are also treatises in which liveries and foreign expenses are distinguished from necessary expenses. The tract which is included in Harleian MS. 667 distinguishes between the "*summa de resumptione totius manerii per annum*" and the "*summa de denariis liberatis resumptionem manerii non tangentibus.*" The first includes the expenses for the upkeep of the manor and the wages of the servants, including the reeve's and bailiff's fees; the second gives the expenses incurred on behalf of the lord or his household, foreign expenses, capital investment and livery. Both sums are added up and deducted from the receipt to show the reeve's liability. We seldom find such very accurate methods employed in the actual accounts. The capital investment, in particular, may sometimes have been very difficult to distinguish from expenses necessary for the upkeep of the manor.

Apart from the account form the treatises contain interesting information about the compilation and the checking of accounts. The auditor is told in great detail how he can discover whether the account has been drawn up correctly. He is instructed, for instance, as to how much salt should be allowed for the salting of a specified quantity of meat, and is told to inquire after the hides and fleeces of beasts which had died during the year, and to compare the corn yield with the seed-corn in the previous roll and with the acreage as shown in the extent.

There does not seem to have been a loophole for the accountant! That there was, nevertheless, is shown in the Carpenter treatise [14] where the author includes some hints as to how the lord could be cheated if the auditors were not very careful. Between the stock and the larder account some advice is inserted on how to render an account " well," that is profitably for the accountant. If he has 150 ewes, and if six have been barren, let him say that nine have been barren; if he wishes to make a fleece look as though the sheep has died of murrain, let him put it in chalky water immediately after the sheep's death . . . and so forth. Such advice was obviously not intended to assist subordinate manorial officials such as bailiffs and reeves to cheat their lord, for they would never have had access to the treatise; but to

---

[14] Mm I 27 (Cambridge University Library).

point out to supervising officials some of the loopholes the neglect of which might result in disadvantage to the lord.

The treatises also contain information about the business of accountancy in general. Several of them include forms showing how to draw up records connected directly or indirectly with the account. The form of a summons to the accountant to appear at a certain date for the audit,[15] examples of acquittances which were issued to the reeve after he had paid his arrears,[16] and forms of the receipt which the reeve would receive after he had fully acquitted himself,[17] are included in different compilations. Three treatises contain lists indicating where the clerk could find the correct designations of beasts according to their ages.[18] Several contain instructions on how to write on tallies, the principal form of receipt. One contains a description of a tally [19] and the size of the incisions in it, similar in fact to the description of an Exchequer tally which is included in the *Dialogus de Scaccario*.[20] Finally, the abacus is described in one treatise [1] while another contains a drawing of it.[2] Very little is said about the audit. Certain questions to which we should like answers, such as who took part in the audit, when it took place and how often, and how the profit could be ascertained, were so dependent upon the methods adopted in the administration of particular estates that it was impossible to give general rules. It is only where a treatise was compiled for a particular estate and was based on its special conditions, as, for instance, the Beaulieu treatise,[3] that some of these questions can be answered.

From a survey of the treatises certain conclusions may be drawn as to their development. The earliest seem merely to have described practices prevailing upon particular estates. Of the four probably written before 1270, for instance, not one is based on more than one system—the two Carpenter treatises reflect the method of accounting which was in use on certain estates in the Isle of Wight, the treatise compiled by J. de Morbiria contains only a specimen account without any rules, and the earliest treatise of all [4] is even less explicit, giving only the beginning of an account form. Out of sixteen treatises which

[15] Hh III 11, fol. 103a (Cambridge University Library).
[16] Hh III 11, fol. 103b, Ee IV 20, fol. 75b, Ee I 1, fol. 231 (Cambridge University Library).
[17] Hh III 11, fol. 103b, Dd VII 6, fol. 60a (Cambridge University Library); Add. 41201 m. 3 (British Museum), etc.
[18] Barlow 49 regula decima (Bodleian Library, Oxford); Mm I 27, fol. 86a, Ee IV 20, fol. 166a (Cambridge University Library).
[19] Mm I 27, fol. 84b (Cambridge University Library).
[20] *Dialogus de Scaccario*, ed. by A. Hughes (Oxford, 1902).
[1] Hh III 11, fol. 102 (Cambridge University Library).
[2] MS. 205/111, CMA 1138 (Caius College, Cambridge).
[3] Printed in N. Denholm Young, *Seignorial Administration in England* (1937), Appendix.
[4] Add. MS. 8167 (British Museum).

were compiled after 1270 there are, however, at least four [5] which not only contain more than one model but also describe different methods. It would therefore seem that in the latter part of the thirteenth century the treatise based only on a particular estate came to be supplemented by compilations based upon the usage of a number of estates. Henceforth these become the commoner form. These compilations took on two forms. One was meant for the use of the auditor and does not distinguish between the different possible methods of drawing up accounts [6]; it consists of a detailed specimen account with instructions inserted between the different chapters to which they apply. The other form was meant to show the different forms of account which were possible. These tracts either enumerate the possible headings in an account or give examples of accounts or use both systems; the forms are seldom complete; in particular the method of drawing up the corn and stock account is often left out, because such variations as existed were not considered significant.

Most of the account forms included in the treatises were compiled in order to show methods of accounting on lay estates, and there is a notable lack of formularies for accounts of monastic estates. This may merely be due to accidental losses, but it is also possible that such treatises never existed, because the clerical departments of such estates trained their own staff and the young clerks learned accounting chiefly by practice and did not need much theoretical instruction. The inclusion of a form of account suited to lay estates in a book which was in the possession of an ecclesiastical institution [7] does not mean that the accounts of that institution were drawn up in accordance with that form of account. Such treatises found their way into the archives of the monasteries through the zeal of the monks for copying; either they were taken away by clerks returning to their monasteries after having served on some seignorial estate, or they were the property of a teacher of accounting who belonged to a monastic body, such as John of Oxford. The specimens which the latter included in his treatise were meant for lay estates, and it is only when he instructs his students how to draw up the headings that he adds an example of how to draft accounts for monastic and episcopal estates.

The teaching of manorial accountancy was evidently a regular

---

[5] Ee I 1, Dd VII 6 (Cambridge University Library); Add. 41201, Harleian 274 (British Museum).

[6] Court of Wards and Liveries, Deeds and Evidences, Box 197, note 5, E 163/24 (Public Record Office); Egerton Roll 2360 (British Museum); Mark G.V. 69 (St. Catharine's College, Cambridge).

[7] Ashmolean MS. 1524 in the possession of Ramsey Abbey. Ee I 1 (Cambridge University Library), property of Luffield Priory. Ee IV 20 (Cambridge University Library), property of St. Albans Abbey. Rawlinson 775 (Oxford University Library), property of the Church of York. Egerton Roll 2360 (British Museum), property of a Church of St. Mary.

branch of the *ars dictandi* at Oxford by the end of the thirteenth
century.[8] Doubtless the adoption of such a study was made easier
by the general rise of culture and learning which is characteristic of
the thirteenth century. The intellectual revival connected with the
friars, which Professor Power believed to have been the cause of the
appearance of treatises on general estate management,[9] may well have
stimulated also the coming into existence of treatises on accounting.
This theory agrees with the fact that so many such treatises were in
the possession of monasteries and that we find monks among their
compilers. That the teaching of estate accounting became desirable
if not necessary was, however, due to the increasing need for trained
clerks in that boom period of demesne farming, the thirteenth
century.[10] While big estates could draw on their own clerical departments, and the increase of the hòme farm provided only a further
stimulus to develop a system of accounting already in existence, the
position was very different for the many small estates which had no
clerical staff of their own. They would have been able to do without
written accounts until the increasing demesne forced them to employ
clerks for accounting, and it was probably in order to meet their needs
that the University embarked upon the training of clerks. These in
their turn applied the forms they had learnt in the University to the
accounting systems of estates which asked them for their help, whether
monastic or lay. As a result of that process we get in the fourteenth
century that form of account which, because it appears on many
estates, seems to be the typical form—with corn and stock account on
the dorse of the membrane and cash account on the front, each part
again being subdivided.

There is no doubt that the teaching of accounting in the University
had its repercussions on the accounting methods of big estates also.
With accounts, as with deeds, there was a marked inclination towards
uniformity and towards stability in forms and wording in the course
of the late thirteenth and fourteenth centuries. This uniformity was
doubtless the result of the scientific study of accounting, but we have
to bear in mind that for big estates the forms as such were not
invented in the University but had their origin in the clerical departments of the different estates, and that the " typical " manorial account
is as much a myth as the " typical " manor.

---

[8] H. G. Richardson, *op. cit.*, p. 12.
[9] Eileen Power, " Discussion on the question of a new edition of Walter of Henley's
    husbandry," *Trans. Royal Hist. Soc.*, xvii (1934), p. 101. See also the recent
    study by Dorothea Oschinsky, " Medieval treatises on estate management,"
    Economic History Review, second series, VIII (1956), pp. 296–309.
[10] M. M. Postan, " The Chronology of Labour Services," *Trans. Royal Hist. Soc.*,
    xx (1937), p. 169.

Cromwell Household Accounts, 1417–1476

E. M. Myatt-Price*

RALPH, Lord Cromwell (1394–1456) [1] gained his experience in financial matters as Lord Treasurer to King Henry VI and as the owner of extensive private estates. It is not surprising to find that he and members of his family kept household as well as estate accounts. [2]

One might expect that household accounts would normally be confined to recording expenditure of a purely domestic nature incurred, for example, in feeding and clothing members of the household, in paying servants, and in buying and repairing household goods. In practice, on a country estate, expenses for manor and household might be set out in the same account. The Cromwell accounts discussed in this chapter include examples of separate household records as well as of estate accounts containing sections relating to household expenses. Whatever form they take, however, the Cromwell records illustrate many points of interest in the history of accounting, the most important of these being the relation of accounting and book-keeping to practical problems of administration.

The accounts studied consist of a day-book (1475–1476), a weekly-book (1447–1448), three annual accounts (1417–1418, 1444–1446, 1450–1451) [3] and a View of account [4] (1418–1419); and they were kept

* Assistant Registrar, London School of Economics and Political Science.

[1] *Dictionary of National Biography, Supplement* vol. II (1901), pp. 90–92. Cromwell is best known for his estimates of 1433 in which he drew up a clear and detailed statement of the country's financial position. (*Rotuli Parliamentorum*, IV, pp. 433–436.)

[2] These are amongst the Penshurst MSS. in the temporary charge of the Historical Manuscripts Commission. They are owned by Lord De L'Isle and Dudley (now Lord De L'Isle) and with his kind permission, which is gratefully acknowledged, I was allowed to consult them in preparing by M.A. thesis *Ralph, Lord Cromwell and his household studied in relation to household accounts in the possession of Lord De L'Isle and Dudley.* (University of London, 1949.) Accounts are available for three members of the family: Ralph, Lord Cromwell; his uncle, Sir William Cromwell; and his niece Joan, Lady Ratcliffe. They are briefly described in the first volume of the Historical Manuscripts Commission's Report on Lord De L'Isle and Dudley's MSS. and are numbered 68, 74, 75, 76, 76A and 76B.

[3] These may be described as annual accounts because of their form and purpose although the periods which they cover are:—
1417–1418: 12 months   1444–1446: 16 months   1450–1451: 15 months

[4] Defined by Walter of Henley as "an inspection of account." (E. Lamond, *Henley (Walter de) Husbandry* . . . [1890].)

by Lord Cromwell and members of his family at Tattershall Castle and at Tydd in Lincolnshire. These books and rolls provide information about the types of account kept in households in the fifteenth century and, being available at intervals between 1417 and 1476, they illustrate accounting practices over a period of nearly sixty years. It is proposed first to consider the records from which the annual accounts appear to have been prepared: the day-book and weekly-book, which have been preserved, and the other books, rolls and papers mentioned in the annual accounts and view but which have now disappeared. It is then proposed to discuss the three annual accounts and the view. This order, rather than date order, has been chosen so as to show the stages in which the accounts appear to have been kept.

The day-book [5] of eleven leaves (twenty-two pages) has been made by folding four sheets of paper in half and stitching them along the left-hand margin to three single sheets. As with all these documents, it is written mainly in Latin, English [6] words being used, presumably, when the writer did not know the corresponding word in Latin. At the top of the first page is the heading:

> Tattershall   Particulars of the account of Richard Parker [7] occupying the
> Castle.   office of steward of the household . . .[8] ending the 17th day
>   of October in the 16th year of the reign of King Edward IV.

The remainder of the page is left blank. Overleaf is a list of moneys which Parker received during the period of the account. His method of recording the first section of these receipts is to list the names of the persons from whom he received various sums, such as the master, the lady and the master's clerk, and to enter the amounts opposite to the name in what might be regarded as a rudimentary money column.[9] He does not always give the date on which he received each sum, but from those mentioned,[10] the list appears to be in date

---

[5] It measures 12″×8⅜″.

[6] The English words introduced were mostly descriptive of fish or game birds. For example " cuniculus " was used for " rabbit " but a " thornback " (fish) and " knots and stynts " (small birds) would be so described.

[7] It should not be assumed that Richard Parker himself wrote this account. It may have been written by one of the professional clerks who could read, write and calculate and may even have studied accounting which was known to have been taught in the University of Oxford in the 13th century. Walter de Reyney, steward of the household of Bogo de Clare, employed a clerk, William de Horton, to write his account for 1285 and paid him 3s. for doing so. (M. S. Giuseppi, " The Wardrobe and Household Accounts of Bogo de Clare, 1284–1285," *Archaeologia*, LXX [1920], pp. 1–56.)   [8] Torn.

[9] A list of items with a money column was not unusual at this period. Similar lists may be found, for example, in *A Roll of the Household Expenses of Richard de Swinfield, Bishop of Hereford (1289 1290)*, Camden Society Publications, Old Series, 59 and 62 (1854); and in M. K. Dale and V. B. Redstone (eds.), *The Household Book of Dame Alice de Bryene, 1412–1413*, Suffolk Institute of Archaeology and Natural History, 1931.

[10] November 23, 1475; May 3, 1476; June 11, 1476.

order. These receipts are then totalled. Details of household products such as hides, bran, and tallow candles, from the sale of which the steward would expect to receive money, are then set out in three continuous paragraphs of items and amounts. Totals or, where relevant, " nothing," are put against each paragraph. It is also recorded that the steward received a total of only 33s. from these sales because some of the servants were given certain products in lieu of their wages. The two groups of receipts—that is, from persons and from sales—are totalled giving a " Sum Total of Receipts." [11]

On the third page, which is headed " Tattershall Castle," begin daily entries from March 1 to 6 and from June 16 to October 17 relating to purchases of food such as fresh fish, meat, milk and butter, together with incidental expenses incurred by the caterer when he made these purchases at Boston, Sleaford and Spilsby. The idea of this section seems to be similar to that of a day-book, insofar as items may have been entered each day, using it as a book of original entry, although they might also have been jotted down elsewhere and written up in this book at a later date. The method of book-keeping employed in this section is to record items of expenditure for each day in a continuous paragraph, totalling at the end the day's expenditure:

Wednesday, 19th June [12]: paid for fresh salmon—6d.[13] In [14] soles purchased—5d. In smelts—1d. In flounders—1d. In whelks—1d. In crabs—7d. In the caterer's expenses at Boston—2d.

Sum 23d.

Thursday, 20th June: paid for 1 sucking-pig purchased—3½d. In 2 capons—7d. Sum 10½d.

Friday, 27th September: paid for turbot—8d. In plaice—8d. In shrimps—1d. In soles—8d. In herrings—8d. In " flatfish " purchased— 4d. In butter purchased—3d. In oatmeal—2½d. In 2 geese purchased —7d. In 10 chickens—7d.

Sum 4s. 7½d.[15]

---

[11] These three paragraphs, the sums of the pages, totals of receipts and payments and the list of purchases for stock (see p. 108) appear to be in a different hand from the opening lists of receipts and the daily entries. See also discussion on audit (p. 112).

[12] The entries are dated clearly with the day of the week, date and month. This accurate method was not always observed elsewhere. In the Countess of Leicester's household accounts for 1265 the heading often consists of the weekday and date without the month being stated. (B. Botfield (ed.), *Manners and Household Expenses of England in the 13th and 15th Centuries*, Roxburgh Club [1841].)

[13] In the account this figure is given in Roman numerals but, in translation, Arabic numerals have been substituted to facilitate reading. This practice is followed in translating all extracts from the accounts in which, with a few exceptions in the book for 1447–1448, Roman numerals are used. For comments on Arabic numerals in the 1447–1448 book, see p. 103.

[14] The writer begins his entries by recording " paid for fresh salmon " but with subsequent items substitutes a brief " in " for " paid for."

[15] Sometimes both quantity purchased and money value are stated so that information is given about prices of goods. As a general rule, however, the quantities purchased are not stated.

At the end of this section is given the sum total of daily payments for the whole period.

The book concludes with a list of other payments which the steward has made, with some attempt at classification under the headings of purchases of stock (that is, consumable stores including grain, salt, salted fish, spices and Paris candles), payment of servants' wages and money paid by Parker into the master's coffers. Each group is totalled; but the entries tail away without any attempt being made to reach a grand total of all payments or to strike a balance between receipts and payments. Parker's purpose in keeping this book seems solely to keep a record of each receipt and payment and so to give a proper account of his stewardship.

The second book,[16] a small paper one of eleven leaves (sixteen pages), bears the heading " Quarterly account of the expenses of Lord Cromwell's servants residing at Tattershall from 26th day of October in the twenty-sixth year of the reign of King Henry VI." In fact, the book contains entries for fifteen weeks in all, eleven weeks from October 29 until Christmas, 1447, one week early in Lent and three weeks around Easter, 1448.[17] It is not clear who was keeping the book,[18] which seems to be a sort of memorandum-book, and which contains a record of purchases of food and of food consumed in the household, as well as of other incidental expenses. Entries are grouped under weeks, each group being headed by the Saint's Day falling in that week. Purchases are then recorded in paragraphs of items and amounts and the total amount of money spent is placed in the centre of the page at the end of each paragraph. It is not clear whether purchases were entered daily or weekly, but the writer has made an attempt to classify expenditure, showing the value of food taken from stock, new purchases, and food left unconsumed at the end of the week (*remanentes*).[19] These entries also include the wages of servants waiting on members of the household. The writer's purpose in keeping this book seems to be to show that each member of the household received meals to the value of the allowance (" commons ")[20] to which he was entitled. The names of those present and those absent are meticulously recorded, sometimes in

---

16 This measures 8½″×5½″ and has been made by folding four sheets of paper in half and stitching them down the middle.

17 It is difficult to suggest a reason for these gaps. Either no account was kept for these weeks or perhaps sheets were lost and the book was stitched together in its present form at a later date.

18 From statements in the book the writer might be either the warden who in Lord Cromwell's absence appears to have been left in charge of the twelve regular members of the household at Tattershall Castle, or the cook or the caterer.

19 He carries forward the total of *remanentes* to the following week, including it with the total of food purchased in that week.

20 For example, the six senior members of the household received food to the value of 1s. per week ; their mates (*famuli*), 10d.

ingenious little tables tucked away in the corner of a page. The allowance due to each, the number of meals provided and the value of the amounts of bread, beer, meat, fish and spices making up meals are also carefully recorded. Rabbits caught or chickens received from the tithe are noted as having been consumed although no money was paid for them. Small memoranda such as " he owes John Brown 2d." or " I paid Agnes Cliffe as a reward for her service—20d." are jotted down at the foot of some pages. No attempt is made at the end of the book to calculate the sum total of purchases or of goods consumed. It is not clear whether money is being handed over in exchange for goods bought or whether they are being bought on credit and the bills settled later. With the exception of the last four pages, each page is scored through, either when the information it contained has been transferred to another account or perhaps when the bills have been paid.

As a general rule Roman numerals are used in the Cromwell accounts, but in this note-book six Arabic numerals [1] (1, 2, 6, 8, 9 and zero, written both as $\emptyset$ and 0) appear occasionally, used in conjunction with Roman numerals. For example, at the end of the second page, having already written the sum of $6\frac{1}{4}$d. in Roman numerals, the writer has made an additional marginal note of the sum with an Arabic 6. He knew how to write Arabic numerals but not fractions, so this sum appears as " 6 qa." (quadrans $= \frac{1}{4}$d.). In his entries for Easter week, the writer lists food left over from the previous week, giving money values in Roman numerals. Instead of putting the total in the centre of the page, he puts it in the left-hand margin and instead of writing Roman numerals, he writes an Arabic " 2s. 9d. ob." (obolus $= \frac{1}{2}$d.). Food purchased during this week is set out in the usual paragraphs and the total written in Arabic numerals in the right-hand margin " 18.10." [2] The total of 2s. $9\frac{1}{2}$d. plus 18s. 10d. is, however, then written in the centre of the page in Roman numerals.

While only two daily books have been preserved it is clear from references in the three annual accounts and in the view described below that a number of other daily account- or note-books were kept in the household. It may be reading too much into them to suggest that these books were the forerunners of books of prime entry but they evidently served much the same purpose. The need for keeping a daily record of purchases was recognised and day-books were kept in most departments of a big household, and the Cromwell accounts

---

[1] The appearance of Arabic numerals (nine numbers and a sign for zero) is unusual at this early date. In his article " The Use of Arabic and Roman Numerals in English Archives " (*The Antiquaries' Journal*, 6 [1926], p. 263), Sir Hilary Jenkinson concludes that the use of Arabic numerals was extremely rare before the last quarter of the 15th century.

[2] An auditor may have made these entries; see p. 112.

contain many references to books of this nature.   On several occasions
in his annual account for 1417–1418 John Horseth [3] refers to the
Journale which, according to his reference, contained "all and
separate purchases of fresh fish, meat and similar things."   Both in
this account and in the view for 1418–1419 Horseth mentions the
"Household Paper" which is said to contain purchases of "divers
necessaries for the household" and also items such as gifts to
messengers carrying letters from lands across the sea (presumably from
Sir William who was fighting with Henry V's army in Normandy) and
locally.   In the household paper is also said to be recorded another
item of miscellaneous expenditure, the payment of one mark (3s. 4d.)
to a certain John Farnton for the care of a goosehawk.[4]   There is
little indication of the form of the household paper, except that an
attempt seems to have been made to group expenditure by setting it
out under headings, or in "parcels" (lists or groups of items), showing
some attempt at classification.   For example, one entry in the view
reads:

> And in making divers gowns and cotton shirts for the lady and for
> Robert Cromwell [5] and other people, as appears under the title of
> Tailoring (*Sissoria*) in the said paper—3s. 7½d.

A "Lady's paper" is mentioned twice in the account for 1417–
1418.   This seems to have been a book in which Lady Cromwell
noted her personal expenses, such as the payment of her debts; but it
also seems to have included some household expenses.

The two annual accounts for Lord Cromwell's household have
many references to other books, rolls and papers, but as these
references usually consist of a bare statement that a particular item
incorporated in the annual account appears in one of these books,
there is not a great deal of evidence about their nature, form and
content.   For example, the "Book of Purchases" (or "Household
Purchases") is mentioned several times in the account for 1444–1446.
Swans bought for Lord Cromwell's table (185 at 2d. each) were noted
in it.   In 1450–1451 veal, wine and unspecified food (*diversa victualia*)
were included in it; and from this account it appears that in the book
of purchases was recorded the cost of food consumed both in "the
permanent household" (probably at Tattershall Castle) and in Lord
Cromwell's other houses in London, at Collyweston and Wingfield.
There is also a reference to food sent to Leicester when Lord Cromwell
went to the Parliament held there in 1450.   It seems likely that

---

[3] Sir William Cromwell's steward.
[4] This was probably the goshawk provided for the King under the terms of a
charter granted by King John to Robert de Tateshale, one of Sir William Cromwell's ancestors.   In return for a well-trained goshawk, he was allowed to hold
a market at Tattershall on Thursdays.   (*The Publications of the Pipe Roll Society*,
LIII, new series XV [1937], p. 238.)
[5] Sir William Cromwell's son.

separate books were kept in each household and the information they contained was incorporated in the account for the " permanent household " which gave the complete picture of total expenditure. From the account for 1444–1446 it seems that all goods bought for the household, not only food, were put down in the book of purchases, and that they were carefully and separately listed:

Household Expenses

He [*i.e.,* George Fishlake] [6] accounts as follows in the expenses of the aforesaid household during the time of this account, namely: in £1,041 12s. 11½d., the sum total of the Book of Purchases of this household, including supplies left over from the last account, as are contained and set out, by parcels, in the same book. . . .

This suggestion is also borne out by the following passage in the 1450–1451 accounts:

Sums owed for supplies left over at the end of William Kempe's [7] account:

And in £112 2s. 9d. received in the price of food and other provisions for the lord's household, left over at the end of the account of the said William Kempe, and contained in parcels in the aforesaid Book of Purchases, and similarly in 1 bill filed with the account of the said William Kempe.

Another small piece of information which can be picked up from the 1444–1446 account, a reference to the " quarter's provisions," suggests that a quarterly account was kept of such items.

There seems to have been another book, the " Book of Provisions," [8] in which, as its title suggests, food consumed in the household was recorded. The only reference to it in the account for 1444–1446 is a note which it contains of the money value of food sent to Lord Cromwell as a present and eaten in the household. The writer of the account comments that the sum quoted appears " in the aforesaid Book of Provisions [it had not been mentioned before] and the Book of Purchases." This comment raises the question of the relation between the book of provisions and the book of purchases, but unfortunately no information can be gleaned from the annual accounts. There is also a single reference to a " Book of Supplies " but all the reference says is that an item for oats supplied to the household was entered in this book. " Daily and monthly rolls " are mentioned many times in the 1450–1451 account as being used to keep a record of purchases of food, but there is no other information about their contents, nor how they were used in relation to the books of purchases, provisions or supplies. Perhaps bulk purchases of food

---

[6] Lord Cromwell's " clerk of the kitchen."
[7] According to the heading of this account, William Kempe was the previous accountant (*immediate computans*) of Lord Cromwell's household. (See, however, p. 100, note 7.)
[8] This seems to have been a sort of drawings account.

were recorded in these three books and the daily rolls recorded how they were used up, day by day. Reference is also made in this account to " day-books." Probably these were similar to the books for 1447–1448 and 1475–1476 already described.

Finally, mention should be made of a Wages Bill and a Wine Cellarer's account, referred to in the annual account for 1450–1451. Their purpose and content can easily be guessed, even if there is little information about the way in which they were set out.

The three annual accounts are made out on rolls and contain both estate and household expenses.[9] It is now proposed to show how the household expenses fitted into the framework of the estate account. The Cromwell accounts are arranged in the same way for both households, in a form which was often used, although one should be wary of describing it as the standard form. The accounts are set out in two parts: the *charge,* consisting of arrears [10] and receipts, and the *discharge,* consisting of payments made by the steward. They are divided again into the money account and the stock account, where it is available; the relation between these two is discussed on page 108. The front or inner part of the rolls contains arrears, receipts and regular expenditure. On the back or outer part of the rolls for 1417–1418 and 1450–1451 are recorded incidental and extraordinary expenses as well as the stock account, fragmentary for the former and full for the latter. The roll for 1444–1446 has only a fragmentary grain account on the back. Household expenses, purchases of food, and servants' wages, are confined to three paragraphs in the account for 1444–1446. In the account for 1450–1451 they are set out in several paragraphs and in that for 1417–1418 they form the greater part of the entries, with the exception of items relating to the receipt of rents and expenses for farm work.

---

[9] The account belonging to Sir William Cromwell consists of a paper roll of four sheets, stitched together, measuring $68\frac{1}{2}'' \times 11\frac{3}{4}''$. It runs from September 29, 1417, to September 28, 1418.

    The two accounts belonging to Lord Cromwell consist of:—
        1. a parchment roll of one membrane measuring $34'' \times 12\frac{1}{4}''$, covering the period September 29, 1444, to May 1, 1446;
        2. a parchment roll of two membranes, stitched together, measuring $59\frac{3}{4}'' \times 11\frac{1}{2}''$, covering the period April 1, 1450, to July 31, 1451.

[10] The nature of the item—*arrears*—has been much discussed. There is ambiguity in its meaning as sometimes it is included in the *charge,* as in the Cromwell accounts, and sometimes it is excluded. In his section on the " System of Account " in *Seignorial Administration in England* (1937) Mr. N. Denholm-Young suggests that arrears may mean two opposite things: bad debts and cash in hand. I am inclined to agree with Dr. D. Oschinsky, who, in *English Manorial Accountancy in England in the 13th and 14th Centuries* (Ph.D. thesis, University of London, 1941) and in " Medieval Treatises on Estate Accounting " (*Economic History Review,* XVII [1947], p. 52) [reprinted in this volume, pp. 91–98, above], comments that arrears seldom meant " cash in hand." In the Cromwell accounts *arrears* seem to mean " unpaid bills from the previous account " or, in modern terminology, " debtors' opening balance."

Returning to the form of the accounts, items are set out under the following headings:

Arrears
Receipts
    Rents from manors
    Foreign receipts (from sales of hides, wax)
      TOTAL
Expenditure
    Household expenses (food, clothing, household goods)
    Outside expenses (journeys, alms)
      TOTAL
      BALANCE

It has already been noted that no attempt is made to strike a balance at the end of the daily and weekly books. In the annual accounts a balance is struck by subtracting the discharge from the charge, leaving a sum which, in the accounts for 1444–1446 and 1450–1451, represents what the head of the household would expect the steward to account for. In the account for 1417–1418 the steward's payments exceeded his receipts and then, presumably, he would have subtracted the charge from the discharge, as the balance left would have represented the amount which Sir William Cromwell owed him. The purpose of the account becomes clear: it is to show the liability of the accounting official at the end of the period, not to find the profit or loss or net income from the activities of the estate. A true profit or loss could not be found from an account which did not include all items of receipts and expenditure for estate and household, but which was confined to recording those items for which the accountant was responsible. This purpose may be the reason why, so far as can be seen from the Cromwell documents, no attempt was made to strike a balance in the household accounts, because, presumably, no one wished to demonstrate with figures that the households were self-supporting.

The steward, however, was careful to clear himself both in the money and in the stock account. This point is illustrated by the closing paragraph of the 1444–1446 account. The steward has previously arrived at the "Sum total of receipts including arrears: £1,087 7s. 1½d." He then concludes [11]:

> Sum total of the aforesaid [items of expenditure]: £995 4s. 9d. And he owes £92 2s. 4½d. Afterwards he answers for 6s. 8d. in a small allowance made to him in the price of food by the said Robert Wimbush, the lord's receiver and John atte Hall, the lord's bailiff at Candlesby . . . and so he owes £92 9s. 0½d. The same accountant paid to himself as Steward of the household 35s. 1½d. which includes amounts owing in arrears; so that, finally, he owes £90 13s. 11d., plus those items on the back of the roll.

[11] This is a fairly free translation designed to clarify the meaning of the final reckoning.

"Plus those items on the back of the roll" appears in the text as
"*plus extra*" as the relevant items are those in the stock account
which appears on the back or *extra* (outside) of the roll. In fact, on
the back of the account for 1444–1446 there are only a few entries for
grain; the annual account for 1450–1451 is the only one which has a
full stock account. This is made up of the following items for which
only quantities and not money values are shown:

	1. Stock remaining from previous accounting period
plus	2. Intake
less	3. Issues
leaving	4. Stock remaining

The stock account does not contain all items of consumption. For
example, it contains items for grain, wine, meat and beer but not for
fish, eggs and spices.

It may be assumed that the intake in the stock account includes
both purchases of items of "stock" and goods produced on the
estates and taken into stock; but the connection between entries in the
stock account and those in the annual money accounts and other
accounting records cannot be established clearly from the Cromwell
documents. The grand total of purchases is incorporated in the
money account, since the steward was accountable for money spent.
But there is no record showing the total value of goods consumed
during the period of the account. The daily books for 1450 have not
been preserved and it is in them that one would expect to find details
of daily purchases and consumption of those classes of goods which
are not included in the stock account. It would, however, be possible,
from information in the stock account and from prices mentioned in
the 1450 money account, to build up a detailed list of at least part of
the money value of total consumption.[12]

There is a great contrast between the style of setting out the
account for 1417–1418 and that of the other annual accounts. In
the first account household expenses are set out in detail by a writer
who had very little idea of classification and gathered many varied
items under headings which did not describe them accurately. The
title of one paragraph is "Purchases of herrings, fish, sprats, hens,
geese and salt," but it also contains payments for spices. The entries
in the two accounts for 1444–1446 and 1450–1451 are better classified
and arranged. They do not contain corrections to subject-matter and
totals, nor are there abacus markings in the margin.[13] In fact, these

---

[12] One would have to assume that there were no changes in the stocks held by
subordinate "accounting officers," such as the cellarer; on this basis issues from
stock can be equated with consumption.

[13] These markings occur frequently in the day-book for 1475–1476 and in the
account for 1417–1418 but only once in the view and do not appear in the weekly
book nor in the two annual accounts for Lord Cromwell's household.

two appear to be copies made for the auditors, identifiable as such because totals and balance are written in the same hand, whereas the account for 1417–1418 might well be an early draft of the final account for that year. The method of book-keeping is to record expenditure in the usual continuous paragraphs, with headings in the left-hand margin. The sum total of each paragraph is put in the centre of the roll and occasionally in the margin.

Walter of Henley, writing in the early thirteenth century, refers to a view of account as follows:

> View of Account.
> Have an inspection of account or cause it to be made by someone in which you can trust, once a year and final account at the end of the year. View of account was made to know the state of things as well as the issues, receipts, sales, purchases and other expenses and for raising money.

A view was arranged, according to the example for 1418–1419 [14] relating to Sir William Cromwell's estate and household at Tydd, in a similar way to an annual account of that period. On the front of the document are entered rents from manors and receipts from sales of wool, with the total of receipts in the margin. These are followed by sums spent in buying food, household necessities and cloth for servants' liveries, in paying wages and in almsgiving. On the back are set out expenses for farming the manor and a note of debts settled during the period covered by the view; there is no stock account. Entries are made in continuous paragraphs, with descriptive titles in the margin, by referring briefly to the original household book in which expenditure could be found:

> And in various necessities bought for the household, as appears, item by item, in the household paper.

Totals of paragraphs are put either in the left-hand margin or at the right-hand side, linked to the paragraph by a bracket, and never as a sum total in the centre of the page. There is no summary of receipts and payments, nor is a balance struck at the end of the view, so that this particular " inspection " does not go very far in showing " the state of things."

What conclusions can be reached about the practice in domestic accounting in the fifteenth century as illustrated by these accounts? It can be said that the need was recognised for keeping accurate accounts, day by day, presumably to prevent loss or theft, and that it was expected that every transaction should be recorded

---

[14] This consists of a paper roll of two sheets, stitched together, measuring $35\frac{1}{2}" \times 11\frac{1}{4}"$. It covers the period September 29, 1418, to September 28, 1419.

and, if necessary, explained.[15]   As a general rule, methods employed
in Exchequer and manorial accounting were applied, suitably adapted,
to household accounts.   A complicated system was necessarily in use
in a big household such as that of Lord Cromwell [16]; the system in
smaller households, such as those of Sir William Cromwell and Lady
Ratcliffe, was less complicated but no doubt suitably adapted to the
household's needs.

It seems likely, at least from the form of the two annual accounts
for Lord Cromwell's household, that the person writing out the

---

[15] This point is substantiated by frequent references to tallies and indented bills.
As a steward recorded purchases or receipts from stock in his day-book or annual
account, so the person from whom he bought or received the goods recorded
this transaction on a tally.   The tally seems to have been used more for stock
records than for money purchases.   For example, in the account for 1417–1418
the following appears in the fragment of a stock account on the endorsement:
> And in 53 quarters 6 bushels of malt received from William de Burton
> bailiff of the manor this year as appears on two tallies between the said
> William & Robert Benet.   [Robert was described as the " baker and butler ".]
In the view for 1418–1419 it was remarked that there were no money payments
to record for corn because it was taken from the farm granary; however, the
amount issued appeared by tally.   Another interesting reference, not strictly
connected with the household, occurs in connection with repairs to ploughs and
carts, performed by one Simon Smith:
> As appears by tally clearly marked up in the presence of the bailiff of the
> manor and as was examined in connection with the account—21s.
In the account for 1444–1446 it is confirmed that the keeper of the granary was
expected, as a store-keeper, to record issues and did so by means of a tally.
References are made to corn for fowls and bran for horses being issued, the
amounts being recorded " according to the tally."
In the book for 1475–1476 is the following entry:
> And paid to Katherine Dawber for light bread bought from her on divers
> occasions for the lady according to a certain tally—20s. 11d.
Presumably the tally was split between the caterer and Katherine Dawber.
The use of bills should also be commented upon.   They seem to have been
used as receipts or as documentary evidence of a transaction, and not, however, as
bills of exchange.   The account for 1444–1446 carefully records the receipt of money
from the Lord's coffers by means of four indented bills and gives the date, place
of issue and amount of each.   In 1450–1451 moneys were received from Lord
Cromwell's receiver in the County of Lincoln by means of two indented bills.
When William Kempe relinquished his office of accountant he handed over
£6 2s. 4½d. " by means of one other bill issued in connection with, and vouched
for in, his account."
It is also worth noting that the keeper of an account might reasonably be
expected to produce evidence of purchases.   The book for 1475–1476 refers to a
bill for spices being available and, in connection with the account for 1450–1451,
the wages bill previously discussed was produced.
Finally, if neither bills nor tallies were used, it was worth remarking upon.
The account for 1450–1451 states:
> Moneys delivered by the Steward to the lord's household for the expenses
> of the same without bills or tallies—60s.
[16] See also A. R. Myers, " The Household Accounts of Queen Joan of Navarre,
1419–1421," *Bulletin of the John Rylands Library*, 24 (1940) and 26 (1941), and
Lord Bagot, " Extracts from the Household Book of Edward Stafford, Duke of
Buckingham.   5th November, 1507–22nd March, 1508," *Archaeologia*, XXV
(1884), p. 311   It would be interesting to know what instructions Lord Cromwell
gave about the keeping of accounts in his household.   In the *Northumberland
Household Book, 1507* (published in 1925, edited by Bishop Percy) instructions
were given about the household accounts to be produced annually at Michaelmas
and at each of the four quarters of the year: " Michalmas, Crystmas, Estur and
Mydsomer," and monthly.

account was a professional man—a clerk—who could read, write, calculate and set out accounts.

A number of memoranda- and note-books were in use, and it seems that payments for food and household necessities were first set down in these or on rolls. The account for 1444–1446 specifically refers to " the said daily and monthly rolls prepared in connection with this account." The following books are mentioned in the view or in the annual accounts:

daily and monthly rolls	book of purchases
day-book	book of provisions
journal	book of supplies
household paper	wages bill
lady's paper	cellarer's account

Apart from the wages bill and cellarer's account, which are clearly specialised, the other books appear to contain purchases of the same miscellaneous nature, presumably because all the persons responsible for keeping the various books in the household made miscellaneous purchases at one time or another.

The first stage in keeping an account seems to have been to enter a purchase in a day-book. The accountant depended greatly upon these day-books and drew upon them frequently when preparing the view or the annual account. The preparation of the view (probably, according to Walter of Henley's description, the next stage)—an interim statement of the financial position at the half-year—illustrates the supervision exercised by the lord of the household and manor over those keeping accounts. This is borne out by the mention, in the account for 1417–1418, of Lady Cromwell's visiting a manor " to take the account there." It has been suggested [17] that on some estates the normal practice was to take a view of account for the current year and to hold an audit of the account for the previous year at the same time. Such an arrangement would make comparison of expenditure easy. The final stage in the Cromwell accounts seems to have been the preparation of an annual account, of which the form and purpose have already been discussed. The process seems to be clear enough, but while this is suggested by evidence contained in the various Cromwell documents, it cannot be demonstrated conclusively, as no day-book, view and annual account, all relating to precisely the same period, have been preserved.

It cannot be claimed that there are any signs of what is now meant by double-entry book-keeping. All that can be said is that, so far as can be seen, records of transactions appear in two places, in the account of the steward and on the tally [18] of the person from whom the goods were purchased or received. This seems to provide a means

---

[17] Denholm-Young, *op. cit.*   [18] See p. 110, note 15.

of stock control or of debtor and creditor recording.   As far as the method of book-keeping is concerned, in the Cromwell accounts items are sometimes listed and sometimes entered in continuous paragraphs of items and amount, the sum total of a paragraph being normally set in the centre of the page.   A similar arrangement is found in other household accounts of the period.   There is some attempt at classification and arrangement, but for the two smaller households, entries tend to be muddled.   The accounts for Lord Cromwell's household are well arranged, with marginal headings and with totals neatly linked to the paragraph by a bracket at the right-hand side.   In contrast, in the accounts for Sir William Cromwell's household, the title of a paragraph does not always accurately describe its contents and similar items are set out under different paragraphs.   It would appear from the frequent references in the annual accounts to particular " parcels " in daily account books that all transactions were easily traceable.

In the accounts there is evidence of the audit: corrections to totals in a different hand and in a different ink, and, in the margin, dots representing calculations by the abacus.   On one or two occasions in the book for 1475–1476 the dots are corrected.   In the same book there appears at the foot of each page the sum of the items on that page.   It may be that the auditor put in this total.   He may also have taken and written down the statement about kitchen products and purchases of stock.   Other evidence that the auditors were at work may be found in an item for 2d. for a meal for the auditor's clerk at Tattershall in 1447–1448.   This item is included in expenses for Easter week, which suggests that the audit took place then.   Apart from this amount there is no mention of any other expenses incurred in connection with the audit, neither is there any evidence, such as the word *probatur,* that the accounts were audited and found to be correct.   In the Cromwell accounts there seem to be no signs of the procedure described elsewhere in connection with estates similar to those owned by the Cromwell family.   From the accounts for the de Fortibus estates, for example, it is shown that as a general rule there was an itinerant audit, that the bailiff waited for the auditors to visit him and that he would then be prepared to supply them with any evidence they might require about expenditure; sometimes a general audit was held at one centre.[19]   There is no indication in the Cromwell accounts of the type of person whom the Cromwells appointed to be their auditors nor whether the head of the household was present at the audit.

In conclusion, it should be stressed that the Cromwell accounts

---

[19] Denholm-Young, *op. cit.*

should not be regarded as typical of household accounts of their period. Only a few of these have been published and they show that practice differed from household to household as, today, from firm to firm. The Cromwell documents are valuable because there is much variety in the material that they contain. When considering this material care must be taken not to try to find fifteenth-century parallels of modern practices, since these accounts were essentially the product of their time and circumstances.

The Development of Accounting Prior to Luca Pacioli According to The Account-books of Medieval Merchants*

Raymond de Roover †

IN recent years Italian and other scholars have done extensive research on medieval business records with the result that we are now much better informed about book-keeping prior to Pacioli than even a decade ago. Under the influence of Fabio Besta, whose treatise first appeared in 1909,[1] the older writers attached much importance to the matter of form and procedure, whereas the younger generation places greater emphasis on accounting as a tool of management and control. While I fully sympathise with this new approach to accounting history, I also believe that form and procedure are not completely devoid of significance and should not be entirely overlooked. One ought not to forget that there is no double entry without the observance of certain strict rules. A necessary prerequisite is that all transactions be recorded twice, once on the debit and once on the credit side. If this requirement is not fulfilled, there is, by definition, no double entry. This principle also involves the existence of an integrated system of accounts, both real and nominal, so that the books will balance in the end, record changes in the owner's equity and permit the determination of profit or loss. It is true that due to errors, medieval balance sheets do not always balance, because the book-keeper was either unsuccessful or neglectful in tracing and

* The author wishes to express his gratitude to the John Simon Guggenheim Memorial Foundation for the fellowship which enabled him to spend over a year in Italy and to collect some of the original material used in this study.
† Professor of Economics in the Graduate School of Boston College, Chestnut Hill, Massachusetts.
1 *La Ragioneria*, 2nd ed., 3 vols. (Milan 1922). The work of Fabio Besta is still authoritative and contains several historical chapters: Vol. I, Book 2, Chap. 7 (On value); Vol. II, Book 3, Chap. 4 (History of inventories); Book 4, Chap. 5 (On reserve accounts); Book 6, Chap. 2, art. 5 (On the meaning of *dare ed avere*, debit and credit), Chap. 3 (On the development of accounting theory), and Chap. 5, art. 3 (On the remote origins of book-keeping); Book 7, Chap. 2, art. 3 (On the development of single entry) and Chap. 4 (On cameralistic book-keeping); Vol. III, Book 9, Chap. 9 (On the development of double entry), Chap. 10 (On the history of accounting literature); and Book 12, Chap. 6 (On the history of auditing).

correcting small differences. Frequently he found it more convenient to eliminate them simply by posting them to profit and loss. However, to have double entry, the procedure must be such that the books would have balanced if no errors had been made.[2] Double entry does not depend in the least upon the form in which the accounts are presented.[3] A recent author, Professor Tommaso Zerbi, admits this point, but he contends that only the bilateral form could logically lead to the spontaneous development of double entry.[4] The trouble is that historical evolution does not always follow the path of logic. In Tuscany, it seems, double entry was achieved before the general adoption of the bilateral, Venetian, or tabular form.[5]

Until recently it was generally believed that double-entry book-keeping originated in Genoa around 1340 and that it spread from there to other trading centres such as Florence, Milan and Venice. This hypothesis has been shattered and its place has been taken by a much more complicated and confused picture. It is now doubtful whether Genoa may be considered as the birthplace of double entry; Florence is henceforth a serious contender to the Genoese claims, but it is even more likely that double entry developed almost simultaneously in several Italian trading centres. Since trade rests on the exchange of goods and services, the duality which forms the basis of double-entry book-keeping is deeply rooted in the nature of business. Is it then surprising that the merchants would eventually hit upon a system founded on an equation between debits and credits? By 1300 the times were ripe; the merchants were already using equity and expense accounts and very little was needed to perfect the system by making it a rule that there should never be a debit without a corresponding credit or vice versa. This result was most probably achieved gradually; double entry did not grow out of any pre-established theory but was developed step by step by a process of trial and error. As improvements were made, they spread from one counting-house to another, until they gained general acceptance.

The three factors which, in the early days, contributed most to the progress of accounting were, without any doubt, partnership, credit and agency. Of the three, partnership is perhaps the most important, since it led to the recognition of the firm as an entity distinct from the owners.

The oldest known business records of the Middle Ages relate to partnership and date from 1157. They are not fragments of an

[2] Raymond de Roover, " New Perspectives on the History of Accounting," *The Accounting Review*, XXX (1955), p. 406. This is a review article devoted to recent Italian publications, including the books of Melis and Zerbi listed in the next footnotes.
[3] Federigo Melis, *Storia della Ragioneria* (Bologna, 1950), p. 429.
[4] *Le origini della partita doppia* (Milan, 1952), pp. 11, 15, 50.
[5] Melis, *op. cit.*, pp. 425 et seq.

account-book, but are made up of a few figures jotted down on three
scraps of paper inserted in the cartulary of the Genoese notary,
Giovanni Scriba.[6]   More elaborate records were deemed unnecessary,
since, in the twelfth century, partnerships were still ephemeral affairs
formed for the duration of a single voyage and dissolved after its
conclusion.   Conditions were to change in the ensuing century as
temporary arrangements gave way to more durable, or terminal,
partnerships, especially in the overland trade between Italy and the
fairs of Champagne.   The immediate result was to make the medieval
book-keeper conscious of the fact that the firm is a unit in itself and
that capital and accumulated profits represent the claim of the owners.
It thus became necessary to keep track of changes in the owners'
equity, either through new investments or withdrawals, and to devise
a system permitting the determination of profit or loss, which was
then distributed among the partners in accordance with the provisions
of the articles of association.   As early as the fourteenth century the
larger Italian mercantile and banking " companies " even set aside
reserves to take care of any contingencies or subsequent readjustments.

Next to partnership, credit certainly played an important role in
the development of medieval accounting practices.   During the period
of the Crusades trade expanded rapidly and business gained in com-
plexity.   Soon mnemonic devices, such as tallies, proved to be
inadequate and the need was felt for a more systematic recording of
credit transactions.   At first such records were kept in paragraph
form: after an initial entry, some space was left blank for making one
or two additional entries—for instance, to add interest—and for
indicating how the settlement was made.   An appropriate formula
usually made clear whether this initial entry was a receivable or a
payable.   As yet there were no accounts current and each transaction
was considered separately.   It was only gradually that all items concerning the same person were grouped together so as to form a
running account.   This result was achieved at first by leaving more
space for additional entries and later by adopting the bilateral form
and putting the debits beside the credits, either on two opposite pages
or on the same page divided vertically into two columns.

The paragraph form is found in the fragment of a Florentine
account-book dating from 1211.[7]   As yet no earlier example of

---

6 See the article on these accounts in this volume: Florence Edler de Roover,
" Partnership Accounts in Twelfth Century Genoa," pp. 86–90.

7 This fragment was first published by Pietro Santini, " Frammenti di un libro di
banchieri fiorentini scritto in volgare nel 1211," *Giornale storico della letteratura
italiana*, X (1887), pp. 161–177, and later republished by Alfredo Schiaffini, *Testi
fiorentini del Dugento e dei primi del Trecento* (Florence, 1926), pp. 4–15. *Cf.*
Mario Chiaudano, " Affari e contabilità dei banchieri fiorentini nel Duecento," in
his *Studi e documenti per la storia del diritto commerciale italiano nel secolo
XIII* (Turin, 1930), pp. 55–64.

medieval book-keeping has come to light.   This account-book is
written in the vernacular and certainly belonged to a company of
bankers which has not been identified because the text gives only the
first names of the partners.   Most of the entries refer to loans on
which interest was charged at the rate of four pennies a pound per
month or 20 per cent. per annum, which, in the thirteenth century,
was by no means extortionate.   Each loan is still considered as a
separate transaction.   Since most loans were paid off by instalments,
the records were intended to show how much was still due at a given
moment.   Repayments are entered one item after the other in chronological order without any separation other than a punctuation mark.
This clumsy arrangement made it difficult to figure out the total
without the aid of the abacus.   Occasionally, more space was needed
than had been anticipated originally, and the book-keeper was forced
to crowd in additional entries as best he could.   In many cases the
text mentions not only the debtor but also gives the names of two
witnesses to the loan contract: shall we conclude therefrom that
business records were not yet acceptable as evidence in courts of law?

   Agency, the third factor which seems to have had a determining
influence on the development of accounting, is perhaps less important
than the other two but may explain the appearance of merchandise
accounts.   After merchants had ceased to accompany their own
goods, they began to conduct their business from the counting-house.
Instead of travelling along with their wares, they preferred to send
them on consignment to foreign correspondents.   The consignees
were, of course, expected to remit the proceeds of their sales to their
principals and, hence, were prompted by circumstances to keep
accurate records of any goods received in consignment.   This was the
first step.   The second was to keep track of all goods coming in or
going out.   In doing so, medieval book-keepers could hardly fail to
notice that receivables were counter-balanced by sales, and payables
by purchases.   Moreover, after a lot of merchandise was entirely sold,
any remaining difference between sales and purchases represented
either a profit or a loss.

   Because of the prevalence of venturing, inventory valuation did
not constitute a problem, and medieval merchants were accustomed
to open a separate account for each lot or consignment and to leave
it open until everything was sold.   In dealing with medieval book-
keeping, one must not lose sight of the prevailing way of doing
business.

   The great achievement of the Italian merchants, roughly between
1250 and 1400, was to fuse all these heterogeneous elements into an
integrated system of classification in which the pigeonholes were
called accounts and which rested on the principle of dual entries for

all transactions. One should not, however, assume that balancing the books was the primary objective of medieval accounting. On the contrary, in Italy at least, the merchants had begun by 1400 to use accounting as a tool of management or control. To be sure, they were not so far advanced as we are today and they were even far from realising all the potentialities of double-entry book-keeping. Nevertheless, they had made a start by developing the rudiments of cost accounting, by introducing reserves and other modes of adjustment, such as accruals and deferred items, and by giving attention to the audit of balance sheets. Only in the analysis of financial statements did the merchants of that time make little progress.

Recently Professor Arrigo Castellani has published nearly all the extant texts in Tuscan dialect prior to 1300.[8] With a few exceptions, which include two important business letters written by the Cerchi company to its agents in England, most of these texts are fragments of account-books. Although a philologist, the editor has made a special and praiseworthy effort to master the secrets of early book-keeping.

Since all the fragments published by Professor Castellani, without a single exception, are still in paragraph form, one may conclude that the bilateral form, with the debit of an account facing the credit, was still unknown in Florence prior to 1300.

One of the most interesting fragments is that of an account-book kept at the Fairs of Champagne by Rinieri Fini and his brothers, who were in the employ of the famous Musciatto and Biccio Franzesi, the bankers of Philip the Fair, King of France (1285–1314). The fragment covers a period extending from 1296 to 1305, but Professor Castellani publishes only the entries up to 1300.[9] This is a regrettable decision because the manuscript is in an advanced state of disintegration and may soon become entirely illegible.

Although kept in paragraph form, the account-book of Rinieri Fini has the distinctive feature of containing accounts for operating results and expenses as well as the usual personal accounts for receivables and payables. Moreover, so far as Professor Castellani was able to ascertain, each entry gives a cross-reference to a corresponding debit or credit, as the case may be. Professor Castellani concludes therefrom that the account-book of Rinieri Fini undoubtedly meets the requirements of double entry. To prove his point, he even publishes an extensive table to show that each transaction is recorded twice.[10] If he is right, double-entry book-keeping would date back to 1296 instead of 1340 and, contrary to

[8] *Nuovi testi fiorentini* (Florence, 1952).
[9] *Ibid.*, pp. 674–696. *Cf*. Melis, *op. cit.*, pp. 481–485.
[10] *Nuovi testi*, opposite p. 10.

prevailing opinion, would have originated in Florence rather than in Genoa.

It seems to me rather dangerous to draw a sweeping conclusion from a small fragment, especially since it contains no indication regarding the procedure used in closing the books. At the end do we have a real balance showing the assets on one side and the liabilities and the owners' equity on the other? Only if this question can be answered affirmatively, is one justified in speaking without hesitation of books kept in double entry.

Accounts for operating results also appear in another fragment published by Professor Castellani. It was part of a ledger belonging to the Farolfi company, a firm of Florentine merchants operating on the confines of Languedoc and Provence, with headquarters in Nîmes and a branch office in Salon. The extant fragment is entirely in the hand of Amatino Manucci, the branch manager, and the entries go from 1299 to 1300.[11] It may well be another early example of double entry, since all the entries, save those relating to cash transactions, have cross-references to corresponding debits or credits.[12] In the case of cash transactions the absence of such references proves nothing, since receipts and disbursements were recorded in a separate book, called *libro dell'entrata e dell'uscita,* which was complementary to the ledger and served both as cash-book and as cash account. Merchandise accounts, it seems, were also kept separately in a *libro rosso* or red book.[13] Of course, sectioning the ledger is perfectly compatible with double entry. It is even indicative of better organisation, since it permits dividing the work among several book-keepers.

Another sign of high technical proficiency is the presence in the Farolfi ledger of a clear example of prepaid rent, which was treated correctly as deferred expense. The case refers to an amount of £16 *tournois* for house rent that was paid four years in advance. At the end of the first year, £4 were written off to Current Expense and the remaining balance of £12 was left on the books as a deferred charge to be extinguished later.[14] The same procedure was followed in connection with prepaid rent of a shop.[15]

Further improvement was achieved by placing the amounts in extension columns instead of inserting them in the narrative Summations were thereby greatly facilitated, but the use of Roman numerals continued to impose the aid of the abacus. It is true that a medieval clerk who knew " the lines," that is, the use of the abacus, could cast

---

[11] *Ibid.,* pp. 708–803.
[12] Such is at any rate the opinion of Prófessor Melis, and he may be right (*op. cit.,* pp. 485–490).
[13] Castellani, *op. cit.,* p. 748, Nos. 364–367 ; Melis, *op. cit.,* p. 485.
[14] Castellani, *op. cit.,* p. 721, Nos. 104–109.
[15] Melis, *op. cit.,* pp. 486–487.

his counters as fast as we can operate today with adding or calculating machines.

Among the other texts published by Professor Castellani only the account-book relating to the estate of Baldovino Riccomanni (1272–1278) and the private memoranda of Gentile de' Sassetti (1274–1310) present any interest. The first opens with a long list of legacies, mourning expenditures, and other charges paid by the administrators of the estate left by Baldovino Riccomanni. Then follows a list relating to the collection of various investments made by the deceased before his death. The third part contains the accounts concerning the funds placed at interest with various banking companies in the name of Baldovino's minor children.[16] Returns on such deposits varied from eight to ten per cent. a year. The private account-book of Gentile de' Sassetti also deals mainly with loans at interest and money invested in a partnership headed by a kinsman, Sassetto di Azzo.[17] On this investment Gentile received a return of eight per cent. plus a share in the extra profits.[18] Neither the Riccomanni nor the Sassetti fragment gives evidence of any progress in the art of book-keeping: accounts are still in paragraph form and no attempt is made to integrate the available data into a cohesive system.

The only point which needs stressing is that interest charges are scarcely concealed. It is true that the word " interest " is not used; it is replaced by various euphemisms: *prode* (yield), *costo* (cost), *guadagno* (gain), *dono* or *donamento* (gift or gratuity), *merito* (reward). The entries reveal that borrowers who made out a letter obligatory for a certain sum actually received less. Thus a villager who borrowed only 60 gold florins from Gentile Sassetti promised by deed to repay 67 florins at the end of a year.[19] After 1300 much greater secretiveness prevails: account-books cease to refer to the taking of interest and sundry devices are used to conceal the matter. This change is certainly due to the influence of a decretal promulgated in 1312 by Pope Clement V, according to which lenders could be convicted of usury on the strength of their own account-books.[20] At that time usury meant any accrual, great or small, above the principal of a loan. True, Clement's canon was rarely enforced, but the possibility was always there; hence the merchants took precautions to conceal any interest received. To protect their customers, the bankers

---

[16] The latest edition of the complete text of this fragment is in Castellani, *op. cit.,* pp. 249–283. *Cf.* M. Chiaudano, " Affari e contabilità," *op. cit.,* pp. 64–74; Armando Sapori, " Il libro di amministrazione dell'eredità di Baldovino Jacopi Riccomanni," in his *Studi di storia economica medievale* (Florence, 1946), pp. 505–523.
[17] Castellani, *op. cit.,* pp. 286–362.
[18] *Ibid.,* p. 296, Nos. 55–65. Sequence of this account on pp. 306, 325, 326, 334, 336–337. This partnership apparently lasted until January 1, 1290.
[19] *Ibid.,* p. 304, Nos. 161–165.
[20] *Corpus Juris Canonici,* Decretals: canon *Ex Gravi,* in Clement., V, 5, 1, § 1.

were even careful to enter as *dono* or *discrezione* any interest paid to depositors. The matter deserves mention, because the question has often been asked why any trace of interest is rarely found in old account-books.

Toward the end of the thirteenth century, Siena—today a slumbering Tuscan town—was the principal banking centre of Western Europe, with perhaps Piacenza as its closest rival. Representatives of Sienese banking houses regularly visited the fairs of Champagne, at that time the great international money and commodity market. Unfortunately, only a few records of Sienese companies have come down to us. A most interesting document is a kind of financial statement regarding the liquidation, around 1281, of a partnership which traded in cloth imported from France and dealt also in armour.[1] For this purpose it maintained an establishment in Siena and another in Pisa. There were several partners, among whom Bernardino Ugolini was the principal one. The inventory or statement in question refers to the shares of two other partners, Manno Squarcialupi and Bartolomeo Aringhieri, in the dissolution of one partnership and the formation of another. It shows, at any rate, that partnership agreements made the preparation of general statements inevitable, at least in the case of dissolution or reorganisation. In this instance it seems that in accordance with Roman law the partners received no payment on their equity until all creditors had been satisfied.[2] After that, as collections of outstanding claims came in, the available funds were distributed rateably among the partners in the form of liquidation dividends. Again in conformity with the rules of Roman law, goods in stock were divided in kind, probably on the basis of a valuation made by outside appraisers. There are plenty of examples of this practice in the Middle Ages. It seems that Manno Squarcialupi, as soon as he received his liquidation dividends, reinvested them in the new partnership, which probably succeeded the old without any interruption in the running of the business. The extant statement suggests that losses were at the root of this reorganisation and that the liquidation resulted in a deficit. Possibly partners responsible for mistaken decisions were dropped, but the statement gives no inkling in this respect. It also gives no clue to the state of Sienese bookkeeping.

On this problem, some information may be gathered from a notebook kept by the representatives of the Ugolini company at the fairs of Champagne (1255–1262).[3] Apparently it contains chiefly a list of

---

[1] Mario Chiaudano, " La divisione della compagnia di Bernardino Ugolini a Siena nel 1281," *Studi e documenti, op. cit.*, pp. 80–113.

[2] *Corpus Juris Civilis*: Digest, XVII, 2 (*Pro socio*), 27.

[3] Chiaudano, " Il libro delle fiere di Champagne della compagnia degli Ugolini, mercanti senesi nella seconda metà del sec. XIII," *op. cit.*, pp. 143–208.

overdue loans, since the entries extend over several fairs. There are no real accounts as yet, only paragraphs separated by blanks which could be used to insert new items regarding the settlement.

An even more important record than the Ugolini memoranda is the cash-book (*livro dell'entrata et dell'escita*) of a Sienese mercantile and banking company which traded with the fairs of Champagne and had branches in Italy (Pisa, Florence and Rome), France (Nîmes) and Greece (Chiarenza). The company has not been identified with certainty, but it is likely to have been the Salimbeni company, one of the most powerful houses in Siena. At any rate, Salimbene de' Salimbeni and Federigo Lei are mentioned so frequently that they were most probably two of the partners. The entries, with some gaps, extend from November 15, 1277, to July 30, 1282. A characteristic of this cash-book is that receipts are recorded on the front pages and expenditures in the rear, instead of being placed side by side, the receipts to the left and the expenditures to the right. The cash balance was computed every Monday by taking the preceding balance, adding the receipts of the week and deducting from this total the expenditures during the same period. During a short absence of the cashier, the cash record was kept for a few days (from December 8 to December 11, 1281) by a substitute who used a loose sheet and placed receipts next to expenditures, as we do today. Upon the return of the regular cashier these items were recopied in the appropriate sections of the cash-book.[4]

From numerous references in the cash-book we learn about the existence of at least a half-dozen other account-books: a *livro a devito e a richolti*, or a debtor and creditor book, which certainly contained chiefly the personal accounts of customers and correspondents; a *livro a vendite*, or sales-book, which probably included not only sales but all.merchandise accounts; a *livro de' provenesgini*, in which were recorded all dealings in foreign exchange and, especially, all purchases or sales of money of Provins, current at the fairs of Champagne; a *livro de la ragione del rame*, which is mentioned only once in the cash-book and was probably used in connection with the company's trade in copper; a *livro dei chapitali*, to which were presumably posted all confidential entries concerning the partners' equity and, perhaps, the salaries of the factors, or employees; and

---

4 Guido Astuti, *Il libro dell' entrata e dell' uscita di una compagnia mercantile senese del secolo XIII (1277-1282)* (Turin, 1934), pp. 536 *et seq.* There are in all five items of receipts and seven items of expenditures, so that this document by no means deserves the importance which Professor Melis (*op. cit.*, p. 429) attributes to it as an early example of the bilateral form. A better case is a statement of account (1288) written on parchment by Cepperello Dietaiuti of Prato, receiver of royal revenues in Auvergne. This statement also has two columns, one for the debit and one for the credit. The text is available in Schiaffini, *Testi fiorentini*, pp. 244-259.

lastly a *livro de le mandate*, the purpose of which is not clear from the rare mentions in the cash-book.[5]

How well these books were co-ordinated into a system is impossible to tell without more information than is available. Whether we are in the presence of double entry is even more conjectural. However, one point is clear: the organisation of the Sienese banking companies had become so complex that they needed several books and that they had to divide the work among several book-keepers.

The company of the Bonsignori, another Sienese banking house, which was the largest of its time when it failed in 1298, also used a great many books, but none have escaped destruction, so that we know nothing of their contents.[6] On the other hand, there still are extant in Belgium two account-books of the Gallerani, also a Sienese company with branches abroad.[7] One of the two is a cash-book of the London branch for the years 1305–1308; it is kept in the same way as the one described above. The other, dating from 1306, contains a list of bad debts which the Paris office was doing its best to collect. Because of the presence of accounts for operating results, a cursory examination led Professor Melis to the conclusion that the Gallerani unquestionably kept their books in double entry. This is possible, but by no means established without more careful study.[8]

From this rapid survey we may conclude that by 1300 the Florentine and Sienese companies, although their accounts were still in paragraph form, had reached a high degree of technical proficiency. Presumably, double entry was achieved in certain cases, but, in view of the fragmentary state of the evidence, it would be incautious to make any categorical statement in this respect.

With the fourteenth century accounting entered into an era of rapid progress. It corresponded to a period of business expansion and population growth which was halted in 1348, when the Black Death swept through Europe. The trends, already in evidence before 1300, continued to favour the ascendancy of the " sedentary " merchant who, instead of travelling with his wares, conducted his business from the counting-house, used common carriers, and relied on partners, agents or correspondents to secure representation abroad. In imitation of the Sienese, the Florentines formed large mercantile and banking companies, among which the Bardi, the Peruzzi, and the Acciaiuoli are the most famous. In 1335 the Peruzzi company, which

---

[5] Astuti, *op. cit.*, pp. xi–xiii.

[6] Chiaudano, " Le compagnie bancarie senesi nel Duecento," *op. cit.*, p. 39.

[7] Publication of these two account-books was planned by the late Georges Bigwood. After his death, his transcripts were turned over to Armand Grunzweig who has not yet published them, although the scholarly world has eagerly awaited them for many years.

[8] Melis, *op. cit.*, pp. 474–475, 479.

was the second largest of the three, had at least fifteen branches scattered all over Western Europe, North Africa, and the Levant, and, according to a reliable estimate, employed a staff of about ninety factors or employees. In the same year its capital amounted to 90,000 florins, or approximately $360,000 at the present official valuation of gold at $35 an ounce. This figure, however, disregards the tremendous difference in purchasing power and is far from representing total investment, since it does not include the deposits by outsiders or by partners above and beyond their quotas of the capital. All three companies failed shortly before the Black Death because they granted excessive credits to Edward III of England and the Angevin rulers of Naples. During the fifteenth century no firm, not even the Medici bank, attained the size of the Bardi or the Peruzzi, described by the chronicler, Giovanni Villani, as the pillars of Christendom.

Besides the "big three," there were several minor companies. One of them was that of the Alberti, which successfully weathered the crisis of 1346–1348 and became quite important in subsequent years until it split into several rival firms because of family quarrels. Only a few fragments of the Alberti account-books have come down to us.[9] The most extensive includes the major part of a *libro segreto* that covers without discontinuity a period from 1302 to 1329. Such a *libro segreto,* or secret account-book, usually contained data on the distribution of capital and profits. In many firms the *libro segreto* also contained the salary accounts of branch managers and factors.[10] Because of the confidential nature of this information it is quite understandable why the *libro segreto,* in Italian companies, was usually kept by one of the partners himself and stored away in a locked chest to which employees had no access. With respect to contents, the *libro segreto* of the Alberti company fits this description. However, in addition to the accounts of partners and factors, it includes about a dozen financial statements—I purposely avoid using the term "balances." There is no doubt that these statements were drawn up at irregular intervals in order to determine profit or loss, which was then divided among the partners and credited or charged to their accounts. According to the secret account-book of the Alberti company, from one to five years were allowed to elapse between two successive settlements or *saldamenti generali.* In the meantime no partner was either admitted or permitted to withdraw. Even death

---

[9] The text has been published in full by Armando Sapori ed., *I libri degli Alberti del Giudice* (Milan, 1952).

[10] In the Middle Ages, the word "factor" (Ital. *fattore*) had only one meaning and always referred to a salaried clerk or employee. In this study, "factor" is always used in the medieval meaning and never in the modern meaning of commission agent or manager of a trading post.

did not automatically dissolve the partnership and the heirs of a deceased partner had to wait until the next settlement to receive their share in the equity and the accrued profits. Apparently each settlement was accompanied by a renewal or an extension of the partnership agreement.

How profits were to be divided was determined in advance by the articles of association and could not be changed as long as they were in force. The rules varied greatly according to time and circumstances. From 1302 to 1323 partners were first entitled to a return of 8 per cent. per annum on *total* investment at the beginning of each year. The remainder of the profits, if any, was then distributed according to an arbitrary ratio determined in the articles. It was only in 1323 that this system was completely altered: a distinct *corpo*, or capital stock, of £25,000 *affiorino* was established, and it was further stipulated that profits were to be shared among the partners in proportion to their quotas of this sum. Any partner—and there actually was one—who failed to supply his assigned quota was charged eight per cent. interest on the deficiency.[11] On the other hand, a partner was entitled to the same interest on any *sopracorpo*, or surplus, invested in addition to his quota of the *corpo*, or capital.[12]

In a recent book on accounting history it has been advanced that the Alberti company kept its books in compliance with "all the canons of double entry," but the *libro segreto* and the other extant fragments do not, in my opinion, afford any evidence in support of such an assertion.[13] Accounts are not yet in bilateral form; instead, the debit is still placed below the credit or vice versa, according to the nature of the initial entry. What is more important, it does not seem that the fundamental rule without which there can be no double entry is strictly observed. In going carefully through the *libro segreto*, I have not found that each transaction is recorded twice. On the contrary, there are many debits without an equivalent credit or the reverse. Furthermore, there is no trace of accounts for expenses or operating results. The financial statements—and there are a dozen of them—are not really balances. Profits were determined by deducting total liabilities and invested capital from total assets including receivables, goods in stock, and cash in hand. Once determined, earnings were distributed among the partners after making a provision for unpaid salaries. While this procedure is correct and betrays a high level of proficiency, it does not prove anything more and it certainly does not justify the conclusion that the Alberti books are in double entry.[14] One point, perhaps, deserves special mention:

[11] See the account of Neri del Giudice (Sapori, *Alberti*, p. 91).
[12] See *loc. cit.*, the account of Alberto del Giudice.   [13] Melis, *op. cit.*, p. 494.
[14] The editor of the Alberti account-books, Professor Armando Sapori, cautiously refrains from advancing such a claim.

at each *saldamento generale,* inventory was taken of all the stock on hand. The Alberti, consequently, did not have a system of venture accounting with separate accounts for each lot of merchandise.

The account-books of the Gianfigliazzi (1320–1325), a firm of moneylenders operating in Dauphiné and Provence, are devoid of interest from our point of view.[15] They do not exhibit any sign of progress beyond the level attained by the Florentine companies in the thirteenth century. The same applies to the fragment of an account-book of the Frescobaldi (1311–1312). Most of the entries refer to expenses in connection with the flight of the Frescobaldi partners and factors from England to Avignon in order to escape arrest on charges of defrauding the English crown.[16] In a brush with pursuers, one of the factors in the party lost his hat and duly charged it to the company!

Of more importance is a set of books belonging to the Florentine company, Francesco del Bene & Co., which was one of the principal importers of " French " cloth and, as such, a member of the powerful Calimala gild.[17] The imported woollen cloth was usually undyed and unfinished and the members of the Calimala gild gave it the beautiful finish for which Florence was then famous. The del Bene company, consequently, combined international trade with manufacturing. It also combined retail and wholesale trade, since it sold by the ell as well as by the piece. The del Bene company, founded in September 1318, was dissolved on August 1, 1322, although the liquidation dragged on until 1323.[18] There were three partners: Francesco del Bene, Domenico de' Bardi (who withdrew in September, 1321), and Perotto Capperoni. The latter probably had little, if any, money invested in the company but assumed the burden of everyday management. The del Bene company used quite an array of books, but only four of them have survived: (1) the ledger or *libro dei debitori e creditori,* (2) the register of purchases and sales or *libro delle comprevendite,* (3) the cash-book or *libro d'entrata e uscita,* and (4) a waste-book called *quaderno del P.,* in which were recorded miscellaneous consignments and merchandise accounts not connected with the trade in " French " cloth. The following are lost: the important *libro segreto,* which probably contained the most vital information on the composition of the owners' equity; the *quaderno delle spese minute,* undoubtedly a record of petty expenses; the *libro*

15 Armando Sapori ed., *I libri della ragione bancaria dei Gianfigliazzi* (Milan, 1943).
16 Armando Sapori, *La compagnia dei Frescobaldi in Inghilterra* (Florence, 1947).
17 The " French " cloth (*panni franceschi*) was bought in France at the fairs of Champagne, but most of it was of Flemish origin. In the beginning of the fourteenth century, England was not yet producing much cloth for exportation.
18 Armando Sapori, *Una compagnia di Calimala ai primi del Trecento* (Florence, 1932).

del taglio or book of retail sales; the *libro delle recate* or general sales-book; the *libro del fondaco,* presumably an expense-book; the *libro di Francesco del Bene proprio* or the personal record of Francesco del Bene; and the *quaderni dei tintori e dei assettatori,* which were books connected with the industrial activities of the firm.[19] At that time piece rates were the rule in the textile industry and the *libri dei tintori e dei assettatori* were used to keep track of the work performed by dyers and finishers, their earnings, and the advances paid as work progressed.

As in earlier Sienese cash-books, the book-keeper of the del Bene company, Lotto Franceschi, places the receipts or *entrate* in the front half and the expenditures or *uscite* in the rear half of the cash-book, an arrangement which made it somewhat clumsy to strike a balance.[20] A similar arrangement was adopted in the ledger, where the debits were placed in the front up to folio 200 and the credits in the rear, after folio 200.[1] A third section, beginning with folio 273, is reserved for expense and profit-and-loss accounts. This presentation constitutes an improvement over the paragraph form, but is less convenient than the bilateral form, with debit and credit placed side by side, which was already being used in Northern Italy.[2]

There are present in the ledger accounts for profits (*avanzi*) and losses (*disavanzi*); however, the procedure followed in closing the books shows that the del Bene did not use double entry.[3] The financial statement drawn up on August 1, 1322, does not balance, but shows that assets exceeded liabilities by nearly £400 *affiorino.*[4] The book-keeper decided that this difference represented a profit, which was duly apportioned between the two remaining partners in accordance with the articles of association, 60 per cent. to Francesco del Bene and 40 per cent. to Perotto Capperoni. Although Lotto

---

[19] *Ibid.,* pp. 223–231; Melis, *op. cit.,* pp. 509–510.

[20] Sapori, *Calimala,* p. 228. This division of the cash-book into two sections, one for receipts and one for expenditures, was common in Tuscany even into the sixteenth century.

[1] The preamble of the account-book states: ". . . and we shall write the debits (*dare*) from this folio to folio 200 and from folio 200 onward we shall write the credits (*avere*)." *Ibid.,* pp. 225–226.

[2] In Genoa the bilateral form was already used by the bankers in 1313, according to the excerpt from a ledger made nineteen years later by a Genoese notary. However, there is no evidence that the Genoese bankers already kept their books in double entry; bilateral accounts and double entry are different things. *Cf.* Robert L. Reynolds, "Bankers' account in double entry in Genoa, 1313 and 1316," *Bollettino ligustico per la storia e la cultura regionale,* III (1951), no. 2, pp. 33–37.

[3] Melis is of the opinion that the del Bene books are in double entry (*op. cit.,* p. 515).

[4] The text is quoted by Sapori, *Calimala,* p. 255: "We find that on August 1, 1322, we have to receive more than we owe, which means that we have earned from September 1, 1321, to August 1, 1322, as shown above and on the next page, *affiorino* . . . £383 9s."

Franceschi, the book-keeper of the del Bene firm, was an able man, he failed to integrate completely the rather complicated accounts of his employers.[5] The registration of operating results was certainly defective. Otherwise the books would have balanced instead of showing a surplus as they actually did.

The reason why the del Bene company kept such elaborate records may be due in part to the fact that it was engaged in manufacturing, which always calls for more detail and stricter control. The great amount of duplication may also have been a clumsy way of providing internal checks, a result which could have been achieved more efficiently by a simpler and more rational system of accounting. However, we should not blame the del Bene book-keeper. His was still a period of experimentation.

With regard to the Bardi, the largest mercantile and banking company of its time, only insignificant fragments of its business records are still preserved in private family archives.[6] They reveal that the company kept a great many books, among which the principal ones were the ledger, the *libro segreto,* and the *libro della ragione.*[7] The latter apparently contained transcripts of the articles of association and copies of periodic financial statements which it would be rash to call balances. The company's standards of book-keeping were certainly high, but the system in use can hardly pass for double entry, since profits were still arrived at by deducting total liabilities, including capital investment, from total assets.[8] In making this computation, bad debts were written off or listed separately as doubtful. If, contrary to expectations, they were recovered at a later date, adjustment was made accordingly, by crediting the partners' accounts.[9]

Next to the Bardi, the Peruzzi company was the most important of the Florentine companies during the period from 1300 to 1343. With regard to the preservation of records, we are a little better off because of the survival of important fragments of a ledger (*libro dell'asse sesto*), of a confidential book (*libro segreto sesto*), and of the accounts kept by two partners, Arnoldo di Arnoldo and Giotto di Arnoldo de' Peruzzi.[10] The latter's records are especially valuable for the detailed

[5] Lotto Franceschi received a salary of 50 florins or about $200 a year at the official gold price of $35 an ounce. This seems to have been normal pay for a book-keeper.

[6] Armando Sapori, *La crisi delle compagnie mercantili dei Bardi e dei Peruzzi* (Florence, 1926), pp. 209–225.

[7] *Ibid.,* pp. 239–241.

[8] This procedure is clearly described in a text quoted by Sapori (*ibid.,* p. 218) and by Melis (*Storia,* p. 505).

[9] An example of such an adjustment is given by Sapori (*Crisi,* p. 238) and by Melis (*Storia,* p. 506).

[10] All this material has been published *in extenso* by Armando Sapori, *I libri di commercio dei Peruzzi* (Milan, 1934).

information they give about the structure of the Peruzzi company and the allocation of the shares in the *corpo*, or capital, among the partners, outsiders as well as members of the family. Up to 1331 the latter retained majority control. Even after losing it, their influence remained decisive and the partner entrusted with the supreme direction of the company's affairs was invariably chosen from their midst. Branches were not separate legal entities and were managed by either partners or factors.[11] Thus, in 1335, partners, and not factors, stood at the head of the more important branches in Avignon, Bruges, London, Naples, Paris and Sicily. It seems that a partner who was at the same time a branch manager received a stipend without prejudice of his share in the earnings.[12]

From the point of view of presentation, the Peruzzi accounts are no longer in paragraph form and not yet in bilateral form. In the *libro dell'asse*, as in the del Bene ledger, debits were placed in front up to folio 131 and credits in the rear from folio 131 onward.[13] Expense accounts—mainly interest paid to depositors—appear in the first section beginning with folio 112. Income received was recorded on the very last folios (218 and following), which have been torn out.

A somewhat different arrangement was adopted in the *libro segreto*. Most probably this book opened with a transcription of the articles of association drawn up in 1335, which occupied the first three folios, now missing.[14] The first section, up to folio 56, contains the accounts of partners or the heirs of ex-partners who, because of drawings, owed money to the company. These accounts are still in paragraph form with the credits placed under the debits. The second section, from folio 56 to 63, is made up of expense accounts, mostly interest charges on *sovracorpo*, or money invested by the partners beyond their capital quotas. The next or third section, extending from folio 65 to 73, gives a list of the salaries earned by factors from July 1, 1335, to July 1, 1343. After a number of blank pages, the

---

[11] According to the *libro dell'asse*, the Peruzzi company had branches in Avignon (Papal Court), Barletta, Bruges, Castello di Castro (Sardinia), Cyprus, London, Majorca, Naples, Paris, Pisa, Rhodes, Sicily, Tunis, and Venice.

[12] There is the case of Pacino di Tommaso Peruzzi, who was manager in Bruges (Sapori, *Libri dei Peruzzi*, p. 378).

[13] This statement, which I made first in my article, " Aux origines d'une technique intellectuelle: la formation et l'expansion de la comptabilité à partie double," *Annales d'histoire économique et sociale*, IX [1937], p. 180, was attacked by Professor Alberto Ceccherelli, " Intorno ad alchuni antichi libri di conti," *Rivista Italiana di Ragioneria*, XXXI (1937), pp. 81–83. I do not see how one can deny the obvious. For example, the debit of the account of Giotto de' Peruzzi e compagni di vecchia compagnia is on folios 2, 3, 4, 5, 6 and 7 recto of the *libro dell'asse* and the credit on folios 131, 132, 133 and 134. Consequently, the debit and the credit are in two different sections of the ledger and not placed on the same page one below the other, which would have been impossible anyhow, considering the length of this account. *Cf.* Melis, *Storia*, p. 387.

[14] Sapori, *Libri dei Peruzzi*, p. xxix.

fourth section starts on folio 109 and goes, with some gaps, to folio 160. It includes only accounts with credit balances and the order of presentation is the reverse of that followed in section one: the credits are placed above the debits instead of below. The fifth and last section occupies only a few pages beginning with folio 177 and is devoted entirely to income from accrued interest on the debit balances in section one.

The private account-book of Arnoldo di Arnoldo de' Peruzzi presents little interest. As already mentioned, the contrary is true of the one of his brother, Giotto di Arnoldo, who had been the chief accountant of the Peruzzi company before the other partners called him, in 1332, to assume the headship left vacant by the death of another brother, Tommaso di Arnoldo.[15] Giotto retained this post until his own death on August 9, 1336.[16] Because of his connection with the Peruzzi company, he was well informed about its accounting and other managerial practices, and his skill shows in his private records.[17]

Like the Bardi, the Peruzzi kept a great many books of original entry, which have been lost in the course of the centuries.[18] The surviving papers are only fragments of the *libro segreto* and the general ledger wherein the data taken from other records were greatly condensed. Despite the presence of income and expense accounts, I should hesitate a great deal to commit myself by asserting, as has been done, that the Peruzzi account-books are a genuine example of double-entry book-keeping.[19] I am not convinced at all that integration of operating results was carried to the point of perfection so as to eliminate any source of unbalance. While references reveal that net profits were certainly determined on the basis of inventories, or financial statements, there is nothing to prove that the procedure followed was consonant with the requirements of double entry. It is more likely to have been the same as that of the Bardi or the Alberti, where profits represented the excess of assets over liabilities plus equity.[20]

Whenever the partnership agreement was renewed, the Peruzzi proceeded to the closing of the books and the drawing up of a general

---

[15] Giotto di Arnoldo's private account-book furnishes the basic material for Sapori's article, " Storia interna della compagnia mercantile dei Peruzzi," *Studi medievale,,* pp. 243–284.

[16] Sapori, *Libri dei Peruzzi*, p. 1.

[17] Melis, *Storia*, p. 494.

[18] Sapori, *Libri dei Peruzzi*, p. xxiv.

[19] This opinion is expressed by Melis who even states that the Peruzzi kept their books in double entry since 1292 (*op. cit.*, pp. 495–497).

[20] This is not mere conjecture but is based on information given in the *libro dell'asse* about the financial statements sent in by the branches. See Sapori, *Libri dei Peruzzi*, pp. 7–9, 191–194.

statement, or *saldamento generale*. For this purpose all the branches abroad were required to send in statements reflecting their financial condition. This happened, for example, on July 1, 1335, when the partnership formed in 1331 was terminated and a new " company " was set up. The *libro dell'asse* shows that the " old " company was charged for any liabilities which were assumed by the new one. On the other hand, credit was given for any assets that were taken over by the newly created *ragione* or entity.[1]

In Lucca, by 1332, accounts were sometimes kept in bilateral form, according to the fragment of a *libro segreto* belonging to a company of silk manufacturers of which the main partner was Princivalle Manni. It is curious that the customary order of debit and credit is reversed, which indicates that there was as yet no uniformity and that the merchants of Lucca were still in a stage of experimentation.[2]

While in Tuscany the bilateral form was still far from prevalent in 1350, it had been common for a long time in Northern Italy. In Genoa, as early as 1327, accounts presented in this form were said to be kept *ad usum banchi* or after the manner of the banks, perhaps because it was first adopted by the banks or money-changers' tables (*tavole*), whence the name of tabular form. As a matter of fact, Genoese bankers were actually using the tabular form in 1313. However, there is no evidence that they were also acquainted with double entry.

The first example of this method in Genoa is found in the accounts of the stewards or *massari* of the Genoese commune for the year 1340.[3] In the books of these public officials, debits and credits are

---

[1] *Ragione* is an expression often used in Italian accounts and business correspondence of the Middle Ages. Its meanings range from a statement of account to a firm as a whole or one of its branches. However, *ragione* always suggests something about accounting and refers either to a single account or a set of accounts. *Saldare la ragione*, for example, means to close the books; *mandare la ragione* may refer to sending a balance sheet or a simple statement; *la ragione di Parigi* may designate the Paris branch, especially as an accounting entity. Florence Edler, " Ragione," *Glossary of Mediaeval Terms of Business, Italian Series, 1200-1600* (Cambridge, Mass., 1934), pp. 236-237.

[2] State Archives, Lucca, Archivio Bottini, No. 1. *Cf.* Melis, *op. cit.*, pp. 432-433.

[3] These famous account-books were first described by Cornelio Desimoni, " Christoforo Colombo ed il Banco di San Giorgio," *Atti della Società ligure di storia patria*, XIX (1889), fasc. 3, pp. 585-623, especially pp. 600-601. They were later re-examined by Fabio Besta, *La Ragioneria*, III, pp. 273-281, and Heinrich Sieveking, " Aus genueser Rechnungs- und Steuerbüchern," *Sitzungsberichte der Kais. Akademie der Wissenschaften in Wien, Philosophisch-Historische Klasse*, 162, fasc. 2 (1909), pp. 15-17; *ibid.*, " Genueser Finanzwesen vom 12. bis 14. Jahrhundert," *Volkswirtschaftliche Abhandlungen der Badischen Hochschulen*, I (1898), pp. 388-389, 481-488. More recently, the account-books of the *Massari*

not only placed side by side like the panels of a diptych, but thorough investigation has brought out that each transaction is recorded twice, once on each side of the ledger.[4] The debit is indicated by the Latin words *debent nobis* (they owe us) in the text of the first entry on the left of an account. Subsequent entries begin with *item*, meaning " the same." On the credit side the first entry starts invariably with the words *recepimus in* (we received from). Without exception, each entry gives the cross-reference to the corresponding debit or credit, as the case may be. Expenses are charged to an account called *Avaria*, a word commonly used in medieval Latin to designate brokerage, weighing, and other costs on goods. Losses on sales of pepper and other commodities are posted to the debit of an account entitled *Proventus cambii et dampnum de rauba vendita* (Income from exchange and loss on sales). The account of the Commune of Genoa functions as a capital account to which the balances of all expense and income accounts are transferred when the books are closed at the end of the fiscal year.[5] The consensus of experts is that the accounts of the *massari* for 1340 meet the requirements of double entry.[6]

One puzzling point, however, may need a word of explanation. The registers of the *massari* contain several merchandise accounts for pepper, raw silk, sugar and wax, on which there is a loss in each instance.[7] One author even states that the Commune of Genoa " took a flyer on pepper," but it seems unlikely that a public administration would be speculating on the rise or fall of the market.[8] The explanation is simply that the Commune of Genoa, in order to raise money, bought goods on credit at a high price and resold them for cash at a lower price. The pepper, for example, was purchased at £24 5s., Genoese currency, per centner and resold *ad numeratum*, i.e., for cash, at £22 14s. 6d. and £22 10s. The transaction is, therefore, a way by which shrewd merchants took advantage of the government's plight. It is also a way of evading the Church's ban on usury. In the Middle Ages, practices of this sort were fairly common. The City of

---

were re-examined by Melis (*op. cit.*, pp. 527–529) and Zerbi (*op. cit.*, pp. 185–204). An English translation of some accounts will be found in Edward Peragallo, *Origin and Evolution of Double Entry Bookkeeping* (New York, 1938), pp. 3–17. The translation is not always reliable.

[4] Sieveking, " Genueser Finanzwesen," *op. cit.*, p. 389; Besta, *op. cit.*, III, p. 279.

[5] Zerbi, *op. cit.*, p. 199. This author has not been content with formal observance of the rules but has investigated carefully the procedure followed in closing the books. The text of the account *Commune Janue* will be found in Sieveking, " Genueser Finanzwesen," pp. 482–485; also in Zerbi, *op. cit.*, p. 200.

[6] Besta, *op. cit.*, III, p. 279; Sieveking, " Genueser Finanzwesen," p. 388; Zerbi, *op. cit.*, p. 203; Melis, *op. cit.*, p. 527.

[7] The text of the pepper account will be found in Besta, *op. cit.*, III, p. 276; Melis, *op. cit.*, pp. 528–529; and Peragallo, *op. cit.*, p. 8. In the latter's text, *valent nobis in* should be emended throughout to read *unde nobis in*. The Chinese silk account is published by Zerbi, *op. cit.*, p. 192.

[8] Peragallo, *op. cit.*, p. 9.

Bruges resorted to the same expedient to replenish an empty treasury. As late as the sixteenth century, distressed sovereigns could only find much-needed cash by accepting part of a loan in overrated jewels or diamonds which they then had to peddle around at disastrous prices.

The ledger of 1340 contains balances carried forward from a preceding one for the year 1339. Unfortunately, no records of the *massari* prior to 1340 are extant in the Genoese archives. Perhaps they shared the same fate as a mass of other papers and were burned by the mob during the riots which, in 1339, marked the overthrow of the aristocratic régime and the election of the first " popular " doge, Simone Boccanegri. It is likely that the introduction of double entry into the Genoese finance administration dates back to 1327 when, because of numerous frauds, the system of book-keeping was completely overhauled and orders were issued to keep accounts *ad modum banchi*.[9]

In general, double-entry book-keeping conflicted with the voucher system favoured by the public authorities and was rarely adopted by governmental bodies. Experiments made by minor officials usually met with rebuttal from higher up. An example is that of an enterprising municipal treasurer of Reggio Emilia who, in 1385, devised a system of double entry to keep the accounts with the central treasury of the Milanese Visconti. He was soon rebuked by the auditor and forbidden to deviate from the beaten path.[10]

In the Genoese archives there are preserved a series of cash-books and journals belonging to the Lomellini bank.[11] The first cash-book dates from 1386. Those for 1390, 1392 and 1394 are also extant, and from 1396 through 1433 the series is complete. The journals cover, with numerous gaps, a period from 1397 to 1431. Unfortunately, no ledgers are included in the series. In the cash-books, receipts are entered in a column to the left and expenditures to the right. In the journals, entries follow each other in chronological order. These records show that payments by book transfer were very common, at least among merchants. In the absence of ledgers, there is no reliable evidence that the Lomellini bank actually kept its books in double entry.

If the records of private banks are incomplete, we are more fortunate with respect to the Bank of St. George, a public bank erected in 1408 in the expectation that it would reduce the burden of the public debt, prevent the malpractices of the private bankers, and

---

[9] Besta, *op. cit.*, III, p. 280.
[10] Zerbi, *op. cit.*, pp. 206–214.
[11] Alessandro Lattes, " Gli antichi registri dei banchieri genovesi," *Rivista del diritto commerciale*, XVII, pt. 1 (1919), pp. 616–618.

halt the rise of the gold florin and the concomitant depreciation of the silver currency. The Bank of St. George is often confused with the *Casa di San Giorgio,* or the Office of St. George, a semi-public organisation of State creditors. Actually, the Bank was one of several agencies created and controlled by this larger and more powerful institution, which even administered Genoese colonies in the Levant. In spite of a chequered career, the business of the Bank grew by leaps and bounds. Had it not been prematurely dissolved in 1444, central banking might have developed much sooner than it actually did.[12] The Bank of St. George was primarily a transfer and deposit bank. Most of the entries relate to transfers from the account of one depositor to that of another.[13] As cheques were not in use, transfer orders were given by word of mouth and written down by the banker in his journal in the presence of both parties: payer and payee. This practice explains the importance attached to the journal, since there was no other record of an otherwise oral agreement.[14] In Genoa, the book-keepers of the banks, private as well as public, were required to be licensed notaries, so that their records had the same value as formal deeds.[15] A banker guilty of tearing leaves out of journals or of tampering with any entries exposed himself to criminal proceedings and severe penalties.[16]

The influence of these medieval practices still lingers on in Napoleonic commercial law, which considers the journal as the only official record and still requires that it be kept strictly in chronological order without any blanks between entries, that the number of folios be stated on the first and last pages, and that each folio be initialled by a judge of the mercantile court. This legislation is still on the books in Continental countries, though it has become inapplicable in the case of large corporations using several books of original entry.

In the records of the Bank of St. George a journal was called a *manuale notularum bancorum,* a name which suggests that its purpose was to "note" or register contracts. From there the entries were

12 Raymond de Roover, " New Interpretations of the History of Banking," *Journal of World History,* II (1954), pp. 56-57.
13 Sieveking, " Die Casa di San Giorgio," *Volkswirtschaftliche Abhandlungen der Badischen Hochschulen,* III (1899), p. 330. According to a Genoese statute, it is clear that bank deposits were payable or transferable on demand. See L. Goldschmidt, *Universalgeschichte des Handelsrechts* (Stuttgart, 1891), p. 324, note 91.
14 Luca Pacioli, *Summa de Arithmetica* (Brescia, 1494), Dist. 9, Tract. 11, Chap. 24. *Cf.* R. de Roover, " The Lingering Influence of Medieval Practices," *The Accounting Review,* XVIII (1943), pp. 148-151.
15 Sieveking, " Casa di San Giorgio," *op. cit.,* p. 331. *Cf.* Henry Harrisse, *Christopher Columbus and the Bank of Saint George* (New York, 1888), pp. 67, 114. Harrisse was really the first to call attention to the books of the Bank of St. George as early examples of double entry.
16 A. P. Usher, " The Origins of Banking: The Primitive Bank of Deposit, 1200-1600," *The Economic History Review,* IV (1934), p. 411.

posted to the *cartularium*, or ledger. This posting was indicated by a cross-mark in front of each journal entry. Cash transactions, however, do not appear in the *manuale*, or journal; they were posted directly from the cash-book to the ledger. As a result, the *manuale* was used only for transfers of credit from one account to another.

The ledger, or *cartularium*, for 1408—and the same arrangement is found in the later ones—is divided into two sections,[17] The first section contains the *rationes de numerato*, that is, the cash account, the general expense account, and the great mass of deposit accounts. All the accounts in this section are in bilateral form with debit and credit facing each other in two columns on the same page. The accounts of the depositors are classified in alphabetical order of Christian names (and not of surnames). Originally, index tabs in the form of strips of parchment protruding from the side of the ledger indicated where each letter began. Thus accounts could be located quickly without first consulting an index.

The second section of the ledger includes far fewer pages than the first and contains only *rationes temporum*, or time accounts originating in credit transactions. In this section, too, accounts are in bilateral form, but debit and credit appear on opposite pages instead of in two columns on the same page. By statute the Bank of St. George was forbidden to extend credit to private individuals by means of overdrafts, but it could lend on security of *loca*, or shares in the public debt.[18] It also made advances to tax-farmers, various government officials, and private bankers. As usual in the Middle Ages, interest is not mentioned; it was perhaps concealed under the form of service charges. Officially at least, the Bank did not lend money at interest.

Apparently the bank did not have any capital other than the support of the Casa di San Giorgio.[19] The first funds, on March 2, 1408, were provided by two private bankers, Raffaello de ' Vivaldi and Antoniotto di Nairono.[20] The first balance was cast on January 1, 1409, after ten months of operation. Because of the numerous deposit accounts, the number of credit items by far outweighs the number of debit items, most of them balances of *rationes temporum*, or time accounts.[1] Total credits, almost exclusively deposits, amount to £54,295 14s. 1d., Genoese currency.[2] Total debits, both *rationes*

---

[17] In the ledger of 1408, the first section occupies 600 out of 719 folios or 1,200 out of 1,438 pages.

[18] Sieveking, " Casa di S. Giorgio," p. 336.

[19] The establishment of the bank was authorised by a decree of January 18, 1408.

[20] The two together supplied over £5,300, Genoese currency.

[1] The credit side of the balance includes more than 310 items, the debit side only 95.

[2] The totals are given by Sieveking, " Aus Genueser Rechnungs- und Steuerbüchern," *op. cit.*, pp. 36–37.

TABLE 1

BALANCE OF THE BANK OF ST. GEORGE ON JANUARY 1, 1409

Allocation of Resources

Explanation	Amount in Genoese Currency			Per Cent. of Total
	£	s.	d.	
Cash on hand	3,013	9	3	5·5
Officium Procuratorum S. Georgii	20,660	14	10	38·0
Loans to private bankers	20,236	15	5	37·3
Other advances	10,204	7	8	18·9
General expense	179	16	3	·3
Total	54,295	3	5	100·0

Source : State Archives, Genoa, Registri Bancorum S. Georgii, Sala 24, Cartularium 1408, fol. 110ᵛ.

de numerato and *rationes temporum,* amount to £54,295 3s. 5d. Consequently, the books balance, save for a small and negligible difference of 10s. 8d.[3] Although the balance is little more than a trial balance, there can be no doubt that the Bank of St. George kept its books in double entry.[4] Table 1 shows the use made of the bank's resources according to the balance of January 1, 1409.

The Bank of St. George expanded very rapidly. By 1421 the ledger was filled in six months and it became necessary to use two a year.[5] In 1425 the *rationes de numerato* and the *rationes temporum* were lodged in different ledgers and reciprocal accounts were created to form the link between the two.[6] By 1439 the volume of business had become so great that the protectors of the *Casa* or Office of St. George decided to open a second " bank " or ledger. In 1441 a third " bank " was set up.[7] These banks, of course, opened clearing accounts to each other to facilitate settlements between their respective customers.

Despite a growing volume of business, the Bank of St. George repeatedly ran into difficulties, perhaps because of excessive advances to the State. In 1415 cash resources ran so low that it was forced to suspend specie payments while continuing to make transfers. As a result, deposits with the Bank of St. George became inconvertible bank money, intrinsically the same as irredeemable paper money. After resuming specie payments, the same difficulties recurred again

[3] To check the books, the bank employed auditors who were paid 10 per cent. of the amount of each error which they discovered. See Balduin Penndorf, *Luca Pacioli, Abhandlung über die Buchhaltung . . . mit einer Einleitung über die Italienische Buchhaltung im 14. und 15. Jahrhundert* (Stuttgart, 1933), p. 5.
[4] Besta, *op. cit.,* III, p. 286.
[5] Sieveking (" Casa di S. Giorgio," p. 338) gives 1424, but this date must be wrong, since two ledgers and two journals for 1421 are extant in the Genoese archives.
[6] This statement is based on my own investigations, as are the figures in Table 1.
[7] Sieveking, " Casa di S. Giorgio," p. 339.

and again; cash resources were drained away either because of Government demands for credit or because of unsuccessful attempts to keep down the rising rate of the florin.   Rather than pursue a ruinous monetary policy, the protectors of the *Casa* decided, in 1444, to surrender their charter and to dissolve the Bank.[8]

In Lombardy, as in Genoa, account-books were commonly kept in Latin instead of in the vernacular.   As a rule, accounts were also arranged in tabular or bilateral form.   Perhaps this uniformity may be due to the influence of the Placentine bankers who, toward the end of the thirteenth century, were serious competitors of the Sienese companies and played a leading part in Genoa and at the fairs of Champagne.   Unfortunately, none of their business records seem to have escaped destruction.   There are extant only two ledgers of a Milanese, Giacomolo di Francesco da Giussano, who was established in Piacenza as banker and treasury agent of the Visconti government. They cover only a short period from 1356 to 1358.[9]

As collector of public revenue, Giussano was in close relations with Beltramolo Leccacorvo, a prominent banker who farmed out taxes, and Tommaso Anguissola, the municipal treasurer, who through relatives participated in the same business.   Since Leccacorvo and Anguissola are names of great bankers' families frequently mentioned a century earlier in the Genoese records, the role of Placentine financiers around 1360 was not yet entirely finished, though, presumably, their activities were no longer international in scope.

The account-books of Giussano shed an interesting light on medieval taxation, mainly indirect, and on the expedients used in financing a war that was then being waged between the Visconti of Milan and a defensive league of neighbours.   From the point of view of accounting history, however, Giussano's account-books are of minor interest.   They are kept in single entry with no systematic endeavour to go beyond the registration of receivables and payables and to determine operating results.[10]

The same defect is found in three ledgers covering the years 1396, 1399 and 1400 of the important Del Maino bank of Milan.   It is quite possible, as Professor Tommaso Zerbi maintains, that this bank originally kept its books in double entry, but that the system broke down because of monetary disorders.[11]   As a result it became increasingly impracticable to keep accounts in one monetary unit when business was actually transacted in two or three rival currencies, which

---

[8] *Ibid.*, p. 357.
[9] Tommaso Zerbi, *La banca nell'ordinamento finanziario visconteo; dai mastri del Banco Giussano, gestore della Tesoreria di Piacenza (1356–1358)*, Università commerciale L. Bocconi, Pubblicazioni, series II, no. 1 (Milan, 1935).
[10] *Ibid.*, pp. 37–38.
[11] Zerbi, *Origini della partita doppia*, pp. 289–292.

fluctuated in price from day to day. For the same reason, the book-
keeper of the Florentine bank, Lippi and del Bene in Padua (1391–
1392), who had started out by keeping his books in double entry, was
forced to give up.[12] It was probably too much of a task to make
constant adjustments for exchange differences as increased monetary
instability aggravated the inconvenience of dealing with competing
currencies. This exchange problem was peculiar to transfer and
deposit banks which, in the Middle Ages, derived most of their profits
from exchange transactions and currently accepted deposits repayable
in different kinds of money. At that time gold and silver coins circulated side by side, but they were not always current at the same rate,
thereby causing a knotty problem for the poor book-keepers. It was
also one of the main reasons why merchants preferred to make their
payments by transfer rather than in coin. Another reason was that
telling money was a time-consuming process, especially because of
the variety of coins in circulation.

Double entry was not unknown in Milan and a perfect example
of it is found in the ledger of a partnership, Marco Serrainerio and
Giovannino da Dugnano, which traded with Catalonia.[13] It lasted
from 1395 to 1397 when it went into liquidation. These proceedings
dragged on for another year. Its capital was about £4,800 *di
imperiali*, Milanese currency, of which the first partner supplied one-
third and the second, two-thirds. The account-book of the
Serrainerio-Dugnano partnership is especially remarkable as a sample
of venture accounting. A separate account is opened to each lot of
merchandise imported or exported. The book-keeper, who was
Marco Serrainerio, made a special effort to allocate expenses to the
proper lot and to determine as accurately as possible the net profit or
loss on each single venture. Unallocated burden or overhead was
thereby reduced to a minimum.

As this survey of the development of accounting in Northern
Italy shows, it did not follow the same pattern as in Tuscany where
the tabular or bilateral form did not win general acceptance until late
in the fourteenth century. On the other hand, the Tuscans were more
progressive in another respect and kept their accounts in Italian,
whereas the Genoese and the Milanese continued to use Latin
throughout the fourteenth century and even later. There were other
differences between trading centres. Not even the terminology was
uniform; and it differed from place to place: a ledger, for example,
was called a *libro dei debitori e creditori* in Florence, a *libro grande*

[12] *Ibid.*, pp. 226–236, esp. p. 235.
[13] The text of this account-book has been published in full by Tommaso Zerbi,
Il mastro a partita doppia di una azienda mercantile del Trecento, Università
commerciale L. Bocconi, Pubblicazioni, series II, no. 3 (Milan, 1936). *Cf.* Zerbi,
Origini, pp. 237–274.

in Prato, a *quaderno* in Venice, a *cartularium* in Genoa, a *liber tabulle* in Milan, a *libro reale* in Arezzo, and a *mastro* or a *campione* elsewhere. In view of this local diversity, it is quite possible that double entry developed independently at about the same time in several trading centres. Such an explanation does not exclude the possibility that one centre borrowed improvements from another. It would, therefore, be inadvisable to attribute the invention of double entry without hesitation to this or that centre. Neither would it be wise to set a definite date. One thing is certain: double-entry book-keeping originated in Italy between 1250 and 1350. The first unquestionable example of it is found in the Genoese *massari* records of the year 1340, but there are indications that it may be older or even that it may have been born in Tuscany, as Professor Federigo Melis claims.

Florence, as we have seen, was rather slow in adopting the bilateral form, which was probably imported from Venice rather than from Genoa or Milan. At any rate, the first mention of it is found in the heading of a ledger dated 1382 and kept by a Florentine merchant, Paliano di Falco Palliani, who declares on the front page that he intends to keep his accounts *alla veneziana,* or after the Venetian manner, that is, " on one page the debit and facing it the credit." [14] Since Paliano's accounts do not come up to the standards of double-entry book-keeping, it is clear that the expression *alla veneziana* refers to the form of presentation and not to the system of accounting.

The transition from single to double entry in Tuscany can best be studied in the records of Francesco di Marco Datini (*ca.* 1335–1410), the famous Pratese merchant-banker, who became one of the richest men of his time and entertained royalty in his palace. [15] Having no legitimate offspring, Francesco Datini left the major part of his fortune, including his palatial home, to a charitable foundation, the Ceppo de' Poveri, with the recommendation that the trustees continue his policy of keeping all his records. [16] The foundation still exists

---

[14] Edler, *Glossary of Mediaeval Terms of Business*, p. 314: " . . . scriverollo *alla viniziana,* cioè nell'una carta dare e a rinpetto l'avere." *Cf.* Besta, *op. cit.*, III, p. 328; Melis, *op cit.*, p. 427; Alberto Tofani, *Alcune ricerche storiche sull'ufficio e la professione di ragioniere a Firenze al tempo della Repubblica* (Florence, 1910), pp. 51–55.

[15] The best study on Francesco Datini is that of Enrico Bensa, *Francesco di Marco da Prato* (Milan, 1928). This book has valuable appendices, including excerpts from account-books. Unfortunately, the legal point of view predominates. In English, there are only two brief articles: Robert Brun, " A Fourteenth-Century Merchant of Italy: Francesco Datini of Prato," *Journal of Economic and Business History*, II (1930), pp. 451–466; Stanley S. Miller, " Business and the Fear of Materialism," *Bulletin of the Business Historical Society*, XXVI (1952), pp. 107–121.

[16] The text is given in the introduction of Cesare Guasti ed., *Ser Lapo Mazzei, Lettere di un notaro a un mercante del secolo XIV* (Florence, 1880), vol. I, p. cxiii. This is a collection of letters addressed to Datini by his notary.

today, and the founder's wish was faithfully carried out, with the result that most of the records, including those of the branches abroad, are in Prato. The Datini archives today are unique for their completeness and fill an entire room in the old palace; they include about five hundred account-books and more than 100,000 business letters, not to mention several bundles filled with bills of exchange, insurance policies, early cheques, bills of lading, and other documents.

Francesco Datini, so the story goes, was a poor boy who lost both parents through the Black Death (1348). Two years later he went to Avignon where he worked his way up from *garzone*, or office-boy, to factor, until he had acquired enough experience to stand on his own feet. In 1363 Datini invested his modest savings in a partnership which throve and grew by reinvestment of earnings. By 1371, at any rate, he was in possession of a sizeable capital that made him a well-to-do, 'if not a rich, man. He married in 1376 a Florentine girl also residing in Avignon, who brought him no dowry. In December, 1382, Datini left Avignon to return to Prato, where he died twenty-eight years later (1410). His managerial talents were conspicuous and his business did not cease to prosper. By 1395 he was at the helm of a firm with headquarters in Prato (1382), an establishment in Florence (1383), and branches in Pisa (1382), Genoa (1392), Avignon (1382), Barcelona (1393), Valencia (1393), and Palma de Mallorca (1395). The network of his correspondents extended from England to the Levant. In London his representatives were for a time Luigi and Salvestro Mannini, a firm which apparently went bankrupt as a result of the downfall of Richard II (1399). Francesco Datini also established a bank in Prato (1398) and was partner in a " shop " (*bottega*) there producing woollen cloth (1384–1400). As a rule branches were autonomous entities, but Datini was careful to keep a controlling interest in the capital and a preponderant voice in the management. His junior partners were little more than executive officers, who were expected to carry out his policies, and woe unto them if they did not. One should read the letters which he wrote in his own hand to branch managers who had dared to transgress his instructions.

In the beginning of his career, while still residing in Avignon, Datini followed the prevailing Tuscan practice and kept his books in single entry, the ledger having split accounts, debits in front and credits in the rear, as in the del Bene and Peruzzi ledgers already mentioned. This form, which belongs to a transitional stage between the paragraph and the bilateral forms, is found in the *libro giallo A*, or ledger A bound in yellow [leather], of Datini's mercery business in Avignon (1367–1372). In an inscription on the front page, after the usual invocation to God, the Virgin, and the Saints, the book-keeper states explicitly that he intends to record systematically all entries involving a debit up to folio 150 and all those involving a credit from folio 151 onward to the end on folio 300.[17]   Thus the debit of Niccolo di Bono's and Puccio Ricci's account is found on folio 2 verso and the credit on folio 151.[18]   To close the account, the total of the debit, or florins 270 14s. 8d. *di camera,* papal currency, was transferred from folio 151 to folio 2 and deducted from the total debit; the remaining balance was then collected in cash.

This system is altered in a later ledger (1383–1386), also a *libro giallo,* belonging to Datini's Pisan branch.   In it the personal accounts for receivables and payables are in bilateral form, but merchandise expense, and profit-and-loss accounts continue to have the credit beneath instead of beside the debit.   The presence of accounts for operating results has led to the conclusion that this ledger is in double entry,[19] but Professor Zerbi, who has examined it carefully, challenges this opinion because of the absence of a cash account, though there is a cash-book which might have been used as a substitute.[20]   Combining the cash-book with the ledger would enable the book-keeper to strike a balance, provided, of course, that he observed the rules in other respects.   The argument, therefore, is not decisive.

Professor Zerbi also intimates that none of Datini's account-books contains a clear-cut example of double entry.[1]   On the contrary, after 1390 this system was certainly applied in most of the Datini branches abroad and at his main office in Florence.[2]   Branch managers were expected to send regularly a copy of the balance sheet to headquarters, and several of such copies are still preserved in Prato.   They show that the books were in balance save for small errors which the book-keepers often did not bother to trace but preferred to adjust by posting them to Profit and Loss.   As further evidence I am publishing in Tables 2 and 3 the balance sheet and the income statement of the Barcelona branch on January 31, 1399.   These tables show beyond any doubt that the books were kept according to the most exacting standards of double entry.   The evidence presented is so conclusive that it settles, I think, the point at issue.

---

[17] Gaetano Corsani, *I fondaci e i banchi di un mercante pratese del Trecento; Contributo alla storia della ragioneria e del commercio* (Prato, 1922), pp. 71–72. *Cf.* R. de Roover, " Aux origines," *op. cit.,* p. 274.

[18] The text (with many errors) is published by Bensa, *Francesco di Marco,* pp. 409–413.

[19] Corsani, *op. cit.,* pp. 82–89 ; Besta, *La Ragioneria,* III, pp. 318–320.

[20] Zerbi, *Origini,* pp. 131–136.

[1] *Ibid.,* p. 136.

[2] Corsani (*op. cit.,* pp. 91–92) gives the following dates : Avignon (from 1398 onward), Prato (the bank of F. Datini and B. Cambioni, 1398 onward), Florence (1386 onward), Genoa (1391 onward), Barcelona (1393 onward), Valencia (1396 onward), and Majorca (1396 onward).

It should perhaps be emphasised that Table 2 is not a reconstruction but simply a condensed balance sheet based on an original, of which there are two different copies in the Datini archives.[3] These original copies are booklets of twelve pages and contain a list of more than 110 items on the assets side and nearly sixty on the liabilities

TABLE 2

FRANCESCO DI MARCO DATINI & CO. IN BARCELONA

Balance Sheet on January 31, 1399

ASSETS

Explanation	Barcelonese Currency						Per Cent. of Total
	£	s.	d.	£	s.	d.	
CASH AT BANK AND IN HAND							
Cash in hand	18	17	2				·1
Deposit accounts	1,242	9	8				8·2
Special account	440	0	0				2·9
				1,701	6	10	*11·2*
RECEIVABLES							
Local tradesmen for goods sold	4,841	14	10				31·9
Local customers for exchange	2,192	19	4				14·5
Local customers for insurance	99	17	11				·7
				7,134	12	1	*47·1*
BALANCES WITH FOREIGN CORRESPONDENTS							
Venice	1,305	5	9				8·5
Genoa	9	7	7				·1
Avignon	6	0					·0
Montpellier	854	15	1				5·6
Paris	19	5	2				·1
Pisa	980	12	7				6·4
Bruges	1,036	2	7				6·5
Florence	520	10	10				3·8
Perpignan	118	18	5				·8
				4,845	4	0	*31·8*
DATINI BRANCHES IN OTHER PLACES							
Majorca	88	9	0				·6
Venice	224	16	10				1·4
Florence	211	16	0				1·4
				525	1	10	*3·4*
INVENTORIES							
Goods in stock				288	0	9	*1·9*
FIXTURES							
Office furniture	95	0	0				·6
Martha, our slave (*Marta, nostra schiava*)	30	0	0				·2
				125	0	0	*·8*
MISCELLANEOUS							
Sundry deferred charges and supplies	112	1	10				·7
Drawing account Simone d'Andrea	25	0	2				·2
Shortage in cash	38	13	0				·3
Sundry adjustments for errors	17	18	6				·1
				193	13	6	*1·3*
BAD DEBTS				384	7	3	*2·5*
UNTRACED ERROR IN CASTING THE BALANCE				11	9	1	*·0*
Total				15,208	15	4	*100·0*

[3] Both are in bundle No. 1165 (old No. 1129 in Nicastro's printed inventory).

TABLE 2 (*continued*)

FRANCESCO DI MARCO DATINI & CO. IN BARCELONA

Balance Sheet on January 31, 1399

LIABILITIES

Explanation	Barcelonese Currency						Per Cent. of Total
	£	s.	d.	£	s.	d.	
PAYABLES							
Local merchants (mostly acceptances)				1,951	2	9	*12·8*
BALANCES WITH FOREIGN CORRESPONDENTS							
Majorca	586	5	6				3·8
Valencia	865	1	9				5·7
Perpignan	3	11	2				·0
Montpellier	91	0	10				·6
Paris	297	0	0				2·0
Bruges	2,848	18	9				18·7
Bologna	570	7	6				3·8
Florence	2,090	12	10				13·7
Genoa	666	12	11				4·4
Pisa	182	7	1				1·2
Venice	59	10	6				·4
				8,261	8	10	*54·3*
DATINI BRANCHES IN OTHER PLACES							
Florence	804	19	1				5·3
Genoa	1,037	13	11				6·8
Avignon	32	17	8				·2
Majorca	510	11	6				3·4
Valencia	171	11	3				1·1
				2,557	13	5	*16·8*
CONSIGNMENT SALES				828	7	9	*5·5*
RESERVE FOR ACCRUED TAXES AND CONTINGENCIES				80	0	0	*·5*
OWNER'S EQUITY							
Francesco di Marco Datini da Prato				768	6	8	*5·1*
Net profit on merchandise and exchange	751	10	7				4·9
Later adjustment	10	5	4				·1
				761	15	11	*5·0*
Total				15,208	15	4	*100·0*

Source : Datini Archives, Prato (Tuscany), No. 1165.

side. To publish this material in its original form would have taken too much space and served no useful purpose. It was, therefore, necessary to condense it by grouping the data under appropriate headings without making any other changes. The procedure followed, in other words, is the same as that currently used by accountants in preparing a condensed balance sheet from analytical data. The last page of the original balance sheet is reproduced as Plate V; as the corrections are in a different handwriting, they show plainly on the photograph.

The income statement presented in Table 3 is based on data supplied by the ledger, *libro verde C*, from which the balance was cast. This ledger, too, is still extant in the Datini archives. As the

TABLE 3

FRANCESCO DI MARCO DATINI & CO. IN BARCELONA

Statement of Profit and Loss

July 11, 1397–January 31, 1399
(*In Barcelonese Currency*)

	£	s.	d.
Profits on trade (*Pro di mercatantie*)	689	11	5
Profits on foreign exchange (*Pro di cambio*)	262	4	0
Credit balance of merchandise expense (*Spese di mercatantie*)	133	13	7

				£	s.	d.
Total of gross profits				1,085	9	0
Deduct expenses:	£	s.	d.			
Rent for eighteen months	60	0	0			
Irrecoverable account	3	8	0			
Convoy expenses (*guidaggio*)	67	12	0			
Living expenses	106	1	5			
Depreciation on office equipment	16	17	0			
Reserve for unpaid taxes and other accruals (*riserbo di spese di lelde a pagare e altre spese*)	80	0	0			
Total expenses				333	18	5
Net income				751	10	7

Source : Datini Archives, Prato (Tuscany), No. 801, Barcelona, *Libro verde C.*

reader will notice, the statement leaves a balance of £751 10s. 7d., Barcelonese currency, which reappears as net earnings on the liabilities side of the balance sheet.[4] We are consequently in the presence of an articulate system of proprietary computations of gain or loss. The puzzling feature that merchandise expense (*spese di mercatantie*) has a credit balance is easily explained; it is simply due to the fact that commissions, brokerage and other fees charged to consigners abroad were credited to this account. Since these credits exceed the amounts actually spent, *spese di mercatantie*, instead of being an expense, turns out to be a source of income.[5] Among the expenses, the profit-and-loss statement includes a charge of £80 for unpaid taxes and other unforeseen contingencies, obviously made to avoid overstating profits. This item is also listed as a reserve among the liabilities. Accrual accounting, therefore, is nothing new; it antedates 1400.[6] So does depreciation, since the statement indicates that £16 17s. were written off on office equipment and charged to expenses. Many more examples of reserves and provisions for unpaid

---

4 The amounts in the balance sheet and the income statement are in Barcelonese pounds. They should not be confused with English pounds, or pounds sterling, any more than it would be advisable today to confuse French and Swiss francs. Around 1400, a Barcelonese pound was worth only 3s. 10d. sterling, English currency.

5 I do not see why Professor Zerbi finds this procedure faulty and strange (*Origini*, p. 135).

6 A. C. Littleton, " Fifteenth-Century Reserves," *The Accounting Review*, XIX (1944), pp. 457–459.

charges can be found in the records of the Medici bank, so that the setting up of such reserves may be considered current practice long before the publication of Luca Pacioli's treatise.

The reader may be somewhat surprised to find among the fixtures an item entitled "Martha, our slave." Throughout the fourteenth and fifteenth centuries, slavery was fairly common in the Mediterranean world. One of the great slave markets was the Genoese colony of Caffa on the Black Sea. In Florence, all the prominent families, among them the Medici, owned one or two slaves, usually women and rarely men.[7]

As the balance sheet shows, the business of Datini's Barcelona branch was very diversified. It combined trade and banking and also acted as a commission agent for foreign correspondents. No interest income appears anywhere, but the profit-and-loss statement reveals that *pro di cambio*, or profits on foreign exchange, was a considerable source of income. Because of the Church's ban against usury, the discounting of commercial paper was ruled out, so that the bankers operated instead on the exchange by means of correspondents abroad. This practice explains the presence in the balance sheet of so many accounts open to foreign correspondents. It also explains the importance of *pro di cambio*. Its balance originated in exchange differences from the *Nostro* accounts of foreign correspondents. *Nostro* accounts, as opposed to *Vostro* accounts, were accounts in foreign currency.[8] They usually had two adjoining columns on both the debit and the credit sides: one for the foreign, and the other for the local, currency. Whenever a *Nostro* account balanced in foreign currency, but not in local currency, the difference represented either a profit or a loss on exchange dealings. To be sure, interest was concealed in the rate of exchange, but it was mixed with other speculative elements. Its presence, however, favoured the lender to the detriment of the borrower with the result that the bankers who lent money by buying foreign bills gained on most exchange dealings. To determine these profits or losses, the bankers used the convenient device of *Nostro* and *Vostro* accounts, *Nostro* accounts when they were actively speculating and *Vostro* accounts when they were passive and carrying out the orders of their foreign correspondents. *Nostro* and *Vostro* accounts are found not only in the *libro verde C* under discussion, but in other Datini ledgers. They are also a common feature in the account-books of other medieval merchant-bankers, including the Medici of Florence and the Borromei of Milan.

---

[7] On this subject there is a recent article, both delightful and learned, by Iris Origo, "The Domestic Enemy: The Eastern Slaves in Tuscany in the Fourteenth and Fifteenth Centuries," *Speculum*, XXX (1955), pp. 321–366.

[8] Raymond de Roover, "Early Accounting Problems of Foreign Exchange." *The Accounting Review*, XIX (1944), pp. 381–407.

interesting examples of job accounting with allocation of burden and indirect labour cost were discovered in the records of Datini's manufacturing establishment in Prato.[9] Cost accounting is, however, outside the scope of this study. I shall, therefore, limit myself to the remark that these cost records do not fit into a comprehensive system of double entry. As already pointed out, the disorderly state of the Florentine monetary system seriously hampered such a development, because the cloth manufacturers bought their raw material and sold their finished product in stable gold currency, but paid their wages in depreciating silver currency. Merchants and bankers, who dealt only in gold, were not confronted with the same problem.

Coeval with the Datini records is an extensive fragment of the ledger of Averardo di Francesco de' Medici (1395). Be it said at once that this ledger, contrary to the assertions of several writers, does not belong to the famous Medici bank, established by Giovanni di Bicci de' Medici in 1397, but to another firm founded earlier by Vieri di Cambio de' Medici, a distant cousin, and continued by Francesco di Bicci, Giovanni's elder brother, and his son, Averardo di Francesco. It was one of the leading banking houses in Florence and had branches in Pisa and in Spain. The extant fragment has 94 folios and contains several examples of *Nostro* and *Vostro* accounts, an insurance account, and sundry accounts for operating results, including an expense account (*Spese di banco,* bank charges), and a profit-and-loss account (*Avanzi e disavanzi*). According to Professor Ceccherelli, this ledger of Averardo de' Medici meets the test,[10] but Professor Zerbi denies its being in double entry on the ground that there are no cross-references in the case of cash transactions.[11] This argument is flimsy but would be difficult to refute, since the extant fragment does not permit us to ascertain the procedure which was adopted in closing the books. In my opinion, it seems improbable that one of the most prominent banking houses in Florence would not be using the most up-to-date methods. In 1395, as the Datini records show, double-entry book-keeping was certainly known in Tuscany. Among the Medici papers there is another fragment of a ledger (1425–1426) of Averardo de' Medici & Compagni. This one belonged to the Pisan branch.[12] It is presumably in double entry and indicates that the firm did not limit its activity to banking or exchange, but also dealt extensively in commodities. One of the

[9] Melis, *Storia della ragioneria*, pp. 558–559, and "La formazione dei costi nell'industria laniera alla fine del Trecento," *Economia e storia*, 1 (1954), pp. 3–72.
[10] Alberto Ceccherelli, *I libri di mercatura della Banca Medici e l'applicazione della partita doppia a Firenze nel secolo decimoquarto* (Florence, 1913), p. 51. This study is almost exclusively devoted to the Averardo de' Medici ledger.
[11] Zerbi, *Origini*, pp. 125, 130.
[12] Heinrich Sieveking, "Die Handlungsbücher der Medici," *Sitzungsberichte der K. Akademie der Wissenschaften in Wien, Ph.-Hist. Klasse*, 151 (1905), pp. 29–33.

accounts in this fragment is that of Donatello, the famous sculptor, who received advances for the purchase of Carrara marble.

Until recently it was generally thought that only insignificant fragments of the account-books of the famous Medici bank had escaped destruction from the mob or from unappreciative custodians. However, in 1950 there turned up in a mislabelled bundle three *libri segreti,* or secret account-books, extending without any break from 1397, when the Medici bank was founded, to March 24, 1451, when a fourth book was started; but this has not survived.[13]   A systematic search of the Florentine archives has also yielded a crop of Medici balance sheets, discovered not only among the Medici papers but also among the records of the Florentine *catasto,* or income tax.   Although this new material is now available, no thorough study has yet been made.   Some of it is used for the first time in this essay.

The Medici material is supplemented by the private account-book of Francesco Sassetti, who was the general manager of the Medici bank from 1470, if not earlier, to 1488, when he went to Lyons to straighten out the confusion created by an inefficient and dishonest branch manager.[14]   He returned to Florence in 1489.   On March 21, 1490, he had a stroke and died within a few days.   Since Sassetti was a partner in both the Lyons and Avignon branches, his private account-book gives valuable information on their profits from 1462 until 1472, when the record ends.   At first it was kept in genuine double entry, but later Sassetti relaxed and became increasingly careless.

At the peak of its prosperity the Medici bank had five branches in Italy (Milan, Naples, Pisa, Rome and Venice) and four beyond the Alps (Avignon, Bruges, Geneva—transferred to Lyons in 1466—and London).[15]   Besides the bank, the Medici controlled three manufacturing establishments in Florence itself: two woollen " shops " and one silk " shop."[16]   Each of the branches and the " shops " was an autonomous partnership, or separate entity, which had its own capital, its own partners, and its own books.   However, the Medici had a

[13] R. de Roover, " I libri segreti del Banco de' Medici," *Archivio storico italiano,* CVII (1949), pp. 236–240.   This article gives an account of this discovery and a brief description of the three parchment account-books.

[14] Florence Edler de Roover, " Francesco Sassetti and the Downfall of the Medici Banking House," *Bulletin of the Business Historical Society,* XVII (1943), pp. 65–80.

[15] R. de Roover, *The Medici Bank; Its Organisation, Management, Operations, and Decline* (New York, 1948).   The appendices of this book contain excerpts from the ledger of the Bruges branch of the Medici (1441) and from the private record of Francesco Sassetti.

[16] These " shops," of course, were not factories or even central workshops, since the prevailing organisation of production was that of the putting-out system. Wool-washers, spinners, weavers, dyers, finishers, and others worked at home or in their own small establishments.   Only a few operations, such as sorting and beating the wool, were performed in the shop itself.

controlling interest—at least fifty per cent. of the capital—in all of
them. The structure of the Medici bank closely resembled that of a
holding company, with this fundamental difference: it was a combination of partnerships rather than of corporations or joint stock
companies.[17]

According to the second of the *libri segreti*, the Medici bank had,
in 1420, a capital of 24,000 gold florins, of which 16,000 florins
represented the share of Cosimo and Lorenzo de' Medici and 8,000
florins that of Ilarione de' Bardi, their partner and general manager.
Of this sum, 10,500 florins were invested in the bank in Florence (see
Table 5), 6,000 florins in the Rome branch and 7,500 florins in the
Venetian branch. The other branches did not yet exist in 1420. This
capital was gradually increased in later years. According to the
closing balance of the third and last of the extant *libri segreti*, the
capital of the " parent " partnership, which controlled all the sub-
sidiaries, amounted, on March 24, 1451, to 72,000 florins. The share
of the Medici in this sum was as high as 54,000 florins; the remainder,
or 18,000 florins, was supplied by Giovanni d'Amerigo Benci, their
general manager. Of course, aggregate capital investment exceeded
the amount of 72,000 florins, which does not include the share of the
branch managers and outside investors in the capital of the sub-
sidiaries. According to a reliable estimate, this aggregate amounted
in 1451 to 83,070 florins. Thus, the London branch was a limited
partnership with a capital of £1,000 sterling. The active partner,
Simone Nori, had an investment of only £200, whereas the Medici
bank had contributed £800. As a silent partner, it was responsible
only up to this initial amount, in accordance with a Florentine law
passed in 1408.[18]

Around 1460 the Medici bank, not counting the workers of the
three Florentine " shops," employed a clerical staff of about sixty
persons of all ranks from branch managers to office-boys and
apprentices. These figures may not impress a modern reader, but the
Medici bank was a giant for its time.

It is not surprising that a firm of its size could not get along with
one wastebook, one journal, and one ledger, according to the description given by Pacioli. Not only did each branch have its own books,
but each used, as a rule, several ledgers that supplemented one
another. This practice, of course, did not prevent the books from
being in double entry, whether or not reciprocal or controlling accounts

---

17 R. de Roover, *The Medici Bank*, pp. 6–7.
18 One thousand pounds sterling was far from being a negligible amount in the
fifteenth century, when the purchasing power of money was several times greater
than today.

TABLE 4

BALANCE SHEET OF THE MEDICI BANK IN FLORENCE

May 30, 1433

LIABILITIES

	F. s. d.	F. s. d. *aff.**
Credit balances taken from:		
the *libro bianco* (white book) marked N	119,781 16 9	
less: reciprocal account	2,224 8 0	
		117,557 8 9
the *libro vecchio* (old book) marked M		800 19 7
the *libro segreto* or confidential book		34,694 20 3
Total		153,052 19 7

ASSETS

	F. s. d.	F. s. d. *aff.**
Debit balances taken from:		
the *libro bianco* (white book) marked N..		119,781 16 10
the *libro vecchio giallo* marked M	8,331 24 1	
less: reciprocal account	2,224 8 0	
		6,107 16 1
the *libro segreto* or confidential book		27,111 12 7
Subtotal		153,000 16 6
Error in casting the balance		52 3 1
Total		153,052 19 7

* The books were kept in Florentine gold florins and *soldi* and *denari affiorino*. The florin was equal to 29 such *soldi* (not the usual 20 *soldi* to one florin), each of which was subdivided into 12 *denari* or pennies.

Source : State Archives, Florence, Archivio del Catasto, No. 470, fols. 541 *et seq.*

were used to link the different ledgers.[19] Both these devices were known, but they were not always adopted. It could happen that all accounts were not housed in the same ledger. In such a case, the *libro dei debitori e creditori*, for example, might not balance, but the gap would be filled by the *libro segreto*. Striking a balance could be accomplished by putting the two ledgers together.

Conclusive evidence is presented in Tables 4 and 5.[20] Table 4 gives a summary of the balance of the Medici bank in Florence (*il banco di Firenze*) as of May 30, 1433. As the reader can see, the balance is taken from three different ledgers: the ledger M, the ledger N, and the *libro segreto* of the Medici bank in Florence (which should not be confused with the still existing *libro segreto* of the Medici concern as a whole). According to the statement of May 30, 1433,

[19] An example of reciprocal accounts was given with reference to the Bank of St. George. See also Table 4. An example of a *quaderno di cassa*, or cash-book, represented in the general ledger by a controlling account, is found in a balance sheet of the London branch (State Archives, Florence, Mediceo avanti il Principato, filza 99, fols. 21 and 22: Bilancio del libro grande, anni 75, 76, 77).

[20] This evidence disposes of the doubts which Zerbi entertains with respect to the Medici keeping their books in double entry (*Origini*, p. 130).

TABLE 5

CREDIT BALANCES IN THE LIBRO SEGRETO OF THE MEDICI BANK IN FLORENCE

May 30, 1433

	F. s. d.	F. s. d. *aff.*
Corpo or Capital Stock:		
Cosimo and Lorenzo de' Medici, Ilarione		
de' Bardi & Co.	10,500 0 0	
Lippaccio di Benedetto de' Bardi	2,000 0 0	
Folco d'Adoardo Portinari	1,500 0 0	
		14,000 0 0
Cosimo and Lorenzo de' Medici, Ilarione de' Bardi & Co., current account		15,500 11 9
Undivided profits of 1431		3,251 19 9
Reserve for bad debts (*Riserbo per cattivi debitori*)		1,046 23 6
Agnolo di Lorenzo della Stufa		94 23 3
Francesco di Giovanni di Guccio di Rimini		801 0 0
Total		34,694 20 3

Source: State Archives, Florence, Archivio del Catasto, No. 470, fol. 546ᵛ.

credit balances of the *libro segreto* amounted to 34,694 florins and 20s. 3d. *affiorino.* Table 5 shows how this amount is made up. It also throws a significant light on the financial structure of the Medici bank. Apparently the capital of its Florentine office was 14,000 florins, of which 10,500 florins were supplied by the " holding " partnership, Cosimo e Lorenzo de' Medici, Ilarione de' Bardi & Co., 2,000 florins by Lippaccio di Benedetto de' Bardi, a nephew of Ilarione, and 1,500 florins by Folco d'Adoardo Portinari. The latter had been the local manager of the bank in Florence but was already dead when the balance sheet of May 30, 1433, was drawn up.[1] Lippaccio di Benedetto de' Bardi was also in some way connected with the Medici bank, but it is not clear in which capacity. As for Ilarione de' Bardi, in 1420 he had succeeded his brother Benedetto, the father of Lippaccio, in the post of general manager of all the Medici establishments, in Florence as well as outside.[2]

Although the surviving records are incomplete, they show that the Medici kept their books in double entry, except perhaps those of the manufacturing " shops." The financial statement of the wool shop attached to the *portata,* or return, of the Medici for the *catasto* of 1427 is not a real balance sheet, since there is an unexplained excess of assets over liabilities.[3] As already pointed out, monetary disturbances account for the retarded adoption of double entry in

---

[1] This Folco Portinari was the father of Tommaso, who later managed the Bruges branch, and of Pigello and Accerito who succeeded each other as managers in Milan. Folco died on December 23, 1431 or 1432.

[2] Ilarione died in 1433. He was succeeded as general manager by Giovanni d'Amerigo Benci (1435–1455).

[3] State Archives, Florence, Archivio del Catasto, No. 51: Catasto di 1427, fols. 1170–1171.

manufacturing. The Medici material is valuable, however, not so much for the information it gives about the diffusion of double entry in Tuscany as for the light it sheds on another and more interesting problem: the use of balance sheets for purposes of management and control.[4]

As a rule, the partnership agreements prescribed that the branch managers close and balance their books each year on March 24, or more often, if so required by the senior partners, that is, the Medici.[5] There is no doubt that this provision was actually carried out and that a copy of the balance sheet was sent every year to headquarters in Florence. Often it was accompanied by a report or comments in the branch manager's hand.

At headquarters, without doubt, the incoming balance sheets were carefully scrutinised. Some of the extant copies still have check marks in the margins. It is true that medieval balance sheets are not systematically arranged and that items are listed more or less in the same order as they appear in the ledger. The Medici balance sheets, like Datini's, are booklets of several pages in which assets and liabilities are listed separately, but without any attempt at further classification.[6] The audit apparently consisted in going over the balance sheet, item by item, in order to detect aging or slow accounts. Bad debts, it is true, were a perennial threat to the solvency of merchant-bankers like the Medici. They were well aware of the dangers involved in letting such debts accumulate or in granting excessive loans to a single individual or firm. One of the principal purposes of the audits was precisely to watch for overdue items or large advances and to ask the branch manager for an explanation. In some instances, each receivable listed in the balance sheet is accompanied by a comment on the prospects of recovery.[7] Such annotations sometimes provide entertaining reading. Thus it is stated in the balance sheet of the Basel branch (March 24, 1442) that there is only a slim chance of collecting a particular sum because the

---

[4] There is on this topic almost nothing save two studies: one by Alberto Ceccherelli in his book, *Il linguaggio dei bilanci; formazione e interpretazione dei bilanci commerciali* (Florence, 1950), pp. 27-56; the other, an article by Balduin Penndorf, " Inventar, Bilanz, und Bewertung in der italienischen Buchhaltung des 14. Jahrhunderts," *Zeitschrift für handelswissenschaftliche Forschung*, XXIV (1930), pp. 489-495. Prof. Ceccherelli writes that he found the word " balance " (*bilancio*) used for the first time in a Medici statement of the year 1495. However, I have found earlier examples of the same word used in the same meaning, namely, in the articles of the London branch (1446), and in those of other branches. *Bilancio* was even used in the sense of any financial statement whether or not it was a real balance as early as 1427 by both the Florentine tax officials and the taxpayers filing returns. The *portate* or returns of the Florentine *catasto* from 1427 to 1480 are full of examples of this usage.

[5] R. de Roover, *Medici Bank*, p. 16.

[6] The assets were usually listed first.

[7] Many examples are found in the balance of the London branch, mentioned above, p. 149, note 19.

principal debtor, a cleric, has been dead for some time and his surety, a layman, is completely indifferent to the penalty of excommunication for his failure to pay the Medici.[8] Perhaps, the note adds, there would be some hope if he were a priest. In their capacity of papal bankers, the Medici could obtain sentence of excommunication against anyone who owed them Church revenues and failed to pay. As the balance sheet illustrates, this dreadful sanction did not always work and left some debtors unperturbed.

From time to time branch managers were called to Florence to report on their management. One may be sure that the latest balance sheet was one of the main topics discussed at these conferences. This is not conjecture but a statement substantiated by the business correspondence of the Medici. For instance, on May 14, 1464, Tommaso Portinari, then still a factor, wrote from Bruges to headquarters that he was sending the balance sheet " with the usual notes and appendices." [9] However, if there should be any further questions, he added, they could be addressed to Angelo Tani, the branch manager, who had gone to Florence to report. In his letter, Portinari, perhaps with the intention of discrediting his superior, whose post he was eyeing, pointed out that the balance was still burdened with many bad debts and many slow items inherited from the preceding partnership, also managed by Tani. Portinari further explained that, profits being small, he had not written the interest due to depositors to the credit of their accounts. So " window-dressing " does not seem to be anything new, either. Apparently the Medici branch managers sometimes tried to make the balance sheet look better than it really was.

Perhaps the Medici system of internal audit had one great weakness: the balance sheets were checked, it is true, but the branches were not visited regularly by inspectors, or travelling auditors—such as the Fuggers, the Welsers, and other South German firms used in the sixteenth century. Someone was sent to adjust matters only after trouble had already developed, which was usually too late. In general, too much confidence was placed in the branch managers. Moreover, Sassetti failed to keep them firmly in hand.[10] His laxity was very likely a major factor in the downfall of the Medici bank, which, in 1492 at the death of Lorenzo the Magnificent, was on the verge of bankruptcy.

In Florence, balance sheets were used not only for purposes of

---

[8] State Archives, Florence, Mediceo avanti il Principato, filza 104, fols. 598–603: Balance of Basel Branch, March 24, 1442 (N.S.). The entry in question is on folio 599ʳ.

[9] Text published by Armand Grunzweig, *Correspondance de la filiale de Bruges des Medici* (Brussels, 1931), I, p. 130. The second volume has never been published.

[10] For example, he gave too much power to Tommaso Portinari, the manager of the Bruges branch from 1465 to 1480, who involved the Medici in speculative undertakings and risky loans to princes.

control but also for purposes of taxation.[11] In 1427, a new tax, the *catasto*, was introduced. It was a hybrid between an income and a property tax. The rate was based on the capitalised value of income from real estate, from shares in the public debt, and from business investments. Most important for our purpose, the law required each taxpayer to file a return listing all his property and to submit a copy of the latest balance sheet of any business firm in which he held a share. So several balance sheets of the Medici were found annexed to their *catasto* reports for 1427 and 1433. As the same is true of many other reports, there are still buried in the archives of the *catasto* hundreds of financial statements which no one has ever bothered to examine.[12] In 1458, the *catasto* on business investments was abolished, because frauds were widespread and difficult to detect. The merchants apparently managed to evade the tax by concealing their profits and tampering with their records. Moreover, the tax was unpopular with the business men, who objected to its inquisitive nature and to letting tax commissioners, who might be competitors, pry into their affairs or their books. This interesting experiment was thus ended, to be revived only in modern times.

It was a standard policy of the Medici bank to set up provisions for accrued wages, bad debts, and unforeseen contingencies before dividing any profits. By means of this procedure profits were deliberately reserved and allowed to accumulate in the form of surplus or *sopracorpo*—the word is actually used in this meaning in the *libro segreto*.[13] This surplus could also be used—and actually was used— to correct possible overstatement of profits in previous years.[14] An interesting example of this practice is given by the private account-book of Francesco Sassetti. In 1467 the profits of the Lyons branch being small, nothing was distributed to the partners and all the net earnings, *écus* 5,575 5s. 11d., were set aside as a provision against contingencies.[15] The next year, it was found that even this amount overrated profits to the extent of *écus* 3,442 9s. 1d. Consequently, this amount was charged to the reserve, leaving a credit balance of *écus* 2,132 16s. 10d., which was carried forward as undistributed surplus.[16] Other examples of the same kind are found by the dozen in the *libri segreti* of the Medici. Reserves for bad debts, as Table 5 shows, were a common feature. Sometimes the creation of such a

11 Sieveking, " Aus Genueser Rechnungs- und Steuerbüchern," *op. cit.*, pp. 89–105 ; Balduin Penndorf, " The Relation of Taxation to the History of the Balance Sheet," *The Accounting Review*, V (1930), pp. 243–251.
12 With the exception of Sieveking, the art historians have been the only ones to dig into this material in quest of information about famous artists.
13 State Archives, Florence, Mediceo avanti il Principato, filza 153, No. 3 : Libro segreto, 1435–1450, fol. 56.
14 Littleton, *op. cit.*, pp. 457–459.
15 The monetary units are *écus* of 64 to the gold mark.
16 R. de Roover, *Medici Bank*, p. 68.

reserve was prescribed in the Medici articles of association, which stipulated that profits were to be divided among the partners only after making due provision for accrued salaries and bad debts.[17] Of course, the piling up of irrecoverable claims was the great danger that threatened to undermine the solvency of medieval merchant-bankers.[18]

The Medici account-books of the Selfridge Collection at the Harvard Graduate School of Business Administration do not belong to the historic Medici but to another and elder branch which, in the eighteenth century, took the name of Medici-Tornaquinci and is still represented today by male descendants. In the fifteenth century this branch was not engaged in international banking but chiefly cloth manufacturing. As was usual in industrial enterprises at this time, the books do not measure up to the standards of double entry, but they are very interesting for the history of cost accounting, a topic which lies outside the scope of this study.[19] One peculiarity deserves attention. In case of dissolution, some of the partnership agreements provided for the division of all assets, not in proportion to invested capital, but according to the quotas set for sharing profits.[20] This arrangement favoured the active partners to the detriment of the investing partners, to the extent that the former received a greater share of the earnings in order to compensate them for their services. Later, toward the end of the fifteenth century, the system was changed. From then on the partnership contracts of this branch of the Medici family provide that partners were first to be paid back their initial investment and that only the surplus was to be divided in the same proportion as earnings.

In Milan, as well as in Florence, double entry seems to have gained a firm foothold during the fifteenth century. Our major source of information is a series of ledgers and other records belonging to the Borromei, a firm of merchant-bankers, who had branches in Venice and in Bruges and, in 1436, opened an office in London.[1] The latter was provided with a capital of £1,600 groat, Flemish currency, equivalent to £1,431 17s. 1d. sterling, English currency.

The surviving account-books include two ledgers (1426 and 1427)

---

[17] State Archives, Florence, Mediceo avanti il Principato, filza 94, fol. 164 and filza 153, No. 3, fol. 2. These are two different copies of the same contract, dated 1435.

[18] In the sixteenth century the Spanish merchant-banker, Simon Ruiz, feared bad debts " like the pest." See Henri Lapeyre, *Une famille de marchands : les Ruiz* (Paris, 1955), p. 74.

[19] See the appendices to Florence Edler's *Glossary*, pp. 335–426. *Cf.* S. Paul Garner, *Evolution of Cost Accounting to 1925* (Alabama, 1954), pp. 7–15.

[20] William T. Baxter, " An investigation into the Dissolution of a Mediaeval Italian Partnership," *The Accountants' Magazine*, XXXVI (1932), pp. 449–455.

[1] Gerolamo Biscaro, " Il banco Filippo Borromei e compagni di Londra (1436–1439)," *Archivio Storico Lombardo*, XL (1913), pp. 37–126, 283–386. *Cf.* P. Kats, " Double-Entry Book-keeping in England before Hugh Oldcastle," *The Accountant*, LXXIV (1926), pp. 91–98.

of the main office in Milan, four ledgers (1436–1439), bound together in one volume, of the London branch, and one ledger (1438) of the Bruges branch.[2]   Apparently, the Borromei bank followed the practice of opening a new ledger each year.   Instead of being kept in Latin like earlier Milanese account-books, these of the Borromei are in Italian.   The technique is far advanced and on a par with the contemporary Medici records.   Since the Borromei were bankers and dealt extensively in exchange, their ledgers contain many examples of *Nostro* and *Vostro* accounts open to foreign correspondents.   There are no original balance sheets in existence, but Professor Zerbi was able to recast the balance of the Milan office (December 31, 1427), of the London branch (December 31, 1436), and of the Bruges branch (December 31, 1438), and to draw up the corresponding operating statements.[3]   The results are particularly illuminating and demonstrate that account-books are among the most precious sources for economic and business history.   According to the operating statement, headquarters at Milan derived most of their profits from the trade in linens, fustians, cotton, and wool; foreign exchange, or banking, was decidedly of minor importance.[4]   The Bruges statement reveals that the business of the Borromei in the Low Countries was not going well and that, in 1438, they lost nearly three-tenths of their capital on exchange with Venice.   Professor Zerbi attributes this loss to a sudden debasement of the Flemish currency which caused the exchange rate of the Venetian ducat to jump suddenly from 47 to 51 Flemish groats.[5]   This may be part of the story, but the Bruges branch suffered such heavy losses chiefly because it took up considerable sums by selling drafts on Venice.   Dr. Zerbi does not explain why the Bruges branch was so deeply in debt toward its Venetian correspondents.[6]

The four ledgers of the London branch undoubtedly contain valuable source material for the history of the City during the fifteenth century, but even Gerolamo Biscaro's excellent article and its English summary seems to have attracted little attention.   While the Bruges branch was having difficulties, the London branch was doing well: profits increased from £24 17s. 8d. sterling in 1436 to £386 12s. 1d. in 1439.[7]   In the latter year gross profits on exchange (banking) and

---

[2] Zerbi, *Origini*, pp. 312, 413–414, 432.
[3] *Ibid.*, pp. 348–351, 420–423, 440–443.
[4] In the Middle Ages banking was tied to foreign exchange, and bills were not discounted.   [5] Zerbi, *Origini*, p. 433.
[6] At that time merchants borrowed by selling bills on other places and granted credit by buying such bills at the current rate of exchange.   The market favoured the lenders to the detriment of the borrowers because interest was concealed in the rate of exchange.   The Borromei lost doubly because speculative losses aggravated the effect of interest charges.
[7] R. de Roover, " Early Accounting Problems of Foreign Exchange," *op. cit.*, p. 397. *Cf.* Zerbi, *Origini*, p. 429.

trade were about equal in importance, with commissions on consignment sales running a close third. The Borromei certainly dealt in wool and they imported spices and merceries; they also granted credit by buying the bills of English wool-staplers and mercers.[8] Among these customers were Robert " Utingham " or Whytingham, Mayor of the Staple, and " Giusfredo Bologna " or Geoffrey Boleyn, mercer, great-grandfather of Anne Boleyn. The interest of account-books is by no means limited to accounting history.

In contrast to Florence, Venice was first of all a trading, rather than a banking, centre. Moreover, this trade was geared to the Levant, where political conditions were always more or less unsettled. The Venetians did not have companies with branches abroad of a size comparable to that of the Medici. As a rule, the Venetian merchants preferred to operate by means of commission agents, often related to them by ties of blood. Kinship was of extraordinary importance in the Middle Ages, even in business. The Venetian type of business organisation probably had deep historical roots and was better adapted to the requirements of the Levantine trade, the mainstay of Venice's prosperity. As one might expect, the Venetian ways of doing business had their effect on accounting procedure. Although the basic principles of double entry remain unaffected, there are marked differences between Florentine and Venetian methods of book-keeping. The most striking of them all is the greater emphasis on venture accounting in Venetians records.[9]

Typical of Venetian accounting are the venture or voyage accounts, which have not disappeared to this day as they are still currently used by shipping companies.[10] These accounts were charged with the value of any goods " recommended " to the care of agents abroad and with any expenses incurred thereon.[11] To offset these charges, such accounts were credited with the proceeds of the sales as detailed in the agent's report. In the trade with the Levant, it rarely happened that " returns " were made in cash or in bills of exchange. As a rule, they were made in eastern wares for which the agent received credit; to this credit there usually corresponded a charge to a newly opened merchandise account, which was not closed

---

[8] Some of the bills bought were payable to the bearer.

[9] Some of the differences are purely formal, such as the wording of journal and ledger entries, but those details are of no consequence.

[10] There is on this subject an excellent article by Frederic C. Lane, " Venture Accounting in Medieval Business Management," *Bulletin of the Business Historical Society*, XIX (1945), pp 164–173.

[11] *Viazo* accounts are found in all the surviving Venetian account-books. A typical heading of a voyage account is, for example, the following: *Viazo da Constantinopoli recommanda a Ser Bartolamio Querin* (Voyage of Constantinople entrusted to Bartholomew Querini).

until each lot was fully sold.[12]   As specie was flowing East rather than
in the opposite direction, it occurred frequently that remittances rather
than goods were sent to agents in Syria or Alexandria.   In such a
case, the procedure remained the same: a voyage account was opened
and not closed until returns were made.[13]

Both voyage and merchandise accounts were closed into Profit and
Loss after each affair was completely finished.   Since agents sometimes failed to report or goods were slow in moving, it happened that
such accounts remained in abeyance for months or even years.[14]   It
was one of the serious drawbacks of the Venetian system.

Whereas the Florentine companies drew up balance sheets every
year or, at least, at more or less regular intervals, the Venetians saw
no point in so doing.   They often postponed casting a balance for
several years and, when they did, it was to see whether debits and
credits were equal rather than to ascertain the state of assets and
liabilities.   In general, Venetian accounting, because of the smaller
size of the business unit, was also less involved than that of the great
Florentine mercantile and banking companies.   Luca Pacioli's treatise
—it is not surprising since it follows a Venetian model—fits the
practice of Venice much better than that of Florence.

The main characteristics of venture accounting are found in all
surviving Venetian and Ragusan account-books.[15]   Of course, as
Professor Frederic C. Lane points out, different merchants, according
to their capacities and to the nature of the problems encountered,
handled the system differently.[16]

If any fourteenth-century account-books have survived in Venice,
they are buried in as yet unexplored archives.   In the present state of
research, the oldest Venetian mercantile account-books are those of

---

[12] See also Frederic C. Lane, *Andrea Barbarigo, Merchant of Venice, 1418–1449*,
The Johns Hopkins University Studies in Historical and Political Science,
series LXII, no. 1 (Baltimore, 1944), pp. 164–168.

[13] *Ibid.*, p. 170. In the example given by Professor Lane, the agent's account was
eliminated and the voyage account was charged for the value of silver sent to
Tunis and directly credited for the returns made, some of them in Sudanese
gold-dust.

[14] *Ibid.*, p. 167.

[15] Lane gives a detailed list of business records in the Venetian archives (*ibid.*,
Critical Note 1, pp. 137–152). The studies of Professor Lane supersede most
earlier works by Vittorio Alfieri, Heinrich Sieveking, and others. On Ragusa
(now Dubrovnik), there exists a series of articles by C. Leyerer, " Aus den
ältesten Handlungsbüchern der Republik Ragusa," *Zeitschrift für Betriebswirt-
schaft*, VI (1929), pp. 13–23, 106–116, 169–179, 253–265, 346–355, and 415–431.
Double entry was already used in Ragusa from 1417 onward (*ibid.*, p. 171) in the
account-books of Niccolò e Luca de Caboga (*ibid.*, pp. 348 *et seq.*). The
accounts of the Ragusan mint (1422) were also kept with rare perfection (C.
Leyerer, " Aus dem Rechnungsbuche der Ragusaner Münze," *Hochschulwissen*,
VI [1929], pp. 353–358 and 430–436). This article reproduces the text (but not the
appendices containing accounts) of a brochure published under the title *Das
Rechnungsbuch deli merchadanti dela Zeccha in Ragusa, 1422* (Brünn, 1914).
Cf. R. de Roover, " Aux Origines," pp. 294–295.

[16] Lane, " Venture Accounting," *op. cit.*, p. 168.

the *fraterna*, or family partnership, in which *ser* Donado Soranzo and his three brothers participated. The *libro reale vecchio,* the first of the two surviving ledgers, contains entries extending from 1410 to 1477. It is extremely doubtful that it is in double entry, since all debits or credits do not have offsetting entries on the other side. The contents of the later *libro reale nuovo* are rather puzzling and appear to be a bringing together of sundry records scattered in other books including the *libro reale vecchio.*[17]   Although some of the entries date back to 1403, the *libro reale nuovo* was certainly compiled several years later, perhaps, as Professor Lane believes, after the return to Venice of Donado Soranzo, who was in Syria from 1410 to 1416. The incomplete records kept in Venice by one partner and in Syria by another partner were then put together. After 1416 the entries continue until 1434. Professor Lane's thesis does not conflict with the fact that the *libro reale nuovo* was laid out in connection with a lawsuit involving the division of the family estate and probably arising out of disagreements among the Soranzo brothers. The difficulties probably originated in the *fraterna's* deficient organisation because the partners abroad failed to send in reports and those at home to consolidate promptly all the records.[18]   After so many years had gone by, it proved difficult to amalgamate the data and to arrive at a satisfactory synthesis of operating results, although the *libro reale nuovo* shows that the book-keeper did not ignore the technique of double entry.

The account-books of Andrea Barbarigo (1431–1449) are far more complete and informative than those of the Soranzo brothers. Venture accounting is still in evidence. When Barbarigo was half through his ledger, he drew up, on February 28, 1435, a balance, or *conto saldo.* Since he reopened all the accounts immediately in the same ledger, his purpose must have been either to make just a trial balance or to get at least a rough idea of the state of his affairs.[19] The latter seems probable, since Barbarigo closed several equity accounts into his capital account with the result that it thereby increased from 200 ducats to 4,435 ducats. In any case Barbarigo's balance is the only Venetian example of one that is not a closing balance drawn up to transfer the accounts from one ledger to the next. The Barbarigo ledger illustrates that certain agents abroad were

---

17 Heinrich Sieveking gives a different view, but it is now seriously challenged by Lane (*Barbarigo,* p. 155) and Zerbi (*Origini,* pp. 371–377). The reference to Sieveking's old study is: " Aus venetianischen Handlungsbüchern ; ein Beitrag zur Geschichte des Grosshandels im 15. Jahrhundert," Schmollers *Jahrbuch für Gesetzgebung, Verwaltung und Volkswirtschaft,* XXV (1901), pp. 1489–1521 ; XXVI (1902), pp. 189–225. Sieveking considers the older Soranzo book as evidence that double entry was not yet widely used in Venice (*ibid.,* p. 1502).

18 Lane, *Barbarigo,* p. 156. *Cf.* Zerbi, *Origini,* pp. 373–374.

19 Lane, *Barbarigo,* pp. 173–175.

not dishonest and duly made returns in goods but were remiss in sending itemised reports, a practice which interfered with orderly accounting procedure.[20]

The ledger kept by Jacomo Badoer in Constantinople (1436–1439) is another illustration of venture accounting.[1] Badoer acted as commission agent for merchants in Venice, but he also did business on his own. He kept his books in perfect double entry: according to the Venetian system he used separate accounts for each venture and each exchange transaction, whether he was principal or agent.[2] Badoer's ledger is the only extensive record that throws any light on the conduct of business in the Byzantine Empire. Because of the ledger's exceptional interest, the complete text will be published in the near future with a volume of commentaries by various authors.[3]

The infrequency of balancing was certainly a serious shortcoming of Venetian practice.[4] From this point of view, the least careless among the merchants whose accounts have survived was Andrea Barbarigo, who drew up balances of a sort in 1431, 1435 and 1440, and then he let his accounts run unbalanced till his death in 1449.[5] But his son went twenty years without ever casting a balance. The early treatises, all of them Venetian, are influenced by local practice and create the impression that balances were cast for the sole purpose of proving the ledger and that this tedious job was often postponed until the books were filled. It should be emphasised that the early treatises do not give a fair account of actual practice in other trading centres. As we have seen, the Borromei in Milan and the Medici in Florence made it a rule to close and balance their books every year. The same rule was undoubtedly followed by others, so that the early treatises, in this as in other respects, fail to give a reliable picture.

In the Middle Ages the leading business men of Europe were the Italians, and their organisation was far superior to that of any of their rivals. It is only in the sixteenth century that the other nations began to catch up, with the Spaniards and the Portuguese in the lead and the others trailing far behind. Throughout the sixteenth century the Italians maintained their hegemony in such fields as international banking. In the Middle Ages, of course, their monopoly was nearly absolute and the Italian banking houses dominated the money market

[20] *Ibid.*, p. 175.

[1] Vittorio Alfieri, *La partita doppia applicata alle scritture delle antiche aziende mercantili veneziane* (Turin, 1891), pp. 45, 56, 82–101.

[2] See example in Besta, *op. cit.*, III, pp. 312–313. The Venetians did not use *Nostro* and *Vostro* accounts like the Florentines, but solved the problem by opening special exchange accounts when dealing in foreign currencies.

[3] T. Bertelè, " Il libro dei conti di Giacomo [*sic*] Badoer," *Byzantion*, XXI (1951), pp. 123–126.

[4] Lane, *Barbarigo*, p. 171.

[5] *Idem.*, " Venture Accounting," *op. cit.*, p. 172.

in London and in Bruges.   Because of their superior organisation, the Italians put some of their competitors out of business.   This happened to the Flemings, whose carrying trade was practically eliminated. Thanks to a strongly privileged position, the English were more or less able to hold their own, but their sphere of action was confined to the Low Countries and to Gascony, an English possession.   Only the Hanseatic League succeeded in warding off any Italian encroachment of its Baltic preserve.   However, in this area, conditions were so primitive that superior organisation did not give to the Italians the same advantage as elsewhere.

In these circumstances it is no wonder that double entry up to 1500 or thereabouts was a business technique known only to the Italian merchants.   Its Italian origin is attested by the fact that, until the eighteenth century, book-keeping " after the Italian manner " and double entry were synonymous expressions.   No trace of this method is found in any medieval account-book that is not Italian.   There is, therefore, no point in discussing whether the merchants of other nationalities kept their books in double entry, since everyone agrees that they did not.   Why?   Probably because they neither knew it nor felt the need of it.   Outside Italy, business organisation was much less elaborate, and the merchants could get along quite well without refined methods of accounting.   It is true that unsystematic records put severe limitations on the size of the business unit; they were adequate up to a certain point, beyond which they engendered such disorder that results might be catastrophic.   This situation partly explains why banking and other techniques remained backward in the Baltic region where the Italians did not penetrate.

For lack of space, it will be impossible to devote much discussion to mercantile account-books in France, Germany, and other countries. Since double entry did not originate there, these manuscripts are less important from our point of view; they lie outside the main trend of development, on a sidetrack which leads to a dead end.   The following remarks will, therefore, not provide much more than bibliographical guidance for those who wish to go deeper into the subject.

In France the oldest extant account-book is a kind of ledger dating from 1320 to 1323 and belonging to an unknown Lyonnese draper, who sold at retail to local customers.   The accounts are in paragraph form and frequently mention the name of a surety who guarantees payment of the debt.   References reveal the existence of a notebook (*quert*) and a red account-book (*paper vermeil*), but nothing is known about their contents.[6]

---

6 Paul Meyer and Georges Guigue, " Fragments du grand livre d'un drapier de Lyon, 1320–1323," *Romania*, XXXV (1906), pp. 428–444.

A different arrangement is found in an account-book (1330–1332) of Maître Ugo Teralh, notary and draper in the small town of Forcalquier in Provence.[7] It has only receivables. Each page is divided into three columns: the first, much narrower than the other two, gives the locality where the debtor resides; the middle one, which is the widest of the three, contains a brief description of each transaction; and the third indicates how the debt was settled. Sometimes the entry in the middle column is written or undersigned in the debtor's own hand. When the customer is a Jew, the entry itself is in Provençal but an acknowledgment of debt is added in Hebrew. Sureties are mentioned if there are any. It is also stated whenever the obligation has been enacted by notarial deed.

The same features as in the book of the Lyonnese draper are found in a fragment (1340–1341) of the accounts kept by Jean Saval, a merchant and draper in Carcassonne.[8] As in the Provençal ledger of Maître Ugo Teralh, the record of a debt was sometimes entered by the debtor himself.

By far the most interesting French account-books of the Middle Ages are those of the Bonis Brothers, merchants and bankers at Montauban in Languedoc.[9] Their activity was very diversified: they sold not only cloth, spices, and pharmaceutical products, but did banking and moneylending on the side. The extant records include the ledger C (1345–1349) and the *livre vermeil des dépôts* (1347–1368) bound together in one volume. As the name indicates, the *livre vermeil des dépôts* contains depositors' accounts. References reveal that the Bonis Brothers also kept journals, or *manoals*, in which transactions were described in greater detail. The accounts are in paragraph form with blank spaces in between to indicate how payment was effected. At the end of ledger C, it is mentioned that a total of £551 2s. 10d. *tournois* is outstanding among customers.[10] A similar inscription in the rear of the *livre vermeil* states that £678 7s. 8d. are due to depositors.[11] No further detail is given, but these totals were probably itemised on loose sheets that are now lost. If so, it proves that the drawing up of financial statements was also practised outside Italy.

---

[7] Paul Meyer, " Le livre-journal de Maître Ugo Teralh, notaire et drapier à Forcalquier (1330–1332)," *Notices et Extraits des Manuscrits de la Bibliothèque Nationale,* XXXVI (1899), pp. 129–170.

[8] Ch. Portal, " Le livre-journal de Jean Saval, marchand-drapier à Carcassone (1340–1341)," *Bulletin historique et philologique du Comité des Travaux historiques et scientifiques,* 1901, pp. 418–449.

[9] The text has been published *in extenso* with an introduction by Edouard Forestié ed., *Les livres de comptes des Frères Bonis, marchands montalbanais du XIVe siècle,* " Archives historiques de la Gascogne," fasc. 20, 23, and 26 (Paris-Auch, 1890–1894), 2 vols. in 3.

[10] *Ibid.,* II, p. 419.

[11] *Ibid.,* II, p. 560.

Unlike the Bonis Brothers, who were local merchants, Jacme Olivier of Narbonne traded extensively with the Levant. In his account-book (1381–1391), we meet the usual venture accounts relating to goods which he entrusted to travelling partners rather than to agents residing overseas, an indication that business organisation in Narbonne was lagging behind Italy or Barcelona.[12] The account-book gives only the amounts invested in each venture and does not disclose how " returns " were made. Perhaps this information was furnished in another book that has disappeared.

According to an investigation made recently, the merchants of Toulouse were in the habit of keeping fairly elaborate records,[13] although none of them have survived, with the exception of a small fragment of what might be called a perpetual inventory (1433–1441) found among the papers of Jean Lapeyre, a draper.[14] Each piece of cloth that he bought was probably tagged and received a number; the number, the purchase price and the length of each cloth were then recorded in his inventory. As pieces were cut off, he wrote down how much they measured and how much he got from his sales. When a cloth was entirely sold, Lapeyre determined his profit by deducting cost from receipts. He thus knew exactly how much he had earned on each single purchase and he could also tell at any time what he had left in stock and what his stock was worth. Lapeyre presumably kept other books, but these have not come down to us.

The account-book (1423–1443) of Colin de Lormoye, a Parisian tailor, presents little interest from our point of view. His purpose in recording claims was chiefly to keep track of what was due to him, since many customers paid by instalments.[15] The same observation applies to the accounts (1520) of Mathieu Dengremont, mercer at Saint-Amand-les-Eaux, a small town near Valenciennes in Hainaut.[16] No less rudimentary are the accounts of Jean Le Clerc and Jacquemin de Moyeuvre, two mercers of Metz, who went to buy spices, caps, purses, and other mercery at the fairs of Bergen-op-Zoom and Antwerp.[17] They use two columns: the purchases on one side and

---

12 Alphonse Blanc, *Le livre de comptes de Jacme Olivier, marchand narbonnais du XIVe siècle* (Paris, 1899), vol. II (only one published). The introduction is in the *Bulletin de la Commission Archéologique de Narbonne*, IV (1896), pp. i–lxxxiv.
13 Philippe Wolff, *Commerces et marchands de Toulouse (vers 1350–vers 1450)* (Paris, 1954), pp. 520–524.
14 *Idem.*, " Une compatibilité commerciale du XVe siècle," *Annales du Midi*, LXIV (1952), pp. 131–148.
15 C. Couderc, " Les comptes d'un grand couturier parisien au XVe siècle," *Bulletin de la Société d'Histoire de Paris*, 1911, pp. 118–192.
16 J. J. Salverda de Grave, " Un livre de compte du XVIe siècle," *Mededeelingen der Koninklijke Akademie van Wetenschappen, Afdeeling Letterkunde*, series B, vol. 70 (1930), no. 9, pp. 259–312.
17 Jean Schneider, *Recherches sur la vie économique de Metz au XVe siècle : le livre de comptes des merciers messins Jean Le Clerc et Jacquemin de Moyeuvre, 1460–1461* (Metz, 1951).

the sales on the other, although the latter sometimes run over into the adjoining column. There is also an expense account, but it is not footed. Neither are most of the other accounts. What is then the use of keeping a record?

Among the French account-books, one should perhaps include two Hebrew registers (1300–1306 and 1310–1318) belonging to a company of Jewish traders and moneylenders who operated in Vesoul (Franche-Comté) and its vicinity.[18] Their records present some analogy with the accounts of Maître Ugo Teralh, since customers are classified according to localities, at least in the earlier of the two volumes. In the later one there is more confusion. The Jews of Vesoul used other books simultaneously but what they contained is not clear from the references given here and there in the extant ledgers.

Outside Italy, by far the most interesting medieval account-books are those of two Bruges money-changers, Collard de Marke and Guillaume Ruyelle.[19] These books are all in French, but Flemish words creep into the text from time to time. Collard de Marke's set includes five ledgers (only two still with indices) and two journals. They extend from Easter (April 6), 1366, to Christmas, 1369, with no interruption in the case of the ledgers. Ruyelle's only extant account-book is a ledger going from January, 1369, to June, 1370. In addition, it contains a fragmentary cash record of daily receipts and expenditures from March 21, 1370, to June 27 of the same year.

Of the two men Collard de Marke was undoubtedly the more important. Indeed, he was one of the three leading money-changers in Bruges and his main customers were the members of the Lucchese colony, including the Rapondi, the Guinigi, and the merchant-banker, Forteguerra di Forteguerra. It is certain that Guillaume Ruyelle failed in 1370, and his colleague, Collard de Marke, presumably shared the same fate. Their activities, of course, were not confined to money-changing but embraced deposit banking. Many payments, at least between merchants, were made by book transfer instead of in specie, a practice which explains the presence in the Bruges account-books of thousands and thousands of transfer entries. A favourite method of granting credit was by means of overdrafts, so that many customers had debit balances.

Collard de Marke and Guillaume Ruyelle kept their ledger accounts *ad modum banchi*, that is, in bilateral form, with each page divided into two vertical columns. The former observes the usual

---

18 Isidore Loeb, " Deux livres de commerce du commencement du XIVe siècle," *Revue des études juives*, VIII (1884), pp. 161–196, and IX (1884), pp. 21–50.

19 A thorough study of these account-books is available in Raymond de Roover, *Money, Banking, and Credit in Mediaeval Bruges : Italian Merchant-Bankers, Lombards, and Money-Changers* (Cambridge Mass., 1948).

order, debit left and credit right, but the latter reverses this. In other words, he puts debit to the right and credit to the left. In the cash-book, however, Ruyelle places his receipts to the left, that is, on the credit side according to his system, and his disbursements to the right, or on the debit side. One would expect the opposite. The result is that payment to a customer was entered twice on the same side: to the debit or right of the customer's account and also to the debit or right of the cash account. I am unable to offer any explanation for this anomaly, except that Ruyelle had not yet a clear concept of what should be debit or credit, especially when applying it to anything as inanimate as cash. In the books of both money-changers descriptions of transactions are laconic to an extreme degree: the date, the amount, and the name of the person to whose debit or credit this amount was transferred. In the case of cash transactions, this mention was replaced by the word *contet* for " counted in specie."

The ledgers are bulky in-folios of about 800 pages, but the journals are small half-folios, oblong in shape. In form and content they resemble closely the journals of the Genoese banks. Entries are strictly in chronological order and are crossed out diagonally to indicate that they have been posted to the ledger. Since cheques were not in use, the journal served to record transfer orders as they came from the customers' lips.

Collard de Marke's ledgers are divided into three sections: the first—by far the largest—contains the accounts of local depositors and customers; the second, the clearing accounts with other money-changers; and the third, the accounts of certain out-of-town customers. They resided mainly in Valenciennes and Hainaut, the region from where Collard de Marke came and where he still had business connections.

Of course, Collard de Marke and Guillaume Ruyelle kept their books in single entry. Their ledgers contain only accounts with persons. Profits on money-changing resulted simply in a cash surplus.

In Ruyelle's ledger there is a loose sheet that bears no date but is of May 24, 1370.[20] It lists all the amounts due to depositors, on the one hand, and resources, on the other hand. The statement does not balance, since liabilities aggregate £946 17s. groat, Flemish currency, against £894 8s. 6d. in cash, overdrafts, and other investments.[1] There is, consequently, a deficit of £52 8s. 6d. groat, which may

[20] R. de Roover, " Le livre de comptes de Guillaume Ruyelle, changeur à Bruges (1369)," *Annales de la Société d'Emulation de Bruges*, LXXVII (1934), pp. 15–95. *Cf.* Lewis Carman, " Researches of Raymond de Roover in Flemish Accounting," *Journal of Accountancy*, LX (1935), pp. 111–122. This old article has not been completely replaced by later studies.
[1] R. de Roover, " Ruyelle." pp. 55–58, 92–95.

explain why Guillaume Ruyelle got himself into difficulties. No similar statement was found thrust in the bindings or inserted among the leaves of Collard de Marke's ledgers. However, on May 20, 1369, when the last of the extant ledgers was closed, aggregate balances due to depositors and transferred to the next ledger amounted to £5,575 6s. 1d. groat. Total overdrafts on the same date were £2,553 11s. 9d. groat.[2] No information is available on cash in hand and other assets. At any rate, these figures show that Collard de Marke was doing more business than Ruyelle. One may also conclude that statements were often established on loose sheets, which have survived even more rarely than account-books. Their scarcity does not prove that the practice of drawing up financial statements was limited to the Italians.

The relatively advanced state of Flemish book-keeping in the fourteenth century is without doubt due to Italian influences. Beyond Bruges, even in Holland, this was no longer true, and business techniques tended to depend upon the practices developed by the Hanseatic merchants.

Hanseatic book-keeping has one thing in common with that of the Venetians: the emphasis on venturing. In all other respects the records of the Hanseatic merchants are very inferior and hardly comparable. It is true that forms of business organisation were less developed in Northern than in Southern Europe. One reason is perhaps that the general pattern was less complicated. Instead of a cobweb of trade routes going in all directions, the Hansa had the advantage of operating on a single axis centring in Lübeck and stretching from London and Bruges in the west to Danzig, Riga, Reval, and Novgorod in the east.[3] There was only one main offshoot reaching out to Bergen in Norway, one of the great fish-markets of the Middle Ages. Like the Venetians, the Hanseatic merchants conducted their business by means of factors or agents in foreign places. A typical institution of theirs was, however, the so-called *gegenseitige Ferngesellschaft*, with one partner in one place and another partner in another place, acting as agents for each other.[4] Although the Hanseatic merchant often stayed at home and managed his affairs from the counting-house, his agents or factors were constantly on the move, travelling back and forth between Lübeck and Bruges or Lübeck and Danzig, as business required. When abroad, the Hanseatic merchants dealt preferably through the host of the inn at

---

[2] *Idem., Banking in Bruges*, p. 254, Table No. 12.
[3] Fritz Rörig, " Die Hanse und die nordischen Länder," in his *Hansische Beiträge zur deutschen Wirtschaftsgeschichte* (Breslau, 1928), p. 157.
[4] Gunnar Mickwitz, " Neues zur Funktion der hansischen Handelsgesellschaften," *Hansische Geschichtsblätter*, LXII (1937), p. 27.

which they were lodged.[5]   As a rule, the host was also the broker and
was privy to all their business deals.[6]   Merchants like Hildebrand
Veckinchusen, who resided permanently in Bruges, were the exception,
and even he was so frequently on the road that it interfered with the
orderly conduct of his business.

This mobility was to a large extent due to surrounding institutional
and economic factors, but it was also the product of unsystematic
methods of book-keeping.   These methods prevented extensive delegation of power and made it necessary for the business leader to
maintain personal contact with his. subordinates.   The aim of
Hanseatic book-keeping was not to give a comprehensive view of a
firm's financial condition but to prepare the necessary data for the
periodic settlement of accounts between partners of a *Ferngesellschaft*
or between principal and agent.   A secondary objective was, of
course, to keep a record of outstanding claims.[7]   Beyond this restricted
goal Hanseatic book-keeping never went.   Because of these limitations, the growth of large companies with permanent branches in
foreign parts, such as existed among the Italians, was precluded among
German merchants from the Hansa towns, and economic progress in
Northern Germany and Scandinavia was slowed down as the
inevitable result.[8]

The typical features of Hanseatic book-keeping are already
encountered in the earliest Hanseatic account-book (1329–1360), that
of Hermann Wittenborg and his son Johann, who became burgomaster of Lübeck in 1360 and ended his life on the scaffold in 1363.[9]
At first it is kept in barbaric Latin but later the book-keeper switches
to Low German.   Paragraphs regarding credit transactions and investments in business ventures follow each other promiscuously.   Between
paragraphs, just enough space is left to add the amounts of partial

---

5   There are many examples in the account-books of two merchants of Amsterdam
who went to trade in Danzig. See N. W. Posthumus, *De Oosterse Handel te
Amsterdam* (Leiden, 1953), pp. 311 (item 1), 313 (item 19), 315 (item 41), etc.
This was the prevailing method adopted by the Hanseatic merchants when doing
business in Bruges. Of course, in London, Bergen, and Novgorod, they did not
stay at inns and business was conducted according to different rules.

6   The attempt made in 1439 by an Act of Parliament (18 Hen. 6, c. 4) to foist
hosting regulations on the Italians proved to be a fiasco, because the Italians
had outgrown this form of organisation.

7   Wilhelm Stieda, " Ueber die Quellen der Handelsstatistik im Mittelalter,"
Abhandlungen der K. Preuss. Akademie der Wissenschaften, Phil.-hist. Klasse, II
(1902), p. 24 ; Balduin Penndorf, *Geschichte der Buchhaltung in Deutschland*
(Leipzig, 1913), p. 36 ; Fritz Rörig, " Das älteste erhaltene deutsche Kaufmannsbüchlein," *Hansische Beiträge*, p. 192 ; Posthumus, *op. cit.*, pp. 5, 7, 22. See
also the article of Nordmann on Veckinchusen (cited p. 168, note 17), p. 117.

8   The German economist, Walter Eucken, writes in this connection : " Where this
knowledge [of double entry] was lacking or slow to penetrate, as in the Hansa
towns, economic development was delayed " (*The Foundations of Economics;
History and Theory in the Analysis of Economic Reality* [London, 1950], p. 282).

9   Carl Mollwo, *Das Handlungsbuch von Hermann und Johann Wittenborg*
(Leipzig, 1901), pp. lxxix–103. *Cf.* Penndorf, *Buchhaltung*, pp. 3–7.

payments without room for details. Once a transaction was terminated, the related paragraph was simply crossed out. Cash transactions are not recorded.

A somewhat better arrangement is found in the Latin account-book of the Rostock merchant, Johann Tölner (1345–1350).[10] At least an attempt at classification is made. Accounts relating to ventures are on the first pages of the book and those relating to credit sales, in the rear. On the other hand, little improvement is noticeable in the account-book (1367–1392) of Vicko von Geldersen, a Hamburg draper, who did not confine his activity to the cloth trade.[11] He combined retailing with import-export of a variety of commodities. His records are partly in corrupt Latin and partly in Low German, sometimes even in a mixture of both.

Some rudimentary classification of similar items appears in a notebook (1330–1336) kept by two brothers-in-law, Johann Clingenberg and Hermann Warendorp, who were both prominent Lübeck merchants.[12] It contains only notes on business transacted by Warendorp while Clingenberg was abroad and then by the latter while the former was away. Apparently, one acted as the representative of the other in case of absence. The purpose is obviously to prepare the necessary data for an eventual settlement of accounts. Despite the enthusiastic admiration of a prominent historian of the Hansa, it does not seem that in this notebook Warendorp and his brother-in-law display great mastery in the art of book-keeping.[13] However, it may have been adequate for its limited purpose.

The accounts (1391–1399) of Johannes Plige, the *lieger* or permanent representative in Bruges of the Teutonic Order, are fortunately of a higher calibre.[14] They are kept with a degree of accuracy and comprehensiveness which is quite unusual among Hanseatic merchants. Presumably they are based on original data that Johann Plige rearranged and reclassified in a convenient form. As *lieger,* he provided for the needs of the Order in Flemish cloth and spices, which were purchased from the proceeds of amber, copper, wax, furs, and other commodities sent from Prussia to Bruges.

The position of Hildebrand Veckinchusen (1365–1426) is quite exceptional among the Hanseatic merchants.[15] Ambitious and full

[10] Karl Koppmann, *Johann Tölners Handlungsbuch von 1345–1350* (Rostock, 1885). *Cf.* Penndorf, *Buchhaltung,* pp. 7–9.
[11] Hans Nirrnheim, *Das Handlungsbuch Vicko von Geldersen* (Hamburg-Leipzig, 1895). *Cf.* Penndorf, *Buchhaltung,* pp. 9–12.
[12] Fritz Rörig, " Das älteste . . . Kaufmannsbüchlein," *op. cit.,* pp. 174–216.
[13] *Ibid.,* p. 191.
[14] C. Sattler, *Handelsrechnungen des Deutschen Ordens* (Leipzig, 1887), pp. 317 *et seq. Cf.* Penndorf, *Buchhaltung,* pp. 18–19.
[15] Luise von Winterfeld, *Hildebrand Veckinchusen, ein hansischer Kaufmann vor 500 Jahren,* Hansische Volkshefte, no. 18 (Bremen, n.d.).

of initiative, he tried to expand his business and to develop direct relations with Venice. For this purpose he established himself in Bruges. Unfortunately, after promising beginnings, his plans went awry and several ventures failed. The Venetian business, especially, caused so many disappointments that it proved to be his undoing. Being unable to pay a Genoese banker, Hildebrand Veckinchusen was cast into the Steen, or prison, of Bruges (1422) and remained in jail for more than three years. After his release he returned to Lübeck, a broken man, and died a few months later.

Besides business letters, ten of Veckinchusen's account-books, extending from 1399 to 1420, have come down to us.[16] They are quite well kept according to the standards of Hanseatic merchants: as usual, they were not intended to be comprehensive but only to facilitate the settlement of accounts with partners or agents.[17] This system was satisfactory as long as business remained small and only two partners were involved, but it broke down as soon as the merchant began to operate with a network of agencies and partnerships became triangular affairs. This must have happened in the case of Hildebrand Veckinchusen. His business outgrew his means of exercising control. He lost his grip, was cheated by his agents, and could not bring his partners to settle accounts.[18] He did not know where he stood and his bills of exchange were returned with protest, because they were refused by his correspondents. Finally, dire consequences ensued as the bankers pressed for payment of the returned bills. Most probably, Veckinchusen's plight is at least partly attributable to the lack of an adequate system of book-keeping.[19] As a matter of fact, his own books disclose that disorder in his records grew with the disorder in his business affairs.[20]

Progress toward more rational classification is evidenced by the account-book (1421–1454) of Johann Pisz, commission-merchant in Danzig.[1] It is divided into three parts: the first contains only sales on credit; the second, purchases; and the third, consignments

---

[16] The correspondence is available in print: Wilhelm Stieda, *Hildebrand Veckinchusen, Briefwechsel eines deutschen Kaufmanns im 15. Jahrhundert* (Leipzig, 1921). Publication of the account-books was also planned before the Second World War, but I do not know what has become of this project.

[17] A description of Hanseatic book-keeping is given in a letter dated September 28, 1412, and written by Syvert Veckinchusen to his brother Hildebrand (*ibid.*, p. 95). *Cf.* Claus Nordmann, " Die Veckinchusenschen Handlungsbücher: Zur Frage einer Edition," *Hansische Geschichtsblätter*, LXV (1941), pp. 79–144, esp. 116–117.

[18] An example of such a settlement is in Stieda, *Briefwechsel*, pp. 14–18 (Letter No. 15).

[19] This point has been stressed by Gunnar Mickwitz in two articles: (1) " Neues zur Funktion . . . ," *op. cit.*, p. 37, and (2) " L'economia medievale nei paesi baltici e nei paesi mediterranei," *Rivista internazionale di scienze sociali*, XLVI (1938), pp. 813–824.

[20] Nordmann, *op. cit.*, p. 121.

[1] Walter Schmidt-Rimpler, *Geschichte des Kommissionsgeschäfts in Deutschland* (Halle a. d. S., 1915), I, pp. 74–76, 311–318; Penndorf, *Buchhaltung*, pp. 20–24.

received or entrusted to others. In all three sections each transaction is described in detail on the left-hand page and payments made or received are entered on the opposite right-hand page. In the records of Johann Pisz accounting technique reaches a level not surpassed by any other Hanseatic merchant.

Although of later date, the account-book (1479) of Heinrich Dunkelgud, a Lübeck mercer, is again a hodgepodge of miscellaneous data.[2] As it is a book which the owner took with him on a pilgrimage to Santiago de Compostella, it contains a copy of his will. His devoutness did not cause him to forget his business and, passing through Bruges, he took advantage of the opportunity to conclude profitable deals. Occasionally accounts are in bilateral form, but Dunkelgud is by no means consistent in following this practice. References to other books show that his business was large enough to require that several be used concurrently.

The notebook kept by Paul Mulich at the Lent Fair of Frankfort-on-the-Main (1495) presents no interest from the point of view of accounting history.[3] Mulich was a commission agent who frequented the fairs to buy luxury wares (velvets, damasks, lighter silks, jewellery, pepper and other commodities) for his brother Matthias in Lübeck. The purpose of the notebook is, of course, to provide the data needed by Paul Mulich to render an account.

In the Middle Ages the Dutch towns near the Zuiderzee had close ties with the Hanseatic League, even if they were not actual members. Business methods also were similar, and so was the book-keeping.[4] Evidence is furnished in the register (1457–1463) kept by an unknown merchant of Hoorn, a small town in North Holland.[5] Paragraphs relating to claims or debts follow each other without apparent order; when full settlement had taken place, an entry was simply crossed out. A special annotation was made whenever a debtor or creditor and the Hoorn merchant had reviewed their account together and reached an agreement about the remaining balance. As in the book of Maître Ugo Teralh, the place of residence is written in the margin in front of each item. No advance is noticeable in the account-book of two Amsterdam merchants, Symon Reyerszoon and Reyer Diricszoon, who made regular trips to Danzig.[6] As is natural, the items relating to the same trip are all together.

---

[2] Wilhelm Mantels, " Aus dem Memorial oder Geheim-Buche der Lübecker Krämers Heinrich Dunkelgud," *Beiträge zur Lübisch-Hansischen Geschichte* (Jena, 1881), pp. 341 *et seq.* ; Penndorf, *Buchhaltung*, pp. 24–26.

[3] Fritz Rörig, *Das Einkaufsbüchlein der Nürnberg-Lübecker Mulich's auf der Frankfurter Fastenmesse des Jahres 1495* (Breslau, 1931).

[4] Posthumus, *Oosterse Handel*, p. 4.

[5] E. C. G. Brünner, " Een Hoornsch koopmansboek uit de tweede helft der 15e eeuw," *Economisch-historisch Jaarboek*, X (1924), pp. 3–79.

[6] Posthumus, *op. cit.* This book includes facsimiles and full text.

The conclusion is clear that Hanseatic book-keeping remained backward up to 1500. If the account-books of Reval merchants may be considered typical, conditions did not even change very much during the sixteenth century and the purpose of keeping records was still to gather data for effecting, sooner or later, a settlement of account.[7] As agreement was difficult to achieve by correspondence, the matter was often put aside until the parties could meet or until one of them died, leaving to his heirs the task of reconciling the differences.[8] Unsystematic book-keeping, in which each merchant followed more or less his own inspiration, was a serious shortcoming of the Hanseatic organisation of trade.[9]

In the fourteenth and fifteenth centuries, South Germany had a business organisation which differed sharply from that of the North. Instead of joint ventures on an informal basis, the South German merchants developed real firms with a style, a capital, and an accounting system of their own. In quite a few cases, these were companies in the Italian sense with a network of permanent branches. The accounting was also on a higher level: not yet double entry; but a well-organised system of single entry can be quite effectively used and not be a serious handicap to expansion, as we have seen in the case of the Alberti, the Peruzzi, and others. Of course, medieval companies, although large for their time, were small units when measured by a modern yardstick.

The first South German account-book recorded in historical literature dates from 1304 to 1307.[10] It is a Latin *Schuldbuch,* or register of receivables, belonging to the Holzschuhers, a family partnership of Nuremberg drapers. It offers little of particular interest and is kept in paragraph form. When full payment was received, the debit entry was simply cancelled by crossing it out with two diagonal strokes or by adding the word *persolvit.*[11] The names of the witnesses to a transaction are often given. A curious feature of this book is that customers are classified according to social rank and grouped in different sections: noblemen (the first thirty folios), clergy (the next six), and burghers (the remaining twelve).[12] In all, over two thousand entries refer to 445 customers, among whom there are 242 nobles, 53

---

7 Gunnar Mickwitz, *Aus Revaler Handelsbüchern; Zur Technik des Ostseehandels in der ersten Hälfte des 16. Jahrhunderts,* Societas Scientiarum Fennica, Commentationes Humanarum Litterarum, vol. IX, no. 8 (Helsingfors, 1938), p. 189.
8 *Ibid.,* pp. 195–199.
9 Heinrich Bechtel, *Wirtschaftsstil des deutschen Spätmittelalters* (Berlin, 1930), p. 151.
10 The text has been published in full: Anton Chroust and Hans Proesler eds., *Das Handlungsbuch der Holzschuher in Nürnberg von 1304–1307* (Erlangen, 1934).
11 *Ibid.,* p. xxv.
12 *Ibid.,* p xi.

clerics and 150 burghers of Nuremberg. Peasants apparently did not buy the quality cloth in which the Holzschuhers were dealing.

Next in chronological order comes the account-book (1383-1407) of Wilhelm and Matthäus Runtinger, father and son, merchants of Regensburg in Bavaria.[13] Their connections extended from Prague to Venice and their servants visited regularly the fairs of Frankfort-on-the-Main. In 1392 Matthäus was appointed municipal exchanger and warden of the mint. Three-fourths of his extant records relate to this money-changing business. The distinguishing feature of the Runtinger book is the gradual emergence of the bilateral form, presumably because paragraph accounting was such a source of confusion.

The fact that the account-book (1426-1435) of Ulrich Starck has debit and credit on opposite pages confirms the impression that the bilateral form was gaining ground in South Germany at a relatively early date.[14] On the other hand, the account-book (1440-1458) of Hans Lerer, a Munich merchant, reverts to the paragraph form with scarcely any attempt at rational classification.[15]

While travelling, the merchant was not relieved from the need of keeping records. This is illustrated by a memorandum book (1444-1458) which Ott Ruland, a merchant from Ulm, carried with him on his extended trips to Bavaria, Austria, Bohemia and the fairs of Frankfort-on-the-Main.[16] Credit transactions are recorded more or less in chronological order, because Ruland jotted them down immediately lest he forget an important detail. Once, when he had neglected to do so, he could not remember later the name of his debtor, but he eventually received his due, since the entry is duly cancelled. Ruland kept other books in his counting-house. Unfortunately, no information is available about their contents.

The account-book (1489-1490) of Hans Keller belongs in the same category as Ruland's. Keller made three trips to Italy for his employer, Ludwig Rottengatter, a merchant in Ulm.[17] For each voyage there is a separate account neatly divided into three parts: receipts, expenditures, and a list of the commodities bought with indication of cost.

---

[13] The text of the Runtinger book has been published with an elaborate critical apparatus by Franz Bastian, *Das Runtingerbuch, 1383-1407* (Regensburg, 1935-1944), 3 vols. The first volume contains a learned introduction, the second the text itself, and the third supplementary source material. Unfortunately, poor organisation and irrelevant detail impair the work's usefulness. *Cf.* A. Luschin von Ebengreuth, " Zur Geschichte der Handlungsbücher in Deutschland," *Bank-Archiv*, IX (1910), pp. 195-198 ; Penndorf, *Buchhaltung*, pp. 13-17.

[14] *Ibid.*, pp. 26-30.

[15] *Ibid.*, pp. 30-31.

[16] *Ibid.*, pp. 31-33 ; K. D. Hassler ed., *Ott Rulands Handlungsbuch* (Stuttgart, 1843).

[17] Adolf Bruder, " Das Reiserechenbuch des Hans Keller aus den Jahren 1489-1490," *Zeitschrift für die gesamte Staatswissenschaft*, XXXVII (1881), pp. 831-851.

No account-books of any of the larger South German firms have reached us; we are nevertheless rather well informed about their accounting procedure. Periodic, if not yearly, inventories and financial statements were drawn up. Thus the firm, Kress of Nuremberg, made it a rule to prepare such statements every two, three or four years. This was done for the first time in 1395 and again in 1397, 1401, 1403, 1407, 1411, 1413, 1415, 1418, 1422 and 1425.[18] The *Grosse Ravensburger Gesellschaft*, or the Great Company of Ravensburg, which had a continuous existence for a century and a half (1380–1530), followed a similar practice.[19] Other firms proceeded in the same way.[20] Since books were in single entry, the financial statement was based on the taking of an inventory, a troublesome job, which may explain why it was not done every year. Profits were presumably determined by deducting liabilities and initial investment from total assets. No complete statement has been preserved. In 1497, however, collective assets amounted to 165,473 Rhenish florins, according to figures scribbled on a scrap of paper by Hans Hinderofen, second in command among the partners.[1] This is an impressive sum for the fifteenth century. In the statements sent by branches to headquarters, sound, dubious and uncollectable claims were carefully segregated.[2] The preparation of the general statement and the probing of the accounts rendered by the branches were accompanied with much ado. For *Die Rechnung*, or periodic settlement of account, the partners—they were rather numerous—assembled in Ravensburg and were entertained for over a month at the company's expense.[3]

Although the book-keeping of the South German companies was on a high level, it still lagged behind the best Italian practice.[4] The accounting of the Ravensburg company, at the end of the fifteenth century, had probably not progressed beyond the standards achieved by the great Florentine companies in 1340.

In Switzerland, conditions were much the same as in South Germany. The account-book (1437–1448) of an unknown merchant in Geneva in still in Latin and contains solely receivables. The only sign of progress consists in the adoption of the bilateral form.[5] The

---

18 Penndorf, *Geschichte der Buchhaltung*, p. 17.
19 Aloys Schulte, *Geschichte der grossen Ravensburger Handelsgesellschaft, 1380–1530* (Stuttgart, 1923), 3 vols.   20 *Ibid.*, I, p. 56.
1 *Ibid.*, I, pp. 58–59.   2 *Ibid.*, I, pp. 103–105.
3 *Ibid.*, I, pp. 56–61. According to an incomplete list (*ibid.*, III, pp. 47–49), there were, in 1497, thirty-eight partners: three general managers, seventeen connected with branches abroad, twelve residing at home (*so husa*), and six on the road (*uff der Straus*).
4 Schulte admits that the books of the Ravensburg company were not in double entry (*ibid.*, I, p. 109).
5 Hektor Ammann, "Genfer Handelsbücher des 15. Jahrhunderts," *Anzeiger für Schweizerische Geschichte*, LI (1920), pp. 12–24.

Geneva Chamber of Commerce possesses in its archives a series of seven account-books, extending from 1483 to 1520, that belonged to the firm, Vuarambert and Sallaz. The set is incomplete. Only one of the books is a kind of ledger; the others are sales-books. The language used was Latin up to 1510, when it was displaced by French. The owners called themselves apothecaries and traded mainly in spices, but they were not specialised in any one line of business and dealt in a variety of commodities, including copper and silver imported from Nuremberg.

For lack of source material there is not much that can be said about the early development of commercial accounting in the British Isles. Prior to 1400 the only manuscript of any interest is the record of a London ironmonger, Gilbert Maghfeld, who had Geoffrey Chaucer among his customers.[6] It is kept in Norman French, interspersed with English words, a fact that should cause no surprise as French was still considered the official language. For our purpose, Maghfeld's account-book is only of slight interest, since no methodic arrangement is apparent. The record was merely intended as an aid to a faulty memory. It is a misfortune that none of the important wool-staplers have left any extensive business records, such as those of Datini. At any rate, business letters of English merchants, such as the Celys, suggest that book-keeping in medieval England did not stand much above that in Northern Germany.

The account-book (1492–1505) of Andrew Halyburton, conservator of the Scottish staple in Middelburg, is rather well laid out, but it is of a late date.[7] As in the book of Johann Pisz, the Danzig commission merchant, purchases and sales are recorded on the left page and payments are indicated on the opposite right page. As a result, debits are placed to the left in the case of a sale or to the right in the case of a purchase and the reverse applies to the credits.

As this survey shows, quite a bit of work has been done on medieval account-books, so that we are well informed about the development of accounting prior to 1500. It is possible that new discoveries of business records will be made in archives or libraries, but it seems improbable that such finds will alter the general picture in the least.

It may be considered a well-established fact that, in the fifteenth century, the practice of the counting-house was far ahead of the rather simple system described in early treatises, including the first

---

6 Public Record Office, E 101/509/19. *Cf.* Margery K. James, " A London Merchant of the Fourteenth Century," *Economic History Review*, second series, VIII (1956), pp. 364–376.

7 C. Innes, *Ledger of Andrew Halyburton, 1492–1503* (Edinburgh, 1867).

and most celebrated one, by the Franciscan, Luca Pacioli. Besides omitting cost accounting, they do not mention many of the refinements—not even those used in Venice, and certainly not those known and currently applied by merchants in other parts of Italy. There is not a word in Pacioli's treatise on simultaneous or subsidiary ledgers, on controlling and reciprocal accounts, on *Nostro* and *Vostro* accounts, on the audit of balance sheets, or on reserves and provisions. The actual records of the merchants clearly show that they were well acquainted with these devices and used them constantly. Certainly, the balance sheet was not used solely to prove the ledger, but it was also an effective instrument of management and control. True, all the possibilities were not fully realised from the start. The Medici records show decisively that the main purpose of auditing balance sheets was to go over them item by item in order to spot bad debts.

Double entry developed in Italy in response to the needs of nascent capitalism. Italian business organisation was already so complex that merchants could not get along without an efficient system of book-keeping. In the rest of Europe, double entry did not penetrate until the invention of printing aided its diffusion. Moreover, in the age of the discoveries, capitalism spread its tentacles to countries which thus far had escaped from its grip or barely been touched.

The fourteenth and fifteenth centuries were perhaps the most brilliant and progressive period in the history of accounting. It was followed by a long period of stagnation that lasted until the nineteenth century.

One final word: up to now the history of accounting until 1500 has been written on the basis of actual records, and thereafter on the basis of treatises. Business records of the later period are abundant in the archives. Very recently, a Frenchman, Henri Lapeyre, has published a most interesting book on the firm of Simon Ruiz (*ca.* 1525–1597) of Medina del Campo.[8] Its archives are only second to those of Datini for their completeness. There are innumerable records that await exploration, including those of the *Insolvente Boedelskamer* in Antwerp, the Capponi, Martelli, Strozzi, and Galli-Tassi archives in Florence, and many others. Perhaps a study of these later account-books will show that the contemporaneous treatises are no more reliable than the earlier ones in giving a true picture of business organisation in the past.

---

[8] Cited p. 154, note 18.

Luca Pacioli

R. Emmett Taylor*

LUCA PACIOLI lived and worked in Italy at a time of great discord and dissension. It was a time when leading families sought to establish themselves firmly, and the struggles among the families and the city-states were likely to arise at any time to upset tranquillity. The shifting alliances among leading families and duchies, and cities such as Urbino, Venice, Milan, Florence and Naples were difficult to follow. The Popes of the period, predominant in the Papal states, often took a firm stand in political as well as spiritual matters. The French on more than one occasion were in occupancy in northern Italy, especially in Milan, and the Spanish were at times in possession of southern Italy. The Turks in the east had taken over control of many of the trade routes, and the Hungarians had edged along the Dalmatian coast across the Adriatic and were in control of such important cities as Zara and Ragusa. Zara in 1409 was purchased from Hungary by Venice and remained Venetian for about four hundred years. Ragusa during much of the period of which we write was listed as a Republic but at the same time was a vassal state of Hungary.

Pacioli was born some time between 1445 and 1450, more likely nearer the first date, in Borgo San Sepolcro, a small town on the Tiber in central Italy, about eighty miles south-east of Florence and forty miles north of Perugia. He was apprenticed at an early age and taken into the family of Folco de Belfolci in his home town. His early training may well have been in the household of this family where training in business was emphasised. At the same time his religious training was acquired from the Franciscan friars in the town.

About the year 1416 Piero della Francesca, the writer and painter, was born in Pacioli's home town. During Pacioli's youthful years in Borgo San Sepolcro, Piero was already a man of standing, and it is possible that Pacioli actually was a student of the latter at an early time. A number of young men learned their perspective and their painting from Piero della Francesca and some of these became more famous than the Master himself. From this artist, who wrote a number of manuscripts and especially one on the subject of perspective, Pacioli got his early start in learning and in writing. Francesca had access to the Court of Urbino only a few miles north-east of

* Emeritus Professor of Business Law, University of Cincinnati, Cincinnati, Ohio.

Borgo San Sepolcro, and there in the famous library he could encourage Pacioli to study the ancient writings upon which later Pacioli was to base his own compilations and calculations.

Pacioli left his home town " when scarcely twenty years of age," and went to Venice where he became tutor to the three sons of a rich merchant, Antonio de Rompiasi. Many tutors in those days were treated very much as ordinary servants, but this was not the case with Pacioli. One person wrote that "Fra Luca Paciolo was the guest of his pupils, the merchant family of Ropiansi." Pacioli remained with this merchant family for nearly six years, and then about the time of his departure in 1470 he dedicated his first manuscript on mathematics to the three Rompiasi sons. This manuscript was done seemingly when Pacioli was scarcely twenty-five years of age. Pacioli was engaged not only in the teaching of the Rompiasi sons, for in his own writing he stated that " on account of this merchant I travelled in ships carrying goods."

During these years Pacioli was improving his own education. In Venice at this time there were public lectures given in the morning and afternoons in philosophy and theology and paid for by the Government. The various public lectureships, or chairs, were much sought after and a candidate had to pass a rigid examination respecting his ability, and in addition, an inquiry into his morals. The candidates often numbered as many as fifteen and the pay was good. Paolo della Pergola publicly taught philosophy, geometry and arithmetic there as early as 1449. He was succeeded by Ser Domenigo Bragadino, a Venetian patrician, chosen by the Signoria as a public lecturer in all the sciences at an ample salary of 150 gold ducats a year. Pacioli went on with his study of mathematics under Ser Domenigo Bragadino. He had as a fellow-student one Antonio Cornaro of the famous family of that name. Cornaro subsequently succeeded their teacher at his post. As students under Bragadino and afterwards, Pacioli and Antonio were to become friends of long standing.

Thus in his early years Pacioli had received training in the religious life among the Franciscan friars of his home town; he had acquired some of his love for books and his desire to write in some measure certainly from the artist Piero della Francesca in his home town; he had gained some experience in business with the merchant Rompiasi in Venice, possibly the greatest trading city of the times; he had encountered sound teachers in the field of mathematics; and he had acquired the knack of associating agreeably with people of all classes.

Pacioli did not neglect his own family, and was especially fond of a favourite uncle, Benedetto, whose surname was Baiardo and who may have been a brother of Pacioli's mother. He followed a military life first as a pupil of the distinguished condottiere Baldaccio d'Anghiari. Benedetto on several occasions was captain-general of the infantry, first under King Alphonso V (the Magnanimous) of the Empire possibly at the conquest of Naples in 1442, with Holy Church when Nicholas V was Pope, then with the Florentines at the siege of Volterra in 1472; he was twice in the service of the Venetians, in 1466 a guard of the City of Padua, and finally captain of the whole Levant. This uncle was a favourite of and had great influence upon the nephew. Much of Pacioli's early knowledge of military matters and especially of architecture, so close to things military in those days, must have come from the uncle. Later, in his books, when Pacioli developed the idea of devising games from practical problems, or of modelling problems on games, he drew upon his discussions with his uncle. The following is an example: The uncle on one occasion asked his corporals which of two things they could do more quickly— pick up and carry to a heap, one by one, a hundred small stones spaced in a straight line at intervals of one pace, or walk a mile. The answer reveals that more than a mile would have to be covered in collecting the stones in the prescribed manner.

Association with Piero della Francesca sooner or later brought Pacioli into contact with Leon Battista Alberti, painter, poet, philosopher, musician and architect and author of books on sculpture and architecture. During the régime of Pope Paul II, still under the guidance of Piero della Francesca, Pacioli went to Rome where he lived with Alberti during the years 1470–1471. In 1470 Pacioli was not over twenty-five years of age while Alberti was sixty-six years of age. Pacioli learnt much about sculpture, painting and architecture from the great Alberti personally and from his manuscripts on these subjects.

It might have been at this period when in Rome that Pacioli decided to join the religious Order of the Franciscans Minor. Alberti, strictly speaking, was not a churchman, though he held various ecclesiastical offices. The death of Alberti in 1472 may have hastened Pacioli in his move, though Pacioli wrote only that he went into the religious Order in " accordance with a vow." It was quite common during the Renaissance for young men to promise to take such a step, particularly if they sought advancement as teachers or writers. It would afford the backing of a strong religious Order and the Church. It would make it possible to improve a person's education and to secure a teaching position which afforded remuneration.

Pacioli first went to teach at the University of Perugia in 1475. " They engaged me for three years and I served them with diligence." Early in 1478 he asked for a raise in salary more in keeping with his position and dignity. The University conformed to his wishes because he was eminently satisfactory both as a man and as a teacher. In 1478 he was reappointed for a two-year period and then in 1480 for an additional year. The last salary payment was on December 11, 1480. Thus on this occasion Pacioli served at the University of Perugia from 1475 to 1480. Early during these years Pacioli was working on his second manuscript which he dedicated to the " Youth of Perugia."

Even before Pacioli went to teach at Perugia, he may have been acquainted with the della Rovere family which had come into great prominence. Francesco della Rovere, a Conventual of the Franciscan Order, taught at Perugia and later became the great Pope Sixtus IV from 1471 to 1484. Francesco sent his nephew, Giuliano, at an early age to be educated among the Franciscans; Pacioli and Giuliano were about the same age and became close friends.

Pacioli's successive appointments at Perugia first for three years, then for two years, and then for one year suggest that he may not have been in the best of health or else he found teaching too burdensome to carry on together with his writing in which he was deeply interested. In a dedicatory letter in one of his books to Cardinal Francesco Soderini years later, Pacioli wrote: " How can I forget that you whom I could hardly approach on account of my ill health after my life had been saved from the shades. . . ." The Cardinal was a member of the famous Soderini family of Florence; he and his two sons were to befriend Pacioli on numerous occasions.

In 1481 Pacioli was at Zara across the Adriatic in Dalmatia. There he worked on his third manuscript, which, he wrote, " I composed at Zara in 1481 about more subtle and advanced problems."

There are indications that Pacioli travelled elsewhere outside Italy during the early eighties, and it may have been during this time that he finished his formal university education. In time pressure was brought upon him by his ecclesiastical superiors to go back to teaching at the University of Perugia. He did so acting especially under the orders of " our present general, Master Francesco Sansoni of Brescia," who was then Head of the Franciscans Minor.

When Pacioli went back to Perugia in 1486 after an absence of six years he put " Magister " to his name. This was the highest title in academic studies and was equivalent to a doctorate, which was not given at the universities except in medicine and in law The " magister " gave the recipient the right to hold a professorial chair. There are records for salary payments from May 1, 1487, through April, 1488. The titles used for Pacioli by him and others usually were " Doctor of Sacred Theology and Philosophy," or " Master Lucas Paciolus, Professor of Sacred Theology."

There at Perugia in the year 1487 Pacioli was asking his readers " to have pity on me who feels the worries, as I feel the burden of daily reading, lecturing, and teaching, here in this beloved August City of Perugia. . . ." He continued that to return to Perugia he had just left " the flower of the world, Florence. . . ." But in spite of his manifold duties Pacioli was still able to get away from his routine. For example, on occasion he renewed his association with the della Rovere family. In the year 1489 he stayed in Rome at the palace of his old friend, Giuliano della Rovere, who was to be the great Pope Julius II from 1503 to 1513.

In 1494 Pacioli published his *Summa de Arithmetica, Geometria, Proportioni et Proportionalita* in Venice. He had been working on this book over a period of thirty years. Pacioli regretted the low ebb to which teaching had fallen and he thought that the fault lay in the use of improper methods and in the scarcity of available subject-matter. He sought to correct these faults in the *Summa*. His division of the material was as follows:

1. Arithmetic and algebra.
2. Their use in trade reckoning.
3. Book-keeping.
4. Money and exchange.
5. Pure and especially applied geometry.

The author stated that up to the time of the publication of the *Summa* he had written four books, that is, manuscripts. His first book was done in Venice in 1470 and dedicated to the three Rompiasi sons. His second book was done in 1476 and was dedicated to the " Youth of Perugia." His third book was done at Zara in 1481. Pacioli does not state what his fourth book was.

Pacioli in Venice was putting the book-keeping section of the *Summa* in shape for publication towards the end of 1493, but that portion was certainly written some time before the date of publication. Venice had granted Pacioli a ten-year copyright on the book. At the expiration of the ten years the portion on book-keeping was published separately in Tuscany under the title *La Scuola Perfetta dei Mercanti*, that is *The Perfect School of Merchants*. The new edition appeared under Pacioli's name and was published by Paganino de Paganini who had also published the *Summa* ten years before.

The *Summa* is by no means an original book. It is a compendium, as Pacioli himself called it. It is a collection of material and ideas from many sources and by many authors. Pacioli wrote that his main source for the *Summa* was the works of Leonardo da Pisa who wrote about the year 1200. In one place Pacioli stated that if he did

not name definitely the author to whom he was indebted then the
reader should understand that he was indebted to Leonardo da Pisa.
At no place did Pacioli claim originality for the double-entry system
of book-keeping which he described. He specifically stated that he
was merely writing down the system which had been used in Venice
for over two hundred years. Pacioli in this and other writings has
been wrongly accused of plagiarism.

Pacioli recommended that all business transactions should be
recorded in a systematic way consisting of the debit (*debito*—owed to)
and the credit (*credito*—owed by). After the merchant takes his
inventory, he uses three books, the memorandum for general information on the business transactions, from which daily such information
is entered briefly in the journal using debit and credit. In Venice they
used *Per* indicating the debtor (*debitore*) and *A* denoting the creditor
(*creditore*). A journal entry then might be *Per Cash// A Capital*, the
debit being first and the two lines separating it from the credit. This
information could then be transferred to the ledger, the debit being
placed on the left under a *Cash* heading and the credit to the right
under a *Capital* heading. At a given time a total of the amounts of
the debits should equal a total of the amounts of the credits, giving
the book-keeper in effect a trial balance.

Even in his earlier years Pacioli had the ability to write upon
subjects as drab perhaps as book-keeping and mathematics and to
enliven them with examples and pithy statements to stimulate the
interest of the students. He would emphasise that " every action must
be determined by the end in view," that " where there is no order
there is confusion," or that " he who does nothing makes no mistakes; who makes no mistakes learns nothing." The chapters are not
without religious admonitions: " Remember God and your neigh-
bour "; " by being charitable you will not lose your riches." When he
speaks of losses he prays " that from them, God may keep every one
who really lives as a good Christian! "

The *Summa* attracted great attention throughout Italy. It caught
the eye of Lodovico, Duke of Milan, who was tireless in advancing
learning at his Court, at the University of Milan, and at the University
of Pavia about twenty miles away. He invited Pacioli to his Court
and Pacioli went to Milan in 1496 to teach mathematics. There
Pacioli had an opportunity to associate with many prominent doctors,
lawyers, architects and painters. Among the last was Leonardo da
Vinci who was then engaged in doing in bronze the huge equestrian
statue for the Duke, which, unfortunately, was never to be completed.
It is said that Leonardo da Vinci learned his " roots " from Pacioli,
and that Pacioli helped him calculate the amount of bronze needed

for the huge statue. Leonardo was also working in Milan on his famous painting, *The Last Supper*. In Milan Pacioli worked on a new book called the *Divina* for which Leonardo prepared some of the drawings. Pacioli wrote that though he had resolved " to pass his years with the others in the open air," when he came to Milan, greatly stimulated by the sciences, he resolved to write a " tractate De Divina Proportione, as a spice " to his other works. He did this in " appreciation of Lodovico's interest in science and mathematics, as a benefit to his subjects, and as an addition to his excellent library " which was " already graced with a countless multitude of volumes on every science and doctrine."

Perhaps it was during the middle nineties, specifically 1495, that the painting of Pacioli attributed to Jacopo de Barbari was done. It hangs in the National Museum in Naples and shows the Friar teaching geometry, that is, Euclid, to his student, Guidobaldo, Duke of Urbino, who had succeeded his father Federigo. The Friar standing behind a table with his student at his elbow is dressed in the garb of his Order. An observer is struck with the stern, serious face and the determined chin of Pacioli, and the marked contrast in colours in the painting. Pacioli's left hand rests upon a page of an open book from which he is lecturing. The subject-matter of the book is geometry and the book may be a copy of Euclid. In Pacioli's right hand he holds a pointer resting on a slate on which is drawn some geometric figures. The slate is marked *Euclides*. A crystal globe is suspended at Pacioli's right above the slate. The painting is sometimes entitled *A demonstration in Mathematics*.

The stay of Pacioli in Milan was brief because at the turn of the century the French captured Milan and drove the Court out before them. Leonardo da Vinci and Pacioli left for Venice but stopped at Mantua for a while. Pacioli later dedicated his book on " Games," mainly on chess, to the Duke and Duchess of Mantua; no copy of this book has survived.

During the early years of the new century Leonardo da Vinci and Pacioli were in Florence where they were closely associated. During these years Pacioli taught at the Universities of Florence, Pisa and Bologna, and also gave public lectures in Rome and in Venice. On one occasion, on August 11, 1508, Pacioli gave a lecture in Venice upon the Fifth Book of Euclid before a distinguished audience said to have numbered five hundred persons. The lecture was delivered in the Church of St. Bartholomew and dealt with the subject of " Proportion and Proportionality." In this lecture he showed first how the subject tied up with religion, medicine, architecture, painting, sculpture, music, law and grammar, and in fact with all the liberal arts as well. He spoke first of his many sources, mentioning the natural philosophers Socrates, Plato and Aristotle, especially the last of these three " whose works are continually in my hands. . . ." The next year in Venice Pacioli was preparing for the publication of his book, the *Divina*, and for his revision of *Euclid*.

At this time Pacioli was possibly in his early sixties. Certainly he was getting tired from his life-long exertions in so many directions. In his current writings he clearly showed a desire to rest after. his many years of work: " Although from my earliest years I have been accustomed to study so much that I have done nothing else from my cradle. . . ." About this time he was made Head of the Monastery in his home town of Borgo San Sepolcro where perhaps he hoped to take life easy for his remaining years. But there was dissension between Pacioli and some of the friars under his supervision so that on at least two occasions the issues were brought before their superiors.

Late in the year 1511 Pacioli went before a notary in his home town and arranged for the making of a will to cover the disposition of his property after his death. The Rule of the Franciscans Minor was that the Brothers should live " in obedience, without property and in chastity." Here then is the " venerable and God-fearing scholar " asserting that he has " full power, right, and authority for making a Will relative to his property up to the amount of three hundred large golden ducats." [1] The authority to hold property was granted to him by a Bull of his old friend Pope Julius II on April 28, 1508, which was seen and read by the notary.

In 1514, Leo X, a Medici who was Pope from 1513–1521, called Pacioli to teach at the Academy in Rome. This appears to be the last definite date we have about Pacioli, but there are reasons to believe that he was still alive in 1523 at the time of the publication of the second edition of the *Summa*.

It is perhaps impossible to over-emphasise the influence of Luca Pacioli. To refer only to the subject of book-keeping, those who are acquainted with the history of the subject can see Pacioli's influence, among others, upon the early German, the Dutch, and the English writers and, indirectly, upon the first American writings. But if one wants to see the full impact of Pacioli upon posterity one must look into the Friar's writings in other fields and especially in mathematics and kindred subjects. Pacioli maintained that many other subjects are related to mathematics. The Friar made it a point to learn all he could about religion, mathematics, architecture, sculpture, painting, military science, business, teaching and writing.

He was so typically a " man of the Early Renaissance." He saw

---

[1] A ducat was a gold coin in value about $2.28, first coined in Venice about the year 1284.

the necessity of collecting knowledge, using some of it and discarding other portions, and putting it in shape for students so that they could learn to apply it in everyday life. He took up the subject of book-keeping from the merchants, wrote upon it and made it available for his students.

Pacioli in one of his works on Euclid apologised to his readers for the use of the native tongue, writing " nor should the vernacular and the language of the country offend you since the subject matter will bear more fruit if there are more people to read it. . . ." This shows Pacioli as the trail-blazer, recognising the kind of material that was important and seeking to present it in a manner that would give the best results to the greatest number.

We think of so many men of the Renaissance as accomplishing great things because they were versatile and acquainted themselves with so many subjects. It may be a great fault in our modern education that we possibly tend to become too specialised and as a consequence are unable to see the field as a whole. Thus our specialisation in accounting might be altogether too narrow, and should carry along with it considerable training in law. Perhaps more training in economics too is necessary for both accountancy and the law. In our lives we draw upon a variety of fields of study; yet when we study them we treat them usually as things apart.

It is of interest to watch Pacioli as he sought to develop the things that he did not know. In the market-place he learned his book-keeping. He saw at once the value of the subject and then tried to put the subject-matter in shape for the use of students. Fortunately just then printing came to his aid. Pacioli understood early the need in society for mathematics and especially a study of Euclid. Here too there was need to determine the significant parts of Euclid's material, already eighteen centuries old, and then to make use of a new device called printing to spread the knowledge. He had the native good sense to see that a printed book in mathematics would not get far unless Arabic numerals were used and unless the native language was resorted to in order to reach the greatest number of students. One must not ' think of Pacioli so much as an originator than as an adapter.

Pacioli made it a point to know everybody and he possessed the capacity to differentiate on the spot between those of ability and the less able. That he had friends in every walk of life is apparent and many of these spoke and wrote of him with affection. One of his students recalled that on an occasion of too much zeal, Pacioli rebuked him with: " Oh you want to know too much! " Another student wrote that Pacioli advised him about teaching: " You have to learn to tell a thousand holy lies." Many students of the period attributed their success in mathematics and in kindred subjects to Pacioli and his writings.

The person who wishes to learn more about Pacioli will find his best and most reliable source in the Friar's writings.[2] There is information about the man in some of his original manuscripts which were never published. Other sources are the records of towns and of universities ·in which Pacioli taught. The histories of art and of mathematics are helpful in learning more about Pacioli and his influence. The thread of Pacioli's life and his influence must be picked up from many sources.[3]

---

[2] There are the two editions of the *Summa*, the first edition published in Venice in 1494 and the second in 1523; the *Divina* published in 1509; and the edition of *Euclid* published also in Venice during the same year.

[3] A full bibliography dealing with Pacioli's life and times is given in my *No Royal Road. Luca Pacioli and his Times* (University of North Carolina Press, Chapel Hill, 1942), pp. 403–411.

Some Tudor Merchants' Accounts

Peter Ramsey*

By the middle of the sixteenth century there were sufficient treatises on double-entry book-keeping for any English merchant to instruct himself in its mysteries if he so chose. It is doubtful, however, whether many Tudor merchants could read the works of Pacioli and Manzoni in the original Italian, and the direct influence of these works must not be exaggerated. It is true that from the 1540's there was available an increasing number of English treatises and English translations of Italian and other foreign books—Oldcastle's work appeared in 1543, and the English translation of Ympyn in 1547—but practical experience was none the less probably more important than theoretical instruction. Italian merchants had long been resident in England before the sixteenth century, and some had practised double-entry book-keeping there. The ledger of the Borromeo Company of London, covering the years 1436–1439, is an example of an advanced technique that was adopted by English merchants only a century later. It has been suggested, indeed, that even the English authors of treatises may have learned from the example of Italian merchants resident in London rather than from textbook writers resident in Venice; the work of Peele has a number of features to be found in the Borromeo ledger and in the accounts of other Lombard merchants but not in the treatises of Pacioli and the Venetian school.[1]

Accountancy might equally well be learned abroad. The first known example of an English ledger in double entry was in fact written in Spain. Spain rather than Italy seems to have been regarded in England as the home of advanced commercial technique in the sixteenth century. Marine insurance was thought to have originated at Barcelona, and even double-entry book-keeping was apparently thought of as a Spanish rather than an Italian invention. In a will dated 1543 an English merchant enjoins his executors to " call oon of them that be parfite in the Reconynges of Spayne to see my bokes and accountes," and the probable implication of this phrase is that these books were kept in double entry.[2] But it was undoubtedly Antwerp rather than Seville that acted as a commercial college for

---

* Lecturer in History, University of Bristol.
[1] P. Kats, " Double-entry Book-keeping in England before Hugh Oldcastle," *The Accountant*, LXXIV (1926), pp. 91–98.
[2] Will of J. Kydermyster, P.C.C. 37 Pynnyng.

most aspiring young English merchants.ˑ It was here that the English cloth trade was mainly concentrated in the first half of the sixteenth century, and here young apprentices came from England to reside while acting as servants or factors to their London principals. Undoubtedly they were sent partly with a view to their business education. As late as 1569, when the connection between London and Antwerp was coming to an end, nine young Englishmen were reported as being in Antwerp " pour aprendre la langue et aulcuns pour aprendre tenir livres de comptes." [3]   In Antwerp, too, the professional accountant had made his appearance before the end of the century: in 1573 John Waddington begged the intervention of the Antwerp magistracy to help him recover his fees for more than a hundred days' work on the books of a certain Baptist van Achelen.[4] If, then, English merchants of the sixteenth century failed to obtain adequate theoretical and practical instruction in the technique of book-keeping, it was not for lack of opportunity.

It is doubtful, however, whether many in fact availed themselves of their opportunities. Ympyn remarks that he had seen in his country merchants' books " so grosly, obscurely and lewdely kept, that after their desease nether wife, seruaunt, executor nor other, could by their bokes perceiue what of right apperteigned to them to be receiued of other, nether what iustly was due by them vnto other." [5] Some exaggeration may be suspected here, since Ympyn was naturally anxious enough to sell copies of his book, and was thus led to enlarge at some length on the evil consequences of negligent book-keeping. It must be admitted, however, that as far as English merchants of the period are concerned, the available evidence largely bears out his strictures. Of the many wills of English merchants of this period only a few refer to accounts in a way that suggests that these may have been kept in double entry.[6] Surviving specimens of actual account-books, even those of the most successful and eminent merchants, often show very elementary technique and slovenly execution. The account-book of Henry Tooley, the most important merchant of Ipswich in the sixteenth century, was little more than a rough-book, whose erasures and cancellations make it nearly indecipherable to the modern researcher.[7] Much the same might be said of the " Boke of

---

[3] O. de Smedt, *De Engelse Natie te Antwerpen in de 16e Eeuw, 1496-1582* (Antwerp, 1954), vol. II, pp. 487-488.   [4] *Ibid.*, p. 489.
[5] Quotations from Ympyn are taken from the English translation of his treatise in *Economisch-Historisch Jaarboek*, 18 (1934), pp. 10-58.
[6] Matthew Boughton (P.C.C. 14 Bodfelde) refers his executors to folio 150 of his " grete boke " for a statement of his assets. Robert Tempest (P.C.C. 30 Bucke) refers to his " Jornall and Legere with other bokes of the Cheste and charges paide oute," and gives a detailed statement of his financial position at the time of making his will in 1550.
[7] J. G. Webb, *Henry Tooley, Merchant of Early Tudor Ipswich*, unpublished London M.A. thesis (1953), pp. 181-182.

Remembraunce " of Sir Thomas Kitson (1485–1540), a sheriff of
London and one of the wealthiest members of the Mercers' and
Merchant Adventurers' Companies; though this is not disfigured in
the same way as Tooley's book, it is very ill-written and unmethodical
—little more, in fact, than a series of jottings.[8]   The accounts of John
Smith of Bristol are a good deal more tidy, consisting of a number of
personal accounts with the debit and credit entries on opposite pages.
But though the format thus has something in common with that of
a double-entry ledger, the absence of any impersonal accounts as well
as the form of the entries makes it improbable that Smith was in fact
using a double-entry system.[9]   Merchants of any substance must
undoubtedly have kept books of some kind, and in this period they
were acquiring increasing importance as evidence in courts of law.
Ralph Goodwin of Ipswich told the High Court of Admiralty in 1538
that the " merchantes of the towne of Ippeswiche do use to kepe
bokes of their Reconynges wherin they do enter all bargaynes that
they do make; unto whiche bokes credence is gevyn because that
merchauntes have allways kept such bokes." [10]   On another occasion
it was even suggested in the Admiralty Court that merchants might
keep duplicate sets of false accounts in order to conceal their goods
from their creditors in case of bankruptcy.[11]   But though the principle
and practice of keeping accounts may have been well established, it
seems clear that in the great majority of cases these accounts were of
a very simple nature, little more than mere lists of purchases and
sales.   Even undoubted specimens of double-entry accounting were
often crude by the best contemporary standards, and their aims were,
as will be seen, rather different from those of modern book-keeping.

The earliest known example of a double-entry ledger in England—
over two centuries later than the first extant Italian example—is the
ledger of Thomas Howell, preserved at Drapers' Hall, London.
Howell was a member of the Drapers' Company, and traded chiefly
to Spain, where he was resident during the period covered by the
ledger.   The entries in this relate to the years 1522–1527, though a
number of accounts in it open with balances brought down from a
previous book (with folio references to the old ledger) and refer to
transactions as far back as 1517.[12]   In the Public Record Office are to

[8] Cambridge University Library, Hengrave Hall Deposit 78(2). This collection
also includes a most interesting series of statements of account presented by
Kitson's factor in Antwerp, though these do not appear to relate to a double-
entry system.

[9] My thanks are due to Mr. T. G. Wyatt for allowing me to see his photostat
copies of John Smith's accounts.

[10] Webb, p. 183.

[11] B. Winchester, *The Johnson Letters (1542–1552)*, unpublished London Ph.D.
thesis (1953), p. 468.

[12] My thanks are due to the Drapers' Company for permission to examine this

be found a ledger and some fragments from the accounts of John Johnson, a merchant of the Staple of Calais in the mid-sixteenth century. This ledger covers the years 1534–1538, when Johnson was acting as factor to Anthony Cave at Calais, and the fragments, all from the years 1543–1545, include two parts of journals and one of a ledger for Johnson's own business.[13]   Also in the Public Record Office are some accounts of Thomas Laurence, a Merchant Adventurer in the reign of Elizabeth I.   These include part of a journal for the years 1565–1569 and a part of the corresponding ledger for 1565–1567 —this being the only case where both the two main books of account for the same period have survived.   There is also a ledger of Laurence's for the years 1574–1581, and a book of expenses for 1581– 1582.[14]   All these last are in good condition, but the extreme brevity of the entries in the second ledger make it very difficult to use in the absence of the accompanying journal.   Finally, in the day-book of Sir Thomas Gresham (1519–1579), now in the possession of the Mercers' Company in London, we have the best-preserved and most interesting example—both from the technical and the historical point of view—of sixteenth-century book-keeping.   Its two hundred closely written folios give a detailed and precise picture of the business activities of one of the greatest merchants of the age and at the same time throw much light on the aims and methods of contemporary accountancy.[15]

It is, then, upon these four merchants' accounts that our understanding of Tudor double-entry book-keeping must be based until more account-books of the period come to light.   It is unfortunate that we have among them no examples of two of the four main books of accounts used at this time.   It is clear that the opening 128 entries in Gresham's day-book were derived from an inventory, but the inventory itself has not survived.   It is possible that the archives of Somerset House may some day yield up further examples of inventories that once were part of sets of accounts, but the inventories there are not at present accessible to the researcher.   It would in any case not be easy to determine whether any particular inventory was part of a set of double-entry accounts or not unless it contained specific references to a journal or ledger—a mere list of stock and debts might

---

document. A non-technical description of its contents is given by G. Connell-Smith, " The Ledger of Thomas Howell," *Economic History Review*, second series III (1951), pp. 363–370.

[13] Public Record Office, State Papers 1/185, ff. 100–127; 1/196, ff. 97–165; 46/5, ff. 2–31

[14] Public Record Office, Exchequer Accounts Various, 520/24–25; 521/10; 521/15.

[15] My thanks are due to the Mercers' Company, not only for permission to examine this document, but also for their generous loan of the microfilm copy that has made possible a full examination.

be composed in many different ways and serve many different purposes. Likewise we have no surviving example of a " memorial," the book in which the merchant made a rough note of his transactions before making the more formal entries into the journal and ledger. It is just possible that Kitson's " Boke of Remembraunce " served this purpose, but throughout its length there is no reference to any journal or ledger, and it seems therefore unlikely that it formed part of a double-entry system. As in the case of the inventory, it would be hard to identify an isolated " memorial " as part of any system, since it was essentially only a book of rough jottings, and such a book would be unlikely to have much technical interest from the accounting point of view.

The accounts of Gresham and Laurence, on the other hand, afford good examples of the day-book or journal in the sixteenth century. It must be remembered that in this period the journal contained a great deal more than its more recent counterpart; it contained the entries for *all* transactions. In addition, Gresham journalises all the opening balances for his new ledger, and also the transfer of balances from one impersonal account to another within the ledger (though not, of course, the transfer of balances from one page to another of the same account). The narrative of the entries gives a good deal of detail, though this would probably not be repeated in the ledger. It is, indeed, this wealth of detail that makes possible a reconstruction of Gresham's business from the journal alone.

The journals of both Gresham and Laurence follow a similar pattern. Gresham's, the more elaborately kept of the two, has a long formal dedication that is absent in Laurence's book: " In the name of God, Amen. This present boke shalbe the Jornall called + apperteyning to me Thomas Gresham of London mercer for therin to wryte with my owne hande or els with the hand of my prentys Thomas Bradshawe alle my hoole trayne and doynges and out of the said Jornall to wryte it into the greate booke called the Leger which shalbe holden by poundes shillinges and pence of money of Englonde. Pleaseth God to geve me profytt and prosperitye to defende me from evell fortune losse and domage. Amen." (See Plate VI.) Such pious expressions are indeed a marked feature of sixteenth-century accounts. Thus Kitson likewise refers to all his cloth shipments as being " by the grace of God," and it was normal practice to inscribe a cross by the date; Ympyn instructs his reader to begin his inventory with the sign of the cross " and writeth by it the name of Jesus for a difference betwene the Turckes and Jewes, whiche do not so." [16] The formal dedication apart, Laurence's book closely resembles Gresham's in its general lay-out. On each folio both books have one column reserved for folio

---

[16] Ympyn, *loc. cit.*, p. 17.

references to the ledger, given in the form of a vulgar fraction of which the indicator gives the folio to be debited, the denominator gives the folio to be credited. Gresham, but not Laurence, has a further column in which the journal entries are numbered serially from 1–6572. In both books there is a further column containing the narrative, each entry beginning with the formula " A oweth unto B," indicating the accounts of A and B to be respectively debited and credited. On the right is a single column for amounts. Thus the first entry in Gresham's day-book reads as follows:

$1\frac{1}{2}$ Chest oweth unto Capital, which   Dlxxv li. viiij s. j d.
is for ready money, £575–9–1.

This indicates that the cash account (on the first folio of the ledger) is to be debited, and the capital account (on the second folio) to be credited with £575 9s. 1d., this being the ready money in Gresham's hands at the time of opening his accounts. It will be seen that no column is supplied for dates, these being entered in the middle of the page above an entry or group of entries. It is also interesting to note that the amount in the right-hand column is written in Roman numerals, while the same sum is stated in the narrative in Arabic numerals. (See Plate VII.) In the mid-sixteenth century it was still apparently felt that Roman numerals, for all their obvious disadvantages, were more proof than Arabic against error and fraud. Johnson, in a fragment of his journal, reverses Gresham's procedure, using Roman for the narrative and Arabic for the amounts column. Laurence, on the other hand, uses Arabic throughout, and it is possible that the use of Arabic numerals in merchants' accounts was becoming more general in England towards the end of the century. The entries in these journals are separated from each other by a line drawn across the page. It is also usual to find that each entry has been cancelled by two short diagonal lines drawn through it, these being made when the posting from journal to ledger had been completed.

As has already been suggested, the contents of a sixteenth-century journal were rather different from those of its more recent successor. One journal only was used for both purchases and sales, and included in it were entries that today would appear only in the cash-book, bill-books, or other specialised books of first entry. The entries appear simply in chronological order, no attempt being made to group them under logical headings in such a way as to facilitate posting to the ledger. Nor was the chronological order very strictly observed in practice. In Gresham's day-book the date above a group of entries indicates the date on which they were inscribed in it, which was not necessarily the date of the actual transactions recorded. Gresham, moreover, was decidedly lax in his dating; entries often run for a page and more without any date at all, though it is clear from the narrative that in some cases the transactions in question took place after the last date indicated. This, incidentally, creates difficulties for the researcher attempting to reconstruct Gresham's ledger and to draw up balance sheets based upon it. It is, for example, not uncommon to find that goods were apparently shipped abroad before being purchased, or sold before arrival in London from abroad, and on some dates there may even be a credit balance in the cash account. Sixteenth-century journals were clearly not as meticulous as the textbook writers would have wished.

Howell, Laurence and Johnson all supply examples of the sixteenth-century ledger. Their books show a general resemblance in form, though it is Laurence who comes nearest to modern practice. In the ledgers of both Howell and Laurence the left-hand page is used for debit entries, the right-hand for credit entries, but Johnson's 1534–1538 ledger oddly reverses what was already the standard practice and puts the debit entries on the right-hand page. All the three ledgers have columns on each page for narrative, references and amounts; Laurence has two further columns on the left of the page for the date of the month, and his column rulings therefore closely resemble those of a modern ledger. (Howell and Johnson put the date above the entry in the middle of the page.) These differences in lay-out, as well as certain differences in the form of the narrative, are perhaps best shown by examples:

An entry on the debit side of a personal account in Howell's ledger will appear somewhat as follows:

<blockquote>
J'hus the 11 May anno 1522

Robert Wheeler oweth to give for 5 broadcloths sold   8 L. xv s. – d. – him at £3, to pay ready money.
</blockquote>

The same entry in Laurence's ledger would appear as:

<blockquote>
11th May   Robert Wheeler is debtor to cloths   8   015   00   0
</blockquote>

The corresponding entries on the credit side of the cloths account would read respectively:

<blockquote>
J'hus the 11 May anno 1522

Broadcloths oweth to have for 5 sold to Robert   14 L. xv s. – d. – Wheeler at £3.
</blockquote>

and:

<blockquote>
11th May   Cloths is creditor by Robert Wheeler   14   015   00   0
</blockquote>

In both examples the column between those for narrative and amounts gives the reference to the corresponding folio in the ledger, not the folio in the journal. It has here been assumed that Robert Wheeler's personal account is on folio 14 and the cloths account on folio 8. In the case of Laurence it has further been assumed that the entries are the first in the two accounts; subsequent entries in the same account omit the title and begin simply " to " or " by," as became the standard practice later. (Howell repeats the title in each entry, but in the first entry it is written in large characters to act as a heading for the account.) Johnson's ledger differs from the others in that it gives references to the entry in the journal, not the corresponding ledger folio, and that these references are given in the narrative, not in a separate column. None of the three uses a column for quantities of goods, though this was recommended in some of the textbooks and is to be found in some contemporary ledgers abroad—for example, in the ledger of the Affaitadi at Antwerp.[17]

Laurence's ledger thus comes nearest of the three to modern practice in the lay-out of his accounts, in the form of his narrative, and in his use of Arabic numerals. It is also noticeable that his entries are considerably less informative than those of Howell, since he reduces his narrative to the bare minimum. This again comes nearer to modern practice, but makes the accounts much less helpful to the modern researcher, more especially as Laurence makes use of comprehensive accounts of a very general nature—" Wares " and " Account of Antwerp "—so that the brevity of the entries makes it impossible to ascertain the nature of the transactions recorded in them.

The ledger in this period consists usually of a single book for all the accounts, and there is as yet little attempt to group them. Each new account is normally entered in the next vacant double page, with no distinction between personal and impersonal accounts. When one page is full the balance on the account is simply transferred to the next empty page, so that the major accounts appear at scattered intervals throughout the ledger. Alone of the three merchants here discussed Johnson makes a slight concession to orderliness by leaving blank pages available for the major accounts, and by keeping his cash account in a separate book; but he is not consistent in this and like the others is quite ready to have more than one account on a page where space permits. This lack of orderliness was apt to make the ledger unwieldy for purposes of quick reference, and the textbook writers therefore recommended the use of an alphabetical index. There is no index extant for any of these three ledgers, though it is possible that they may once have existed. But as none of the three is very large, it is likely that someone familiar with the contents would not have felt the need for an index very seriously. Nor, it

---

[17] The Affaitadi ledgers, of which four volumes survive for the 1550's, are magnificent specimens of sixteenth-century book-keeping at its most advanced level, and give a detailed picture of the workings of a great international trading and banking house of the period. They are preserved in the archives of the city of Antwerp (Stadsarchief Antwerpen, Insolvente Boedelskamer 1097).

might be added, are modern ledgers necessarily kept in better order than those of the sixteenth century, in spite of the advent of the loose-leaf book.

Of the actual accounts to be found in these books little need be said of the personal accounts, which were not materially different from those in a modern system. The most distinctive feature, perhaps, is that entries for goods may appear on both sides of a personal account—that is to say that in the case of a customer who was also a supplier the sixteenth-century book-keeper used only the one account to cover both aspects of his relationship with the business, a natural consequence of the fact that there was only the one ledger for both customers and suppliers. Another feature is the slowness with which Tudor merchants seem to have settled their debts, and the fact that a considerable number seem never to have been paid at all. Howell's ledger opens with thirteen balances brought down from a previous ledger, totalling £126 11s. 3d., which appear never to have been settled; Gresham's book likewise opens with a long list of debts already overdue. But this was not, of course, due to the accounting methods in use, nor was it an exclusively sixteenth-century failing.

The impersonal accounts show greater differences. The cash account is the only one kept on lines closely similar to those of modern book-keeping. It is variously styled " Cash " by Howell, " Chest " by Gresham and Johnson, and " Money " by Laurence, and all except Johnson keep it as an account within the ledger, not in a separate cash-book. The entries in it are for the most part very brief and the sums entered often very small—in some instances only a few shillings. Since, however, the total number was small as compared with the cash entries of any modern firm it was not necessary to keep a separate petty cash account. Gresham does, however, appear to have kept something of that nature for his household expenses, for which substantial sums are credited to the cash account at intervals of some months, but without any details being given.

The treatment of purchases and sales was substantially different from modern practice. There was more than one trading account in the ledger. In each of these related purchases, sales and expenses were recorded, the basis of the classification taking one of two forms. In the one case an account was allotted to a particular venture or to a particular consignment of mixed goods sent to or received from a given market. Thus a consignment of soap, oil and iron from Spain might be allotted to an account headed " Voyage of Seville." This account would be debited with the purchase price of the goods on arrival, and credited with the selling price of the various articles as they were disposed of. When all the soap, oil and iron had been sold the account would be closed, and the balance on it would represent the profit or loss realised on this particular venture. Such an account had the disadvantage that it was difficult to ascertain the relative profitability of different commodities comprised in it; on the other hand it was very suitable to the needs of a merchant who was experimenting with new markets and was therefore interested in the relative profitability of markets rather than goods. This, of course, was the case with at least some of the Tudor merchants, as it was later to be the case with the earlier settlers on the North American continent, whose accounts employed similar devices.

The other method was to assign an account to each of the commodities in which a merchant regularly dealt, regardless of their provenance or destination. An English merchant of this period might have separate accounts for the cloths and kersies that he exported, and likewise for the velvets, linens and fustians that he imported. In this method too the account would be debited with purchases and credited with sales, with the difference that the account would run continuously throughout the period covered by the ledger. The use of the two forms of account was not mutually exclusive. Howell used both, having a continuous account for the broadcloths that he exported to Spain, but also an account entitled " Voyage of Danzig " for a particular shipment of goods. Gresham, on the other hand, kept separate accounts for each commodity in which he dealt, even for those of which only one small consignment is recorded, and Johnson and Laurence follow on similar lines, though without Gresham's meticulous differentiation. It is probable that the general trend was from the first to the second form of trading account. The latter would be more appropriate to the needs of merchants trading to fixed markets, like the Merchant Adventurers and members of the later Tudor trading companies.

A further distinctive feature of the accounts is the inclusion in them of certain expenses. All charges specifically relating to the venture or commodity in question are debited to the account. Freight charges and customs duty on exported cloths, for example, would be debited to the account for cloths. Rebates might also be charged or allowed to these accounts, though here the practice seems to have varied. Thus the balance on one of these accounts, after due allowance had been made for stock in hand, represented the net profit or loss made on the venture or commodity in question. Similarly, if all the balances on these accounts were taken at a given date the sum total represented the net trading profit or loss of the whole business.

Some expenses, however, could not be conveniently allocated in this way, and some other account had to be used for them. The treatment of these miscellaneous expenses forcefully illustrates one of the most radical differences between Tudor and modern accountancy. In the earlier system no distinction is made between the private affairs of the merchant and those of his business, and the identification of the two affected not only the treatment of expenses, but also, as will be seen, the estimation of profit and loss. Howell's "Expenses" account consists chiefly of his personal and household expenses. Gresham, though keeping a separate account for household expenses, includes other personal expenses in an account which contains also the wages of servants and the travelling expenses of his factors besides much other miscellaneous matter. Johnson likewise keeps a separate account for household expenses, but combines all the rest in an account called "Expenses ordinary and extraordinary." Laurence has a single account for "Charges" in his second ledger, but the brevity of the entries makes it impossible to determine what exactly was included under this heading; his first ledger seems to have no separate provision for expenses at all. Thus all the English double-entry accounts of this period show some confusion in their treatment of expenses, and in this respect are inferior to the best contemporary examples abroad. The ledger of the Affaitadi, for example, distinguishes clearly between business and household expenses, and even has separate accounts for household furniture and for postal charges. Nor was this a recent Italian innovation; the ledgers of the Borromeo Company of London had the same subdivisions more than a century before.

A further account had to be provided for miscellaneous incomings and outgoings—such items as gifts and bequests and the interest on loans—which could not logically be entered in any other impersonal account. This was provided by the Affaitadi in an account called "Avanzi di nostro conto," by Gresham in a "Damage and Gain" account, by Johnson in a "Gains" account, and by Laurence in an account called "Profit and Loss." (It must be noted that this last had practically nothing in common with the modern account of the same name.) All four merchants use this account also for balances transferred (at irregular intervals) from the other impersonal accounts —the trading accounts. The account is thus made to serve two distinct purposes; profits and losses are confused with all manner of miscellaneous entries, though it is true that if the posting of balances were done systematically the balance on this account would represent the net profit or loss of the merchant over a given period. None of the four merchants did transfer his balances in anything like a systematic manner, however, so that in practice the account served simply as a dumping-ground for items that the book-keeper could not fit in anywhere else. Gresham's account is peculiarly unsatisfactory in that it includes more diverse matter than any of the others; into it went many of his business and personal expenses (the latter include even his gambling losses), gifts donated or received, income from manors, interest payments and bad debts written off. This accumulation cannot be held to have served any useful administrative purpose. It is worth remarking, however, that as late as the eighteenth century a writer referred to the profit and loss account as a repository for "refuse and dregs."

Gresham's ledger is the only one of the four with a capital account, and even in his case it serves only a very limited purpose. The opening entries in the ledger (journalised in the day book) are debited or credited to "Capital." Thereafter no further use is made of this account, beyond the addition of a few items apparently omitted when the books were opened. On the one occasion that he tries to calculate his profit the resultant figure is not posted to "Capital," and it must therefore be concluded that this account did not serve the same purpose as the modern capital account. It is also interesting to note that in the opening entries no accounts are raised for the fixed assets, such as manors, in Gresham's possession. In thus omitting fixed assets, however, Gresham was only following a practice illustrated in at least some of the early textbooks; one published in 1586 showed that it was quite possible for a non-commercial institution such as a monastery to show a negative capital in the ledger.[18] However, fixed assets, such as houses, bought by Gresham during the period of the account-books are entered to the debit of appropriately titled asset accounts, presumably to act as a double-entry counterweight to the required credit entry in the cash account. On the other hand, lands in Yorkshire inherited from his father, Richard Gresham, do not give rise to the opening of an asset account, presumably because there is no pressing need to credit any account as neither cash is paid nor a debt incurred. Though some of the fixed assets are excluded from the ledger, all incomes derived from them are recorded and find their way into the "Damage and Gain" account. It would therefore be inappropriate to compare the recorded net income with the value of the recorded net assets since this would overstate the rate of return on his capital.

The character of Tudor accounts suggests that they were intended to serve purposes rather different from those of a modern double-entry system. The difference is most marked in the calculation of profit and loss, and here the sixteenth century merchants do not seem to have made full use of the double-entry system. One of the main features of this system today is the preparation of a periodic profit and loss account and of a balance sheet, both of which indicate the position of the business as distinct from that of the proprietor in his

---

[18] P. Kats, "Early History of Book-keeping by Double Entry," *Journal of Accountancy*, XLVII (1929), pp. 206 and 275.

personal capacity. These documents are normally cast after the accuracy of the book-keeping has already been checked by the trial balance. None of this applies in sixteenth-century England.

In the first place there is no evidence in any of the accounts here discussed that the accuracy of the postings was ever checked. Pacioli recommended that two apprentices should between them carry out such a check either every year or whenever a new ledger was opened, and that each entry in the journal should be marked with two ticks to show that the postings to both debit and credit accounts had been checked and found correct. There are no such physical marks to indicate a check in the journals of Gresham and Laurence, and it is therefore at least doubtful whether any check was ever made. Perhaps their apprentices found, to quote Ympyn's phrase, that " it should bee to painfull and busy to kepe a reconyng after suche maner." [19]

Sixteenth-century textbooks did provide a means to calculate profit and loss, but only if certain rules were strictly observed. First the stock in hand had to be checked, and then after due allowance had been made for this the balances on the trading accounts could be transferred to some form of " Damage and Gain " account. To this account must also be transferred the balances on other impersonal accounts such as those for expenses and miscellaneous incomings and outgoings. (In Gresham's accounts these were in any case all grouped together.) The balance on this account would then represent the increase or decrease in the net assets at book values. It would not, however, represent profit or loss in the modern sense, since included among the expenses and miscellaneous accounts were many entries relating to the private and domestic affairs of the merchant. In other words, money drawn from the business by the proprietor is reckoned into the profit and loss account and not entered separately into the capital account.

This process also seems to have proved " to painfull and busy " for sixteenth-century book-keepers. Gresham did at intervals ascertain the balance on one or several of his trading accounts—for this purpose stock seems to have been valued at cost price. But he never did this systematically for all the accounts on a single day—at least he never journalised such a proceeding—and it would therefore not be possible for him to estimate his profit or loss in the way indicated. In any case, the result thus obtained would have been most unsatisfactory in the eyes of a modern accountant. For one thing Gresham habitually anticipates profits, crediting the " Damage and Gain " account with rent payments six months and more before they are due

---

[19] Ympyn, *loc. cit.*, p. 57.

and entering interest payments in it at the time the loan is made.[20]
It might be inferred that Gresham was more concerned with having a
suitable record of the moneys due to him than with calculating his
profit accurately. As for Howell's ledger a number of the columns
are not even totalled, and there is no positive evidence that either
Johnson or Laurence made the attempt. Some other method of
calculating profit and loss must have been used in the Tudor period if
any such calculations were made at all.

One possible method, and perhaps the most likely one, was the
compilation of periodic inventories analogous to the modern balance
sheet. In his will of 1568 Henry Becher refers to the " Inventaryes I
have kepte from yere to yere for sixtene yeres paste Excepte that from
Anno 1565 untyll Anno 1568 there was none made The laste of the
same Inventaryes beinge finisshed and made the laste daye of December Anno Domini 1567 The whiche I used to make yerely for the
better understandinge of myne estate." [1]   Other merchants may well
have done likewise, though whether this was a general practice, and
whether December 31 was the usual date chosen, we have no means of
knowing. To compose an inventory the merchant had only to value
his stock and to compile a list of the debts owed to and by him.
Successive inventories would enable the merchant to ascertain directly
the increase or decrease in his net assets from time to time, provided
the personal accounts had been properly kept. There are, however,
three points to observe. In the first place the sixteenth-century inventory supplied no statement of the profit or loss of the business as such.
Secondly, there was in this method of ascertaining profit no inherent
check on the accuracy of the book-keeping, and if errors had been
made in the personal accounts the final result might be a great deal
out. Since, however, the accounts were few and simple by modern
standards the possibility of error was probably not very great in practice. Thirdly, if this was indeed the method used by Tudor merchants,
then the use of double entry was a quite unnecessary complication,
since all the book-keeping information necessary for an inventory
could be derived from a single-entry system with a cash account and
personal accounts. It must be suspected that those English merchants
who did adopt double entry in the sixteenth century did so without
any clear idea of the advantages to be derived from it. And since
most merchants could obviously well afford to do without it, it is
hardly surprising that it was not widely adopted.

It remains to be considered whether these accounts could be used
by the modern researcher for the preparation of final accounts.

[20] For example, Day Book entries nos. 1715, 1716 and 723. No adjustment is made
for such items in the only profit calculation recorded in the day-book.
[1] Will of Henry Becher, P.C.C. 10 Holney.

Howell's ledger lacks any account for those miscellaneous items that we should expect in any business, and it must therefore be suspected that it does not contain all the relevant information required. Johnson's ledger of 1534–1538 lacks a cash account, though it is just possible that this might be reconstructed from the entries in other accounts; his other books are far too fragmentary to be serviceable. There remain the accounts of Gresham and Laurence.

Gresham's accounts are undoubtedly complete enough for the attempt to be made, but present considerable difficulties. For one thing, it is difficult to estimate his stock at any given date, though the entries in the day-book give sufficient detail for it to be possible to obtain reasonably accurate figures by laboriously totalling the quantities of all goods purchased and sold. It is impossible, however, to make any allowance for depreciation of stock or, of course, for the depreciation of fixed assets. Much more serious are the problems presented by the " Voyages " account. This was the account of Gresham's resident factor at Antwerp. To it were debited all goods shipped from London for sale in Antwerp, and to it were credited all goods received from Antwerp for sale in London. If this were all no great difficulty would arise; a credit balance on the account could be regarded as the profit realised on foreign trade, and though it would be impossible to assess accurately the value of the stock in hand at Antwerp this would not seriously affect the balance over a long period of time.

Unfortunately the " Voyages " account is also used for exchange dealings. When Gresham borrows money in London to be repaid in Antwerp by his factor, the cash account is debited and the " Voyages " account credited with the sum in question—the factor being answerable not to Gresham but to some foreign merchant for repayment of the debt. Similarly when Gresham repays in London money that has been taken up by exchange in Antwerp the " Voyages " account is debited and the cash account credited. In the former case, the more common of the two, there is no indication in the " Voyages " account when, if ever, the money was repaid. Most bills of exchange between London and Antwerp were repayable after one month, but it cannot be certainly assumed that repayment in fact took place after that time. Moreover, any debts contracted by the Antwerp factor that did not involve bills of exchange on London—for example, the purchase of goods on credit—do not feature in the account at all. It is therefore not only the stock but also the credit situation that cannot be ascertained with any certainty. A credit balance on the " Voyages " account may thus represent a combination of profit and liability from the point of view of the business, and can be regarded as pure profit only on the dangerous assumption that all debts payable in Antwerp have in fact been paid at the date of closing the accounts. Hence a really accurate balance sheet cannot be constructed from Gresham's day-book, since essential information on stock and debts is lacking. The information was presumably available to Gresham, to whom the factor would periodically present detailed accounts—like those that Thomas Kitson's factor Thomas Washington presented for his dealings at the Antwerp marts. From these an accurate figure for profit or loss on dealings in Antwerp could be derived. It is interesting to note, however, that Gresham's one apparent attempt to calculate his profit is based solely on the London accounts—he in fact simply takes the balance on the " Damage and Gain " account, and he appears to have made no attempt to incorporate into the reckoning the profit or loss on dealings by the Antwerp factor. The resultant figure is inevitably quite out of touch with reality.[2]

Laurence's two ledgers could not, for different reasons, be used as a basis for final accounts on the modern pattern. The entries in the second ledger are far too brief to convey a clear idea of their meaning in the absence of the accompanying journal. The first ledger, where the accompanying journal is still extant, is unusable for another reason. Contrary to one of the most fundamental requirements of double-entry accounting—in the sixteenth century as today—Laurence uses two different currencies in this book, English and Flemish. It is true that he does not confuse the two in any one account, and the value of the ledger as a record of transactions is thus relatively unimpaired, but this confusion makes it virtually impossible to calculate Laurence's profits and cast balance sheets. It also reinforces the general conclusion that Tudor book-keepers regarded their double-entry books as records of transactions rather than as a basis for synoptic final accounts.

It would clearly be dangerous to draw any very hard and fast conclusions about Tudor accountancy from the fragmentary evidence available, but the foregoing discussion nonetheless suggests a number of interesting points. It seems fairly clear that the main principles of double-entry book-keeping were well known in sixteenth century England, even if there were few practitioners of it and the technique of those few imperfect even by contemporary standards. The books of account were fewer in number and more simply and crudely kept than those of a modern firm, but on the whole the differences in form are relatively unimportant. Much more distinctive is the confusion between the affairs of the business and those of its proprietor, a confusion which comes out strikingly in the treatment of expenses.

---

[2] Day Book, entry no. 1499. Gresham estimates his net loss for the period April 26, 1546–April 22, 1547, as £74 7s. 3d., though he states that this relates specifically to his trade in England.

The sixteenth century also had much to learn on the subject of balancing the books and casting final accounts, and its weaknesses in this sphere suggest not only a difference in aim in keeping accounts but also a failure to understand or make use of the particular advantages of the new technique of double entry. On the other hand, the distinction between business and private affairs would have seemed meaningless to a sixteenth-century merchant, who was not accountable to anyone but himself. The absence of the modern profit and loss account and balance sheet, in fact, mattered little before the advent of the modern shareholder and tax-collector. The experienced Tudor merchant undoubtedly had a perfectly clear idea of the progress of his affairs, whatever the technical deficiencies of his book-keeping. It would be presumptuous and absurd for the twentieth-century critic to suppose that he could conduct the affairs of Gresham and his contemporaries better than they themselves.

The First English Books on Book-keeping*

Cosmo Gordon †

DOUBLE-ENTRY book-keeping satisfies a common but by no means universal human instinct for orderliness and balance in the affairs of life, and its practice has proved delightful or tedious according to people's differing tastes. To the ordinary citizen double entry has a slightly comic flavour and is held to have been invented about 1860 by some Italian warehousemen with the object of ensuring that fraud in accounts, rampant in other countries, should be from henceforward impossible within the limits of the British Empire.

More serious inquiry places the emergence of the double-entry technique in Italy and rather before than after the year 1300. In the course of foreign trade the method came at length to England and the manuscript ledger of a London merchant, Thomas Howell, for the years 1519 to 1527 is kept in this way. This book is now in the possession of the Drapers' Company.

Towards the end of the fifteenth century there were already one or more manuscript (possibly even printed) textbooks or simple sets of directions for the practice of double entry in circulation in North Italy, though no copies of such a text seem to have survived. One of these manuals was incorporated by the Franciscan, Luca Pacioli, in his comprehensive work on mathematics entitled *Summa de Arithmetica, Geometria, Proportioni et Proportionalità*, a folio printed at Venice in 1494. Pacioli has consequently had credit for the authorship of the first printed work on book-keeping, but it is much more likely that he adopted ready made this short treatise on a branch of applied mathematics just as we know that he did adopt, as part of the same section of his book, a treatise on foreign exchange. A separate edition of the latter manual printed at Florence thirteen years earlier is in existence.

The importance to us of Pacioli's *Summa* is that his book-keeping text formed the basis of books on double entry published in several other countries, among them England. The first of these recensions of " Pacioli " was published, of course without acknowledgment, by Hugh Oldcastle, a draper (or more accurately " shearman ") of Coleman Street, in 1543. No copy has, so far as is at present known,

* From *Accounting Research*, vol. 5, no. 3 (July, 1954), pp. 215–218, with amendments by the author.
† Former Librarian, Institute of Chartered Accountants, London.

been preserved, though one was still in existence in 1779, when it was sold by auction with the property of the collector and antiquary, Edward Rowe Mores. The sale catalogue, carefully prepared, as was his wont, by the auctioneer, S. Paterson, gives the cumbrous title of this earliest English work on accounting:

> *Here ensueth a profitable treatyce called the instrument or boke to learne to knowe the good order of the kepyng of the famouse reconyng, called in latyn Dare et Habere, and in Englyshe Debitor and Creditor,* b.l. impr. by Johan Gough, 1543.

The disappearance of this book is the less to be regretted as it had been reprinted in 1588 by John Mellis and copies of the re-issue are to be found in the British Museum and the Huntington Library as well as at the Institute of Chartered Accountants.

Shortly before the original publication of Oldcastle's book an Italian manuscript work on book-keeping came into the hands of a merchant of Antwerp, Jan Ympyn Christoffels, who published a Flemish version in 1543. From this a French translation was printed in the same year and it was from the French that an English translation was made and printed in 1547. The only known copy of the English translation was for many years preserved in the public library of the Esthonian town formerly known as Reval, now Tallin. In or before 1934 the book was removed to Russia, where it has lately come to light through the activity of Mr. R. R. Coomber. A microfilm copy has been furnished by the Russian authorities and is now in the British Museum. The text was, however, already known from Dr. P. de Waal's reprint in the *Economisch-Historisch Jaarboek* for 1934, reproduced in *The Accountant* with remarks by Mr. P. Kats in the same year. The book now consists of three gatherings of six leaves each (A B C) and one odd leaf, D 1: the examples called for in the text are missing. The small practical illustrations given in the text are dated 1547 and presumably the missing examples were also revised.

The book was printed by Richard Grafton, treasurer of Christ's Hospital and later Master and is the first of three manuals of double-entry book-keeping emanating from the Hospital within the next thirty years. Its title page is adorned with a woodcut border showing the descent of Henry VIII from John of Gaunt.

We now come to the earliest printed book-keeping text of purely English origin:

> *The maner and fourme how to kepe a perfecte reconyng, after the order of the moste worthie and notable accompte, of Debitour and Creditour, set foorthe in certain tables, with a declaracion therunto belongyng, verie easie to be learned, and also profitable, not onely unto suche, that trade in the facte of Marchaundise, but also unto any other estate, that will learne the same. 1553. Imprinted at London, by Richard Grafton, printer to the kinges Maiestie. Cum privilegio ad imprimendum solum*

Of this book the Institute of Chartered Accountants secured an almost perfect copy in 1913 from the estate of Karel Petr Kheil, a banker of Prague, and there is another copy, very defective, in the British Museum.

The author, James Peele, was for many years clerk at Christ's Hospital and the printer is again Richard Grafton. It seems, however, according to McKerrow and Ferguson's *Title Page Borders* (Bibliographical Society, 1932), that only the title-page was printed by Grafton, the rest of the work having been executed by other printers named J. Kingston and H. Sutton. This change can be readily explained as Grafton had been imprudent enough to print the proclamation of Lady Jane Grey as Queen and thereby brought down upon himself the vengeance of Queen Mary I. Kingston and Sutton, who formed a partnership to print Catholic service books in the same year, were obviously under no such displeasure and some arrangement must have been come to that they should finish the impression of Peele's book.

The copy of the *Maner and Fourme* belonging to the Institute of Chartered Accountants was bound in calf in the early part of the nineteenth century, probably for Tho. Kinnear whose signature is at the top of the title-page. The volume has been heavily pressed: the sewing of the quires is not visible and has been overcast for extra strength and consequently the collation long remained something of a puzzle. Signatures begin regularly A–B⁶, but thereafter cease except for a few odd ones. There are 87 leaves remaining and their order, judging by the text, is correct. Is the book complete, and what is the collation?

The most likely solution, that the book consisted of fourteen sixes with a four at the end, will not do because it does not fit the few remaining signatures after B6. Nor does a collation in fours or in alternate sixes and fours prove satisfactory. The correct collation was finally ascertained in the following way. The book is a folio and as usual each conjoint pair of leaves has a watermark in one leaf, the other remaining blank. Thus in a gathering of six leaves, if leaf 1 has a watermark, leaf 6 has not; if 2 has, 5 has not; if 3 has, 4 has not; and vice versa. In the book under consideration let us try to apply this to leaves 13–18, that is the part of the book immediately after the regular signatures stop. Alas! there are two leaves Ff. 14 and 17 which should, if the section is complete, be conjoint leaves, but neither of them has a watermark!

The solution was found by starting from the end of the book and assuming that the last section was perfect. All went well working backwards through 5 sections of sixes to L1. Conjoint leaves showed the watermark on one half and no watermark on the other. The next section, K, proved by the same method to be a four and the previous 7 sections, C–I, sixes with one leaf missing at the beginning of C. The absence of C1 was the root of the trouble and prevented the " watermark collation " from starting consistently.

The collation and contents then are as follows:

> *Collation:* A–I⁶ K⁴ L–P⁶ : 88 leaves; C1 missing.
>
> *Contents:* A1 *title,* A1b *contents,* A2 *dedicatory epistle to Sir William Densell,* A3 *preface,* A3b–B5 Necessary Rules or observacions of remembrance to be practised of a faithfull keper of his accoumpte, B5b An exhortation to learne sciences especially of the accompt in the trade of marchandise (*in verse*), B6 1553. Maye XXV. daie+The Journal . . . , B6b Rules to be observed (*in verse*), C1 missing (? blank), C2–D1 The Inventorie, D2 The Quaterne+, D3–H1 *index to the ledger* (+), H1b–K4 *the ledger* (+), L1 The Quaterne (A), L2–O5 *index to the quaterne* (A), O5b–P6 the quaterne (A), P6b The Jornall.

The British Museum copy of *Peele* is, as has been said, very defective and has been made up by photographs of the missing leaves taken from the copy at the Institute of Chartered Accountants. But the Museum copy even now does not contain the right number of leaves. A considerable proportion of Peele's book consists of leaves which are entirely blank except for a letter of the alphabet in the margin. These are leaves of the ledger index and from one of them in the Institute copy even the guide letter has been shorn away. The Museum photographer, weary in well doing, or perhaps not sharing the Bellman's taste for " a perfect and absolute blank," has failed to photograph this leaf or to insert a leaf of paper in its place!

The disappearance or extreme rarity of all of these earliest accounting books is easily explained. They were intended as instructional textbooks, proved unexpectedly popular and were used until they fell to pieces. Later books were no doubt printed in rather larger editions and, though all the sixteenth-century ones are very rare, they are not beyond all hope for the would-be collector.

James Peele himself published another more elaborate work on accounting in 1569, of which several copies are known. One of them has had a curious history. When the Huntington Library acquired the Bridgewater collection, complete with its original catalogue, Peele's second book was found marked as having been removed by the estate steward. Some years later the Huntington Library bought a copy of this book of Peele's from another source and it was found to contain the signature of the Bridgewater steward. Let us not be censorious after all these years. He may have made the entry in the catalogue himself and a servant of a family or institution will sometimes write his name in an official copy of a book in the hope that it will remain on his own desk and not wander to the desks of other servants of the same master.

Hugh Oldcastle and John Mellis*

R. R. Coomber †

THE first known book-keeping text in the English language was a book, the full title of which is *Here ensueth a profitable treatyce called the instrument or boke to learne to knowe the good order of the kepyng of the famouse reconyng, called in latyn Dare et Habere, and in Englyshe Debitor and Creditor.* No copy of it is known to have survived to the present day and the last known reference to it was in the catalogue issued in 1779 of the books belonging to Edward Rowe Mores, F.S.A., an actuary and one of the founders of the Equitable Life Assurance Society. It was a black letter quarto book, printed by one of the earliest of English printers, John Gough, in 1543.[1] By 1779 the book was already a rarity, and its title did not in fact figure in the first edition of Ames Typographical Antiquities in 1749, but was added by William Herbert after it had appeared in the Rowe Mores Catalogue. No name is given in the catalogue for the author of the book, and it was not until 1852 that B. F. Foster[2] added the name of the author as Hugh Oldcastle and thus identified it with the work which had been reprinted by Mellis in 1588.

Hugh Oldcastle[3] was the youngest son of Richard Oldcastle, a shearman carrying on his trade in Coleman Street in the City of London. The will of Richard Oldcastle has been traced and it appears that Hugh was alive when the will was made in 1510 although the exact date of his birth is unknown. Richard Oldcastle died in 1520 and by his will left to Hugh, his youngest son, certain property in Almeley in Herefordshire which formerly belonged to Sir John Oldcastle the martyr, an ancestor of the family. Hugh does not appear to have taken possession of his inheritance, for he figures in 1533 in a Chancery action claiming the delivery of evidence which would enable him to obtain possession of the property and in another action for the delivery of evidence which would enable him to obtain

---

* From *Accounting Research*, vol. 7, no. 2 (April 1956), pp. 201–216.
† Chartered and Incorporated Accountant.
1 Gough put out most of his printing and the *Profitable Treatyce* may well have been printed for him by John Mayler (see E. Gordon Duff, *A Century of the English Book Trade* [London, 1948], pp. 58 and 110). Gough died in October, 1543.
2 *The Origin and Progress of Book-keeping* (London, 1852).
3 Most of the biographical details on Hugh Oldcastle appeared in an article in *The Accountant*, March 23, 1940, by Mr. Cosmo Gordon and myself under the pseudonym Paul Sutherland.

206

possession of certain other lands at Benthall in Shropshire. In neither of these actions does he seem to have been successful. About the same time his name is mentioned as presenting a supplication to Thomas Cromwell, and two more entries record in 1538 payments to him of 10s. and 20s. by Thomas Avery, Cromwell's clerk.

The Oldcastle family were thus people of substance; Richard Oldcastle, apart from his claim to the Almely property, owned land at Eltham in Kent, which was left to Hugh's eldest brother Henry, who inherited it and was buried in the parish church where a memorial was formerly erected to him. Henry Oldcastle's will is registered in the Rochester probate records. It was proved in 1523 and is of interest in that Henry is described as of Eltham and St. Olave's next the Tower of London, the parish in which, according to Mellis, Hugh Oldcastle lived; one of the overseers appointed by Henry for the execution of his will was Richard Homan whose name figures in Richard Oldcastle's will as the latter's godson and servant. The curate of St. Olave's was a witness.

Hugh Oldcastle appears to have died early in 1543 for there is a record in the index of the Commissary Court of London of the grant of administration to his widow, Anice, of " the goods of Hugh Old-castle, of the parish of St. Olave in Hart Street, who recently died intestate "; the entry is dated the last day of February, 1542, *i.e.*, 1543 New Style.[4]

It is a curious fact that the character Falstaff was first named Oldcastle by Shakespeare, and there is still a reminder of the original name in *Henry IV* where Falstaff is referred to as " my old lad of the castle." It has been suggested that the alteration of the name was at the instance of some member of the family of sufficient importance at that time to secure it.[5] The fact that the alteration was secured gives some evidence of the standing of the family of which the book-keeping author was a (possibly humble) member.

The only other information we have about Hugh Oldcastle is that according to Mellis, who issued a reprint of his work, he taught arithmetic and book-keeping in the Parish of St. Olave's, Mark Lane (or Hart Street), and that his book was published on August 14, 1543.

---

4 This was a fairly recent find, and in commenting on it Mr. Cosmo Gordon says in a letter to the author: " The fact that Hugh died intestate adds to the picture of him as a rather disappointed man since he had been unable to establish his right to the property at Almeley and not bothering to make a will as he had little or nothing to leave." The administration is recorded in the Story register of the Commissary Court of London, p. 27, M.S. 9171/11.

5 Sir Sidney Lee, *A Life of William Shakespeare* (London, 1915). Sir Sidney Lee suggests that this was Lord Cobham, but the Elizabethan Lord Cobham was not a descendant of Sir John Oldcastle, who was Baron Cobham only by right of his wife; in a private communication Professor Taylor of Clemson has suggested that it was more likely to have resulted from representations by descendants of Sir John's brother and sister who, he states, included the Earl of Essex and Baron Hunsdon.

The date of publication is thus some six months after Hugh Oldcastle's death, and publication must therefore have been arranged by his widow. It seems that the book was used in manuscript form for teaching purposes by its author who may or may not have intended publication. In Chapter 14 he says he has only written this treatise for a direction or instruction to a greater matter; the meaning of the sentence is rather obscure, but could indicate that the manuscript used by his pupils was intended to be succeeded by a more extensive treatment of the subject which might or might not be published.

It is a curious coincidence that in the precise year that Hugh Oldcastle's work was published presumably on behalf of his widow, another widow, in Antwerp, was arranging for the publication of another book on book-keeping (in Flemish and French) left by her husband, Jan Ympyn.

Thomas Mellis, who republished the Oldcastle text in 1588, was a schoolmaster and teacher of arithmetic in another London parish of St. Olave's—St. Olave's, Southwark, where for some years he lived at Mayes Gate, near Battle Bridge. He was at one time assistant to Dr. Forth at Cambridge; he was responsible for the reissue and enlargement of a standard book on arithmetic, Robert Record's *Arithmetick or the Ground of Arts*. In the preface to the reader in the reissue of Oldcastle's work, which was then entitled *A briefe instruction and maner how to keepe bookes of Accompts after the order of Debitor and Creditor*, he said: " And knowe ye for certaine, that I presume ne usurpe not to set forth this worke of mine owne labour and industrie, for truely, I am but the renuer and reviver of an auncient old copie printed here in London the 14 of August 1543. Then collected, published, made and set forth by one Hugh Oldcastle Scholemaster, who as appeareth by his treatise then taught Arithmetike and this booke in St. Ollaues Parish in Marke lane." It is curious, by the way, that Mellis was able to find this in the old copy of the *Profitable Treatyce*, for Paterson who compiled the Rowe Mores catalogue in 1779 did not even trace the name of the author. It might be, of course, that the (front) page containing this information was missing in the copy owned by Rowe Mores. It is almost certain, however, that Mellis was working from a copy of the *Profitable Treatyce*, for later he says: " with these three bookes " (*i.e.*, the ledger, the journal and the memorial) " is this famous reckoning ordered and guyded which reckoning in the parts of Italie is named Dare & Habere. Which in our language of English is called Debitor and Creditor "; the echo in this sentence of the title of the *Profitable Treatyce* given above is unmistakable.

The evidence that the author of the book republished by Mellis was in fact the Hugh Oldcastle referred to in the Oldcastle wills is strong; the identity of this book with the *Profitable Treatyce* rests on the date of publication (1543) and this echo of the title in Mellis's preface to the reader.

By the time the book was reissued in 1588 other books on book-keeping had appeared in the English language, namely the translation of the work by Ympyn in 1547, the two books by Peele of 1553 and 1569; and Mellis, who said that he enlarged and beautified the original, is almost certain to have been influenced by them and also possibly by Pacioli's treatise of 1494 which may or may not have been known to Oldcastle himself. Mr. P. Kats, in an article in *The Accountant* in March, 1926, attempted by a careful comparison of the text of Mellis/Oldcastle with those of Pacioli and Peele to distinguish between Oldcastle's original work and the grafting of Mellis. The extent of Mellis's additions is difficult to assess however; he certainly added a fairly full example of a set of accounts at the end of the text " for the better and plainer understanding and practice of these rules "; various illustrations in the course of the text also bear dates of 1587, most likely indicating that they were not in the original. In Chapter VII there is an illustration of a memorial relating to the affairs of Philip Mellis.

The registers of the Stationers' Company do not start until 1554, and therefore contain no references to the publication of the *Profitable Treatyce*; there are three entries relating to the reissue by Mellis: the first in 1587 records the payment of VId. by Wyndet and Singleton for printing; the second in 1611 records the acquisition by William Stansby of the printing rights of this and other books belonging previously to Windett; the third is in a list of publications in 1588 where Mellis is described as the editor, with a note of the first edition on August 14, 1543, by Henry Oldcastle (*sic*).[6]

As noted above it was not until 1852 that Oldcastle was first stated to be the author of the *Profitable Treatyce* identifying it with the book reissued by Mellis. Benjamin Franklin Foster, in his book *The Origin and Progress of Book-keeping,* seems to imply in the preface [7] that he saw it with other old book-keeping texts through August de Morgan who in his own list of books on arithmetic [8] coupled the Mellis reprint with the *Profitable Treatyce* but without naming the author. An attempt to trace Foster's own books in case they included

---

[6] Transcript of Stationers' Registers, vol. V, 3548. The incorrect reference to Henry Oldcastle is curious; the brother of this name died in 1523.

[7] Foster says that the books dealt with by him in the work were all in his possession with the exception of " Oldcastle 1543; Mellis 1588; Collins 1652 and Peele 1659 (*sic*) "; he continues: " but these I have seen as well as the two celebrated works of Pacioli and Simon Stevin and I am indebted to the politeness of Professor de Morgan for an opportunity of inspecting several of the above rare and curious publications."

[8] *Arithmetical books from the invention of printing to the present time* (London, 1847).

Oldcastle has not succeeded; after practising as a teacher of writing and book-keeping in the Strand in London Foster emigrated to America and the latest information obtained about his books was that there was a " legend " that a large case containing them was lost at sea! Whether Foster did in fact see the original *Profitable Treatyce* is open to doubt; if he did, he obtained and passed on nothing about the contents, and one would give a lot to have had even a manuscript copy such as was made of the English translation of Ympyn when it was found about sixty years ago in Russia.

Oldcastle's book and its influence

Owing to its similarity to the text of Pacioli, it was formerly thought that Oldcastle's work was a more or less direct translation of the former. There are, however, a number of differences both in style and content. As Kats showed, some of the chapters in Pacioli's book are completely missing in the Mellis/Oldcastle work, and the latter also has many phrases and precepts in Latin which are absent in Pacioli. The suggestion has been put forward that both Pacioli's and Oldcastle's books derive from a (possibly manuscript) set of rules or tract, in Oldcastle's case probably written in Latin, and which Pacioli embodied in his *Summa de Computis et Scripturis,* in both instances the debt to the author of the tract being unacknowledged. It could possibly have been derived from a copy of the work of which no example has survived, by Juan Paolo di Bianchi, which Ympyn said that he had translated from Italian into French.[9] A book by Cotrugli, although published in 1573, had existed in manuscript form since 1458 and thus pre-dated Pacioli's work.

Oldcastle's book consisted of twenty-five chapters. In the course of them various examples are given of journal entries and the like, all with dates of 1587 bearing witness to the revision by Mellis. The book of 1543 appears also to have contained no worked example such as were given later in the books by Ympyn and Peele,[10] for at the end of the twenty-fifth chapter Mellis, after the word " Finis " adds " Here endeth my Authour, and for the better and plainer understanding and practice of these rules, I have hereunto added a little Inventorie, Journal, and Leager, as followeth; with a briefe Treatise of Arithmetick." Mellis finishes with the words: " If wishes might

---

[9] Ympyn's work published by his widow appeared in Dutch and French in 1543 and in English in 1547. In the prologue appear the words " it fortuned me to get a copy of the work of the said Juan Paolo written in his language which I translated into French."

[10] According to Professor R. de Roover the first textbook to include a practical example was by G. A. Tagliente, published in Venice in 1525. (See R. de Roover, *La Formation et l'Expansion de la Comptabilité à partie double* [Paris, 1937], p. 34.) There was, however, a worked example, although not of the full double-entry system, in a book by Heinrich Schreiber published in Nürnberg in 1518.

serve, I would I were present with any learner that is at a stay or in doubt. Iterum Vale. John Mellis." The example concerns the affairs of " N. A. Citizen and N. of London " [11] and commences with an inventory dated August 8, 1587, which, contrary to the practice recommended in parts of the text, but following Ympyn and Peele, is posted direct to the ledger and not by means of journal entry; only the net difference between the total of the inventory and the debts due by the merchant is posted to the credit of stock (or capital) account.

In his preface to the reader Mellis says that he had kept Oldcastle's book by him for thirty years for his own " private knowledge and furtherance " and because " this small volume is a jewell so commodious " at the earnest request of a friend he now published it. Its worth either in its original or republished form does not appear to have been widely recognised; Peele's work (1553) contains many passages closely similar to the Oldcastle book but this may result from a common derivation; Dafforne writing in 1636 refers to several earlier writers on book-keeping including James Peele, but not Oldcastle. On the other hand a book by John Carpenter published in 1632 contains passages from Oldcastle including the eighth chapter almost literally, but without acknowledgment. No further reference has been traced to the book until Kelly writing in 1801 mentioned it, giving the title of Oldcastle's work as republished by Mellis. Nevertheless, although not directly acknowledged, Oldcastle's book may have had considerable influence on other writers of his day. Mellis, who speaks so warmly in praise of it, can hardly have been alone in his appreciation.

Some Account of the Work

The system of book-keeping is based on the use of three main books: the memorial (or waste-book), the journal and the ledger, although it is noted (Chapter V) that some merchants in a small way of business use only the journal and the ledger.

The process started with the taking of an inventory, setting out all the merchant's substance (not merely his trading assets), his movable and immovable property, debts due to him, gold and silver, and deducting the amounts he owed to arrive at his net stock (or capital). It is recommended that the inventory should be recorded in a " secret quaire " or book and entered directly from there to the journal for posting to the ledger and not via the memorial which came to the sight of many persons.

The memorial or waste-book was entered by the master or his servants and anybody of the household who could write, and records

---

[11] This is a very early example of the use of initials in the description of the trader keeping books. The " N " in the description refers probably to N.A.'s trade.

the daily business in simple terms. The need is stressed for the book to be marked *A* (*cf.* Pacioli who suggested a cross for the first set, then *A*) and the first leaf to contain the date and title. From the memorial or waste-book the entries are to be transcribed to the journal in a form suitable for posting to the ledger. The memorial and the inventory needed no special ruling but a fair space to set the sums. The entries in the memorial are to be detailed and at length, not only as regards the subject of the transaction but also the terms and conditions of payment.

The second book, the journal, is to be marked and have its leaves numbered like the memorial. The entries are to be made in terms of the currency of the merchant, entries in the memorial being converted into this where necessary. The journal is provided with one money column, and each entry is a simple one with one debit and one credit posting to the ledger, the folios being shown in the form of a fraction in the margin. Two terms are noted here—" capsa " being chest or ready money and " capital " the substance of a man's goods or his stock. The journal is to be written in shorter terms than the entries in the memorial. In entering the journal the debtor is described as the name of the debtor, receiver or borrower; the creditor as the name of the creditor, deliverer or lender, and the rule is given that all things received, or the receiver, must owe to all things delivered or the deliverer.

The entries are in a narrative form and this, for example, is the record in the journal of the money in hand at the time the inventory was taken: —

> Chest or money is Debitor (or oweth) [12] to stock belonging to mee, M.N., and is for pounds, shillings and pence, so many etc., or duckets so many etc., expressing the name, number and value as appeareth in such a leafe or folio of your Inventory etc., amounting to the summe of £00 00s. 00d.   li.   s.   d.[13]

Again, if money is received of any man, the debtor and creditor relationship is to be expressed by saying, " Money owes to William

---

[12] An alternative wording given elsewhere is " Chyst or ready money ought to give me."

[13] The entry made by Pacioli in the journal to record the same matter was the following:

8th of November MCCCCLXXXXIII. Venice

" Per " Cash " A " Capital of myself for so much

Debitor 1   cash etc., which I have in such and such a place, in gold, coin, silver, and copper of various coinage as appears in the Inventory sheet posted in cash,

Creditor 2   in all so many ducats in gold, and in coins, so many ducats. In our Venetian money it is all valued in gold, that is, in *grossi* 24 per ducat, and in *picioli* 32 per grosso, so many gold *lire*.

L . . . S . . . G . . . P . . .

No money column is provided. (P. Crivelli, *Pacioli's Treatise on Double-Entry Book-keeping* [London, 1924], p. 26.)

Hall "; if money is paid, " James Wilch owes to money "; if goods are sold, " Henry Par owes to cloths."

It is recommended that the entries in the memorial should be entered in the journal within five or six days.

The third principal book is called the ledger, to be marked like the memorial and journal and with its leaves numbered. The left side is debtor and the right creditor, and a small space provided towards the left hand on each side is to serve to record the number or quantity of cloths or hogs-heads, etc. There is no provision in the system for a cash-book but it is suggested that the first leaf in the ledger should be used for the account of money or chest as this is the most occupied. The debit side of the chest account records " what money you borrow or receive " from any person or for any goods sold; the credit side shows in brief sentences where the estate of the chest is bestowed—what money you deliver or pay out to any person. The entries in the ledger are to be referenced not to the journal folio, but each to the other's ledger folio.

The name of the account is not set out at the head but contained in the opening words of the first entry, debit or credit. Thus, for example, the first two entries on the credit side of the cash account are:

1587 fol. 1

August 12

The accompt of the chyst or ready money is due to have li. s. d. and is for so much lent R. Bas in his accompt in debtor folio   li.   s.   d.
As more li. s. d. for so much paid to W.C. as in his accompt in debtor folio   li.   s.   d.

When the debit or credit side is full, the balance is transferred to a new folio and marked " R " for rest.

In addition to the personal accounts, the ledger contains: (a) an account for each main type of goods which were dealt in, the account being debited with the cost of purchases and credited with sales, the final balance representing loss or profit; (b) an ordinary expense account containing costs and expenses of merchandise, such expenses being ultimately posted to the appropriate goods accounts, and also extraordinary expenses such as " flesh, wines, ale, beer, rent, etc." ultimately transferred from this account to profit and loss account; (c) a profit or loss account or otherwise lucrum or damnum; and (d) a stock or capital account. Entries are made in the money column in Arabic numerals, with Roman numerals in the body of the entry; totals in the ledger are inserted, in Arabic numerals, not in the money columns but in the middle of the narrative space. This contrasts with Pacioli who used Roman numerals only; on the other hand Ympyn used Arabic numerals in the text and Roman in the money column.

The books are to be balanced when a new ledger is started which might be done annually or when the old ledger was full (Chapters VI and XXI). Chapter XXI contains directions for checking and calling over the postings from the journal to the ledger. In Chapter XXV the making of a trial balance on a sheet of paper is described; if the sum of the debtor balances is equal to that of the creditor balances, " than is your ballance well, and appeareth evidently, that your bookes have been orderly kept & governed." In the example which Mellis added, borrowing from later practice, he introduced a balance account in the ledger itself, to which all accounts were closed at the time of balancing, the accounts being reopened at the commencement of the new period.

On the debit side of the profit and loss account in the ledger the. author places all losses sustained and on the credit all things gained. The account is debited or credited with the loss or profit when any account of goods in the ledger was all sold. Profit and loss account was also charged with any extraordinary expenses (see above). At the time of closing the books the profit and loss account is to be cleared by a transfer to stock (capital) account.

The conception of an annual measurement of profit or loss was not, at least in theoretical book-keeping, a primary concern. Trade consisted in many cases of a series of ventures of greater or less duration, and the need for a strict computation of net worth arose only on the occurrence of an unusual event such as death or a dissolution of partnership. Problems such as those arising out of the accounting records for depreciation are not considered although in the worked example in the account for household implements covering the period August 8 to October 9, 1587, the opening balance is shown at £69 9s. 4d.; the closing balance is £58 19s. 4d. The difference of £10 10s. is described as " for so much as I doe finde at this day to be consumed and worn, which said Xli. Xs. for the decay of the said householde stuffe is borne to profit and loss in debtor." It is not clear whether or not the closing balance represents a fresh appraisal; it seems unlikely in view of the short period covered by the account and the point is not dealt with in the text.

Oldcastle gives rules for the keeping of the books of a company (or partnership); they consist either of a full separate set of books, or of accounts within the individual's own book-keeping system. Operations in partnership, however, seem to have been exceptional and for a limited period or purpose.

Origin of the Trial Balance

Edward Peragallo*

DOUBLE-ENTRY book-keeping and its procedures found their inception in the spectacular expansion of commerce that occurred in Italy after the Crusades. The inadequacy of the crude record-keeping procedures in use at that time made it imperative to devise more efficient methods of book-keeping to record the increasing flow of complex transactions of a fast-growing foreign trade. From this mammoth growth of business, double entry gradually evolved. It is fairly well established that it originated and developed in Italy during the thirteenth and fourteenth centuries, though the exact time, manner, and locality are a matter for conjecture. The paucity of merchants' records which have survived from this early period is the reason for this uncertainty.[1]

Because of this lack of basic business data, scholars have turned to the study of the works of the early writers on double-entry book-keeping. The first known work of importance to appear was Pacioli's *Summa*, published in 1494, in which he includes a treatise on the double-entry system then current in Venice.[2] This, however, was at the end of the fifteenth century and double entry had already been in use for a long time. The earliest known double-entry records, fragmentary though they be, are the " Massari Ledgers " of 1340 [3] of the Commune of Genoa, which date a century and a half earlier. Pacioli's *Summa*, because of its late appearance, yields very little light on the origins of double-entry procedures. The system he describes is a mature system, fully developed and thoroughly tested by the exigencies of trade.

The ambiguity of terminology in the works of the early writers on book-keeping has caused confusion among recent writers about the nature of some of the recording procedures and the manner in which

---

* Professor and Chairman of the Department of Accounting and Economics, College of the Holy Cross, Worcester, Massachusetts.
[1] E. Peragallo, *Origin and Evolution of Double Entry Bookkeeping* (New York, 1938), p. 1.
[2] Luca Pacioli ; *Summa de Arithmetica Geometria Proportioni et Proportionalita. Distintio Nona-Tractatus XI, Particularis de computis et scripturis* (Venice, 1494).
[3] Raymond de Roover states that additional original sources have recently been uncovered in Florence which, if they prove to be double entry, would date the earliest known double-entry records as (at least) 1296 instead of the 1340 of the Massari Ledgers. (" New Perspectives on the History of Accounting," *Accounting Review*, XXX [1955], pp. 405–420.)

they were applied.   The trial balance is one such procedure.   Lack of clearness in Pacioli's text is responsible for the belief that both the *bilancio del libro* (balance of the ledger) and the *summa summarum* (sum of sums), as described by Pacioli, were trial balances and that the two terms refer to the same book-keeping procedure.   But this is not so.   They refer to two separate and distinct procedures.   To clear the issue, both procedures will be described and traced through the writings of the principal authors of the fifteenth and sixteenth centuries.

The *bilancio del libro*, as explained by Pacioli, concerns the basic characteristic of duality of entries in the ledger kept on a double-entry basis, and the check on this duality of entries by a trial balance.   In Chapter 14 of his *Summa*, Pacioli clearly delineates the need to maintain the duality of entries when he says: " . . . and therefore never must an amount be entered in credit which is not also entered in the same amount in debit." [4]

The duality of entries of the ledger thus established, Pacioli then turns his attention to the trial balance as a check on the equality of the debits and credits.   In Chapter 36 he says: " The [trial] balance of the ledger is understood to be a sheet of paper creased lengthwise on the right hand of which are copied the credits of the ledger and on the left hand the debits; and check if the sum of the debits is the same as that of the credits, and if that is so the ledger is correct." [5]   The same point is made, but less succinctly, in Chapter 14.

Despite previous statements of the writer to the contrary,[6] it is obvious that Pacioli was fully aware of the true construction and function of the trial balance.   Yamey stated this correctly, but unfortunately referred to Manzoni's *summa delle summe* as a proper trial balance.[7]   Hatfield also made the same mistake when he identified Pacioli's *summa summarum* as a trial balance.[8]

Pacioli uses his *summa summarum*, literally the " sum of sums," as a final proof of the closing of a ledger whose balances are transferred to a new ledger.   He explains this closing procedure at some length.   In Chapter 32 he begins by saying: " . . . now one must state the method of transferring one ledger to another, when one wants

---

4 Pacioli, *op. cit.*, Chap. 34: " . . . e cosí mai si deve mettere cosa in avere che ancora quella medesima con suo ammontare non si metta in dare."
5 Pacioli, *ibid.*, Chap. 36: " Il Bilancio del Libro s'intende un foglio piegato per lo lungo sul quale dalla mano destra si copiano i creditori del Libro e dalla sinistra i debitori; e vedi se la somma del dare é quanto quella dell'avere, e allora il Libro sta bene."
6 Peragallo, *op. cit.*, p. 64; and " Origin of the Trial Balance," *Journal of Accountancy*, LXXII (1941), p. 448.
7 Basil S. Yamey, *The Functional Development of Double-Entry Bookkeeping*, Accounting Research Association Bulletin no. 7 (London, 1940), p. 22.
8 Henry Rand Hatfield, " Neither Pietra nor Flori," *Journal of Accountancy*, LXXV (1943), p. 165.

to change ledger because it is full, or because of a new year, the latter
being customary to do in famous places, where leading merchants
observe the practice every year. And this act together with the
following is called the balancing of the ledger [*bilancio del libro*]." [9]
This latter, incidentally, illustrates another use of the term *bilancio del
libro*. The variety of meanings which Pacioli attached to this term is
probably the reason for some of the confusion that has occurred.

In Chapter 34 of his *Summa* Pacioli gives a detailed exposition of
the ledger-closing procedure. He begins with the closing of accounts
which are to be transferred direct from the "Cross" ledger to the
"A" ledger,[10] such as cash, capital, merchandise, fixtures, establishments, debtors, creditors, etc. But, says Pacioli, there are certain
accounts which one may not wish to transfer to the new ledger, such
as expenses and income. These accounts are of a private nature and
should therefore be closed into the profit-and-loss account, the latter
in turn being closed into the capital account. The capital account,
following the similar treatment of the asset and liability accounts, is
then closed and its balance transferred to the new ledger. This is
usually the last entry, which finally closes the old ledger.[11]

At this point Pacioli introduces his *summa summarum*. He says:
" And in this manner, [as set out in the preceding paragraph] is closed
all of the first ledger with its journal and memorandum book. And
so that this will be clearer, the following additional check of ledger-
closing will be made: That is, add all the debit entries [of each
account] of the Cross ledger [the old closed ledger] and place them on
the left-hand side of a sheet of paper, and add all the credit entries [of
each account] and place them on the right-hand side; and now add these
other sums and the total sum of all the debits will be called *summa
summarum,* and the same will be done of all the credits which total

---

[9] Pacioli, *op. cit.*, Chap. 32: ". . . bisogna ora dar modo al riporto di un Libro
in altro, quando volessi mutar Libro per cagion che fosse pieno, ovvero per
ordine annuale di millesimo, come il piú si costuma fare per luoghi famosi, che
ogni anno, massime a millesimi nuovi, i gran mercatanti sempre lo osservano.
E questo atto insieme con li seguenti é ditto *Bilancio del Libro*."

[10] It was the practice in early double-entry book-keeping to distinguish the ledgers
of succeeding periods with letters, the first one beginning with + (the sign of
the Cross), the next with *A*, and the rest following alphabetically.

[11] Pacioli, *ibid.*, Chap. 34: " E così anderai saldando tutte le partite nel Libro
croci, che tu intendi portare in Quaderno A, di Cassa, Cavedal, robe, mobili,
stabili, debitori, creditori, uffici, sensarie, pesadori di comune, ecc. coi quali si usa
alle volte andare a conto lungo. Ma quelle partite che non volessi portare in
ditto Quaderno A (che potrieno essere quelle che solo a te s'appartengono, e non
sei obbligato a segnare conto ad alcuno, come son spese di mercanzia, spese di
casa, entrata, uscita e tutte spese straordinarie, fitti, pensioni, feudi o livelli . . .)
queste simili convengonsi saldare nel medesimo Libro croci nella partita del Prò
et Danno . . . E così tutte le avrai saldate in questa del Prò et Danno, dove subito
poi, somando sua dare e avere, potrai conoscere tuo guadagno e perdita . . .
E veduto che avrai per questo l'utile e danno tuo seguito, allora questo salderai
nella partita del Cavedale, dove nel principio del tuo maneggio ponesti lo
inventario di tutta la tua facoltà. . . .'"

will also be called *summa summarum*; . . . Now if these two *summe summarum* are equal . . . it will be reasoned that the ledger was well managed, kept and closed . . . but if one of the two *summe summarum* is larger than the other then that would denote an error in the ledger." [12]

At first this may appear to be a trial balance, but a closer examination will disclose that this is not the case. Pacioli makes the *summa summarum* after the balances of all open accounts, with the exception of the nominal accounts, have been transferred direct to the new ledger, without first routing them through the capital account or any formal balance account. After this the old ledger is bound to balance in all cases, even if it had been full of errors, because the two sides of each account have been made equal by inserting its balance to transfer to the new ledger. A trial balance of a closed ledger is no trial balance at all.

This obviously means that Pacioli used his *summa summarum* to serve exactly the purpose he intended, which is to prove the correctness of the closing of the ledger, and not for the purpose of a trial balance in the modern sense. If one takes a supposedly closed ledger and adds up all the debits on the one hand and all the credits on the other and there should happen to be among these an account not yet closed, it is obvious the two totals will not be equal. Naturally, this will indicate that the ledger is not completely closed. This is exactly what Pacioli wanted to find out with his *summa summarum*. It is the last step in his ledger-closing procedure, and it is not in any sense a trial balance as we understand it.

Pacioli, however, was also aware of the use of the trial balance as a guide for the transferring of accounts from one ledger to another. In the last few paragraphs of his last chapter, he says: " If the ledger is filled or old, and you want to transfer its accounts to a new ledger, proceed as follows: . . . take off the trial balance [bilancio del libro] of the old ledger and be certain that it is correct and equal, as it necessarily must be, and from this trial balance copy all the credits and the debits into the new ledger, all in the order they appear in the

---

[12] Pacioli, *ibid.*, Chap. 34: " E così sia saldo tutto il primo Quaderno con suo giornale e Memoriale. E acciò sia più chiaro, di ditto saldo farai questo altro scontro: cioè sommerai in un foglio tutto il dare del Quaderno croci e ponlo a man sinistra, e sommerai tutto suo avere e ponlo a man destra; e poi queste ultime somme risommerai e farane di tutte quelle del dare una somma che si chiamerà *summa summarum*, e così farai una somma di tutte quelle dell'avere che si chiamerà ancor lei una *summa summarum*; ma la *1a* sarà *summa summarum* del dare, e la *2a* si chiama *summa summarum* dell'avere. Ora se queste due *summe summarum* saranno pari, cioè che tanto sia l'una quanto l'altra uguali, quella del dare e quella dell'avere, arguirai il tuo Quaderno essere ben guidato, tenuto e saldato, per la cagione che di sopra nel capo 14 fu ditto; ma se l'una di ditte *summe summarum* avanzasse l'altra dinoterebbe errore nel tuo Quaderno."

trial balance, leaving sufficient space between each account as you think will be needed. . . . In this manner the old ledger is transferred to the new ledger. Now in order to cancel the old ledger it would be wise to close each open account using the trial balance as a guide, that is, if an open account in the old ledger is a credit, as you will notice in the trial balance, debit it saying: ' the credit balance of this account is entered as a credit in the new ledger on page . . . ' And in this manner you will have closed the old ledger and opened the new ledger." [13]

In effect, Pacioli uses the trial balance in this instance as a balance account, the only difference being that it was not included as an account in the old ledger, but was drawn up as a separate statement outside the ledger. It should be observed, however, that in practice, book-keepers were already using the balance account as an account in the ledger for a good many years before Pacioli. Andrea Barbarigo, a Venetian merchant, used such an account in his records of 1434.[14] Apparently both procedures were in use at that time.

It may be of interest to note that the type of *bilancio del libro* we are considering is also a post-closing trial balance, because it is drawn up after the nominal accounts have been closed into the capital account. Furthermore, it should also be noted that in the ledger-closing procedure described by Pacioli, the trial balance (*bilancio del libro*) is drawn up first before the transferring of the accounts, whereas the *summa summarum* is prepared from the accounts of the old ledger only after they have been closed and their balances transferred to a new ledger. This should be convincing proof that Pacioli was describing two separate procedures when he was writing about the *bilancio del libro* and the *summa summarum*.

It is, therefore, evident that Pacioli fully understood the trial balance and its uses as a check on the equality of the debits and credits and as a guide for the transferring of accounts from one ledger to another. It is also evident that the trial balance was fully known and in general use at the end of the fifteenth century, since Pacioli himself says that he is merely describing the Venetian method of

---

[13] Pacioli, *ibid.*, Chap. 36: " Quando il Libro fosse tutto pieno o vecchio, e tu volessi ridurlo a uno altro Libro nuovo, fa così: . . . E di poi levare il Bilancio del Libro vecchio che sia giusto e pari, come debbe essere, e da quello Bilancio copiare tutti i creditori e debitori in sul Libro nuovo, tutti per ordine come elli stanno in sul Bilancio, e fare i debitori e creditori ciascuno da per sè e lascia tanto spazio quanto tu arbitri avere a travagliare con seco. . . . E così è ridotto al Libro nouva. Ora per cancellare il Libro vecchio ti conviene a ciascun conto acceso, ispengnerlo con lo Bilancio sopra ditto, cioè se uno conto del Libro vecchio sarà creditore, che lo vederai per lo Bilancio, faralo debitore, e dirai: per tanti resta avere a questo conto posto debbe avere al Libro nuovo segnato B a carte. . . . E così avrai spento tutto il Libro vecchio e acceso il Libro nuovo.
[14] Fabio Besta, *La ragioneria* (Milan, 1929), vol. 3, p. 308.

book-keeping, " which among all others it is certainly the best." [15]
What is not so clear is whether use was made of Pacioli's *summa
summarum* in the book-keeping of the day.   Whereas the trial
balance remained an accepted book-keeping procedure, the *summa
summarum,* as it had originally been conceived, seems to have had
a short existence.

Manzoni, who published his *Quaderno Doppio* in 1540, continued
to use the *summa summarum.*[16]   His work is important because of
the set of double-entry books which accompany his text, the latter
itself being nothing more than a copy of Pacioli's with minor changes.
This should not be surprising considering that plagiarism was a
common practice until recent times.

A study of his double-entry books shows that Manzoni clearly
understood the basic characteristic of duality of entries.   However
one looks in vain for a trial balance.   Curiously, he correctly describes
it in his text, but, since it is taken verbatim from Pacioli, it is to be
wondered if he really understood it.   Furthermore, in Chapter four,
where he describes the trial balance [*bilancio del libro*], he refers the
reader to his *summa delle summe* in his worked example as an illustration of it.   This is nothing more than Pacioli's *summa summarum,*
the last test of a closed ledger, worked out exactly according to
Pacioli's instructions.   It is not a trial balance at all.[17]

It seems rather odd that, having understood the basic characteristic
of duality of entries, Manzoni should not have fathomed the true
nature of a trial balance.   But that seems to have been the case.
Nowhere in his set of double-entry books does he have a trial balance.

Three years later in England, Oldcastle (as reprinted by John
Mellis in 1588) [18] correctly reiterates the description of a trial balance.
He says in Chapter 25: " The ballance of your booke is to be under-
stoode, a leafe of paper disposed and made in length and cressed in
the middes, in such wise that it haue two faces in plaine sighte, uppon
which leafe on the right side, yee shal copy al the Creditors, with the
restes according to your Leager, and uppon the left side the Debitors,
with their rests according.   That don, beholde if that the summe of
the Debitor, be as much as is the summe of the Creditor, and yf the
summes of money, of Debitor and Creditor bee like, than is your

[15] Pacioli, *ibid.,* Chap. 1: " E servaremo in esso il modo di Vinegia, quale certa-
mente fra gli altri è molto da commendare e mediante quello in ogni altro si
possa guidare."
[16] Domenico Manzoni, *Quaderno Doppio col suo Giornale, secondo il costume di
Venezia* (Venice, 1540).
[17] An extract of a *summa del summe* from Manzoni's worked example is reproduced on p. 64 of my book. This shows that every entry has debit and credit
equal, and the same account title (*e.g.,* cash) often appears more than once, as
balances have been carried forward from one page to another in the ledger.
[18] On the works of Oldcastle and Mellis, see pp. 206–214, above [Eds.].

ballance well, and appeareth evidently, that your bookes haue been orderly kept & gouerned." Manifestly, Oldcastle, as Manzoni did before him, based his work on Pacioli's or some version of it. This is an eloquent testimony to the wide appeal of double-entry book-keeping and of its spread throughout Europe in the wake of trade.

. In the same year, 1543, Ympyn published his noteworthy *Nieuwe Instructie* in Antwerp. It was immediately translated into French in 1543, with the distinction of being the first book on double entry to be published in that language, and was also rendered into English in 1547. As in the case of Oldcastle, Ympyn correctly describes the trial balance. In Chapter 25 of the English version he writes: " And this ballaunce shall ye make in suche maner as the exemplary shall shewe you, where ye shall finde all parcelles brought together as it wer on an heape in one shete of paper, that is to saie, al that is owyng on the one side, and al that is to discharge it withal on the other side. When ye haue doen this, then shall ye note in a paper the somes on bothe sides, and if the somes come bothe a like, then is there none error or faute committed in your boke, which seldome happeneth. . . ." [19]

Ympyn, however, is the first author to use the balance account proper as an account in the ledger. An example appears in his set of books which accompany the text.[20] The procedure he uses is simple and direct. He first of all transfers the balances of the various merchandise accounts to a " remaining goods " account. He then transfers all the nominal accounts to the profit-and-loss account, the latter then being closed into the capital account. He finally transfers all the remaining open accounts to the balance account, thus closing the ledger. The sum of the debits and the sum of the credits of the balance account are each labelled *somma sommarum*. Thus, Pacioli's old *summa summarum* is now, quite logically, identified with the balance account. The former originally was devised to test the accuracy of the ledger-closing and since the balance account does that much better and in addition closes the ledger, it is only natural that it should supplant the old procedure and take its name. Casanova in 1558,[1] Pietra in 1586,[2] and all later writers use the balance account as the generally accepted procedure. Pacioli's awkward *summa summarum* is no longer used.

[19] The text of the English version of the *Nieuwe Instructie* was published in *Economisch-Historisch Jaarboek*, 18 (1934), with notes by P. G. A. de Waal.

[20] The illustrative set of books found in the Dutch and French editions is missing from the only known surviving copy of the English edition.

[1] Alvise Casanova, *Specchio Lucidissimo* . . . (Venice, 1558). Casanova is also the first author to introduce the " opening balance account " in starting a new ledger. (Peragallo, *op. cit.*, p. 69).

[2] Angelo Pietra, *Indrizzo degli Economi* (Mantua, 1586).

In conclusion it may be recapitulated that Pacioli, as the first author of importance on book-keeping, did know the true function and construction of the trial balance. His *summa summarum,* which has been mistaken for a trial balance, is nothing more than a device to test the closing of the ledger and it eventually gave way to the more efficient balance account. Why Pacioli did not use the balançe *account* is not clear, since it was in current use at the time he wrote. Moreover, the manner in which he employs the trial balance in transferring accounts from one ledger to another strongly suggests that he was aware of its existence.

It is obvious that the book-keeping procedures described by Pacioli did not originate with him. The accounting literature of the period was more intent on setting forth the book-keeping practices of the day than in formulating theories or creating new procedures. The origin of the trial balance, therefore, is to be found only in the actual business practices of the period. This, however, is difficult to establish, because, as previously mentioned, few book-keeping records of the period have survived, and many of the survivals are incomplete.

Evolution of the Journal Entry*

A. C. Littleton †

THE journal entry is an important book-keeping mechanism which serves as a means of converting a non-technical statement of a transaction into a species of technically formed, intermediate statistical records. It is, moreover, particularly characteristic of double entry—more characteristic perhaps than the ledger entry—because it so clearly expresses the inevitable duality which is present in all transactions.

The importance of the journal entry in modern practice seems to be somewhat on the decrease, at least in America. Whether or not the processes of evolution will finally remove it altogether, no one knows. But one can say that it is not indispensable, and consequently it might conceivably disappear altogether from book-keeping practice.

It is easy to become curious about this element of book-keeping method, which probably was added to the structure after double-entry account-keeping was quite well worked out and might sometime drop off the structure again—an outgrown appendage like a polliwog's tail.

The earliest journal entries were not what one would perhaps be inclined to expect in view of the early characteristics of the ledger account. Ledger entries, as has already been pointed out, were at first complete sentences—whole transactions entered twice *in toto*. But the earliest journal entries that we know of were not sentences to be rewritten in the ledger. On the contrary, they were, even in the first appearances, quite technical in form and phrasing. The uninitiated might understand a ledger entry, for the wording expressed a complete thought, but they could hardly grasp the meaning of a journal entry unaided, for the expression of thought was very much abbreviated.

Before speculating upon the origin of the peculiarities of journal-entry form, let us examine some typical journal entries of the fifteenth and sixteenth centuries.

---

* From *Accounting Evolution to 1900*, New York: The American Institute Publishing Co., Inc., 1933. (Chap. VIII.)

† Emeritus Professor of Accounting, University of Illinois, Urbana, Illinois.

JOURNAL ENTRIES OF THE FIRST TYPE [1]

ORIGINAL	TRANSLATION
(1430)	
1. *Per* Cassa le contadi *a* ser franzesco baldi e fratelli— per resto de zafaran 0 0 0	1. *By* ready money *to* Franzesco Baldi and Brothers —for balance of saffron ... 0 0 0
(1494)	
2. *Per* Ser Zuan d' Antonio da Messina: *A* Cassa contati a lui per parte de'sopra ditti zuccari secondo la forma del mercato 0 0 0	2. *By* Zuan Antonio of Messina: *to* cash, paid to him for part of the above mentioned sugar according to the terms of the agreement 0 0 0
(1525)	
3. *Per* Bancho di Cappelo e Vendramine, *a* chavedal i quali me trovo aver nel detto bancho come per suoi libre apar 0 0 0	3. *By* Cappelo and Vendramine's Bank, to Capital, which I find I have in the said bank per their books 0 0 0
(1540)	
4. *P(er)* Pro e Danno // *A* spese diverse per piu spese fatte l'anno presente, come in esse appar, per saldo suo 0 0 0	4. *By* Profit and Loss, *to* Sundry Expense, for various expenses made in the present year, as appears in the balance of that account 0 0 0
(1543)	
5. *Per* profyt ende onprofyte / *aen* Capitael van my Nicolaes Forestain somma sommarum dat ick bevinde gheprofiteert te hebben binnen den tijt gheduerende disen boek 0 0 0	5. *By* profit and loss *to* capital of myself Nicholas Forestain, the sum total that I have profited within the period of this book ... 0 0 0
(1549)	
6. *Für* Ingwer // *an* nutz und Schaden für nutz und gewin ich an dem Ingwer gehabt 0 0 0	6. *By* Ginger, *to* Profit and Loss, for loss and gain I have had on Ginger 0 0 0

All these examples, in whatever language they are written, exhibit the same technical characteristics. The typical form in all of them is:

By A——, to B——

(with more or less detail of explanation).

This is a technical form, first, because the meaning is not obvious in the wording—something is left to be implied or understood; and, second, because the prepositions " per " and " a " have been given a special significance not in common usage. The old textbooks are very careful to point out that " per " must come first in the journal entry and that it indicates, or labels, the debtor. The creditor is always to be named next and is indicated by " a." Thus a rule explains the usage but not the significance. The writers do not explain how

---

[1] Sources are cited at the end and numbered to correspond with the entries.

" per " and " a " came to be associated with " debtor " and " creditor " respectively.

The absence of any authority showing how these technical meanings came about throws the matter open to conjecture and inference. The question is interesting enough to be discussed.

A hint of a possible starting place may be found in the phrasing of some of the early German journal entries. Even though the German examples are dated later than many of the Italian entries in the established form, these particular German entries are not cast into the same earlier technical form. The following is a sample entry by Mathew Schwartz, the chief book-keeper for the famous Fugger family of German merchants. It is dated 1516.

ORIGINAL	TRANSLATION
Uns soll herr Jacob Fugger duc. 85, die *sollen wir* a Cassa, umb souil hat Matheus Schwartz hie zu Venedig für sich gebraucht	*To us* Mr. Jacob Fugger *shall* [give] 85 ducats, which *we shall* [give] to cash, for as much as Mathew Schwartz has used here at Venice ...

The words in italic type are the ones which have technical significance; the words in brackets in the translation are added to the original to complete the obvious meaning. Thus completed, the journal entry assumes the form of a simple sentence quite devoid of technicalities and therefore understandable by anyone who reads it. The word " give " is not in the original entry of 1516, and without that word even this entry becomes semi-technical, since a missing word is to be implied.

Back in 1440–1444, however, unsystematised memoranda of the time (as Penndorf shows in his *Geschichte der Buchhaltung in Deutschland*) contained the phrases " *er sol geben*," " *ich hab im gegeben* " (" he shall give," " I have given him ") and the like. Thus it seems clear that the Germans had started with complete sentences, but by 1516 had begun to drop words out of the book-keeping entry so that the record was already becoming technical. But the process had not yet gone so far as to make the full sentence hard to reconstruct.

On the other hand, the entry given above (No. 6) was only thirty-three years later (1549) and, it will be noted, its form was already so technical as to have been hard for the uninitiated to understand. It is not a whole sentence, whereas the entry of 1516 was very nearly a complete sentence. The entry of 1549 is, moreover, identical with the Italian form. This leads to two suggestions. The first is that the established Italian form probably did not make itself felt in Germany until some time later than its early use in Italy (1430). The second suggestion here is that the technical Italian form of journal entry might possibly be experimentally reconstructed into a complete

sentence which could have been so changed in the course of time by
dropping out words as to produce in the end the brief, technical
expression used in the Italian entries, namely:

By A——, to B——.

In order to follow up this thought, it is necessary to start with a
hypothetical ledger account in the early Italian manner.

On the cash page, debit side, it might read:

> " Cash shall give the stated amount to
> Francisco at his pleasure for coins
> this day deposited."

On Francisco's page, credit side, it might read:

> " Francisco shall have (*i.e.,* receive) the
> stated amount at his pleasure for cash
> this day deposited in coins."

Certain conditioning factors must now be taken into consideration:

1. The journal was developed *after* the ledger, presumably for the
purpose of systematising the day-book memoranda preparatory to
entry in the ledger. Consequently, journalising would be then as now
a process of translating the occurrence into ledger terms. Therefore
it would have been natural at first to state the journal entries in
phrases used in the ledger.

2. The only words in the ledger entries which do not vary
according to the details of the transaction are: " shall give " and
" shall have," and " to " and " for " (*per* = for or by). Therefore
these words at least would have to appear in every journal entry to
put it into association with the ledger.

3. The debit item (here " cash ") appears twice in the old form
of ledger entry: once as the first part of the entry on the debit page
and again as the second part of another entry (the contra). The same
is true of the credit item, reversed of course. Thus in the above
example, " Cash shall give " appears again as " for cash " in the
other account, and " to Francisco " appears a second time as
" Francisco shall have " in the contra account.

4. The modern entry for the receipt of cash on deposit from
Francisco would be

Cash 0 0 0
Francisco 0 0 0

But in the old ledger both debit and credit from the journal were
shown twice, that is to say, the *whole transaction* was written in both
of the accounts concerned. Therefore, the old journal entry would
need some unmistakable indication of a " four-element posting."
Consequently, the old journal entry would have to have two elements

not shown in the modern journal. In essentials, the only thing the old entry had that the new has not are the words " by " (or " for ") and " to." These constitute the third and fourth elements, and produce the form: By cash, to Francisco.

On the basis of these factors the situation seems to be as follows. It is possible to reconstruct a fully worded journal entry to express the facts of the transaction in accordance with what would seem from the German examples to have been a very probable form of entry before technical omissions began to be made. This hypothetically reconstructed journal entry is as follows:

> For cash deposited this day, Francisco
> shall have the stated amount, etc., and
> to Francisco, cash shall give the stated
> amount at his pleasure.

If omissions or reorganisation of the wording then appeared, the entry might next have been reduced to the type:

> For cash, Francisco shall have;
> To Francisco, cash shall give.

And if still later the duplicated phrases were neglected, the form might result in this type:

> For cash, to Francisco.

This form expresses the technical essentials of the journal entry of 1430 and for a long time thereafter. Why such a change should take place it would be hard to say; perhaps it seemed to simplify the record and reduce the work of recording—a reason no doubt as satisfactory to scribes of that day as it still is to book-keepers now. The essential facts for the ledger—to anyone who had been instructed in the book-keeping of the day—were still quite plainly discernible. They were a debit to a named account (and a contra), and a credit to a named account (and its contra)—four elements.

1. " Cash " by its position first in the entry gives the name of the account which " shall give " (*i.e.*, which is to be debited).

2. " Francisco " by its position as second in the entry gives the name of the account which " shall have " (*i.e.*, which is to be credited).

3. " For " may be regarded as the symbol of the contra entry of cash in the credit account (Francisco).

4. " To " may be regarded as the symbol of the contra entry of Francisco in the debit account (cash).

Thus it will be seen that the journal entry in its technical abbreviation names two things in its left member: 1. the account debited (cash) and 2. the contra or explanation entry (by or for cash) belonging to the other account concerned. In its right member it names: 1. the account to be credited (Francisco) and 2. the contra or explanation entry (to Francisco) belonging to the other account concerned.

This technical form of journal entry would clearly state (to a trained book-keeper) the whole transaction in duplicate and in terms already in use in current ledger practice. It would form a perfect bridge of the gap between the memorandum record and the ledger. But there is nothing authentic in this explanation of the origin of the form which the entry took; it is only an attempt to piece together a plausible hypothesis out of the information available. There is really nothing definite to show that. journal entries were ever made in the complete-sentence form as here reconstructed. If they had been, they must have evolved into the recognised abbreviated form (By A——, to B——) within a period of about one hundred years. Double-entry ledgers are first found complete in the middle of the fourteenth century, say by 1340, the date of the accounts of the stewards of Genoa (there could have been no urge to construct journal entries of any kind before double-entry ledgers were in use) and the technical abbreviated form [2] of journal entry is definitely known to have appeared by 1430. Whether or not that is a long enough period for such an evolution to take place—even assuming a great stimulus from the Renaissance background—is an unanswered question.

In regard to the later development of journal entries, much less speculation is necessary, for many examples are available and the forms in use are much less technical and therefore easier to understand.

One of the most interesting facts about the old practices of double-entry book-keeping is the existence at the same time of two strikingly different types of journal entry, one of which has already been presented here. Yet different as they are in wording and technicalities, and different undoubtedly also as to origin, they nevertheless could serve the same function equally well without, apparently, introducing any confusion.

This other form of entry may prove to be even more interesting than the one first discussed, because in some ways it is closer to modern forms, or, perhaps it would be better to say, because the modern journal entry in English seems to evolve more naturally out of the form now to be considered than out of the " by and to " type of entry.

[2] A people which in 1494 favoured the almost excessive use of abbreviations in place of complete words, which is evident in Pacioli's *De Computis*, probably earlier than this would have been inclined to accept as reasonable, perhaps even as desirable, the outright omission of repetitive phrases in book-keeping entries where the meaning could be imputed into the words remaining, thus producing the technicality of form here discussed.

JOURNAL ENTRIES OF THE SECOND TYPE

(first variation)

ORIGINAL   TRANSLATION

(1491)

7. *Faro debetore* Tomasone del Buono *e creditore* spese di mercanzie di s. iiij d'oro per spese fatta a un fardello di panno corsato mandato da Lucca da Bonaccorsi a Libro 203/100 0 0 0

7. I *make debtor* Tomaso del Buono and *creditor* Merchandise Expenses for 4 s. in gold, for expenses incurred on a bale of cloth sent by Lucca da Bonaccorsi, in the book 203/100 0 0 0

(1550)

8. Cassa *est debiteur* adj ditto L. 987.13.4 Je Pierre du Mont ay receu de mon maistre Nicolas de Reo en argent contant L. 987.13.4 pour luy seruir au train de marchandise dieu me donne la grace de bien servir
    Nicolas de Reo *est Creditor* 0 0 0

8. Cash *is debtor* on this day [for the] L. 987.13.4 I, Pierre du Mont, have received from my master Nicholas de Reo L. 987.-13.4 in ready money to be employed for him by way of business. God give me grace to serve well.
    Nicholas de Reo *is Creditor* 0 0 0

(1559)

9. *Fa debitore* Michele Gharo Nestri a di 2 di maggio di s3 d xv posto a lui detti Contanti per sua provvigione del mese passato di aprile e *fa creditore* Cassa 0 0 0

9. *Make debtor* Michele Gharo Nestri on May 2nd for s3 d15 posted to his debit account for his provisions of the past month of April and *make creditor* Cash 0 0 0

(second variation)

(1553)

10. Devonshire Kerseys *is debitor to* Laurance Fabian, draper, and is for 10 pieces at 36 s. a piece—etc. 0 0 0

10. (English in the original)

(1595)

11. Cassa van ghereden ghelde *is schuldich aen* Cappital van my 8000 guld. Ende is voor verscheyden penninghen van gout ende silver, so ick in mynen handen hebbe, omme daermede te dryuen den handel van coopmanchap. Godt wil my verleenen ghewin, ende behaeden voor verlies. Amen 0 0 0

11. Ready money *is indebted to* Capital for my 8000 guilders. And is for different coins of gold and silver that I have in hand to use in pursuing the trade of merchandise. God will grant me profit and preserve me from loss. Amen 0 0 0

(1613)

12. Meale in Barrels *is debitor unto* stocke for 16 tuns remaining in the house 0 0 0

12. (English in the original)

(third variation)

(1567)

13. Caisse d'Argent comptant es mains de Pierre Savonne *doibt* 12450£ 10s 6d qu'il met pour compte de son capital, *credeteur* ledit Savonne 0 0 0

13. Ready money in the hands of Pierre Savonne owes 12450£ 10s 6d which he places in his capital account, *Creditor* is Savonne 0 0 0

(1570)

14. Roggen *soll an* Hering, hab ich mit Andreas Klur von Thorn einen stich getroffen—etc. 0 0 0

14. Rye *owes to* Herring, which I have bartered with Andreas Klur of Thorn— etc. 0 0 0

(1588)

15. Chest or money *is Debtor* or *owes to* stock belonging to me, M. N. and is for— etc. 0 0 0

15. (English in the original)

(1594)

16. Casse *sol* m.11437.8 Per Capital. So viel befind ich bey dem Inventario an bahrschafft so ich dato zum glücklichen aufang dieser· handlung in Cassa leg 0 0 0

16. Cash *owes* m.11437.8 for (to) Capital. As much as I find of ready money in the inventory I place in the cash box this day for the prosperous beginning of this business 0 0 0

(1606)

17. Cassa *is schuldig* für fl. 8560. welche ich N. N. eingelecht habe in cassa zu handeln. *Creditor* mein Capital 0 0 0

17. Cash *is indebted* (owes) for fl. 8560 which I, N. N., have invested in cash for trade. My Capital (is) *Creditor* 0 0 0

(1608)

18. (original not available)

18. Trading Expenses debit per cash, for payments during the month as shown by the memorandum book 0 0 0

It will be noted in the examples of journal entries of this so-called second type that not all the cases run true to form; the wording is such as to produce three varieties of entries which, while slightly different in phrasing, are still basically related. The characteristics of these journal entries may be generalised as follows:

First variation: A is debtor / B is creditor

Second variation: A is debtor to B

Third variation: A owes to B

The second and third variations in form seem rather similar on the ground that, if A " is debtor," he likewise " owes," since by definition " debtor " is one who " owes." [3] Perhaps they are both also

---

[3] Yet one can hardly escape the feeling that this third variation is somehow related to the underlying phrasing of entries of the first, since the latter used (or implied) the technical words from the ledger (" shall give," etc.), and since the root word translated as " must " or " shall " also means " owe." The Latin *debet* from *debeo*, the Italian *deve* from *dovere*, the French *doit* from *devoir*, and the German *soll* from *sollen* all mean " he must " as well as " he owes."

similar at heart to the entries of the first variation, since one might say: " A is debitor to B (who is creditor)."

But whatever virtue (or lack of it) there may be in grouping entries of the second type into three sub-classes, it is clear enough that entries in this list are radically different from those in the first list in both form and phrasing.[4] The first type was probably derived from the wording of the ledger entries of the time and obviously led to the use, much later, of " to " in the debit and " by " in the credit of the English ledger entries. The second type of journal entry, on the other hand, would seem to be one to grow more naturally out of the " day-book " record of personal-account transactions, and it is quite clearly a closer antecedent of modern journal entries than the first type.

This last point is demonstrated not only by the form of the entry itself, but also by the fact that entries of the first type soon drop out of use. If some twenty-five journal entries from various sources, including those reported above, are arranged into columns according to type and in chronological sequence, it will be observed that the first type of entry predominates prior to 1550 (the entry in the Medici books of 1491 are the only example in the list of the second type to appear prior to the middle of the sixteenth century) and that after 1550, entries of the second type strongly predominate. Thus, while the real origins of the journal-entry forms are not known, the direction taken by their evolution is unmistakable. The method of which Pacioli thought so highly was proved in the sequel to be inferior, for it was driven out of use by the other form.

But the evolution of the journal entry was by no means complete at the date of the last example given above (1608). The developments of the next three hundred odd years can be traced through journal entries in English alone. Since the changes which took place can therefore be easily read from the entries themselves, the discussion accompanying the examples will be brief.

---

[4] The sharp contrast in the two styles of journal entry raises the interesting question of whether or not such a difference could be the principal factor distinguishing the methods used in different localities. Pacioli says in the first chapter of *De Computis*, " This treatise will adopt the system used in Venice, which is certainly to be recommended above all others, for by means of this, one can find his way in any other." (Geijsbeek, *Ancient Double Entry Bookkeeping*, p. 33.) Hence, one may conclude that the journal entry of the form:

By A—— to B——

was the Venetian method, and perhaps it may be that the entry in the form:

A is debtor to B

was the distinguishing characteristic of the Florentine method. Certain it is that this form was used in Florence by the Medici family in 1491.

ENGLISH JOURNAL ENTRIES AFTER 1600

(1684)

19. George Pinchback Debitor to Kettles £75–8d. for 5 barrels
—etc. ....   75/—/8

(1717)

20. P. Q. at Gibralter my accompt current Debtor to Voyage to
Gibraltér, consigned to P. Q. £322.9.7½—etc. 322/ 9/7½

(1754)

21. William Wife £360 to Sherry for 10 pipes delivered to him
in barter ....   360/—/–

(1788)

22. Charges merchandise Dr. to paper taken for use in shop ......   —/10/6

(1841)

23.   Dr.   Cr.
Mdse. 1000   B/P 500
                                         Cash................................. 500

(1848)

24. Cash to Sundries	1590	
to Bills Receivable		1500
Profit and Loss		90

(1864)

	Dr.	Cr.
25. Merchandise Dr.	5000	
to James Munroe		5000

(1900)

26. Merchandise	400	
to Cash		400

Slight differences in the wording used by the different entries are
apparent, especially in examples 19 to 22. The word "debitor" in
one entry is "debtor" in another or is wholly omitted in a third
(No. 21). In still other cases the abbreviation "Dr." takes the place
of the word itself.[5] These changes, however, are of relatively little
significance. But subsequently—beginning a little before the middle
of the nineteenth century—a more pronounced change appears. The
tendency is for the entries slowly to swing back again into a technicality of form; not the same technicality of

By A——, to B——

which had almost disappeared by 1550, but a technicality almost
altogether of position. The debits and credits are now entered in
separate columns and the name of the account credited is indented
below the debit item. Sometimes the abbreviation "Dr." is retained,

---

[5] This abbreviation is found as early as 1690 in *Debtor and Credltor Made Easie*
by Stephen Monteage (3rd ed.). In the years around 1800 its use as in entry
No. 22 was quite general; see Thomas Dilworth, *The Young Bookkeeper's
Assistant* (London, 1792); William Jackson, *Practical Bookkeeping* (New York,
1816); Patrick Kelly, *The Elements of Bookkeeping* (London, 1833) (10th ed.).

sometimes it is omitted; the word " to " is retained, however, as the sign of the credit. But even this word " to " disappears entirely before long, and debit or credit is read into the entry purely by the position of the words and figures. Not even the columns are labelled " Dr." and " Cr."

The form of the eighteenth century—" John Doe is debtor $1000 to Stock "—was a plain statement of fact which had to be posted in two places, but these two places were not forcefully indicated. The later developments improved the mechanics of book-keeping by stating two distinctly separate facts, each to be posted according to its name and its debit or credit characteristic. The procedure now leads one to think of *debit-entries* waiting to be posted, not *debts* or *debitors*; that is, to think of " accounting units " to be transferred or tabulated and not of personified obligations. The journalising process under modern usage becomes a matter of sorting wholly impersonal facts in a manner designed to increase the accuracy of the sorting (posting).

Practice has passed from one definite stage to another: 1. a time of no journal entries, when the full statement of the transaction was probably entered directly in the two ledger accounts concerned; 2. a period (say 1430 to 1550) with a highly technical form of journal entry preparatory to the record in the ledger; 3. a long interval in which the journal entry expressed more or less fully a complete thought; and 4. the modern period—now quite technical in form again—when the focus is the accurate sorting of accounting units.

But the end is not yet, for evolution is carrying this book-keeping process still deeper into technicalities. Even the journal entry itself is dispensed with for a great many transactions recorded in numerous subsidiary books of original entry. Posting is made directly to the ledger from the column totals of various special books for most of the transactions of modern American business; only a minor portion of the ledger details comes through formal debit and credit journal entries. Furthermore, some large organisations have abandoned the time-honoured left and right, debit and credit, divisions of the ledger account itself; a wide sheet becomes an account, its columns are sub-accounts and entries in them are black and red instead of debit and credit.

Most of the clerks thus have no need to know book-keeping as such. But for the persons charged with assembling the final book-keeping data, the process is even more technical than any form of journalising yet conceived. Only a complete knowledge of the whole ledger and of the characteristics of every book of original entry in the whole elaborate system enables one to bring the many separate debit and credit classifications and summaries together into a unified whole.

As a result, the modern book-keeper—the one who is responsible for uniting the maze of detail into a coherent whole—has a task the like of which none of his predecessors ever faced, and the very act of learning book-keeping is harder than ever before. Book-keeping has become a real technology instead of a simple clerical routine.

NOTE ON THE SOURCES OF THE JOURNAL-ENTRY EXAMPLES

(a) The sources of the several journal entries of the first type are as follows:

1. From the account-books of Andrea Barbarigo, 1430. Entries in similar form from the books of the Barbarigo family appear for 1457, 1482, 1496, 1507, 1537. See *La Partita Doppia*, by Vittorio Alfieri, p. 60.

2. From Luca Pacioli's *De Computis*, the first printed textbook on book-keeping. See *Trattato de' Computi e delle Scritture*, by Prof. Vincenzo Gitti (1878).

3. From a text by Antonio Tagliente. See *La Ragioneria*, by Fabio Besta, Vol. III, p. 380.

4. From a text by Domenico Manzoni. See the photo-reproduction of a journal page in *Ancient Double Entry Bookkeeping*, by John B. Geijsbeek, p. 82.

5. From *Nieuwe Instructie*, by Jan Ympyn Cristofle. See *Van Paciolo tot Stevin*, by Dr. P. G. A. DeWaal, p. 118. For other entries in English from the 1547 edition of Ympyn's book, see *The Accountant*, August 20, 1927, pp. 261–268.

6. From *Zweifach Buchhalten*, by Wolfgang Schweicker. See *Geschichte der Buchhaltung in Deutschland*, by Dr. Balduin Penndorf, p. 126. Other entries in similar form by Dutch writers are given in DeWaal, *op. cit.*; Van Hoorebeke, 1599 (p. 253); Van Renterghem, 1592 (p. 230); Van den Dycke, 1596 (p. 242).

(b) The sources of the several journal entries of the second type are as follows:

7. From the account-books of the Medici Bank in Italy. See Besta, *op. cit.*, p. 325, there citing A. Ceccherelli *I libri di mercatura della Banca Medici*; also see Penndorf in *The Accounting Review*, September, 1930, p. 247.

8. From *Practique brifue pour tenir livres de compte*, by Valentin Mennher de Kempten. See Besta, *op. cit.*, p. 392. For other entries by the same author dated 1565 see DeWaal, *op. cit.*, p. 139, also *Maandblad voor het Boekhouden*, October 1, 1926, and *Die Zeitschrift für Buchhaltung*, V. 7, p. 37.

9. From the account-book of Benvenuto Cellini, in Ceccherelli, *op. cit.*

10. From *The maner and fourme how to kepe a perfect reconyng*—etc., by James Peele. See *The Accountant*, January 16, 1926, pp. 91 *et seq.*

11. From *Boeckhouwen op die Italiaensche maniere*—etc., by Claes Pietersz. See DeWaal, *op. cit.*, p. 164.

12. From *The Pathway to Knowledge*—etc., by John Tapp. See *Maandblad voor het Boekhouden*, March 1, 1926, p. 172.

13. From *Instruction et maniere de tenir livres*—etc., by Pierre Savonne. See DeWaal, *op. cit.*, p. 147.

14. From *Buchhalten Durch Zwey Bücher*—etc., by Sebastian Gammersfelder. See Penndorf, *op. cit.*, p. 142.

15. From *Briefe Instruction*—etc., by John Mellis. See *The Accountant*, May 1, 1926, pp. 64 *et seq.*

16. From *Buchhalten fein Kurtz Zusammen Gefasst*—etc., by Passchier Goessens. See Penndorf, *op. cit.*, p. 150.

17. From *Schöne Forma des Buchhaltens*, by Ambrose Lerice. See Penndorf, *op. cit.*, p. 215.

18. From *Coopmansbouckhouding op de Italiaensche wyse,* by Simon Stevin. See *The Institute of Bookkeepers Journal,* December, 1927, p. 322.

(c) The sources of the English journal entries are as follows:

19. Richard Dafforne, *The Merchant's Mirrour* (entry for January 30, 1633) reprinted in *Lex Mercatoria,* by Gerard Malynes (London, 1686).

20. Thomas King, *An exact guide to Bookkeeping* (London, 1717), p. 3 of the journal.

21. William Weston, *The Complete Merchants Clerk* (London, 1754), p. 2 of Journal A.

22. Robert Hamilton, *An Introduction to Merchandise* (Edinburgh, 2nd ed., 1788), p. 293.

23. Thomas Jones, *Principles and Practice of Bookkeeping* (New York, 1841), p. 58.

24. P. Duff, *Bookkeeping* (New York, 10th ed., 1st edition 1848), p. 29.

25. Bryant & Stratton, *Bookkeeping* (New York, 1861), p. 12.

26. Williams & Rogers, *Introductive Bookkeeping* (Chicago, revised edition, 1900), p. 22.

Simon Stevin of Bruges

O. ten Have*

SIMON STEVIN lived in a turbulent age of economic, cultural and political change. The Dutch Republic, engaged in a seemingly endless struggle with Spain (1568–1648), was in its infancy, though destined within a few decades of its birth to become the centre of the world and remain so for almost a century. After 1587, when the Earl of Leicester returned to England, the Republic was left to manage its own affairs without direct help from other countries.

In its difficult formative years it was materially sustained by the capital accumulated in commerce, and was further fortunate in its leaders, among whom Oldenbarneveldt was the leading statesman of high ability, and Prince Maurice of Nassau the brilliant military leader. Prince Maurice (1567–1625) gained his victories with a highly mechanised and modernised army, well disciplined and well trained, equipped with standardised weapons and supported by a sound financial administration. The reorganisation of army transport and of military engineering—the soldiers had to make their own fortifications—made a significant contribution towards his successes.

The many-sided Stevin, the brilliant scientist, mathematician, natural philosopher, physicist, engineer and financial expert was the tutor, counsellor and friend of the Prince. The ties between the two were partly official; Stevin had an official position as engineer in the army and was also administrator of the royal domains. But Stevin, who was the Prince's senior by almost twenty years, was also the trusted friend of his royal patron.[1]

Simon Stevin was born in Bruges in 1548, the illegitimate child of Anton Stevin and a gay woman who also had two illegitimate daughters by the burgomaster of the city. Little is known of his

---

* Head of the Department of Social and Economic Statistics, Netherlands Central Bureau of Statistics, The Hague.
[1] In presenting this account of Stevin's life and work, the author has made extensive use of the following publications:

E. J. Dijksterhuis, *Simon Stevin* (The Hague, 1943).

A. J. J. van de Velde, *et al.*, *Simon Stevin, 1548–1948* (Brussels, 1948).

E. J. Dijksterhuis and C. de Waarde, *Simon Stevin, 1548–1620, en Isaac Beeckman, 1588–1637* (1941). Reprinted from *Archives du Musee Teyler*, series 111, part IX.

P. G. A. de Waal, *De leer van het boekhouden in de Nederlanden tijdens de zestiende eeuw* (Roermond, 1927).

Jan and Annie Romein, *Erflaters van onze beschaving* (*Deel I, 14de–16de eeuw*) (Amsterdam, 1947), pp. 246–284.

Volume I of *The Principal Works of Simon Stevin*, edited by E. J. Dijksterhuis and translated into English by Miss Dikshoorn, has appeared recently.

education. He knew Greek and Latin. In his early years he served as book-keeper and cashier of a trading firm in Antwerp, and it is possible that he learnt book-keeping at one of the private book-keeping schools of which there were several in the Netherlands. It is not known whether he attended the University of Louvain, at the time the only university in the country. But even if he had studied there, his search for knowledge in the exact sciences would not have been satisfied at this Catholic university. Its outlook was practically medieval and the sciences had a small place in its curriculum. More-over, the sciences were rigidly incorporated in a set system, accepted by the Church, and derived with little change from the work, for example, of Aristotle, Archimedes and Galen. There was no opportunity in this system for developing the exact sciences by the process of practical experimentation and empirical research giving rise to new hypotheses and new theories.

However, leading scientists were already challenging the generally accepted ideas and theories at the time of Stevin's birth, and were not content to repeat what had been handed down and made authoritative by the approval of the Church. In 1543 Vesalius published the result of his work in medical science and in the same year Copernicus gave the world his new system of the universe, a system which Stevin, a first-rate expositor, was to explain and defend in a masterly way in some of his writings.

The new University of Leyden in the United Provinces was a cradle for the new sciences and the new scientific outlook. This university was founded in 1575, in honour of and as a reward for the brave behaviour of the citizens of Leyden during its siege by the Spaniards when one-third of the population succumbed from starvation and plague. The practical aim of its foundation was to provide a training ground in the new Republic for theologians, jurists and physicians since the previous contacts with the Universities of Louvain and Paris could no longer be maintained. But the new university was not bound by the old traditions of the schoolmen, and there were wide possibilities for investigation and research in the natural sciences. It proved to have a strong attraction for all those who sought freedom in the pursuit of knowledge, including many who were considered as heretics, or at least as dangerous men, in their own countries.

The new movements in scientific thought, originating in the crisis in the world of science, were strongly stimulated by the pressures of practical needs. Students in a number of fields hoped to discover the solutions to their practical problems in the new learning. The new Republic was faced with a number of such issues: the political struc-ture of the republic; its financial management; the development of its external trade and navigation; the reorganisation of the army, and so on. The search for knowledge to further practical ends is illustrated by a well-known print of this time, entitled *The School of Navigation,* which shows the reverend minister Plantius giving lessons from a church pulpit to an audience of seamen and merchants. The number of schools for commercial subjects, including book-keeping, was also increasing. All this was a prelude to the seventeenth century, a century known in the history of the Netherlands as the Golden Century.

After having worked as book-keeper and cashier in Antwerp, Stevin went back to his native Bruges, where he was employed for a time in the municipal administration. Eventually he left the southern Netherlands; he probably was one of the group of people who left the South to find greater freedom, or in many cases refuge, in the United Provinces. In 1581 he was in Leyden as a teacher and student at the University, where he met, probably for the first time, Prince Maurice, who also was a student.

Stevin did not remain for long at the University, but he did not leave the United Provinces. He worked in the service of Prince Maurice and was very influential. He also worked privately as an engineer and concerned himself with a host of technical problems. Rather late in life, in 1614, he married Catharina Cray of Leyden, and had four children. He died in The Hague in 1620.

Apart from the few facts given above, there is little else available to detail and document the course of his career and his life. Neither diary nor correspondence exists. An estimate of his achievement must therefore be formed on the basis of his publications which were copious by the standards of his time. The flow of writings started in 1582 and continued till after his death when his son published some of his work. The publications were generally treatises on specialised subjects, the main exception being his most voluminous work, of about 1,500 pages, which contains the text of lessons he gave to Prince Maurice. Originally these lessons were in manuscript only. But the Prince, who took them with him on his numerous campaigns, feared that they might be lost, and it was decided to print them. The *Wis-constighe Ghedachtenissen* was published between 1605 and 1608.[2] Later the book was translated into Latin as *Hypomnemata Mathematica,* and parts into French with the title *Memoires Mathematiques.*

This enormous work contains the results of his most important researches in the sciences. It may be described as a sixteenth-century encyclopaedia of mathematics, mechanics and astronomy. In

[2] It is difficult to find an exact equivalent in English for this title. The word " ghedachtenissen " in Stevin's time meant " range of thought " or " sphere of ideas." Perhaps the nearest direct translation would be " range of thought on mathematics." In the recent English translation (see note 1, above), the title is rendered as " Mathematical Memoirs."

general, Stevin was well acquainted with what had been written on the various subjects, and it is not always easy to distinguish in his work between what already had been known before his time and what sprung from his brilliant and fertile mind. From a pedagogic point of view the lessons are excellent; often Stevin expounds with greater clarity and order what others had already published.

In the course of his writings Stevin gave his views on the functions of science. He believed that a rational person should not adopt a course of action without understanding the fundamentals on which it was based. However, the necessity for action did not permit him to be satisfied with theoretical speculation alone. Theory and practice had to be combined. But purely theoretical speculation was not to be ignored, because the fruits of the work of the pure theorist could be used by practical men. He was firmly of the opinion that observation and research had to be extended. His general attitude is summed up in his device, " Wonder en is gheen wonder," which may be rendered as " Marvel and yet no marvel "—the marvels of this world could be explained. The theoretical works of Stevin are nearly always combined with accounts of practical applications. Often his studies are composed of two parts, first the theoretical considerations and then the applications based on the theory. Very often a practical problem caused him to engage in theoretical speculation in search of a workable solution.

In Stevin's time Latin was the universal language of the scientists. This facilitated communication among them across national frontiers, but at the same time restricted the dissemination of knowledge outside the narrow circle of the learned. It is not surprising, therefore, that the new tendencies in the study of the sciences went hand in hand with the more frequent use of national languages by scientists. Stevin was a fervent advocate of the use of Dutch. He thought that Latin was very appropriate for the study of theology and law and for learned quotations in literature, but impossible for use in the exact sciences, for which he believed the Dutch language to be particularly suitable. He was the first teacher to give lectures (for instance on trigonometry) in Dutch at the University of Leyden; he also was entrusted with organising the school of engineering in the University, in which instruction was given in Dutch. The language was not sufficiently developed for its new task, and Stevin was obliged to make up a large number of new Dutch words and expressions. He enriched the language considerably, though many of his words and expressions have since gone out of use and now are difficult to interpret.[3]

[3] J. Row Fogo (in R. Brown's *History of Accountancy and Accountants* [Edinburgh, 1905], pp. 138–140) misunderstood the position taken by Stevin. He wrote of Stevin's " gallant attempts to preserve the dignity of the Latin language." Perhaps the misunderstanding arose out of Row Fogo's acquaintance with the

Stevin's publications cover a vast area of knowledge and deal with subjects falling in the following categories: mathematics, mechanics, hydrostatics, astronomy, physical geography, navigation, engineering and technology, military science, accounting, architecture, theory of music, political theory and logic. Before considering his writings on accounting it will be useful to give a brief indication of his achievements in some of these other fields.

Stevin published the first tables of interest, though such tables had previously been used by book-keepers and others; his purpose was to spread useful knowledge. He also published an important treatise on decimal fractions; he advanced the knowledge on this subject and extended its applications. He was convinced that the use of decimal fractions would become universal in all fields such as currency, surveying and astronomy. Stevin did not reach the stage of introducing the decimal point; this final development was achieved by the English mathematician, Briggs.[4]

Before Stevin, algebra was difficult to handle because a suitable notation was lacking. Stevin evolved a system of symbols which proved to be adequate for the needs of eminent mathematicians after him, such as Descartes and Newton. He also made important advances in the theory of equations.

In mechanics Stevin's achievement was immense, and his work on statics, which he developed into an autonomous field of science, was of lasting importance. Among his many contributions was the statement of the conditions for equilibrium which hold for the inclined plane, and, ultimately, he arrived at the law of the parallelogram of forces. He also demonstrated that the velocity of a freely-falling body was independent of its mass (contrary to the traditional view traceable to Aristotle) by experiments performed with Joh. Grotius, the father of the eminent jurist, in Delft, before Galileo's famous experiments.[5] The subject of hydrostatics was also developed by Stevin. He was aware of the so-called hydrostatic paradox, *viz.*, the law that the pressure exerted by a column of liquid is independent of its shape,

Latin version of Stevin's work only, and his ignorance of the fact that it was a translation from the original Dutch.

In his writings on book-keeping Stevin used " un-Dutch " terms such as " credit " and " balance " because, he explained, if his pupil, Maurice, were to adopt the system for his own affairs, he would have to make use of experienced book-keepers who would be familiar with such foreign terms and would have had difficulty with newly invented Dutch equivalents.

$$\begin{array}{ccc}(0) & (1) & (2)\end{array}$$

4 Stevin wrote 378·54 as 378   5   4.

5 Stevin was also responsible, as might be expected, for a number of practical applications in the field of mechanics. One of these may be mentioned here, not so much because of its intrinsic importance but because it illustrates an aspect of the relationship between Prince Maurice and Stevin. The Prince asked Stevin to investigate the working of a bridle-bit. As a result of this work, he had a special bridle made according to Stevin's design.

and depends only on the area of the surface under pressure and the height of the column above it. Stevin was also acquainted with the principle that the pressure at any point in a liquid is the same in all directions, a hydrostatic law which was to be formulated much later by Pascal.

Stevin's studies in physical geography, on the formation of and changes in the earth's crust, were prompted by concern with military problems, such as the collapsing of earthen ramparts. His publications on engineering deal mainly with the struggle against water, the hereditary enemy of the Dutch. He made a number of plans for regulating the flow of water not only for several Dutch cities but also for Calais and Danzig and other towns in Prussia. He wrote on the construction of mills and gave the first systematic treatise on locks. Nine letters-patent were issued to him, mainly in connection with the construction of mills and sluices. In passing may be mentioned the invention of his " zeil wagen " (sailing chariot), which achieved contemporary fame. In this vehicle Prince Maurice and members of his court made journeys at high speeds (high for the seventeenth century) on the beach at Scheveningen.

In the study of the science of warfare Maurice, the general, and Stevin, his practical scientific adviser, were known the world over. Gustavus Adolphus of Sweden came to Stevin for advice, for example, on the most efficient way of digging, and on the deployment of infantry. Tristam Shandy's military uncle, Toby, in Sterne's novel, was a warm admirer of Stevin in the world of fiction, while in the world of reality German military circles also were interested in Stevin's work until shortly before the outbreak of the Second World War. Stevin was a pioneer in his work on fortifications, and on most aspects of warfare, from administration to the technique of fighting, he made useful contributions. Finally, Stevin's versatility is brought out by the fact that he could be the practical innovator in matters of grim warfare and yet also make contributions to the theory of music.

Prince Maurice was aware of the unsatisfactory financial administration of his royal estates and of the army; so he asked Stevin whether it was possible to use the Italian system of book-keeping, as practised by business people, in the management of his affairs as ruler and head of the army. Stevin set out to answer this question in a treatise of about 100 pages on double-entry book-keeping.[6] The publication

---

[6] The work, included in the *Wisconstighe Ghedachtenissen*, falls into four parts, the titles of which may be freely translated as :
   (i) Commercial book-keeping in the Italian way.
   (ii) Book-keeping for domains in the Italian way.
   (iii) Book-keeping of the royal expenditures in the Italian way.
   (iv) Book-keeping for extra-ordinary finance (*i.e.*, war finance) in the Italian way.

takes the form of a series of questions and answers, Stevin replying in turn to the many questions put to him by his talented royal pupil. This system of giving instruction by question and answer was in vogue in treatises during the seventeenth century. But in one important respect Stevin's work was superior to those of most of his contemporaries. Most writers on book-keeping in the sixteenth and seventeenth centuries attempted to deal with the subject by explaining and illustrating the appropriate entries for each of the many possible kinds of business transactions. Stevin, on the other hand, attempted to explain the more general principles for analysing transactions into debit and credit, so that the pupil or reader himself could arrive from first principles at the book-keeping solution to each practical problem; his exposition of double entry is in terms of the " beginning " (appearance) and " ending " (disappearance) of items of property considered from the point of view of the firm.[7] It may be added that Stevin recognised the distinction between the capital of an enterprise and that of the owner—the distinction between commercial and private capital. This was unusual at a time when the private or domestic affairs of the owner generally were recorded in the set of accounts that contained his commercial transactions.

Stevin played an important part in the development of accounting. Dr. de Waal, the well-known Dutch authority on the history of accounting, went so far as to express the view that the development of the theoretical side of accounting until the nineteenth century was based on the writings of Pacioli and Stevin.[8] The influence of Stevin on many subsequent writers is undeniable, even though the debt was not always acknowledged. The important seventeenth-century work by Richard Dafforne, *The Merchant's Mirror*, which was the first English work to go into several editions, was based fairly directly on the work of Stevin and some other Dutch writers. Dafforne mentioned several of these writers and referred to Stevin as " a good friend of mine," and his short chapter on the " origin of bookkeeping antiquity " is a literal translation of Stevin's account.[9]

Some special features of Stevin's treatment of double entry may be noted. Stevin uses the customary three books, journal, ledger and

---

[7] Consequently, entries in the journal are made only when there are changes in assets and liabilities. Stevin was consistent in following his theory to the extent that no entry would be made in the books when a merchant sent goods to a factor, for the goods would not have changed hands. His contemporaries would have credited the appropriate goods account and debited a factor's account or account for goods with factors.

[8] P. G. A. de Waal, *op. cit.*, p. 289.

[9] D. Murray, *Chapters in the History of Bookkeeping and Accountancy* (Glasgow, 1930), pp. 244–247.

On the general influence of Dutch book-keeping texts on English writings, see P. Kats, " De invloed der Nederlanders der 16e en 17e eeuw op de Engelsche literatuur van het boekhouden," *Maandblad voor het Boekhouden*, 1925, pp. 160–176.

memorial, the first of which he says is the most important. But his use of the memorial differs in two ways from its general use in contemporary practice. First, not all the entries appearing in the journal are first written in the memorial. Preliminary entries in the memorial are made only when a servant handles a transaction; the servant writes up the details in the memorial, from which the owner or his book-keeper later makes the systematic entries in the journal. Second, unimportant transactions such as small loans for short periods are noted in the memorial, without corresponding entries in either the journal or the ledger. The object was to avoid the bother of making formal entries for minor matters and yet to have a suitable record.

Stevin also tried to minimise the work involved in book-keeping in other ways. Where possible, he combines several entries to form a single " compound " entry in the journal and ledger. For instance, if several lots of goods are bought at the same time from one supplier, there is one journal entry in which the several merchandise accounts are debited with their respective amounts and quantities, and the account of the supplier is credited with the single grand total. Stevin explained that this was not the normal practice, but that it saved work and also made the entries clearer. The use of compound entries had already been described in a Dutch treatise by Claes Pietersz (Nicolaus Petri Daventriensis, 1550?-1602?), but seems to have become more common only much later; de la Porte, for example, writing in the first half of the eighteenth century devotes several pages of his *La Science des Negocians et Teneurs des Livres* to illustrate compound entries.[10]

Stevin was one of the first to dispense with the custom of prefacing account-books with pious invocations in which, generally, the Almighty was implored to bless the transactions which were to be entered in the books.[11] It may be that this deviation from common usage reflects no more than Stevin's wish to save time in the counting-house. But it is at least possible that it was influenced by his general attitude of indifference towards religion.

An interesting variation in Stevin's treatise concerns the closing of

---

[10] The treatise by Pietersz was translated into English by " W.P." in 1596 (reprinted in 1613) under the title *The Pathway to Knowledge* . . .

The use of compound journal entries had previously appeared in English book-keeping literature in James Peele's *The Pathewaye to Perfectness, in th' accomptes of Debitour and Creditour* . . . (1569). He used the term " reperticion appertaining to sundry accounts " for the sundry accounts involved in the collective debit or credit. Dafforne avoided the use of compound entries in his book because it was designed for purposes of instruction, though he acknowledged that their use " would much *abridge* the prolixity of my Journal passages." " As for the word *Repertition*, used at present among Merchants," Dafforne objected pedantically that it should not be used since no account with this title appears in any " leager " or " Kalendar " (index to ledger).

[11] For an example in Sir Thomas Gresham's books, see p. 189, above. [Eds.]

the accounts. Stevin effects this by making a " Staet " or " Staet-proef " (the term " staet " can be translated as " sheet " or " list "). When the owner wishes to know his profit or loss, he draws up a statement on a separate sheet listing all assets, debts and liabilities. The balance (*i.e.*, net assets) he compares with the corresponding figure produced at the previous closing; the difference is the profit or loss for the period. This calculation is checked by means of the " sheet proof," which aggregates the gains and losses on the various accounts in the ledger.[12] Contrary to the practice of other contemporary writers, the listing of the assets and liabilities, etc., is not done through the medium of a balance account recorded in the ledger; it is something derived from but outside the books of accounts. A further peculiarity is that in Stevin's " sheet " the assets are listed on the right-hand (" credit ") side, and the liabilities on the left-hand (" debit ") side, as in the modern English practice. Stevin also recommended that the balancing should be carried out whenever it was thought desirable to ascertain the profit or loss; many writers of his time required the balancing process only when the set of books was to be discontinued and the account balances transferred to a new set.

Stevin also set out a system of accounts by double entry suitable for use in public administration. The administration of the royal domains was to be reorganised, taking effect from 0 January 1604—Stevin explained that the beginning of the year is not the first of January. In his manual instructions are given to guide the newly appointed book-keepers and to regulate the settlement of the accounts by the stewards. However, the book-keeping methods of the stewards were not to be altered, for both Prince Maurice and Stevin thought it not practicable to instruct all these officials in the niceties of Italian double entry. Stevin also worked out projects for keeping accounts of the royal households by double entry, and likewise in connection with war expenditures.

Maurice applied Stevin's plans and nominated special book-keepers for the purpose, and the city of Amsterdam also used his system for a period of years. Unfortunately no trace of the records of the reformed financial administration has survived. A similar system of public accounts came into use in Sweden in the seventeenth century, the " general ledger " of 1623 marking a revolutionary change—the application of the double-entry system to government

12 The procedure has some similarity with that used in the earliest German texts on book-keeping, those of Heinrich Schreiber (Grammateus), first published in 1518, and of Johan Gottlieb, the first of which appeared in 1531. (See B. S. Yamey, " Notes on the Origin of Double-Entry Bookkeeping," *Accounting Review*, XXII [1947], pp. 266–267.)

accounts.[13]   Since that year the Swedish government accounts have been on a double-entry basis, and several cities followed the example of the central government (Stockholm being the first, in 1643).[14]

The reform in Sweden was a product of the programme of reorganisation implemented in the reign of Gustavus Adolphus (1611–1632).   As double entry was little known or used in Sweden, the government called upon a prominent Dutch merchant, Abraham Cabeljau, to introduce the plan.   Cabeljau was born in Leyden in 1571 and had been a merchant in Amsterdam.   He lived in Sweden from 1607 to 1617 and again from 1621 to his death in 1645, and held several prominent positions in the service of the government of his adopted country.   He apparently had no previous experience of government accounting but was recognised as being a successful administrator as well as an expert on double entry.   There is no conclusive proof that Cabeljau was acquainted with or influenced by the writings of Stevin; nevertheless, it is probable that this was the case.   Both were Dutchmen; Stevin was the first to advocate the use of double entry in government accounting; and there were frequent links between Sweden and Holland.   (It will be recalled that Gustavus Adolphus had consulted Stevin on certain military problems.)   The presumption that Cabeljau was influenced by Stevin is strengthened by one particular feature of the Swedish ledger of 1623.   Stevin recommended that in public financial administration the accounts should not be closed off at the end of the financial year, but that the period should be extended so that receipts and payments pertaining to a particular year but made after the end of that year could be included.   Stevin recognised that this extension of the accounting

---

[13] See V. A. Hanner, *Rikshuvudboken, av år 1623.*   The book includes a short summary in English, which has been reprinted in *Accounting Research*, 6 (1955), p. 58.

[14] Dafforne, writing in 1636, observed that Prince Maurice had followed " Simon Stevin, his Mathematician " and adopted his book-keeping system for dealing with the Princely Revenues and " exercised the same in his Court, which still (as I have been informed) is there in use, as also in the Swethian Court, and else-where."

Row Fogo, in R. Brown, *op. cit.*, pp. 138–139, was mistaken in stating that Stevin's work in the field of public accounting was unsuccessful, since his plans were in fact adopted.   Row Fogo was of the opinion that " the fault lay with the subject, for while double entry may be serviceable where the state administers domains or engages in commercial enterprises, the system is altogether unsuited for the simple transactions connected with the collection and spending of taxes, which can be tabulated clearly with much less expenditure of labour."   However, the saving in labour is not likely to be significant.   Moreover, the transactions are not simple, certainly not from the administrator's point of view.   In the sixteenth and seventeenth centuries the administration involved the delegation of the exercise of taxing rights and privileges to private individuals, a process giving rise to much the same accounting problems as those connected with dealings in goods on consignment or commission which were common in international trade in those centuries.   It is of interest that one of the oldest ledgers before 1494, in the archives of San Giorgio in Italy, is that of the cashier of the city and has several of the features of the double-entry system.

period was not in accordance with commercial accounting practice, but urged that it had two advantages in that it avoided the labour of transferring numerous balances and also secured closer correspondence between the data in the accounts and those in the original budget. This procedure, which caused an overlapping of successive accounting periods, was adopted on Cabeljau's advice in the General Ledger.[15]

---

[15] Ludovici Flori, a Jesuit, who wrote his *Trattato del modo di tenere il libro doppio domestico* (1633) for the benefit of Sicilian monasteries, may also have been influenced by Stevin. Peragallo writes that he " mentions the placing of transactions in their proper fiscal periods; Flori makes it one of the principal points of his book." This seems to be an echo of Stevin, who was mentioned by Flori as a writer on administrative (in contradistinction to mercantile) bookkeeping. Peragallo notes that " Flori follows up Simon Stevin's ' compound entry ' " in the journal, though Kats (*op. cit.*, p. 175) inclines to the view that Flori's type of entry, particularly in the method of indicating the folios of the accounts, resembles Peele's " reperticion " entries (note 10, above) more closely than Stevin's compound entries. Kats thinks it is likely, since Flori was almost certainly unaware of Peele's book, that each had found the procedure used in practice. (Flori's book is described in E. Peragallo, *Origin and Evolution of Double Entry Bookkeeping* [1938], pp. 82–89.)

The Goldsmith Banker*

S. W. Shelton †

IN 1924 Glyn, Mills & Co. purchased the business of Child's Bank and thus acquired what is probably the oldest existing bank in the country. Its origins as a goldsmith business date back to 1559, to the days of Queen Elizabeth I, when it was owned by John Wheeler who lived in Cheapside. About 1620 the business was transferred to the present premises at the " Marygold," No. 1 Fleet Street, and in the middle of the seventeenth century passed by marriage into the hands of Robert Blanchard and Francis Child.

Although there had been a crude form of moneylending and money-changing in Elizabethan times, and goldsmiths seem to have been moving towards some form of banking, " The crucial innovations in English banking history seem to have been mainly the work of the goldsmith bankers in the middle decades of the seventeenth century," as a recent writer has pointed out.[1]

Before the Civil War it was the custom for London merchants to use the Mint (then in the Tower) as a repository for their surplus cash. But when, in 1640, Charles I requisitioned some £200,000 which had been thus deposited, they naturally began to seek elsewhere for a place safe from such royal interference. The goldsmiths, with the facilities which they had for the safe storage of their own valuables, were a logical choice, and their acceptance of money deposits in trust, returnable on demand, was really the first stage in the evolution of goldsmith into banker. From " working " goldsmiths—jewellers and makers and sellers of gold and silver ware—providing safe custody facilities, they developed into bankers in the modern sense, and by 1694, when the Bank of England was founded, banking as we now know it was recognisably in being.

The earliest surviving ledger of Child's Bank covers the period 1662–1670, and the numbering of subsequent ledgers indicates that it was number 3 of a series. It seems reasonable, therefore, to assume that No. 1—the first methodical record of their banking transactions— must have started in the mid 1650's, almost exactly 300 years ago.

An analysis of these ledgers shows quite clearly the change from goldsmithing to banking. In 1663, 60 new accounts were opened, of which 41 were goldsmith accounts, 9 banking and 10 mixed accounts

* From *The Three Banks Review*, No. 27 (September, 1955), pp. 42–52.
† Archivist, Messrs. Glyn, Mills & Co., London, Bankers.
[1] D. M. Joslin, " London Private Bankers, 1720-1785," *Economic History Review*, second series, VII (1954).

—containing entries of both types of business. The following year the figures were 48, 25 and 16 respectively, indicating that the business was expanding in an encouraging manner. But disaster was at hand. December of 1664 saw the beginning of the Great Plague of London, and its effect was such that the number of new accounts opened in 1665 dropped to only 9. True, the numbers grew slowly each succeeding year, but it was not until 1679 that the figures rivalled those of the years before the Plague. And by that time the growth of new business had shown a definite change of pattern. Whereas in 1663–1664 the majority of the accounts were devoted entirely to goldsmith business, by 1667 purely banking accounts exceeded the purely goldsmith accounts, and in 1679 the figures for new accounts opened were—banking 206, goldsmith 27 and mixed accounts 20. Despite this change of emphasis, however, the older traditional side of the business remained an important factor until the end of the century.

In the initial stages the goldsmith merely accepted money for safe custody and gave in exchange a receipt which took the form of a promise to pay on demand. But the practice soon developed of these receipts being presented from time to time for part payment; the face value of the receipt being reduced on each occasion. Thus it was that the goldsmith bankers became known as " keepers of running cashes."

The following is an example of this simple type of early " running cash " account; the forerunner of the modern current account.

MR. MARTYN

Cr.			*Dr.*		
1663			1663		
July 30 Recd. being left here	£56		Oct. 4 Payd Mr. Martyn	£16	
			1664		
			Jan. 9 p. himselfe	10	
			23 pd. more	10	
			May 16 pd. in full	20	
				———	
				£56	

The growth of this practice of keeping " running cashes " led to the goldsmith receipts becoming assignable and passing from one party to another with their eventual development into the modern bank note, the wording of which has changed surprisingly little since those early days.

Novr 28: 1684

I promise to pay unto ye Rig^t Honble ye Ld North & Grey or bearer Ninty pounds at demand———

for Mr. ffran Child & my Self
JN^o ROGERS

£90———

Another point of interest is that in the modern bank note the letters " I " and " P " of the words " I Promise to pay " are linked together in a rather peculiar form. In fact many people do not realise that the letter " I " is there at all. This method of writing it dates back to the earliest days and a scrap of paper in Francis Child's own handwriting, bearing the date " Mar. 25th 1685," shows his attempts at design. The first printed bank notes were issued in 1729, but even on these the amount and payee's name were still written by hand.

A further method by which a customer could withdraw money was by writing a " note " requesting a sum of money to be paid to a third party, or to bearer, adding " and place it to my accompt," or " the receipt shall bee yr. sufficyent discharge." These " drawn notes " were the forerunners of the modern cheque but, though there is an isolated reference in the ledger for 1680 to such a " checque," the expression does not appear to have become current usage until very much later.

This method of operating an account is demonstrated in the following letter to Francis Child, written by George Evelyn, brother of the diarist.

Sr

Haveing occasion for yt little Sume of Money yt lyes in your hands, I have ordered the bearer hereof my servt Chapman to receave it. There is still in your hands 122l 06s 06d for when I left the Towne you had of my monys 150l. Since wch I have rec. upon two notes I sent you 27l 13s 6d the first note was 10l payd to Susan Scoggs my mayd Servt the other was 17l 13s 06d payd lately to Mr Spencer by my Lre to you– Both these Sums comes too 27l 13s 06d so yt remaynes in yr hands 122l 6s 6d which when my Servt hath recd from you, I have ordered him to deliver up to you the Note yr partner gave me when I came out of Town: I shall desire yt the two receipts or notes my mayd Servt & Mr Spencer left wt you (when they recd the moneys I have here mentioned) may be given to my Servt yt their may be no mistake hereafter, when all accounts are made even between us.

– Se I did expect more moneys to be payd unto you this Tearme for my Use; but my Creditor fayling me; I shall have occasion for 40l which if you please to Accomodate me at 6l ye cent. till my own moneys be paid to you by my order, I shall take it as a favor, and when my Servant Chapman the bearer hereof receaves it from you, be pleased to make a Bond for it for 3 months, and send it down to me, & I will Syne & Seale it, and return it up to you wt all Speed. I have no more to add, but my service to yu I am

Sr

Yr humble Servt,
GEO. EVELYN

Wotton 24
Novb [16] 84

The purely goldsmith accounts operated as one would expect, customers being debited for plate or jewels supplied—often with a charge for making or engraving—and credited either with cash which

they paid in or allowances for old plate returned. The account of
Francis Wyndham, for example, was debited July 31, 1663,

for the silver of 6 forged forkes wt. 12. 9. at 5s. 2d.	£3	4	3
for makeing them		15	0

On the same date his account was credited with

Old Spoones & forkes wt. 54. 14. at 5s. 2d.	£13	2	7

A fascinating variety of items may be noted from the various
accounts, such as

1673 (Countess of Devonshire)			
A warming pan wt. 79 oz. 7dwt. at 6s.	£22	6	0
For handle and graveing		7	6
1686 (H.R.H. Prince George of Denmark)			
24 Trencher Plates wt. 505 oz. at 5s. 8d. p. oz.	143	1	8
A stewing pan wt. 112 oz. 5dwt. at 6s. 4d. p. oz.	35	10	11
1686 (Duke of Beaufort)			
For a chamberpott & cover 38 oz. 7 dwt.	11	10	0
1687 (Earl of Kingston)			
For a gold plate wt. 31oz. 00dwt. 12gr. at 4¹ 5s. p. oz.	131	17	0

When the plate was out of fashion and they wanted a change, or
some ready cash was needed, customers would sell it back or, alternatively, make use of another facility provided by the goldsmith banker,
and pawn the plate, receiving a loan against its deposit. These
" pawnes " were a common feature of the business and the records
show that the facility was availed of by many customers, including the
famous " Nell " Gwyn, for whom there are several entries, including—
" Nov. 26. (1685) Lent on plate £4,600,"[2] for which she paid interest
at 6 per cent. Eventually all loans, of whatever description, were
entered in a separate " P " or " Pawns " ledger, a practice which
continued until well into the present century.

There are isolated instances of mortgages on property in the
early days, but they all occur in Francis Child's " Own Posting
Book," and appear to have been undertaken by him as a private
venture rather than as part of the normal business. This book also
contains details of exchange accounts showing dealings in foreign
bills, as well as references to his " Adventures " in the East India
trade.

Acting as goldsmith and banker to many national figures of the
period, the firm's ledgers contain a large number of interesting
accounts, amongst them being that of King William and his Queen,
Mary. The first entries on the debit side of this account, dated May
17, 1689, are

For Loan of Jewells for ye Coronation to ye Queen	£222
For a pre. of Diamd. Earings to ye Queen	300

---

² The security for this loan appears to have been over-valued, for when she died
two years later, in debt to the bank, they purchased the plate in part settlement
for the sum of £3,791 5s. 9d. only.

In his own personal account-book, Francis Child records £10 18s. 6d. " Paid for a Place att ye Coronation," while a later entry, dated April 30, 1691, records the receipt of £50 " Recd. of ye Queen to be given away."

The ledgers, then called posting books, varied considerably in size and shape, being referred to as " ye greate poaste Booke," " little Posting booke," " long new Po. Booke," etc. The earliest surviving ledger for 1662–1670 contains 235 accounts and occupies 514 pages. Most of these are simple accounts consisting of only a few entries each. The second ledger, running concurrently with the first—from 1663 to 1679—is a larger volume of 656 pages but contains only 18 accounts. Of these, three alone occupy two-thirds of the ledger; Christopher Cratford has 205 pages, Roger Jenyns [3] 100 pages and Lord Herbert (subsequently Marquess of Worcester) 106 pages. This division of the accounts into active and non-active seems to have been the regular practice, for the ledgers show a similar pattern throughout the whole of the seventeenth century. Taking one year with another, 11 per cent. of all the accounts were those of ladies.

The standard of book-keeping was decidedly poor. The writing was often very bad, items being entered and then crossed out or altered in a rough and heavy hand, while the spelling of the names was more often than not purely phonetic, varying even from page to page. The account of John St. Leger, for example, is carried forward as " Sellinger," while there are many variations of such names as Beauvoir, Villiers, Wolseley, etc. This question of spelling was not all one-sided, however, for we find Sir Benjamin Maddox originally signing his account as " Maddoks," changing later to " Maddox."

Accounts, particularly the goldsmith accounts, often ended with a small balance either way. If it was a credit balance it was usually ignored; if a debit, it would be balanced by an entry " amount abated." In the case of purely banking accounts the records are rather franker. That of the Dowager Lady Anne Brooke, for example, contains a credit entry, " Per Mistake some way to Ball. £5. 4. 3.," while another account, that of John Mawson, was balanced by the entry, " Recd. I suppose though not posted before ... £436. 16. 6."

At this early stage in the development of banking there were no passbooks and it was the practice for the customer to call from time to time and check his account in the actual ledger in the presence of one of the partners. Having agreed his account, the customer would

---

[3] Cousin of the celebrated Sarah, Duchess of Marlborough.

append his signature at the foot, and the partner present would often append his as well. A typical form of wording was

Feb. 17. 1688. I allow of this acct. there
resting due to mee £640. 17. 7.
JOHN HARVEY

In this particular case, however, the customer seems to have been aware of the fact that mistakes were often made, for he adds—" errors excepted."

By the 1680's the practice had developed of sending the customer a copy of his account on a sheet of paper, similar to the modern statement of account. The ledger would be balanced and a note made that the account had been sent. The Earl of Danby's account, for example, was balanced on November 9, 1686, and the entry made—" By an acc^t then dell^d his hon^r there rested due to his hon^r £2362.–.9¼." An entry in another account, dated March 22, 1686–1687, records the sending of the account " with all his Vouchers since Aprill the 2d." The issue of passbooks was a logical development of this practice and the earliest mention of these is found in the records in 1715.

Balance night, for so long a headache each half-year to banking staffs, was a very different affair in the seventeenth century. Then known as " Casting up ye Shop," it was done at very irregular intervals, varying from eighteen months to as long as eight years. Individual accounts were not necessarily balanced on these occasions, this usually being done only when an account was asked for, or the customer called to agree and sign the ledger. Records of these periodic assessments of the state of business survive from 1686 onwards and, in most cases, sufficient information is available to draw up fairly accurate balance sheets. It is interesting to note that the dates chosen for this irregular " Casting up ye Shop" usually bore some relationship to national events. For example, William of Orange landed at Torbay on November 5, 1688, and James II abdicated on December 11; the books were balanced on December 8. Similar action was taken six days prior to the final incorporation of the Bank of England on July 27, 1694.

The balance sheets reveal that the ratio of cash to deposits was normally about 35 per cent. On two occasions, however, in September, 1697, and again in October, 1712, it rose to over 50 per cent. Today the corresponding figure is under 10 per cent., but the higher figure then is understandable. The comparative newness of the system, together with the fact that the times were uncertain, made it difficult to assess just what demands would be made by customers withdrawing their cash, and the banker of the day had to keep a large stock of actual cash in his strong-room ready to meet any eventualities.

Apart from actual cash, the assets included the stock of jewels, gold and plate held in the shop, and the figures show very clearly the decline in this side of the business as the partners concentrated more and more on banking. From 1686 until 1696 the ratio of these assets to deposits averaged just over 17 per cent. In 1697 and 1704 they were 7 per cent. and in 1712 only 1 per cent. On two occasions the assets included an item " Sweep " of £40 and £220, obviously referring to the sweepings from the goldsmith's workshop.

The total of deposits varied fairly considerably, being £109,000 in 1694 and again in 1712, while the figure rose to £160,000 in 1690 and to £177,000 in 1704.

In 1686 the balance sheet shows liabilities exceeding assets by £39 0s. 11d., but thereafter a credit balance was maintained varying up to £8,500. Only once—in 1697—do the balance sheets mention any division of profits. On that occasion the amount divided was £2,250 and at the same time £1,878 8s. 5d. was allocated as " Provision for Bad Debts." Some idea of the profits, however, can be obtained by reference to the partners' own accounts. Francis Child joined Robert Blanchard as a partner in the goldsmith business at about the time he married Blanchard's step-daughter, Elizabeth Wheeler, in 1671, and we find him credited with £50 on October 22, 1674, " p. Pfitt to Mich. 74," with a further £50 a year later. No further entry can be found until 1697, by which time Blanchard had died and Sir Francis Child (he was knighted in 1689) was the senior partner. In September of that year, as has already been stated, £2,250 was divided, of which Sir Francis received £1,000. There is then a further gap until 1701 from which year the figures are more regular—and astonishing, considering the size of the business. In August, 1701, he was credited with £3,000; October, 1702, with £4,000; February, 1704, with £8,000 together with a further £4,000 in the July of the same year. From that time until his death in 1713, Sir Francis took a smaller share in the profits amounting only to £1,200 a year: a further £1,000 being divided between the other partners. It is of interest to note that throughout this latter period the entries always record the same detail—" Recd. on acct. of profits of ye Shop since Mich. 1704," confirming the fact that there was no " Casting up ye Shop " during the intervening years.

Sir Francis Child kept accounts in his books for a number of his fellow goldsmith bankers, entries in which show that they were in the habit of paying each other's notes and leaving amounts with each other to meet such liabilities. Examination of these accounts raises an interesting question as to their business arrangements. It would appear that while not actual partners in their business as bankers, they did, in fact, combine for the purpose of their goldsmith business in some form of co-partnership. The ledger for 1669–1679, for example, contains a lengthy and detailed account, headed by the clerk— " Inventory of Dyamonds and Jewels betweene Mr. E(ast) and my M(aste)r." And for the better identification of these partnership assets there are appended several pages of drawings of individual items with a note of their value and eventual disposal.

In the same ledger is the account of this John East—who carried on his business in the Strand, only a few doors away from Child's— and this is debited and credited with " ½ pte " of sales and purchases of jewels. As an instance of the way this worked, Robert Flatman's account with Child's is debited September 30, 1670, with £23 10s.— for a diamond ring; John East's account being credited the following February 22 with £11 15s.—" ½ pte of a ring sold Mr. Flatman." Similarly, debit entries in John East's account, such as " Pd. by ½ pte of a Ring he sold of ours," shows that the partnership operated both ways.

Contemporary with these accounts, but in the ledger for 1677–1682, there is a further account of " Dyamonds bought betweene Mr. Mawbert, Mr. Churchey, Mr. East and ourselves," and Mr. Churchey's separate account in the same ledger is debited and credited with items " in pte of " various transactions.

As has already been said, the prominence of the goldsmith side of the business diminished considerably towards the end of the seventeenth century, but cheques continued to be addressed to " Sir Francis Child & Compy., Goldsmiths " until well into the next century, and it is not until 1729, the year they first issued printed bank notes, that we find a cheque addressed to the firm as " Bankers."

The personal banking, started so many years ago, is still carried on at Child's Branch on the very same site where it started, and among the bank's customers are many who can find the accounts of their ancestors in the early ledgers. These contain not only much material of considerable banking interest, but they also have a lighter side. What could be more human, for instance, than the little note penned by the young son of the 1st Duke of Beaufort in 1686—when he would have been about eighteen—addressed to his father's banker?

> Pray do mee the favour to pay this bird-man four guineas for a paire of parckeets that I had of him. Pray dont let any body either my Ld. or Lady know that you did it and I will be sure my selfe to pay you honestly againe.
>
> ARTHUR SOMERSET
>
> Chelsey
> the 23d. of September 86

A Bookseller's Memorandum Book, 1695–1720

Cyprian Blagden*

SOME evidence of the way in which, at the beginning of the eighteenth century, a small tradesman kept a record of his business has recently been brought to light in Somerset House [1] by Colonel Le Hardy. It is a Memorandum Book of 184 leaves, 16 ins. by 6¼ ins., kept by Henry Rhodes, a Fleet Street bookseller, from 1695 to 1720; and I believe, from a detailed study of the variety of the entries and from the continuity in the dates, that it is the only permanent record which Rhodes had for his business. There must have been an earlier volume of a similar nature, to which occasional reference is made; and there were perhaps cash-books for retail shop business, of which there is no mention. But, though I believe that Rhodes kept only one book of accounts, I cannot claim that this gives anything like a complete picture. I cannot understand why some transactions are entered and others, of a similar nature, are relegated to pieces of paper kept in his "scrutore," and I have therefore chosen to call the document a memorandum-book, rather than a ledger which suggests completeness and periodic balancing; moreover, it is a book of first entry in which appears the handwriting of his servants and, I expect, of Mrs. Rhodes, and in which other booksellers and their servants sign for goods received. But there is no aspect of his working life as a bookseller which does not find some mention and there are a few entries which throw a little light on his private affairs; there are notes of the lending of money to his maids, the record that he and not the bookseller at Eton had paid his son's coach-fare in July, 1705, and a note that he had instructed Mr. Appleyard to pay £1,000 into the Exchequer on his behalf a month later.

Henry Rhodes was made free of the Stationers' Company by redemption on March 26, 1680, and shortly afterwards set up at the Star, which stood on the corner of Bride Lane and Fleet Street. In this shop he conducted the four main branches of his business: he

---

* Executive, Longmans, Green & Co., Ltd., Publishers, London.
[1] I am grateful to the Senior Registrar both for his assistance in making this document easily accessible to me and for his permission to quote from it. Since I wrote this article, Colonel Le Hardy has found another memorandum-book which Rhodes began to keep as a result of his quarrel with Mrs. Harris (see below p. 261) and which deals solely with the printing and distribution of the periodical, *The Monthly Mercury*.

sold new and old books retail (his own publications and those of other booksellers); he managed and distributed periodicals (both wholesale and retail); he acted, in a small way, as a wholesale supplier of London books to the country trade; and he managed the printing and distribution of those books in which he owned the copyright.

Cash sales to retail customers are not mentioned in the memorandum-book, but credit accounts for about 250 "Gentlemen" occupy, among entries of many different kinds, a large amount of space—particularly on the earlier leaves. One opening (ff. 56ᵛ and and 57ʳ) will illustrate what sort of accounts these are. The first entry, dated August 19, 1699, is a record of five lots of cheap books sold to Peter Parker, a bookseller, and paid for the same day. Rhodes perhaps expected Parker to come back for more since he made the next entry in time (August 23) some inches lower down the page.² By August 26 he must have decided that Parker was not going to return immediately (he did not buy again till October 19) for he used the space for six volumes of Tillotson's *Sermons* sold to "Mr Turner yᵉ Silkman" for £1 10s. On August 28 he sold four copies of *The Devout Companion*, bound, to "yᵉ French Gentleman Mr Meidgs friend," and on September 4 he began an account for "Mr Wise Minister at Richmond" which jogged on with small entries until September 3, 1700, and only amounted to 15s. At the top of the right-hand page he opens with Dr. Atterbury of Highgate. Half a page is left for him, which lasts until June 4, 1701, where his account runs into that of John Slatter, bookseller of Eton, dated September 5, 1699, the day on which Atterbury's account was opened. A cash account of September 8 for Nicholas Boddington, another bookseller, completes the page. When accounts are settled Rhodes lightly crosses them through, and he usually adds, for trade accounts, the date of settlement. There is no index and the leaves are not numbered. There is a rough system of cross-reference by date. Rhodes goes about as far as he can towards *not* following the simple rules for keeping accounts laid down in one of his own publications, *The Exact Dealer*.

For his established "Gentlemen" customers, like Nathaniel Axtel

---

² The following is an exact transcript of this entry, which is crossed through:

	To Mr Gately Apothecary Augᵗ : 23ᵈ			
	1 Ett[m]uller abridg'd	–	–	0 5 6
	1 Lat. Com. Prayʳ wʰ Psalms	–	0· 3 6
Dec 9	1 Cambdens Brittania	–	–	1 10 –
1700				
Jan 17	For 1ˢᵗ paymᵗ for Colliers Dictʸ qʳˢ			0 16 1

As confirmation of the crossing through habit, I find that another bookseller, Samuel Smith, in writing (December, 1684) to a customer who has just paid his bill, says: "I have crossed ye booke."

and Mr. Digby, Rhodes devotes a whole page and allows the account to run for about a year; along with the sales of books he records exchanges and borrowings.   He is ready to sell any books, new or not so new, which are available in London; when the second-hand books are not worth listing he lumps them together as " a Parcel of books." Though he naturally tends to sell, retail, proportionately more copies of books like Collier's *Dictionary* and *Letters writ by a Turkish Spy* in which he holds a share of the copyright, he also deals in many hundreds of other books and gives us the varying prices at which they were sold, bound and unbound.

These accounts show how one bookseller kept a record of his retail credit transactions.   They suggest that quite an ordinary bookseller had a wide range of customer—the local tradesman, church-warden, parson and lawyer, the schoolmaster in the suburbs, the M.P. and the country gentleman, and even members of the aristocracy: there is no hint of specialisation either in the kind or in the geographical situation of Rhodes's customers.   They emphasise (what is well known) that 250 years ago a bookseller, in addition to acting in all respects as a bookseller would today, lent books from his stock, lent money and acted as a commission agent in London (by buying lottery tickets, for instance) for his country customers.   They provide evidence for establishing the ratio between retail and trade prices, and for estimating the costs of binding.

Rhodes's handling of periodicals is treated in the memorandum-book exactly like his handling of pamphlets or cheap books, except that, in addition, he records (when cash is not paid) the charges for advertisements.   In April, 1704, for instance, Dr. Atterbury was to pay 5s. for three notices " of an Inn " and Mr. Watts 12s. 6d. for a quarter's " Advᵗ of Teeth " in *The Flying Post*, which came out three times a week.   But much the most interesting is the agreement which he made on May 20, 1700, with Richard Smith, another bookseller,

to Print Once a Week for this year an Advertisemᵗ in the Flying Post Giving an Invitation to Persons to sell him Parsells or Librarys of Books, for wᶜʰ he is to pay Mr Rhodes by Quarterly Paymᵗˢ from this day at 25ˢ per Quarter till the year is up 5ˡ five Pound and he has paid this day in pᵗ: five shillings and I likewise Promise that there shall be no such Advertisemᵗˢ with my knowledge put in Relating to buying of books wᵗʰout Mr Smiths Consent.

Witnest our Hands

[signed] Hen. Rhodes
Richard Smith

What follows this entry is a perfect example of the incompleteness of Rhodes's records.   There is no mention of the £1 due to balance the first quarter; on September 7 Smith paid the 25s. due on August 20, and on February 24, 1701, he paid 30s. " in full." The account is then crossed through.

As a third side to his business Rhodes has dealings with over a dozen provincial booksellers but, with few exceptions, he sells them only his own books or periodicals. The name of the carrier, the inn where he puts up and the day when he sets out are always clearly recorded; but the repeat orders seldom come; wholesaling to the provincial trade was not one of Rhodes's successful ventures. With John Slatter of Eton, however, he has a close association lasting for ten years and sometimes resulting in well over £20 worth of business in twelve months. The first account, to which I have already referred, consists almost entirely of binding 500 books for £3 19s., and every year there are large sums charged for binding (usually school-books) or notes of amounts paid to Mr. King the binder on Slatter's behalf. As time goes on Rhodes supplies, in addition to his own publications, both cheap school-books (which he had at first been merely having bound for him) and more expensive theological and classical works. From 1708, however, this side of the business with Slatter began to decline (perhaps young Rhodes had ceased to be the connecting link); the last account, which runs from July 14 to December 29, 1709, contains no items but two of Rhodes's monthly periodicals.

I come now to those entries which reveal Rhodes's activities as a proprietor of copyrights; these fall, with one exception, into four categories: his relationship with authors, his dealings with printers and suppliers of paper, his instructions to binders, and his complicated sales arrangements with other London booksellers who probably had the same general pattern of behaviour as he had.

The exception occurs when Rhodes is acting outwardly as a proprietor but in reality as an agent for someone else; and such agency is not always for the sale of books. Rhodes was one of the booksellers entitled to deal wholesale in " Stoughton's Elixir "; he received as many as seven dozen of this mixture in May, 1704, but leaves no note of how or when he disposed of them. On January 18, 1700, he records the receipt from Mr. Inglish of five boxes of pills at 2s. a box, which he is to sell at 2s. 6d. In the course of the summer of 1702 he receives from Mrs. Wroth two dozen bottles of liquid snuff to retail at 6d. a bottle; he puts two advertisements in *The Flying Post* at 2s. 6d. a time and his apprentice records the payment of 2s. 6d. to Mrs. Wroth on September 16; the balance, 4s. 6d., is presumably his profit on this transaction (over and above the concealed profit in the advertising). A year later he receives from Mr. Emmet " 12 Pictures of our Steple for wch I am to allow him 8s per doz when sold; 1 in frame besides, return'd again." These were probably engravings of St.

Bride's steeple, which was completed in 1701 and at the foot of which stood Rhodes's shop.

There are several examples of similar bargains made with the authors of books. Sometimes Rhodes is only one of the distributors, as he is in November, 1699, when he receives from Dr. Maynwaring twenty-five copies of his *Ignota Febris* in quires and a further six bound in sheep, " To be pd for as used or else return'd "; and as he is in November, 1704, when he receives from Colonel Parsons two copies of a *Book of Cyphers*, bound and lettered, to sell to booksellers at 9s. 6d. each and to " Gentlemen " at 12s., and a further two copies in quires to sell at 7s. 6d. and 10s.

Sometimes he is the sole distributor. Nearly two pages are devoted to the account of Dr. William Cole's *Consilium Aetiologicum*, which is advertised among the Reprints in the *Term Catalogue* for Hilary, 1703, as " sold by H. Rhodes . . . Price 2s bd." Rhodes records receipts and deliveries in the same column; but it is possible to discover that between August, 1702, and February, 1709, when the account is " Even'd and Paid," Rhodes received 650 copies in quires from Wilde the printer, who still had fifty left at the end. Far and away the best customer for the book was the author; Rhodes arranged for the delivery of over 300 copies to him, six or a dozen at a time, through the binders King and Gathorn who put the books up in calf or sheep; and there is a note that on April 2, 1703, the " Dr had 100 for Holland from my house " in quires. The editor of *The History of the Works of the Learned* is sent a copy for review; so pleased is Dr. Cole with the four-page result that he buys twenty-five copies of the September issue. The rest of the account is taken up with notes of the advertisements arranged by Rhodes (like most authors, Cole was a great believer in space advertising) and of the few other books sold to the doctor. There is no mention in the account of the total number of copies of the *Consilium* sold by Rhodes nor of the financial return to either party.

Most of the books in which Rhodes himself owned the copyright, wholly or in part, were first published before the date of the earliest entry in the memorandum-book; there is therefore little evidence of payments to authors. The few fees which are set down are either for editorial work or for translations. David Jones was the editor of the annual publication, *The Compleat History of Europe*, and Rhodes carefully notes the loan to him in November, 1704, of Clarendon's second volume " to goe on wth History of Europe for Mr Nicolson Mr Bell & my self," and the payment of 2s. coach-hire at the same time and on the same account; but the main arrangement with Jones must have been made by one of the other partners.[3]   It is likewise impossible even to guess at the terms agreed with Jeremy Collier either for the new editions of his *Dictionary* or for the *Supplements* to it, though Rhodes did pay him £10 in January, 1715.   There is an entry for February 11, 1706, which is encouragingly headed " The Acco^t: of ye Managem^t of the Tongue."   Of the twelve lines in the account, which lasts till April 16, three record payments to Mr. La Roche for translating (£5 and £3, and £1 1s. 6d. " Presented him wth over "), one is for 12s. 6d. spent at the Oxford Arms with the translator, one is a 10s. advertisement in the *Gazette*, six are for copies of the book presented to various people and one for 10s. " Pd Mr Froude [4] Postage for Original."   A similar account is started at about the same time for *The Memorial from Holland* and plenty of space is left for its completion; but the only item of interest is that Mr. Ridpath was paid 30s. for his part in the translation.

Rhodes's arrangement with William Salmon for one of his books is dealt with in the following note: " Then even'd & P^d Mrs Gray the whole Acco^t for Dr Salmons writeing The Herbal, ye Febr 9th: 1716 [1717]. . . ."   The printing of the *Herbal* was done by Ichabod Dawks, with whom a final settlement was made three years later and recorded in the same general and unrewarding terms.   The only details which Rhodes does record with great care are of the rent paid for warehousing the book and of the stock he draws from the warehouse; it is probable, therefore, that his partner in this venture, William Taylor, kept the main account and acted as " manager."   If we assume that Rhodes's memorandum-book was typical of the records kept by his colleagues in the London trade at this time, and if we put the lack of detailed information about certain transactions with the number of signatures (of other booksellers and their servants) which Rhodes's book contains, it seems reasonable to hazard this suggestion: of the two parties to a normal credit transaction—the creditor and the debtor—the creditor was responsible for keeping a record of it which would be open to the debtor's inspection and, in many cases, signed by him as a true statement.   The debtor might, as Rhodes often did, keep a memorandum of what happened and when; but he would be saved time and trouble by omitting altogether the recording of some transactions (as when he made an " exchange " in another's shop [5]) and by reducing the recording of other transactions

---

[3] Partners, not in Rhodes's business, but in the undertaking of individual book-producing ventures.

[4] He was Controller of the Post Office and a customer of Rhodes's but he did not always release foreign packets as speedily as he ought.   " It was in town a fortnight before " is Rhodes's irritated comment on receiving from Froude the February issue of *Les Clefs des Cabinets* on March 15.

[5] See below, pp. 262–263.

to a brief note (as when he had signed for deliveries from a printer or when he knew that the details had been written down by his partner). As a creditor—when selling to other booksellers or to private customers—Rhodes would be responsible for recording the smallest item for which cash was not paid. His agreement with Richard Smith about a series of advertisements (which I quoted earlier) is an example of the care he takes when he is the interested—and therefore the responsible—party; in the same way he makes Francis Bugg write and sign the following note in the memorandum-book:

> Aprill ye 19th 1699 I doe Agree to take of Mr. Rhodes: three pence half peny: A book Intituled Quakerisme exposed: . . . & he is to sell them at 6d: And, when you want, send to Mr Jeneway book binder . . . And hel furnish you at all times.

This theory—that the creditor's record was normally enough for the book trade—holds good for the printers with whom Rhodes has dealings. When he lends money, as he does to Jenour in May, 1717, or sells books, as he does to Everingham in 1696 and 1698, he keeps a careful note; but he only reveals the facts that Croome printed *Funeral Gifts* for him in December, 1703, through a note of the sales of copies which he, Rhodes, never handled; and that Bowyer was printing part of the *Supplement* to Collier's *Dictionary* by a note of the withdrawal, in January, 1705, of some of the paper from Bowyer and its redelivery to Wilde and Broomhead. In this last example Rhodes is acting, so to speak, as a paper-supplier and feels obliged to keep the record in case any dispute should arise.

His own records of dealings with paper-merchants are confined (as we should expect) to sales of waste—bundles of *The Flying Post* to Samuel West of Southwark or Mr. Tysum of Cripplegate in 1707 and 1708, and various quantities and varieties of waste to Mr. Banks of Newgate between 1716 and 1719—and to incidental revelations of the books which Wilde and Mrs. Snowdon printed and for which Hoole supplied the paper.

Normally, and no doubt for the reason I have suggested, Rhodes does not record the receipt of stock from printers: one knows when stock has been received because one finds its being sold; but there are two sets of exceptions. For his monthly periodicals he keeps at different times careful notes of stock received and, for the *Monthly Mercury*, notes of the numbers printed. I think that the reasons for this are partly suspicion of his partners (particularly Mrs. Harris with whom he had a tremendous row) and partly the need to keep separate the drawing off of back numbers. These reasons also operate with the second set of exceptions. Stocks of big books like the *Supplement* to Collier's *Dictionary* could not be taken into his own shop as soon as they were printed; they had to be warehoused with the printer, or with a binder or another bookseller who had space to hire. It was therefore essential to ensure, by keeping a careful record of copies delivered to him, that neither his untrustworthy partner, Maurice Atkins, nor the man providing warehouse accommodation should acquire books for which Rhodes had paid.

As I have already said, Rhodes records no purchase of a copyright from an author, nor have I found any reference to his buying even a share in one from another bookseller. He did, however, occasionally sell his own shares—a third share in three of Mrs. Behn's Plays to James Knapton for £3 6s. in 1697, a third share in *Love's Last Shift*, with 300 copies [6] of the book, to Lintot for £10 in 1701, and, in 1714, the whole copyright of Flavell's *Balm of the Covenant* to Cliff for £3 10s., which he had to share with Mrs. Newborough.

Rhodes's dealings with his fellow booksellers were mostly on an "exchange" basis. John Dunton [7] has described the advantage, particularly to a young bookseller, of being able to stock his shop with a variety of books exchanged for copies of one of his own publications. Such an arrangement in the book trade was probably almost as old as the introduction of printing, and in the early Registers of the Stationers' Company licence to enter books is occasionally given on condition that the copyright owner " shall not refuse to exchange these bookes with the company for other good wares." The practice lived on well into the nineteenth century.

Rhodes's entries of exchanges fall broadly into two categories,[8] which can best be described, contradictorily, as " cash " and " credit." On March 12, 1697, Rhodes's wife or apprentice records the exchange of six of his books for six of Crouch's, a direct and immediate exchange of books of the same kind and price, each party providing three bound and three in quires. On September 22, 1698, Rhodes exchanges six copies of *The Royal Mistresses* (two in quires) and four of *The Devout Companion,* for one each of South's *Sermons,* Vol. 3, and Salmon's *Dispensatory* from Francis Saunders. These " cash " exchanges were completed on the day of entry and are recorded, I think, for the exchange rates. The " credit " arrangements, on the other hand, sometimes spread over several years. For the copy of Phillips's *A New World of Words,* in quires, which he supplied to Samuel Buckley on April 28, 1699, Rhodes did not receive his part of the bargain—two copies of Bysshe's *The Art of English Poetry,* also in quires—until August 26, 1703. In February, 1698, Richard

---

[6] Since the trade price had been 1s. 2d., this was not a profitable transaction.

[7] *The Life and Errors* (new ed., 2 vols., 1818), p. 62.

[8] It can, I think, be assumed that there would be similar categories in the records of other booksellers for transactions, in their shops, with Rhodes or one of his servants.

Greenaway, as the servant of Matthew Wotton, took and signed for a copy of Hale's *Contemplations,* in quires, for which Rhodes is to have a copy of the second part of Echard's *The Roman History* " when printed "; this account is " evend " but there is no indication when.

The " credit " exchanges were, of course, not all as simple as these. On February 25, 1703, Rhodes begins an account for Timothy Goodwin which was not settled, and signed for by both parties, until August 7, 1707. There are several points of interest in this account. All the deliveries made by Rhodes have their exchange prices noted and nearly all are signed for by Goodwin's apprentice, Edward Valentine. It does not of course matter how exchange prices are fixed so long as the principle is the same for all books. I should have thought that in order to reduce the number of prices to be carried in the head it would have been sensible to make the exchange the same as the trade price for a single copy. But for a reason, which is no doubt both good and old, the exchange was higher than the trade price: 4s. 9d. to 3s. 10d., 2s. 6d. to 2s., 5d. to $3\frac{1}{2}$d. In the middle of the Goodwin account there is a charming sidelight on human nature; against February 28, 1705, Rhodes records: " Rec^d 2 Dionis Anatomy qr   he brought 3 but I returned 1."

There remains one aspect of Rhodes's business of which he made careful notes in his memorandum-book. One such is against December 5, 1704:

Gave Mr Cholmley a Note to Receive 600 Witts Cabinets of Mr Barber to deliver to ye Subscribers of it

Return'd 25			all pd
24 Jan: Recd. of him in Mony	5	0	0
1 Feb: — more — in full	2	0	0

Cholmley was a bookbinder who acted as a Town Traveller for Rhodes. He must have collected, during November, the names of those booksellers who were prepared to " subscribe " for *Wit's Cabinet* (price to the public 1s. bound) at the pre-publication rate of 3d.—and the numbers they signed to take. He received the due number of copies from the printer, Barber, delivered them to the subscribers, and, after the agreed period of credit, collected the money and handed it over to Rhodes. It is again typical of the incompleteness of the records that Rhodes does not mention, as he does on some other occasions, the commission earned by Cholmley. The method was also employed at the launching of more expensive books. The following extract, besides being an example of one such subscription, happens—exceptionally—to show how Rhodes paid his bills and to suggest what profit he made on one of his publishing ventures.

		To M[r] Woodward Febr 23[d] 1709/10		£	s	d
		For 700 Salmons Family Dict[ry] at Subscription 4[s] p Quartern [9]		112	0	0
1710		of M[r] Woodward	£ s d			
July	8	Rec[d] & p[d] to Mrs Snowdon	15 : 0 : 0			
—	15	Rec[d] & p[d] to Mr Hoole	15 : 0 : 0			
Aug	17	Rec[d] & p[d] to Mrs Snowdon	15 : 0 : 0			
—	17	Rec[d] & p[d] to Mr Hoole	15 : 0 : 0			
Oct	6	Rec[d] & p[d] to Mr Hoole	20 : 0 : 0			
Nov	29	Rec[d] & p[d] to my Self	14 : 0 : 0			
Mar	10	Rec[d] & p[d] to my Self	08 : 0 : 0			
—	15	Rec[d] & p[d] to my Self in full	10 : 0 : 0			
		Sum	112 : 0 : 0			

P[d] for his Subscribing them & Receiving the mony
4£ 10[s] 0[d]

Like Cholmley, Woodward was a bookbinder; Mrs. Snowdon was the printer and Mr. Hoole the supplier of paper. Rhodes made no profit from this source until he received the last three payments; but more than 700 copies were printed, and other sales, to the trade and retail, were made. As usual there is insufficient evidence, and a full profit and loss account for the book cannot be made. But, on the subscription sales alone, Rhodes cleared £27 10s. after he had paid for paper and print and for the subscription commission. Assuming that the printing number was 1,000 and that the balance was sold at the subscription rate (*i.e.*, taking the worst view, for the book was reprinted), Rhodes would have made a profit of £77 10s., a sum very nearly equivalent to his original investment of £80 [10]; there was the additional, and considerable, advantage that he only had to find the cash for his outlay as the receipts from sales came in.

I have dealt at some length with the main aspects of Rhodes's business, partly in order to establish my point that the memorandum-book was the only permanent record he kept of them, and partly because they determined the manner of his record-keeping. His was a small and personal business conducted, almost certainly, on the ground floor of the house in which he lived. The differentiation between his private and his commercial life—even between his private and commercial expenditure and income—was ill-defined; those who helped him in his business, his wife and his apprentices, were members of his household and worked directly under his instructions

---

[9] For every four copies bought at 4s. each, a fifth copy was given free; the subscription price therefore worked out at 3s. 2d. per copy.

[10] Since this was a reprint, authorship charges probably did not arise. The retail price was 5s., the price to booksellers 3s. 6d.

and, most of the time, under his eye. Moreover, there was no out-sider, no shareholder or income-tax inspector, for whom he had to provide evidence of the state of his business; I doubt if the officials of the Prerogative Court of Canterbury, who were responsible for the survival of the memorandum-book, could have learnt from it much about the value of his estate.

By the same token, I believe that Rhodes himself would have been hard put to it to draw up a balance sheet for a given twelve months. He must have inherited certain book-trade rules of thumb about the relationship between wholesale and retail prices, about costs of production and subscription rates, about handling commissions. Most of the vital information he could carry in his head: his house-hold expenses, his rent, his servants' wages, probably even his indebtedness to printers and paper-suppliers; most of his stock was on his shelves and required no more recording than its daily use imprinted on his memory (what was warehoused elsewhere he care-fully noted). What he did write down was what someone else owed him and, where there might be future argument, the debt was signed for.

Rhodes's knowledge of the relationship between income and expenditure was, I take it, empiric. So long as the cash coming in was at least sufficient for the private and trade demands on it, the business was satisfactory; if the cash accumulated in the till, the surplus was invested in Government securities or, perhaps, in copy-rights, which could be sold in times of difficulty. I doubt if he differentiated between capital and income and, though he might figure out the gross return to him on a certain transaction, he would have thought it unnecessary to calculate, for all aspects of his business, the profit he had made in a given financial year.

Mr. Chest and Mr. Box*

THE deeper roots of present-day banking in England are to be sought not in the eighteen-thirties, when the big banks of today were founded, but a century earlier, when country banking first established itself as a business in its own right, and the country bankers, who were to play so important a role, appeared on the scene. Through the kindness of a reader of this *Review* we have lately had the opportunity of studying three old books of account, which give glimpses of a country banker's affairs at intervals between 1707 and 1777, and offer as clear a picture of the development of banking in that important period of industrial and commercial growth as one might hope to find.

The books belonged to the Derby family of Crompton, whose banking business, founded at the beginning of the eighteenth century —or perhaps even earlier—descended through the generations of the family until, as Crompton, Newton & Co., it was combined with W. & S. Evans & Co. to form Crompton and Evans' Union Bank, Ltd. In 1914 that bank was merged with Parrs Bank, one of the larger of the group of banks which, after amalgamation, ultimately became the Westminster Bank.

Samuel Crompton, of Derby, who died in 1757, was probably the first of his line to confine himself exclusively to banking. The books do not cover a continuous period, and do not bear the names of the owners, but entries dated 1725 in the earliest of the three serve to fix Samuel Crompton as its owner and as proprietor of the business at that time. The following entry provides further confirmation:

> 24th December [1726] paid William Holme for making
> Sam a suit   8s.

Besides throwing a ray of light on the cost of living in the eighteenth century, this entry, supposing it to refer to the proprietor's eldest son, introduces Samuel Crompton II, who was evidently senior partner forty years later, when the second book was in use. Entries indicate that in 1765 Samuel Crompton II had already brought into the business his own eldest son, Samuel Crompton III. By the time the third book came into use the firm appears to have consisted of Samuel II and his four sons. In December, 1779, just before the records cease, the father drew from the business £1,177, his eldest son,

---

* From *The Westminster Bank Review*, August, 1952, pp. 14–17. A reproduction of two pages of the cash-books referred to in this article and a genealogical table of the Cromptons have been omitted.

Samuel III, two-thirds of that sum, and his other three sons, John, Joshua and Gilbert, one-third each. An annual profit of over £3,000 was a very respectable one in 1779.

It was John, one of the sons, who bought " The Lilies " at Windley, where the old account-books were found; and the family connection with the business seems to have been maintained through him, and through his grandson, John Gilbert Crompton, also of " The Lilies." The latter, who was Chairman of Crompton and Evans' Bank, is still remembered in Derby as an elderly man; he died not long before 1914, aged over ninety. Many parallels could be found for the story of this fine old family banking business, extending from the early eighteenth century, through 200 years of growth and development, until its identity was lost—and who will not feel a pang of regret?—by a merger with one of the big banks of the present century.

The earliest entries in the first of the three books do not, however, relate to banking. The book was started in 1707 as a wool-merchant's delivery-book. The following is a typical entry:

> November the 28 [1707] sent Mr. Daws a packe of Good Jarsy Woole at 6. 10. 0 at Derby.

Only about twenty pages had been filled with entries of this kind when the book was put aside in 1709. It was not used again until 1725, when it was opened once more, this time as a banker's cash-book. As there is no reason to think that it had not remained in the possession of the family in the interval, it may be that, by a stroke of luck, we have a clear example of the transition from merchanting to banking that so many firms made at that time. First started as a side-line, banking became the more profitable part of these businesses as the demand for banking services grew, and finally ousted the rest.

It is fortunate that the books, which have survived the chances of 200 years, were cash-books; most of a banker's dealings in the eighteenth century involved cash, and a record of receipts and payments therefore gives a remarkably clear picture of the various classes of business. The entries of 1725 contain a pleasant sprinkling of private affairs; for if, as we suppose, the business then had a sole proprietor, there would have been no essential reason for keeping them separate. So besides the reference to Sam's suit we find payments of £1 to " Cousin Katharine for House "; 10s. to " Ed. Granger for taking care of my Horse "; 12s. 6d. to " John Cross for a pr Boots "; and so on. The following payments speak for themselves:

To Cousin Katharine a quarter's wages		15s.
To Betty	do.	11s. 3d.
To Hannah	do.	10s.
To Milk woman [quarterly]		7s. 7d.

But the first book ended in 1726, and the second did not start until 1765. By then, the business had grown; and as it had become a partnership, there was no place in the cash-book for purely personal entries. No longer written up by the proprietor himself (in the first person singular) but in the neat hand of a clerk, the books had become more business-like—and much less human.

The method of keeping the cash account in these books remained uniform and has nothing remarkable about it to the modern eye. Receipts are entered on the left and payments on the right. The cash was not agreed every day but every three or four days, the balance on hand on the previous occasion (sometimes called the " Last Cash ") being brought forward under the receipts, and the present balance being inserted under the payments, so that the two sides agreed within a few pence. A summary of the cash on hand was written in the margin showing the items separately—G[old], O[dd], S[ilver], B[rass]. " Gold " was a round amount probably made up in a separate bag; " Odd " would be the remainder of the gold guineas, half guineas, quarter guineas, and so on, and possibly foreign coins valued by weight. That the tribulations of bank cashiers have not changed much is shown by such entries as:

Wanting in a £500 bag	5s.
Over 27/- in the Cash	£1 7s. 0d.

But it is to be hoped that the following did not happen often:

Wanting 1s. which a man stole at the counter.

Here was another tiresome incident:

6/9 wanting which I paid to Stephen Seal the 19th which he said was paid him short this Stephen Seal paid the 19th June having found the 6/9 piece in Gillott's House—put it to Pettits

If Pettits was the petty cash, he probably did the best thing.

When the second book was in use the surplus of cash not required from day to day was evidently kept in a chest and a box, the larger part in the chest. Records of transfers to and from this reserve appear among payments and receipts respectively; but there was some reluctance to make these entries too clear. No doubt the custody of the cash was an anxious business in those times, and there was every good reason why as few people as possible should know how much there was; but the method of concealment was not very good:

Rd from S[amuel] C[rompton] C . . . st	£1,000
Paid to the B . . x	£1,500

Whenever the cash was agreed, a summary of the contents of the chest and box was shown separately in the margin, this reserve not being included in the ordinary balance of cash on hand.   Here also a cryptic style was used, with dots instead of zeros:

```
S:   C:   3 . . .
L:   C:   1 . . .
B–x       5 . .
```

The reference to "L.C." is puzzling.   Could there have been a partner named L. Crompton at the time (1766), to whom part of the cash reserve belonged specifically?   It is rather unlikely, since there is no evidence elsewhere of the existence of such a person.   Or were there two chests, Samuel Crompton having custody of one and "L.C." of the other?

In the 1777 book, the chest and box had become "Mr. Chest" and "Mr. Box," and transfers to and from the reserve were shown as receipts from and payments to these fictitious characters.   What is the explanation of this device?   Did it grow out of the former practice of inserting the name of the custodians of the chest (or owners of its contents)?   Or was it that double-entry accounts had been opened for the cash reserve and been given these personal designations?   The chest and box disappeared from the records altogether later in 1777.

When we analyse the classes of transactions in the three books, we come to some facts of great importance in the history of the development of banking methods.   The first things we should look for in a banker's books are records of deposits and withdrawals.   It was the custom at that period to issue a numbered "note" in exchange for every separate sum deposited, the note embodying a promise to repay the depositor, or order, on demand.   In 1725 each sum deposited was entered in the cash-book among the receipts, with the name of the depositor set against it.

From May 22, 1725, only the total of deposits received was entered, with the consecutive numbers of the notes issued, each time the cash was agreed.   On presentation of the note the deposit was repaid in whole or in part with interest, and the payment was entered in the margin separately on the payments side with the year-date and the number of the note.   The total of repayments was carried into the payments column for the purpose of balancing.   The rate of interest allowed appears to have been $3\frac{1}{2}$ per cent.

We may deduce from these facts that in the country at least the idea of a current account had not yet taken shape; the deposit of each sum was regarded as a separate transaction.   The "notes" were certainly used to some extent for payments to other persons, but the main purpose of using a bank was to have a safe place for one's money and to earn interest.   The question of making payments to third parties was a secondary consideration.

The transfer of money from one part of the country to another was a risky business in the early eighteenth century. Payments between provincial towns may not have been very heavy, but many people had occasion to remit money to London. Apart from purchases of goods there was a steady flow of money to the capital representing income (largely rents) for investment or for spending there. In 1725 Cromptons, like other country bankers, regularly accepted funds for transfer to London at a charge (" return ") which seems to have varied between ½ per cent. and ¾ per cent.

> Aug. 6 [1725] Rd of Brown for London 40*l*. retn 5/–   40.5.0

Having accepted the money, the banker had to put his London agent in funds, and he did this as far as possible by buying bills of exchange drawn on merchants in the City. Consignments of produce, such as wool, to London merchants gave rise to a supply of bills, drawn by the sellers on the merchants and then sold to the local bankers. Discount was deducted, but as the usance of the bills was not shown in the Crompton books, it is not clear what the rate was.

The supply of bills was inadequate in 1725 for all the payments it was desired to make in London, and therefore it was necessary for Cromptons to send a consignment of gold from time to time.

> June 6 [1726] for Lo: in Box directed for Mr. Benson in Star Court, Brd St, Lo: in it 1000 Gns, 10 Moidrs [Moidores?] 2 fr [French?] Gns. 1065.10.0

By 1765, however, the growth of commerce had been so great that the supply of bills was sufficient and there are no records in the second and third books of consignments of gold. Money is no longer entered as received " for London "; instead we find records of sales of bills to customers, who presumably sent them to creditors in London and elsewhere by messenger or by post. The supply of bills was augmented by the " notes " of the Bank of England, which were used freely in London as a means of payment and found their way into the country in fair numbers. These were not bank notes in the present-day sense of promissory notes payable to bearer, but were similar in form to the notes issued by the country bankers against deposits. The Cromptons bought and sold them and also Bank Post Bills, which were bills issued by the Bank of England to customers as a rather safer means of remitting money than bankers' notes.

Cromptons had a particular reason for making heavy payments in London. At some time in the middle of the century they became Receivers (Tax Collectors) for the county. In April and October, when they collected the Land Tax and Window Tax, they had about £3,000 to send to London, and they did this by buying bills to the required amount from Messrs. Wilkinsons, Bankers, of Chesterfield.

The evidence seems to show that in the middle of the eighteenth century bills of exchange were still primarily a means of safe and convenient payment; their function as credit instruments was still in course of development.

The Cromptons lent money, of course, and the books show that they did so on mortgages and bonds; but the day-to-day method of lending seems to have been against the customer's " note." The term " note " was applied to an acknowledgment of indebtedness whether from customer to banker or vice versa. The rate of interest charged was 5 per cent.

Other business carried on by the firm included the collection of dividends for customers and the purchase and sale of securities. There were not many Stock Exchange investments available in those days, and the ones we find referred to are Bank of England Stock, East India Stock, South Sea Stock, and Government annuities.

An interesting feature of the business was that the Cromptons were pay-agents for the militia, and the record of transactions under this heading includes payments for " clothing the militia," many payments of £1 for " Deserters warrants," and the following:

19 May 1779 Pd Major Revell the Militia Marching Guineas   £559.13.0

A brisk business was done in State lottery tickets, and it is pleasing to note that Christmas, 1777, was cheered by two of the brothers receiving a prize of £19 12s.

Such are a few of the facts and impressions yielded by a preliminary study of these interesting and valuable relics of an important chapter in the long history of English banking. Did Mr. Granger (salary £50 per annum) ever dream that the entries he made in his excellent handwriting would make such fascinating reading 200 years later?

Accounting in Colonial America[1]

W. T. Baxter*

MOST people who have lived in a small country town can still remember cases of " book-keeping barter." Perhaps for instance the dairy-farmer sent milk each day to the tailor. The latter did not bother—and was hardly expected—to pay cash, but ran up his account indefinitely. Then, when the farmer needed a new suit, he ordered it from the tailor. With luck the two sets of sales would more or less cancel over the years, so that both men avoided the distasteful task of settling accounts by paying money.

This modified version of barter seems to have been the essence of much colonial trade, to judge from surviving account-books.

BARTER

In the eighteenth century, barter was still practised to some extent in Britain[2]; in America, it was very common. For this there were several reasons. First, each community was small in numbers; and, if a market consists of few dealers, the chances are high that A will both sell to and buy from B—particularly as both men may be somewhat unspecialised and so have a wide range of wares on offer. Second, money was scarce and bad.[3] Britain would not let the colonies make their own coins; and any British coins that reached America were soon sent home again to pay for much-needed manufactures. So, though the colonists calculated and bargained in terms of pounds, shillings, and pence, these were somewhat abstract moneys of account

---

* Professor of Accounting, London School of Economics and Political Science.
[1] My interest in this subject was roused by research on the records left by the Hancocks of Boston ; a description of that firm's accounts is given in my *House of Hancock* (Cambridge, Mass., 1945), and " Credits, Bills, and Bookkeeping in a Simple Economy " in *Studies in Accounting* (London, 1950), edited by me. To find whether the Hancock's methods were typical, I have lately looked at over fifty other sets of accounts, for firms scattered from New Hampshire to Virginia—and in one case at Nevis. The evidence appears consistent and convincing. However, there are few sets of records that include, for any one firm, both (a) correspondence, orders to pay, etc., and (b) complete accounts, *i.e.*, day-book and ledger for the same period. Particularly for (a), the Hancock MSS. are still the least fragmentary collection that I have seen.
[2] The writers of accounting textbooks deemed it worthy of mention, *e.g.*, John Mair's *Book-keeping Modernized*, 6th ed. (Edinburgh, 1793) has a section on " Debtor and Creditor applied in Bartering," p. 28.
[3] See, *e.g.*, C. P. Nettels, *The Money Supply of the American Colonies* (Madison, 1934) ; A. M. Davies, *Currency and Banking in the Province of Massachusetts Bay* (New York, 1901) ; and W. B. Weedon, *Economic and Social History of New England, 1620–1789* (Boston, 1890).

rather than real coins; their nearest equivalents today are perhaps the " guineas " 'that generous British donors send to charities, or the " bits " that sometimes crop up in American speech. When hard money was in fact available, it was likely to consist of a motley collection of foreign coins, such as Spanish dollars, which the colonists gained by trade with the West Indies. The dollar, worth 4s. 6d. in sterling, was declared by each colony to be worth such-and-such a number of its own imaginary shillings (for example, Massachusetts at one stage valued a dollar at six local shillings). The colony that put the biggest value on the dollar hoped to attract most coins to its ports; they argued that this kind of inflation would lure silver from Spaniards, pirates, and other holders of dollars. But the inflow of coins proved erratic. Moreover they were often light-weight and mutilated; their sizes did not make up a convenient range of values; and in any case they seldom circulated in a colony for more than six months before they too were exported to pay British debts.

In an attempt to make good the shortage of coins, the colonists issued various kinds of paper money. Their schemes were apt to be ingenious rather than sound. In Virginia " tobacco notes " were based on tobacco in warehouses. In Massachusetts, groups of private persons formed a " land bank " and a " silver bank " to emit notes. The provincial government might issue notes—with no special backing, but with a promise that they would be accepted in payment of tax. These flows of paper sometimes led to inflation, and widened the disparity between the money-units of the different colonies.

Under such handicaps, even a rich and provident man was apt to be perennially short of sound money. He might look on coins not as the inevitable means of paying for commodities but as one of the commodities themselves—and one whose supply was exceptionally fickle. " Bring all the money you can for it is scarce and in good demand " wrote a Canadian settler in 1773.[4]

In these circumstances some form of barter was inevitable.

" Barter " is apt to call up mental pictures of a savage trying to swap a pig for a spear. Such an exchange, simple though it sounds, must in fact present awkward problems. The savage has to find a seller who

(a) owns a spear just equal in worth to the pig; and

(b) wants a pig on just that day.

The value of colonial accounts is that they show how men over-came these difficulties. Barter became plain sailing when traders could appraise goods in common terms, and still more when they

---

[4] Frederick Moore, a loyalist *émigré* whose letter is preserved at the East Pulteney Tavern Vermont.

could stretch the exchange over a long time.   Money—even though it was too scarce to be always available as the unit of exchange— provided the common unit of value; and book-keeping gave the means for remembering and proving the details of a lengthy exchange.   Thus the farmer of colonial New England was able to sell his pig in Boston for a money-credit in the storekeeper's books; he could then take supplies as and when he wanted them, while the storekeeper charged up his account.   If the farmer could also on occasion *assign* his credit to third persons—so that the storekeeper acted in effect as his bank— then barter became a tolerably flexible and efficient means of trading.

In discussing colonial trade we must evidently distinguish between what we may call:

(1) truck, *i.e.*, the simultaneous exchange of goods; and

(2) book-keeping barter, *i.e.*, an exchange with a time-lag.

Both types of barter appear to have flourished.   The colonists were not much given to compiling statistics of their doings, and so a quantitative description of their different ways of trade is hard to come by.   But one exceptional man did make and bequeath to us an analysis of his sales.   He was Adam Stanton, who kept a general store at Clinton, Connecticut.   His surviving records [5] include pages ruled with columns in which he splits up his " sails " for each week from 1796 to 1801.   The columns are for:

" Truck "   —   presumably straightforward barter;

" Charged " —   presumably credit sales, which might be paid for later either in cash or by book-keeping barter.

" Cash "   —   presumably cash sales.

His total for the three items averaged about £40 a week.   A little more than 10 per cent. of these sales were for truck, over 60 per cent. were charged, and under 30 per cent. were for cash.

Unfortunately, Stanton does not tell us what fraction of his charged sales was eventually paid for in cash and what by barter.   This was a bit of information that could hardly be foreseen at the date of sale. Even a search through the accounts in many ledgers, long after they have been ruled off, does not yield satisfactory statistics on the point (mainly because the involved nature of some transactions defies analysis).   But, as a rough guide to the quantities at stake, I would hazard a guess that about one-third of total indebtedness was dis- charged in cash, and two-thirds by more roundabout means such as book-keeping barter.

The books of most traders seldom mention truck; men less fond than Stanton of statistics may have thought that crude barter called

---

[5] At Yale Library.

for no entries. But Ninian Boog of Virginia kept a household expenses account,[6] which shows that much of his food was got by bartering wares from his store:

	£	s.	d.
To 1 dozen pipes for 1 dozen eggs			4
4 penknives 2s. 1 lace 9d. for 2 turkeys		2	9
1 quart rum for 4 chickens		1	3

and so on, at the rate of about twenty purchases a month. When the wares from the store did not quite balance the food received, a little cash was thrown in as the needed make-weight.

BOOK-KEEPING BARTER

If most traders did not trouble to mention truck in their accounts, they were at pains to record more sophisticated exchanges. Indeed, I fancy that the main purpose of colonial book-keeping was to lubricate barter.[7] Ledgers contained practically nothing save accounts for persons; apparently colonial merchants for the most part saw no point in keeping any other records. Further, these accounts cannot readily be divided between those of debtors and creditors. A modern firm can split up its personal accounts into two clear camps: its debtors (goods on the left, cash on the right), and its creditors (goods and cash the other way round). The colonial merchant bought from, and sold to, the same man, and so an account in his ledger might well have goods on both sides. Perhaps he could mentally distinguish between " suppliers " (often the British exporters who sent manufactures to him) and " customers " (*e.g.*, the smaller storekeepers of the villages); and it may be that he tended to be in debt to his suppliers, and that his customers were usually in debt to him—though a balance might well swing the other way after a large remittance in kind. Perhaps too he could divide goods into (i) those which it was his primary aim to handle, and (ii) those staples—beef, timber, tobacco, etc.—which passed more as commodity-money than as merchandise.[8]

The evidence on this point is overwhelming. Though cash is

---

[6] His ledger (1748–1751) lies in the library of William and Mary College.

[7] It would be an interesting task, if one had the skills of a medievalist, to find out whether the same generalisation holds for the earliest examples of book-keeping in Europe. There is a certain plausibility in the notion that the American colonies were, in such matters as currency shortage and lack of specialisation, nearer to the thirteenth than to the twentieth century. And European textbooks of the seventeenth—still more, those of the sixteenth—century suggest that the colonists were faithfully copying the ways of European traders—with a time-lag of a century or so.

If there is anything in this idea, it may help to explain the development of both double entry and bills of exchange.

[8] Strictly, " commodity money " means goods that were acceptable by government in payment of tax. Here I use the phrase to describe goods that were commonly taken and given by merchants to square off debts. For such settlements, the goods were valued at the current market rate ; so a journal may show them being " bought " and then " sold " *without any profit*.

CAPTAIN

	Dr.		
1730			£
	To Sundries as per ledger A fol. 192	36
May 28	Wheat, corn and bacon as per waste	22
June 4	Cash paid £50 (5) 1 pen knife 2/6	50
	[There follow numerous items of stationery, etc.]	
Feb. 3	1 ream paper 45/– (6) To 3 account books 66/–	5
6	Cash £20	20
	1/4 part of oil and bone the 16 June	51
13	100 quills, 12/–. Mar. 9 1 quire paper 2/–	
	1 barrel pork omitted Oct. 2nd	9
	1/5 of 6 bags cotton	29
	1/8 of the balance of sloop Dolphin	15
	Captain Harris's set of books	3
			434
Mar. 10	Balance due per adjustment	129
			£563

BENJAMIN HORROCK

	Dr.		
1730			£
Apr. 22	To Mr. Clark's bill of exchange on Mr. Wilks	19
Feb.	Mr. Caner's bill on Tryon	20
	Gold and silver sent per Carey	33
	53 oz. silver sent per Captain Homans (Boston May 10)	14
1731		
Aug. 3	My note on Messrs. Sam Sheafe account to pay	50
Feb. 24	1 bill of exchange drawn by Apthorp	20
Mar. 20	1 do. drawn by ———— on F. Mills Jr.	25
Feb. 28	91½ oz. silver 16 moidores,* 1 guinea sent per Alden	
1734		
May 18	Oil and bone sent per Homans	
Nov. 9	80 oz. silver sent per Homans	
22	16 barrels oil per Bennett	
Mar. 7	48 barrels oil sent per Scott	
May 15	5 tons logwood per Homans	
June 14	10 moidores 5 pistols and 11/– sterling per Bennett	
	tons cwts. qrs. lbs.	
	12 14 0 21 logwood per Quince	
Sept. 19	2 notes of Gordon for £5 9s. 9d. sterling	
Dec. 8	Sundries as per waste per Shepherdson	
1736		
Dec. 3	Bill of exchange of J. & J. Gerrish £55 5s. 4d. sterling	
1737		
Oct. 29	Cash to Saint, New England currency £50	

Note that the calendar year does not end on 31 December (but on 25 March).
* One Moidore was equal to 6 Spanish dollars.
This account was kept in sterling, and the fact that many of the figures are not c
at balancing is of course impossible. The names are chiefly those of ship's capt

RISH & COMPANY

		Cr.		
		£	s.	d.
	By foot of account in ledger A fol. 192	525	11	4
	Short credit in invoice of books	4	10	0
	So much due on guns		8	4
	Russian linen	2	0	9
	1 barrel oil	3	15	0
	6½ yards Whitney	3	5	0
	My part of fitting out sloop Raven	23	17	9
	Omission		7	8
		£563	15	10
10	By balance due per adjustment	129	9	9
4	1 barrel bread	2	0	1
		131	9	10
21	By balance due as per adjustment transferred to fol. 120	14	9	8
		£145	19	6

DON, STERLING ACCOUNT

		Cr.		
30		£	s.	d.
12	By balance due	83	14	1¼
	Interest to Feb. 10th	4	10	3
20	Freight of money per J. Carey		13	10
6	A parcel of goods per Bayley	70	9	1
23	Freight of silver per Homans		5	6
26	Goods per Capt. Foster	19	13	0
3	do. Capt. Homans	8	3	0
19	do. Capt. Crocker	22	18	4
29	do. Capt. Webster	9	13	2
on				
3	do. Capt. Bonnor April	97	5	11

asizes the difficulties of keeping accounts when exchanges were uncertain ; any attempt mentioned in most accounts, its appearances tend to be erratic, belated, and inadequate. Innumerable accounts display a jumble of goods or services on both sides. An innkeeper charges his customer with " a bowl of toddy," and credits " a bushel of rye "[9]; a blacksmith charges for ploughing and gets back molasses[10]; and the accounts of a trader had to encompass not only his sober merchandise but also such items as " a little pig," " one day's mowing," " writing a very long petition to the General Assembly," " seven fowls to balance," and the like.

As an example of the roundabout flows that seem to have been normal, consider the accounts kept by Daniel Henchman. He lived in Boston from 1689 to 1761, and was a bookseller of note.[11] Besides books, he imported a wide range of wares from London. His customers were both fellow-Bostonians and village storekeepers. The latter might pay in country produce, *e.g.*, by sending rye and pork on a coastal sloop; in such cases the accounts show a fairly clear flow of manufactures out of Boston, and of produce into Boston. The flow between Henchman and other Boston merchants is not so clear; probably it depended on household wants, the need to settle old debts, and the fitting-out of joint trading ventures. Often the ventures were voyages to the West Indies, where the produce of New England was exchanged for Spanish and other foreign coins, logwood, and bills on London. These provided Henchman with a means of repaying part of his debt to his British supplier; the rest of the debt might be squared with exports of whale oil.

Two personal accounts from Henchman's ledger are given on pages 276 and 277); they have been slightly simplified and modernized. (See also Plate VIII for a reproduction of the first account.) The accounts are, respectively, for Captain John Gerrish, a Boston merchant, and Benjamin Horrocks, a Londoner. Gerrish's account is mainly concerned with the fitting out of a joint-venture; the debits seem to be a mixture of genuine sales (of Henchman's stationery) and of commodity-money and cash (perhaps transferred to Gerrish to finance the venture). The British agent is credited with supplies, freight, and interest; he is charged with bills, specie, and the proceeds of goods (such as whale-oil) consigned to him for sale in London.

ACCOUNTING METHODS

As trade was so largely based on book-keeping barter, many people (including petty shopkeepers and farmers) had to keep accounts. What sort of system did they use?

---

9 Stratton's ledger (1788–1814), Essex Institute.
10 Harvey's ledger, in New York Public Library. These entries are as late as 1837.
11 W. T. Baxter, " Daniel Henchman," *Essex Institute Historical Collections*, LXX (1934).

The answer is clear. Everyone in business had some inkling of standard double entry, and took its form as his model; but remarkably few seem to have had the skill—or felt the need—to push the system to anywhere near its full perfection. Crude single entry was overwhelmingly the rule. I have not come across any colonial ledger that is certainly complete.[12] In the great bulk of cases a trial balance was patently impossible, as most of the impersonal accounts are lacking, the personal accounts are not ruled off, and the work abounds in arithmetical slips and other blemishes. Some of the accounts may be in the currency of a sister province or of Britain, or a debit may be in £ s. d., and the credit in lbs. of tobacco.[13] Even in the rare cases where full and logical entries in a copper-plate journal hold out promise of completeness, the ledgers do not in fact fulfil this promise [14]—though the deficiency may conceivably be due to a book or pages having been lost.

There is, of course, nothing surprising about the colonists' nodding acquaintance with the standard ledger. European textbooks were available to them; for example, Obadiah Brown of Providence, R.I., used one entitled *A Guide to Book Keepers according to the Italian Manner* (London, 1729); his copy has survived, with his diary when a ship's captain written on its blank pages.[15] Further, the bigger firms had each one or more correspondents in Europe, whose frequent statements of account mirrored their ledgers. In some cases, a colonial merchant's son was sent overseas for a spell of training in the correspondent's counting-house.[16]

We can guess some of the reasons why colonial traders fell short of full double entry. Their whole method of business was often lax and careless, so precision in their accounts was hardly to be looked for; moreover, the snail-like pace of transport gave a good excuse for

---

12 But possibly the sample offered by American libraries is biased. Mair, *op. cit.*, Chap. VII, describes how factors were shipped out from Britain to keep stores in Virginia, and then would send home accounts to their employers in complete double entry. In such cases there would indeed be unusually strong pressure to keep full records. On the other hand, Mair was apparently painting his picture of colonial trade from his study in Perth, Scotland.

13 See, for instance, Ninian Boog's ledger, 1748–1751 (William and Mary College). This has a few personal accounts with double columns, in some cases headed " tobacco " and " cash," in others " sterling " and " cash." The tobacco and sterling balances may in the end be translated, at suitable rates, into the currency column.

14 Thus an entry in Hancock's journal may debit cash or merchandise, and credit a person. But the items composing the debits are so odd and varied—sterling bills of exchange, cash collected in London, the cost of hiring a sloop or buying a house—that one suspects the words " cash " and " merchandise " were used ritually when the book-keeper could think of nothing else with which to round off the entry; if cash and merchandise accounts existed, they must have been meaningless hold-alls.

15 James E Hedges, *The Browns of Providence Plantation* (Cambridge, Mass., 1952), p. 6.

16 The general statements made in this and the next two paragraphs are supported in W. T. Baxter, *The House of Hancock*, especially in Chaps. XI and XVI.

dilatory book-keeping. Few if any professional book-keepers were at hand to help. And traders must have felt it pointless to record matters that they could, thanks to the tiny scale of business, keep under close watch.

PROFIT CALCULATION

There was another—and perhaps a more weighty—reason for not keeping full accounts: a colonial trader was not obliged to calculate his year's income in order to please tax officials or stockholders. So he had little need for sales and expense figures; nor was there much point in closing off his ledger at regular yearly intervals.

Some scholars have argued that profit calculation, and therefore double entry, are essential tools of the successful capitalist.[17] Such a theory naturally commends itself to accountants like myself, since it bestows still further prestige upon our craft. Unhappily the book-keeping of the colonial merchant (who was often a remarkably successful capitalist) does not lend colour to this flattering view. He apparently felt that profit figures were not worth their keep. True, he may conceivably have worked out his profit by drafting a single-entry balance sheet; but his failure to rule off ledgers once a year makes even this compromise improbable.

It might, on the other hand, be argued that for an eighteenth-century trader the annual profit of his whole business was not the vital figure—that what he needed to know was the outcome of various lesser enterprises as each reached its end. For, if he was a man of substance, he tended to engage in many short-lived ventures as side-lines to his principal business—perhaps to get rid of commodity-money, and perhaps because there was no stock-market through which to invest his surplus capital. From time to time he might send off a parcel of fish on consignment to his agent in Spain, or fit out a whaler, or experiment with the making of candles or potash; and he might well keep an account for the consignment, voyage, or manufactory.[18] Such atomised profit-and-loss statements may perhaps be regarded as the eighteenth-century counterpart of today's cost accounts. Yet even here we cannot be sure that profit calculation was always the motive for keeping the account. When such enterprises were afoot, the

[17] This view is explained and criticised by B. S. Yamey, " Scientific Book-keeping and the Rise of Capitalism," *Economic History Review*, second series, I (1949), reprinted in W. T. Baxter (ed.), *Studies in Accounting*.

[18] *e.g.*, Jenkins' day-book, 1747 (Rhode Island Historical Society) mentions accounts for voyages, Fowle's ledger, c. 1822 (New York Public Library) for consignments inwards, and Ridgeley's ledger, 1765–1769 (Maryland Historical Society) for shoe-making and a plantation. Apart from these venture accounts, there was not much liking for the many different merchandise accounts featured in contemporary textbooks.

A good example of an account for a shipping venture is reproduced in Richard Pares, *Yankees and Creoles* (London, 1956), p. 140. It cheerfully confuses successive voyages, and also capital and revenue items.

trader was apt for safety to join with other men; thus he might at any time hold shares in half a dozen brief partnerships. Or an agent or captain might be mixed up in the affair (*e.g.*, receiving a commission on the proceeds). In such cases profit had to be known—or, at least, a cargo, etc., had to be split up—in order that settlement could take place. In short, personal relations might here again be the chief spur for keeping accounts, not a love for profit figures in the abstract.[19]

One more question poses itself. How would a colonial accountant with a taste for theorising have defined profit? Clearly, there would be small point in his talking about realised gains and losses; debts were apt to turn into pork rather than cash. In such circumstances final " realisation " might take place only if the pork was transferred to the family dinner-table, or if a debtor furnished the trader's wife with a new bonnet. Nor could the theorist have taken refuge in phrases about matched flows of receipts and expenditure. To measure his profit, the trader would have had to estimate the net appreciation on a host of commodities and unfinished ventures, and appraise the probability that each debtor would pay in some acceptable medium. This approach might have left a salutary imprint on accounting theory. But the work and mental strain of the calculations would have been a sore burden. The colonists perhaps showed a true sense of economy in declining to measure profit.

Personal Accounts

From what has been said, it follows that the overwhelming majority of accounts in a colonial ledger are for persons. The degree of care with which they were written up varied greatly; occasionally they are elegant (notably in the books of the wealthier merchants), but often they are slovenly. Many contain wording that strikes the modern reader—used to the drab products of book-keeping machines and their operators—as quaint and pleasing. The narrative rambles over the small incidents of everyday life:

> To cash paid in the street,

or (from a kind of cash-book kept by Jefferson)[20]:

> Gave in charity . . . . . . 3d.

or, on the credit side of an account:

> The latter part of May my negro wench scoured at his house 3 days at 2 per day charged on other side

and, sure enough, the correct debit has been put in.[1]

---

[19] But how (it may be asked) were good relations maintained when the main business was run by a permanent partnership? I do not know the answer. Perhaps the partners hoped to straighten matters out with occasional single-entry balance sheets. Perhaps—as the indices of ledgers suggest—such partnerships were rather rare, and tended to be confined to a closely knit family group.

[20] Massachusetts Historical Society.

[1] Evert Wendell's ledger (early eighteenth century), New York Historical Society.

Once a debt had been created, a quick settlement was hard to accomplish. Payment might consist of a long-drawn-out series of petty instalments. Thus a merchant credits Doctor Greenough with two year's service ($100), and the doctor then takes driblets of goods from the store, and cash in single dollars.[2] Accounts often span periods of many years—perhaps with long breaks during which the balance lies fallow. For example, the ledger of an Albany merchant has an account, starting in 1711, that drifts on—with many gaps—till 1757, when at last his heirs put in a note to say that settlement has been reached.[3] A contemporary writer describes a store's life as being endless—" the debts are so small and numerous that it requires posterity to finish a concern." [4]

Sometimes the two men concerned would meet to scrutinise the details in an account; and then—no doubt after a good deal of debate and head-scratching—the balance would be agreed by both the parties. A note might be inserted:

> He produced his book to me and found the balance due to him £1 10. 10,

or

> This I took out of his book.[5]

One or both parties might sign under the agreed balance, *e.g.*:

> Then made all accounts even from the beginning of the world to this day to our satisfaction as witness our hands
>
> Joel Canford
> Joseph Peck [6]

In one case, the parties must each have employed an auditor:

> Then we the subscribers reckoned and found due from Thos. Cobb Esq. to Mr. John Adam sixteen shillings and 3d. witness our hands
> On behalf of Mr. John Adam, Wm. Crocker.
> On behalf of Thos. Cobb Esqr., Joseph Crocker.[7]

SPECIALISED DAY-BOOKS

In general, traders do not seem to have kept any books of original entry except an omnibus waste and/or journal. But there were exceptions. The records of a Nevis planter include a cash book of 1703; receipts are listed at one end of the book, and payments at the other.[8] Special needs might give rise to other books, *e.g.*, an iron-founder's papers include a " time-book." [9]

By the start of the nineteenth century, cash-books were getting not

---

[2] Ledger of Parker, Aikens, & Co., in Essex Institute.
[3] Evert Wendell's ledger, New York Historical Society.
[4] Quoted by Albert J. Voke, in " Accounting Methods of Colonial Merchants in Virginia," *Journal of Accountancy*, XLII (1926), p. 5.
[5] Both from Evert Wendell's ledger, New York Historical Society.
[6] Peck's ledger (1793), Yale University.
[7] Cobb's ledger (1766-1784), New York Public Library.
[8] Pinney papers, University of Bristol, England.
[9] Ridgeley papers, Maryland Historical Society.

uncommon. Thus in 1816 a Salem firm had both a cash-book and a sales day-book.[10]

CREDIT TRANSFERS

Notes payable in goods

Credit transfers, the historians of early accounting tell us, played an important part in the birth or growth of double entry. They certainly are an outstanding feature in colonial ledgers. Thanks to these transfers, colonies with little cash and no banks contrived to build up a supple system of trade.

Consider a simple transfer, involving three parties. A country storekeeper buys produce from Farmer Giles, and sells it to a city merchant. Neither creditor pays. When next the farmer goes into the city, the storekeeper furnishes him with a letter to the merchant: " Please let Farmer Giles buy £*x* of goods in your shop." So two debts are settled by a short-circuit, and not one penny of cash is used.

John Hancock kept a big store at Boston, and here is an example of the " orders " that he received by the dozen:

Boston May 27 1766

John Hancock Esq.
Sir
Please to let Mr. John Moore have Four pounds one shilling lawful money out of your store in such goods as he shall chose on account of your humble servant

Thomas Atkins

On getting the goods, Moore signs the back of the order by way of receipt. Hancock's clerk methodically docquets it " Thomas Atkins note to John Moore," and debits Atkins " for his note paid John Moore." [11] Presumably Atkins must in his ledger credit Hancock and debit Moore; it is in just such a credit transfer (we may surmise) that double entry had its genesis.

Notes payable to order

It may be too that these notes to pay in goods—a blend of the modern cheque and the letter to a mail-order firm—can suggest the origin of the bill of exchange. They undoubtedly performed many of the bill's functions. Thus, by adding " or order " to the wording, the colonists could stretch the cycle of credit transfers:

April 27 1770

John Hancock Esq.
Sir Please to pay out of your store to Captain Adino Paddock or order £13. 6. 8 and etc.

Thomas Dawes

---

[10] Parker & Company's records, at the Essex Institute (which also has one or two other cash-books from different firms).
[11] Harvard Business School, Hancock MSS. This collection has also examples of even simpler letters, in which the creditor asks that goods be given to an agent (not to an independent third-party) such as his wife or a ship's captain.

On the back is written

> Please to pay the within to Mrs. Mary Hatch
>
>   Adino Paddock
>
> Received the contents
>
>   J. Hatch.

In Hancock's journal, the entry this time runs:

> Sundry accounts debtor to Merchandise
>   Thomas Dawes—paid his order to Adino Paddock   £13. 6. 8.

Orders often did in fact circulate from hand to hand; they thus provided a private source of paper-money, based on a merchant's credit and his goods.   The resulting journal entries may be somewhat formidable (particularly as they were apt to stray far afield from our textbook precepts):

> A and Company dr. to B for their acceptance of a note drawn by C on them in B's favour and by him indorsed to me.[12]

The beginning of a series of order transactions can be seen in this narrative, written by Brown (of Providence) in his account for Chauncey (of Hadley):

> Settled the above account and there is due to balance £108—19—6 which I promise to ship in sugar @ £15 per hundred-weight on account of the said Chauncey to his order in Newport as witness under hand
>
>   Obadiah Brown
>   Josiah Chauncey.[13]

Later debits show that this arrangement was carried out—*i.e.* Chauncey from time to time sent orders, and Brown met these by issuing sugar.

Variants.   Notes payable in money

The procedure varied greatly from case to case.   The man who penned such primitive instruments felt himself free to change their wording according to taste and circumstance, and few of them (except those for foreign exchange dealings) fall clearly into the categories now recognised by bill of exchange law; nor had he any prim ideas about such formalities as presentation for acceptance, etc. Sometimes the notes were payable in unspecified goods up to a given value, sometimes in specified commodity-money at a given rate.   Or a note might be payable in cash; when it was met, the drawee would charge the drawer's account with " cash paid—per your order." Occasionally the note was payable half (or some other fraction) in money and the rest in goods.   Even if the note did not state that payment was to be made in goods, the journal may show that goods were in fact the final means of settlement.   The drafter seldom

---

[12] Brown's Ledger 4 (1740–1752), Rhode Island Historical Society, has entries in this style.
[13] *Ibid.*

bothered to specify any payment time; when he did observe this formality, the order might be payable on demand or at a date as remote as three years later.[14]   On occasion, all writing might be dispensed with, and settlement contrived by word of mouth alone— hence entries like:

To Timothy Gilbert's Verble Order [15]

By the beginning of the nineteenth century some accounts are treating the orders in a more orthodox way, suggesting that the formal bill of exchange has arrived in ordinary trade.   The payee of a bill may on occasion be charged with an " advance " that varies with the nearness of the due date (*e.g.*, $8\frac{1}{2}$ per cent. if the bill is payable at once, and 6 per cent. if in sixty days).[16]

Promissory Notes

Besides the notes ordering a debtor to pay, the colonists made some use of documents resembling promissory notes.

It was fairly usual, after two men had agreed the amount due between them, for the debtor to give a promissory note (or occasionally a bond) for the balance.   This balance might be still carried forward in the creditor's ledger; the note was regarded more as a proof of debt than a guarantee of payment on a certain date.   Thus Wendell remarks, when writing up Fitch's account, that the two men have settled and found that Fitch owed a balance of £14, " as may appear by his note of hand "; three years later comes the sequel: " I gave Fitch up his note of hand and he paid me in goods." [17]

There were many variants to the procedure.   A promissory note might carry interest.   Its holder might get paid by instalments (acknowledged on the back in some such words as " Received on this note six dollars by me ").   It might be drafted specially for triangular settlement, as in this example addressed to one Hill:

I promise to pay Benjamin Hand two pounds lawful money.   Charge me with the same and you will oblige

July 18, 1787 [18]   David Lyman

---

[14] See Ridgeley's accounts (mid-eighteenth century), Maryland Historical Society.
[15] Cobb's ledger (1766–1784), New York Public Library.
[16] See the books of Lawrason & Fowle (Alexandria, Va.) in the New York Public Library—for instance :

Nov. 14, 1816	Jacob Hoffman dr. to Sundries		
	Thomas Thaxter for our draft on him at		
	1 days sight in favour Jacob Hoffman		1200
	Advance $8\frac{1}{2}$ p. ct.		102

[17] Wendell's ledger (entries of 1791–1794), New York Historical Society. See also Pinney's Ledger 3, at the University of Bristol. In May, 1774, Pinney owes Stanley £232 " for which I gave my [promissory] note payable on demand "; in June, Stanley's account opens with this credit balance, and is charged with four payments (to third parties) of cash and rum ; £106 of " balance due on my note " is carried down to the credit of the next account, which then starts: " By my note for the balance having taken up the above [note] ———— £106."
[18] Examples from a packet of documents with the Lyman day book, Yale.

Settlement by book entry alone

On occasion, traders managed to effect a settlement by the neat device of book-transfer alone, *i.e.,* no goods or cash changed hands. Here some friendly merchant made a cross-entry in his books on behalf of the two parties; he thus acted exactly as a modern banker who, on receipt of a cheque, credits one customer's account and debits another. Such jugglery seems to explain entries like:

> To amount of your debt due this day to Anthony Gibbons on bond assumed by me,

and—to square off a long-standing liability for freight and turtles—

> To William Cohen paid him the amount of this account in full by a deduction from your bond to him.[19]

The use in notes of phrases such as " please to pay or discount with " suggest the same procedure. " Discount " is here used in its old sense of a set-off to debt:

> Sir   Please to discount one dollar with Captain Strong if it is convenient and you will much oblige your humble servant
>
> Elizah Cornwal
>
> To Colonel David Lyman
>   Middletown   September 2 1800 [20]

Other orders run " please to pay to or discount with ——."

Importance of notes

Credit transfers of one kind or another played a substantial part in colonial trade. Many accounts are freely sprinkled with references to them. Their number must have been great—*e.g.,* an important merchant like Hancock might well receive several notes in one day from the same customer. Even humble labourers (whose counterparts today would not recognise a bill of exchange in the unlikely event of their seeing one) were adepts at handling such papers; thus the ledger of a trader in Taunton, Mass., has an account for " Gambo Negro," who got advances of cash, rum, and iron; Gambo is then charged with " your order to Philip King, paid to John Adam "; and the account is ruled off when Gambo gives his note of hand for the balance.[1] At the other end of the scale, we find also a municipality using paper to settle for the shovels that it buys.[2]

THE END OF THE SYSTEM

What I have called " colonial accounting " in fact out-lasted the colonial period by many years. The transition to modern methods varied in its speed from case to case. By say 1820, the modern look

---

[19] Pinney papers (c. 1770), University of Bristol.   [20] Lyman MSS., Yale.
[1] Cobb's ledger (1766–1784), New York Public Library.
[2] This was the town of Newburyport (see its account in Greenleaf's ledger, Essex Institute). In 1814 it still paid with a " town order " and bills on third persons.

is beginning to creep in: cash appears more often, debtors can some-times be distinguished from creditors, and the double-entry structure is less incomplete. Twenty years later the change has become marked; nevertheless colonial traits still crop up in some ledgers.[3]

The date at which a book-keeper switched from £ s. d. to $ was entirely a matter of his own whim. The change was usually made at some point during the fifteen years between 1795 and 1810. The break was not always a clean one; a few accounts might still be kept in the old units after the others had been changed to the new. An inner column was sometimes used for $s and an outer column for the £ equivalents; or the narrative might state the amount in $s, whereas the column translated these figures into the more traditional and respectable units.

We can readily guess what were the factors that put a stop to colonial methods. Growth in population encouraged more specialised trade. The currency was disciplined, and coins were issued in plenty; by the early nineteenth century, a cash account—or even a cash-book—was becoming feasible and useful. Banks appeared in the same period, and with them came bank accounts; the cheque drove out the order payable in pork.

Perhaps these economic factors tell us everything that is needed to explain the change. But I am not quite sure. May not the character of colonial life—for instance, a relaxed tempo in business, and a relish for negotiation—have had something to do with financial methods? Attitudes on such points still vary from place to place. The modern visitor to South Africa (where coins and banks are plentiful enough) is struck by the widespread habit of putting off settlement; shopkeepers politely assume that even well-to-do cus-tomers will not pay till the end of the month. In the American colonies, money cannot have been unobtainable always and every-where. For instance, Massachusetts printed paper money wholesale to finance expeditions against the French; and Rhode Island was even more reckless in her emissions. Ledgers show the results of this inflation clearly—in the sense that prices soared to many times their former level; but, though the provincial notes must presumably have circulated freely and abundantly in those years, there is scant sign of any fall in the volume of barter. We are thus left wondering how far the colonists' roundabout trade sprang from economic forces, and how far it mirrored a more easygoing way of life.

---

[3] Thus an order in kind is mentioned in 1842 (Barbour's books, New York Public Library). A ledger from Hanover, N.H., still has the full colonial flavour at its end, in 1834 (E. Miller's books, in the same library).

The History of Methods of
Exposition of Double-entry
Book-keeping in England

J. G. C. Jackson*

THE great majority of sixteenth- and seventeenth-century authors of book-keeping texts were primarily teachers of their subject. The method of exposition which they adopted was influenced by both the contemporary attitude to the teaching of academic subjects and the theory of accounts which, consciously or unconsciously, the authors held.

The journal was the keystone of the Italian three-book system of accounts and the principal aim of book-keeping instruction was the " right ordering of debit and credit " in that book. A journal entry was something to be made " with all the Consideration and Discretion imaginable; and it will not be done hastily unless it be a very plain Matter; but requires the Solitude of a Compting-House, or Retirement from all Manner of Interruption." [1] The history of the teaching of book-keeping until almost the end of the nineteenth century consists essentially, therefore, of the evolution of methods of explaining how to find which accounts to debit and credit and how the entry was to be made in the journal. The usual method followed by textbooks up to the eighteenth century was to present a great mass of rules applicable to the particular cases of a large variety of transactions. The outstanding exception was, strangely enough, the first English book-keeping text, that by Hugh Oldcastle, known to us through Mellis's edition. Each journal entry, he says has

> two denominations: to wit, by Debitor, and Creditor, whereof the first is the name of the Debitor, receiuer or borrower: and the other of the Creditor, deliuerer, or lender. To the furtherance whereof there is a Rule, which beeing well understood, will aide you greatly: which Rule is to bee learned as well by rote, as by reason, which is thus.
> > All thinges receiued, or the receiuer must owe to
> > all thinges deliuered, or to the deliuerer.[2]

It is difficult to find any improvement on this rule for two centuries.

---

* Inspector of Further Education, London County Council.
[1] R. North, *The Gentleman Accomptant or . . . An Essay to unfold the Mystery of Accompts* (London, 1714), p. 33.
[2] H. Oldcastle, *A briefe instruction and maner how to keepe bookes of Accompts . . .* (London, 1588), Chap. 11. The original edition appeared in 1543.

Kats,[3] having noted that this rule was not in Pacioli's treatise, is of the opinion that it was filched from Peele whose first text was published in 1553. Be that as it may, Peele's contribution is much more in the style of the remainder of the seventeenth- and eighteenth-century authors. Peele's method was to give a specimen transaction (forty-four of them in all) and follow it with the journal entry required, making reference to an example " parcell " [entry] in the long set of books which followed. Here are three successive specimens:

> Money receiued of a debitour.
> You shall make the money receiued, debitour to the man that did pay it, as in the 37 parcell.
> Money paied to the Creditour.
> You shall make contrarwise the man debitour to the money paied to hym, as in the 38 parcell.
> To deliuer a Debitours bill, to a Creditour.
> You shall make the man that receiueth the bill, debitour to the other man, that ought [owed] you money by the bill, as in the 39 parcell.[4]

In his larger work of 1569 the general rule is repeated by the " Scholemaster " in almost the same words as were used in Mellis's edition of Oldcastle but the " scholler " replies, " I am alreadie able to aunswere the same by rote, but the reason thereof I understande not." [5] And well might this candour be justified for the examples, each followed by its debit and credit entry, are expanded to number 187.

By the following century the general rule had lengthened but the number of " cases " or examples did not diminish. Dafforne, in a book which was the first in the English language to go through several editions, gave fifteen " Rules of aide " and they give a clear picture of the teachers' attitude of mind and method of presentation. The first four rules were as follows:

> Rules of aide, very requisite in Trade continuance, to be learned without booke.

1. Whatsoever commeth unto us (whether Mony, or Wares) for Proper, Factorage, or Company account, the same is . . . Debitor.	1. Whatsoever goeth from us (whether Mony, or Wares) for Proper, Factorage, or Company account the same is . . . Creditor.
2. Whosoever Promiseth, the Promiser is . . . Debitor.	2. Unto whom we Promise, the Promised man is . . . Creditor.
3. Unto whom we pay (whether with Mony, Wares, Exchanges, Assignations) being for his own account: that man is . . . Debitor.	3. Of whom we receive (whether Mony, Wares, Exchanges, Assignations) being for his own account: that man is . . . Creditor.
4. Unto whom we pay (as above) for another mans account: The man for whose account we pay is . . . Debitor.	4. Of whom we receive (as above) for another mans account: The man for whose account we receive is . . . Creditor.[6]

[3] P. Kats, " Hugh Oldcastle and John Mellis," *The Accountant*, LXXIV (1926).
[4] J. Peele, *The maner and fourme how to kepe a perfecte reconyng* . . . (London, 1553), Chap. 3.
[5] J. Peele, *The Pathewaye to perfectnes*, . . . (London, 1569), Preface.
[6] R. Dafforne, *The Merchant's Mirrour* . . . (London, 1636), p. 19.

The rules were clearly intended to cover all types of transactions which the young book-keeper might be expected to meet and comparable attempts to extend rules for this purpose are common until the end of the eighteenth century. In his *Apprentices Time-Entertainer . . .* [7] Dafforne doubles the number of his " rules of aide." He does, however, appear to appreciate the memory load involved for after them he quotes a translation of Johannes Buingha's rules [8]:

Who the Debitor is, or oweth		Who the Creditor is, or must have	
1. What we have		1. Whence it arriveth	
2. Whoso receiveth		2. Whoso giveth out	
3. What we buy		3. Of whom we buy	
4. Unto whom we sell		4. That which is sold	
5. For whom we buy	Is Debitor	5. They of whom we buy	Is Creditor
6. Whoso must pay		6. They that must have	
7. For whom we pay		7. Wherewith we pay	
8. What we cause to be insured		8. The Assuror	
9. For whom we insure		9. Insurance reckoning	
10. Whither-wards we send		10. What we send away	
11. That which is gained upon		11. That which is lost	
12. Profit and Losse		12. Profit and Losse	

The tradition of including numerous " cases " or examples was continued into the eighteenth century. Edward Hatton [9] presented twenty-nine cases for " Proper [*i.e.*, sole trader's] accounts in Domestick Trade," eighteen cases for " Accounts proper in Foreign Trade," six cases for " Factorage [*i.e.*, agent's] Accompts in Domestick Trade," five cases of " Factorage Accompts in Foreign Trade " and sixteen cases for " Company [*i.e.*, partnership] Accompts." Snell, a contemporary of Hatton's, and a well-known teacher, having published his *Rules for Book-keeping . . .* [10] which consisted of eleven pages of rules numbering seventy in all, followed it up with *The Merchants Counting-House*, [11] the entire contents of which was made up of sixty-nine rules! Only twenty-one rules were given by William Taylor, [12] perhaps because he covered both single and double entry in but twenty-three pages. J. H. Lewis, on the other hand, having pointed out in his preface that students " have been discouraged in their first attempts to acquire a knowledge of the art, as they were confounded by the multiplicity of rules and examples . . ." and that " for the sake of such, the Author of this work has therefore made the examples few,

[7] R. Dafforne, *The apprentices Time-Entertainer accomptantly* . . . (London, 1640).
[8] J. Buingha, *Oprecht fondament Ende principalen inhout van het Italiaens Boeckhouden* (Amsterdam, 1627).
[9] E. Hatton, *The Merchant's Magazine* (London, 1701).
[10] C. Snell, *Rules for Book-keeping* . . . (London, 1701).
[11] C. Snell, *The Merchants Counting-House* (London, 1718).
[12] W. Taylor, *A Complete System of Practical Arithmetic* (Birmingham, 1783).

and the rules for posting and balancing plain and easy to be comprehended " [13] then proceeded to give forty-seven rules.

Authors were not, however, unaware of the difficulties of learning the subject by means of rules and we find them attempting to improve the presentation of rules in at least three ways. In the first place they began to display them more clearly; secondly, they rendered them into verse; and thirdly the rules were classified.

John Collins,[14] for example, had obviously spent a great deal of thought in the setting out of his " analisis " of the rules governing the recording of the various sections of book-keeping but for typographical or other reasons Collins's pioneering work in lay-out was not followed up. Much the more popular was the concocting of doggerel verse as an aid to the memory.

Versification has a long and honourable history in book-keeping. Manzoni put his rules into verse [15] and this memory crutch was, of course, common in other subjects; but undoubtedly the father of British double-entry versification is James Peele. Father of George Peele, the well-known Elizabethan dramatist, he needed no excuse to lapse into verse. At the beginning of his journal he wrote:

> Rules to be observed
> If that in this accompt, these precepts ye observe,
> Than I you wel assure, no part thereof shall swerne (*sic*)
> To make the things Recieuyd, or the receiver,
> Debter to the thinges delivered, or to the deliverer
> And to receive before you write, and write before you paye,
> So shall no parte of your accompt, in any wyse decaye
> Observe wel these few rules, your Journall boke throughout,
> So shall you make sure worke, of that you go about.

Dafforne's verse, which is to be found at the beginning of the ledger, is rather simpler.

> In Brief
> The owner, or the owing thing,
> Or what-so-ever comes to thee:
> Upon the LEFT hand see thou bring
> For there the same must placed be.
> But
> They unto whom thou dost owe,
> Upon the RIGHT let them be set:
> Or what-so-e'er doth from thee go
> To place them there do not forget.

Although reduced in extent and simplified in vocabulary, verses of one sort or another became more and more common during the

---

[13] J. H. Lewis, *The Quick and Easy Method of Teaching Book-keeping* (14th ed., London, c. 1860), p. xiv.

[14] J. Collins, *An Introduction to Merchants Accompts* . . . (London, 1653).

[15] D. Manzoni, *Quaderno doppio* . . . (Venice, 1534). A translation of them appears in J. B. Geijsbeek, *Ancient Double Entry Book-keeping* (Denver, 1914), p. 84.

nineteenth century. Dr. Kelly's *Elements of Book-keeping* . . . ,[16] a standard work of its period, contained:

> By Journal laws, what I receive
> Is debtor made to what I give;
> Stock for my Debts must debtor be,
> And Creditor my Property.
> Profit and Loss Accounts are plain
> I debit Loss and credit gain.

Boulter [17] in quoting the verse, goes on to explain that pupils were made to copy a set of transactions into a waste-book, and thence transfer them into the journal with the aid of this " kind of verse." Jingles of this kind are quoted in professional accountants periodicals to this very day.

The third and major improvement that teachers were able to effect in the use of rules was by means of classification. This movement marks the beginning of that search for the holy grail of book-keeping—the single, general rule which is applicable to all transactions.

Carpenter, for example, classified his rules into many groups and I quote only the first three of them in the section dealing with " Of receiving and buying money by bils of Exchange " by way of illustration.

> 1. If any one deliver you a Bill of exchange, which you send to another; you are to make him to whom you send it, Debtor to him that underwrit it.
> 2. Contrarily; if you deliver a Bill of Exchange to any one, which you have taken up upon another, you shall make him to whom you deliver it, Debtor to him upon whom you have charged it.
> 3. When [any] one accepteth a Bill of exchange which is sent to you, you are to make him who accepteth the same, debtor to him who sent it you.[18]

Another pioneer in the field of classification was Thomas Browne,[19] who taught " accompts for merchants " to the orphans at Christ's Hospital. He drew up an " Analysis " which covered a double page of foolscap size covered with small print in an attempt to reduce a multitude of rules to a meaningful classification. For instance, he brought together all the rules concerning " wares or goods " and then analysed those that referred to purchases in the following way:

Bought
- For ready Mony. Debitor, the Wares bought.
  Creditor, Cash . . .
- For Time. Debitor, the Wares bought.
  Creditor, the party of whom bought . . .
- For part Mony, part Time.
  Debitor, those Wares bought
    - Creditor, Cash for so much ready Mony paid
    - Creditor, the party of whom bought the remainder.
- In Barter for Wares. Debitor the Wares received.
  Creditor, the Wares delivered. If both of equal value.

---

[16] P. Kelly, *Elements of Book-keeping* . . . (Edinburgh, 1801).
[17] G. H. Boulter, *Course of Book-keeping* (London, 1859), Preface.
[18] J. Carpenter, *A most excellent Instruction* . . . (London, 1632), p. 57.
[19] T. Browne, *The Accurate Accomptant* (London, 1670).

Mathew Quin, too, was following a similar path towards classification and simplification in the use of his " six plain cases " [20] each of which exemplified a section of the book-keeping theory.   However, it was not until well into the nineteenth century that the three golden rules, one for each of the main classes of account, became generally recognised as the usual method of exposition.

The method of teaching which went with the " journal approach " to book-keeping and the application of rules or cases was as follows. First find the " case " or rule in the textbook which fits the transaction to be entered, look up the waste-book folio beside it, and trace the example through the journal and ledger.   Such is the gist of Thomas King's instructions.[1]   The " Directions to Teachers " given by Dr. Robert Hamilton are typical.

> The chief point is to convey to the learner a distinct notion of the nature of Dr. and Cr. and the contents of the accompts in the ledger. After he has been thoroughly instructed in the eight principal rules for journalizing and has carefully perused the detail of the ledger accompts he is to proceed to transcribe a portion of the waste-book, and try the computations; then he is to write in a scroll-book that part of the journal which is printed in italics, which expresses the Drs. and Crs. of the several articles.   When this is done, it is to be compared with the printed journal, or examined by the teacher then the narrations are to be filled up, and a fair copy of the whole transcribed into the journal.[2]

Instruction by repetition by rote, making, as Dafforne put it, " A Booke full of Writing, and a Head void of Knowledge " [3] appears to have been the main method of instruction.

Questioning in class, when it was used, followed the same pattern. John Matheson submits the following method of exercising the pupil " for the inspection of the ingenious Instructor " [4]:

> Q. Sold A. B. ten puncheons of rum, per bill at six months, required the Journal Entry?
> A. Bills Receivable Dr. to Rum, because a bill is received in payment of goods delivered, per rule 4th.

The significant pedagogical features of the first 250 years of book-keeping instruction are here wonderfully exemplified.   First, the emphasis on the journal as the important book of record and secondly the use of rules to determine the required entry.   It is not surprising that book-keeping was " the soonest of all other things forgot." [5]

Yet at the same time authors and teachers were gradually evolving improved methods of instruction which would reduce the grosser

---

[20] M. Quin, *Rudiments of Book-keeping* (London, 1776). His six cases were 1. Inventory and debts; 2. Buying; 3. Selling; 4. Receiving; 5. Paying; 6. Balancing. (p. 6.)

[1] T. King, *An Exact Guide to Book-keeping* . . . (London, 1717), pp. 6–8.

[2] R. Hamilton, *A Short System of Arithmetic and Book-keeping* (London, 1788), Introduction.

[3] R. Dafforne, *The apprentices Time-Entertainer* . . . (London, 1640), Foreword.

[4] J. Matheson, *The Theory and Practice of Book-keeping* (London, 1818), p. 73.

[5] W. Webster, *An essay on book-keeping* . . . (London, 1719), p. 84.

limitations of their method.   In particular, the development of pupil's exercises is of interest.   In the earliest texts the theory of the subject was generally followed by a " set " of books consisting of a waste-book, journal and ledger but almost 150 years were to elapse before the value of the waste-book as a student's exercise came to be appreciated.   At the beginning of his *Merchant's Mirrour* (1636) Dafforne wrote an epistle " To the Book-keeping Teachers " in which he said:

> I dedicate the First and Second Waste-bookes unto you, not as teaching, but necessary assisting bookes: especially for such as have no opportunity to compile a Waste-booke for their Schooles proper use. Here you have matter to exercise your Scholars in diversities of accompts, and after severall manners of entrances, for the effecting of the same: the like (though spoken by me) I have not seen presented to my Nation.

The first book-keeping exercise had been born.   A few years later in the foreword to his *Apprentices Time-Entertainer* (1640) he refers to his two " Waste-Bookes for exercises," adding of them parenthetically that " by the scarcity of them in generall, seeme to bee very difficult in their Composition; else they would bee more common in ovre Schooles."

In the following century Malcolm suggested that the pupils should use the waste-book examples as " so many questions proposed, in order to find the Debtors and Creditors; . . . and in the Journal they have the Solutions." [6]   Half a century later Hamilton followed with his " Sets for Practice " and as an improved method of presentation placed his specimen waste-book and journal on opposite pages " that the learner may easily compare them." [7]   By the end of the century the waste-book has become generally recognised as an exercise.   J. H. Wicks " Master of the Boarding-School, Englefield-House, Egham, Surry " included as a matter of course in his textbook of 1797 a " second Waste-Book, for the use of those who may be desirous of further practice." [8]   He further promised to publish a " distinct Journal and Ledger, for the ease of the preceptor only," but I have not been able to trace such a publication and the honour of having published the first teacher's answer-book must be bestowed elsewhere.

The waste-book exercises were, however, extremely long, and the practice of following the theory of the subject with a complete set of books and one or more long waste-books continued well into the nineteenth century.   For example, Hamilton and Ball's textbook [9] which achieved a popularity between 1870 and 1890, which was not unconnected with the fact that they were Society of Arts examiners, contained only one long exercise.   This included a large variety of

6 A. Malcolm, *A Treatise of Book-keeping* . . . (London, 1731), p. 35.
7 R. Hamilton, *An Introduction to Merchandize* (Perth, 1777), p. 29.
8 J. H. Wicks, *Book-keeping reformed* . . . (Egham, 1797), Dedication.
9 R. G. Hamilton and J. Ball, *Book-keeping* (Oxford, 1869).

transactions all of which had been worked out in their entirety. Long exercises were in fact so common up to the beginning of the present century that Thornton [10] considered it worthy of remark that he had given, " instead of a long series of eighty or a hundred transactions, taking six months to get through, a very short series of only three to begin with " and, at about the same time, G. F. C. Vernon published a book of exercises each of which was short enough to be " properly worked within the limits of one or two lessons." [11]   By the beginning of the present century then, the waste-book, the first book of the Italian system, had been transformed from a record of a multitude of miscellaneous transactions into a series of short exercises directly related to the chapter in the textbook.   It is interesting to speculate on the extent to which the evolution of the waste-book into a textbook exercise has resulted in the existing practice of teaching book-keeping from textbook transactions instead of from specimen documents. This teaching technique has but widened the gulf between the class-room and the business house.

The Personification of Accounts

Exposition by means of repetition of a set of rules concealed the fact that the authors of textbooks held, consciously or unconsciously, one of two distinct theories of accounts.   This becomes apparent on the relatively few occasions when authors attempt to explain or rationalise their rules.   On the one hand was a group which sought to personify the accounts, whilst on the other hand we find the very small group whose influence was to be greatest in the United States of America and who held what may be described as an " ownership " theory of accounts.

The attribution of a living, independent personality to accounts must have had its roots in the very earliest forms of book-keeping. The theory may have had at least two sources.   In the first place there is little doubt that the first ledger accounts were those showing personal debt relationships between merchants. [12]   With the development of the double-entry system, the terms " debtor " and " creditor " were extended first to accounts of objects (real accounts) and later to abstract classifications (nominal accounts).   It therefore became the practice to extend the meanings of the terms " debit " and " credit " beyond their original personal connotation and to apply them to inanimate objects and abstract conceptions and by that very process a ready-made teaching device was forged.

Another source from which the conception of personification may

---

[10] J. Thornton, *First Lessons in Book-keeping* (London, 1879), p. 5.
[11] G. F. C. Vernon, *Sets for practice* (London, 1893).
[12] E. Peragallo, *Origin and Evolution of Double Entry Book keeping* (New York, 1938), p. 1.

have developed is the practice of recording the financial relationship between the owner of an estate and his bailiff or " accountant " in the form of an account of " charge and discharge." The bailiff " charged " himself with that portion of the estate entrusted to him including all receipts accepted on behalf of the lord and " discharged " himself with all expenditure made on his master's behalf and money paid over to the estate owner. The use of the term " charge " was extended from its personal application to that of " charging " accounts, *i.e.*, debiting them. Whatever may have been its origin, the practice of explaining the entries to be made in the ledger by means of personifying the accounts is found in the very earliest British texts and must be closely linked with the very origin of the system of book-keeping.

Three main forms of personification can be traced. In the first the account is thought of as an independent, living entity. In its second form the account is conceived as representing the owner of the business. Finally, there is a combination of these two forms in which the account is imagined to be an individual apart from the owner yet accountable to him. These three forms are often inextricably interwoven in any one text and historically they developed and expanded contemporaneously with one another, each borrowing a little from the others.

The original Venetian form of journal entry was to preface the account to be debited by " per " and the creditor account by " a." These words were purely technical terms which had lost their grammatical significance. On translation, however, authors found no corresponding existing English terms and were apparently loth to coin new ones. They therefore fell back on a more general translation of the old Italian " debito " and " credo " as " oweth " and " trusts "; terms of relationship which, of course, are applicable only to persons. Entries which in Pacioli's treatise were in the form " Per Cash, a Capital . . ." after translation took the form " Money oweth to Thomas Lee " in Oldcastle's manual. " Money " was given a theoretically independent personal existence. James Peele followed a similar sequence of words whereas " W. P." [13] made his ledger entries in the form " Peter Garetson ought to give to money . . ." when debiting the personal account. He used the words " ought to have of " when crediting accounts. These phrases clearly indicate the mental image the authors had of the cash and other real accounts as possessing human qualities.

By the beginning of the seventeenth century the journal entry had assumed a close approximation to its modern form of " X Debtor to Y " and from the technical form of the entry followed the explanation. In Dafforne's dialogue between " Philo-Mathy," the teacher, and

---

[13] W. P., *The Pathway to Knowledge* (London, 1596).

" School-Partner," the pupil, the question is asked why cash in hand is journalised as " Cash Debitor to Stock " and the teacher's reply is: " Because Cash (having received my mony into it) is obliged to restore it again at my pleasure." [14] The cash account, which Pacioli called " cassa " and which was translated by Oldcastle as " chest," was the account easiest to personify since the receptacle for the storage of coin could be visualised mentally and could be thought of as " receiving " and " paying."

The personification concept was extended to apply to inanimate objects (real accounts) in what Alexander Malcolm calls an " artificial and improper sense." " When any Thing becomes mine," he wrote in 1731, " I consider it as a Subject which owes, or is accountable to me." [15] Peele's " scholemaster " was more explicit.

> Marke me well, [he admonishes] and I will declare the same to you in fewe wordes. Where as I saide before, that the thinges receaued must owe, I meane therby that the goodes bought, or monie receaued of anye man, muste in all percelles be made debetour, (that is to saye) to owe vnto the parties of whom it is receaued or bought. As for example, Imagine that you haue bought clothes of William Jones, then to observe the rule, you must enter the percell in your Journall sayinge, Clothes oweth to William Jones etc.[16]

An explanation or rationalisation of this method of exposition is given by Benjamin Donn in *The accountant and Geometrician . . .* :

> As I may expect to make of [*i.e.*, sell] my Goods as much as they cost me, they are in Effect the same to me as if their Value was due to me from some person; and as, in such Case, that Person would be 'Debtor, so I may make the Goods in my Possession Debtor for their first Cost.[17]

Another development of the personification principle was the evolution of the idea that accounts (other than personal accounts) represented the owner himself. Degrange senior was amongst the first to put it into words: " Débiter l'un de ces comptes, c'est débiter le négociant lui-même sous le nom de ce compte en particulier." [18] The basic idea, however, as Professor Littleton has shown, may be derived from the form of the earliest known examples of double-entry book-keeping.[19] The proprietor was conceived as entering twice into each transaction. For example, if goods were bought on credit from Z, the analysis would be, " Goods shall give to proprietor, Z shall have or receive from proprietor." An extension of this concept made by the younger Degrange was that the proprietor enters into each and every transaction and that to avoid overcrowding the proprietor's personal account with an entry for every transaction he proposed his

---

[14] *Merchant's Mirrour*, p. 9.
[15] Malcolm, *op. cit.*, p. 12.
[16] Peele, *op. cit.*, Introduction.
[17] B. Donn, *The accountant and Geometrician* (London, 1765), p. 5.
[18] E. Degrange, *La Tenue des Livres rendue facile* (Paris, 1802), p. 6.
[19] A. C. Littleton, *Accounting Evolution to 1900* (New York, 1933), p. 46.

well-known five "comptes généraux," all of which "représentent le négociant." [20]

The notion that the accounts represented the proprietor soon gained ground in Great Britain and by the middle of the nineteenth century James Henry Lewis was able to explain that this "ingenious and useful fiction," which had "long been employed in book-keeping," by which the article received was always made debtor to the person from whom it was received, meant that "instead of the merchant's name standing as Debtor or Creditor in his own books, he is personated by the goods." [1]   An excerpt from Crellin's book shows the direction of the development of this idea:

> It is the trader himself who is the owner of this property, it is he who receives and parts with it, and it is he who, it may be thought, should be debited and credited rather than "Goods." But the trader, it must be remembered, has several kinds of goods, has cash, and bills, and fixtures, and leases etc; and if all the transactions occurring in these various forms of property were brought together into one account and entered under his name, it is evident that it would be very voluminous, and that it would be impossible without great waste of time to ascertain particulars regarding any one of them. Hence the advantage of sorting these several items, bringing together all that relate to the same thing, naming the accounts correspondingly, and treating them in the way of debiting and crediting as if they were living persons having charge of, and responsible for, the property to which they refer.[2]

For the origin of this most extreme form of personification we must retrace our steps a little.

The most complete theory of personification arises when the accounts are given a personal identity which is "accountable" or responsible to the proprietor yet completely independent of him materially.   A short appendix which first appeared in the fifth edition of the famous Augustus de Morgan's *Arithmetic* entitled "On the main principle of Book-keeping" [3] was, in its effect on the teaching of book-keeping, probably the most influential piece of writing to be found during the nineteenth century.   In personification it made explicit and expanded to its logical conclusion that which had previously been implicit in teaching methods and it initiated the movement which finally resulted in the rejection of the journal, the stumbling block to the learning of the subject.

Traces of de Morgan's idea of clerks representing accounts can be found as early as 1731.

> Now observe that each of those Particulars your Inventory does consist of, are therefore made Debtor to Stock [*i.e.,* Capital] in your

[20] E. Degrange, *Eléments de la Tenue des Livres* (Paris, 1850), p. 4.
[1] *Op. cit.*, p. 41.
[2] P. Crellin, *Book-keeping for Teachers and Pupils* (London, 1892), p. 26.
[3] A. de Morgan, *Elements of Arithmetic* (5th ed., London, 1846).   All references are to the sixth edition, 1876, Appendix VII.

Leger, because they are in Effect so many Stewards to whom you intrust your Estate, and each of them are accountable to you for their several Parts of it.[4]

In the following year, in a book no copies of which now appear to exist, the complete personification theory was expressed in these words:

Let it be supposed that the account of Stock [*i.e.,* Capital] is a real person employed to take care of my estate and to render an account of the improvement he has made of it. In a like manner, Cash, and all other accounts which I may have occasion to keep, may be considered as persons employed by Stock to take care of that part of my estate with which they are entrusted.[5]

De Morgan's brief appendix on book-keeping which proposed the complete personification of every account in the person of a " clerk " was not, therefore, entirely a pioneer work. It was, however, expounded at a time which was ripe for the embracing of new methods of teaching and de Morgan's eminence in related fields undoubtedly did much to encourage the acceptance and development of the idea:

The accounts are kept as if every different sort of account belonged to a separate person, and had an interest of its own, which every transaction either promotes or injures. If the student find that it helps him, he may imagine a clerk to every account: one to take charge of, and regulate, the actual cash; another for the bills which the house is to receive when due . . . and so on.

All these clerks (or accounts) belonging to one merchant, must account to him in the end—must either produce all they have taken in charge, or relieve themselves by shewing to whom it went. For all that they have received, for every responsibility they have undertaken *to the concern itself,* they are bound, or are *debtors*; for everything which has passed out of charge, or about which they are relieved from answering *to the concern,* they are unbound, or are creditors. . . . To whom are all these parties, or accounts, bound, and from whom are they released? Undoubtedly the merchant himself, or, more properly, the *balance-clerk.*[6]

Both Collier (in 1884) and Dyer (in 1897) appropriated the notion utterly and completely, the latter acknowledging his debt to de Morgan. " We have appealed strongly to the imagination to create an array of clerks," wrote Collier, " who must be anything but dummies, and we have reasoned out everything from the principles enounced. . . ." [7] These principles were that

the whole business is *supposed* to be carried on by *clerks.* There is supposed to be a clerk called Capital or Stock who represents the owner of the business (or the Firm). There is supposed to be a clerk called Goods who takes charge of the merchandise. There is supposed to be a clerk called Cash who takes charge of the money. There is supposed to

---

[4] R. Hayes, *Modern Book-keeping . . .* (London, 1731), p. 4. The book was " written originally for the use of his own Pupils."

[5] J. Clark, *Lectures on Accompts* (London?, 1732), quoted in B. F. Foster, *The Origin and Progress of Book-keeping* (London, 1852).

[6] De Morgan, *op. cit.,* p. 181.

[7] J. Collier, *Book-keeping by Double-Entry* (London, 1884), Preface.

be a clerk called Bank who represents the firm's banker. There is supposed to be a clerk called Bills Receivable who takes charge of all " Bills " payable to the Firm. . . . There is supposed to be a separate clerk for each and every person or firm with whom the Firm has credit transactions. . . . There is supposed to be a clerk called Profit and Loss. . . .

N.B.—These clerks mind their own business and do not interfere in another's department. Thus, if perchance, " Goods " receives some money he instantly hands it over to " Cash " because he himself has no business with money.

All transactions were analysed in terms of movements of value between the " clerks." For example, his first rule was: " In every transaction there is a clerk (A) who *gets* something of a certain value from clerk (B). Then A is *Debtor* to B and B is *Creditor* by A for tha amount." As a method of exposition which he had used for twenty-five years, Collier had " found it to be the enlightening fact to the learner, and the progress has commonly been in proportion to the learner's grasp of this notion." Dyer, using exactly the same method, called it the " Common Sense Method of Double Entry." [8] The acceptance of outright personification was in accord with the general revolt against teaching by rote which took place in the latter half of the nineteenth century.

By explaining the structure of accounts in the form of relationships of indebtedness, teachers were indicating the difficulty in presenting book-keeping procedures in personal terms. Although somewhat inadequate even for the explanation of the entries to be made in personal accounts, the meanings of the terms " debtor " and " creditor " have to be stretched to absurdity when dealing with real and nominal accounts. Edward Thomas Jones, the first accountant to make a head-on attack upon the established system of double-entry book-keeping, naturally poked fun at these methods of exposition. Of the current method of journalising a credit sale to A.B. as " A.B. Dr. to Wine," he asks, " Now, if A.B. owes wine money, why not let Wine call for payment? But if A.B. do not owe Wine money, why make the entry in such way as only tends to confuse the mind of a person . . . ? " [9] B. F. Foster, who was anxious to advertise the advantages not only of his textbooks but of his method, taught exclusively at his " establishment " 161a, Strand, London, disdainfully reproduced such confusing examples as that of Daniel Sheriff's elucidations [10]:

Robert Henderson Dr. to Bills Payable ... £337.10. Elucidation —Henderson is debtor because he *owes us*, we having paid him the

---

[8] S. Dyer, *A Common Sense Method of Double Entry Book-keeping* (London, 1897).
[9] E. T. Jones, *English System of Book-keeping* . . . (Bristol, 1796), p. 24.
[10] D. Sheriff, *The Whole Science of Double Entry Book-keeping* . . . (London, 1850), p. 24.

amount that *we owed* him. Bills payable are creditor, because the note to which that title is given has paid Henderson for us; therefore *we owe* it.[11]

Similar examples can be culled without end from contemporary textbooks. Even when using de Morgan's complete personification Collier is forced to explain that " when we write ' Cash debtor to Goods £50 ' it does not necessarily mean that the cash-clerk *owes* the goods-clerk £50; nor does it mean that the goods-clerk (the creditor) has discharged a debt of £50 owing by him to the cash-clerk. It means that the cash-clerk has *got* (or received) £50 from the goods-clerk and of course that the latter has *parted with* £50 (or its value) to the former." [12] In other words the accepted meaning of " debtor " and " creditor " is not really satisfactory even in this context. It was, of course, very easy to ridicule the personification method of exposition. Charles Sprague, in America, could write a pointed skit on balancing the ledger with a cast including " Stock, a merchant; Balance, his accountant; Cash, keeper of the money chest; William Receivable, protector of the portfolio " [13] and others. This piece of fooling was hardly so far from the truth when compared with the textbook.[14]

The explanation of nominal accounts is, however, the *bête-noire* of the personification approach, for these accounts are mere abstractions. The problem of their explanation did not arise as a matter of urgency until the middle of the nineteenth century for up to that date trading was treated, in textbooks at any rate, as a series of " ventures " each with their respective expenses " charged " to them. Implicitly, appeal was made to the " charge " and " discharge " technique which had arisen in the financial relationships of principal and agent. It is, however, impossible to explain profits and expenses in terms of personal debt relationships and after much abortive discussion they came finally to be explained in terms of parts of the capital account.

Exposition by means of personification of the accounts was but one aspect of the attack on the journal method of teaching book-keeping with its concomitant rote learning by rhymes and rules. There had been sporadic criticism of learning by rote from the earliest textbook authors. In 1714, Roger North said he would not " labour very hard, or penetrate deep, by exaggerating Multitudes of Rules and perplexed Examples, as most Writers of this subject have done," [15] yet succeeded in preparing a very readable account of elementary book-keeping. Malachy Postlethwayt, who in the middle of the

---

[11] Foster, *op. cit.*, p. 31.
[12] Collier, *op. cit.*, p. 10.
[13] C. E. Sprague in *The Bookkeeper* (New York, 1882), quoted in Littleton, *op. cit.*, pp. 59–61.
[14] It may be compared with Collier's version (pp. 299–300, above).
[15] North, *op. cit.*, p. 10.

century published the " blue-print " of his ideal " institution for the education of merchants," required that his book-keeping instructors should " in a natural progression, proceed to explain systematically the axioms, and rational maxims and principles . . . according to the method of double-entry. . . . This inimitable method of accounts being founded on the principles of reason, will prove a kind of practical logick to young people, when it is rationally and methodically communicated, not mechanically, and by rules depending on the memory only, which latter does not merit the name of instruction at all." [16]

The rote method of teaching book-keeping was so prevalent that some authors were chary of including the subject in their works. " As book-keeping is a Subject which has not hitherto been inserted in any Course of the Mathematicks," writes Benjamin Donn quite incorrectly, " some perhaps may not consider it as a Part thereof. . . . But if they would but consider, that, though Book-keeping has commonly been treated of and taught by Way of Rote, or arbitrary Rules, without shewing the Reason of them; yet as the Subject is of great Utility, is now introduced and taught in all our Academies which qualify Youth for Business, requires no inconsiderable Knowledge of Numbers, and is capable of being treated of in a rational Manner," [17] he felt he was justified in including it in his arithmetic-book. Malcolm too, in his earlier book wished to make the practice of the rules " a work of Judgment rather than of Memory." [18]

Nevertheless, although attacking the learning of the subject by rote, teachers limited their aim to making the *application* of the rules a matter of reason. The premises and justification of the rules themselves did not arise. " The learner must exercise his judgment to determine, *by the rules*, in what book each transaction is to be entered " wrote Bryce in 1860.[19] Perhaps the clearest denunciation of this approach is in a passage quoted by B. F. Foster:

> It is only from a series of particular facts, that the mind ascends to general truths. All rules being but general truths, or inferences, deduced from observations of particular facts or examples, it is clear the former cannot be understood, unless by means of a minute analysis and explanation of the latter. According to the existing modes of instruction, however, it would seem that rules are not inferences but self-evident principles. For the pupil first learns the rule, and then applies it to an example. It would be a matter of astonishment indeed, if a mode of proceeding so directly opposed to the order of nature, as this is, were unattended with difficulties.[20]

[16] M. Postlethwayt, *The Merchants' Public Counting-House* (London, 1750), p. 23.
[17] Donn, *op. cit.*, Preface.
[18] A. Malcolm, *A New Treatise of Arithmetick and Book-keeping* (Edinburgh, 1718), Preface.
[19] J. Bryce, *Treatise on Book-keeping* (Edinburgh, 1860), Preface. (Author's italics.)
[20] B. F. Foster, *Double-Entry Elucidated* (London, 1863), p. 4n.

The Journal Approach v. *The Ledger Approach*

The conflict between those teachers who favoured the journal and those who preferred the ledger as the book through which the subject should be approached is the translation to practical classroom procedures of the conflict between the rote and rational approaches to book-keeping. Teachers who used the journal as the introduction to the subject were forced to the use of rules. Those using the ledger might also use rules but could develop comparatively rational principles, if they wished.

The struggle between these opposing methods was as fierce as that which had taken place nearly two centuries earlier between the " ancients " and the " moderns " on the question of the Grammar School curriculum and raised issues vital to the teaching of book-keeping. It resolved itself into a battle between the " ancients " who favoured the journal and the " moderns " who preferred the ledger. It resulted in the vanquishing of the journal as the main book for the presentation of book-keeping principles and its relegation to an insignificant position as a technique of teaching. This banishment was not however the result of purely pedagogical pressures but was greatly hastened by the fact that the journal was rapidly disappearing from the business world. The supporters of the ledger approach were therefore doubly reinforced—by pedagogical advances towards rational teaching methods and by changes in the demands of business.

Although the journal had held the field as the " chiefest booke " for almost 350 years before the rumblings of the attack could be heard in the middle of the nineteenth century, it had not always found favour. Criticisms of the encouragement it gave to rote repetition of rules and copying have already been given. These criticisms could be levelled with justification at the greater part of the nineteenth century instruction in other subjects too.

In book-keeping it was common to find that the " Plan of Tuition " was " to read over and over again and again, very attentively, the entire of my General Instructions." [1] These " Instructions " consisted of twelve large pages of small type! Alternatively, the pupil might be condemned to the drudgery of " copying a multitude of similar examples, which gives him employment for some months, before he learns the manner of balancing a single account." [2] " If the learner is not quite master of the subject, after writing up the first Set of Exercises once," writes Theodore Jones, " he is recommended to write it again and if necessary, repeat it till he has acquired such proficiency as to be able to write up and balance the first set complete." [3]

---

[1] P. Comins, *The Science of Commerce* (Dublin, 1814), p. 30.
[2] R. B. Roe, *An Introduction to Book-keeping* (London, 1825), Preface.
[3] T. Jones, *Jones Exercises in Book-keeping for Schools* (? London, c. 1840), p. 2. Theodore was son of the famous Edward Thomas Jones and this school-book

It must be agreed, in fairness to the teachers of the period, that both Comins and Theodore Jones were practical men from the business world; but this attitude of mind was just as prevalent amongst teachers.   The Reverend Ebenezer Cobham Brewer,[4] whose output of school textbooks on a variety of subjects was tremendous, expected his pupils to " copy out " his book filling in the blanks for practice in arithmetic.   Fortunately for the teacher a " key " was available.   A good deal of the copying was, of course, aimed at improving the students' writing and James Dimelow's *Practical Book-keeping made Easy* published in 1876 is the supreme example of this type of approach.   Its pages are foolscap in size with beautiful copper-plate writing on each left-hand page to be copied on the leaf facing.

The type of book-keeping taught and the prevailing method of teaching satisfied none but the teachers.   In the course of a review of a book-keeping textbook in *The Times* it was said (in 1845):

> There needs little observation to know that the manner in which merchants' accounts are taught in the generality of schools is tedious, defective and unsatisfactory. The pupil is disgusted, because the systems adopted are incomprehensible, or so perplexed with difficulties that the reason is fettered, and all attempts at deductions from the premises are futile, and so much labour lost.[5]

The decisive factor in the substitution of the ledger for the journal as the main book for the presentation of the system was, however, that by the beginning of the twentieth century the journal as a sole book of original entry hardly existed in the business world.   Whatever may be its educational value, book-keeping as a subject rests upon vocational foundations and if the foundation changes its form then the superstructure must change too.

Apart from the vocational reasons, what pedagogical grounds existed for preferring the ledger to the journal for purposes of presentation?   Quite briefly, that the journal entries were records about which decisions could not be made without understanding their effect on the ledger.   The journal entries were in fact the ledger entries in a technical form and it was the attempt to get behind the technicalities of the subject which finally led to the decline of the use of the journal as a teaching technique.   In what is probably the first treatise on the teaching of book-keeping B. F. Foster [6] wrote:

---

was an attempt to encourage the use of his father's " English " system of book-keeping in schools.

[4] E. C. Brewer, *An Entire New System of Book-keeping by Single Entry* (London, 1850).

[5] Quoted in Foster, *op. cit.,* p. 51. For later comments, see the remarks of S. Latham reported in the Proceedings of the Fourth Meeting of the International Congress on Technical Education, London, June, 1897.

[6] Foster had a school in U.S.A. as well as in London and it is claimed by some to have been the first business school in America. See H. C. Bentley, *Brief Treatise on the Origin and Development of Accounting* (Boston, 1929), p. 24.

The ordinary mode of teaching book-keeping is to commence by copying from some popular treatise a series of transactions, such as receipts, payments, purchases, sales, consignments and the like. After being wearied, *secundum artem*, with this work, the student is made to construct a journal; that is, to narrate under what heads in the ledger the respective items are to be placed, the substance of his instruction being, that " the thing received is debtor to the thing delivered "; but as to the object of making one *thing* debtor to another, he must be totally ignorant; for every journal entry has reference to the ledger, and the ledger is a sealed book to him. His whole progress through the journal, is, therefore, a blind process of guessing; and when, ultimately; he transfers these items to the ledger, and balances his books, he does so more like an automaton than a rational being.[7]

Putting the matter more directly in his *Double Entry Elucidated*, he wrote:

It is impossible to comprehend the technicalities of journalising, unless we are previously familiar with the design and use of each account in the ledger. Hence, the ledger should be the *first*, and not the *last* book to which the learner's attention is directed.

A similar attack on the journal approach appeared somewhat earlier in the United States of America in which Thomas Jones took a leading part. Professor Littleton quotes a letter written by B. F. Foster to Thomas Jones in which the latter is given the honour of having originated the method of beginning the " explanation of the theory with the ledger." [8]

However, the appreciation of the primacy of the ledger for teaching purposes was not a spontaneous discovery of the mid-nineteenth century. Malcolm, writing in 1731, considered that the " Leger-Book is the principal Book of Accounts " and treated the ledger before the journal. A widespread appreciation of the importance of the ledger in the teaching of the subject is not met, however, until we reach the nineteenth century. James Morrison was amongst the first to realise its importance. " We shall next consider the Ledger," he wrote in 1825, " because though the Journal comes before it in the order of writing, yet the Journal cannot be well understood until the nature of the Ledger be explained." [9] It was not, however, until de Morgan allied himself to the " Ledger school " that there was an expansion in the number of books using this approach.

As a result of de Morgan's emphasis on the nature of double-entry book-keeping through the personification of accounts he was quite logically led to the position where he was able to announce with the whole weight of his authority in the academic field that " the only book that need be explained is the ledger." [10] It will be remembered

---

[7] B. F. Foster, *Remarks on the ordinary modes of teaching Writing and Book-keeping* (London, 1846), p. 4.
[8] Littleton, *op. cit.*, p. 181.
[9] J. Morrison, *The Elements of Book-keeping* (London, 1825), p. 36.
[10] De Morgan, *op. cit.*, p. 183.

that de Morgan's appendix on book-keeping did not appear until 1846 and is unlikely to have become widely known until it reached its next edition thirty years later.   During this intervening period of three decades the author has been able to find only one newly published book using a ledger approach, that by Henry Manly " Principal Writing-Master and Teacher of Book-keeping in the City of London School [11]; but after the 1876 edition of de Morgan's " Arithmetic " progress was a little more rapid.   In 1879, Thornton [12] and in 1894, Lisle [13] published books which taught all transactions through the ledger before dealing with the journal.   The latter acknowledged his debt to de Morgan.   In the nineties the question had clearly become one of considerable interest and de Morgan's name was frequently mentioned.   Whitfield, for example, refers to him and goes on to say that " the disrepute into which Book-keeping as a school subject has fallen down to a recent period is traceable to the mistaken postpone-ment of work upon the ledger to the detailed consideration of other books of account." [14]   *Double-Entry Book-keeping* by Andrew Sarll,[15] which was recommended by Beard [16] for public examinations, used the ledger approach so that by the beginning of this century this method of presentation must have been well known in teaching circles.

The Ownership Theory of Accounts

The chief rationalisation of book-keeping entries until the nineteenth century was, as has been shown, in terms of account per-sonification.   This is, however, but one of the " theories " of accounts which has, consciously or unconsciously, influenced the method of exposition.   An alternative theory may be called the " ownership " theory of accounts.   This theory is concerned with the meaning of accounts from the owner's point of view and is the method of exposition now used in the majority of American textbooks.

Technically, the " ownership " theory of accounts involves a balance sheet or " balance sheet equation " approach because the centre of discussion and the point of origin from which the teaching starts and finishes is the balance sheet.   This is a radical departure from the debt relationship concept of accounts in which the balance sheet is the final result of account entries.   In the case of the owner-ship theory, on the contrary, the balance sheet is conceived rather as the activating mechanism than the final repository.   It is a logical extension and development of the idea of tracing a transaction

[11] H. Manly, *Principles of book-keeping* . . . (London, 1864).
[12] Thornton, *op. cit.*
[13] G. Lisle, *Elementary Book-keeping* (London, 1894).
[14] E. E. Whitfield, *School Introduction to the Commercial Sciences* (London, 1892), p. 118.
[15] A. Sarll, *Double-Entry Book-keeping* (London, 1897; first published 1881).
[16] W. S. Beard, *Guide to Employment for boys on leaving School* (London, 1890).

" cycle." The balance sheet is thought of as the crystallisation of the financial position of the business. Instead of tracing all transactions through to their effects on the balance sheet as in the " cycle " method, the transaction is analysed in order to determine the changes in the financial structure which it will entail, *i.e.*, what the new balance sheet will be, and the account entries are formulated as a result of this analysis. It is a complete reversal of approach to the subject. Attention is focused not on " exchange " between accounts but on the *transformations* of each side of the balance sheet. Transactions are analysed in terms of mutations of assets and liabilities of the firm and their effect on the profit aspect of ownership. Discussion is in terms of conversions rather than debt relationships; of impersonal statistical relationships rather than personal relationships; of analysis rather than rule and rote. Accounts are " increased " or " decreased " rather than " debited " or " credited." Emphasis is transferred from book-keeping fictions to book-keeping realities.

Although Baker appears to suggest [17] that the " ownership theory " with its resulting balance sheet approach is the result of the development of recent American teaching techniques, its origin can in fact be found much earlier than the present century and its early progress makes fascinating reading. In essence the complete theory with its resultant teaching techniques can be found as long ago as 1735, expounded by a teacher who also made up (*i.e.*, adjusted) " all kinds of intricate and confus'd accounts." His name, Hustcraft Stephens, deserves to figure much more prominently than is now the case.[18]

Stephens succeeded in extricating himself from the quagmire of personification at a time when no alternative was known or contemplated. His approach was so novel that he was forced to coin new words to express his ideas and from the point of view of teaching his method of exposition was quite a century before its time in its emancipation from rules. His design was " to offer no Rules, until he has shown them to be Consequences of Conclusions, plainly drawn from Self-evident Principles."

In his introduction he lays the foundation for his theory of the mutations of the assets and liabilities by defining capital as an abstraction separate from the business.

> That Portion of Things which a Man possesses, or has otherways belonging to him, as a Security, taken all together, I call the Estate, and the Worth of a Man's Estate, consider'd abstractly from the Things which are valued, I call the computed Value or Extent of a Man's Estate.

In general he uses the term " Condition " for what today would be called " assets " and " Extent " for " liabilities." Both are words of

[17] J. W. Baker, *A History of Book-keeping Instruction in the United States* (1935), p. 19.
[18] H. Stephens, *Italian Book-keeping Reduced into an art* (London, 1735).

specialised reference because of lack of suitable existing terms.   The aim of book-keeping, he says, quite simply is to find the " Condition and Extent of a Man's Estate."   His next step is to classify transactions into three categories according to the way in which they affect assets alone, liabilities alone, or both assets and liabilities.   He further introduces the idea, also quite novel in that period, of the owner being a creditor of the business.[19]

Hustcraft Stephens's explanation of the function of accounts shows a complete understanding of their use as an arithmetical device for showing variations of individual assets or liabilities.

> I say, the various Securities [debit balances] must be so divided, that when by any Transaction it becomes necessary to add to, or take from them respectively any Quantity, Number, or Sum, we may do it so, that the remaining Quantity, Number, or Sum, with the Alterations that produced them, may appear.

In turn he goes on to show the effect of sales, purchases, and the receipt and payment of cash upon the financial position of the business.   For example, the sale of 500 lbs. of sugar for £50 and the purchase of 3,000 lbs. of sugar for £150 is shown as follows:

Second Account

Sugar bears Part of the Condition of my Estate		l.	s.	d.
I have - - - - - - -	1,000 lb. for	100	0	0
Alter. 1. Sold out - - - -	500 lb. for	50	0	0
First Remains -	500 lb. for	50	0	0
Alter. 2. Bought - - - -	3,000 lb. for	150	0	0
Second Remains -	3,500 lb. for	200	0	0

Third Account

Money bears Part of the Condition of my Estate			
I have - - - - - - - - -	200	0	0
Alter. 1. Receiv'd for Sugar - - - - -	50	0	0
First Remains - - - - -	250	0	0
Alter. 2. Bought Sugar; for which I paid - - -	150	0	0
Second Remains - - - -	100	0	0

Continuous addition and subtraction is tedious, he points out, " whereas were all these Alterations which cause an Increase of the Condition, and those which likewise bear a Part of the Extent, respectively gather'd together, they might at Pleasure be compar'd by one Subtraction after their Sums were severally added up " and so we arrive at the normal form of the two-sided account.

Stephens's book marks a complete departure from the prevailing

---

[19] It is interesting to note that the word " proprietor " is used for what today would be called " creditor " indicating how Stephens conceived of the liabilities side of the balance sheet as being in the nature of a list of " sources "; he gets away from the conception of book-keeping as the recording of debt relationships.

explanation in terms of personification.   Although no reference is made to his book by later authors and his underlying ideas were not developed for over three-quarters of a century, the framework for an impersonal, statistical approach to the subject with a complete exposition of the arithmetical function of the account had been provided. It is in the latter direction that Stephens's contribution to teaching method is so outstanding.

It was not until the turn of the century that this view of the structure of accounts was to be developed.   James Williamson Fulton, a book-keeper with the Board of Revenue, Bengal, India, had been struck by the great difficulty in obtaining a rapid general view of a person's or firm's financial position under existing methods of keeping accounts.   The aim of his book [20] was therefore to expound a method of keeping accounts so that " the progressive effect of all transactions on the General Stock daily or monthly " was immediately available. By reason of his approach to the problem he had grasped an important aspect of the " ownership " theory of accounting, *i.e.*, that the accounts were a method of recording changes in the assets and liabilities of the person or firm and that all such changes would be reflected in the balance sheet.

Fulton insisted that basically it is necessary to distinguish only between the stock (capital) account and the totality of all other accounts because the capital account " is not composed of a particular independent property, like each of the other accounts, but arises from the state of all these collectively taken, which thus form merely the particulars of it: and the grand aim of double entry is, to ascertain the true state of the stock account."   He goes on to point out that the equality of debits and credits is never disturbed.   " If a *gain* be made, the Cr. side of the stock account is thereby increased, . . . but at the same time the Dr. side of cash or some other, one or more, accounts must be *equally* increased.   A *loss* will increase the Dr. side of stock, and increase in an *equal* degree the Cr. side of some other account or accounts."   He recognised and stressed that the balance of the capital account was not only the difference between assets and liabilities but also the original balance together with the net effect of changes arising from profits and losses.   By means of additional columns to his journal, Fulton, by distinguishing between capital and revenue items, was·able to analyse the net effect on capital of all transactions and thus enabled to extract the net balance of capital at any time and equate it with the net effect of changes in other account balances.   Whatever may have been the practical value of his suggestions, Fulton's work was a further step iṇ the building up of a new way

---

[20] J. W. Fulton, *British–Indian Book-keeping* (London, 1800).

of looking at the aim and purpose of keeping accounts and at the inter-relationships between the various accounts in a ledger.

Eighteen years after the appearance of Fulton's book the exposition of the " ownership " theory was completed by F. W. Cronhelm.[1] Cronhelm's contribution lay in his enunciation of the abstract nature of capital as a " whole," its differentiation from its constituent " parts " and the inevitability of the " equilibrium " of the " whole " with the " parts." Apart from occasional lapses into personification his, also, is a mathematical approach.

From the very beginning Cronhelm, like Stephens and Fulton, looked upon book-keeping as a method of recording property and changes in property rather than debt relationships.

> The purpose of Book-keeping as a record of property is to shew the owner at all times the value of his whole capital, and of every part of it. The component parts of property in trade, are in a state of continual transformation and change; but, whatever variations they undergo, and whether the whole capital increase, diminish, or remain stationary, it is evident that it must constantly be equal to the sum of all its parts. This Equality is the great essential principle of Book-keeping.

Stemming from this approach no account could be regarded as " fictitious " or " imaginary "; all were equally " real " and a source of great confusion which had arisen from the personification theory was abolished.

Having abandoned personification the way was open for an abstract mathematical approach to the subject:

> The introduction of Credit and Bills into commerce produced two kinds of property directly contrary in their natures:
> 1st. Positive Property, consisting of Goods, Cash, Bills Receivable and Debts Receivable.
> 2d. Negative Property, consisting of Bills Payable, and Debts Payable.
> And as these two kinds of property mutually destroy each other, it is evident that the Stock or entire Capital, must always be equal to the difference between them.

From the idea of the capital account as a mathematical equilibrating device it follows logically that it must be a credit item:

> Should it be inquired why the Stock [capital] appears to be negative when the property is positive, and positive when the property is negative, this seeming contradiction will be removed by the following consideration. In these general relations of Debtors and Creditors, the estate or concern itself is abstracted from its proprietor and becomes a whole, of which the Stock or Proprietor's Account is now also one of the component parts . . . and he classes among its other Creditors.

Not only capital, however, but all accounts can be thought of as equilibrating factors.

> When we thus abstract a Concern from its Proprietor, and place the account of Stock or entire capital among the component parts, the

---

[1] F. W. Cronhelm, *Double Entry by Single* (London, 1818).

Concern itself is constantly neutral, consisting of a mass of relations between Debtors and Creditors, in perpetual and necessary equilibrium. The Concern thus abstracted, is always a cypher; and all its component parts are equally and mutually dependent upon each other, and upon the whole. It is no longer merely the Stock which is the result of all the other Accounts collected together: every Account has the same property, and may be found or proved in the same manner.

In Cronhelm's algebraic form and notation: if a, b, c . . . are " positive parts " and 1, m, n . . . are " negative parts " and s is capital or proprietor's real worth, then

$$a + b + c \ldots - l - m - n \ldots = \pm s$$

By transposition he reaches the general equation of the abstract concern:

$$a + b + c \ldots - l - m - n \ldots \mp s = 0$$

Here, he observes that " the transposition of s changing its sign, explains the reason why the Stock, when positive in itself, becomes negative or creditor as a component part of the estate."
By transposing *any* of the terms it can be shown to equal the remainder, for example:

$$b + c \ldots - l - m - n \ldots \mp s = -a.^2$$

That is to say

any debtor or creditor in the books is equal to the collective result of the other debtors and creditors, an affection which has been commonly supposed peculiar to the stock [capital] account.

This general equation, however, is a static conception and when transactions take place an exposition in dynamic forms is required. The component parts are continually changing. At this point Cronhelm develops an " ownership theory " of transformations of property from one form into another.

In purchases cash is converted into goods; and in sales, goods are re-converted into cash . . . [credit] purchases create personal creditors and goods, sales convert goods into personal debtors; receipts convert personal debtors into cash; whilst payments destroy cash and personal creditors.

He goes on to apply this system to profits and losses, viewing them as increases or decreases of capital. The function of the profit and loss account was therefore seen as a method of collecting together the individual augmentations and diminutions of capital so that the general result might be transferred to the capital account in one sum.
The basic principles of the " ownership theory " were therefore expounded clearly and simply by 1818. These were, the complete

---

[2] It is a matter of some surprise that this idea of a fundamental equation was not followed up and developed by mathematicians. Pierre Jocet wrote his *Théorie algébrique et idéologique de la tenue des livres* in 1898 and developed a superstructure of equations from his " équation fondamentale " which was similar to Cronhelm's. This book is little known however.

separation of the owner from the business, the fundamental equation of ownership, and the conception of transactions affecting this equation by increasing or decreasing assets, liabilities or capital.   This method of explaining and teaching book-keeping then almost completely disappears from view in Great Britain and it requires diligent research to find even a passing reference to this way of looking at the accounting problem.[3]

The astonishing feature of this depersonalised, mathematical approach to book-keeping is that, although it is the principal current method of exposition in the United States of America and several European countries, it was not until 1949 that it was adopted in a twentieth-century British book-keeping textbook.

---

[3] The approach by way of the " ownership " theory is used in the following works in the nineteenth century: P. C. L. Vautro, *A New System of Book-keeping* (London, 1828), J. H. Chauvier, *The Perfect Book-keeper* (London, 1849), R. Y. Barnes, *A Treatise on book-keeping . . .* (London, 1867), and P. Child, *Book-keeping and Accounts* (London, 1891).

Edward Jones and the
Reform of Book-keeping, 1795–1810

B. S. Yamey

IN 1795 Edward Thomas Jones, an accountant in Bristol, announced in a lengthy prospectus the forthcoming publication of his English system of book-keeping which he guaranteed would measure up to the most exacting standards and supply what the commercial world, we may be sure, had long been seeking—an infallible system of book-keeping.

The prospectus [1] heralded the coming of a new method of book-keeping by *single entry*, which would be simple to understand and operate, enable all errors to be detected without much delay or trouble, provide valuable information not yielded readily by the double-entry system, and, finally, would banish the possibility of fraudulent book-keeping entries. The panegyrics lavished by the author on his new system were coupled with an intemperate attack on the so-called Italian system of double entry, which, in the course of a lengthy castigation, was said to be delusive, conducive to error, and capable " of being converted into a cloak, for the vilest statements that designing ingenuity can fabricate." As the result of the shrewdly composed prospectus, the recommendations of well-known gentlemen (including D. Giles, Governor of the Bank of England, and Robert Peel, M.P.), the high promises held out by Jones, and the prestige of having obtained patent rights in respect of some features of the new system, there were over 4,000 subscriptions to the first edition of the English system published in 1796.[2] Further editions were brought out, and an American edition was published in 1797.

The invention and publication of the English system proved to be a great financial success for Jones. But his preposterous gibes at the

---

[1] The full title is *An Address to Bankers, Merchants, Tradesmen, &c., intended as an introduction to a New System of Book-keeping in which it is impossible for an error of the most trifling amount to be passed unnoticed*.

    Quotations from the *Address* as well as from the introduction to the *System* itself are given by J. Row Fogo in R. Brown, *A History of Accounting and Accountants* (Edinburgh, 1905), pp. 160–163, and in my " Edward Jones's ' English System of Bookkeeping,' " *Accounting Review*, XIX (1944), pp. 407–416.

[2] The full title is *Jones's English System of Book-keeping by Single and Double Entry, in which it is impossible for an error of the most trifling amount to be passed unnoticed; Calculated effectually to prevent the evils attendant on the methods so long established; and adapted to every species of trade* (Bristol, 1796).

expense of double entry drew forth a sharp counter-attack by its
defenders.   In 1796 and 1797 five publications appeared in England,
exposing the hollowness of the extravagant claims made by Jones for
his system (and especially of the boast that it made it impossible for
fraudulent errors to remain undetected) and vindicating the Italian
double entry.[3]   His system appears to have been thoroughly discredited in the land of its birth and from which it took its name.   It
was left to Jones himself to come to the rescue of his system, and he
published a 100-page reply to his English critics[4]; but this did not
have any effect in rehabilitating his prestige.

In the meantime, and even after he and his system had been
ridiculed in England, his fame spread abroad; his book undoubtedly
was the first English work on accounting to achieve international
renown.[5]   Translations appeared in German, Dutch, Danish, French,
Italian and Russian.   Some of his translators, while generally in
favour of the English system, nevertheless were displeased with its
inventor's boasting,[6] or unhappy about his criticisms of double-entry
book-keeping, which one of them described as an " invention which is
a tribute to the human intellect."[7]   Some, too, were aware of
deficiencies in his otherwise esteemed system and incorporated
improvements in their versions of it.[8]

On the Continent, as in England, the publication of Jones's system
caused acute controversy which persisted for several years.   There
were scathing criticisms of his work, some even questioning his

3 The five works are: James Mill, *An Examination of Jones's English System* . . .
(London, 1796); Joshua Collier, *A Defence of Double Entry* . . . (London, 1796);
Thomas Knolles Gosnell, *An Elucidation of the Italian Method of Book-keeping*
(London, 1796); *A Letter to Mr. T. Edward Jones . . . , by a Merchant* (1796);
and J. H. Wicks, *Book-keeping Reformed* . . . (Egham, 1797).
    I have not been able to locate copies of the works by Mill, Collier and " A
Merchant."   Some detail of these publications can be obtained in book reviews
in *Analytical Review*, 23 (1796); J. W. Fulton, *British-Indian Book-keeping* . . .
(London, 1800); and B. F. Foster, *The Origin and Progress of Bookkeeping* . . .
(London, 1852).
    James Mill was an " accountant and notary public," and not the economist,
as I mistakenly wrote in an earlier article (referred to in note 1, above), misled
by a sentence in Brown's *History* . . . , p. 167.   Alexander Bain, the biographer
of James Mill, the economist, noted and corrected earlier incorrect attributions
of the anti-Jones pamphlet.   (See *James Mill* [1882], p. 51n.)
4 This 100-page *A Defence of the English System of Book-keeping* . . . was
noted and discussed in *Analytical Review*, 25 (1797), pp. 649–650.   I have not
been able to locate a copy of this publication by Jones.
5 J. Row Fogo in Brown's *History* noted than Jones's work " is the most widely
known book on the subject in the English language " (p. 159).
6 For example, N. A. Vestieu, *Wederlegging der Ingebragte Bezwaaren tegen de
nieuwe Methode van Boekhouden* (Amsterdam, 1802), pp. 11 and 24.   This work,
by the Dutch translator and advocate of Jones's system, dealt with Dutch and
German criticisms of the system.
7 A. Wagner, *Eduard T. Jones neuerfundene . . . Englische Buchhalterey* . . .
(Leipzig, 1801).   Wagner, one of two German translators of Jones's work, later
repudiated the system in his *Buchhalterei für das gemeine Leben* . . . (Leipzig,
1810).
8 See below, pp. 316, 319.

competence as an accountant and the authenticity of the testimonials published in his support.[9] However, three of his translators, in particular, came to his defence.[10] In the course of the debates several opponents of Jones brought out their own " systems " of account-keeping; two German systems, and French, Belgian, Swiss and American systems eventually also saw the light of day. Rivalry and attempted innovation in accounting matters flourished greatly in the years of the Napoleonic wars.

Shorn of its author's bombast and extravagance, Jones's volume of 1796 advocates a system of modified single entry as well as certain changes in the organisation of books of account. The latter alterations were designed to reduce the possibility of errors in posting from the journal to the ledger. First, the book of original entry, the day-book—Jones did not approve of separate waste-books and journals—has three columns: when a transaction takes place, the amount is entered in the centre column, irrespective of debit and credit; then, when the merchant or book-keeper has more time, he enters the amount to be debited to a ledger account in the column on the extreme left-hand side of the page, and the credit in the third column on the other side of the page. The " new disposition " of columns, by which " the Debits are far removed from the Credits, and can never meet " [11] was said to prevent confusion in posting to the ledger by indicating debits and credits clearly, and to be an improvement on the customary journal which had merely one money column.[12] This innovation was adopted, without acknowledgment, by several of Jones's most vehement critics.[13] It is probable that this trifling improvement was to some extent adopted in practice.[14] It certainly appears as if the

---

[9] Among the critics were J. G. Meisner (*Neuerfundene Deutsche Buchhalterey* . . . [Breslau, 1803]) in Germany, M. Bataille in Belgium (see p. 322, note 14), and E. Degrange (*Supplément à la Tenue des Livres rendue facile* . . . [Paris, 1804]), J. Rodrigues, and A. Mendes (*Examen d'un ouvrage* . . . [Bordeaux, 1803] in France.

[10] Notably N. A. Vestieu (see note 6, above) in Holland, and J. G [abriel] (*Méthode simplifiée de la tenue des livres en partie simple* . . . [Paris, 1803]) and B. Delorme (*Nouveau système de tenue de livres d'après Jones* . . . [Avignon, 1808]) in France.   [11] Gosnell, *op. cit.*, p. vi.

[12] For examples of the single-column journal, see the reproduction of the first page of Sir Thomas Gresham's journal, 1546 (Plate VII), and of a page of the 1701 journal of the Darien Company, in Brown's *History*, opposite p. 158.
    In some eighteenth-century journals (for example, those of the East India Company) additional columns were sometimes added to the main column to list details. Fulton, writing in 1800, noted that extra columns in the journal for the details of compound entries (*i.e.*, entries with more than one debit or credit) had been in use in the " Factory Books of Dacca for 1787–8, and those of the Salt Department, for some successive years before."

[13] Collier, Gosnell and Wicks. Fulton (*op. cit.*, p. 25) noted that Gosnell " has condescended unacknowledgedly to adorn himself with a feather plucked from the wing he assisted to clip."

[14] Kelly observed (*The Elements of Book-keeping* . . . [London, 1801], p. ix) that " some of the columns [of the English system] have been adopted in Counting-houses and even by subsequent Writers."

modern double-column journal dates from the early nineteenth
century.

The second major alteration in the arrangement of the books was
designed to make it easy to compare the totals of debits and credits
entered in the day-book with the totals of items posted to ledger
accounts in a given period. For this purpose Jones invented his
much-derided patent ledger which, besides the usual money-columns,
has four extra ones on each side, a set for each quarter of a year.
Entries in the ledger are repeated in the appropriate quarterly columns.
These could be totalled page by page without examining the contents
of individual ledger accounts, and the quarterly grand totals compared
with the totals in the debit and credit columns of the day-book
balanced quarterly. Errors and omissions in posting would then be
discovered and located.

This check was also considered useful by some of his critics.[15]
But it was generally felt that the multiplicity of columns in the ledger
was too high a price to pay for it. His second French translator,
Delorme, regarded the multi-columnar ledger as the obstruction which
impeded the practical application of Jones's system; he discarded the
patent ledger and instead made use of an additional column on each
side of the ledger for bringing out monthly totals. Vestieu, the Dutch
translator and adapter, pointed out that Jones's arrangement necessi-
tated a new ledger or new ledger accounts each year with more work
in consequence. Instead he proposed the use of an additional column
on each side for quarterly totals, to be checked against the day-book
totals. Jones later recognised the shortcomings of his form of ledger,
which, he said, "though correct in principle, was inconvenient in
practice."[16] He therefore devised alternative systems to provide the
check on the correspondence between the entries in the book of
original entry and those posted to the ledger. In these can be seen
the beginnings of modern systems of sectional balancing and control
accounts. In all, Jones's proposals in the field of book-keeping
techniques foreshadow later developments, and he may be regarded
as one of the "inventors" of tabular book-keeping and sectional
balancing procedures.

On the *contents* of accounts, as distinct from their form and
organisation, Jones's proposals were far more heretical and therefore
more irksome to his critics. He was an outspoken enemy of double
entry and put forward a plan for a modified form of single entry. In

---

15 In the review of Jones's volume in the *Analytical Review*, 23 (1796), p. 415, the
check was said to be useful, but it was added: " The originality of this disposition
of columns in the ledger has been disputed, but when we consider the great
labour attending such a variety of additions and arrangements, we do not know
that the invention is worth contending for."

16 *The Science of Book-keeping Exemplified.*(London, 1831), p. 30.

his system there is no place for impersonal accounts, with the exception of those for cash and bills payable. (The former was explained to be a personal account in the name of the cashier, and the latter was presumably to be explained in similar terms.) The ledger therefore contains only personal accounts of debtors and creditors, the capital accounts of the two partners in Jones's illustrative worked example—Bold and Wise in the original, Hardy and Sage in Gabriel's French version—and cash and bills accounts, with one other, for unsold merchandise at balancing date, which Jones was obliged to introduce, but did not bother to explain.

It follows that the entries in the day-book and ledger are not in full double entry, and the check on the accuracy provided by double entry is lacking.[17] Jones claimed that his truncated system of entries had the major advantage that the ledger (and he could have added the day-book as well) showed, when posted, " the exact difference between what a person owes, and what is owing to him; and that without being at the trouble of ascertaining the balance of one single Account—Surely this is attaining *valuable* information, by a process as EXPEDITIOUS, as it is UNPRECEDENTED." [18] However, this claim is not quite valid, even in respect of Jones's simple example which excludes opening assets and liabilities and dealings in fixed assets; for the ledger includes both capital and cash accounts. But it is true that, provided simple adjustments are made for these items and for fixed asset accounts (if any), the balance of the English ledger entries at any time gives the firm's net position *vis-à-vis* third parties. Whatever may be thought of this particular plan, it was an early attempt to arrange accounts so that key aggregates could be made to appear without detailed balancing of individual accounts.

Jones claimed another advantage for his system of entries—the " plain and simple manner in which the profit or loss in any concern may be ascertained, *precludes* the *possibility* of the most ingenious man deceiving his partner, if possessed only of common understanding."

---

17 Jones attacked the facile acceptance of the trial balance as a " proof " of double-entry records: " How is it that Men of common understanding can believe that the Debits and Credits of a Ledger balancing or agreeing in amount, is a proof of it being a fair and correct representation of the Day-book ; which, surely, is the most material point in Book-keeping! Would two pictures being exactly alike, prove that they were a correct copy of the original? Or would my putting two guineas of equal weight into a balance, prove that they were weight by the standard? "

18 Delorme was particularly impressed by this feature of Jones's system.
Wicks, an opponent of Jones, had a journal much like Jones's day-book, save that from its columns were omitted the amounts of all entries affecting personal accounts, other than capital accounts. He left out what Jones put in, and vice versa. In consequence the quarterly balances showed what was " owing to Antonio Prettyman and Co. more than is due to them," or vice versa, an excess of debits indicating net indebtedness by the firm, and conversely for an excess of credits. Fulton correctly pointed out that the two plans (those of Jones and Wicks) were " the *type* and *impression* of each other."

The calculation of the profit at the end of the year in Jones's uncomplicated example is indeed simple, though it is doubtful whether it would have been plain to all his readers, since Jones did not reveal its rationale. The procedure is to debit the day-book, and a " stock of goods unsold " account in the ledger, at the end of the year with the value of unsold merchandise. The excess of the year's debits over credits is the profit for the year. This calculation gives the correct result. As the day-book contains only entries affecting personal accounts, capital, cash and bills accounts (entered to debit or credit as in orthodox double entry),[19] the difference between total debits and total credits reflects the *net* amount that would have been credited to the nominal accounts (including individual merchandise trading accounts) if these had been kept. The final debit for the unsold stock (the only other asset) makes the only necessary closing adjustment. Cronhelm, writing in 1818, pointed this out by describing the day-book " as an account of Merchandise," [20] or, as we would say today, a combined trading and profit-and-loss account (though with the important differences that the sides are reversed, and the entries refer not to categories of incomes and expenses but to movements and changes in assets and liabilities).

Jones did not explain or illustrate how the profit calculation would be affected if there was a stock of goods on hand at the beginning of the trading period. Cronhelm elucidated the required adjustment in his critical commentary on Jones: " Had Mr. Jones understood the nature of his book [day-book] as an account of Merchandise, he would have carried down the stock of goods in the book itself as its proper balance [*i.e.*, to leave a *credit* balance as the opening stock entry for the next period], and not have let it abscond to a sinecure account in the Ledger, either to be fetched back again to its appropriate station, or to disconcert the next year's result by its elopement." Again, Jones did not explain how the presence of other assets (for example, houses, investments) would affect the calculation. He did write: " The first thing requisite to be attended to, is to state in a Day-Book a true account of the stock or property with which he [the trader] commences trade." However, this would have involved ledger accounts for fixed assets, etc., contrary to Jones's specific prescriptions elsewhere in his volume. Moreover, an opening day-book entry comprehending all assets and liabilities would have given the wrong results, since it is necessary to begin the " account of merchandise " for the new period with a net credit for the opening stock of goods.

---

[19] For example, the purchase of goods on credit would lead to a single entry, a credit to the supplier's personal account ; the subsequent payment of the account would give rise to a double entry, a debit to the personal account and a credit to cash.

[20] F. Cronhelm, *Double entry by single* . . . (London, 1818), p. 25.

This effect two of Jones's translators and adapters, Vestieu and Delorme, achieved in their more realistic worked examples by having orthodox " double-entry " opening entries for capital, assets and liabilities except that the *value* of the merchandise was deliberately omitted from the money column, thereby causing the credits to exceed the debits by the appropriate amount.

The profit calculation of the English system does not show the profits or losses on individual ventures or lots of merchandise, nor the totals of particular classes of expense. These omissions, and more particularly the former, were considered to be a serious deficiency by several of his critics and translators; the first-mentioned type of information was available in double-entry accounts as these were commonly kept.[1] Once more some of his translators tried to remedy this defect. Vestieu advised that " some " nominal accounts should be kept, the elimination of the others being an important source of economy; in his worked illustration he had an account for transactions concerning a part-interest in a ship and another for discount on bills, the profit in each case being entered, oddly but correctly, on the debit side of the day-book. Wagner, who arranged and annotated one of the two German editions of the English system, prescribed the use of a " merchandise book," the accounts in which gave the profit or loss on each venture or lot and were not linked up with the " English " profit calculation.[2] Delorme went further by arranging his ledger with complete double entry, while keeping the day-book on " English " lines. This modified English system was in fact much the same as

---

[1] On the other hand, De la Porte (*La Science des Négocians et Teneurs de Livres* [new ed. Paris, 1753], p. 188) wrote that there were two ways of keeping accounts for the control (" pour la régie ") of merchandise in double-entry book-keeping, *viz.*, either by having separate accounts for each sort of goods, or by having a single account for all goods. He added that the latter was customary " for those who trade in many kinds of goods, and who sell at retail and at wholesale " and that the single account was more common in practice than the system of separate accounts. However, most of the book-keeping manuals and the discussions of Jones's system point to the prevalence, at least in England, of the system of particularised goods accounts. It may well be that it was mainly merchants operating on a large scale who employed double entry and hence satisfied the conditions mentioned by De la Porte as suitable for the use of separate goods accounts. The general disappearance of particularised goods accounts seems to have occurred only in the nineteenth century.

Benjamin Booth (*A complete system of book-keeping by an improved mode of double-entry* . . . [London, 1789]) advocated a single goods account in the ledger instead of what he said was the current practice ; he contended that owing partly to the introduction of so great a number of these nominal accounts the " bulk of traders . . . prefer the plain, simple method of single entry. . . ." But Booth did not decry the use of individual profit calculations for separate lots of goods ; he advised merely that these should go elsewhere and not clutter up the ledger.

[2] Jones may be said to have anticipated this modification. He wrote: " . . . if it be required to know the profit or loss of any particular speculation or article, a Sales Book, distinct from the Ledger or Day Book, may be used, which will fully answer the purpose." But he did not describe or illustrate this Sales Book, and the general tenor of his argument was against the keeping of such accounts.

Daniel Richter's German system of book-keeping published in 1803, and as Wicks's system of 1797.[3]

It has been shown that it was necessary for the profit calculation in the English system to introduce the value of unsold stocks, and some of his critics wondered how Jones obtained the necessary data on unsold quantities in the absence of goods accounts. The reviewer of his book in the *Analytical Review*[4] argued that if his system relied solely on 'an annual stock-taking, " which is at best but a troublesome and precarious task," it "can furnish no proof or criterion" on whether goods had been pilfered or otherwise lost,[5] whereas the double-entry system, as then practised, gave the information provided by a perpetual inventory system.[6]   On the other hand, "if Mr. Jones mean to open a book for sales, then this is virtually double entry, and nothing is gained by the new system." Fulton believed that Jones, to ascertain the closing stocks, must have had supplementary records, so that "the principles of the Italian system are unavoidably adhered to" though, because of the "absurd attempt . . . to conform to single entry" "we look in vain for that connection and symmetry which reign throughout and characterise a regular plan of double entry; and of course, in vain also for that important check arising from this very coalescence or dependence, consistently with which but few probable instances of unintentional error can well occur." [7]

It is unlikely that the English system was widely employed at any time in England.[8]   The best proof of the inadequacy of the system is

---

3 D. Richter's *Deutsches Buchhalten* (1803) is described in K. Bes, *Bijdragen tot de Geschiedenis en de Theorie van het Boekhouden* (Tilburg, 1908), pp. 142–144.
   A somewhat similar arrangement is in the Rev. Denis Ferrall's *A New System of Book-Keeping, by Double Entry* . . . (Dublin, 1809), in which it is claimed: "That which Mr. Jones promised to do, and has not done, is now performed in this Work."
4 Vol. 23 (1796), pp. 413–416.
5 Mill, in his examination of Jones's system, discovered that in the illustrative example ten pieces of calico were lost. The reviewer in the *Analytical Review* stated this error "seems to complete the climax of absurdity."
6 From about the middle of the sixteenth century textbooks prescribed the use of quantity columns in the ledger accounts for merchandise, so that the owner could keep track of his assets. Thus De la Porte (*op. cit.*, p. 188) dealing with the contents of accounts where separate accounts are kept for each *sort* of goods (see p. 319, note 1), described how inner quantity columns are necessary so that it can be seen readily "if all is sold or not." Malcolm (*A Treatise of Book-keeping* [London, 1731], p. 45), after explaining that it may be convenient to group several "species" in one account, added: ". . . then, that the State of the Account may be distinctly and readily found, by the Comparison of the two Sides, it is necessary to make a Quantity Column for every Species, and set its Name on each Side on the Head of it."
7 Fulton, *op. cit.*, pp. 21–22.
   Jones did refer to the possibility of keeping a sales-book (p. 319, note 2).   He also illustrated, without explanation, a " Monthly Statement of [Bold and Wise's] Partnership Accounts," a cryptic sheet which contains details of physical quantities bought and sold as well as some Jonesian calculations.
8 It has been ascertained that, despite the testimonial given by its Governor to Jones, the Bank of England did not adopt the English system.
   Vestieu, writing in 1802, observed that "it appears from reports that the

provided by the fact that by the 1820's Jones himself had discarded it, and the false prophet had become a supporter of the true faith of double entry. The very failure of his own system to supplant Italian double entry was regarded as a proof of the virtues of the latter. Though some of his work may be interpreted as early models of methods which later came to be widely used, perhaps Jones's most lasting influence was that the publication of his system gave rise to " much useful enquiry and investigation on the subject of Merchants Accounts." [9] In the concluding section some of the results of this activity are indicated briefly.

Jones had made use of " perplexed numerous ledger columns " [10] to bring together the entries of each quarter for checking against the day-book totals. Collier, one of his English critics, also made use of an array of columns, in his case in the journal, each column " intended to record the same particular species or article of commerce. This prevents repetition, and saves the trouble of making separate entries in the ledger, for thus the aggregate sum of each column is posted into the ledger in one line." [11] Though his critics, in turn, believed that the variety of columns would " tend to promote errour and perplexity " and require to be managed by a person possessing " more Knowledge, Steadiness, and Skill, than falls to the Share of Clerks in general," [12] Collier's plan for economy of effort on posting to the ledger can be recognised in Isler's so-called Swiss system of book-keeping published in 1810.[13] Another critic, Fulton, Book-keeper in the Office of the Accountant to the Board of Revenue, Bengal, also advised the use of columns for analysis of data. There were to be two sets of columns in the journal, one for debits and credits to " real accounts," and the other for decreases and increases of stock (capital)

English system, notwithstanding the laudatory testimonials given to Jones by Bristol merchants and the directors of the Bank of England, is little used in England, from which can be concluded that the testimonials do not count for much there, for the system, in my opinion, would otherwise be more highly valued, particularly because the inventor is an Englishman. I can think of no explanation of the hesitancy of the English to adopt the system other than that there is an obstinate prejudice in favour of double entry. . . ." (*Wederlegging* . . . , p. 30).

An account of the English system of book-keeping is given, after that of double entry, in the 1810 and 1817 editions of the *Encyclopaedia Britannica*. This suggests some lasting interest in the new method.

The author of the first French translation of Jones's volume, Gabriel, remarked that " during a visit to the United States in 1798, we saw that the [English] method was generally adopted." There is no corroboration of this report in other sources.

[9] Kelly, *op. cit.*, p. ix.
[10] So described by Fulton, *op. cit.*, p. 31.
[11] Review in *Analytical Review*, 23 (1796), p. 416.
[12] Gosnell, *op. cit.*, postscript.
[13] This work also shows the influence of Degrange's " French " system, described in the text, below.

to provide, in effect, a running balance of the profit to date for each accounting period.

The use of multi-column accounting records for the purpose of grouping data analytically and for presenting them in compressed form was developed by two of Jones's continental critics, Bataille and Degrange, who published their systems almost simultaneously in 1804; each was provoked by the initial success of the English system to announce his own system and to demonstrate its superiority.

Bataille, a Belgian, explained that his new system [14] differed from single entry only in that he provided four sets of columns on the right-hand side of each journal page. Transactions which would involve debiting or crediting impersonal accounts in double entry were recorded in one or other of these four sets of columns, assigned, respectively, to merchandise, gains and losses, cash and bills. The ledger contained personal accounts only. The profit and loss of the business was calculated from time to time in a so-called inventory book, from information yielded by the totals of the four sets of columns in the journal and the separate data of opening and closing assets (as in single entry). A special virtue of the procedure was that only the custodian of the inventory book need be aware of the profit figure. Bataille also explained how the accuracy of the books could be checked, the check being based on the fact that for every transaction there were two entries in the ledger and/or the supplementary journal columns.

Bataille's ingenious system, which was a decided improvement on single entry or on Jones's modified single entry and probably quite suitable for small concerns, appears to have had little influence on subsequent works. The system of the Frenchman Edmond Degrange, a member of the *Société Académique des Sciences de Paris,* was far more productive of progeny.

In 1795 Degrange had published a treatise entitled *La Tenue des Livres rendue facile, ou Nouvelle Méthode* . . . , a popular work which appeared in nine editions before the author's death in 1818. In this work he elaborated his view that a business has five " objets principaux " and that, in addition to personal accounts, there were five major classes of account, namely, merchandise, money, bills receivable, bills payable and profit and loss. This is the basis of the five-accounts theory which was hotly debated in the nineteenth century

---

[14] A Dutch translation by Vestieu (Jones's translator) of the treatise written in French appeared in 1805. I have not been able to ascertain the title of the original work, which is not listed in G. Reymondin, *Bibliographie Méthodique des Ouvrages en langue française parus de 1543 à 1908 sur la Science des Comptes* (Paris, 1909). This Bibliography has an entry for another publication by Martin Battaille, which, according to the description given by Bes (*op. cit.,* pp. 152–153) differs from the 1804 work and seems to have been influenced by Degrange's work.

by its supporters, called the *cinquecontisti* in Italy, and their critics. In 1804 Degrange brought out a slender volume entitled *Supplément à la Tenue des Livres rendue facile*, which, in the words of its sub-title, described a new method for keeping books by double entry, through the medium of a single account-book which could be balanced daily without the necessity of having to call over ("point") the details. The single account-book was the celebrated journal-ledger, combining the journal and the ledger.[15] Degrange explained that he developed this book to keep track of his own business affairs at a time when he was very fully occupied looking after the affairs of others. He tried to limit his own book-keeping to those particulars which were indispensable for double entry, and in the process he discovered that his solution had other virtues in that it gave a quick review of his business position at a glance, made daily balancing possible and exposed errors without recourse to detailed pointing.

The left-hand page of Degrange's single book was a conventional journal. The right-hand side contained seven sets of columns in debit and credit. The first five were assigned to the five "objets principaux" identified by Degrange in his earlier work. Items affecting personal accounts were entered in the sixth set, entries in this set relating to a particular person being indicated by a number in an inner reference column so that, when necessary, the state of any one personal account could be ascertained separately. The seventh set of columns ("Total au Grand-Livre") was intended for such calculations and for general balancing purposes. Degrange also illustrated how the six "accounts" could be balanced in a neat and orderly manner.

Apart from the cumbersome procedure for determining individual personal account balances, Degrange's method may have been suitable for small and simple undertakings (and perhaps also for teaching purposes). In any event the idea expounded by him appeared in a number of variants as new "inventions" in many systems of columnar accounting published in the succeeding hundred years.[16] Indeed, a

---

15 The idea of merging two of the three "essential" books of "classical" double entry seems to have been anticipated by some merchants in eighteenth-century England, the two books being the waste-book and the journal. In the revised arrangement the waste-book is on one side of the page (or pair of pages) and the journal, with abridged entries, on the other, as it were in the margin. Alexander Malcolm recommended this "new Method, which I have found practised by some eminent Traders," as being "very much shorter." He preferred the use of this "Marginal Journal" to a system without any waste-book at all for "this would by no Means be convenient, because the Discovery of the true Debtors and Creditors being the great Difficulty, must not be done in a Hurry; as this [latter] Method would often occasion. Or if, to prevent this Effect, the Journal is filled up more slowly, then there is danger of forgetting" (*op. cit.*, pp. 28–33).

16 For an account of many of these variants, see K. P. Kheil, "Uber 'Amerikanische' Buchführung," *Zeitschrift für Buchhaltung*, XVI (1907), and J. F. Schär, "Väriationen in der praktischen Verwendung der amerikanische Journale," *Zeitschrift für handelswissenschaftliche Forschung*, I (1906–1907). Schär explained

324 Edward Jones and the Reform of Book-keeping

burning desire for novelty, real or spurious, useful or useless, seems
to have agitated many of the writers on book-keeping and its practitioners in the nineteenth century.[17] The name of American
book-keeping came to be given to all the systems based on the
combined journal-ledger, though America had no hand in its birth.
The appellation, apparently of German origin, is probably to be
explained on the ground that the names of the more relevant countries
of western Europe had already been appropriated and attached to
one or other of the systems of " national " accounting that came in the
wake of Jones's pioneering effort with his English product.[18]

that he wrote his classificatory account of " American " systems to forestall the
patenting of variations of the basic system deriving from Degrange; he gave
examples of some recent systems which had been patented.

[17] A French writer, Vannier, protested in 1845 against this tendency by warning his
readers in a preface that they would not find in his work a " journal-ledger-
balance " or other products of the imagination but only an account of double
entry as it exists in commerce. (Reymondin, *op. cit.*, p. 111.)

[18] Similarly, Isler's " Swiss " system had no connection with Switzerland; it was
created by a Belgian in a work published in Antwerp.

Some Early Australian Accounting Records[*]

Louis Goldberg [†]

A FEW hours spent among the available early Australian accounting records is an interesting, profitable, and, in some respects, chastening experience. In the Mitchell Library, Sydney, there is quite a variety of accounting records, and even a rapid and inadequate survey of some of them has convinced me that there is here a fruitful field for research by an accountant with some feeling for historical background or for a historian with some knowledge of accounting procedures.

The earliest of these records appears to be the ledger of T. Abbott, evidently a merchant. The first entry in the book—a personal ledger —is dated March 15, 1805, but on p. 63 entries dated March 4, 6, 22 and April 8, 1799, appear in an account headed " William Stevenson on acct. of Mr. Simeon Lord." As this is the only account in the book prior to 1805, one wonders whether it was written up much later than 1799 from an earlier record, especially as the first entry on p. 1 shows a balance forward from a previous ledger. Apart from this account, the entries run from 1805 to 1811.

This " ledger " contains a number of debtors' accounts in double journal form; payments and other credits are shown on the credit side and ruled off where the account is balanced or deducted from debits where they are set off but are not sufficient to balance the account. A number of accounts are crossed thus: settled.

The business of Mr. Abbott was evidently not highly specialised— he sold such commodities as brandy, muslin, tobacco, rum, wine, shoes, soap, cashmere (" 6 yds. Cassimere @ 14/- "), tea (at 12s. per lb.), etc. One customer, within a period of three months in 1806, bought, *inter alia*, thirty gallons brandy (for £67 10s.), ten gallons brandy (£23 10s.), one gallon rum (£2 5s.), one gallon three pints brandy (£3 16s.), and on December 25 (whether for Christmas celebration or for re-sale we cannot tell) ten gallons wine (£12 10s.) and one cask porter, together with a pair of shoes (8s.) and one lb. soap (2s.). Quite likely this customer was also a merchant—at least it is to be hoped that not all the liquor bought was for personal

---

* From *The Australian Accountant* (October, 1952), pp. 346–355.
   The article has been abridged by the author.
   The original documents and records referred to in this article are all located in the Mitchell Library, Sydney.
† Senior Lecturer in Accountancy, University of Melbourne.

consumption.　In fairness to him, it should be mentioned that in the same period he is credited with £10 for four gallons rum which he had evidently bought in a previous period and returned in this one. These accounts abound in interesting details.　In the first account in the ledger, for instance, there are total debits, between March 15, 1805, and July 15, 1807, of £33 9s., less a credit of £9, leaving a balance of £24 9s., with the notation against it, " Bill deliv^d. March 1808 " (credit control rather lax, perhaps).　Then appears a credit " By 12 Bushels of wheat £5/8/-," and " Balance due £19/1/-." Following this is a note " Settled by an execution," and, remembering the troubled state of the colony at the time, one is moved to hope that the execution was a legal rather than a mortal one.

Abbott also had dealings with a Captain William Collins, who bought a mare in 1810 for £150, ran an account for over two years, and was charged interest (£11 18s. on £71 4s. for two years, which was probably compound interest at 8 per cent. per annum), and was also debited with £84 2s. 10d. for " Amt. of goods retain^d by yow at the Derwent."

Consignments to the Derwent (where the settlement at Hobart Town had been founded) were a feature of some of these merchants' activities.　In the account-book of W. H. Mansell (1809–1812), which also comprises a number of personal accounts, there are given details of the contents of several trunks and cases consigned to Hobart. These were of considerable value; for example, in one case there was a total value of £2,303 11s. ½d., including " Sundries from Mr. Hook 1570.11.6."　In this book there is an account headed " Mr. W. H. Mansell," evidently the owner.　This account shows details of goods on the debit side, with credits mostly for wine and cash; at the bottom of the page there is a good deal of pencilling, as if an attempt had been made (rather unsuccessfully, it would appear) to determine the proprietary capital.

In this book there is also a promissory note pasted into one page, which, I think, is worth reproducing as it there appears:

June 8th 1817

6 months after deat I promas to pay to thomas abbot or odear the sum of 5 pounds sterling for value received by me neal Mack Cloud his X mark.

The account-book of D'Arcy Wentworth, which runs from 1812 to 1820, contains a simple list of entries covering amounts of weekly expenditure by Wentworth, with no evidence of posting or any other further use in a book-keeping system.　Wentworth was a government surgeon and father of William Charles Wentworth.[1]

---

[1] The explorer (1793–1872) who, in company with Blaxland and Lawson, crossed the Blue Mountains in 1813 and opened up the possibility of utilising the rich pasture land which lies west of that range. He later became a prominent figure in politics and public affairs.

Historical figures stalk through the pages of one of the Burdekin account-books of the period 1832 to 1835: Capt. Sturt (fo. 129, 162), Major Mitchell (fo. 212), Dr. Redfern (fo. 213), W. C. Wentworth (fo. 283), J. Blaxland (fo. 437) [2] were some of the well-known people in whose names accounts were opened in this record. This is a large volume, whose last page is numbered 996, but as a fault occurred in the numbering of the pages (fo. 509 is followed by fo. 600 instead of fo. 510) the actual number of account folios is 906. It is a personal ledger, with references which suggest postings from a cash-book and other records; but there is also an account for the Bank of Australia, so that the cash-book may have been used purely as a book of original entry. The record is, however, short of being a double-entry ledger, as there are no income or expense accounts contained in it.

That the colony was becoming a thriving centre for traders is evidenced by an entry showing the purchase on July 1, 1832, by one W. Macdonald of goods priced at £13,120, which was settled by a number of weekly payments of £57 13s. 10d. or multiples thereof, with some amounts of £58—and one of £56 9s. 2d. That some of the conditions of trade in the 1830's were akin to those of the 1930's is shown by an account headed " Wm. Kaye. Shopman, absconded," in which the items are all debits " To Cash." Several other accounts also show debits without any credits, but not all of these were necessarily bad debts. For, in one account (fo. 927) there appears a debit of £80 16s. 5d. dated December 19, 1832, " To P/Note @ 4 m/d " against a credit of the same amount dated December 20, 1832, " By Hoop Iron," and a further debit dated March 15, 1833, " To P/Note @ 4 m/d " £72, after which appears a pencil note by the accountant: " N.B. I should think as a Bill was given goods were obtained altho' no note taken of this. Wm. Smith." Mr. Smith was also evidently puzzled by another account in which the following pencil note appears: " Memo. All transactions with Warne appear to have been settled but I cannot ascertain exactly in what way. Wm. Smith."

Another record—the ledger of J. D. Lang—contains a medley of items. In addition to personal accounts of debtors for printing, advertising, etc., it contains pay-rolls with employees' signatures, some correspondence of a private nature, and numerous newspaper cuttings. Towards the back of the book there are several journal and ledger entries dated 1774, which, if authentic, would make this the earliest Australian accounting record by far, antedating the first settlement by

---

[2] Sturt and Mitchell were explorers; Redfern was an emancipated transportee who preceded D'Arcy Wentworth as doctor at Norfolk Island and later built up a very successful practice in Sydney; J. Blaxland, brother of the explorer Gregory Blaxland, was a pioneer in cattle raising in the colony and a member of the Legislative Council for fifteen years.

several years. I suspect, however, that these entries are merely exercises from some early textbook on book-keeping. For example, there are some five pages of a cash journal, followed by two pages of ledger accounts, four accounts on each page. These accounts are for Baillie and Bell, Borrowstoness (two debit entries); Jan Jonker, Rotterdam (one debit), Clover Seed (three credits), John Scott (one debit), Share of Ship Hazard (one debit), William Ainslie (one credit), Linseed (one debit and two credits), Train Oil (one debit). One James Boswell, merchant, Edinburgh, also figures in this portion of the book, and this makes one suspect even more strongly than ever that he is one of those fictitious characters so often portrayed in book-keeping textbooks—a device to which textbook writers and examiners have regular recourse even in these days. Although these few pages contain some aspects of double entry, the procedure is not fully carried out, and the impression is strong that they are the scanty fruit of an uncompleted course of self-training in double-entry recording.[3] The period of authentic entries in this book lies between 1837 and 1843.

The account-book of Imlay Brothers, 1837 to 1840, also contains, for the most part, personal accounts, but there is also a summary of a wool clip (on p. 32) and details of whaling expenses for each of the years 1837 (p. 136) and 1838 (p. 90). In addition to serving an accounting purpose, this book was later useful as part of somebody's liberal education, for in various parts of it there are such things as a short biography of Sir Walter Scott, some snippets from French history, geography revision lessons, and the like.

The account-book of Rev. T. Williams, which records, over a lengthy period from 1839, the receipts and payments of a Wesleyan missionary, contains much matter of human interest and constitutes something of a saga in its way. An account on the first page, headed " Account of Outfit and Travelling expenses allowed T.W. and M.W. in 1839," opens the story. This account, with receipts on the left-and payments on the right-hand side, has as its first item dated " Aug[st] 9 " an amount of £30 " Received of the Rev[d] E. Hoole (in the vestry of Liverpool chapel) for Wes[n]. Miss[y]. Committee." Then comes a credit of £15 on Aug[st] 13, " Paid Miss M. Cottingham (afterwards Mrs. Williams)," and several dated Aug. 20: " To Mr. J. Akrill of Horncastle for shoes. See bill £2 2. 0 "; " To Mr. W. Seargents of Horncastle for articles of clothing. See bill £8. 19. 6 "; " Travelling expenses during the months of Aug[st]. and Sep[r]. Journey from

---

[3] Since this article was first published, I have seen a copy of Robert Hamilton's *An Introduction to Merchandise*, published in 1788 (second edition), and the people, commodities, etc., indicated in these pages of Lang's ledger appear in the specimen accounts shown in Hamilton's book, Part IV—Italian Bookkeeping—Chap. I—General Principles and Rules.

H.Castle to Liverpool £2. 10. 6 "; " D⁰. from Liverpool to H'castle £2. 0. 6 "; and " Coach fare &c. for Mrs. W. & Self from *H.Castle to Bristol £6. 4. 6." This last entry has the footnote: " *From Peterborough to Bristol: my dear Father paid our fare from H.C. to Peterborough. T.W." Then, on the debit side, dated Sep. 4, we have " Received of Revᵈ. E. Hoole (in the vestry of St. Philips Chapel Bristol) for Wesⁿ. Miss. Comᵉ., for Traveˡ. Expences, &c. £6. 17. 0." The account is closed with totals of £36 17s.

The first account on the next page (the pages are not numbered) is brief. The title is " Thoˢ. Williams in Accᵗ. with the Wesⁿ. Missʸ. Committee. London. Per Rev. E. Hoole. 1839.," and the entries comprise one debit, " Sepʳ. 4 Advanced for 2 Qrs. salary i.e. Sepʳ. and Decʳ. by the Revᵈ. E. Hoole £17. 0. 0 " and one credit " By Sepʳ. & Decʳ. Quarterage £17. 0. 0." Then comes (on the same page) a slight change in procedure—receipts are shown on the credit, payments on the debit side. The account is headed " Thoˢ. Williams in Accᵗ. with the Wesⁿ. Missy. Comᵗ. Per Revᵈ. J. Archbell 1839 and 1840." The debits comprise: " Sepʳ. 10 & 26 Washing at Bristol and Milford 6/4 "; " Oct. 17 Sundries at Bristol, Milford and Maderie £2. 3. 5½ "; and on the same date, " Stuff for Pillow Cases 9/4 "; total £2 19s. 1½d. On the credit side we find: " Oct. 17 By Cash £1. 8. 5½ "; " Febʸ 7 By D⁰. £1. 1. 4," and " Cr. for Pillow cases 9/4 "; total £2 19s. 1½d. This account is continued on the next page with amounts of £2 19s. 1½d. brought forward on each side. The debits here are: " Feby 6 Private Stores £3. 19. 3 "; " Jan. 8, 12 & 31 Cape Washing £4. 8. 10 "; and " Balance £10. 0. 0.," while the credits comprise three items of cash for £8 0s. 0d., £2 0s. 0d. and £8 8s. 1d. on January 28, February 7 and 11, respectively.

As the information in this account looks as if it may refer to the voyage out from England, it may have been thought that book-keeping procedure should be reversed on the way to the Antipodes, although after arrival procedure reverted to the original by September, 1840. Thus the next account is " Thoˢ. Williams in Account with the Lakemba Circuit. Sepʳ. 29 1840," and this starts with a debit balance of £10, to which are added the following items: " April 11 Cash advanced at Hobart Town by the Revᵈ J. Waterhouse £50. 0. 0 "; " Subscriptions to Preachers fund for the years 1840 and 1841 £12. 12. 0 "; " Schools do. do. £1. 1. 0 "; and " Mrs. W. class and Ticket money 5/0 "; total £73 18s. 0d. On the credit side we find, all under the date Sep. 29, the following: " Quarterage for March & June £26. 0. 0 "; " Quarterage for Sepʳ £13. 0. 0 "; " Board for do. £7. 10. 0 "; " Stationery £1. 0. 0 "; " Lying in expences £2. 2. 0 "; " Quarterage for one child £3. 10. 0 "; " Washing at Hobart Town £1. 6. 8 "; " Postage 2/4 Packing Case 5/- . . . 7/4 "; " Box of

Candles 31¾ lb. at 2/3 per lb. £3. 11. 6 "; " Medicines £9. 3. 2 ";
" Iron & tin goods £4. 7. 4 "; " To balance £2. 0. 0."; with the total
shown at £73 18s. 0d.

There are several pages after this style, with a balance (usually
representing an excess of expenditure over receipts) carried forward
from quarter to quarter. The story, commencing thus in 1839, is
carried on in this fashion over many years, and it is apparent that Mr.
Williams was later officiating in Adelaide in 1856, Brighton, Ballarat,
Geelong (1864), Melbourne, and Colac (1867). There is also another
account-book of his, containing personal accounts of transactions with
other clergymen.

A " ledger " kept by the Sydney Railway Co. in 1850–1852 is anything but a ledger in the modern, technical sense. It contains some
personal accounts (often with no indication of their settlement), pay-
roll details, details relating to clearing and fencing land, and so on, but
there is nothing that suggests the application of double-entry procedure.
A typical contract was that with John Tuck " for fencing in the
Terminus of Railway Station £10. 0. 0." The pay-roll record from
September 25 to October 3, 1850, reveals that employees engaged in
boring were paid at the rate of 6s. and 3s. 6d. per day.

A ledger of E. S. Antill, running from 1850 to 1864, contains a
number of personal accounts, some of which are interesting because of
a touch of cynical realism which they portray. M. Ryan's account on
p. 16, for example, after recording a number of items supplied over a
period for a total of £2 10s. 6½d., less £1 3s. 4½d. for bedding returned
and £1 4s. 5d. for wages for twenty-six days (a daily rate of less than
one shilling!), records against the balance, " Loss for having a lunatic
discharged 2/9." And on the same page is the account of Patrick
Kelly, who ran up a total debt, over a period of some months, of
£18 9s. 1½d., against which is credited " Wages to this date £11 2 0,"
so that he was " In debt when he absconded £7 7 1½." Under each
of the accounts of Michael Cleary (p. 45) and Thomas Merit (p. 48)
appears the single, expressive word " Bolted "; under that of one
McCarthy (p. 128), the words " Overdrawn and Bolted 7/2." No
messing about here with provisions for doubtful debts, no finessing
between " reserves " and " provisions " and " allowances." The facts
are disclosed—simple, stark, and convincing.

In the Wyndham day-book for 1868 we can see an example of a
pre-journal record in the paciolian tradition. The first entry, for
example, dated January 1, 1868, shows " Cash. Dr. to Mrs. Wilkin-
son " on one line, then " Cheque . . . £36. 12. 0 " on the next, with
the amount extended to the right on a third line. On the left of the
entry is a folio column and on the left of this again appears the word

" Journal," no doubt to indicate that a journal entry had been made in another record. The second entry is under the same date and in similar form: On the first line is " Cash. Dr. to Thos. Bird "; on the second, " Post O. order £5. 0. 0 "; on the third, " Stamps 8d "; and on the fourth is the total, £5 0s. 8d., extended to the right. The word " Journal " again appears on the extreme left of the page alongside the entry and outside the folio column. Thus this record appears to be an example of the waste-book, which was a feature of early double-entry recording, at least according to the textbooks of a century or more ago. Some of the entries, presumably, were not taken to a journal, since they have " nil " instead of " Journal " written alongside. This record, which goes up to November 30, 1868, suggests a double-entry system, but the evidence is inconclusive in the absence of other records of this firm.

This does not purport to be an essay in historical research: the investigation made into these records was purely an exploratory one, and the results given here are just a few points of interest taken from some of our early records. It is not pretended that anything more than a cursory examination of an almost random selection has been made.

One observation of a general nature may, however, be made. In no instance among the records examined was a set of double-entry records discovered. This, of course, does not prove anything but that a century ago the gospel according to Fra Lucas Pacioli had not yet conquered the whole of " the great south land." It is, nevertheless, a chastening reflection for us as accountants to consider that not one out of the thirty or so samples of accounting records investigated was what we would now call a satisfactory, systematic record by even the simplest of professional standards.

A further, concluding observation is that the preservation of these early records is a matter of considerable historical and cultural interest. There is little doubt that the incinerator and the pulping machine have already claimed many valuable historical records. It is important that any which may still survive should be preserved, especially as the machinery for their preservation is now available in State and Federal archives offices, administered by competent and conscientious officials. Before the destruction of any documentary material, whether of a financial or other character, it would be a national service to consult these archives officers or the universities. And this is valid not only for century-old records. We must remember that yesterday is already history, and that by tomorrow today will be. Economic historians are even now looking for documentary material relating to the 1920's and 1930's; it will not be long before they will require it for the warring forties.

Aspects of Railway Accounting Before 1868[1]

Harold Pollins*

THE Railway Age in Britain, when about three-quarters of the country's route-mileage were built, may conveniently be limited to the four decades between 1830 and 1870. Near the end of that period, in 1868, the Regulation of Railways Act was passed, and for the first time railway companies were given fairly detailed guidance as to the form and content of published accounts.[2] In particular they were required to adopt the " double-account " system[3] for their published accounts, and uniformity as between one company and another was secured after many years of chaos. While the Act did not settle all the problems and difficulties of railway accounting,[4] the form of accounts which it prescribed remained unchanged until the Railway Companies (Accounts and Returns) Act of 1911; in general the Act of 1868 marked a turning point in the history of railway accounting after a long period of uncertainty.

* Historian, at present with London Transport Executive, London.
1 The research on which this paper is based was done during the currency of a grant from the Houblon-Norman Fund. I should like to thank the Archivist of the British Transport Commission and his staff for making available the material in their charge, as well as for suggesting lines of thought. I have also benefited from the criticisms of Prof. David Solomons and Mr. S. A. Broadbridge.

Note on sources
The most obvious sources for the study of railway accounts are the published *Reports and Accounts* of the companies, copies of most of which are in the custody of the British Transport Commission. A few are to be found in other places such as the British Library of Political and Economic Science. The volumes of *Reports and Accounts* often include reports of the shareholders' meetings (*viz.*, the chairman's speech and shareholders' comments), extracts from which have been quoted in this article. Before the Act of 1911 railway accounts were made up twice yearly, normally for the six months ending June 30 and December 31, respectively. However, some companies published annual accounts and others balanced their books at dates other than in June and December. The company *Reports and Accounts* and reports of shareholders' meetings were also printed, in varying degrees of detail, in the railway periodicals, such as *Herapath's Railway Journal, The Railway Times, The Railway Record*, and *The Railway News*.
2 The Act was generally welcomed at the time: see, for example, the views of one accountant, H. Lloyd Morgan, *Accounts and Audits : Remarks on the new " Regulation of Railways Act "* (London, 1868). A short note on the origins of the Act is to be found in the Report of the Departmental Committee on Railway Accounts and Statistical Returns, B.P.P. (1910) LVI (Cd. 5052), pp. 405-406. See also C. C. Wang, *Legislative Regulation of Railway Finance in England* (Urbana, Illinois, 1918).
3 So called because, under this system, the balance sheet is divided into two sections, one dealing with fixed capital and the other with circulating capital.
4 See the Departmental Committee on Railway Accounts, B.P.P. (1909) LXXVI (Cd. 4697) and (1910) LVI (Cd. 5052).

There are many topics of interest to students of history and accounting which it would be worth while examining in the formative period of railway history before 1868.[5] One might try to trace the origins and development of the double-account system. The history of railway auditing is also of importance.[6] Again, the development of the organisation and methods of the accounting departments of the railway companies would repay study. Many of the companies were large; some in the 1860's had a paid-up capital of as much as £30–£40 million. They needed highly elaborate systems of accounting and financial control to avoid misappropriation of resources. Not all of them had the necessary safeguards. Several published *Reports and Accounts* reveal that the secretary or treasurer had absconded with the funds, and registrars misappropriated dividends by forging stock. Leopold Redpath, the registrar of the Great Northern Railway in the 1850's, who after his conviction in 1857 was transported for life, was a notable example.[7] A study of the methods adopted by the companies to prevent financial irregularities would usefully add to our knowledge of the history of financial administration in business concerns.[8]

However, in this article it is not intended to do more than discuss certain accounting practices affecting the determination of profits, primarily those concerned with the distinction between capital and revenue receipts and expenditures, and with the depreciation of fixed assets. On the basis of this discussion it will be possible not only to exhibit differences in the accounting practices of different railway companies, and the changes over a period of years, but also to suggest their significance for accounting and economic history.

Although it is possible to indicate some general lines of development, the very multiplicity and variety of the accounting practices

---

[5] It is not always very profitable to date periods in economic history, but it is interesting to observe that one eminent railway historian dates the virtual completion of the British railway network at 1868: L. M. Jouffroy, *L'Ere du rail* (Paris, 1953), p. 78.

[6] S. 30 of the Railway Companies Act of 1867 (30 & 31 Vict. c. 127) raised the status of auditors by providing that:
   " No dividend shall be declared by a company until the auditors have certified that the half-yearly accounts proposed to be issued contain a full and true statement of the financial condition of the company, and that the dividend proposed to be declared on any shares is bona fide due thereon after charging the revenue of the half year with all expenses which ought to be paid thereout in the judgment of the auditors."
Any difference between the auditors and the directors over the deduction of expenses from revenue was to be decided by the shareholders; but " if no such difference is stated, or if no decision is given on any such difference, the judgment of the auditors shall be final and binding."

[7] See C. H. Grinling, *History of the Great Northern Railway* (London, 1898), Chap. 11; and D. Morier Evans, *Facts, Failures and Frauds* (London, 1859), Chap. 9: " The Great Northern Railway Frauds and Forgeries by Leopold Redpath." See also a letter to *The Railway Times*, August 14, 1869, p. 788.

[8] In this connection see a description of the financial methods of Thomas Brassey, the great railway contractor, in A. Helps, *Life and Labours of Mr. Brassey* (London, 1872), Chap. 9.

adopted by the several hundred companies before 1868, for which they were notorious, make a comprehensive treatment of these matters quite impossible. Walter Bailey, the accountant of the Midland Railway, wrote in 1914 that " the accountants of those days [*sc.* before 1868] must have been giants indeed if they were able to make useful comparisons with each other's accounts from the published material at their disposal. There is scarcely an account, abstract, or statement, in either of these early half-yearly reports which is paralleled by a corresponding account, abstract, or statement in the report of another company." [9] In addition, it was said, railway accounts were " so intricately framed that they are calculated either to conceal the truth, or to lead to erroneous conclusions." [10] In 1850 *The Times* referred to the financial affairs of the Caledonian Railway Company in these terms: " The Caledonian Railway Company, the work neither of lawyers, nor of old women, nor spendthrifts, but of shrewd middle-aged mercantile men, is just such a tangle as one might dream of after supping on lobster salad and champagne." [11] This kind of comment was constantly made throughout the nineteenth century about railway finance and accounts.[12] Professional accountants too were criticised for their inconsistency.[13]

The Railway Age

Railways had a long history before the introduction of the locomotive; the use of rails has been traced back to the sixteenth century. But railway history has little significance before the 1820's when important developments in the locomotive led to the success of George Stephenson's *Rocket* in 1829, at the Rainhill Trials,[14] organised by the Liverpool and Manchester Railway. In 1830 that line was opened and was immediately successful, paying good dividends at once.[15] The Railway Age had begun, although the locomotive required further development and improvement before it could completely supersede other forms of traction. By the middle of the 1830's Acts of Parliament had been passed to authorise the incorporation of many main

---

[9] W. Bailey, " Railway Accounts—Old and New," in *Jubilee of the Railway News* (London, 1914), p. 78.

[10] H. Ayres, *The Financial Position of Railways* (London, 1868), p. xxv. See also a letter to *The Railway Times*, September 23, 1843, p. 1060: " I fear that deceptive Reports and deceptive balance-sheets are a growing evil."

[11] *The Times*, September 30, 1850, p. 4, leading article.

[12] For some further references see my " A Note on Railway Constructional Costs, 1825–1850," *Economica*, XIX (1952), pp. 400–401.

[13] *Herapath*, September 27, 1851, pp. 1051–1052.

[14] On October 6, 1829, " date marquant véritablement le début de l'histoire des chemins de fer proprement dits." (J. Dessirier, " Chemin de fer et progrès technique," *L'Année Ferroviaire* [Paris, 1952], p. 25.) The trials lasted several days.

[15] H. Pollins, " The Finances of the Liverpool and Manchester Railway," *Economic History Review*, second series, V (1952).

line companies, and by the late 1830's and early 1840's their lines had been built and opened (apart from one or two which, for financial reasons, had abandoned part of their route).

Railway promotion and construction came in bursts. There was a mania of railway company promotion in 1835 and 1836. Then between 1837 and 1842 hardly any promotion took place, but in the mid-1840's the famous " railway mania " led to the promotion of about a thousand companies. Lines were promoted throughout the country; shares were at enormous premiums; high guaranteed dividends were promised by main line companies to small branch line companies with little regard to earning capacity. In 1847 financial conditions adversely affected the raising of capital and in subsequent years share prices fell as dividends fell, partly because construction was proceeding faster than the increase in traffic. Between 1847 and 1851 there were few promotions of new companies, and much authorised mileage was abandoned. However, the most significant feature of railway history in the 1840's was the extensive mileage that was built despite financial difficulty. The mania added about 5,000 miles of railway, but it also resulted in the downfall of one of the major characters involved, George Hudson, the " Railway King." In the late forties most railway companies appointed some sort of committee of inquiry to investigate alleged frauds, scandals and abuses or to prove that the particular company had been free from irregularities. Judging by the course of share prices, and the comments of such observers as Herbert Spencer,[16] railways were no longer the favourite child of investors or the public.

Nevertheless, some 8,000 miles were built between 1850 and 1870, part of this having been authorised in the mid-forties. Improved trade in the early fifties led to a veritable boom in 1852 and 1853, and again in 1856 (the Crimean War intervening). After the financial crisis of 1857 the period of 1858–1865 was full of railway excitement, particularly in 1863–1865, and by 1870 some 15,000 miles were open in the United Kingdom.

Though an extensive mileage was built between 1850 and 1870, the period was one of financial difficulties for the railways. Dividends rose only slightly despite continuous increases in the traffic carried, and equity share prices hardly improved until the sixties. There was a shortage of equity capital and some companies had to resort to unusual methods of finance, for example, paying contractors in the company's shares, usually at a discount. The financial crisis of 1866 showed up not only the imperfections of the " contractors' lines " but also the unsoundness of many apparently solid railway companies.

---

[16] H. Spencer, *Railway Morals and Railway Policy* (London, 1855).

In particular their habit of over-issuing short-term debenture debt left them, in 1866, when rates of interest were high, unable to renew their debt on favourable terms, or indeed on any terms. One effect of the crisis and depression was the hasty conversion of short-term mortgage debentures into long-term debenture stock. Another was a series of legislative enactments laying down more detailed rules for railway companies to follow.[17]

Railway Legislation

Railway companies were statutory companies, their powers being conferred directly by Parliament. Each company had to obtain an Act of Parliament to give it authority, amongst other things, to build the line and to raise capital. The clauses in these Acts came mainly from two sources: the Standing Orders of both Houses of Parliament, and various general Railway Acts. Standing Orders had little to say on accounts,[18] and it was not until 1844 and 1845 that general Acts were passed which affected railway accounts.[19] These were: the Railway Regulation Act (1844) (7 & 8 Vict. c. 85); the Companies Clauses Consolidation Act (1845) (8 & 9 Vict. c. 16); and the Railway Clauses Consolidation Act (1845) (8 & 9 Vict. c. 20). Of these the most important for present purposes was the Companies Clauses Consolidation Act.

Before the general Acts were passed the accounting provisions in the various private Acts were not uniform. It was normal for them to require that accounts should be kept, but often they demanded little beyond that. There was seldom any reference to auditors. For example, the Act incorporating the Stockton and Darlington Railway in 1821 [20] consisted of 104 sections, but the only reference to accounts was the requirement that the company should keep " proper Books of Account " (s. 56). The company was empowered to pay dividends: " All Persons . . . who shall severally subscribe for One or more Share or Shares . . . shall be entitled to and receive . . . the

---

[17] For more details and discussion of the development of railways in the period under review, see H. G. Lewin, *Early British Railways* (London, 1925), and *The Railway Mania and its aftermath* (London, 1936); J. H. Clapham, *Economic History of Modern Britain* (3 vols., Cambridge, 1930–1938); G. H. Evans, *British Corporation Finance 1775–1850* (Baltimore, 1936); L. H. Jenks, *The Migration of British Capital to 1875* (London, 1938); R. C. O. Matthews, *A Study in Trade Cycle History 1833–1842* (Cambridge, 1954); G. Cohn, *Untersuchungen über die englische Eisenbahnpolitik* (3 vols., Leipzig, 1874–1883); B. C. Hunt, *The Development of the business corporation in England 1800–1867* (Cambridge, Mass., 1936); and T. Tooke and W. Newmarch, *A History of Prices* (vol. 5, London, 1857).

[18] See O. C. Williams, *The Historical Development of Private Bill Procedure and Standing Orders in the House of Commons* (London, 1948–1949); F. Clifford, *History of Private Bill Legislation* (London, 1885–1887).

[19] See Wang, *op. cit.*; C. H. Newton, *Railway Accounts* (London, 1930); A. M. Sakolski, " Control of Railroad Accounts in Leading European Countries," *Quarterly Journal of Economics*, xxiv (1910).

[20] 1 & 2 Geo. 4, local Act, c. xliv.

entire and net Distribution of an equal proportionable Part, according
to the Money so by them respectively paid, of the net Profits and
Advantages that shall and may arise and accrue by the Rates and
other Sums of Money to be raised, recovered, or received by the said
Company, by the Authority of this Act " (s. 38). There is no
reference to a balance sheet or to the shareholders' right to examine
the accounts. Indeed this company as well as some others did not
publish accounts at first.[1]

Another company, the Liverpool and Manchester, obtained its Act
in 1826. This time the Act was more specific as to dividends. In
order to reduce the possibility of excessive profits the company's
charges were to be related to its dividend. If the dividend exceeded
10 per cent., the rates charged by the company were to be reduced by
5 per cent. for each 1 per cent. of dividend above the 10 per cent.[2]
But nothing was said as to the method of determining the net profit.
A later, and larger company, the Great Western, though its Act contained 251 sections, had only a little more detail in it on accounting
matters. Accounts were to be made up half-yearly and to be laid
before the half-yearly general meetings of the company; if the shareholders at the meeting considered the accounts to be unsatisfactory,
they could appoint a committee to examine them and make a report.[3]
Dividends could be declared from the " clear Profits " of the company,
provided that " no Dividends shall be made exceeding the net Amount
of clear Profit at the Time being in the Hands of the said Company,
nor whereby the Capital of the said Company shall in any degree be
reduced or impaired " (s. 146).

Gradually more detail was included in these private Acts so that as
early as 1842 (three years before the general Acts were passed) a body
of regulations had been built up which the general Acts took over.
Thus the various sections, relating to accounts, in the Warwick and
Leamington Union Railway Act of 1842 [4] were similar to those, to be
quoted below, of the Companies Clauses Consolidation Act of 1845.
By 1844 the clauses in the new private Acts were virtually identical
with those to be prescribed in 1845.[5]

There was little in the private Acts to guide railway companies on
the keeping of accounts or the determination of profits. However, it

---

[1] H. Scrivenor, *The Railways of the United Kingdom Statistically considered*
(London, 1849), p. 533, says that no accounts of the Stockton–Darlington Railway
had been published. The earliest accounts of this company preserved by the
British Transport Commission date from the 1850's.
[2] See the discussion in H. Pollins, *loc. cit.*, pp. 93–94. At least one other railway
company had a similar limitation: Garnkirk & Glasgow Railway, 7 Geo. 4, local
Act, c. ciii (1826), s. 88.
[3] 5 & 6 Will. 4, local Act, c. cvii (1835), s. 145.
[4] 5 & 6 Vict., local Act, c. lxxxi, ss. 103–107, 111–113.
[5] See, for example, the North Wales Mineral Railway Act, 7 & 8 Vict., local Act,
c. xcix (1844), ss. 106–110, 114–115.

should be mentioned that gross income was regulated in part, since each Act laid down maximum charges that could be made, and interest on loans was declared a prior charge. Sometimes part of the gross profit had to be reserved as a contingencies fund.[6]

The following changes were introduced by the general legislation of the 1840's. Under sections 115–119 of the Companies Clauses Consolidation Act of 1845 a book-keeper was to be appointed to " enter the accounts . . . in books," and accounts were to be kept and books were to be balanced at the prescribed periods. " On the books being so balanced an exact balance sheet shall be made up, which shall exhibit a true statement of the capital stock, credits, and property of every description belonging to the company, and the debts due by the company at the date of making such balance sheet, and a distinct view of the profit or loss which shall have arisen on the transactions of the company in the course of the preceding half-year." The balance sheet was to be examined by at least three of the directors and signed by the chairman or deputy-chairman. The directors were to produce the balance sheet at shareholders' meetings. The balanced books and the balance sheet were to be available to shareholders at the company's office fourteen days before the shareholders' meeting, and for one month after it. Auditors, holding at least one share in the company but not holding any office in it, were to be appointed.[7] They were to receive the accounts from the directors fourteen days before the shareholders' meeting " and to examine the same." They could make a report or simply confirm the accounts (ss. 101–108).[8] They did not have to sign them, though in fact auditors often did.

This was the sum and substance of the statutory provision governing railway accounts during the most important period of railway development. Clearly it did not amount to very much.[9] Although there was government supervision of railways in such matters as safety in operation, as far as accounts were concerned the companies had only to deliver copies of their balance sheets to the appropriate government department, together with other prescribed

---

6 An analysis of the Acts relating to twenty-six railway companies, contained in Appendix 31 to the Second Report from the Sel. Comm. on Railways, B.P.P. (1839) X (517), pp. 449–541, shows that there were important variations in these enactments.

7 Some of the major companies in fact also employed full-time professional accountants, as permitted by the Act.

8 This Act applied to companies incorporated thenceforth. Many of the older companies did not appoint auditors until after the crises and scandals of the late 1840's.

9 Sometimes other Acts of Parliament affected railway accounts. Thus the Stage Carriages Act (2 & 3 Will. 4, c. 120 [1832], ss. 50, 51) and the Railway Passenger Duty Act (5 & 6 Vict. c. 79 [1842], s. 4) required railway companies to keep books giving details of passenger receipts. Copies had to be sent monthly to the Commissioners of Stamps and Taxes. This was for the purpose of assessing liability for passenger duty.

statistical information. The officially published annual railway returns invariably contained a pathetic statement to the effect that the statistics printed were those given by the companies, and the compilers of the returns had no responsibility for their accuracy or for their completeness; and there were always delinquent companies which did not bother to deliver any information at all.

A great deal of latitude was left to the companies in the calculation of profit, with little power of control by auditors or by the government. This was realised at the time. Thus Gladstone's Act of 1844,[10] which provided for the eventual purchase of new lines by the State at prices to be based on their annual divisible profits, was criticised at the time for not " establishing a systematic control over the method by which profits were calculated." [11]

Although throughout the early period of railway development there were few legislative and administrative changes affecting railway accounting, it is convenient to draw a dividing line at about 1850. Before that time there was little experience on which the companies could draw, and the majority were cavalier in their attitude to railway finance and accounts. After 1850 there were attempts to improve matters, at least on the part of some of the major companies. In the late forties, too, public concern about railway matters led, amongst other things, to the appointment of the Select Committee on the Audit of Railway Accounts.[12] Dionysius Lardner's book entitled *Railway Economy*, which was published in 1850, was perhaps the first attempt to lay down principles for railway administration and accounting.[13] Both the Select Committee and Lardner scrutinised past practices and tried to establish some principles that companies ought to follow.[14]

The Distinction between Capital and Revenue

In the discussion of the determination of the amount of net profit available for distribution as dividend, the most important question was the allocation of items of expenditure between the revenue and capital accounts. Net profits could be increased, and the rate of dividend raised, by debiting capital with expenses which should have been debited to revenue; and vice versa. Until the Regulation of Railways Act of 1868 the law did not attempt to detail or specify the items of expenditure which belonged in each of the two accounts; and in

---

[10] 7 & 8 Vict. c. 85.
[11] E. Cleveland-Stevens, *English Railways. Their Development and their Relation to the State* (London, 1915), p. 111.
[12] Its report is in B.P.P. (1849) X (371) (421).
[13] For a note on Lardner's work, see M. Robbins, " Dr. Lardner's ' Railway Economy,' " *Railway Magazine*, March, 1950.
[14] Other writers of that period were Mark Huish, *On the Deterioration of Railway Plant and Road* (London, 1849), and Samuel Laing, *Report on the Question of Depreciation and on the Policy of establishing a Reserve Fund* (London, 1849).

practice there was no uniformity in the treatment of important expenditures before that date.[15]

It should be stressed that contemporary opinion realised the necessity of keeping separate the two accounts of capital and revenue. The separation was emphasised over and over again in the evidence submitted to the Select Committee on Audit of 1849. Throughout the nineteenth century one of the recurring themes of the pamphleteers was that railway companies had not properly kept the two accounts separate. One commentator wrote of the important Lancashire and Yorkshire Railway Company, in the late forties, when railways were in the doldrums: " No one can examine the capital accounts with any degree of attention without being impressed and—were it not for the *declarations* of the Chairman to the contrary—being convinced that this Company paid all dividends out of capital." [16]   This was not an isolated case. The recent accounting habits of one company were summarised in 1867 in these terms: " Dividends have only been paid by a wholesale system of charging to Capital not only interest on new lines, but repairs, renewals, law charges, and other accruing expenses on completed lines." This was the London, Brighton & South Coast Railway, whose accounts had been specially audited in that year by Price, Holyland and Waterhouse.[17]   The flexibility in the treatment of items of expenditure naturally lent itself to fraudulent management. The most notorious case was that of the Eastern Counties Railway which, between 1845 and 1848 (when George Hudson was Chairman), paid out in dividends some £115,000 more than the " accounts in their books stated they had earned," by the conscious transfer of items from revenue to capital account; " traffic accounts were altered, and the expenses were squared to suit the dividend." This was in addition to some £200,000 " improperly charged to capital." [18]   Some companies may even have paid dividends directly from moneys raised to defray capital expenditure; although it is difficult to find specific evidence of this,[19] some contemporary comments seem to imply it. " So long as

---

15 There was room for discussion even after 1868 ; see, for example, the complaint of lack of uniformity in the treatment of expenditures in *The Railway and Tramway Express*, April 4, 1885, pp. 216–217.

16 Arthur Smith, *The Bubble of the Age* (London, 1848), p. 49.

17 London, Brighton & South Coast Railway, *Reports and Accounts* for the period ending June 30, 1867.

18 Sel. Comm. on Audit, Appendix A (Report of the Committee of Investigation), p. 362. The Report of the Committee of Investigation is reprinted in the Sel. Comm. on the Eastern Counties Railway, B.P.P. (1849) X (366). The published reports of both these Select Committees include a full report on this railway by a firm of accountants, Quilter, Ball, Jay & Crosbie. The amount improperly charged to capital included interest on lines in operation.

19 This appears to have been the burden of the complaint against the Liverpool & Manchester Railway in the 1830's (H. Pollins, *loc. cit.*). In the 1860's the Metropolitan Railway intended paying a dividend out of funds applicable to the construction of a branch line ; directors' and auditors' fees and office expenses were also charged to capital. (See H. Godefroi and J. Shortt, *The Law of*

you have a capital account open, you have two sources of receipts, one a much larger source of receipt than the other; and I am afraid, that with the best intentions, even on the part of such a Board as the London and North-Western, they can hardly avoid occasionally a little tripping, in spite of themselves." [20]   Another factor making for imperfect accounts was the inefficiency of the clerks; details of this sometimes 'appear in the companies' minutes.

Most companies seem to have been aware of the difference between capital account and revenue account.   The assistant accountant of the ill-fated Eastern Counties Railway, who was in charge of the construction ledger, explained that " blue checks are issued for traffic, and red checks for construction expenditure."   It was true that " some of the blue checks were afterwards charged to capital, and portions of others; whether properly or not, I cannot say." [1]   The point is that the company did draw a distinction between revenue and capital expenditure, though sometimes it took little notice of that distinction.

Many companies opened part of their line for traffic while the rest was under construction, and did not have a separate revenue account until the whole was open.   The income and expenditure on current working were entered in the capital account.   When the line was fully opened, the accumulated revenue items were transferred to the revenue account.

During the period of construction interest was paid on long- and short-term loans, sometimes on all calls paid by shareholders (until this was prohibited in 1847), and on calls paid in advance; interest was meantime earned on temporary balances.   The amount paid in interest was usually greater than that earned.   These interest payments had to be made while the company was building, when there was no revenue; they had, therefore, to come out of capital.   Most companies seem to have debited their current interest payments to revenue account once the line was opened, leaving the amount previously paid as interest in the capital account.[2]   Although one firm of accountants in 1849 thought that such accumulated interest should eventually be written off in the revenue account,[3] only one example has been found where a company subsequently transferred the interest paid out of capital to the debit

---

Railway Companies [London, 1869], p. 112 for a discussion.)   The Companies Clauses Act of 1845 (s. 121) specifically prohibited the payment of any dividend by railway companies " whereby their capital stock will be in any degree reduced."
[20] Sel. Comm. on Audit, Q. 1110 (Mihill Slaughter, of the Stock Exchange).
[1] Committee of Investigation, p. 367.
[2] For example, London & Birmingham Railway, *Reports and Accounts*, December 31, 1838.   Line opened throughout on September 17, 1838 ; interest paid after that date debited to revenue.
[3] Quilter, Ball, Jay & Crosbie in Appendix to Sel. Comm. on Audit, p. 389.   One journal said it was illegal not to pay it back from revenue : *The Railroad Quarterly Journal* (London), January, 1841, p. 117.

of revenue.[4]   At the other extreme the London, Chatham and Dover Railway Company was still debiting interest against capital account after the line was open, because, the company explained, there was insufficient revenue to cover it.[5]

Some companies drew a distinction between " productive " and " unproductive " capital, *i.e.*, between capital invested in lines earning revenue and that spent on branch lines still in course of construction. The interest on money borrowed to build the revenue-earning lines came from revenue, while that on the uncompleted branch lines was charged to capital.   In 1845, for example, the *Report* of the South Eastern Railway Company stated: " The Directors recognise the propriety of the principle . . . that the net [6] revenue on the Main Line should be divided among the Proprietors, and should not be charged with the interest on the capital employed in constructing Branches, and other ancillary works, while in progress." [7]   On the other hand, the London and South Western Railway Company in 1849 charged all interest to revenue, even though some of the capital was " unproductive." [8]

The costs of obtaining a company's Act of incorporation were invariably debited to capital, but the costs of unsuccessful applications to Parliament as well as the costs of opposing the Bills of other companies were sometimes charged to capital and sometimes to revenue. The object of opposing other companies' Bills was to prevent possible competition.   In 1853 the London & South Western Railway charged capital with all parliamentary costs; three years later the costs of opposition were debited to revenue.[9]   In 1853 the auditors of the South Eastern Railway thought that the costs of parliamentary opposition should be debited to revenue.[10]   Eventually the best railway practice was to charge expenditures on successful applications to capital and those on unsuccessful applications and on opposition to Bills to revenue.[11]

---

[4] Great Western Railway, *Reports and Accounts*, December 31, 1840.   Transfer of net interest.

[5] London, Chatham & Dover Railway, *Reports and Accounts*, June 30, 1861 (statement of the secretary at shareholders' meeting).   One of the reasons given for the fact that the nominal capital of this company was in excess of the amount actually received and spent on construction was the large amount charged to capital for interest and commission: L.C.D.R., *Committee of Investigation* (1866), p. 13.

[6] The *Report* gives " next."   This is probably a misprint for " nett."   *The Railway Times* (March 22, 1845, p. 394) reprinted the *Report* and gives this word as " net."

[7] South Eastern Railway, *Reports and Accounts*, January 31, 1845.

[8] London & South Western Railway, *Reports and Accounts*, December 31, 1849.

[9] London & South Western Railway, *Reports and Accounts*, December 31, 1853; December 31, 1856.

[10] South Eastern Railway, *Reports and Accounts*, July 31, 1853 (Auditors' Report).

[11] J. A. Fisher, *Railway Accounts and Finance* (London, 1891), pp. xii–xiii.

Depreciation

Although the accounting treatment of the depreciation of fixed assets is frequently referred to in the *Reports and Accounts* of the various railway companies, as might be expected, little was said about it in the Acts of Parliament governing railways. Perhaps the nearest reference to it was contained in the Companies Clauses Consolidation Act of 1845 (s. 122):

> Before apportioning the Profits to be divided among the Shareholders, the Directors may, if they think fit, set aside thereout such Sum as they may think proper to meet contingencies, or for enlarging, repairing, or improving the Works connected with the Undertaking, or any part thereof, and may divide the balance among the Shareholders.

But this gave no detailed guidance to railway directors and accountants, and in practice a variety of methods of accounting for depreciation were adopted.[12] It is true that the important case of *R.* v. *Grand Junction Ry.*[13] upheld an order of quarter sessions that in assessing a railway company for a poor rate, the proper measure of the rateable value was the gross receipts less various items of expenditure (interest, working expenditure) including a percentage on the capital invested in the movable stock for the annual depreciation beyond the ordinary annual repairs. But the railway companies did not necessarily take note of the fact of depreciation, much less the sum proposed in this case (*viz.*, 12½ per cent. of the capital sum).

The variety of methods illustrated in this section followed not only from the lack of experience in matters such as the life of assets but also from the absence of any clear definition of what was meant by depreciation. Some meant a fall in the market value of the assets when they spoke of depreciation (thus when the price of locomotives rose some companies assumed that their assets had improved); others meant no more than current repairs and maintenance; others again were concerned with replacement.

In the discussions of depreciation, a difference of emphasis can be detected as between the years before the mania of the mid-forties and the subsequent period. Before the mania the discussion chiefly concerned rolling stock; afterwards the emphasis shifted to depreciation of rails. In 1850 Lardner wrote about rails as follows: " The prevalent opinion, countenanced and supported by the most eminent practical engineers, was, until a late period, that the duration of a railway was secular, and that the wear and tear of the rails was so utterly insensible, that for all practical, financial, and economical purposes it might be totally disregarded. Thus, it was said, that the

---

[12] Similarly American railway accounting at this time showed important variations in the treatment of depreciation; see the quotations and extracts collected by Perry Mason, " Illustrations of the Early Treatment of Depreciation," *Accounting Review*, September, 1933.   [13] (1844) 4 Q.B. 18.

rails of a properly laid line would last from one hundred to one hundred and fifty years."[14]   It was probably for this reason that the first discussions of depreciation centred on the rolling stock and not on rails.   Although the rails of the Liverpool & Manchester Railway (opened 1830) required replacing very quickly, later rails lasted longer.   The consulting engineer of the London & South Western Railway reported in 1858 that on sixty miles of the line the rails were still in use after eighteen to twenty years.[15]   Locomotives, on the other hand, obviously needed repairs and replacements from the time a railway was opened.

In the late thirties and early forties the lines which had been authorised in the early and mid-thirties were opened, and the companies were immediately faced with problems of large-scale railway administration of which, so far, few people had any experience. Maintaining the rolling stock in good order was one problem which demanded attention at that time.   For example, in a discussion of the payment of dividends out of capital by the Durham & Sunderland Railway, *The Railway Times* in 1841 wrote: " We hope and believe that the practice of knowingly declaring fraudulent dividends is not common with Railway Managements.   At the same time care must be taken that deception of a similar kind is not incurred through incaution, or from any other cause.   The declaration of a dividend without making allowance for depreciation of stock, cannot in our opinion be regarded as other than fallacious. Some Companies, we fear, are running out their perishable stock, thereby exhibiting an appearance of a low scale of expenditure, and a rate of dividend not warranted by the profit really made, and thus leaving a succeeding set of proprietors to make up from their income the replacing of the exhausted stock."[16]   Later the same journal pointed out that a depreciation fund was more than a fund for the replacement of parts: " The machine as a whole is gradually and certainly, though insensibly, going to decay; and a time comes at last, when the replacement of parts will not maintain its efficiency, and then it must be cast aside altogether."   It went on to note that at the moment the amount set aside each half-year could only be a guess until sufficient knowledge of the life of rolling stock was available.[17]

---

14 Lardner, *Railway Economy*, p. 42.   This was, of course, apart from repairs of faults, fractures, etc.
15 London & South Western Railway, *Reports and Accounts*, December 31, 1857. His report is dated February 1, 1858.
16 *The Railway Times*, October 30, 1841, p. 1142.   *The American Railroad Journal* for November and December, 1843, made similar comments about the practices of American railway companies: " There is not now to be found in the country a single road which has renewed its iron out of the proceeds of transportation." (Quoted by Perry Mason, *op. cit.*, p. 212.)
17 *The Railway Times*, March 4, 1843, p. 262.

But although the problems of maintenance and replacement were realised to be important, the solutions adopted by the different companies varied considerably.   There were some companies which did not include any provision for depreciation in their accounts.   The reasons given by the Chairman of the London & South Western Railway (W. J. Chaplin) were these: " If I can show you—but I would rather go beyond showing, for I have no objection to hold myself personally responsible—that the locomotive business of this Railway may be conducted, for the next ten years, for less money than it has been conducted for the last half-year, and delivered up, at the end of that ten years at its present full value, what occasion can there be to trouble ourselves with this phantom fund for depreciation? " The permanent way was being maintained by responsible contractors, and the rolling stock was in a more efficient state than it had been three months after it was paid for; the stock had had to be altered " entirely " soon after it was bought, and should last ten years.   In any case it was better to introduce new stock " instead of vamping up the old." [18]   A year later he explained that the " whole expense both of repair and restoration, was entirely charged to the current revenue." [19]

This company was basing its actions partly on a valuation of the rolling stock, and other companies valued their rolling stock at regular intervals, for example, the Grand Junction Railway, the Liverpool & Manchester Railway, and the North Union Railway.   The Grand Junction Railway valued its rolling stock according to its current market value [20]; the change in value, credit or debit, was entered in the revenue account.   Thus in 1839 £5,000 was debited to revenue and credited to a " Stock Account " to reflect the previous six months' depreciation.[1]   That sum, intended " to meet depreciation in value of stock previously to that date, has enabled the Company to reduce the expenditure of Capital in the purchase of stock to that extent." [2]   In 1841 its practice of " debiting or crediting (as the case might be) the Half-year's Receipts with the balance of a comparative valuation " [3] was challenged at a shareholders' meeting,[4] and the practice was discontinued.   Instead, a depreciation fund was instituted; this was intended " for the improvement of the stock, and to meet that insensible but sure decay which is perpetually going on, and which no

[18] London & South Western Railway, *Reports and Accounts*, December 31, 1841 (Report of chairman's speech).
[19] *Ibid.*, December 31, 1842.
[20] Grand Junction Railway, *Reports and Accounts*, June 30, 1838 (Resolution of shareholders' meeting).
[1] *Ibid.*, June 30, 1839.
[2] *Ibid.*, December 31, 1839.
[3] *Ibid.*, June 30, 1841.
[4] Report of meeting in *The Railway Times*, August 14, 1841, pp. 864–865.

care or expense can prevent." [5]   The accounts from June 30, 1842, include a " Depreciation and renewal of Stock Fund " [6]; eighteen months later it was hoped that the current allocation of £5,000 would be the last necessary to build up a fund.[7]   In the meantime the *Accounts* show various items of expenditure from this fund, " to replace Stock worn out." [8]   In addition the company established a reserve fund to meet contingencies, primarily to avoid fluctuations in dividends.[9]

The practice of valuing rolling stock on the basis of *current market prices* was disputed by *The Railway Times* in 1841 [10] and later by Lardner.[11]   *The Railway Times* favoured a half-yearly valuation " provided a right principle were adopted.   The market price or selling value of the articles should have nothing whatever to do with it, but the original cost of the stock being assumed as the starting point, the only consideration is the amount of depreciation from the wear and tear unrestored by repairs at the end of the period."   It was thought possible to do this in two ways: by the " North Union plan " of taking the exact sum which the valuation each half-year showed to be required, or by the London & Birmingham Railway's method of debiting a regular percentage of cost to provide a fund to meet the occasional heavy outlays (apart from ordinary repairs) which were due to " the gradual destruction of parts than cannot be immediately replaced."

The London & Birmingham Railway, indeed, had established a " Reserved Fund (for Depreciation of Stock) " in 1838, before the line was wholly open.[12]   From 1839 the company regularised the depreciation at 5 per cent. each half-year " on the actual Cost," [13] and later it was explained that the principle of the fund had been adopted " with a view of providing the means for making the receipts of each half-year bear more equally their proper share of charge, and of maintaining the Carrying Stock on an effective and uniform footing." [14] A year later the chairman of the company, George Carr Glyn, gave more details of the purpose of the depreciation fund: " In making up our account we have pursued the plan . . . of setting aside a fund to meet the unavoidable depreciation of stock. . . .   The plan which we in this Company follow, and the plan which is virtually followed in

---

[5] Grand Junction Railway, *Reports and Accounts*, December 31, 1841.
[6] This included the sum set aside for this purpose in the previous half-year.
[7] Grand Junction Railway, *Reports and Accounts*, December 31, 1843.
[8] *Ibid.*, June 30, 1843.
[9] *Ibid.*, December 31, 1839.
[10] *The Railway Times*, November 6, 1841, p. 1167.
[11] Lardner, *op. cit.*, pp. 119–121.
[12] London & Birmingham Railway, *Reports and Accounts*, June 30, 1838.
[13] *Ibid.*, December 31, 1839.
[14] *Ibid.*, June 30, 1840.   But part of the fund was used to pay the dividend.

almost every other Company,[15] is to appropriate a portion of the profits of every half year to meet the depreciation which has taken place during that period in the value of the Company's stock—a depreciation which it is clear must be made good either from the profits of working, or defrayed from the capital of the Company. The course adopted in this Company is to set aside from the profits of every half year a certain percentage on the capital originally invested in the purchase of Stock . . . and in the ' Capital Ledger ' to write off against it the amount of such per-centage." [16]   Another main line company, the Great Western, similarly preferred a fixed amount to be set aside, and accounted for depreciation by appropriating annually £20,000 for ten years " to redeem the depreciated value in the first cost . . . the Directors do not think any benefit is derived from pretending to ascertain periodically the opinions of parties, however competent, as to the then supposed value of such property." [17]   This practice lasted until 1846 when it was suspended " until some of the Extension Lines . . . are finished." [18]

During the mania, and for a few years after it, accounting for depreciation seems to have been dropped by some companies, presumably in order that the revenue account should be relieved of charges so that dividend rates could be more easily maintained.[19]   When the companies settled down again after the excesses of the mania they once more recognised the need to allow for depreciation in the accounts.   In the Report of the Select Committee on Audit of 1849 there are several references to this, and in its third report the Committee stated that the idea of a depreciation fund " seems now to be generally admitted as necessary, and in some instances, the Committee rejoice to observe, it is practically adopted." [20]   And some of those who gave evidence also stressed its desirability; for example, Sir John Easthope, formerly of the London & South Western Railway,[1] William Quilter,[2] a London accountant—" the practice of my firm I believe to be the most extensive in England " [3]—and Peter Blackburn (Chairman of the Edinburgh & Glasgow Railway).[4]

---

[15] In fact, as is shown, this was not the case. Many important companies did not set aside part of their profits.
[16] London & Birmingham Railway, *Reports and Accounts*, June 30, 1841, Chairman's speech.
[17] Great Western Railway, *Reports and Accounts*, December 31, 1841.
[18] *Ibid.*, December 31, 1846. Auditors' Report.
[19] Thus the London & North Western Railway, newly formed in 1846, made no allowance for depreciation. This company was an amalgamation of, amongst others, the Grand Junction and London & Birmingham companies, which had had depreciation funds. One of the reasons for dropping depreciation on the part of some companies may simply have been that their numerous activities in promoting new lines, building extensions, amalgamating with other companies, etc., led to a state of accounting indigestion.   [20] B.P.P. (1849) X, Third Report, p. x.
[1] *Ibid.*, Q. 2638.   [2] *Ibid.*, Q. 2255.
[3] *Ibid.*, Q. 2215. The firm was Quilter, Ball, Jay and Crosbie.
[4] *Ibid.*, QQ. 3260, 3261.

The South Eastern Railway did not have a depreciation fund until one was recommended by a Committee of Investigation and adopted by the Directors in 1849, when they referred to the fact that " the soundness of the principle is universally admitted," and established separate accounts for the depreciation of permanent way and of rolling stock.[5] The year before the Midland Railway had adopted a " fund for the renewal of Permanent Way " in order to avoid large, sudden payments which would result in fluctuations in dividends. (However it did not bother with one for rolling stock on the ground that the expenditure was more stable.) [6] But neither of these depreciation and renewal funds survived for long. The South Eastern's fund for rolling stock disappeared from the *Accounts* in 1851 [7] and that for rails in 1854 (when it was exhausted and overdrawn). The Midland withdrew its permanent way renewal fund in 1857 (it was then in debit).[8] It had never seen fit to provide for depreciation of its rolling stock and asserted, in a report to its shareholders, that those companies which had adopted the plan of a depreciation fund for rolling stock " have abandoned it, and now repair and renew their Rolling Stock from Revenue each half-year as the necessity arises." [9] The Midland may have been basing its generalisation on the London & North Western Railway. In 1847 that company had reintroduced depreciation funds for the renewal of rails and stock.[10] But the amount deducted from revenue account for the depreciation of stock was almost at once considered to be unnecessary, and in the next account was transferred to a reserve account.[11] Six months later the directors stated that " the practice of the . . . Company is to maintain the working plant at its full effective value, repairing it as required, and replacing it when worn out, from the current revenue." [12] All this was in line with the view of *Herapath* which, in the course of an article on " Reserve Funds " stated: " The shareholders are entitled at the end of every half-year to divide amongst themselves *all* the profits their Companies have realised during that period." [13]

---

5 South Eastern Railway, *Reports and Accounts*, July 31, 1849.
6 Midland Railway, *Reports and Accounts*, December 31, 1848.
7 The newly appointed auditors had recommended that the rolling stock be kept up out of revenue: Auditors' Report, September 11, 1850.
8 In an article on " Maintenance of the Seven Great London Railways," *Herapath* (March 8, 1856, pp. 282–283) noted that only three of them had renewal or reserve funds (*viz.*, London & North Western, Eastern Counties, and London, Brighton & South Coast), and that these were spending an increasing amount from revenue rather than from the reserve funds. The other four companies were: South Eastern, Great Northern, Great Western, and London & South Western.
9 Midland Railway, *Reports and Accounts*, December 31, 1849.
10 London & North Western Railway, *Reports and Accounts*, December 31, 1847. Part of the chairman's speech explaining the need for the funds is given in Perry Mason, *op. cit.*, p. 213.
11 London & North Western Railway, *Reports and Accounts*, June 30, 1848.
12 *Ibid.*, December 31, 1848. Additions to rolling stock were charged to capital at this time.   13 *Herapath*, May 28, 1853, p. 574.

Lardner thought that in depreciation policy a distinction had to be made between rolling stock and permanent way. Stock was being repaired continually, parts of locomotives replaced and new stock added. This did not result in large sudden demands on revenue, as did the relaying of permanent way, which therefore required a depreciation fund.[14]   In 1849 the chairman of the London, Brighton & South Coast Railway (Samuel Laing) wrote a *Report on the Question of Depreciation and on the Policy of establishing a Reserve Fund* which similarly made a distinction between renewal of rolling stock and renewal of permanent way and buildings.   " The alternative evidently lies between the adoption of a reserve fund, future creations of capital, or future fluctuations of dividend."   Given a closed capital account at that date, and the undesirability of unstable dividends, the best alternative was to make appropriations from revenue.   This applied to the rails.   Rolling stock should be kept up out of revenue (pp. 15–16).   But on this there were differences of opinion.   *Herapath* noted that the Lancashire & Yorkshire Railway had dropped their " road renewal fund " and rejoiced that the directors had " discovered the absurdity of this fund and abandoned it. . . .   Keep the stock and road in repair, and away to the winds with all ' road renewals ' and ' stock depreciation ' whims." [15]   Other companies which discontinued the practice of providing for the depreciation of rails—for example the Midland and the South Eastern—have already been mentioned.   But the London & North Western continued it until 1865 when, the directors explained, the amount being spent equalled the amount being credited to the fund.   In future the directors would charge annually the amount actually spent.[16]

Clearly the adoption of depreciation accounts from the late forties was a reaction to the scandals of the mid-forties, as well as a desire to keep dividends stable.   That they did not last long was due to the increase in traffic in the fifties and sixties, when companies found that their past allocations to depreciation reserves were inadequate. Increasingly companies turned to the practice of not providing for depreciation as such but of debiting the actual expenditure on maintenance and renewals to the periodic revenue accounts.

Capital extensions debited to revenue

In the late forties, particularly after the financial disaster of 1847, the main line companies found themselves burdened with heavy programmes of capital expenditure.   Their dividends were falling, their shares were no longer in favour with the investing public, and the shareholders of many companies asserted themselves and called a halt

---

[14] Lardner, *op. cit.*, pp. 114–115.   [15] *Herapath*, March 5, 1853, p. 267.
[16] London & North Western Railway, *Reports and Accounts*, June 30, 1865.

to capital expenditure.   Henceforth any capital expenditure was to be specially authorised by the shareholders, which meant a stop to new promotions and an abandonment of some previously authorised branches.   The list of companies which set limits to their capital expenditure in an attempt to close their capital accounts included: the London & South Western,[17] the London & North Western,[18] the London, Brighton & South Coast,[19] the Midland,[20] the Edinburgh & Glasgow,[1] and the South Eastern.[2]   George Carr Glyn, the chairman of the London & North Western Railway said in 1851: "My opinion is, that no large undertaking is firmly based and placed in a proper position until the capital account is closed."[3]   And the London, Brighton & South Coast Railway boasted that "there is no large Railway Company which has so small an extent of works in progress or in prospect."[4]   Joseph Locke, the engineer, agreed that it was desirable to close capital accounts,[5] as did also *The Railway Times,*[6] the reformed Board of the Eastern Counties Railway,[7] and *The Railway Chronicle.*[8]

By the early fifties most of the companies had slowed down if not actually stopped expenditure charged to capital account.   But capital accounts could not be closed entirely if traffic increased and facilities were to be extended to satisfy the additional demands.   Lardner, writing in 1850, already had pointed out that it "would be utterly impracticable, unless it were deliberately intended in future to feed capital at the expense of revenue."[9]   In fact the secular increase of traffic, the Great Exhibition traffic of 1851, together with the minor railway boom of 1852 and 1853, resulted in more capital expenditure by the old companies, partly in order to protect their territories.   Thus in 1856 the auditors of the Midland Railway said that the company's capital accounts had increased by nearly £4½ million since 1849 instead of by the budgeted amount of £770,000.   After giving the details they said that "these being *additions,* are properly chargeable

---

[17] London & South Western Railway, *Reports and Accounts*, December 31, 1849.
[18] London & North Western Railway, *Reports and Accounts*, December 31, 1849.
[19] London, Brighton & South Coast Railway, *Reports and Accounts*, December 31, 1848.
[20] Midland Railway, *Reports and Accounts*, June 30, 1849.
[1] *The Railway Times*, March 10, 1849, p. 250.
[2] South Eastern Railway, *Reports and Accounts*, June 21, 1853. Special General Meeting.
[3] London & North Western Railway, *Reports and Accounts*, December 31, 1850. His speech was made on February 21, 1851.
[4] London, Brighton & South Coast Railway, *Reports and Accounts*, June 30, 1848.
[5] Sel. Comm. Railway and Canal Bills, B.P.P. (1852–1853) XXXVIII (736), Q. 2931 *et seq.*
[6] *The Railway Times*, September 29, 1849, p. 996.
[7] Sel. Comm. on Audit, p. 365.
[8] *The Railway Chronicle*, September 23, 1848, p. 675.
[9] Lardner, *op. cit.*, p. 118.

to Capital, so long as it shall not have been decided to pay everything from Revenue." [10]

Nevertheless some companies decided to deal with extensions occasioned by increased traffic by charging the cost to revenue account. Sometimes the cost was spread over the revenue accounts of several successive accounting periods, the " unrecovered " balance being accommodated in a suspense account. In 1851 the auditor of the London & North Western Railway reported that the amount spent on additions to works and stock was to be charged to revenue account over a period of five years.[11] Similarly, after the limit set by the London & South Western Railway for capital expenditure had been reached, expenditure on additional rolling stock was " recovered " from revenue by instalments over a period of years.[12] This system was later extended to stations and sidings.[13]

It is not surprising that resolutions to close the capital account or, as an alternative, to write off the cost of extensions to revenue account over a short period, were not followed rigorously for long. Only eighteen months after the London & North Western Railway had decided to charge new rolling stock to revenue over a period of five years through the medium of a suspense account, the auditors suggested a modification of the plan.[14] A year later the idea of a closed capital account was dropped. It had been assumed, the directors explained, that additions to traffic would be slow and steady; but they had been frequent and heavy and the company could no longer continue to charge revenue with additions to stock, stations and sidings. This would be unfair to those who were interested in current dividends rather than in the long-term value of the railway. Further, the chairman (General George Anson, M.P.) was in favour of a fixed rather than a fluctuating dividend. He said: " Why, gentlemen, it is impossible to expect that this enormous increase of traffic can be carried on, and that the charge for all the engines, carriages, and waggons that are to produce these receipts is to be debited against profits. I think it must be quite evident to everyone that it is not fair upon the present Proprietors that the whole of this sum should be charged to revenue.... If I had remained in the position I have now the honour to occupy,[15] my object would be to endeavour to maintain

---

[10] Midland Railway, *Reports and Accounts*, December 31, 1855. The auditor's report is dated February 12, 1856.
[11] London & North Western Railway, *Reports and Accounts*, December 31, 1850. The auditor's report is dated February 14, 1851. But see below for the subsequent reversal of this policy.
[12] London & South Western Railway, *Reports and Accounts*, June 30, 1851.
[13] *Ibid.*, December 31, 1851.
[14] London & North Western Railway, *Reports and Accounts*, June 30, 1852. The Directors extended the period of liquidation to ten years: *ibid.*, December 31, 1852.
[15] This was his farewell speech.

for you a fixed dividend. . . . And I would not be induced to change that decision by any temporary variation that might take place in the revenue. . . ." The directors recommended that the balance of the suspense account should be transferred to the debit of capital account; in future any proposed capital expenditure would be submitted to the shareholders for their prior approval, in detail.[16] Similarly, the London & South Western Railway in 1853 decided to extend the period for the recovery from revenue of expenditure on new rolling stock.[17] However, the shareholders went further and asked that this expenditure and that on extensions to sidings and stations be charged to capital.[18] The directors agreed to charge the cost of new stock to capital because of its great amount.[19]

Betterment

One of the most interesting and lengthy discussions in railway financial history has been that concerned with the treatment of the expenditures on improved and more costly replacements. This problem of betterment or improvement arose almost as soon as the early railways were opened, because in the experimental years of the 1830's and 1840's some equipment had to be replaced quickly and at higher cost on account of increased weight and other improvements. The experience of the Grand Junction Railway is interesting. The line was opened in 1837, and in a subsequent *Report*[20] the directors stated that nearly all the locomotives had been found deficient, and some had been almost wholly rebuilt, at a heavy cost. " It appeared unreasonable to charge the income during this period with an outlay not partaking of the character of current expenses or ordinary repairs, but occasioned by original defects in the Engines." Part was therefore charged to capital, " being regarded as an addition to the capital outlay of the Company, in the increased effective value of the Engines." This was probably the first time that betterment was charged to capital; at any rate this was the first company to make a coherent statement on the subject.

By the late forties the idea gained ground that the increased cost of replacements should be charged to capital. Capt. J. M. Laws, in

---

[16] London and North Western Railway, *Reports and Accounts*, June 30, 1853. In the meantime the General Finance Committee of the company, on examining an estimate for expenditure on new works, had " apportioned in each case, the sums which, in their judgment should be charged to capital—to Revenue direct—or to Deferred payment." They thought that if the suspense account were to be discontinued it would be desirable " to substitute a depreciation Fund to accomplish to a considerable extent the same objects." General Finance Committee Minutes, February 11, 1853 (minute 906).

[17] London & South Western Railway, *Reports and Accounts*, December. 31, 1853.

[18] *Ibid.*, June 30, 1854. Auditors' report.

[19] *Ibid.* Directors' Report.

[20] Grand Junction Railway, *Reports and Accounts*, June 30, 1838.

1849, said that the whole cost should not be charged to capital, only
the difference between original cost and replacement cost.[1] Similarly,
Joseph Locke thought that this difference should be charged to
capital.[2] But company practices varied on this as on other matters.
Thus the auditors of the London & North Western Railway reported
in 1867 that the cost of a wide range of improvements, as well as
additions, had been met out of revenue. These included the
" renewal " of old by improved engines, many of the former remaining
in use, additions to tools, machinery, carts and horses, additions to the
permanent way, and the replacement of timber bridges by more
substantial structures.[3]

Conclusion

It was stated at the outset that there were many differences in the
accounting practices and " principles " followed by the railway
companies. This has been demonstrated by the discussion of selected
topics and the illustrations presented in the preceding sections, which
also make the point that companies from time to time changed their
practices and the bases on which profits (net revenue) were calculated.
Nevertheless, despite the diversity and variation, it is possible to offer
some generalisations.

It seems clear that in general the early accounting practices and
changes in the bases of profit calculations were not designed principally
to produce statements drawn up in accordance with preconceived
definitions or concepts of " profits," " income " or " asset values."
It is possible that at first lack of experience may have been·partly
responsible for changes in the accounting treatment, for example, of
depreciation.[4] But later changes in accounting policy cannot be
explained in these terms. It is more realistic to recognise that in
practice the calculation of profits was often influenced significantly by
changing financial circumstances and the dictates of management
policy. Thus in the mid-forties some companies stopped providing
for depreciation in their revenue accounts apparently simply in order
to pay high dividends. On the other hand, stringency in the capital
market and an attitude of caution seem to have been responsible for
highly conservative treatment of important items (in the sense of
understating profits) in the years following the mania. It is not
possible to detect dominant aims or attitudes of railway directors in

---

[1] Sel. Comm. on Audit, Q. 2992.   See also QQ. 1263 and 3259.
[2] Sel. Comm. Railway and Canal Bills, 1852–1853, Q. 2877.
[3] Auditors' Report to the Shareholders' Audit Committee, January 7, 1867.
(Printed with London & North Western Railway, *Reports and Accounts*, December 31, 1866.) Twenty years earlier the extra cost of heavier rails had been
charged to capital: *Reports and Accounts*, December 31, 1847 (Chairman's
speech).
[4] Noted by Lewin, *Railway Mania*, p. 353.

the period under review, since these were influenced by the changing economic scene as well as by the circumstances of particular companies. However, there is some evidence to suggest that many railway directors as well as shareholders wished to have regular rather than fluctuating dividends, and the entries in the final accounts may very well have been influenced by the desire for a record of stable earnings and dividends. The fact that many items appearing (or not appearing) in the revenue accounts involved personal judgments, and that there was not yet a generally accepted body of accounting doctrine, made it easy for the preparation of the final accounts of even the most conscientiously conducted company to be influenced by considerations of management policy.

The nature of the accounting practices in operation at a particular time may perhaps in part have reflected the composition of the shareholding body. Lardner, writing in 1850, divided railway shareholders into two main groups, permanent investors and temporary investors (including speculators). " Now, the class of proprietors first mentioned have less regard to the amount of present dividends than to the permanent value of the stock, and they chiefly expect from the directors of the railway a due regard to the efficient maintenance of the permanent way and the movable stock out of revenue, before any surplus be appropriated to dividend. On the other hand, the latter class, and especially the speculators, care nothing for the permanent value of the concern, and look only to the present amount of dividend." [5] The relative importance of these two broad groups changed from time to time, and such changes may have affected the treatment of items bearing on the calculation of profits. Thus the widespread practice in the early fifties of charging items to revenue that would normally have been chargeable to capital may have been induced not only by the difficulties of raising capital for the railways; it is likely that there had been a reduction in the number of short-term speculative holdings of the shares of railway companies in the crises of 1847 and the subsequent slump, and that the remaining shareholders were investors who were interested in the long-term prosperity of the companies and willing to forgo current dividends in order to safeguard future dividends. This would help to explain the tendency at the time to substitute deliberate under-statement of current profits for the deliberate over-statement which had been prevalent during the preceding mania.

It has been shown that the basis for the allocation of certain important items between capital and revenue accounts was not the same in all companies, and that the allocation was not carried out in a consistent manner by any major company. The close connection

---

[5] Lardner, *op. cit.*, pp. 116 *et seq.*

between the accounting treatment of these items and the declaration of dividends has also been noted. It will, therefore, be clear that any attempt to use the information in railway accounts before 1868 in order to assess the amount of annual investment and capital formation in railways has to contend with the difficulties and inconsistencies of the kind described in this article. These may have been less in evidence after the Act of 1868 and it is perhaps thanks to this that Professor Cairncross has been able to use railway accounts to compile annual railway investment statistics for the period after 1870.[6] But it may be added, as a qualification, that the legislation of 1868 did not work wonders at once, and complaints about railway accounting practices affecting profit calculations continued.[7]

---

[6] A. K. Cairncross, *Home and Foreign Investment* (Cambridge, 1953), pp. 135–141.
[7] See, for example, the comments of *The Railway Times* (January 12, 1878, p. 30) on the occasion of an increased dividend paid by the Metropolitan Railway: " Could we divest ourselves of the idea that the dividends that Sir Edward Watkin has each succeeding half-year to dispense are pre-arranged, and depend rather upon considerations of financial policy than the result of an actual profit and loss balance, we should hail the announcement of the Metropolitan with unalloyed satisfaction." *The Accountant*, in an editorial (November 12, 1887, p. 618) went further: " . . . when railway accounts are being discussed the question is not the profit shown, but the elements in the account by which that profit has been derived ; and particular regard is paid when looking at the amount spent on renewals and maintenance to see whether the line has or has not been ' starved,' and whether or not the next succeeding dividend will suffer in consequence. The style in which railway accounts are reviewed testifies to their utter uselessness and unreliability as revenue accounts in the proper and only true sense of the term." In 1903 *The Economist*, in discussing the half-year's accounts said (August 15, 1903, p. 1432): " The fact that the chief increase of expenditure occurred in the maintenance of way department is not unsatisfactory, since it may be taken to imply that the companies took the opportunity of a fairly good half-year to improve their permanent way, though it will be seen that not much more was spent [in comparison with the corresponding half-year of 1902] on renewals of carriages and wagons, which is one of the departments in which the line between expenditure that ought to be met out of revenue and that charged to capital is apt to become a little shaky and difficult to distinguish."

British Company Accounting and the Law 1844–1900

H. C. Edey* and Prot Panitpakdi †

Much of present-day company accounting law and practice is explicable only in terms of historical development.[1] Perhaps this is the best justification of this essay, which is devoted to some of the salient features of British company accounting law in the nineteenth century.

The period we have chosen runs from 1844 to 1900: from the year of the Act that introduced the principle of general incorporation by registration, to the year that marked, after a long period of " non-interference " in accounting matters, a decisive step towards the detailed regulation with which we are now familiar. Our account does not purport to be a complete history of company accounting, even for this limited period. We have, for example, made no attempt to study closely contemporary events in the field of company finance—events that must have been of great importance in the formation of public opinion with respect to the need (or lack of need) for accounting legislation. We have excluded the development of company winding-up legislation as this affects the accountant—a complex field of study in itself. Nor have we considered the rôle of the accountant with respect to accounting reports in company prospectuses (a historical study of which would take one back far earlier than 1928, the year in which these reports first received statutory attention). Again, although we refer to the legislation affecting parliamentary companies, we have made no attempt to cover it generally.

Incorporation by registration (but with unlimited liability) was first made possible by the Joint Stock Companies Act of 1844.[2] The accounting clauses of the Act were surprisingly modern in outlook. Books of account were to be kept and provision was to be made for their periodical balancing. A " full and fair " balance sheet was to

---

* Reader in Accounting, London School of Economics and Political Science.
† Assistant Lecturer in Accounting, Chulalongkorn University, Bangkok.
[1] This is true not only of company accounting law but also of the general body of company law. (See L. C. B. Gower, *The Principles of Modern Company Law* [London, 1954], p. 21.)
[2] 7 & 8 Vict. c. 110. Before this the only methods available were *ad hoc* incorporation by Royal Charter or Letters Patent or by special Act of Parliament. Banks and friendly societies were excluded from the Act's provisions. For a discussion of the events that led up to this Act see Gower, *op. cit.*, Chaps. 2 and 3, and the references therein.

356

be prepared and presented to each ordinary meeting of the shareholders. The balance sheet was to be sent to every shareholder before the meeting unless the deed of settlement (which took the place of what are now the memorandum and articles of association) negatived this. The Act did not, however, require the preparation of a profit and loss account and specified neither the form of the balance sheet nor its contents. Nor did it require the date of the balance sheet to be related in any way to the date of the annual meeting.

Auditors were to be appointed, and were to be given full access to the books and all the assistance they needed from officers and servants of the company. They were required to report on the balance sheet and their report was to be read at the meeting. The audited balance sheet was to be filed with the Registrar of Joint Stock Companies. It seems, however, that the auditors contemplated by the Act would not in general have been professional accountants. No doubt it was expected that the auditors would, if they thought fit, employ accountants to assist them.[3]

The direct precursor of the 1844 Act had been the report of the Select Committee on Joint Stock Companies, 1841–1844,[4] which was set up as the result of the unsatisfactory state of the law relating to large, and necessarily unregistered, joint-stock partnerships, which had facilitated a good deal of fraud.[5] The Committee reported, among other things, that " Periodical accounts, if honestly made and fairly audited, cannot fail to excite attention to the real state of a concern; and by means of improved remedies, parties to mismanagement may be made more amenable for acts of fraud and illegality." [6]

That the Committee, while recommending accounting publicity, did not deceive themselves about some of the limitations of accounting documents is evident, though it is not clear how much weight they attached to these limitations. They appreciated, for example, that accounts might not be of help to people inexperienced in business, but this, it was thought, would not matter if business men were, as a result of legislative regulations including accounting and auditing provisions, put on inquiry so that investigation followed [7]—a point perhaps not fully appreciated even today.

---

3 See pp. 359 and 366, below.
4 British Parliamentary Papers (1844) VII. (Gladstone became its chairman in 1843.)
5 Among " modes of deception " used in various frauds were " . . . the making up of fraudulent accounts . . . facilitated sometimes by the accounts not being audited . . ." and " By declaring dividends out of capital, on false representations of profits realised." (*Ibid.*, p. ix.)   6 *Ibid.*, p. v.
7 *Ibid.*, p. vi: " . . . probably the greatest benefit in this direction will be produced by enabling the share-brokers and other persons professionally employed in making investments . . . to learn more easily and more accurately the real nature of these Companies; so that, at least, the ignorant may not be so much misled . . ."

The Committee seem to have been doubtful, on the other hand, whether the payment of dividends out of capital was susceptible of sufficiently accurate determination to be legislated upon,[8] and they made no recommendation on this.[9]

A point of considerable interest raised in the evidence related to the payment of dividends out of reserves at a time when the company was making losses. A witness replied, in answer to a question, " . . . there could be no reasonable objection to paying the shareholders a dividend out of the reserved fund . . . only let it be so declared, and let the public not be deluded into the belief that that dividend was paying out of the then gaining profits (*sic*)." [10] This precise point was to be the essence of the prosecution's case in the *Royal Mail* case nearly 100 years later.[11] However, the Committee made no recommendation on this either and the Act was equally silent.

Mention has already been made of the Companies Clauses Act of 1845. In addition to the section already referred to, this Act included sections that required the keeping of " full and true accounts," and the preparation, audit, and presentation at the ordinary meeting, of a balance sheet showing " a true statement of the Capital Stock, Credits, and Property of every Description belonging to the Company, and the Debts due by the Company . . . and a distinct View of the Profit or Loss . . . of the preceding Half-Year," [12] while before every ordinary

---

8 *Ibid.*, Evidence, qq. 1255–1280.
9 This is interesting because the very real difficulties of defining the maintenance of capital in terms that can be applied in practice—difficulties so great that even today no theoretical definition of profit or income is to be found in most accounting textbooks or in the company legislation—were presumably considered susceptible of solution in practice when the Companies Clauses Act of 1845 (8 & 9 Vict. c. 16) was drafted. (The latter provided model clauses to be included in the regulations of companies incorporated by Act of Parliament. This form of incorporation was still needed after the 1844 Act in the case of enterprises of the public utility type which required special powers not capable of being provided by general incorporation statute.) S. 121 of the 1845 Act provided that no dividend was to be paid that would have the effect of reducing the capital stock. In this context the following extract from a leading article in the *Morning Chronicle* of May 17, 1845, quoted by B. C. Hunt in *The Development of the Business Corporation in England 1800-1867* (Cambridge, Massachusetts, 1936), p. 112, note 92, is particularly interesting: " What are the precise criteria which distinguish revenue from construction charges [in railways] it is no easy matter to determine . . . At present there is great room for controversy, but this, at least, will be generally agreed to, that the principle adopted by any company in the distribution of its expenditure between the two accounts is of comparatively minor importance, provided that the system pursued be distinctly avowed and understood by the shareholders." It is interesting to compare this passage with one from the summing-up of Humphreys J. in 1950 in the *Crittall* case (which was concerned with a prospectus fraud), in which the judge approved the following words of an accountant witness: " . . . the great, important thing to aim at in accountancy . . . is to let people know exactly what you are doing, and that you must leave it to them to judge what they will do finally. Let them understand the figures which you are putting before them." (*The Accountant*, CXXIII [1950], p. 139.)
10 *Ibid.*, q. 1288.
11 See Dicksee's *Auditing* (17th ed., London, 1951), pp. 790 *et seq.*
12 Half-yearly meetings were required.

meeting at which a dividend was to be declared, a " scheme " showing the profit since the previous dividend payment and the appropriation of the dividend therefrom had to be prepared and submitted to the meeting. The auditors could merely confirm the accounts or could report on them; their confirmation or report was to be read at the meeting. The arrangements laid down for the appointment of the auditors included provision for the employment by them of accountants to help them at the expense of the company.

In 1844 another Act [13] made provision for the incorporation and regulation of joint stock banks (which, as already noted, were not covered by the 1844 Joint Stock Companies Act). This Act required the company's regulations to provide for the supply to shareholders of an annual balance sheet, in this case with a profit and loss account as well. Provision was also to be made for the appointment of auditors and for an annual audit of the accounts of the company. In addition, a monthly statement of assets and liabilities was to be published by the bank.

Thus the accounting requirements of the first Joint Stock Companies Act did not represent an isolated phenomenon.[14] The main aims of the contemporary legislators in framing accounting requirements seem to have been: (a) to provide the creditors and shareholders of companies with statements of assets and liabilities that would give indications of the solvency of the companies, and (b) in the case of some classes of companies to prevent actual and potential shareholders or creditors from being misled as the result of dividend distributions made out of capital—which, in effect, means made at the expense, in some sense, of the future of the company without this fact being known. In the case of the Joint Stock Companies Act of 1844, the main consideration was solvency, and no direct attention was paid to the second point. This emphasis on solvency may have been attributable to the prominence of life assurance companies among the unregistered partnerships in which the pre-1844 malpractices had occurred. Life assurance is a business where, *par excellence*, long-run solvency of the company is important. It would not be surprising if

---

[13] The Joint Stock Banking Act, 7 & 8 Vict. c. 113.
[14] The idea that accounts might be useful instruments of control of companies from the viewpoint of creditors and shareholders was not new in 1844. In order to connect historically the accounting provisions of the Acts of 1844 and 1845 with the sources from which they drew their inspiration it would no doubt be necessary to turn to the earlier experience of individual chartered and parliamentary companies and of unregulated partnerships. It is interesting to note that in the evidence given to the 1841–1844 Committee it was stated that it was to the advantage of respectable life assurance companies to publish adequate accounts. (The Report, Evidence, qq. 659–662. Included as exhibits are: the General Cash Account of the Equitable Society for 1840, drawn up in very considerable detail; a detailed list of the assurances, classified by ages of the lives assured; the actuarial valuation at December 30, 1829; and the valuation balance sheet, showing the surplus, at January 1, 1830.)

the Committee had taken the view—not unreasonable at that time—that the joint stock company with a large number of " partners " or " shareholders " was a business form not likely to be relevant to the greater part of the country's business. The question of providing information on earnings for the benefit of shareholders may well have seemed less relevant in the case of companies formed under the general registration provisions than in the case of the parliamentary companies formed to build and operate railways and other public utilities, whose stocks and shares then represented a considerable part of the total quantity of non-government marketable securities.

The possibility of deliberate under-statement of income did not receive attention in the legislation, though the fact that profits of earlier years—possibly undisclosed at the time they were made—might be used to deceive the investing public later when profits were lacking did not, as we have seen, escape all notice. The emphasis, however, was on securing minimum disclosure rather than on achieving knife-edge accuracy of valuation and profit calculation. Where the provision of profit statements was made a legislative requirement, it seems that what was intended was little more than a figure of net profit for the accounting period, together with appropriations to dividend account and to reserve account.

Again, though the legislators (or their advisers) believed, if we may take their words and actions at their face value, in the merits of accounting disclosure, they omitted to define in any clear way the form or content of the accounts that were to be prepared, or the valuation principles that were to be adopted. Nor were the duties of auditors laid down in any detail. This lack of precision was probably attributable to the combination of: (a) a desire not to interfere too closely in matters of private enterprise; (b) an undeveloped state of accounting techniques with respect to the presentation of information and to rules of procedure for the valuation of assets and liabilities and the measurement of profit (or at least a lack of a widespread knowledge of those that had been developed [15]); and (c) the absence of an established code of auditing rules built on professional practice and legal precedent.

There seems little doubt that it was an easy matter for the unscrupulous to violate the spirit of the legislation. We learn, for example, that balance sheets filed with the registrar under the 1844 Act might be " manufactured for the very purpose of the return " or

---

[15] It would not be correct to say that the form of final accounts at that time would necessarily be crude. Some at least of the accounts presented by contemporary railway companies, for example, were in complete double-entry form, and included a detailed revenue account. See, for example, the accounts of the London and North Western Railway, half-year to December 31, 1848, Select Committee on Audit of Railway Accounts, First Report, Appendix H, pp. 276–281, B.P.P. (1849) X.

" unexplainable." [16]   Similar defects existed in the other legislation
we have mentioned.   Railway accounts could be uninformative, failing
to comply even with the limited requirements of the 1845 Companies
Clauses Act, and the audit could be ineffective.[17]   Bank audits also,
it seems, might be purely formal.[18]

No action was taken to remedy the defects of the 1844 Act.   The
tendency was indeed in the opposite direction.   In 1855 when general
registration with limited liability was introduced for the first time,[19]
no attempt was made to strengthen the 1844 accounting or auditing
provisions, although support was not lacking for the proposition that
the privilege of incorporation with limited liability demanded in return
the obligation of providing publicly information on the state of the
company's capital.[20]   In the Joint Stock Companies Act that replaced,
in 1856,[1] the 1844 and 1855 Acts, compulsory accounting requirements
and compulsory audit for registered companies were abandoned.   The
resultant state of affairs was to endure until 1900 for all such companies except banking and insurance companies,[2] and deposit,
provident or benefit societies.

The abandonment seems to have been the result of the strong
contemporary feeling that matters of accounting should be dealt with
by private contract between shareholders and directors,[3] combined with
the ineffectiveness, in the absence of the intervention which was so
disliked, of the kind of provisions written into the 1844 Act.   The
original Bill of 1856 envisaged indeed that an annual balance sheet
should be filed with the Registrar of Companies in a prescribed form
—one of the conditions needed to make the 1844 provisions effective—
but this proposal was abandoned in committee.[4]   It may be noted that
the 1855 and 1856 Acts had excluded insurance companies from the
privilege of limited liability and that when this right was granted to
them in 1862, a special duty was then imposed upon them—along with

---

[16] Select Committee on Assurance Associations, Report, pp. iii and iv, and Evidence,
qq. 66–79, B.P.P. (1852/3) XXI.
[17] Select Committee on Audit of Railway Accounts, Third Report, p. iv.
[18] The *Bankers' Magazine*, XVI (1856), p. 7.
[19] By 18 & 19 Vict. c. 133.
[20] *Cf.* J. S. Mill: " The law is warranted in requiring from all joint-stock associations with limited responsibility . . . that such accounts should be kept, accessible
to individuals, and if needful, published to the world, as shall render it possible
to ascertain at any time the existing state of the company's affairs, and to
learn whether the capital which is the sole security for the engagements into which
they enter, still subsists unimpaired: the fidelity of such accounts being guarded by
sufficient penalties." (*Principles of Political Economy* (Ashley's edition), p. 900.)
[1] 19 & 20 Vict. c. 47.
[2] We use the term to include life assurance companies.
[3] There was not lacking, however, even in the 1840's, evidence that with a large
body of shareholders the close control over the management possible in a small
partnership was illusory. (See Select Committee 1841–1844, Evidence, q. 169.)
[4] See Hansard, CXL (1856), col. 134 and CXLII (1856) col. 634.

banking companies and benefit societies—to publish half-yearly statements of assets and liabilities and authorised, issued and called-up capital.[5] It is not likely that there would have been much public demand for the protection of investors in other types of registered companies, which still represented only a relatively small section of the business of the country,[6] and it may well have been thought that their creditors—who would in most cases be business men themselves—ought to look after themselves.

Although the 1856 Act contained no compulsory accounting or audit provisions, it did include, unlike the Act of 1844, a model set of articles,[7] which were to apply to all companies registered under the Act who did not register their own particular articles. These model articles, whose adoption was therefore not mandatory, were in Table B of the 1856 Act (later to become Table A of the 1862 Act and, in amended form, of the later consolidating Acts up to and including that of 1948).[8] Table B included accounting and auditing clauses considerably more advanced than those written into the 1844 legislation. These are sufficiently modern in their general import to justify their reproduction:

Dividends

64. No Dividend shall be payable except out of the Profits arising from the Business of the Company:

65. The Directors may, before recommending any Dividend, set aside out of the Profits of the Company such Sum as they think proper as a reserved Fund to meet Contingencies, or for equalising Dividends, or for repairing, or maintaining, the Works connected with the Business of the Company, or any Part thereof; and the Directors may invest the Sum so set apart as a reserved Fund upon such Securities as they, with the Sanction of the Company, may select.

Accounts

69. The Directors shall cause true Accounts to be kept,—
    Of the Stock in Trade of the Company;
    Of the Sums of Money received and expended by the Company, and the Matter in respect of which such Receipt and Expenditure takes place; and,
    Of the Credits and Liabilities of the Company:
Such Accounts shall be kept, upon the Principle of Double Entry, in a Cash Book, Journal, and Ledger: The Books of Account shall be kept at the principal Office of the Company, and subject to any reasonable Restrictions as to the Time and Manner of inspecting the same that may be imposed by the

---

5 See note 20, below.
6 See Clapham, *An Economic History of Modern Britain, Free Trade and Steel 1850–1886* (Cambridge, 1932), pp. 133 *et.seq.*
7 Companies registered under the 1844 Act were required to register a deed of settlement which became the company's constitution.   From 1856 to the present day this has been replaced by two documents, the memorandum and the articles of association.   The main internal regulations of the company were, and are, to be found in the articles.
8 There is some doubt whether many companies in fact adopted Tables B or A (*cf.* 1877 Select Committee on the Companies Acts, Evidence, q. 1947, B.P.P. [1877] VIII).   Nevertheless the precedent set by these Tables may have influenced the form of companies' particular articles.

Company in General Meeting, shall be open to the Inspection of the Shareholders during the Hours of Business.

70. Once at the least in every Year the Directors shall lay before the Company in General Meeting a Statement of the Income and Expenditure for the past Year, made up to a Date not more than Three Months before such Meeting.

71. The Statement so made shall show, arranged under the most convenient Heads, the Amount of gross Income, distinguishing the Several Sources from which it has been derived, and the Amount of gross Expenditure, distinguishing the Expense of the Establishment, Salaries, and other like Matters: Every Item of Expenditure fairly chargeable against the Year's Income shall be brought into Account, so that a just Balance of Profit and Loss may be laid before the Meeting; and in Cases where any Item of Expenditure which may in Fairness be distributed over several Years has been incurred in any One Year the whole Amount of such Item shall be stated, with the addition of the Reasons why only a Portion of such Expenditure is charged against the Income of the Year.

72. A Balance Sheet shall be made out in every Year, and laid before the General Meeting of the Company, and such Balance Sheet shall contain a Summary of the Property and Liabilities of the Company arranged under the Heads appearing in the Form annexed to this Table, or as near thereto as Circumstances admit.

73. A printed Copy of such Balance Sheet shall, Seven Days previously to such Meeting, be delivered at or sent by Post to the registered Address of every Shareholder.

Audit

74. The Accounts of the Company shall be examined and the Correctness of the Balance Sheet ascertained by One or more Auditor or Auditors to be elected by the Company in General Meeting.

75. If not more than One Auditor is appointed, all the Provisions herein contained relating to Auditors shall apply to him.

76. The Auditors need not be Shareholders in the Company: No Person is eligible as an Auditor who is interested otherwise than as a Shareholder in any Transaction of the Company; and no Director or other Officer of the Company is eligible during his Continuance in Office.

77. The Election of Auditors shall be made by the Company at their Ordinary Meeting, or, if there are more than One, at their First Ordinary Meeting in each Year.

78. The Remuneration of the Auditors shall be fixed by the Company at the Time of their Election.

79. Any Auditor shall be re-eligible on his quitting Office.

80. If any casual Vacancy occurs in the Office of Auditor, the Directors shall forthwith call an Extraordinary General Meeting for the Purpose of supplying the same.

81. If no Election of Auditors is made in manner aforesaid, the Board of Trade may, on the Application of One Fifth in Number of the Shareholders of the Company, appoint an Auditor for the current Year, and fix the Remuneration to be paid to him by the Company for his Services.

82. Every Auditor shall be supplied with a Copy of the Balance Sheet, and it shall be his Duty to examine the same, with the Accounts and Vouchers relating thereto.

83. Every Auditor shall have a List delivered to him of all Books kept by the Company, and he shall at all reasonable Times have Access to the Books and Accounts of the Company: He may, at the Expense of the Company, employ Accountants or other Persons to assist him in investigating such Accounts, and he may in relation to such Accounts examine the Directors or any other Officer of the Company.

84. The Auditors shall make a Report to the Shareholders upon the Balance Sheet and Accounts, and in every such Report they shall state whether,

in their Opinion, the Balance Sheet is a full and fair Balance Sheet, containing the Particulars required by these Regulations, and properly drawn up so as to exhibit a true and correct View of the State of the Company's Affairs, and in case they have called for Explanations or Information from the Directors, whether such Explanations or Information have been given by the Directors, and whether they have been satisfactory; and such Report shall be read, together with the Report of the Directors, at the Ordinary Meeting.

Article 72 refers to the standard form of balance sheet annexed to Table B. This balance sheet, reproduced on page 365, provides for the analysis of assets and liabilities in substantial detail, and its form compares very favourably with the customary form of present-day published balance sheets.

Particularly noticeable is the careful classification of assets and liabilities by type, an essential condition to proper interpretation of the data. Trade and expense creditors are, for example, separated from bills payable, interest due, debts for law expenses, and so on. There is no explicit current asset—fixed asset distinction, but a division of the assets is made into the three significant classes of *property* (*i.e.*, titles to real resources), *debts*, and *cash and investments*.

It will be noticed that in the case of all the real resources, including both plant and stock, the form of balance sheet provides for the statement of the cost figure with a deduction for " Deterioration in Value," that is, for depreciation—a requirement that goes further than the provisions of 1948, when similar requirements first became mandatory, for even then these were applied only to fixed assets.[9, 10]

Debts are divided into good and bad, secured and unsecured, another feature not required under the current law. On the other hand, no provision is made for stating the value of investments.[11] A statement of contingent liabilities is provided for, and there is also provision for a note about " claims against the Company not acknowledged as Debts."

The surplus over subscribed capital is divided simply into a profit and loss balance and a reserve fund, a much more sensible arrangement than the present proliferation of reserve balances which have little or no meaning and are likely to confuse readers.

---

[9] And even in the case of fixed assets the present requirements can be avoided by showing assets at a current valuation. (Companies Act, 1948, 8th Sched., para. 5.)

[10] It is interesting to note that the text in the 1856 form of balance sheet suggests that the deterioration in value might be charged alternatively to the " reserve fund " or to " profit and loss." This might be interpreted to mean that the draftsmen did not attach great importance to theoretical precision of measurement of any one year's profit, in which case it would be inconsistent with the provisions of Article 71 of Table B, which laid stress on this point. On the other hand, it might be no more than a recognition of the fact that certain types of losses of an exceptional nature may conveniently be charged direct to reserve in order to avoid distortion of current profits.

[11] It was perhaps assumed that they would be shown at current values; it is not clear whether the " rate of interest " on investments to be stated represented a current market yield or merely a coupon rate on the par value.

C.47.   **19° & 20° VICTORIÆ.**   **A.D. 1856.**

Joint Stock Companies.   (*Table B.*)

FORM of BALANCE SHEET referred to in TABLE B.

Dr.   Cr.

BALANCE SHEET of the .... Co. made up to 18

CAPITAL AND LIABILITIES

£ s. d.   £ s. d.

I. CAPITAL - 1. The total Amount received from the Shareholders; showing also:
   (a) The Number of Shares
   (b) The Amount paid per Share
   (c) If any Arrears of Calls, the Nature of the Arrear, and the Names of the Defaulters
   Any Arrears due from any Director or Officer of the Company to be separately stated.
   (d) The Particulars of any forfeited Shares.

II. DEBTS AND LIABILITIES of the Company
Showing:
2. The Amount of Loans on Mortgage or Debenture Bonds.
3. The Amount of Debts owing by the Company, distinguishing—
   (a) Debts for which Acceptances have been given.
   (b) Debts to Tradesmen for Supplies of Stock in Trade or other Articles.
   (c) Debts for Law Expenses.
   (d) Debts for Interest on Debentures or other Loans.
   (e) Unclaimed Dividends.
   (f) Debts not enumerated above.

VI. RESERVE FUND - The Amount set aside from Profits to meet Contingencies.

VII. PROFIT AND LOSS - Showing: The disposable Balance for Payment of Dividend, &c.

CONTINGENT LIABILITIES - Claims against the Company not acknowledged as Debts. Monies for which the Company is contingently liable.

PROPERTY AND ASSETS

£ s. d.   £ s. d.

III. PROPERTY held by the Company -
Showing:
4. Immoveable Property, distinguishing:
   (a) Freehold Land
   (b) ,, Buildings
   (c) Leasehold ,,
5. Moveable Property, distinguishing:
   (d) Stock in Trade
   (e) Plant
   The Cost to be stated with Deductions for Deterioration in Value as charged to the Reserve Fund or Profit and Loss.

IV. DEBTS owing to the Company -
Showing:
6. Debts considered good for which the Company hold Bills or other Securities.
7. Debts considered good for which the Company hold no Security.
8. Debts considered doubtful and bad -
   Any Debt due from a Director or other Officer of the Company to be separately stated.

V. CASH AND INVESTMENTS 9. The Nature of Investment and Rate of Interest.
10. The Amount of Cash, where lodged, and if bearing Interest.

It is interesting to note that the present-day English convention of showing assets on the credit side of the balance sheet, and liabilities on the debit side, is followed.

Table B did not provide for a standard form of profit and loss account but, as readers will have noticed, the textual provisions contained some important points strongly reminiscent of the 1948 accounting provisions. These included the requirement that the several sources of gross income should be distinguished (which, if interpreted liberally, goes well beyond the requirements of the 8th Schedule of the 1948 Companies Act), the requirement that the balance of profit and loss for the period should be a " just " one (compare the " true and fair " clause of the 1948 Act), and the explicit requirement that where expenditure was being spread over more than one year, this should be stated, for which there is no precise counterpart in the 1948 Act, but which is evidently related to the idea of a " just " or " true and fair " statement of profit.

Specially interesting to students of accounting history is the requirement in Article 69 that books should be kept on double-entry principles in " a Cash Book, Journal, and Ledger."

Any student of company accounting law will be struck by the remarkably modern ring of the clauses relating to audit. Perhaps the most significant difference from the provisions of the 1948 Act is the permissive clause in Article 83 allowing the employment at the expense of the company of " Accountants or other Persons " to assist the auditor in investigating the accounts, showing that the appointment of professional auditors as a matter of course was not yet envisaged.

Although the adoption of these articles was not obligatory and although the provisions relating to the balance sheet and profit and loss account provided by no means as complete a scheme as is to be found in the 1948 Act—a state of affairs hardly to be expected without the background of a good many years of company accounting experience —they embodied admirably the spirit underlying the provisions of that Act.

The 1856 Companies Act also made provision for the appointment by the Board of Trade, at the request of a specified number of shareholders,[12] of an inspector to investigate the affairs of the company. This provision (a similar one had been suggested in evidence to the Committee of 1841–1844 [13]) seems to have been regarded in some quarters as a substitute for a compulsory annual auditing provision,[14] acceptable no doubt where the latter was not, because its operation depended upon positive action by shareholders rather than upon outside interference. It has remained on the Statute-book, with some

---

[12] One-fifth in number and value.
[13] Evidence, q. 2276.   [14] See Hansard, CLXVI (1862), col. 545.

amendment in matters of detail, until the present day, and undoubtedly fulfils a useful purpose, particularly in the strengthened form it has taken under the Companies Act, 1948.[15]   By its nature, however, it is a power that is unlikely to be exercised until the need for such action has become patent; it is, therefore, hardly an adequate substitute for a routine audit.

The failure in 1856 of the Royal British Bank (which had been incorporated under the Joint Stock Banking Act of 1844), following substantial falsification of balance sheets by the directors coupled with the payment of dividends in the absence of profits and the issue of new shares to the public,[16] did not convince prevailing contemporary opinion that compulsory accounting provisions and compulsory audit were desirable.   On the contrary, it was suggested that these, while having the effect of causing people to relax their vigilance, would, at the same time, be avoided by the unscrupulous.[17]

In the event the main accounting provisions of the 1844 Joint Stock Banking Act were abandoned when, in 1857, the special incorporation law for banks disappeared and these businesses were added to those that could be incorporated under the general company law.[18] Nevertheless, certain minimum requirements were reintroduced for banking companies in the following year when the right to register with limited liability (other than in respect of any note issue) was extended to them.[19]   Every such company had to display half-yearly in its registered office and in every branch office a statement of assets and liabilities, together with a summary of the nominal capital, authorised and issued, and calls made and received.[20]

Thus, despite the contemporary objections to interference in the affairs of private business, prevailing public opinion was prepared to accept some State control of this kind for certain types of companies the effect of whose failure was likely to spread more widely, and cause more incidental damage to the economy, than would have been the

---

[15] See Gower, *op. cit.*, pp. 515–516.
[16] See *R. v. Esdaile*, 175 *English Reports* 697.
[17] See, for example, *The Economist*, XV (1857), p. 59, and XVI (1858), p. 250.   It is interesting to contrast *The Economist's* dubiety concerning the usefulness of a compulsory audit with the same journal's recent comment in connection with an insurance underwriting fraud: " If Lloyd's Committee had had in the past an expert who performed this duty under their authority, auditing a set of accounts here and a set there . . . it is probable that no fraud ever would have been attempted. . . ." *Ibid.*, CLXXV (1955), p. 106.
[18] 20 & 21 Vict. c. 49.   At first banks could only register without limited liability.
[19] By 21 & 22 Vict. c. 91.
[20] This requirement was to be repeated in the 1862 Act (25 & 26 Vict. c. 89) when the same provision was applied to insurance companies to which the right of limited liability was then extended.   Deposit, provident and benefit societies were also included in this provision, which now appears as the 13th Sched. of the 1948 Act (though it no longer applies to companies to which the Life Assurance Companies Acts apply).

case with the average business.   On the other hand, by rejecting compulsory auditing provisions the principle of non-interference may have reduced the practical value of such concessions as were made to the principle of accounting publicity.[1]

While the law makers of the period were not prepared to impose compulsory publicity on the general body of corporate business they did not hesitate to strengthen the sanctions of the law against fraud. The Punishment of Frauds Act of 1857[2] made it a specific offence for any director, officer or manager of a company to falsify or tamper in any way with the company's books and accounts for fraudulent purposes or to circulate or publish any written statement or account knowing it to be false in any material particular with intent to defraud any member or creditor of the company or to induce any person to invest money in the company either as a shareholder or a creditor. These provisions were later embodied in the Larceny Act, 1861.[3]   It was under section 84 of that Act (formerly section 8 of the 1857 Act) that, seventy-five years later, Lord Kylsant was to be successfully prosecuted in the *Royal Mail* case.[4]

A few years later the general company law was consolidated in the Companies Act, 1862[5]; this was to remain the main Companies Act until 1908.   Apart from points already noted, the 1862 Act made no material change in the part of the law with which we are concerned. The model articles were now included in Table A; the accounting and auditing clauses which had appeared in Table B of the 1856 Act were substantially the same and the model form of balance sheet was again reproduced; an interesting minor change was the omission of the requirement that the books of account should be kept in double-entry form.[6]

After 1862 a number of attempts were made to reintroduce compulsory accounting and auditing provisions into the company law, at first without success.   The usual accounting features of the Bills introduced into Parliament between 1862 and 1900 were provisions for the keeping of proper books of account, for the publication (by way of distribution to shareholders, deposition at the company's office or by registration with the Registrar of Companies) of balance sheets and profit and loss accounts in prescribed forms, and for audit.

Forms of balance sheet attached to the draft Bills tended to be rather less workmanlike than the form in Table A.   The prescribed

---

[1] The compulsory auditing regulations in the Companies Clauses Act were **not** abandoned.
[2] 20 & 21 Vict. c. 54.
[3] 24 & 25 Vict. c. 96.
[4] *R.* v. *Kylsant* [1932] 1 K.B. 442.
[5] 25 & 26 Vict. c. 89.
[6] See p. 366, above.

balance sheet under an 1877 Bill,[7] for example, has no reference to deterioration in value or depreciation of the fixed assets, and stock is to be shown merely " as per inventory and valuation." On the other hand, in a later Bill, that of 1884,[8] the part relating to fixed assets specifically provides for separate statement of the figures " as per last year's balance sheet " or " as per valuation," with separate figures for additions and—if not " by valuation "—for depreciation during the year. Table B's explicit threefold division of assets into property, debts, and cash and investments, is not made in either Bill. Both Bills include forms of profit and loss account, but these amount to little more than appropriation accounts, though they do provide for the disclosure of interest paid on fixed loans and of directors' and auditors' remuneration. In both cases the auditors' certificate refers to the profit and loss account as well as the balance sheet.

Up to 1879 the weight of opinion still seems to have been against accounting legislation of this kind. A Bill[9] which provided for publication of balance sheets was rejected in 1867; the Select Committee on Limited Liability Acts of the same year made no recommendations on accounts and audit.[10] Ten years later the 1877 Bill already mentioned was examined by another Select Committee on the Companies Acts,[11] with a similar result. *The Economist* was among those who were then of the opinion that it was undesirable to impose a form of account on companies.[12]

After about 1880, however, the importance of the company form of organisation was growing rapidly, both from the point of view of business organisation and from that of the securities market.[13] It seems reasonable to suppose that the growing activity in the latter was likely to increase the demand for more reliable accounting information.[14] By 1888 *The Economist*, while still opposed to the compulsory publication of a profit and loss account, was prepared to give measured support to the disclosure of a statement of assets and liabilities.[15]

---

[7] B.P.P. (1877) I.   [8] B.P.P. (1884) II.
[9] B.P.P. (1867) V.   [10] B.P.P. (1867) X.
[11] B.P.P. (1877) VIII.   [12] *The Economist*, XXXV (1877), p. 296.
[13] See Clapham, *An Economic History of Modern Britain, Machines and National Rivalries (1887–1914)* (Cambridge, 1938), pp. 201 *et seq.* and pp. 295–297.
[14] It is perhaps significant that in 1895 an objector to the principle of compulsory publication of accounting information—a partner in a well-known firm of solicitors, who must have been in close touch with financial affairs in the City of London—commented that the " outcry for publication " came chiefly from the financial press and a section of shareholders. (Appendix to the Report of the Davey Committee, p. 76, B.P.P. [1895] LXXXVIII.) It may be noted that even when companies do not wish to tap the market directly for new funds, it may be in the interest of existing family and other owners of their securities to establish a good market in these. A study of the extent to which the pressure of the market brought about voluntary improvements in the presentation of corporate accounting information in the late nineteenth century, anticipating the later legislation, is one of the many opportunities for research in this field.
[15] *The Economist*, XLVI (1888), p. 277.

Y.   24

An event that must have contributed to the change in outlook was
the catastrophic failure in 1878, in a setting of directorial mismanagement and falsification of accounts, of the City of Glasgow Bank, which
had been registered—but without limited liability—under the Companies Act, 1862. By over-valuing assets, undervaluing liabilities and
—particularly significant in a bank—misdescription of balance sheet
items with the object of maintaining the company's credit standing,
directors had for a number of years successfully concealed its
insolvency while continuing to pay dividends, a fraud for which they
received in due course terms of imprisonment.[16]

This fraud was followed by the Companies Act, 1879,[17] which
made it possible for unlimited companies to re-register as limited [18]
and introduced a compulsory annual audit for all banking companies
registered thereafter with limited liability. The provisions relating to
the appointment, duties and powers of the auditors were in general
similar to those contained in the model clauses of Table B of the
1856 Act [19] and Table A of the 1862 Act. No provision was made,
however, as in 1856 and 1862, for the employment of accountants by
the auditors at the company's expense. This suggests that the
appointment of professional auditors was becoming more usual.[20]

The original 1879 Bill required the submission of an annual
balance sheet to the company in general meeting and contained a
simple form of balance sheet,[1] but all this disappeared in the process
of enactment.

It is interesting to note that *The Economist* was prepared to
support the imposition of accounting and auditing regulations on
banking companies and was indeed prepared to regret the loss of the
uniform prescribed balance sheet.[2]

The Accountant regretted a phrase in the auditing section of the
Act (which had not appeared in Table A): " as shown by the books
of the company "; this, it was suggested, might limit the auditors' work
on the balance sheet to mere mechanical checking of figures.[3]   This

---

16 For an account of the fraud and trial, see *Trial of the City of Glasgow Bank
Directors* (ed. W. Wallace, Glasgow and Edinburgh, 1905).
17 42 & 43 Vict. c. 76.
18 The principle of reserve liability (now provided by Companies Act, 1948, s. 60)
was also introduced. The new provision allowed a company if it wished to have
a specified, and therefore limited, uncalled liability on its shares which would only
be available for call in the event of liquidation. This device made possible the
combination of limited liability for shareholders with the protection of creditors
that uncalled capital was supposed to provide and which, when unlimited, had
been so disastrous for the City of Glasgow Bank shareholders.
19 See pp. 363, 364, above.
20 It was still possible sixteen years later, however, for a representative of the
London Stock Exchange giving evidence before the Davey Committee to say that
at least *one* of the auditors should be a professional accountant. (Appendix,
p. 84, q. 10.)
1 B.P.P. (1878–1879) I.   2 *The Economist*, XXXVII (1879), p. 935.
3 *The Accountant*, V (1879), pp. 4–5.

seems, however, to have been an unfounded interpretation. The Act specifically called upon the auditors to report whether the balance sheet was " full and fair." That this required active verification of the company's position, going beyond what was merely recorded in the books, was given judicial recognition in 1895.[4]

Special treatment in accounting matters was not confined to banking companies. Under the Life Assurance Companies Act, 1870,[5] every company carrying on life assurance business was required to prepare, file with the Board of Trade, and make available to shareholders and policy holders annual revenue accounts and balance sheets in prescribed forms. The statutory quinquennial actuarial valuation was introduced at the same time. No special auditing provisions were imposed, however, on these companies.

Public utility companies, too, continued to receive special treatment. The Regulation of Railways Act, 1868,[6] provided for the publication and filing with the Board of Trade of detailed accounting statements including a revenue account and balance sheet in prescribed forms.

Similar arrangements for the preparation and publication of accounts in prescribed forms were made for other public utilities, for example, in the Gas Works Clauses Act, 1871,[7] and the Electric Lighting Act, 1882.[8]

Thus by about 1880 the principle of compulsory publication of accounts in uniform style, and (except for life assurance companies) compulsory audit by auditors elected annually by shareholders, had been accepted for these " special " types of company.

The extension of the compulsory annual audit to all registered companies followed an extensive inquiry conducted by the Company Law Amendment Committee of 1895.[9] The Committee's report, which included a draft Bill,[10] was followed by the submission of the Companies Bill of 1896[11] to a House of Lords Select Committee, which sat during the following three years.[12] Finally, in 1900, an amended Bill became law as the Companies Act, 1900.[13] This Act contained no explicit provisions for the regulation of company accounting,[14] but it did, for the first time since 1856, make an annual audit obligatory for all companies registered under the Companies

---

[4] *Re London and General Bank (No. 2)* [1895] 2 Ch. 673, see *per* Lindley L.J. at pp. 682–683.   [5] 33 & 34 Vict. c. 61.
[6] 31 & 32 Vict. c. 119.   [7] 34 & 35 Vict. c. 41.
[8] 45 & 46 Vict. c. 56.   [9] The Davey Committee, B.P.P. (1895) LXXXVIII.
[10] Most of the draft clauses in the Bill were extracted from one or other of the numerous Bills introduced since 1862. (*Ibid.*, p. v.)
[11] The 1896 Bill was reprinted in *The Accountant*, XXII (1896), pp. 320 *et seq.*
[12] B.P.P. (1896) IX, (1897) X and (1898) IX.
[13] 63 & 64 Vict. c. 48.
[14] Except with respect to the Statutory Report, mentioned below.

Acts, and thereby imposed, by inference, an obligation to prepare an annual balance sheet.[15]

The auditing requirements of the 1900 Act followed the same general lines as those for banking companies under the 1879 Act, and as those of Table A of the 1862 Act, though the wording of the auditors' report to the shareholders differed in some respects; it is doubtful, however, whether this difference had any legal significance.[16]

The Act also required that at the first meeting of a company (the " statutory meeting ") there should be submitted a " statutory report." The latter was to contain a summarised account of the receipts and payments on capital account from the date of incorporation of the company to the first formal meeting of the shareholders. It was also to provide information about the issued and called-up capital, about preliminary expenses, and about the company's contracts. The capital receipts and payments, including the cash receipts from share allotments, and the information relating to the issued capital, were to be certified as correct by the company's auditors.[17]

Although the Act contained no new accounting provisions in the strict sense (apart from the statutory report), the evidence given to the Davey Committee, and the Committee's report, indicate that opinion was becoming increasingly favourable towards placing on directors the specific obligation to prepare annual accounts. The evidence shows, on the other hand, that opinion was still divided on the question of public registration of balance sheets. This was probably due in part to the growing importance of what was becoming known as the private company: the compulsory filing of accounts with the Registrar of Companies would have made generally available a good deal of information about what were often essentially family businesses trading for convenience in corporate form. It is significant

---

15 See *Newton* v. *Birmingham Small Arms Co., Ltd.* [1906] 2 Ch. 378, *per* Buckley J. at p. 387.

16 The phrase " full and fair " relating to the balance sheet was omitted. It still had to show a " true and correct view of the state of the company's affairs." It is of interest to note that in addition to the report the auditors were required to append to the balance sheet a certificate stating whether or not their requirements as auditors had been complied with. The present-day equivalent is now included in the form of report.

17 The statutory meeting had been considered by the Davey Committee as an occasion on which shareholders could review the good faith of the undertaking and the prospects of the company and decide whether or not it should continue in existence. •(The Report, para. 39.) This recommendation was undoubtedly related to the large number of frauds that had occurred in company promotions. The Committee considered that the doctrine *caveat emptor* had only limited application in this context, where buyers had practically no opportunity of making independent inquiries before coming to a decision. (*Ibid.*, para. 3.) After 1907, when private companies were first legally defined as a separate class of company, the statutory meeting and report applied only to public companies. This particular provision of the company law has become practically a dead letter since nearly all companies begin life as private companies, being thereafter converted, if need be, to public companies.

that when the compulsory filing of annual balance sheets was finally introduced, in 1907, this type of company was exempted from the provision and was, as a necessary consequence, given a statutory definition.

The Davey Committee, while recommending that the directors should be required to make provision for proper books of account and to submit annually to shareholders (or deposit at the company's registered office) a balance sheet containing certain minimum information, were nevertheless opposed to public registration of accounts.[18] As we have seen, this view was accepted by Parliament. It is interesting to note, however, that the original 1896 Bill included a clause whereby the annual balance sheet was not only to be submitted to the shareholders but was also to be filed with the Registrar of Companies (where it would be open to public inspection). Speaking on the Bill in the House of Lords, Lord Dudley, Secretary to the Board of Trade, said that the principle upon which the Bill was based was that of publicity in the interests of the shareholders and the creditors. It was impossible to protect people against the consequences of their own folly, but it was possible to place prudent people in a position to determine whether they could safely invest their money in these concerns.[19] Publication had also been advocated by Vaughan Williams J., a member of the Davey Committee, who dissented from the views of the majority on this question. In his addendum to the Committee's Report,[20] he was, however, more concerned with publicity for the accounts of private companies than of public companies, his emphasis being thus more on protecting creditors than on providing information for investors. As a witness to the Committee had pointed out, it was illogical to require publication of information about a company's issued capital if provision was not also made for the publication of data—in the form, for example, of a statement of assets and liabilities—on which creditors might judge what had happened to the assets acquired with that capital.[1] *The Economist*, too, could see no reason why special privileges should be given to private companies.[2]

However, the balance sheet clause did not survive the Parliamentary process, and indeed even in 1956 personal private companies[3] are still exempted from filing their accounts with the Registrar of Companies, though not from the preparation or submission of accounts to shareholders and debenture-holders.

The original Bill would also have imposed certain minimum

---

[18] *Ibid.*, paras. 51 and 52.
[19] Hansard, XXXVIII (1896), col. 1321.
[20] The Report, pp. xxii and xxiii.
[1] *Ibid.*, Appendix to the Report, pp. 68 *et seq.*
[2] *The Economist*, LIV (1896), p. 552.
[3] In technical terms "exempt private companies" as defined in Companies Act, 1948, s. 129.

requirements with respect to the contents of the annual balance sheet, namely that it must show:

(a) The amount of share capital issued, paid-up, and in arrear, distinguishing payments in cash and other payments;
(b) debts due by the company, distinguishing mortgages, debentures and floating charges;
(c) debts due to the company after deduction for bad and doubtful debts;
(d) the bases on which assets were valued: whether at cost, by valuation or otherwise; the percentage or amount of depreciation which had been written off; and what other provision, if any, had been made for depreciation.

The Bill did not provide, however, for a standard form of balance sheet: instead it directed that the form should be as laid down in the articles or by a resolution of the company. The evidence given to the Davey Committee had, indeed, shown that there was a good deal of opposition to the idea of a standard form and the Committee had reported against its introduction on the rather unconvincing grounds of the diversity of business carried on by companies.

It may be noted that the data to be disclosed under the Bill was a good deal less comprehensive than had been proposed in some of the evidence given to the Committee. Suggestions had been made, for example, that the cost of assets, and the accumulated depreciation thereon, should be disclosed; that goodwill should be valued separately; that the main classes of asset and liability should be distinguished; that loans to directors and officials should be disclosed. One witness had even favoured a balance sheet valuation based on the saleable value of the assets.[4] *The Accountant*, too, commented adversely on the lack of a more detailed classification of assets, without which the usefulness of the information which the Bill required about the valuation bases and about depreciation would be reduced.[5]

Although these accounting clauses were not enacted, it is of interest that the requirements concerning depreciation bases should have been inserted in the Bill, for it suggests that increasing attention was being directed towards the question of profit measurement. This was probably attributable in part to the interest that had been raised by the series of judgments during the last twenty years of the nineteenth century on dividend distributions, which are discussed below. It may also have had some connection with attacks that had been made on joint-stock cotton spinning companies in Lancashire in the 1880's: these companies had been charged with contributing to the depression and in particular with failing to provide proper depreciation or charging revenue expenditure to capital—an early example of charges

---

[4] Evidence, pp. 84, 98, 137.
[5] *The Accountant*, XXII (1896), p. 331.

of " unfair competition " on costing grounds.⁶ Proposals then made included suggestions that these limited companies should be required to publish accounts and disclose the principles adopted in accounting for such matters as depreciation of plant and machinery and treatment of capital expenditure.⁷

Although the 1896 Bill, by requiring the disclosure of the basis on which assets had been valued, would (had this clause become law) necessarily have provided some information on the method of profit calculation used, the Bill—and here again the Parliamentary drafts-men were in accord with what appears to have been the prevailing climate of opinion—did not call for either the publication or the supply to shareholders of a detailed profit and loss account.⁸

On one subject—the desirability of audit—there was a substantial measure of agreement including a good deal of support for the inclusion among the auditors of at least one professional accountant. The compulsory audit recommended by the Davey Committee was written into the Bill, but, also following the Committee's Report, without the proviso that professional accountants should be employed. As we have seen, the auditing proposals became law in 1900.⁹

---

⁶ See Royal Commission on the Depression of Trade and Industry, Second Report, Appendix A (9), pp. 378, 379, B.P.P. (1886) XXI.

⁷ *Ibid.*, Evidence, qq. 5813, 5865–5868. The abortive Bill of 1888 provided for an annual balance sheet in which would be disclosed, *inter alia*, the rate and amount of depreciation deducted from the preceding balance sheet value of plant or property owned, together with a statement giving the cost of additions to capital account since the issue of that balance sheet. (*The Economist*, XLVI [1888], p. 790.)

⁸ The Davey Committee had not recommended the provision of a profit and loss account. The profit and loss account *balance* would presumably have appeared in the balance sheet; but as no information on dividends would have appeared it would not have been possible to make (by comparing successive balance sheets) a good estimate of the profit of any given year; and even had the dividends been known, the absence at that time of established rules on secret reserves would in any case have made it impossible to decide by how much the profit, however calculated, had been reduced by appropriations to " contingency " reserves and so on.

⁹ Two auditing requirements that were in the 1896 Bill and are now part of the law, but which failed to reach the Statute-book in 1900, would have imposed upon auditors the duty of ascertaining whether the books of the company had been properly kept and likewise of reporting whether the balance sheet had been drawn up in accordance with the provisions of the Act. These requirements, *inter alia*, were criticised by the Council of the Institute of Chartered Accountants on the grounds that the auditors' work would thereby be made unduly onerous (*The Accountant*, XXII [1896], pp. 418–419). Another interesting suggestion of the Davey Committee which failed to reach the Statute-book was that the directors should, for the purpose of the audit, supply the auditors with a " private balance sheet," giving the full details upon which the balance sheet to be issued to the shareholders was founded, and which would be signed on behalf of the Board. The object of this proposal, said the Committee, was to secure increased care and attention on the part of the directors, and to bring home to their minds their responsibility with respect to the issued balance sheet so that more care would be taken in seeing that the summary results exhibited to the shareholders were founded upon sufficient and trustworthy materials, and at the same time to preserve evidence of the manner in which the directors and auditors had performed their duty (The Report, pàra. 55). The Council of the Institute took the view that this provision was redundant (*The Accountant, ibid.*).

This concludes our sketch of the development of statutory company accounting law between 1844 and 1900. It is appropriate, however, to direct some attention to the case law on distributable profits.

The legality of dividend payments in company law may be said to raise two questions. First there is the problem of profit measurement, which, for formal solution, requires the two steps of (a) setting up or defining a profit concept, and (b) applying that concept to actual situations. Secondly, given the measurement, the question arises of the relationship to be recognised by the law between (a) measured profit, and (b) the amount that may be legally distributed by way of dividend.

As a matter of fact it is not possible to keep those two questions wholly separate in studying the development of the law relating to dividends.[10] It is, however, useful to distinguish the two aspects of the problem for purposes of discussion. Indeed, the case law explicitly recognises this distinction by making it clear that it does not follow because certain types of loss or expense may be ignored without breaking the law when a dividend is declared, that these same losses or expenses may be ignored in the accounts.[11]

How dividends shall be related to the amount of the profit, that is, of the surplus, however defined, over paid-in capital, is a matter of national economic policy, though the legal rules adopted, whatever they may be, are relevant in accounting and auditing practice, as is the disclosure of the relation of the dividends paid by a company to its calculated profit. The manner of the profit calculation, and the principles on which it is based, are essentially economic problems of the firm, within the province of the accountant as theorist as well as practitioner.

As we have seen,[12] these questions were live ones at the very beginning of our period. If we abstract from problems of price level changes, we may conjecture that profit would then (as now) have been conceived by most business men in terms of the surplus remaining after the rough maintenance of the money value of the business (allowance being made for payments-in and withdrawals). Where it was difficult to consider the capital value of the undertaking in terms of the saleable value in the market of the separate assets, because assets were rather specific (as in the case of a railway) or because goodwill—the established knowledge, habits and connections of the organisation—had a significant effect on profits, maintenance of the

---

10 For a fuller discussion of this topic see B. S. Yamey, "Aspects of the Law Relating to Company Dividends," *Studies in Accounting* (ed. W. T. Baxter, London, 1950), and Gower, *op. cit.*, Chap. 6.
11 See *Verner* v. *General and Commercial Investment Trust* [1894] 2 Ch. 239, *per* Lindley L.J. at p. 267.   12 See pp. 357, 358, above.

value of the business would no doubt tend to be considered in terms of the maintenance of dividend-paying capacity; the latter in turn might be interpreted as the maintenance of the business assets in roughly the same physical condition—by no means the same thing in theory, but probably often near enough for practical purposes. These general and necessarily rather fuzzy ideas are, if we allow for accounting conservatism, discussed below, on the whole consistent with the practical rules which have been applied for many years in the preparation of business profit and loss accounts.[13]

There is, in fact, little doubt that this general idea of profit measurement as a comparison of valuations in successive periods [14] was accepted from the beginning of our period. Thus, in a report by accountants to the Committee of Investigation on the accounts of the Eastern Counties Railway Company, made on April 16, 1849, we find the words:

> One of the necessary incidents of traffic being the depreciation of the working stock and permanent way of the line, the outlay incurred in keeping them up to their original value, whether by means of repair or the purchase of new stock and materials, is of the character of working expenses, *and is therefore properly chargeable against that Revenue, in the production of which such depreciation is caused.*[15] (Our italics.)

In an early income tax case we find judicial recognition of the same idea.[16]

This is not, of course, to assert that ignorant or unscrupulous people never overlooked or deliberately ignored, for example, the necessity for making in the profit calculation an allowance for permanent deterioration in the value of assets. Nor does it imply that a logically complete and satisfactory definition of business profit as it was usually calculated existed before 1900; but then nor does it now.

What influence did the dividend law have on profit computation in practice? It followed from a number of judicial decisions [17] that in principle dividends could not legally be paid out of capital. This might reasonably have been interpreted as meaning that no dividend could be paid in the absence of a surplus over and above the money value of the capital funds paid in by the shareholders—the nominal

---

[13] The question of a divergence between money values and real values raises additional issues which we have not attempted to follow up here.

[14] Adjusted, of course, for payments-in or withdrawals.

[15] Select Committee on Audit of Railway Accounts, Second Report, Appendix A, p. 389, B.P.P. (1849) X. See also Appendix H of the First Report, pp. 276–281, where the Revenue Account of the London and North Western Railway contains a provision "for Renewal of Rails £10,250." For further evidence see the quotations in A. C. Littleton, *Accounting Evolution to 1900* (New York, 1933), Chap. XIV.

[16] *Knowles* v. *McAdam* (1877) 3 Ex.Div. 23, 1 T.C. 161.

[17] For example, by the Court of Appeal in *Flitcroft's Case* (1882) 21 Ch.D. 519 and by the House of Lords in *Trevor* v. *Whitworth* (1887) 12 App.Cas. 409. An earlier case was *MacDougall* v. *Jersey Hotel Co., Ltd.* (1864) 34 L.J.Ch. 28.

paid-up capital. Indeed, this interpretation seems necessary to explain the need for those provisions of the Companies Acts of 1867 and 1877 [18] which made it possible by formal legal process to " reduce " capital in various ways.[19]

This interpretation of the law relating to dividend distributions was rendered invalid, however, by the well-known series of judicial decisions beginning in 1889 with the decision of the Court of Appeal in *Lee* v. *The Neuchatel Asphalte Co.*[20] whereby the " maintenance of capital " was so interpreted as to exclude, in certain cases at least, the maintenance of wasting and other fixed assets, or of capital lost before the accounting period for which the dividend in question was to be paid.[1] These decisions amounted to judicial legislation on economic policy, for, as we have already pointed out, the question of what dividends may legally be paid is in theory independent of whatever concept of profit is adopted. On the latter question the courts tended to accept commercial accounting practice as they found it. Nevertheless, their attitude has not been without its effect on accounting doctrine.

This is partly because the court's views on capital maintenance led accountants to place special emphasis on the valuation of current, as distinct from fixed, assets. Again, one of the features of the dividend cases was the stress they laid on the importance of disclosure and of honest and reasonable behaviour. This undoubtedly influenced auditing practice and thereby, indirectly, accounting practice. The cases also, because the stress was on capital maintenance; caused emphasis to be placed on the avoidance of over-statement in profit calculation and in balance sheet valuation. The emphasis on conservatism still persists in company accounting practice (as perusal of any standard auditing text will show), despite the more recent movement in the direction of avoiding *under-* as well as *over-*statement of profits, a movement which owes much to the *Royal Mail* case and which has found expression in the Companies Act, 1948.[2] Even today the law goes little beyond restraining the deliberate under-statement of the profit *as it would be calculated under accounting rules of long*

---

[18] 30 & 31 Vict. c. 131 and 40 & 41 Vict. c. 26.
[19] See *Re Ebbw Vale Steel, Iron and Coal Company* (1877) 4 Ch.D. 827, and Buckley, *The Companies Acts* (7th ed., London, 1897), p. 639. See also R. S. Edwards, " A Note on the Law Relating to Company Dividends," *Economica*, VI (1939), p. 176.
[20] 41 Ch.D. 1.
[1] See Yamey, *op. cit.* The result of these decisions seems to have been to render the process of reducing lost nominal equity share capital to a mere formality, the only practical use of which is to make it possible to issue additional equity shares at the new par (or above) in cases where otherwise no issue could be made (because market saleable value was below the original par) without going through the cumbersome process of obtaining judicial permission to issue shares at a discount (a seldom-used process first legalised by the Companies Act, 1928).
[2] See Companies Act, 1948, 8th Sched., para. 27.

standing, themselves highly conservative. In this context the influence of the dividend cases must be considered together with the effect of the nineteenth-century environment in which the accounting principles developed. No great pressure had yet arisen for the provision of precise profit reporting for the benefit of professional investment analysts while, on the other hand, the period was one in which reckless and fraudulent over-statement of balance sheet values (or under-statement of liabilities) was commoner than it is now.

It seems, in fact, that the cases contributed relatively little towards the settlement of general principles of profit calculation: such influence as they had on accounting practice—and it was probably substantial [3]— was rather in the direction of crystallising certain existing valuation rules-of-thumb with a heavy accent on conservatism—for example the " cost or lower market value " basis of stock valuation—and the creation (or preservation) of the sharp distinction between so-called fixed and current assets. This distinction seems unfortunately to have led accountants to under-estimate the importance to a business of the value of its fixed assets, an attitude which, among other things, begs the very important question of whether the company—or its directors —are justifying the use they are making of the economic resources in their hands.

It is of interest to note, in conclusion, that the 1895 Davey Committee (who had among other things taken evidence on foreign company law practice) recommended the appointment of a small body of experts to consider the conditions under which dividends might be distributed.[4] No action has yet been taken.

---

[3] It is interesting to speculate on the extent to which this influence arose from the weight placed by the earlier writers of the textbooks read by those entering the accounting profession on the dicta of the various judges, as distinct from the exercise of independent thought on the problem of providing the data most useful to those interested in the fortunes of companies. This, in turn, is connected with the relatively large part played by auditing in professional accountants' practices.

[4] The Report, para. 56. The Committee were able to remark that although the court had been strict in enforcing the personal responsibility of directors who had fraudulently, wilfully, or even negligently, without exercising their judgment, paid dividends out of capital, it had been slow to make directors who had exercised their judgment liable for miscalculations, sanguine estimates, or errors of judgment.

The Early History of
Double-entry Book-keeping in Japan

K. Nishikawa*

THE earliest reference to merchants' account-books in Japanese history occurs in A.D. 1520, when rules were prescribed for making use of pawnbrokers' books (*tokuracho*) in connection with law-suits. The oldest books of accounts that have survived until today are dated 1615 and 1634 respectively. It is believed that at first merchants kept only one book, called *daifukucho*, the function of which was similar to that of the ledger of present-day single-entry book-keeping. As the scale of individual business firms grew, other books were added, such as a purchases-book (*kaicho*), a sales-book (*uricho*), a cash-book (*kingindeiricho*), etc. That the indigenous system was adequate for contemporary purposes is suggested by the observation of François Caron, director of the factory of the Dutch East India Company in Hirado from 1639 to 1641, that "they have not the Italian Manner of Keeping Books, and yet fail not in their Calculations." [1]

Some of the larger merchants evolved more complex systems of recording to serve their needs. The most elaborate system of books developed before the modern era is that called " Izumo book-keeping " by Professors Y. Hirai and K. Yamashita of the Kobe National University. They have described the books of accounts of the Tanabe family in the early years of the nineteenth century. The family had operated more than twenty iron forges in Izumo Province in the north-western part of the mainland of Japan, long known for the production of iron. At one of their works more than thirty books were used from which so-called " inventories " were prepared half-yearly. Each " inventory " contains particulars of cash, iron, rice, wages and other charges. Three statements were also prepared, one of assets and liabilities, and the other two concerning profits and losses; the first of the latter shows summaries of revenues, expenses and operating results, and the other shows the same net result calculated by comparing opening and closing balances of assets and liabilities. The Tanabe businessmen called the two profit-and-loss statements " double-sided " accounts. It is of interest that they include adjustments for prepaid and accrued expenses and that purchases of equipment were

---

* Director and Comptroller, Mitsubishi Oil Company, Tokyo.
[1] *Description of Japan*, English Translation, 1671.

treated as expenses when incurred. Nevertheless, however elaborate and cleverly arranged the " Izumo book-keeping " was, basically it was nothing but traditional Japanese book-keeping, a sort of single entry. Many books were used but none with the functions of the ledger of double-entry book-keeping.

It may be surmised that some of the first Western visitors to Japan brought with them books expounding Italian double-entry book-keeping. A little more than a century after the publication of Pacioli's treatise the following entry was made in the Diary of Richard Cocks, Director of the English East India Company's factory in Hirado:

> March 9, 1616. I lent my book of St. Augustyn City of God to Mr. Wickham, and the Turkish History and *a book of forme of debitor and creditor* to Mr. Nealson.[2]

There is some evidence, also—though it refers to later centuries—that some Japanese had knowledge of, or interest in, Western accounting methods before Japan was opened to foreign traders under the Treaty of Peace and Amity made with the United States in 1854. Thus an entry dated February 17, 1778, in the official diary of the Dutch factory in Nagasaki indicates that one Herman Köhler, assistant to the director of the factory, gave lessons in *Vlissingen's book-keeping* to Japanese student-interpreters.[3] Again, the library of the Nabeshima family includes one Dutch work on book-keeping which at one time belonged to a V. Borst, a member of the Dutch factory in Nagasaki around 1847. The Shizuoka library contains two Dutch books on Italian book-keeping, which originally belonged to the library of the Tokugawa Shogunate.[4]

The early contacts with double-entry book-keeping did not lead to the use of the system by Japanese businessmen. The local methods were quite suitable for firms in a largely feudal economic system in which the production and distribution of goods were organised on a small scale and business transactions were generally small and simple. The more elaborate and systematic method of book-keeping by double entry came into its own, and then only gradually, after the modern capitalistic economy had been established and expanded. The feudal economic structure began to collapse towards the close of the Tokugawa régime; its more complete replacement by a capitalistic economic system proceeded apace after the Restoration of the Imperial régime in 1868.

---

[2] It cannot be determined which of the early book-keeping treatises is indicated by the description *book of forme of debitor and creditor*. Peele's volume published in 1553 is the only work the title of which includes the words " fourme " as well as " debitour and creditour."

[3] No book answering this brief description appears to be recorded in the standard works on the history and bibliography of accounting in the Netherlands.

[4] Both the libraries mentioned include a work by W. Oudshoff, an important and influential Dutch writer of the first half of the nineteenth century.

After the opening up of Japan to foreign influence in 1854, modern book-keeping was imported into Japan simultaneously from several countries. Printed treatises played an important part. Not only American and British works, but also French and German, and even Russian books, were introduced. In addition, several Western accounting experts and teachers, drawn from several countries, were invited to design accounting systems and train Japanese accountants and book-keepers for industrial and commercial concerns established on Western models. A few of these experts also wrote treatises on accounting while in Japan.

The Yokosuka Steel Works, the precursor of the Yokosuka Arsenal of later years, was founded in 1865 and was one of the first modern factories in Japan to adopt double-entry book-keeping. The organisation plan for the Works was drawn up in 1865 by the then French minister-plenipotentiary and a French naval engineer in collaboration with senior officials of the Shogunate Government. It was provided that all books of account should be kept in both the Japanese and French languages by the Japanese and French officials. Also, a French naval accountant came to Japan to take up the post of chief accountant at the new Works. He remained for five years, and was succeeded by another Frenchman whose duties were handed over to a Japanese accountant in 1873.

Another important instance of direct foreign influence occurred in 1871. The Japanese Government bought old equipment of the former British Mint in Hongkong, and erected a mint in Osaka. They engaged several former employees of the British Mint, including William Kinder as the director, to man the new venture. A Portuguese, Vicente E. Braga, was employed as chief accountant. Braga and two assistants, an Englishman and a Portuguese, kept all the books of the Mint in English; these were then translated into Japanese, thus making complete sets of books in each of the two languages. Braga remained in Japan until 1878 during which time he drafted an accounting and book-keeping system for the Japanese Government, and gave courses in accounting which were attended by several pupils who later became teachers and writers on book-keeping. His personal influence was so great that his style of penmanship was practised in the Mint long after he had left it.

Braga can be regarded as the first of the three Westerners who filled the most crucial roles in the early development of double-entry book-keeping in Japan. The second was an Englishman, Alexander Allan Shand (1844–1930), who had been employed by the Chartered Mercantile Bank of India, London and China in Yokohama from about 1867. In 1872 the Japanese Government engaged him to compile a treatise on book-keeping to be used by the new national banks which were to be established on the pattern of the national banking system of the United States. The resulting work, entitled *Ginko-bokiseiho*, was published by the Finance Ministry in 1873; it served as the source for bank book-keeping, and the methods it describes remain in practical use to this day in Japan. In April, 1874, the Currency Department of the Finance Ministry started a lecture course in banking and commercial book-keeping, and Shand's *Ginko-bokiseiho* was the obvious textbook chosen for bank book-keeping. In this way his influence spread beyond the confines of banking. Shand continued to serve the Japanese Government as financial adviser and instructor in banking and finance until 1877.

The third important figure was William Gogswell Whitney (1825–1882), the proprietor of the Bryant, Stratton and Whitney Business College in Newark, New Jersey. He came to Japan in 1875 to teach in the first commercial school in Japan, which later was to become the Hitotsubashi University. He stayed in Japan as teacher for five years and wrote a short textbook for use in his school. His disciples contributed more than ten volumes to the early Japanese literature of book-keeping.

The changing influence of different countries on Japanese practice is well illustrated by changes in the form of published financial statements. The first of these to be seen in Japan were the statements, published in English newspapers, of foreign banks which had been established in Yokohama before 1868. In 1873 the Japanese Government adopted for its new national banks the uniform accounting system drawn up by the Englishman, Allan Shand. The prescribed balance sheet was in the English form, with assets on the right-hand (" credit ") side. (Arabic numerals were used in statements submitted to the government, but those published in the press were written vertically using Japanese numerals, with capital and liabilities in the upper part and assets in the lower.) The English form of the balance sheet was prevalent for some time. But most of the first Japanese textbooks on accounting were devised from or based upon American works (apart from those on bank book-keeping stemming from Shand's *Ginko-Bokiseiho*) in which the assets are listed on the left-hand (" debit ") side of the balance sheet. Gradually the American form replaced the English, and towards the end of the century this process was accelerated when the American form was adopted officially for the statements of the national banks. By the end of the century the English form had disappeared from commercial usage in Japan, except among small firms using the " cash method " of book-keeping which is described below. However, the vertical arrangement of balance sheets, using Japanese numerals, in newspapers remained until quite recently.

The influence of the Bryant, Stratton and Whitney College preceded the arrival in Japan of W. Whitney, for the first Japanese text on accounting was a translation of Bryant and Stratton's *Common School Book-keeping, embracing single and double entry*. This translation, made by Yukichi Fukuzawa, was published in Tokyo, the first part in June, 1873, and the remaining part in the following year. Fukuzawa's influence was immense. Apart from being responsible for the adoption of Western book-keeping methods in many firms, he also publicised them at his school and at others with which he was connected. Many commercial teachers and writers on book-keeping received their tuition from him. Dr. Kiyoshi Kurosawa of the Yokohama National University has recently written that it is not too much to say that Fukuzawa's book was as significant in Japan in the early years of the Meiji era as Luca Pacioli's treatise had been in Italy several centuries earlier.

A succession of books on book-keeping in Japanese by Japanese authors appeared after Fukuzawa's pioneer work. By the end of the nineteenth century works on book-keeping by more than ninety authors had been published (some running into several editions), as well as a few specialised works on book-keeping for farms, breweries and railways. It is of interest that in 1886 a short pamphlet on the history of book-keeping appeared, one of the earliest studies on this subject to be published anywhere in the world as a separate work.

Many of the early books on book-keeping were translations or adaptations of published works by English and American authors, usually with additional material by the Japanese author. Some were compounded of extracts from a number of sources [5]; and some works were translated and published by several different authors.[6] Although quite a number of foreign works had been imported into Japan by the last quarter of the nineteenth century, the majority of Japanese texts were based on a small group of foreign texts. The works of Bryant and Stratton, C. C. Marsh, E. G. Folsom, W. Inglis and Charles Hutton were among the most frequently used as bases for the Japanese publications, with American models predominant.

Numerical notation presented one of the greatest difficulties encountered by the early writers. In Japan the numerals, written vertically, were traditionally represented by Chinese characters,

---

[5] For example, T. Zushi states in the preface to his *Bokiho Genri* (1881): " I compiled this book, translating passages from several American and British authors such as Folsom, Foster, Barnes, etc., and also adding my own ideas . . . ," and in the title the work is described as " Translation by T. Zushi of selected passages." The book is now commonly referred to as a translation of Folsom's *Logical Bookkeeping* (New York, 1873).

[6] In this early period copyright and translation rights were not effectively protected by law.

denoting respectively, one to nine, and ten, hundred, thousand, etc.[7]
But there was no cypher. Fukuzawa, the first author, introduced a
novel notation by having a zero and nine characters for one to nine,
but he did not depart from the traditional way of vertical writing.
Subsequent authors followed his innovation. Arabic numerals were
first used in a published work by Usagawa in 1878, and in the same
year Fujii introduced horizontal writing in his text on book-keeping.[8]

The development of the so-called " cash method " or " receipt and
payment " book-keeping is an interesting aspect of the early practice
of double entry in Japan. This method derives ultimately from two
sources, of which the first was Fukuzawa's pioneer textbook of 1873.
In it the author explained to those not familiar with Western accounting that it could be understood more readily by considering all
transactions as being analogous with money transactions and by
substituting the terms " receipts " and " payments " for " debits " and
" credits." Fukuzawa himself used the terms " debit " and " credit "
rather than his own suggested terminology " in view of increasing
dealings with foreigners." However, some of his students and
followers were later to adapt his ideas and to introduce his
terminology.

The second source was Shand's *Ginko-bokiseiho,* published six
months after Fukuzawa's volume. This work, it will be recalled, was
designed to furnish a system of accounts for banks. Shand advised
the use of a cash day-book (with three columns on each side: cash,
transfer and total) to record all transactions, both cash transactions and
those transfers, etc., not involving the passing of cash. A cash day-
book of this kind had been described by William Gilbart in his *A
Practical Treatise on Banking* as one of the various systems then in
general use among banks in Great Britain. It may be presumed that
Shand took Gilbart's description as his model.

In the writing up of the cash day-book and the ledger Shand made
use of credit slips for money received and debit slips for money paid.
The former would be recorded on the debit side of the day-book and
posted to the credit side of the personal account (for example) in the
ledger; the debit slips would be treated in the converse manner. The
terminology was no doubt confusing to the uninitiated in that the

---

[7] In the traditional way numbers are written as they are read. For example, to
write 5,398 the characters representing thousand, hundred and ten are placed
between the characters representing 5, 3, 9 and 8.

In early account-books which have survived entries for deductions or decreases
are sometimes marked with a Japanese character to signify their nature. But
often the original entries are simply struck out, or marked with a symbol
resembling an inverted L, instead of making contra entries.

[8] Horizontal writing of Fukuzawa's numerals had already appeared in the translation of Shand's text on bank book-keeping in 1873.

credit slip had its counterpart in an entry on the debit side of the cash day-book, and vice versa. The translation of Shand's manuscript, which was written in English, was entrusted to five officials of the Finance Ministry, two of whom were graduates of Fukuzawa's school and influenced by his writings. They translated "credit slip" as "receipt slip" and "debit slip" as "payment slip." Also, the appropriate columns of the cash day-book were designated "Cash Receipt" and "Cash Payment" in lieu of Shand's own "Dr. Cash" and "Cr. Cash."

Shand did not have "transfer slips" as vouchers for non-cash transactions; nor did he give any special explanation of the rationale of the cash day-book entries for non-cash items. These gaps were filled by later writers. Fujii, another of Fukuzawa's pupils, in his book of 1878 was the first to introduce the "transfer slip." Following his teacher's ideas he designated the left-hand side of his transfer slip (indicating the ledger account to be credited) "receipt," and the other side "payment." A later author explained the basis for the recording of non-cash transactions in the cash day-book. A purchase of goods on credit is considered as if it were two cash transactions: a purchase of goods for cash, and the receipt of cash from a creditor. This explains why in the cash day-book—which is also in effect the cash account—"merchandise" appears as an entry on the credit side and the creditor on the debit side, that is, reversing the entries as they would be made in an orthodox journal. (Since the "cash account" is both debited and credited, the balance on this account is, properly, not affected at all.) The postings to the ledger would be conventional. This method of journalisation is known as "indirect journalisation."

Later authors discontinued entirely using the terms "debit" and "credit" in favour of the terms "receipt" and "payment." At the same time the writing up of the ledger from the day-book was altered. The entries on the debit side of the day-book were posted to the left-hand side of the ledger account, and conversely for the entries on the credit side. Therefore, in the final version of "receipt and payment" book-keeping the entries in the ledger are the reverse of those in the usual practice of double entry, though there is complete duality of entries.

Fujii, who introduced the "transfer slip" in 1878, also adapted the system of the cash day-book, devised by Shand for banking businesses, for other commercial enterprises. For over fifteen years no one followed Fujii's example. Then several books on corporation book-keeping were published in quick succession, and almost all of them dealt with Shand's system applied to general business trans-actions. From this it can be deduced that this system, an early form of the " receipt and payment " system, was gradually spreading among comparatively large business firms.   Later the fully developed system continued to gain in popularity and was adopted extensively by many small-scale merchants and co-operative societies, presumably because it was easier to understand than orthodox double entry, particularly as this was generally taught by way of the personification theory.   In more recent years " receipt and payment book-keeping " has progressively lost its adherents, and it can be expected that this system will sooner or later cease to be used and be replaced by the method of double entry as practised throughout the world.

Index

Three classes of entry are listed: accounting records (in *italic* type); authors of textbooks or treatises on accounting (in **bold** type); and authors of books or articles on the history of accounting or dealing with particular accounting records.

Parker, Aikens & Company, 282n.
Parthenon, building accounts, 23–24, 25
Pasion the banker, 27–28
Peele, J., 204–205, 209, 211, 243n., 246n., 289, 297
Penndorf, B., 10n., 136n., 151n., 166n., 167n., 168n., 169n., 171n., 172n., 225
Peragallo, E., 132n., 215n., 216n., 220n., 246n., 295n.
Percy, Bishop, 110n.
Peruzzi company, 128–131
Pietersz, C., 234, 243
Pietra, A., 221
Pinney, 282n., 285n.
Pisz, Johann, 168–169
Plige, Johannes, 167
Portal, C., 161n.
Porte, de la, 7, 319n., 320n.
Postlethwayt, M., 7, 302
Postumus, N. W., 166n., 169n.
Preisigke, F., 33n., 35n., 68

Quin, M., 293

Ragusan Mint, 157n.
Ratcliffe, Joan, Lady, 99–113
Reyerszoon and Diricszoon, 169
Reymondin, G., 322n., 324n.
Reynolds, R. L., 127n.
Rhodes, Henry, 255–265
Riccomanni, Baldovino, 120
Richter, D., 320
Roe, R. B., 303
Roover, Florence Edler de, 86n., 131n., 139n., 154n.
Roover, R. de, 2n., 5n., 63n., 64n., 115n., 129n., 134n., 145n., 147n., 155n., 163n., 164n., 210n., 214n.
Rörig, F., 166n., 167n., 169n.
Row Fogo, J., 239n., 245n., 313n., 314n.
Ruiz, Simon, 154n., 174
Ruland, Ott, 171
Runtinger, Wilhelm and Matthäus, 171
Ruyelle, Guillaume, 163–165

Salimbeni company, 122
Sapori, A., 120n., 124n., 125n., 126n., 127n., 128, 130n.

Sarll, A., 306
Sassetti, Francesco, 147
Sassetti, Gentile de', 120
Sattler, C., 167n.
Saval, Jean, 161
Schär, J. F., 323n.
Schiaffini, A., 116n., 122n.
Schmidt-Rimpler, W., 168n.
Schnebel, M., 68
Schneider, J., 162n.
Schreiber, H., 210n., 244n.
Schulte, A., 172n.
Schwartz, M., 10n., 225
Serrainerio-Dugnano partnership, 138
Shand, A. A., 383, 385
Sheriff, D., 300
Sieveking, H., 131n., 134n., 153n., 157n., 158n.
Smith, C. A., 40n.
Smith, John, 187
Smith, K. L., 12n.
Snell, C., 290
Sombart, W., 3, 9
Soranzo, Donado, 158
South Eastern Railway, 342, 348, 349, 350
Sprague, C., 301
Stanton, Adam, 274
Starck, Ulrich, 171
Stephens, H., 307–309
Stevin, S., 4, 19n., 235, 236–246
Stieda, W., 166n.
Sydney Railway Co., 330

Tagliente, G. A., 210n., 234
Tanabe family, 380
Tapp, J., 234
Taylor, R. E., 184n.
Tempest, Robert, 186n.
Temple of Delphi, 23n.
Teralh, Ugo, 161
Theophanes archive, 43n.
Thornton, J., 295, 306
Tjäder, J. O., 20n.
Tod, M. N., 23n., 25n., 26n., 28n., 52n.
Tölner, Johann, 167
Tooley, Henry, 186

Ugolini, Bernardino, 121

Vannier, H., 324n.
Veckinhusen, Hildebrand, 168